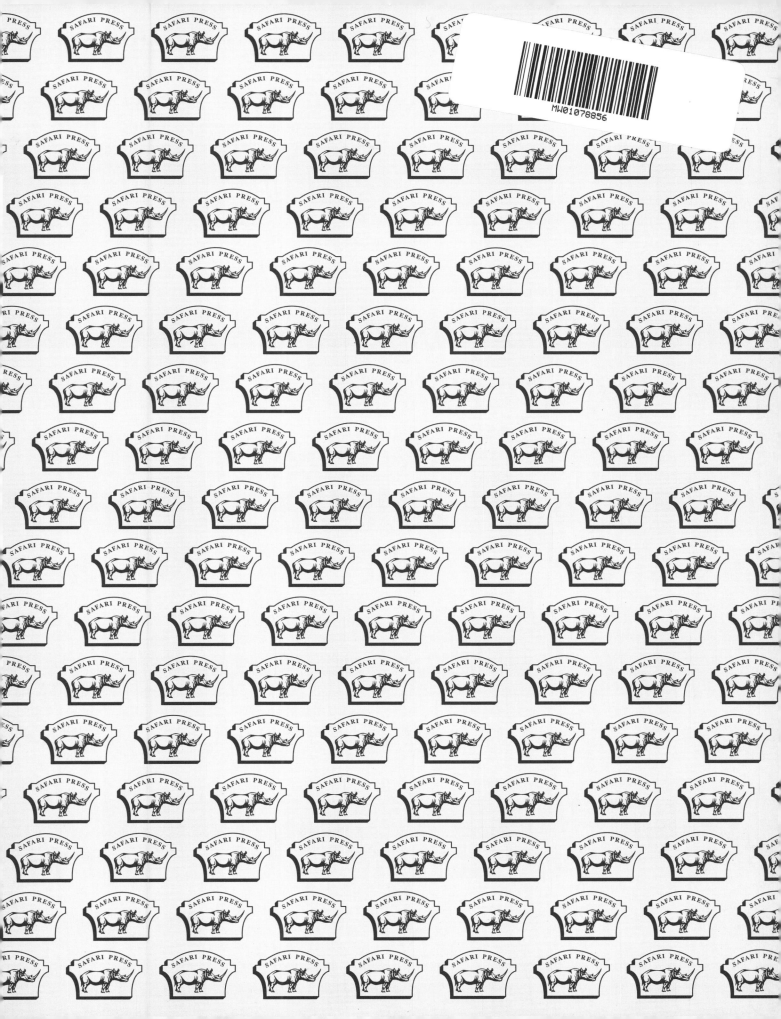

BROWNING®

Sporting Arms of Distinction

1903-1992

By Matt Eastman

The trademark Safari Press ® is registered with the U.S. Patent and Trademark Office and in other countries. Browning ® and the Browning logo are registered trademarks of the Browning Arms Company.

Eastman, Matt

First Safari Press edition © 1998

Safari Press Inc.

1998, Long Beach, California

ISBN 1-57157-114-0

Library of Congress Catalog Card Number: 98060903

10 9 8 7 6 5 4 3 2

Printed in China

Readers wishing to receive the Safari Press catalog, featuring many fine books on big-game hunting, wingshooting, and sporting firearms, should write to Safari Press Inc., P.O. Box 3095, Long Beach, CA 90803, USA. Tel: (714) 894-9080 or visit our Web site at www.safaripress.com.

Table of Contents

Foreword

There has been so much written about John M. Browning that anything I say here is probably redundant. There is no doubt in my mind, however, that if Mr. Browning were still alive and working, he would be designing guns that would adapt to today's manufacturing techniques, and they would function as well and look as good as the originals.

Mr. Browning, who had started with Winchester as the company's chief designer, had Winchester so scared of his designing capabilities that he and his brothers would go to New Haven, Connecticut, each year with an armload of designs and there collect hundreds of thousands of dollars from Winchester for inventions they knew would never be manufactured. It became a personal laughing matter to the Browning brothers who would joke about it among themselves. Just before their annual trip East, they would get busy and finish up seven or eight designs to take with them, knowing it would fatten their take on the trip home.

When Mr. Browning died, he was credited with or had helped design 128 firearm patents, of which only 80 were ever produced. Also, many other companies took advantage of his designs. I was so impressed with this that I have chosen to include it here in a book that was basically written as a guide to Belgium [Belgian] Brownings. You, the reader, will find the additional designs as interesting as I have.

Introduction

Firearms have played a dominant role in the history of humankind from the fourteenth century until this very day, which includes the settling of America. Browning guns, from the beginning of Jonathan Browning's innovative inventions through his son's 129 firearms patents, are still making history. Some of these guns even played a role in Desert Storm. They are still influencing American history and probably will as long as cartridge arms are used by man. Although this book covers the sporting side of Browning guns in this country, the military use of these fine firearms cannot be ignored.

The very name Browning has become synonymous with fine guns. While watching a rerun of "Eye of the Tiger," I noticed that one of the bad guys said he wanted to prove himself as good and brave as his brother, so he bought a "Browning." He was actually saying he wanted the best. Browning guns are respected worldwide as the best in design and workmanship for the sportsman, the police, and the military. If you collect or shoot a Browning, you have a gun in which to take much pride.

When this book was first conceived in 1985, it was originally meant to be a guide for only the Belgian-made models. Since then, many new models made in Japan have been introduced; some of these have become collector's models. In 1987, I wrote that many times I was asked, "Well, why isn't a Japanese-made variation just as good as a Belgian gun?" And I usually answered, "If you only want to hunt with the gun and don't want to look for a Belgian-made model, then go ahead and buy a Japanese model. But, if you want to make an investment that you can enjoy, I recommend that you spend a little more on a Belgian-made gun and get something you'll be able to hand down to future generations."

This is now incorrect. Some Japanese guns are already becoming collector's items: The sidelock doubles come to mind. These are now valued at more than $3,000.00 and getting higher almost monthly. I look for other models made in Japan also to increase in value, so I would advise the astute investor to determine which these are and start collecting them. As a result of this, I have added a lot of information about the Japanese models in order to bring each one up-to-date. The other day, at one of my gun shows, I noticed a Browning BSS that was new to me; *it was made in Belgium*. So my fellow gun collectors, there is always something new when collecting Brownings and just because a particular model was made in Japan doesn't mean it is not desirable to a Belgium Browning collector.

While we're writing about collecting, another point of information needs to be brought to the attention of Browning collectors, especially beginners. Some of the original workmen from Belgium are upgrading guns and creating some rare or hard-to-find variations. To a knowledgeable collector, these guns are not worth as much as an original. If you are a beginning collector, do not let an unscrupulous dealer tell you that just because it duplicates an original, it's the same in value. I have included a lengthy discussion in this book on how to detect a phony.

This book is a culmination of many years of research, note taking, collecting information, and compiling data. It is the result of the need to have this type of information at gun shows for quality dealing—especially since there was little information available about these guns. We begin with the history of the Browning family and carry on with the first inventions fo Jonathan Browning and his son, John. All models are covered: the Auto-5, the Superposed, Double Automatic, bolt action rifles, Auto 22, and all handgun models, including all Japanese guns introduced in the country up until 1992. In the general section is information pertinent to Browning guns including engravers, serial numbers, salt wood, and grading. Collectors, hunters, and shooters will all benefit from the information in this book on Browning firearms. I hope you enjoy this book as much as I enjoyed writing it.

Acknowledgments

There are many people who have contributed to the research of this book. A special thanks goes out to Richard Bauter, Jack Lanhem, Rob Sheerin, Vearl Brown, and Paul Thompson, all of the Browning Arms Company, for all their help and cooperation. Others that have contributed are Jim Allyn, Dave Banducci, Col. Reid Betz, George Boyd, Harvey Broome, Loyd Crede, Morris Hallowell IV, Judge C. Anthony Harris, Art Isaacson, Charles L. Lee, Ron Moore, C. A. Parker, Fiore Passaro, Bill Schwarz, Homer Tyler, Tommy Wilder and others too numerous to name.

This book is lovingly
dedicated
to my
wife and daughter,
Paulette and Mande,
for all of their
support.

Chapter One

The
John M. Browning Armory
and
His Greatest Inventions

As a tribute to Mr. Browning's contributions in military weapons the John M. Browning Armory in Ogden, Utah was dedicated to him in 1959. As part of this dedication, the booklet that appears in this chapter was published by the Browning Arms Company. It is presented here with their permission.

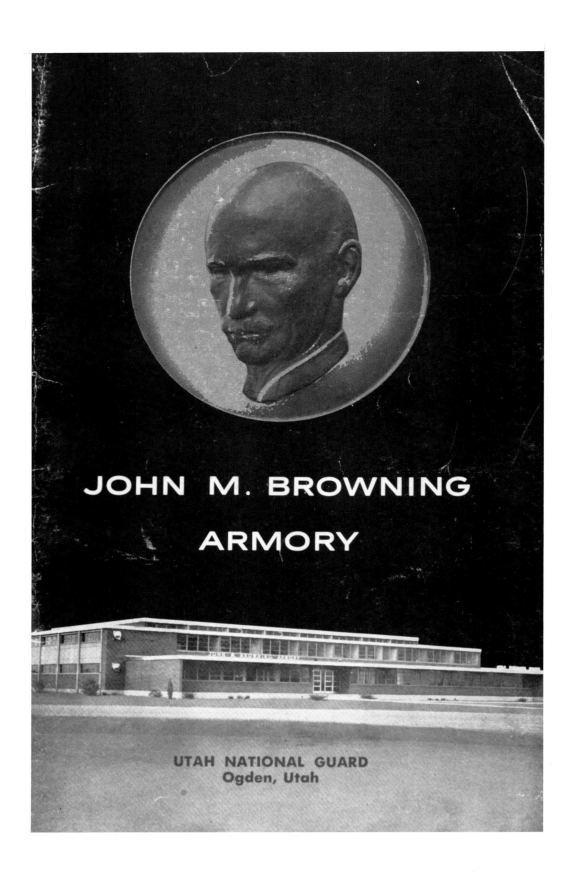

JOHN M. BROWNING

ARMORY

UTAH NATIONAL GUARD
Ogden, Utah

JOHN M. BROWNING ARMORY

1855 - 1926

THE STATE OF UTAH is proud to recognize John M. Browning as one of its most distinguished citizens. It is proud, also, to participate in the perpetuation of his memory with the John M. Browning Armory.

The ingenuity and creative ability of this great man typify the resourcefulness and initiative of the pioneers who settled and developed this great State. The State of Utah is proud that the achievements of this great Utahn may now be shown to countless numbers of his fellow countrymen who will come from far and wide to view the famous Browning Arms Collection. In this way they will be able to become more intimately acquainted with this outstanding American whose contribution to progress has been of such great magnitude.

It is our sincere hope that the contribution of John M. Browning may be indicative of the capacity of this State for contribution to the economic development of the United States of America.

GEORGE DEWEY CLYDE
Governor
State of Utah

THE UTAH NATIONAL GUARD is honored to be able to participate in providing a monument to John M. Browning.

We think it is particularly fitting for a Military organization to participate in the perpetuation of the memory of this great American.

He utilized his special gift of creative ability to provide weapons for United States Service Forces which have contributed materially to their success in the preservation of the Democracy which fosters incentive for creative effort.

It is our hope that the countless numbers who view the Browning Arms Collection will be cognizant of the contribution of this great American.

His mechanical wizardry has had profound effect upon the progress of mankind, providing instruments for sporting diversion, and for deterring aggression which would smother Freedom, and oppression which would bring enslavement.

MAXWELL E. RICH
Major General
Adjutant General, State of Utah

Foreword

I wish to express the sincere gratitude of the Browning family to the Utah National Guard for this Memorial to my father.

John M. Browning was not a man who looked for recognition and during his life did much to minimize his achievements. However, of the many honors accorded him, I am sure none could have meant so much or been so deeply appreciated as this Memorial, in the city of his birth where the major portion of his work took place.

Many of the fine museums in our country have in the past requested this collection of John M. Browning's work. It is not with regret that we have retained it until this occasion. Indeed it seems appropriate that it should become part of Ogden's heritage.

Perhaps a few words about this collection will supplement your interest and understanding.

The collection includes a sizable number of John M. Browning's original models as well as corresponding production models. Those so designated as his originals were made in their entirety by John M. Browning, or under his direct supervision, in his workshop here in Ogden.

In commencing a new gun, it was his usual procedure to make rough, free-hand sketches to clarify mechanical combinations in his mind, but rarely was a gun design completed on paper before realized in metal. In a few instances, wooden mock-ups were made to demonstrate possible exterior lines and appearance. Often cardboard and sheet metal templates were made as a guide to a form of the work or for the location of centers, angles of cams, and lengths and positions of levers. Thus aided, the general picture developed in his mind by dint of long, persistent periods of thought and imagining.

Then, from chunks of metal, through hand forging, milling, lathe turning, drilling, chiseling and filing, these working, shooting models were produced.

The metals used were chosen carefully in advance from what was available in a frontier town. The receivers and some of the parts, for instance, came from old railroad car axles chosen for toughness and resistance to shock. Many of the parts here exposed had clicked thousands of miles over the first transcontinental railroad (completed when John was 14 years of age) before assuming their present everlasting form.

Through industrious self-education, since instruction was not available in that period, he learned how to forge and machine the various types of steel then obtainable and, of greatest importance, became an expert in his day in the art of heat treatment, hardening and tempering of steels.

Many of the details of design and construction were worked out as a model progressed, and it was surely his attention to detail that was largely responsible for the final excellence of his creations.

When the various components of a new model seemed to be working harmoniously as a whole, the gun was submitted to rigorous firing tests under all imaginable conditions. These trials often caused him to make changes here and there, but when he was finally satisfied, one could be certain a fine new firearm had come into existence.

Models such as these shown here were for proving an idea, making production drawings and for technical reference and assistance in manufacturing the guns commercially. When their usefulness in this respect ended, he frequently lost interest in the model and abandoned it, sometimes with its parts scattered throughout various departments of a factory.

I have gathered as many of these as I could in various arms factories where they were used, but of course a goodly number are not obtainable. Many of his models with their patents were sold outright to a manufacturer but never produced and marketed, so even commercial prototypes are not available.

Nevertheless, I am sure the representative number exhibited here adequately illustrate his extraordinary ability and capacity in his chosen field.

Although this booklet contains considerable background and historical data, space limitations necessitated that it pertain primarily to the identity and description of the various models in this collection.

For this reason, much of the Browning story could not be included. Although little reference has been made to John M. Browning's brothers, Matthew and Ed, or others of the organization, I wish to take this occasion to eulogize their important and significant role in the Browning enterprise.

To reflect on that which has been done is of most value if stimulating to future, worth-while effort, irrespective of the field of endeavor. It is hoped the humble circumstances and obstacles which did not deter John Browning will serve as encouragement and inspiration to other generations of our democracy.

"We feed on genius," said Emerson. "Great men exist that there may be greater men."

Sincerely,

Val A. Browning

The Greatest Gun Inventor the World Has Ever Known

In an adobe home of a pioneer settlement, in the vast emptiness of the untamed West, John Moses Browning was born January 21, 1855. His birthplace, known as Ogden, was nestled in a rather barren valley at the foot of the rugged Wasatch Mountains. To provide just food and shelter was no easy task for these early settlers and the gun, in quest of wild game or against the peril of Indian raid, was as important to these pioneers as the plow.

In his early life, the breech loading firearm was still in its infancy and he was to witness much of the transition from the powder horn and ramrod. He learned to use the new and the old and to repair them under the guidance of his father Jonathan, a gunsmith by trade, who had moved West with the Mormon migration in 1851.

As his knowledge increased, he became acutely aware of the limitations of even the most modern firearm of the day, and it seemed, with the gradual perfection of the gas tight cartridge, the profusion of ideas that had been forming in his mind were triggered into reality.

At first thought, the frontier seemed hardly the place to nurture an inventive genius. Educational opportunities were meager at best. Equipment, tools and materials were limited to the bare necessities brought in by wagon. Yet John M. Browning was to mold, perhaps more than any other individual, the remarkable changes that were to come within a century . . . the story of his life is the story of the evolution of modern firearms.

The entire array of types and classes of breech loading firearms have benefited from his fertile imagination, exceptional mechanical sense and tireless persistence. His 128 different patents cover a total of at least 70 complete and distinct firearm models. They include practically every caliber from the .22 short cartridge through the 37mm projectile; they embrace automatic actions, semi-automatic actions, lever actions and slide actions; they include guns that operate by gas pressures, by both the short and long recoil principle and by the blowback principle; they include models utilizing sliding locks, rotating locks and vertical locks.

The many of his models on display at this Utah National Guard Armory are a composite of these developments. They have defended our country, contributed greatly to America's industrial economy and afforded millions of our sportsmen added pleasure in the Nation's second largest participating sport.

In viewing that part of this collection which is specifically military, one might find it difficult to realize that it comprises the prototypes of millions used by our combined Armed Forces and those of our Allies; that these have been the basic automatic weapons of our Armies in every military conflict since the Boxer Rebellion of 1900; that his machine guns, 41 years later, in World War II proved outstandingly superior to those of our enemies.

However, even these are but a comparatively small part of the prodigious work of John M. Browning. His first interest was sporting guns and, as his many designs bear witness, it was to these he allocated most of his time. One might even conclude that more American game, both large and small, have fallen to Browning designed guns than to most other makes in America combined.

Practically every improvement in lever action repeating rifles since 1886 found its origin from his basic patents. In this collection you will see America's first successful, semi-automatic, high power rifle and the first successful, repeating shotgun. His pump action shotgun has established a standard of performance for all such guns since 1893. No other successful semi-automatic shotgun was developed for 54 years after his first was introduced. His small bore rifles outsold all others combined for decades. His automatic pistols were the first ever to be produced in America and today are believed to have been made in greater numbers than all other designs in the world combined. The Browning .45 caliber still serves as the side arm of our Army, 48 years after its introduction. His 9mm Parabellum pistol has been adopted by most NATO Nations.

Many of his models are being manufactured today in greater numbers than ever before, one continuously for 70 years, one for 63 years and many for over 50 years. It is often remarked that John M. Browning was years in advance of his time. Surely the immunity to retirement of his vast and varied developments would confirm this to be a valid statement.

Authorities of many nations recognize John M. Browning as "The greatest firearms inventor the world has ever known." Few men have been accorded such international esteem . . . and few men have contributed so much to the national security of their country.

Though the work of John M. Browning represents a good deal more than this collection, it is from just these models that upwards of 30 million reproductions have thus far been born. Indeed it can be said that John M. Browning has left his mark in history.

John M. Browning loved his home in this valley with its magnificent surrounding wilderness and from them derived inspiration throughout his entire career. Even in the midst of acclaim, when the finest model shops in the world were at his disposal, he preferred his small shop here in Ogden. Embarrassed by praise, indifferent to fame, he ended his career as humbly as it started.

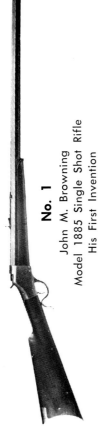

No. 1

John M. Browning
Model 1885 Single Shot Rifle
His First Invention

This was the first of the many models invented by John M. Browning. He was only 23 years old at the time. Patents were filed May 12, 1879. Patent No. 220,271 was granted October 7, 1879.

In a small factory in Ogden, Utah, nearly 600 of these rifles were manufactured by John M. Browning and his brothers before manufacturing and sales rights were sold to the Winchester Repeating Arms Company in 1883. The model exhibited is one of the original 600.

This model later became known as the famous Winchester Single Shot Model 85 and first appeared in their catalog of 1885. It is accorded the unique distinction of having been adapted to more calibers than any other single shot or repeating rifle, here or abroad. It was made in more than 33 different calibers, handling loads as small as the .22 short and as large as the .50-90 Sharpe's caliber. The Model 85 was the first Winchester rifle capable of handling the most powerful metallic cartridges of the period.

The acquisition of this rifle by Winchester was the beginning of an alliance between John M. Browning and Winchester which lasted 17 years. It was the first of some 41 Browning-invented sporting arms sold to the Winchester Arms Company.

The Single Shot is a lever action, hammer type and solid frame rifle. The hammer drops down with the breechblock when the rifle is opened and is cocked by the closing movement. It can also be cocked by hand.

In 1910, additional modifications brought forth the takedown model. Through the years of its production, it was provided in sporting models, carbines, special target and Schuetzen type rifles. Weights varied from 4½ pounds in the .44 Carbine to 13 pounds in the Schuetzen model. It was furnished with or without set triggers and with barrels of many lengths and weights.

In 1914 the Single Shot was also made into a shotgun chambered for a 3 inch, 20 gauge shell. At about this time a special military target model was developed for military training and named the Winder Musket in honor of Colonel C. B. Winder. The Winder Musket was used in large numbers for training U. S. Troops during World War I. This Single Shot was discontinued in 1920, except for the Single Shot Musket which was produced for some time beyond that date.

The Model 85 is so noted for its accuracy it is still highly valued by precision target shooters today.

No. 2

Production Model of John M. Browning's 1885 Rifle
Known as the Winchester Single Shot
1885 to 1920

No. 3

John M. Browning
Model 1886 Type Lever Action Repeating Rifle
Inventor's Model

This was John M. Browning's first repeating rifle. The Model 1886 was invented in 1881; Patent No. 306,577 was acquired in October 1884. This rifle was bought by Winchester October 14, 1884 and was known initially as the Winchester Model 86, first appearing in their catalog in October of that year.

It is a lever action type with exposed hammer and tubular magazine in a solid frame. About 1894 it was converted to a takedown model. This model was the first repeating rifle to successfully employ sliding vertical locks which effectively sealed the breech and barrel of the gun and was the forerunner of all later Browning lever action type rifles. Mr. Sharpe, a noted authority on rifles, had this to say about the Model 86:

"It is probably the smoothest job ever developed in a lever action gun. It functions practically without effort."

This rifle was first adapted to the Government .45-70 cartridge, carrying a 405 or 500 grain bullet and later to ten others of the heaviest caliber cartridges of the time. It has been said that practically every improvement in lever action, repeating rifles has been taken from its basic patents.

The cartridges are carried in a tubular magazine under the barrel; a lever operates the mechanism, opens the breech, cocks the gun, ejects the empty cartridge, picks up and inserts a new cartridge into the chamber, closes the breech and securely locks it, and in less than a second's time the trigger finger is in position for the next shot.

In 1936 this model was slightly modified to handle the .348 Winchester cartridge and was carried in the Winchester line as the Model 71. It was not discontinued until 1958, a life of 74 years.

No. 4

Production Model of John M. Browning's 1886 Rifle
Known as the Winchester Model 86
1886 to 1958

If any one rifle could be designated as the most famous sporting rifle ever produced, it is this lever action Model 94, also known as "The Winchester .30-30." Although it resembles in appearance Mr. Browning's Model 92, it differs from all previous models in being the first sporting repeating action rifle adapted to handle smokeless cartridges. The Model 94 and the .30-30 cartridge developed especially for it, practically revolutionized everyone's idea of what could be expected of a sporting rifle. It was the first popular rifle using a small caliber smokeless cartridge, having the striking energy of former large, black powder loads.

Made in both sporting rifle and carbine models, the 94 became especially popular in the West where, by this time, game was becoming less plentiful and more wary. There was a great demand for a longer range and more accurate rifle. It soon became standard equipment of the Western pioneer, hunter and rancher.

Still being produced, it has been said the Model 94 has outsold any other rifle ever manufactured by the Winchester Company.

In addition to the better known .30-30 caliber, it was produced in the .32-40, .38-55, .25-35 and .32 Special.

It is estimated, to date, close to 3,000,000 have been manufactured. Winchester's 1958 advertisements represented it as "the most popular hunting rifle ever built — bar none!" and the description in their 1958 catalog states, "probably more deer have fallen to this old favorite in the past six decades than to all other rifles combined."

It holds this position of popularity 63 years after its introduction.

No. 8

Production Model of John M. Browning's 1894 Rifle
Known as the Winchester Model 94
1894 to Present Time

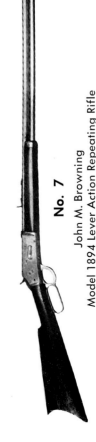

No. 9

John M. Browning
Model 1895 Lever Action Repeating Rifle
Inventor's Original Model

The U. S. Patent Office assigned Patent No. 549,345 to John M. Browning on this model November 5, 1895. It was first manufactured by Winchester in February, 1896. It was the first non-detachable, box type magazine rifle, designed to handle the jacketed, sharp nosed bullets.

-9-

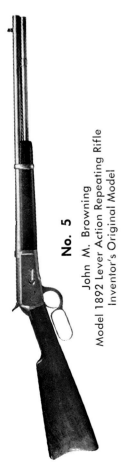

No. 5

John M. Browning
Model 1892 Lever Action Repeating Rifle
Inventor's Original Model

The Model 1892 is similar in basic design to the Model 1886. It incorporates most of the features of the Model 1886 action and double-locking system. Patent No. 465,340 was acquired December 15, 1891.

It was first produced by Winchester in May, 1892 and made available to the consumer in July of that year at a price of $18.00. This particular model was specifically designed for smaller caliber bullets than that of its predecessor, the Model 86, and was best known in the .44-40, .38-40, .32-20 and .25-20 Winchester calibers.

It was manufactured in three styles, the sporting rifle, carbine and musket, first made with a solid frame and later in a takedown model which first appeared about October, 1893.

Some measure of the demand for the Model 1892 is shown by the fact that approximately 735,000 had been sold by the end of 1914.

In December, 1932 the Winchester Company presented a beautifully engraved model bearing the serial number 1,000,000 to Patrick J. Hurley, then Secretary of War. It was discontinued in 1941. Later, modified versions known as Winchester Models 53, 64 and finally 65, which primarily gave increased magazine ecapacities, were introduced and continued until 1947.

No. 6

Production Model of John M. Browning's 1892 Rifle
Known as the Winchester Model 92
1892 to 1947

No. 7

John M. Browning
Model 1894 Lever Action Repeating Rifle
Inventor's Original Model

Patent No. 524,702 was issued to John M. Browning on this model August 21, 1894. Manufacturing and sales rights were granted the Winchester Repeating Arms Company and it was first made available October 20, 1894.

-8-

The 95 is a hammer type lever action model which is loaded by pushing the cartridges into the box magazine when the action is open and the lever in its downward position. The cartridges are held in single column in this magazine and fed into the action by spring tension under the magazine follower.

Its necessity originated with the demand for a rifle to accommodate the larger caliber, smokeless type cartridges then being developed. It handled all of the heaviest cartridges then manufactured. It was a great favorite among both North American and African big game hunters and extensively used by President Theodore Roosevelt, Colonel Townsend Whelan, Major Charles Askins and many other famous hunters of the era.

The 95 was manufactured in a sporting rifle, carbine and musket type and was chambered, among others, for the U. S. Army .30-40 Krag, the Government .30-06 and .405 Winchester. It varied in weight from a 7¾-pound carbine to the hefty 9¾-pound U. S. Army Musket complete with bayonet, scabbard and strap sling. Many thousands were manufactured for use in the Spanish-American War. It was discontinued in 1931 when approximately one-half million had been manufactured.

No. 10

Production Model of John M. Browning's 1895 Rifle Known as the Winchester Model 1895 1896 to 1931

No. 11

John M. Browning
Semi-Automatic High Power Rifle
Inventor's Original Model

John M. Browning acquired patents to this revolutionary new rifle under Patent No. 659,786, October 16, 1900. Manufacturing and sales rights were sold to Remington Arms Company and the rifle first entered the market in 1906, known first as the Model 8.

The rifle is a recoil actuated, auto loading type with a barrel sleeve around the barrel. The barrel sleeve contains a bushing which acts as a bearing surface for the recoiling barrel. The magazine is a fixed box type holding five cartridges. The breech is locked by the turning bolt which locks close against the head of the cartridge as in military type rifles, permitting the shooting of high power cartridges with perfect safety. At the time of its introduction, other auto-loading

types did not use the locked breech, merely depending upon the inertia of a heavy breechblock to support the cartridge.

It is recognized as the first successful auto-loading, high power rifle in America, and for many years one of the preferred hunting models in this country.

Unusual accuracy is attained by two features: The bolt has two lugs on its front end locking into each side of the barrel extension thereby eliminating unequal strains. The barrel is also free to recoil in a straight line, having practically no tendency to whip or switch as do rifles with barrels fixed permanently to the receiver. Law enforcement agencies still use this rifle extensively.

It was manufactured in calibers .25, .30, .32, .35 and .300 Savage and was in continual production by the Remington Arms Company, either as the Model 8 or Model 81, until about 1950. This rifle was also manufactured in Belgium by the Fabrique Nationale d'Armes de Guerre from the period September, 1910 to October, 1931.

No. 12

Production Model of John M. Browning's Semi-Automatic High Power Rifle, Known as the FN Caliber .35 Automatic Rifle — 1910 to 1931

No. 13

Production Model of John M. Browning's Semi-Automatic High Power Rifle, Known as the Remington Model 81 1906 to 1950

No. 14

John M. Browning
Model 1887 Lever Action Repeating Rifle
Inventor's Original Model

This rifle was invented by John M. Browning in 1887. Patent Number 376,576 was acquired January 17, 1888.

This rifle is a lever action with an exposed hammer but operates quite differently from most lever actions. It is of very simple construction with the locking mechanism arranged entirely within the breech piece. The breech piece is hung to the receiver by a link in such a manner that the opening movement causes the rear end of the breech to drop, thereby unlocking the piece while the forward end is guided longitudinally in the receiver. The swinging movement of the link acts as a cam to throw the hammer to full cock position. A carrier which is combined with the breech piece receives a fresh cartridge from the magazine and positions it for feeding into the barrel chamber with each operation of the lever.

When in closed position, the rear end of the breech rests squarely against a recoil bearing surface in the receiver, locking the front end of the breechblock against the barrel. The purpose of this construction was to provide a short receiver adaptable to the longest cartridge, thus reducing the weight of the rifle from that necessary in models with the breechblock moving horizontally within the receiver.

The operating cycle of this rifle is the same as for most lever action rifles. With each operation of the lever the fired cartridge is extracted and ejected, the hammer cocked and a fresh cartridge fed into the chamber.

While very sound in design and operation, this rifle is one of many of Mr. Browning's designs never produced because manufacturing facilities could not keep pace with his inventive capacity.

No. 15
John M. Browning
Model 1887 Lever Action Repeating Shotgun
Inventor's Original Model

This model was the first lever action repeating shotgun made in the United States and on which Patent No. 336,287 was issued February 16, 1885. Patent rights were sold to the Winchester Repeating Arms Company in 1885, and it was first announced by that Company in June, 1887, as the Model 87 Shotgun.

It is a lever action, hammer type repeater with solid frame and tubular magazine.

Other types of repeating shotguns had been made in this country prior to this gun's development, but Mr. Browning's lever action type is recognized as the first successful repeating shotgun. The action is simple and rugged and the gun was a great favorite in this country until early in the 20th Century. The gun carries four shells in the magazine positioned under the barrel and one in the chamber, providing a five-shot capacity. It was made in both 12 and 10 gauge models, weighing approximately 8 pounds in the 12 gauge model and 9 pounds in the 10 gauge model. More than 65,000 were manufactured until production was discontinued on the 12 gauge in 1901. In 1902 the Model 1901 was introduced which was the 10 gauge model of the 87. This model continued in production until 1920.

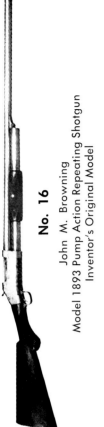

No. 16
John M. Browning
Model 1893 Pump Action Repeating Shotgun
Inventor's Original Model

This model was invented by John M. Browning in 1890. Patent No. 441,390 was granted November 25 of that year. Production rights were acquired by Winchester in 1893. The gun was first placed on the market in April, 1894. It was the first shotgun with a sliding forearm or pump action ever listed by Winchester.

The 1893 Model was a solid frame which continued in production until 1897 when Mr. Browning modified it to a takedown model known as the Model 1897. The Model 93 and its Model 97 counterpart soon became the most popular shotgun in America and established a standard of performance by which other kinds and makes of shotguns were judged for years. Few have carried such reputation for simple, rugged construction and unfailing reliability.

A short barrel variation was widely used as a riot gun by law enforcement agencies. The American Express Company at one time armed all of its messengers with this firearm. During World War I a considerable number were used by American troops as trench guns with exceptional success. It was also used by skilled shots who were positioned in trenches to fire at enemy hand grenades in mid-air and deflect them from falling into the American trenches.

The magazine capacity of most models was five shells in either 12 or 16 gauge. Approximately 35,000 of the Model 93 were manufactured followed by an estimated 1,000,000 of the Model 97. The Model 97 was not discontinued until 1958.

No. 17
John M. Browning
Model 97
Personal Trap Gun

Mr. Browning could find relaxation through a hike in the mountains or a hunt on the marsh, possible for him in no other way. Often a new design kept him at his bench or drawing board continuously for more than 24 hours, and on many occasions he was to remain within the proximity of his work bench for days at a time.

When pressures reached the bursting point, he would seek the out-of-doors "to clear the cobwebs," as he put it.

In the Wasatch range, just east of Ogden, deer, elk, bear, grouse, quail and sage hens were plentiful. The expansive marsh lands west of Ogden offered some of the finest water fowl shooting in North America.

During off seasons he participated in varied target shooting, traps being one of his favorite sports. As early as 1892, the famous "Four B's" were widely recognized for their skill and wrote national history at the traps. The squad included G. L. Becker, John M. Browning, A. P. Bigelow, and Matt S. Browning.

No. 18
Production Model of John M. Browning's 1897
Pump Shotgun, Known as the Winchester Model 97
1897 to 1958

No. 19
John M. Browning
Hammerless Pump Action Shotgun Model 1903
A Production Model Known as the Stevens Model 520
Original Model Not Available

The principle of the repeating shotgun was fascinating to Mr. Browning. In view of the overwhelming success of the Model 97 he set about developing one with a solid streamlined breech, hammerless type, that could be easily taken apart for convenience in transport. He completed this work in 1903 and acquired Patent No. 781,765 on this model February 7, 1905.

The new repeater was placed on the market by the Stevens Arms Company in early 1904 as the Model 520.

In this gun, firing is impossible until the action is completely closed and locked. Disassembly is fast and simple; merely by pushing a release lever it separates into two sections, stock and action one piece—barrel, magazine and action slide another.

The Model 520 has a rather abrupt angle at the rear of the receiver, later modified to a more streamlined version known as the Model 620. The magazine capacity of this gun is five shots. Loading is accomplished by feeding the shells into the magazine from the underside of the receiver. Ejection is through the opening on the right side of the receiver.

It was made in 12, 16 and 20 gauge models and weighed from 7¾ pounds in the 12 gauge to approximately 6 pounds in the 20 gauge.

The 520 is basically the same gun still in production by the Savage Arms Company.

No. 20
John M. Browning
Model 1917 Pump Action Shotgun
A Production Model Known as the Remington Model 17
Original Model Not Available

June 15, 1915, Mr. Browning received U. S. Patent No. 1,143,170 on his last repeater type shotgun. The Remington Arms Company purchased the manufacturing and sales rights to this model, introducing it in 1921 as the Model 17.

It is a hammerless pump or slide action repeater and has one of the fastest, smoothest actions ever developed in a gun of this type. Made only in 20 gauge, it weighs just 5½ pounds and has such nice balance it immediately became a small gauge favorite for upland game. Unusually trim and streamlined, it is constructed with solid breech, proper safety features and but one opening in the receiver, located on the underside, through which the gun is loaded and the empty shell ejected.

By operating the sliding forearm, an empty case is withdrawn from the chamber and ejected downward; a loaded shell is, in turn, released from the magazine and positioned in the chamber. It has a five-shot capacity with four carried in the tubular magazine underneath the barrel. Takedown is accomplished merely by unscrewing the magazine cap and turning the barrel one-quarter turn.

Production was discontinued in 1933. Since patent expiration, the design has been used with marked success by various manufacturers in all gauges. The Ithaca Model 37 Pump, still in production, is of the same basic design.

It is interesting to note that in the late '90's an underloading and ejecting model was sold to Winchester. It was never produced but was doubtless the first of this type ever made.

No. 21
Production Model of John M. Browning's 1917 Pump Shotgun
Known as the Ithaca Model 37
Presently in Production

one-third were ever produced, but Winchester evidently deemed it more profitable to buy them than permit their acquisition by a competitor.

Winchester had no strong convictions on the success of an automatic shotgun but, conversely, feared it might obsolete models in which they had expensive tooling. Mr. Browning, on the other hand, knew he had an exceptional product and was insistent that it be manufactured, and under royalty arrangements.

Other manufacturers, for one reason or other, were unable to consider the gun at the time. Remington, specifically, due to the death of its president, was confronted with reorganizational matters.

The Brownings had no production organization; nor were conditions such that facilities could be provided readily, especially in the far West during that period. It was only natural then that Mr. Browning would seek out the one place in the world where the gunmaking craft was considered unequalled, the Liege Valley of Belgium, noted as the gunmaking center for centuries.

This was the difficult way by which the Browning Automatic was introduced, a memorable circumstance nevertheless since it integrated the Browning organization and was the beginning of its own line of products appearing under the Browning name.

The gun was first introduced in 1903, being manufactured by Fabrique Nationale d'Armes de Guerre de Liege. The Remington Arms Company later settled their internal problems and were licensed to manufacture and sell the Automatic in 1905, known as the Model 11.

Combined production figures on this gun cannot be even estimated. It has been copied by manufacturers in many countries of the world and even today is being produced with no variance in basic design by Remington, Savage, Franchi, Breda and several others. It would suffice to say several millions have been manufactured. The Browning Arms Company has determined that over a million of the guns under their own name are currently seeing service.

The current production model of the Browning Company is made in an adjustable friction brake and shock absorber which, with one in 12, 16 and 20 gauge and 3" Magnum 12 gauge. It is offered in 72 different specifications.

No. 23 on display is his first version, a link-action model.

No. 22 on display closely resembles the final model, except the breech bolt has no operating handle. The device for opening the breech is positioned on the underside of the stock.

No. 24 is the final prototype and is essentially as the gun was first produced.

Nos. 25, 26, 27, 28

Current production models of the Browning Automatic-5, showing in numerical sequence the 12 gauge 3" Magnum, the Lightweight 12 gauge, the Lightweight 16 gauge so well known as the "Sweet 16" and the Lightweight 20 gauge.

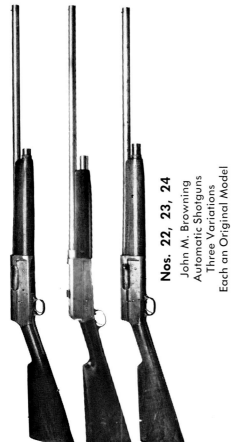

Nos. 22, 23, 24

John M. Browning
Automatic Shotguns
Three Variations
Each an Original Model

October 9, 1900, Mr. Browning was granted Patent Number 659,507 on his autoloading shotgun, considered by him his most difficult invention, and by others one of his greatest achievements.

This shotgun took more time and patience to perfect than any other of his numerous inventions. Perhaps one explanation why no other successful functioning autoloading shotgun of different design was developed until 54 years after his was introduced.

To make a shotgun perform all of the operative functions automatically, leaving only the pulling of the trigger to the shooter, was much more difficult with shotgun ammunition than would be the case with a specific caliber, metallic cartridge, for instance, since the shotgun had to accept a wide variety of loads inconsistent as to pressures generated. Even black powder loads were common during the period of its development.

Mr. Browning ultimately solved the problems by the utilization of an adjustable friction brake and shock absorber which, with one single adjustment, permitted the autoloader to handle either light or heavy loads dependably.

The Automatic utilizes the forces generated by firing the cartridge to eject the empty case, reload, and cock the gun automatically. This complete cycle of operation occurs during a mere fraction of a second — the gun doing all the work, leaving the shooter free to devote his full attention to aim and swing, merely pulling the trigger with each shot. The Automatic will fire five shots as fast as the trigger can be pulled.

It was the Browning Automatic which terminated the alliance of 17 years' duration with the Winchester Company. Even though Winchester had been unable to produce and absorb into its own line his numerous inventions as fast as they were being proffered, manufacturing and sales rights had been acquired outright on 41 designs. Less than

No. 29
Production Model of John M. Browning's Semi-Automatic Shotgun, Known as the Remington Model 11
1905 to 1948

No. 30
Fancy Model 11 Remington Automatic Shotgun Presented to John M. Browning, Its Inventor, By the Remington Arms Company

No. 31
John M. Browning Superposed Shotgun No. 1 Production Model

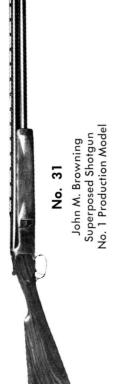

The Superposed "Over-Under" Shotgun was invented in 1925 and Mr. Browning was granted Patent Numbers 1,578,638-39 March 30, 1926.

This gun was the culmination of Mr. Browning's achievements. He laid down his tools for the last time shortly thereafter in 1926. In the Superposed he had created another masterpiece, appropriately a final memorial to the work of a great inventor.

The Superposed is a two-barreled gun with standing breech whereby the action pivots away from the barrels for loading and ejection of empty cases. It can be quickly disassembled into two parts for convenient carrying or storage. The barrels are mounted one above the other, rather than side by side, to permit the improved accuracy of a single sighting plane.

It was first produced by Fabrique Nationale d'Armes de Guerre in 1927 and appeared in the Browning Arms Company line in 1928.

First models had double triggers. Later John M. Browning's son, Val A. Browning, designed twin single triggers for the gun and ultimately the single selective trigger. The twin single triggers differed from the double triggers in that after selecting and shooting the round in one barrel, a second pull on the same trigger would fire the remaining barrel, thus eliminating the necessity of moving the finger from one trigger to the other. In the final version, the single selective trigger fires both barrels, either barrel first by merely moving a thumb selector one way or another.

Automatic ejectors flip out the spent shells when the gun is opened. Unfired shells are retained in the chambers and merely elevated for easy removal by hand if desired.

The Superposed Shotgun is one of the most widely used sporting arms in the world and considered one of the most functional, durable and dependable ever designed.

It was initially provided only in 12 gauge in this country. Val A. Browning later designed the 20 gauge version. Presently the gun is offered in 12, 20, 28 and .410 gauge models as well as in extra barrel sets with extra barrels of same gauge or different gauge. It is made in a 3" Magnum 12 gauge gun for long range shooting, models for field, marsh, skeet and trap. Including the choice of two different weights, six different grades, and various barrel lengths and chokes, 269 specifications are currently manufactured.

No. 32
Current Production Model
Browning Superposed Shotgun
Grade V – 20 Gauge

One of the unique characteristics of all Browning guns is the hand engraving appearing on every model in various degrees of complexity. Steel engraving of this type is done with a light hammer tapping against chisels that are moved about in continuous action. By this means the design is developed much as one might draw it. The engraver begins his work on bare metal; mind, eyes and hands are unassisted by preplaced patterns.

This world of automation has brought about nearly total abandonment of this artistic skill. The makers of Browning guns have preserved this fine art and in the process gathered together perhaps the largest group of qualified engravers found anywhere.

To acquire the skill represented on this model takes years of painstaking experience. It is a craft demanding nearly the ultimate, not only in artistry, but flawless execution. One does not erase steel.

No. 33
Current Production Model
Browning Superposed Shotgun
Grade I – 12 Gauge

Nos. 34, 35, 36, 37
Browning Double Automatic Shotgun
Current Production Models
Inventor, Val A. Browning

Although these models are not those of John M. Browning, it is believed appropriate that they be displayed in this collection to continue the story of Browning guns through the current date and further exemplify the fact that three generations of the Browning family have developed new designs in the field of firearms.

Val A. Browning is now president of the Company founded by his father and has spent all of his working years either in development work or in guiding the operations of the Browning organization.

Val was only 31 when the final salute was fired in honor of John M. Browning. He had worked closely with his father through all of Mr. Browning's later years.

Since the age of 16, Val A. Browning has designed many of the refinements and modifications appearing on Browning guns. In 1954 production commenced on his Double Automatic, not necessarily his most notable achievement but indeed the most unique, both in comparison to earlier Browning models and to all guns of the day.

The Double Automatic, like the Browning Automatic-5, is a recoil operated, semi-automatic shotgun but contains many unusual innovations. It operates on the short recoil system rather than the long recoil principle generally utilized on his father's automatic weapons.

A strong braking system, combined with this principle, contributes to a very soft recoil and permits a reduction in the weight of the gun of more than one pound less than the average for a 12 gauge model. It carries the most compact receiver ever designed in an automatic or repeater type shotgun which, with the addition of a carefully distributed recoil mechanism, gives the Double Automatic exceptional balance very comparable to that of a fine double gun.

The loading principle is entirely new with the port in the left side of the receiver, permitting the introduction of new loads without switching hands or turning the gun on its side. This principle facilitates extremely fast loading and, with the provision of a central safety makes the gun equally convenient for right or left hand shooters.

The mechanism is so designed that the gun shoots all of the large variety of 2¾", 12 gauge loads without adjustment of any kind.

Takedown is accomplished by merely depressing the rear of the forearm and lifting out the barrel. Interchanging barrels is similarly convenient and fast.

For the first time in the history of firearms came the innovation of colors with the Double Automatic. The gun's functional properties permitted the use of lightweight metal alloys in the receiver and the utilization of an annodizing process to infuse a layer of the metal with rich, durable color. The method provides an extremely hard and durable surface which actually wears longer than the customary blued finishes.

No. 35 is especially interesting in that it contains a lightweight alloyed barrel as well as receiver. It has been produced in limited quantities, primarily for experimental purposes, since 1954 and has not been offered for general sale. With this barrel the gun weighs only about 5 pounds.

When absence of weight would take precedence to other features for a more specialized sporting gun, it would serve most effectively. For an all-round sporting gun where balance, swing and recoil must also be considered, the present lightweight steels are, thus far, considered the better compromise.

Three models of the Double Automatic are in current production, the Standard at 7½ pounds, the Twelvette at 6¾ pounds, and the Twentyweight at approximately 6 pounds — all are 12 gauge.

No. 38

John M. Browning
Model 1890, .22 Caliber Pump Action Repeating Rifle
Inventor's Original Model

On June 26, 1888, Patent No. 385,238 was granted to Mr. Browning covering his Model 1890 Repeating Rifle. The Winchester Company purchased rights to the rifle and started producton November, 1890, introducing the gun as the Model 90, .22 Caliber Pump Repeater.

The 90 was the first repeating pump or trombone action model of any kind manufactured by Winchester. It came into being when the Winchester Company asked John Browning if he could design a repeating rifle that could handle the .22 short cartridges. Mr. Browning sent drawings of the proposed model but shortly thereafter received a letter from a Company official stating that he had best discontinue his efforts along the lines proposed since the gun could not possibly work.

Mr. Browning then made the working model here exhibited, according to the plans submitted. He returned it to the factory with the appropriate comment to the Company technicians: "You said it wouldn't work but it seems to shoot pretty fair for me."

The new model was first made to accept either .22 short, long or long rifle. In 1906 it was modified to accept any of the .22 cartridges interchangeably. First manufactured with solid frame, it was converted to a takedown model in 1893.

The radical improvement in this rifle over all previous .22 caliber repeaters was the carrier mechanism. Previously no positive method of handling the small .22 caliber cartridges had been developed. This was accomplished in the Model 90 by two steel fingers that gripped the head of the shell at the rear of the magazine, drawing only one shell from the magazine while ejecting the spent shell and infallibly positioning the fresh cartridge so the breechblock would carry it into the chamber.

The action is of the exposed hammer type and is so smooth, swift and certain that it has become a pattern for gunmakers throughout the world.

The manufacture of the Model 1900 was discontinued in 1902 when the trigger guard shape was modified and thereafter it was known as the Model 1902 over the Model 1900 were a shorter trigger pull, steel butt plate, rear peep sight and slightly heavier barrel.

In July of 1904 another slightly modified version of the M/1900 and M/1902 was introduced as the Model 1904. The primary changes were a longer, heavier barrel and differently shaped stock.

In 1928 and the years following, Winchester announced other variations of the Model 1900, 1902, 1904 type which were known as the Models 58, 59, 60 and 68 Single Shot. The combined production of these models amounted to well over a million units.

Winchester also made a shotgun version similar to the Model 1902 Single Shot Shotgun which was called the Model 36 Single Shot Shotgun. The Model 36 was the only shotgun made in the United States chambered for 9mm paper shot shells. It was discontinued in 1927 after more than 20,000 had been produced.

In conjunction with the Model 1900, Mr. Browning provided another interesting and unique development which became known as the Winchester Thumb Trigger Rifle. It was void of either trigger or trigger guard. Just behind the cocking piece on the bolt was a button called the thumb trigger. When in shooting position, the shooter merely pressed downward on this button with the thumb to release the firing pin.

Although extremely sound in principle as an accuracy feature, it was never very popular in this country. Surprisingly, it became extremely popular in Australia and large quantities were shipped to that country.

No. 42

Production Model of John M. Browning's 1900 Bolt Action Rifle
Known as the Winchester Model 68
1899 to 1953

No. 43

John M. Browning
Semi-Automatic .22 Caliber Rifle
Inventor's Original Model

John M. Browning invented this trim little autoloader in 1913 and was granted U. S. Patent Numbers 1,065,341-2 June 24, 1913 and 1,083,384 January 6, 1914.

It has a tubular magazine positioned under the barrel with a cartridge capacity of 11 to 15 depending on the size shell for which the rifle is chambered. The later model which accepted any .22 cartridge holds 14 long rifle and 20 short.

It is a great favorite in shooting galleries and all types of plinking and target shooting. For many years it outsold all other .22 rifles combined.

The Model 06 was introduced in 1907 and possessed a 20 inch round barrel instead of the earlier 24 inch octagon.

In 1932 the Models 90 and 06 were renamed the Model 62 which is the same basic rifle with slightly different barrel dimensions. The Model 62 is still in production as of this printing and still a great favorite at the age of 70.

No. 39

Production Model of John M. Browning's 1890, .22 Caliber Rifle
Known as the Winchester Model 90
1890 to 1932

No. 40

Production Model of John M. Browning's 1890, .22 Caliber Rifle
Known as the Winchester Model 62
1932 to Present Time

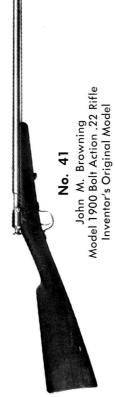

No. 41

John M. Browning
Model 1900 Bolt Action .22 Rifle
Inventor's Original Model

John M. Browning was granted Patent No. 632,094 August, 1899, for his Single Shot Bolt Action Rifle. It was listed in the Winchester 1899 catalog as the Winchester Model 1900 Single Shot Rifle. The action, of the bolt type consisting of very few parts, features simplicity in design, sturdiness and the usual reliability so characteristic of all his guns.

The rifle is cocked by pulling rearward on the firing pin which has a knurled knob to afford a good grip. The construction is so simple and inexpensive to produce that it has since been greatly copied by arms manufacturers all over the world.

It was produced as a take-down model and was designed to handle .22 short or .22 long rim fire cartridges and later for the .22 long rifle.

No. 44
Production Model of John M. Browning's Semi-Automatic .22 Rifle
Known as the F. N. .22 Caliber Automatic Rifle
1914 to 1957

No. 45
Production Model of John M. Browning's Semi-Automatic .22 Rifle
Known as the Remington Model 24 Automatic Rifle
1922 to 1935

No. 46
Production Model of John M. Browning's Semi-Automatic .22 Rifle
Known as the Remington Model 241 Automatic Rifle
1935 to 1951

No. 47
Current Production Model
Browning Semi-Automatic .22 Rifle
Grade I — .22 Long Rifle Caliber
1956 to Present Time

No. 48
Current Production Model
Browning Semi-Automatic .22 Rifle
Grade III — .22 Long Rifle Caliber
1956 to Present Time

No. 49
John M. Browning
Trombone Action .22 Caliber Repeating Rifle
Inventor's Original Model

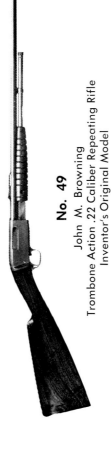

John M. Browning was not satisfied to stop with his extremely successful Model 90 .22 caliber Repeater and set about making a hammerless model which was completed in 1919 under Patent Number 1,424,553 granted August 1, 1922.

This happens to be one of the very few of his designs never produced or sold in this country, even though it has been in continual production by Fabrique Nationale d'Armes de Guerre of Liege, Belgium since October, 1922. Its distribution has included most of Europe, South America and Canada where it has been especially popular.

- 25 -

This rifle again illustrated the sound logic of its inventor since it was designed to specifically handle the small .22 caliber cartridge and possessed none of the characteristics essential only to a heavy caliber rifle.

Thus it possesses ideal proportion, neat slender lines, extremely compact action, light weight and such precise balance that trick shots often demonstrate their skill shooting it as if a pistol.

It is a non-mechanically locked, semi-automatic rifle in which the recoil is used to activate the breechblock in such a way that, when the bullet has left the barrel and no harmful gas remains in it, the mechanism ejects the empty shell, cocks the firing pin and introduces a fresh cartridge into the barrel.

After firing the first shot, the rifle is always cocked and ready for firing. Shooting continues as fast as the trigger can be pulled and released. Initial loading is through a port in the stock which houses the magazine.

The receiver is completely closed on the top and both sides; the bottom is covered by the trigger plate, but a small aperture in the plate permits ejection of the empty cartridges.

The barrel and forearm separate from the receiver in one simple movement so the over-all length of the gun, when taken down, is only 19¼ inches. Another feature of the model is the facility with which it can be stripped for cleaning in a matter of seconds without the aid of a single tool.

The rifle was first manufactured by Fabrique Nationale d'Armes de Guerre in 1914 for .22 caliber short and long rifle ammunition and produced continuously until December 31, 1957, by which time some 200,000 had been made.

Production rights for the United States were granted to the Remington Arms Company which first produced the rifle in 1922. The Remington rifle, known as the Model 24, was in continuous production until 1935 when a slightly modified version called the 241 took its place.

The 241 carried the identical mechanism but was made heavier and with a 24 inch barrel. The 241 was discontinued in 1951.

This Browning autoloader has always been one of the favorites in North America and Europe and practically held a monopoly as the shooting gallery preference.

The fact that ejection is downward prevents the hazard to gallery operators of having hot ejected shells flipping to the right where another shooter may be standing.

The Browning Arms Company reintroduced this autoloader to the United States with further refinements in 1956, this time in its own line. It was surprising to learn, after all its previous years of production in this country and ultimate discontinuance by Remington, that its popularity has continually accelerated, necessitating many successive increases in production facilities.

- 24 -

It is an unusually streamlined little rifle without exposed hammer and has one of the most convenient facilities for quick takedown yet to appear on a repeater. A large knurled screw head on the left side of the receiver is merely loosened and the repeater separates into two halves. Still, assembled it is uniquely rigid and gives excellent accuracy.

The rifle functions by loading the magazine tube, pumping rearward on the forearm, thereby releasing a cartridge from the spring loaded tubular magazine into the action carrier which, as the forearm is moved forward, elevates the cartridge so the breechblock can push the shell forward into the chamber. The gun is cocked during this operation.

After the rifle is fired, the empty shell is extracted from the chamber as the forearm moves rearward. As the breechblock reaches its open position, the ejector flips the spent shell through the ejection opening on the right side of the receiver.

All .22 rifle cartridges may be fired interchangeably in the rifle. It carries a 22-inch barrel and weighs approximately 4¾ pounds.

No. 50

Production Model of John M. Browning's Trombone Action
.22 Rifle — Known as the F. N. Trombone .22 Caliber Rifle
1922 to Present Time

No. 51

Jonathan Browning's Lathe

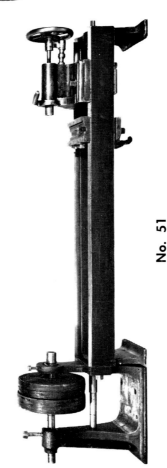

This lathe was hauled across the plains from Iowa by ox team on Jonathan Browning's trek to Ogden in 1851. It was for many years powered by a foot pedal and later adapted to operate from a small steam engine.

One might marvel even more at the accomplishments of John M. Browning when it is realized that this small lathe was one of the more modern pieces of equipment in the Browning shop throughout the development of many of John M. Browning's earlier models.

No. 52

John M. Browning
Machine for Loading Machine Gun Ammunition Belts

Inserting cartridges by hand in the web belting which feeds the ammunition to the machine gun was a slow and painstaking process. As Mr. Browning became more deeply involved in his development work on the machine gun, every functional test included the tedious task of hand positioning each cartridge in the feed belts.

He soon set about eliminating this time consuming operation. In 1899 he completed this machine which was the first suitable method of machine loading fabric ammunition belts.

The cartridges are supplied to the feed chute on the top of the loader and, by turning the crank, mechanically inserted and positioned in the belting.

Patent for this machine was filed November 15, 1899, and Patent Number 660,244 was granted October 23, 1900.

It is officially known as "Belt Loading Machine, Caliber .30."

No. 53

John M. Browning
Browning Automatic Rifle (B. A. R.)
Inventor's Original Model

The B. A. R. was invented just prior to the entry of the United States into World War I in 1917. United States Patent Number 1,293,022 covering this rifle was granted to John M. Browning February 4, 1919.

On April 6, 1917, when the headlines of our newspapers proclaimed that a state of war existed between the United States and the Imperial German Government, the combined Armed Forces of the United States had in their possession a total of 1,100 machine guns, all admittedly of outmoded design. At the same time, our Military's conservative estimate of its requirements was 100,000.

The situation was similarly serious with our Allies. The automatic machine type weapons of France and England were pitifully inadequate for their needs and furthermore considered inferior to the German guns in fire power.

By comparison, when the German Government declared war three years earlier, their armies possessed an estimated 62,000 highly improved Maxim type automatic weapons. By the time the United States entered the conflict, the German Armies' automatic fire power was at a staggering figure.

Thus the urgency on behalf of the United States and its Allies was perilously evident. John M. Browning had already anticipated the serious deficiency. When Government trials were called he brought two brand new guns to the competition. One he called the "Browning Heavy Water Cooled Machine Gun," and the other the "Browning Machine Rifle" (later known as the "Light Browning" and ultimately as the "Browning Automatic Rifle," or more commonly the "B. A. R.").

The B. A. R. was specifically designed to give our ground forces "Walking Fire" so urgently requested by the U. S. Ordnance Command.

The first public demonstration of the B. A. R. took place just outside of Washington, D. C., at Congress Heights, February 27, 1917. There were about 300 people present including many Senators, Congressmen, news reporters and high ranking military personnel from the United States, Great Britain, France, Belgium and Italy. The splendid performance of the B. A. R. at this showing led to its immediate adoption by our Government. Our Allies were equally impressed and immediately placed orders for large quantities of these rifles.

Production commenced quickly thereafter and Mr. Browning spent much time working with the Colt Company, Winchester and the Marlin-Rockwell Corporation, all of which were tooling up to make the rifle. From the date of the rifle's adoption to the signing of the Armistice the following year, over 52,000 B. A. R.'s had been shipped to the combat areas.

The B. A. R. saw first service in the hands of the United States 79th Division. An interesting observation is the fact that John M. Browning's son, Val A. Browning, was the first man to fire a B. A. R. in action against the German Armies.

The B. A. R. is an air-cooled, gas actuated automatic rifle. Chambered for the .30-06 cartridge, it can be fired from either the shoulder or hip. A lever on the receiver permits the rifle to be fired full automatic or semi-automatic. On full automatic the B. A. R. can be fired at a maximum rate of *480 rounds per minute* and its 20-round magazine can be emptied in 2½ seconds. The unloaded magazine can be detached and a fresh one inserted for resumption of firing in about the same time.

On this rifle Mr. Browning employed a gas port 6 inches behind the muzzle of the barrel which allows the powder gases following the bullet to escape into the gas cylinder and expand against a piston. The expanding gases force the piston rearward thereby operating the mechanism which feeds, fires, extracts and ejects the cartridge automatically. The B. A. R. weighs 17 pounds 6 ounces and its sights are graduated up to 1,600 yards.

An outstanding quality of the rifle was the simplicity of design — so simple that trained operators were able to dismantle and assemble the Browning rifle blindfolded. Its 70 pieces can be completely disassem-

bled and reassembled in 55 seconds. This simplicity was invaluable, under the circumstances facing our Government in World War I, implementing mass production of the rifle quickly.

After World War I production rights reverted to the Colt's Patent Firearms Company in the United States per previous arrangements with Mr. Browning. Fabrique Nationale d'Armes de Guerre was licensed to produce the rifle for Europe in 1920.

Many European countries acquired considerable quantities of the rifle. It was made for the Swedish Armies in 6.5mm, France in 7.5mm; England used American calibers and the Polish Army acquired models in caliber 7.92mm. It has been copied by other nations; many, regrettably, were produced by the Japanese in World War II.

In 1933 the Colt Company produced a peace time model for police and bank guard use called the Colt Monitor. It contained a shorter barrel and compensator.

The World War II "B. A. R.," marked the M 1918 A2, is heavier than the earlier models, weighing 19 pounds, and is equipped with flash hider and bipod. It carries the conventional stock without pistol grip. A decelerating device permits either a high or a low cyclic rate of fire, high at a rate of 550 rounds per minute, low at a rate of 350 rounds per minute. No mechanical provision is made for semi-automatic fire but, at low rate of fire, single shots can be discharged by pulling and quickly releasing the trigger.

Needless to say, the B. A. R. has proved to be a most effective, reliable and rugged weapon. The known results of infallible performance under actual combat conditions and the many voluntary testimonials from soldiers and marines extolling its dependability or accrediting it with having saved their lives and those of their buddies, could alone fill a volume.

Production is estimated in the millions.

No. 54

The F. N. — Browning
Light Automatic Rifle
Caliber .308

This rifle is included in this display as a subject of interest for those who may want to know more of modern developments in infantry weapons. As a result of the experiences gained on all the battle fronts during the second World War, the NATO Nations (North Atlantic Treaty Organization), within their broad defense plans, recommended certain uniformities in types of weapons, eliminating many of the complex problems of logistics ordinarily unavoidable during unified actions of different governments. These recommendations included a single infantry rifle and identical cartridge for all member nations.

The rifle was to be lightweight to serve better the increased mobility requirements of today's infantrymen. It was to provide full and semi-automatic firepower. It was to fire the lightest possible cartridge

John M. Browning
Automatic Machine Guns

In 1889, while attending a shoot at the Ogden Rifle Club, Mr. Browning became unusually interested in the movement or swaying of the foliage near the muzzle of a rifle after each shot was fired. He had seen this same movement many times before, but on this particular day it suddenly meant wasted energy to him, energy that might be harnessed to perform some of the operative functions of a gun.

This then was how he first conceived the idea which at the age of 34 stirred his interest in developing a fully automatic gun, one that would fire continuously as long as the trigger was depressed and a supply of cartridges could be fed through the action.

Within a month he had developed his first experimental model. On this model he used a concave cap with a hole in the center of it which fit directly in front of the muzzle. When a bullet was fired and passed through the hole in the cap, the expanding gases following the bullet forced the cap forward (just as they had forced the foliage forward in his earlier observations). A rod connected this cap to a spring loaded operating lever attached to the action. As the cap moved forward, it pulled the operating lever forward. Then the spring would return the lever rearward to its locked position and the cap to the front of the muzzle. The result was a mechanism performing the identical function of a hand-operated lever action repeater, automatically.

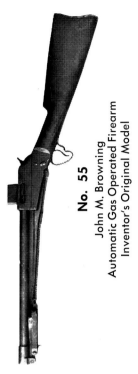

No. 55
John M. Browning
Automatic Gas Operated Firearm
Inventor's Original Model

His second experimental model followed almost immediately. In this model Mr. Browning drilled a hole through the underside of the barrel to permit the gas pressure to enter and activate a small lever connected to the action.

As the lever moves downward and forward in an arc, then back to normal position, the cycle of extraction, ejection, loading, locking, cocking and firing takes place. The action is continuous as long as the trigger remains depressed.

Such is the appearance and function of the world's first successful automatic, gas operated firearm. It could fire 16 shots a second using caliber .44-40 black powder cartridges.

providing effective stopping power at relatively close ranges and still satisfactory accuracy up to 600 yards. It was to incorporate a larger magazine capacity and the ammunition was to serve both for rifles and machine guns.

After much discussion, the member nations settled on the .308 caliber (7.62mm) cartridge with a 144 grain bullet and a cartridge length of 2.8 inches.

The respective NATO Nations have yet to settle on a preference of rifle, although many thus far favor and have placed large orders for the model displayed here.

This model will fire either semi or full automatic, each magazine holding 20 rounds. The rifle is gas operated with an adjustable regulator to insure smooth operation without excessive recoil. The breechblock is mechanically locked during firing and does not unlock until the bullet has left the barrel. The breechblock is in forward position when the trigger is pressed, thereby avoiding disturbance to aim caused when a breechblock must move forward.

The complete cycle of firing, extraction, ejection, cocking and loading is continuous. Due to the placement of the gas cylinder above the barrel and other design characteristics, the rifle has unusual stability with no tendency to jerk skyward as automatic fire continues. Stripping for cleaning and maintenance requires no tools. Accessories include bayonet, flash hider, grenade launcher and folding tripod.

This rifle is now in production at Fabrique Nationale d'Armes de Guerre where it was designed.

One might wonder as to the name since neither the Browning family nor Company claim any credit for its design or have a financial interest in its production. Perhaps the following excerpt from the descriptive brochure on the rifle will best explain the name "F. N.— Browning":

"The designer of this weapon is Mr. D. D. Saive, Chief of Weapon Design and Development at F. N., who, in the course of his career has been able to gain an extensive experience in automatic weapons. For many years he collaborated with the great inventor, J. M. Browning. It is not surprising therefore that one finds in the rifle in several places, features which first appeared in Browning mechanisms (gas intake and piston, wire spring actuated extractor, recoil spring housed in the buttstock) and thus it can be said that the weapon is of Browning inspiration, — a natural consequence of more than fifty years of continuous collaboration between the F. N. and Browning companies.

"In addition, the manner in which it fulfills the needs and desires of the man who actually fires the gun relates it to the family of arms created by the great American inventor, all possessing this quality to the highest degree which explains the favor they continue to enjoy long after their creation."

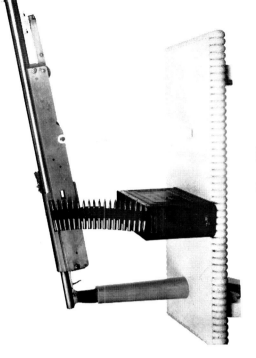

No. 57

John M. Browning
Model 1895 Automatic Machine Gun
Inventor's Original Model

From this prototype came the Browning Model 1895 Machine Gun. Patent Numbers 544,657-61 were granted on this gun August 20, 1895. Arrangements were made with the Colt's Company for its manufacture the same year. This gun, like its forerunner, was a gas operated automatic type, firing over 400 rounds per minute.

It employs a gas port in the underside of the barrel near the muzzle, like his second experimental automatic gun, which allows the expanding powder gases following the bullet to push against a piston which is hung beneath the barrel. The force acting on the piston pushes it downward and rearward in an arc and thereby operates the mechanism through a series of connecting rods, levers and springs. When the mechanism is activated, it feeds, fires, extracts and ejects the cartridges automatically. The firing cycle is continuous as long as the trigger is depressed and ammunition is supplied.

The unusual movement of the piston which swings in a half arc beneath the barrel accounts for the nickname, "Potato Digger." It has a very heavy barrel to prevent heating too rapidly and was adapted to both the .30-40 Krag and the 6mm Lee cartridges.

The Model 95 was tested by the Navy in competitive trials in January, 1896. Following completion of the tests a report was submitted by the Inspector of Ordnance to the Secretary of the Navy which stated in part:

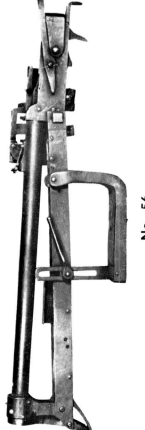

No. 56

John M. Browning
First Gas Operated Machine Gun
Inventor's Original Model

Through further experiments, Mr. Browning refined the principle and in 1890 produced his first gas operated machine gun. He was granted Patent No. 471,783 March 29, 1892. It fired the Government .45-70 cartridge at the rate of six shots per second. With mount it weighed 40 pounds.

On this model Mr. Browning incorporated a bracket on the muzzle end of the barrel on which a lever is hung on a pivot so that one end of the lever forms a cap which faces over the front of the muzzle. Somewhat similar to his first experimental gun, this cap contains an aperture corresponding to the bore of the barrel to allow passage of the bullet. The muzzle bracket acts as a spacer to keep the lever cap a short distance forward of the muzzle, thereby forming a small enclosed gas chamber between the end of the barrel and the cap.

When a shot is fired the expanding gases following the bullet force pressure against the cap, pushing it forward. The cap lever in turn is connected to the action by a series of connecting rods and levers. Thus the forward motion of the muzzle cap is the initial impetus which carries through the mechanism, permitting extraction, ejection, feeding, loading and firing of the cartridges automatically.

The model on display was brought to the attention of Colt's Patent Firearms Company by a hand written letter dated November 22, 1890. It was demonstrated at the Colt factory shortly thereafter. Even in that day this forged blackened and anvil marked piece of equipment presented a somewhat dubious appearance to the Colt and military officials present. Web belting to hold the cartridges had been made by an Ogden tent maker named John Hoxer.

The rate of fire had been stepped up to between six to ten rounds per second for this test. During the test, the barrel turned a luminous blue from the intense heat of continuous firing, but in little more than three minutes 1800 rounds of ammunition had been fired without a single stoppage. Needless to say, a formerly equivocal audience stood temporarily in frozen amazement before genuine elation took hold of everyone. It was quite a startling exhibition for a group of men who had theretofore been familiar with nothing more automatic in type than the hand-cranking Gatling gun.

"The Colt gun is exceedingly simple in construction, and has not more than 100 separate parts, a surprisingly small number, considering the type. It has been designed with great care and with due attention to the often conflicting requirements of lightness and strength, so that with maximum weight of 40 pounds no part, with the single exception of the extractor, has been known to break in the course of a number of very severe tests . . . In the course of the experiment, for marking the sight, several hundred shots were fired, with most gratifying results as to accuracy."

Shortly thereafter the Navy submitted an initial order for 50 of these guns from the Colt's Company. This was the first purchase of a fully automatic weapon ever made by the United States Government. These guns, in the hands of the Marines, saved the Foreign Legation in Peking during the Boxer Rebellion. They were also used by the Navy in Cuba during the Spanish-American War. The Model 95 was soon to acquire a new name, that of "The Browning Peacemaker."

At the outbreak of World War I, the Model 95 comprised a great portion of the United States machine gun arsenal. However, these guns were soon replaced with a much superior Browning recoil operated machine gun, known as the Model 1917 Browning Heavy Water-Cooled Machine Gun, Caliber 30.

No. 58

John M. Browning
Model 1917 Browning .30 Caliber Machine Gun
Inventor's Original Model

No. 58 is the inventor's original model.

No. 59 is the first Factory Tool Room prototype of the Model 1917. It was the first Browning Machine Gun to arrive in France during World War I, and was used by Lieutenant Val A. Browning, son of the inventor, to instruct Machine Gun Crews of the American Expeditionary Force.

The Browning Heavy Model 1917 Machine Gun was actually a slightly modified version of Mr. Browning's Model 1901 which he invented in 1900. United States Patent No. 678,937 was granted July 23, 1901. All of the basic features of the Model 1917 were specified in this earlier patent. However, lack of interest by the United States Government in military weapons at that time and the demand for Mr. Browning's services in the development of sporting arms prompted him to set aside further work on the Model 1901 until 1910.

At this time he changed it to eject the fired cartridge from the bottom instead of the right side and increased its rate of fire above that of his first model. An additional Patent No. 1,293,021 was granted Mr. Browning, February 4, 1919, to cover these improvements on this gun.

The 1917 is a short recoil operated, fully automatic machine gun chambered for the .30-06 cartridge and capable of firing more than 600 rounds per minute. In the short recoil system, the barrel and the breechblock are locked together when the gun is fired and are allowed to recoil together for a short distance to permit the bullet to clear the barrel and the gas pressure to diminish. They are then unlocked and the breechblock alone continues to recoil during which energy is stored in the springs which return all parts to their normal or battery positions.

During the recoil of the breechblock, the fired case is extracted from the barrel, ejected downward, and a fresh cartridge is fed into the chamber and fired as the breechblock returns to battery. The firing cycle is continuous as long as the trigger is depressed and a supply of ammunition is available.

The barrel is encased in a jacket which is filled with water to prevent the barrel from over heating. With water jacket filled, the gun weighs only 37 pounds, thereby giving it excellent mobility.

In early 1917 when it was inevitable that the United States would be an active participant in World War I, the Government sent an urgent request to gun designers for a new machine gun to replace a very inadequate and outmoded arsenal.

Mr. Browning took his heavy water-cooled machine gun, along with the B. A. R., to Washington, D. C., where he publicly demonstrated them at Congress Heights on February 27, 1917. The B. A. R. was immediately adopted, but the Government wanted to give the water-cooled gun more extensive tests because of the more severe treatment this weapon would likely receive in service.

In May, 1917, an official test was held at the Government Proving Grounds, Springfield Armory. The Browning Water-Cooled Gun exceeded all expectations by firing 20,000 rounds at a cyclic rate of over 600 per minute without a single malfunction or broken part. Mr. Browning then proceeded to fire an additional 20,000 rounds with the same results. The extraordinary showing led some to believe that the weapon was specially prepared for the test to achieve such results. To expel possible doubt, Mr. Browning called for a second model which actually bettered the original test by operating continuously for 48 minutes and 12 seconds.

After this astounding demonstration, a board appointed by the Secretary of War to study the problem of machine gun supply recommended the immediate adoption of the Browning Heavy .30 Caliber Model, stating that it, and the already accepted B. A. R. were the "most effective guns of their type known to the members." Not only was the ruggedness and performance of the new gun outstanding, but again its simplicity of design further influenced the Government in its adoption. It contained a minimum of parts and like the B. A. R. was so easy to assemble and disassemble operators were taught to perform the function blindfolded.

The Government contracted with three companies for the production of the Browning Water-Cooled Model: Colt's, Remington and Westinghouse. Surprisingly, Westinghouse had the best production record, although production differences were not a true measure of performance. Remington was delayed due to previous contracts for arms with Russia. Colt's similarly had a contract to complete with the British Government. In addition, Colt's spent a great deal of time in the preparation of drawings and precision gauges for the other two manufacturing plants.

Between the tests in 1917 and the Armistice, just over one year later, approximately 43,000 of these machine guns were delivered. Westinghouse accounted for 30,150, Remington 12,000 and the Colt's Company 600.

The first combat use of these weapons was by the 79th Division. The following report was sent to General Pershing by the Commanding Officer of a small detachment of this Division:

"During the five days that my four guns were in action, they fired approximately 13,000 rounds of ammunition. They had very rough handling due to the fact that the Infantry made constant halts, causing the guns to be placed in the mud. The condition of the ground on these five days was very muddy, and considerable grit and other foreign material got into the working parts of the gun. The guns became rusty on the outside due to the rain and the wet weather, but in every instance when the guns were called upon to fire, they fired perfectly. During all this time I had only one stoppage, and this was due to a broken ejector."

The .30 Caliber Browning Heavy Machine Gun had hardly been introduced overseas in 1918 when General John Pershing, Commanding Officer of the American Expeditionary Forces, called for a much heavier and more powerful machine gun cartridge than the .30 caliber to meet the increased threat of armored combat vehicles.

A .50 caliber cartridge was finally developed which gave an 800 grain bullet a muzzle velocity of 2,750 feet per second. To shoot this powerful load Mr. Browning developed the Browning .50 Caliber Water-Cooled Machine Gun.

It had the same basic features of operation as the .30 Caliber, but through the use of a unique oil buffer the necessary strengthening

of the gun was accomplished without a nearly proportional increase in weight, an important factor which increased the gun's utility. The oil buffer absorbed the excess energy of recoil thereby effectively reducing undue strain on the parts. In addition, the buffer provided a means of controlling the rate of fire.

Mr. Browning also incorporated double spade grips on the .50 Caliber instead of the pistol grip used on the smaller .30 Caliber. The original .50 Caliber Browning Water-Cooled Machine Gun without mount weighed 82 pounds when the 16-pint water jacket was filled.

This .50 Caliber version was developed by Mr. Browning, including the completion of successful firing tests, in slightly over one year, even though the cartridge it was to shoot had not yet been developed at its commencement. It was at the termination of successful Government trials that he made his now famous reply to the query of the press as to what he attributed this achievement:

"One drop of genius in a barrel of sweat wrought this miracle."

Mr. Browning continued his development work on the automatic guns even though World War I came quickly to an end. "There will come another war," he firmly maintained, "and the skies will swarm with warriors. This country must not once again be caught without the very latest defensive weapons, and pay the terrific price of trying to do, in a few short months, what other nations have spent long patient years in doing."

He had already made an air-cooled model of his .30 Caliber Machine Gun, weighing only 22 pounds with a rate of fire increased to approximately 700 rounds per minute. This weapon was the first in this country to be successfully affixed to pursuit planes so that the pilot could look along his sights and aim the gun by maneuvering his ship. To do this the firing mechanism of the gun was synchronized with the motor of the plane so that the stream of bullets could pass through the revolving propeller without hitting the blades.

Later the .50 Caliber Browning was converted to an air-cooled model. Much lightened in weight, the .50 Caliber fired an 800 grain bullet at a muzzle velocity of 2,700 feet per second — sufficient to penetrate a 1 1/8-inch piece of armor plate at 25 yards.

Both models, known as the Browning .30M2 and .50M2, were exclusively the aircraft machine guns of our Air Force throughout World War II as well as more recent campaigns and to this date continue as part of our Air Force armament.

A report from the Commanding Officer of the Army Air Force dated November, 1943, specifically pointed out the performance of these guns. With particular reference to the .50 Caliber, this report states the following:

"This weapon, together with its ammunition, is the backbone of offensive and defensive guns for American aircraft and was brought to such a state of perfection by

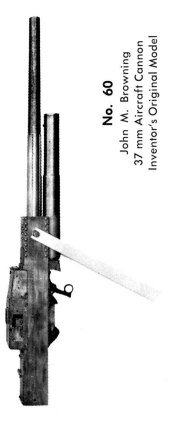

No. 60
John M. Browning
37 mm Aircraft Cannon
Inventor's Original Model

Before World War I had officially ended, Army Ordnance commenced work toward the development of a 37mm Aircraft Cannon. Many difficulties were encountered as its design progressed, and nearly three years later they still found it impossible to fire over six or seven rounds through the model without a stoppage.

On November 29, 1920, at the request of Chief of Aircraft Armament Design, Mr. Browning went to Washington, D. C., accompanied by Fred T. Moore, production manager of the Colt's Company, to visually inspect the model and see if they could suggest changes to improve its function.

After a close examination of the model, it was concluded by both Mr. Browning and Mr. Moore that the design was unworkable. Their recommendation to the Army was to discontinue further work on the model and start anew.

John M. Browning, then 65, was not anxious to undertake such a project on top of his other work, but at the insistence of General Williams, Chief of Ordnance at the time, he finally agreed to give the matter further thought.

He returned to Ogden and, as it turned out, commenced designing the model on display here almost immediately. It was completed in early 1921 just about three months from the date he undertook the project. The Cannon was first tested just east of Ogden. During the tests the projectiles were fired against the imposing quartzite cliffs readily visible from the city.

Shortly thereafter it was demonstrated to Army officials at the Aberdeen Proving Ground in Maryland. It is interesting to note that from the first trial the Cannon encountered no functional difficulties.

Patent Nos. 1,525,065-66 and 67 cover this model and subsequent models. This Cannon fired a one pound projectile having a muzzle velocity of 1,400 feet per second at the rate of 150 rounds per minute.

Shortly thereafter Mr. Browning designed two additional models each firing heavier projectiles, the first at 2,000 feet per second, the second at approximately 3,000 feet per second.

the Ordnance Department during the years of peace prior to the present conflict that it has enabled the Army Air Force, the U. S. Navy and Marine Corps to show a definite superiority in aircraft gun power throughout the global war."

Similar reports were received during the Tunisian Campaign when 72 enemy aircraft were destroyed by 35 fighter planes with less than 200 rounds of ammunition expended per gun.

An interesting sidelight relative to its effectiveness was discovered in correspondence recovered in Germany after World War II. It was part of a congratulatory message from Field Marshal Goering to General Rommel on one of Rommel's brilliant maneuvers during the African Campaign resulting in the capture of Tobruk. Along with its capture, Rommel seized thousands of Browning .50 Caliber Machine Guns just unloaded from an Allied convoy. In so many words, the congratulatory message stated: "If the German Air Force had had the Browning .50 Caliber, the Battle of Britain would have turned out differently."

In correspondence with George M. Chinn, Colonel U. S. Marine Corps, who authored the comprehensive and authentic volumes of "The Machine Gun" for the Bureau of Ordnance, Department of the Navy, he passed along the following information which reveals a closely similar appraisal to that of Goering's: "Students of warfare are generally in agreement that the most far-reaching single military decision made in the 20th Century was when a small group of British officers, shortly before World War II, decided to mount ten caliber .303 Brownings on their Hurricane Fighters. This single act undoubtedly brought about the turning point of the War."

Other highly effective models of the .50 Caliber Browning are the Water-Cooled Infantry, the Water-Cooled Anti-Aircraft Single and Twin Mount, and the Air-Cooled Tank Guns. Latest aircraft models have been stepped up to a cyclic rate of fire of 1,300 rounds per minute in the .30 Caliber and 950 per minute in the .50 Caliber.

To date not less than 66 known and different models of the Browning recoil operated machine gun have been made for the U. S. and 13 Allied Nations.

During World War II it was produced by the following Companies: Colt's Patent Firearms Company, High Standard Company, Savage Arms Corporation, Buffalo Arms Corporation, Frigidaire, AC Spark Plug, Brown-Lipe-Chappin, Saginaw Division of General Motors Corporation, and Kelsey Hayes Wheel Company. Total production figures are not available but estimated in the millions. General Motors alone produced more than 1,000,000.

It is now quite unanimously recognized that most John M. Browning designs were far in advance of his time. When one realizes that this basic machine gun was invented three years before Orville Wright flew the first airplane and a number of years before Henry Ford's Model T became greatly recognized, one has an interesting gauge by which to measure the unique capacity of this man.

However, it was at about this time that all interest in military weapons in this country ceased. No monies had been allocated for such projects and, in fact, general hostility was in evidence against any advocation of military preparedness.

All drawings and the three successful models of Mr. Browning's Cannon were merely filed away by the Army for future need. Accordingly, as Mr. Browning had predicted before starting on his first model, he never saw his Cannon in actual production.

It was not until 1935 that the United States Government renewed interest in the Cannon and the first were produced. The World War II model was known officially as the M-9 and was principally used for aircraft. It was either mounted to fire through the hub of the propeller or from the wings. With little modification, it could be fed from either right or left.

Operation is on the long recoil principle. Both recoil and counter recoil are controlled by a hydro-spring buffing mechanism. The breech lock is of the vertical, sliding wedge type. When the projectile is fired and driven down the bore of the barrel, the barrel, breechblock and locking frame, all locked together, recoil rearward ten inches before the breechblock cams downward. In turn, the hammer is cocked, the empty case ejected, a new shell loaded, the mechanism locked and again readied for firing.

The Browning Cannon was actually used in rather limited quantities by the Army Air Corps which had ultimately determined that such heavy armament was not entireley practical or essential on its planes. Higher altitude flying had become more and more necessary as War progressed, thus it was important that weight be kept to the absolute minimum. The Aircraft Cannon weighed 405 pounds, more than that of eight Browning .50 caliber Aircraft Machine Guns.

The Cannon saw much use in the hands of the Russians and, during their more critical defensive combat periods with Germany, became their primary aerial cannon. Many thousand were sent to Russia by our Government along with the Bel Aircobra planes on which they were mounted. The high velocity, armor-piercing projectiles used in the Cannon proved most effective against the heavy German tanks.

John M. Browning Automatic Pistols

Mr. Browning became interested in automatic type hand guns in 1894 and completed his first prototype in early 1895. Up to that date and for some years thereafter, no pistols of this type, properly termed semi-automatic, other than of his design, were manufactured in America. A few designs had been made in Europe in small quantities, but they were heavy and cumbersome and had received very little favorable recognition. So he had again pioneered an untouched field and in a very short time, through his prolific and varied developments, started a new industry on two continents.

Since the Colt's Patent Firearms Company had already established a close working relationship with Mr. Browning in producing his machine guns, it was natural that this Company become the manufacturer of his automatic pistols in this country. This arrangement had its origin with an agreement dated July 24, 1896, and from that date to the present no known Colt automatic pistol has been of other than John M. Browning design.

Fabrique Nationale d'Armes de Guerre of Liege, Belgium, was licensed to manufacture his pistols for the European market. Although Mr. Browning's first four designs were licensed to the Colt's Company, the Belgian manufacturer was the first to commence production. Their first model, a .32 caliber, appeared on the market in 1899.

The Colt's Company followed quickly with a .38 caliber which reached the market in early 1900.

These two Companies produced practically all of the Browning designs, and it can be concluded that a major portion of all automatic type pistols produced in the world were made by these Companies for many years.

It has been said that as patents expired on his many models Mr. Browning's hand guns have been copied by more manufacturers and in more countries than is believed the case with most other firearms combined.

All of his many models manufactured by the Colt's Company were identified by the Colt name, but for many years also carried the words "Browning Patent."

Fabrique Nationale, on the other hand, chose to designate his pistols of their manufacture by the name Browning, as they have all of his many guns to this date. For this reason, the name Browning became far more widely known in Europe than in this country. Since shortly after the turn of the century, the word "browning" has appeared in French dictionaries as a common noun, defined as an automatic pistol.

As seems apparent with most of Mr. Browning's designs, the following descriptions of his pistols will further emphasize their immunity to age and obsolescence.

It is generally accepted that more pistols of Browning design have been manufactured since the origin of the semi-automatic than all other makes in the world combined.

No. 61

John M. Browning
First Semi-Automatic Pistol
Inventor's Original Model — Invented 1895

Mr. Browning completed this pistol quickly after his first in the latter part of 1895. It is interesting to note that patents covering his first model, this pistol and four subsequent designs were all issued on the same day, April 20, 1897. This model is identified by Patent No. 580,926.

This pistol differs from his first hand gun in that operation is accomplished by the blow back principle whereby the expanding gases of the fired cartridge act directly on the breechbolt through the cartridge case, forcing both rearward, effecting extraction, ejection and cocking during the movement. An action spring located above the barrel provides the energy to return the breechbolt to its forward position, and in the fractional interval during its forward motion, a fresh cartridge is picked from the magazine and chambered for immediate firing. The process is continuous until all ammunition in the gun is expended.

The slide and breechbolt are integral and, as with any blow back action, must provide sufficient inertia to delay rearward movement until the bullet leaves the barrel and gas pressures have partially diminished.

This gun was test fired by Colt officials at Hartford, Connecticut, January 14, 1896, after which Mr. Browning returned to Ogden to make minor modifications. It was again delivered to the Colt's Company May 3, 1896, in its present form.

This design was never manufactured but is very similar in operation to the first Browning pistol manufactured by Fabrique Nationale d'Armes de Guerre, the .32 caliber hammerless, No. 66.

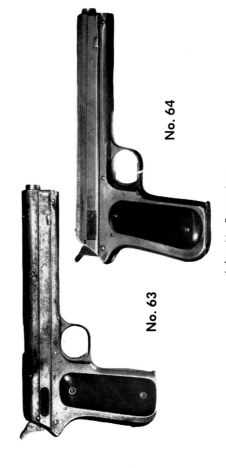

No. 63

No. 64

John M. Browning
Forerunners of the Colt Model 1900
Inventor's Original Models — Invented 1896

These two pistols were invented by Mr. Browning in 1896 and are covered by U. S. Patent Numbers 580,924 dated April 20, 1897, and 708,794 dated September 9, 1902.

This was the first of Mr. Browning's many semi-automatic pistol designs, invented in 1895 and covered by Patent No. 580,923 issued April 20, 1897. Old records reveal that this model was shown to the Colt's Company on July 3, 1895, and test fired on that day in Hartford, Connecticut, by John M. Browning and Colt officials, J. H. Hall and C. J. Ehbets. Hall was then President of the Colt's Company.

It is a .38 caliber, gas operated type with exposed hammer. A gas vent is located on the top of the barrel a short distance from the muzzle over which is positioned a piston lever, linked to the breechbolt. As the expanding powder gases pass through the vent sufficient pressure is exerted on the lever to force it upward and rearward in an arc. This rearward movement opens the breechbolt, causing it to extract and eject the fired cartridge and cock the hammer. Then as the lever and breechblock return to their forward position, a fresh cartridge is fed into the chamber, readying the pistol for the next round.

The design proved very successful in operation, and production rights were acquired by the Colt's Company. Had not Mr. Browning so quickly developed other designs, it probably would have been commercially produced, but it was, nevertheless, the corner stone of the agreement with the Colt's Company which led to their production of great numbers of his designs.

No. 62

John M. Browning
Second Semi-Automatic Pistol
Inventor's Original Model — Invented 1895

No. 66

John M. Browning
Model 1900, .32 Caliber Semi-Automatic Pistol
Known as the F. N. .32 Caliber M 1900
Inventor's Original Model — Invented 1897

This design was completed by Mr. Browning in 1897. U. S. Patent Number 621,747, of March 21, 1899, identified this pistol.

It is a semi-automatic, hammerless type utilizing the blow back action described under Mr. Browning's second pistol (No. 62). It contained numerous improved modifications, however, particularly suited to a smaller caliber hand gun. It provides a magazine capacity of 7 cartridges, has a 4 inch barrel and weighs 22 ounces.

Mr. Browning first showed this model to officials of the Colt's Company on September 21, 1897. He then sent the model to Fabrique Nationale d'Armes de Guerre (F. N.) in Liege, Belgium. This Company was licensed to manufacture the pistol for all markets outside of the United States and actual production commenced in 1899.

Thus this model was the first Browning designed automatic pistol to be manufactured.

It was immediately popular and sold in great numbers, but one incident greatly enhanced its popularity shortly after its introduction. This occurred when a band of French Apaches or bandits, armed with the gun, were able to withstand for many days a siege by Parisian police armed with old fashioned revolvers.

The pistol was rather quickly adopted by the Belgian police force and army and was extensively used by the police of other nations throughout Europe. It was manufactured until 1910 when it was replaced by a more modern design of Mr. Browning's.

No. 67, on display, is the actual 100,000th production model completed by F. N. This production figure was attained on August 4, 1904.

No. 68, on display, is the actual 500,000th pistol from the F. N. factory, completed in 1909.

This .32 caliber automatic pistol was the first Browning product manufactured by the Belgian factory and the first of his designs to be manufactured outside of the United States. It marked the beginning of a friendly and successful association between Mr. Browning and Fabrique Nationale d'Armes de Guerre which has continued between the Browning Arms Company and the Belgian factory to this day.

They are the first Browning designs to employ a positively locked, recoiling barrel. The top of the barrel has transverse ribs and recesses which fit into corresponding ribs and recesses in the slide. Each end of the barrel is attached to a link which, when the barrel is in battery position, presses the barrel tightly upward against the slide and thereby interlocks these ribs and recesses. Thus, at firing, the barrel and slide are locked together with a secure seal at the breech.

Upon firing, the barrel and the slide recoil, locked together, for a short distance until the bullet has left the barrel and gas pressures diminish. Then barrel links draw the barrel downward out of the locking recesses, freeing the barrel. The slide alone continues to move rearwardly accomplishing the extraction, ejection and cocking functions in the process. The slide returns to its forward or firing position by spring tension chambering a new cartridge from the magazine during this forward movement.

Both of these pistols are designed to eject from the top and were later modified to eject from the side. They were the prototypes closely followed in the design of Colt's first pistol, the Model 1900.

No. 65

John M. Browning
Model 1900, .38 Caliber Semi-Automatic Pistol
Known as the Colt .38 Caliber M 1900
Inventor's Original Model — Invented 1896

Invented in 1896 and covered by U. S. Patent Number 580,924 issued April 20, 1897, this model became the first commercially produced semi-automatic pistol in America.

This design was submitted to Colt's Patent Firearms Company June 29, 1896, and fired by Colt officials on that day. It was then shown at the Mechanical Fair in Boston and returned to the Colt Factory on March 28, 1898. Mr. Grover, then President of Colt's, selected this model to become the first Colt produced semi-automatic pistol.

It was first manufactured as a sporting type hand gun and in 1902 a military version, known as the Model L Military, was introduced. Late in 1903 a shorter barrel design, named the Pocket Model, was placed on the market.

All three models, as commercially produced, had an exposed hammer and were chambered for the caliber .38 A. C. P. cartridge. The design incorporated the locked breech, operated on the short recoil principle and, excepting that it ejected the spent cartridge from the side rather than the top, was closely similar functionally to its forerunners, Numbers 63 and 64, just described.

No. 69
John M. Browning
Model 1903, "Pocket" .32 Caliber Semi-Automatic
Known as the Colt Model 1903 "Pocket" .32 and .380
Inventor's Original Model — Invented 1901

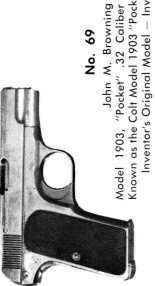

In initial negotiations with Mr. Browning the Colt's Company had decided to manufacture his designs of the recoil operated, locked breech type. This brought about Mr. Browning's decision to provide his .32 caliber blow-back design (No. 66) for Fabrique Nationale's manufacture. However, as discussed earlier, the F. N. model had proved a fantastic success and the Colt's Company quickly became interested in a blow-back version to complement their .38 caliber model.

Early in 1901 Colt's asked Mr. Browning if he could provide them a .32 caliber design with the blow-back type action. The displayed model (Patent Number 747,585 of December 22, 1903) was submitted to Colt officials on July 16, 1901, and immediately accepted.

The agreement between the Brownings and the Colt's Company on this particular pistol was quite unique in that, in addition to the usual clauses, it stipulated certain standards in materials and workmanship and further specified that the Colt's Company would endeavor to sell the pistol at a price successfully competitive with revolvers of the period.

This automatic was first placed on the market in June of 1903 and became an immediate success. An identical model in the .380 caliber was announced in 1909.

The M 1903 is very similar in operation to Mr. Browning's Model 1900, .32 caliber (No. 66) but contains several improvements.

It is very easily assembled and disassembled. The barrel is above the reaction spring and locked to the frame by a threaded section. Unlocking is accomplished by a partial turn of the barrel, although this is not possible unless the slide is drawn nearly all the way rearward. In this pistol Mr. Browning first employed his now well known grip safety and a manual thumb safety on the left side of the frame.

This design carries a magazine capacity of 8 cartridges, has a 3¾ inch barrel and weighs only 24 ounces.

Colt's finally discontinued production in 1946 after close to one million had been manufactured.

No. 70
John M. Browning
Model 1903 Military Semi-Automatic Pistol
Adopted as Official Swedish Military Model
Inventor's Original Model — Invented 1901

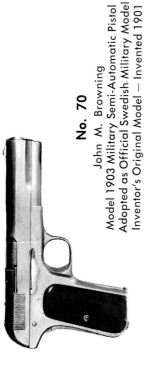

From the records it is hard to determine whether this model, produced by F. N., or the Colt "Pocket" 1903, just described, was developed first by Mr. Browning. Both are closely identical and were submitted in the same year, 1901.

In this year F. N. was anxious to place a military style pistol on the market, and John M. Browning responded with this version.

As with the 1903 Colt "Pocket" Model, this pistol has the quick disassembly feature, the mechanical safety and grip safety. A hammer is provided but is fully enclosed by the slide. It weighs 32 ounces and has a 5 inch barrel. Also, the slide is made to stay to the rear after the last shot is fired. It is closed mechanically by an action release lever located on the right side of the frame.

Fabrique Nationale ammunition technicians developed a new cartridge for this pistol, a 9mm rimless type called the "9mm Browning Long."

The pistol was equipped with a lanyard loop and later with an attachable stock holster. Throughout Europe it was generally known as the "Pistolet Automatique Browning Grand Modele."

The pistol was adopted as the official Swedish military side arm and manufactured by Swedish Government Arsenals as well as Fabrique Nationale d'Armes de Guerre.

Several thousand of this model were supplied to Russia during the Russo-Japanese War.

No. 71
John M. Browning
.45 Caliber Military Model Hammerless
Inventor's Original Model — Invented 1905

United States Ordnance commenced to show interest in a .45 caliber automatic pistol as early as 1905. This model, invented in 1905, was one of a number of prototypes developed by Mr. Browning leading up to the design ultimately accepted by the Army, Navy and Marine Corps.

This design is basically similar to the Model 1911 (No. 72) except that it employs an internal hammer rather than external.

At the insistence of the United States Cavalry, the Government selected the exposed hammer type as the ultimate official U. S. Government sidearm.

This pistol was never commercially manufactured.

No. 72

John M. Browning
Government .45 Caliber Automatic
Model 1911
Inventor's Original Model — Invented 1905

Invented in 1905, this is the original or pilot model of what has become the official U. S. military side arm for 48 years. Patent Numbers 984,519 and 1,070,582 pertaining to this pistol were issued to Mr. Browning in February, 1911, and August, 1913, respectively.

The Colt's Company commenced commercial production in late 1905 with first models reaching the market in the spring of 1906.

Government trials on various automatic type pistols commenced as early as 1907. Minor design changes were made on this model in 1909 and 1910 until finalized and officially accepted in 1911.

This model is a semi-automatic, short recoil type pistol utilizing a locked breech and exposed hammer. When fired, the slide recoils rearward and remains locked to the barrel for a short distance. Then the barrel unlocks from the slide which continues its rearward movement, ejecting the fired case and sliding over the exposed hammer, thus cocking it. Returning to its forward position under spring tension, the slide picks a fresh cartridge from the magazine and chambers it ready for firing. The magazine, housed within the grip, holds seven cartridges. The model incorporates many safety features including the unique Browning grip safety which prevents firing unless pressure is exerted at the rear of the grip. Safety release is accomplished automatically when the gun is gripped in actual firing but makes it most difficult to otherwise or by accident discharge the gun.

At the competitive trials held on March 3, 1911, under the supervision of the Ordnance Command, the following stipulations were set down: Six thousand rounds were to be fired through each type of

pistol under consideration. Firing was to take place in **series** of 100 after which the arm was permitted to cool for five minutes before the next series commenced. After each 1,000 rounds each pistol was to be cleaned and oiled.

The Browning model completed the test without a single malfunction. Then freak loads were tested including underloads, overloads and cartridges with thin primers. The model was then made to rust and finally subjected to fine sand and grit tests. Through all this, no failure to operate occurred and upon careful inspection not a single part showed signs of deterioration. It was the first time a small arm had completed an official government test with a perfect record.

The report of the examining board submitted March 20, 1911, reads as follows: "The Board recommends that the Colt Caliber .45 Automatic Pistol of the design submitted to the Board for tests be adopted for use by foot and mounted troops in the military services in consequence of its marked superiority to the present service revolvers, and to any pistol, of its extreme reliability and endurance, of its ease of disassembly, of its accuracy and of its fulfillment of all essential requirements."

Orders from the Chief of Ordnance of the General Staff and Secretary of War dated March 29, 1911, made the adoption of the Model 1911 official.

Between this date and the beginning of World War I, few more than 100,000 had been taken by the U. S. Armed Forces. Confronted with a determined need for some 2,000,000 pistols and with Colt's capacity at maximum only 30,000 a month, the Ordnance Department quickly made provisions for the following companies to tool up and commence production in the following quantities:

Remington Arms Co.	150,000
Winchester Arms Co.	100,000
Burroughs Adding Machine Co.	250,000
Lanston Monotype Machine Co.	100,000
National Cash Register.	500,000
A. J. Savage Munitions Co.	100,000
Savage Arms Co.	300,000
North America Arms Co. — Canada	50,000
Caron Brothers Mfg. Co.—Canada	300,000

It can be concluded that some of these companies barely entered production as the war ended.

In World War II between 1940 and 1945, an estimated 1,800,000 of these Automatics were made. Colt's and Ithaca each produced about 400,000, Remington-Rand, Inc. 900,000 and the Union Switch & Signal Company 50,000.

So this .45 caliber Automatic, designed by Mr. Browning, has seen thus far 48 years of continuous military service, and proved a most reliable and indestructible weapon through two world wars.

No. 74

The One Millionth F. N. Made Browning

The millionth Browning Pistol was manufactured by F. N. in 1912. On January 31, 1913, an elaborate banquet was arranged at the factory to honor Mr. Browning and celebrate this production accomplishment.

The actual millionth pistol was presented to John M. Browning on the occasion but has since been lost.

The souvenir model in the display was given to his son, Val, at the banquet.

It was at this celebration that John M. Browning was decorated by King Albert as a "Chevalier de l'Ordre de Leopold."

The Belgians also presented to him a beautiful bronze statue in recognition of his genius; the symbolic work was that of the famous sculptor Rousseau. It was unveiled at the banquet to the strains of "The Star-Spangled Banner," rendered by a 30-piece orchestra. The actual medal pinned on him that night is shown. It represents the "Cross of Knighthood of the Order of Leopold."

At an even earlier date, however, Mr. Browning had received notable recognition for his work in Automatic Pistol development. In 1905 the City of Philadelphia, upon recommendation of the Franklin Institute, presented to John M. Browning the John Scott Legacy Medal for his achievements in perfecting the Automatic Pistol.

No. 73

John M. Browning
Semi-Automatic Pistol Model "Vest Pocket"
Caliber .25
Inventor's Original Model — Invented 1905

This pistol was also invented by John M. Browning in 1905 and was first patented in Belgium in that year. Mr. Browning was later granted U. S. Patent Number 947,478 on January 25, 1910, covering this pistol.

It is semi-automatic, hammerless and operates on the blow-back principle. It employs the Browning grip safety as well as a manually operated thumb safety. It has a 2-inch barrel and weighs only 13 ounces. It was first manufactured by Fabrique Nationale d'Armes de Guerre in 6.35mm caliber in 1905 and became an immediate success. Approximately 100,000 of these pistols were sold by F. N. within five years.

Mr. Browning licensed Colt's Patent Firearms Company to produce this pistol in the United States and Colt's started production in the latter part of 1908. Colt's offered this pistol, chambered for the .25 caliber A. C. P. cartridge, for general sale in 1909 about the same time that Mr. Browning applied for his United States patent. Over a million of these "Vest Pocket" models have been sold by F. N., and Colt's produced approximately 500,000 before discontinuing the model in 1946.

After World War II the pistol was redesigned to make it smaller and lighter by the Browning Arms Company and is now called the Browning .25 Caliber. Cartridge capacity is 7. An additional safety feature prevents its being fired when the magazine is removed. A cocking indicator enables the user to determine if the pistol is ready to fire, even in the dark. Weight has been reduced to 10 ounces in a standard model and 7¾ ounces in a lightweight model. Total length is 4 inches.

After the expiration of Mr. Browning's patent, many imitations have appeared on the market.

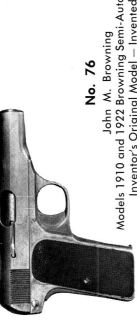

No. 76
John M. Browning
Models 1910 and 1922 Browning Semi-Automatic
Inventor's Original Model — Invented 1910

Mr. Browning completed this pistol design in 1910 and it was patented in Belgium shortly thereafter.

It contains the blow-back type action and its function is basically the same as that of his earlier Model 1900 .32 caliber, which it replaced. New modifications included a magazine safety which prevents firing with the magazine removed or, upon its insertion, without first releasing pressure on the trigger. The grip safety was also added.

The action spring is placed around the barrel in this model, rather than above it, thereby giving the pistol a much more streamlined appearance.

The 1922 Model, introduced in 1922, is merely an enlarged version of the 1910. The barrel was lengthened to four and one-half inches and its magazine capacity was increased from seven to eight cartridges by lengthening the grip.

One or the other of these models has been adopted as the official police side arm in many European countries.

Fabrique Nationale d'Armes de Guerre began the manufacture of this pistol in 1912, and over one million were produced by 1935. It is made in calibers 7.65mm (.32 A.C.P.) and 9mm Browning Short (.380 A.C.P.). It is currently produced by Browning Arms Company and sold in the United States in the .380 caliber, and in Canada in both .32 and .380 caliber.

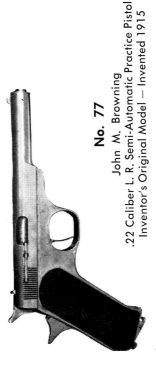

No. 77
John M. Browning
.22 Caliber L. R. Semi-Automatic Practice Pistol
Inventor's Original Model — Invented 1915

Shortly after the Ordnance Command adopted the 45 caliber Model 1911 Service Pistol, they expressed interest in a similar design cham-

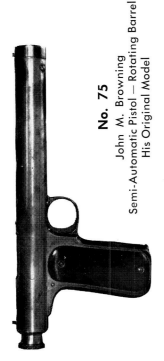

No. 75
John M. Browning
Semi-Automatic Pistol — Rotating Barrel
His Original Model

John M. Browning invented this pistol in 1896 and was issued U.S. Patent Number 580,925 on April 20, 1897.

It is a semi-automatic pistol which operates on the short recoil principle. In this pistol Mr. Browning employs a rotating barrel which locks to the slide. It consists of a cylinder shaped frame which contains a cylinder shaped slide. The barrel, encased by the recoil spring, is wholly contained in the slide. Located near the breech end of the barrel are three pairs of locking lugs which fit into corresponding grooves in the slide, thus locking the barrel and slide together.

When the gun is fired, the barrel and slide recoil together for a short distance. As the barrel and slide recoil, two camming studs near the muzzle cause the barrel to rotate and disengage the locking lugs from their grooves. This allows the slide to separate from the barrel and continue to recoil alone, effecting the extraction and ejection of the fired cartridge, and cocking. The slide is then returned to its forward position by spring tension, picking up a fresh cartridge from the magazine and feeding it into the barrel chamber ready for firing. This, it should be noted, is the first pistol in which Mr. Browning employed his grip safety.

Mr. Browning submitted this model to officials of Colt's Patent Firearms Company in the spring of 1896 at about the same time this Company was considering his double barrel link models (Nos. 63 and 64). The pistol was subjected to thorough tests by Colt's and, although its performance was excellent, Colt's finalized on the double link model and this pistol was never manufactured.

In 1906 during a patent infringement case against Albert H. Fuke, this pistol was used as evidence. The frame was cut through to expose to view the grip safety latch underneath the sear point.

bered for the .22 Long Rifle cartridge. Their objective was to have a pistol of similar weight and handling characteristics to the big .45 for practice shooting.

Three or four different designs were proffered prior to World War I, this model being the last. The project was dropped due to the war emergency.

This pistol has a full slide encasing the barrel, an exposed hammer, and an overhang on the rear portion of the frame to give it the feel and balance of the Model 1911.

Some of the features appearing on this pistol were employed on Mr. Browning's Woodsman Model.

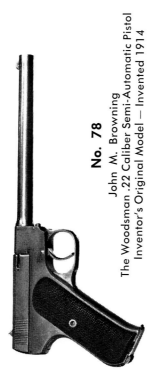

No. 78
John M. Browning
The Woodsman .22 Caliber Semi-Automatic Pistol
Inventor's Original Model — Invented 1914

This pistol was invented in 1914. United States Patent Number 1,276,716 which covers this invention was issued to John M. Browning on August 27, 1918. Colt's Patent Firearms Company was licensed to manufacture the pistol and production commenced March 29, 1915. It was called the Colt Woodsman.

The Woodsman is chambered for the .22 caliber Long Rifle cartridge and operates on the blow-back principle whereby the inertia of the slide or breechblock is utilized to seal the breech end of the barrel until the bullet escapes. By this time the energy from the fired cartridge has overcome the inertia of the slide and pushes it rearward. The rearward movement extracts and ejects the fired case and recocks the mechanism. The slide is then returned to its forward position under spring tension and at the same time picks up a fresh cartridge from the magazine and feeds it into the chamber ready for firing.

Unlike many pistols, the Woodsman Model utilizes a "½ slide" which completely separates from the breech end of the fixed barrel. The magazine has a ten cartridge capacity. The Colt Woodsman is noted for its extreme accuracy and has been widely used in competitive matches.

Still in production, it is estimated that about one million have been manufactured since 1915.

Nos. 79, 80
John M. Browning
Semi-Automatic Pistol — 9mm Parabellum
Inventor's Original Models — Invented 1923

In early 1923 Mr. Browning was informed that the French Ministry of War was interested in obtaining a semi-automatic pistol chambered for the 9mm Parabellum cartridge (same as 9mm Luger) and of large magazine capacity. In just a few months he completed these two models.

No. 79 was first and was designed on the blow-back principle. On this model, however, the barrel is adapted to move rearwardly a short distance in a line parallel with the movement of the breechblock and slide without being locked to the breechblock. The pistol was not patented and was never produced commercially.

The second design, **No. 80,** was Mr. Browning's last pistol development. His application for a U. S. patent was filed on June 28, 1923, and Patent Number 1,618,510 was issued on February 22, 1927, three months after his death.

On this model he employed the locked breech, short recoil type action. The visible ribs on the breech end of the barrel are engaged by corresponding grooves in the slide which securely lock the two together upon firing. The breechblock is demountably fixed to the slide so that the breechblock effectively seals the breech against the forces of the fired charge.

Recoil continues in this locked position until the bullet leaves the bore. Then the rear of the barrel is tilted downward by a camming action which disengages it, freeing the slide and breechblock to continue rearwardly alone. The mechanics of ejection, cocking and loading are closely similar to his other locked breech type pistols.

With a full magazine and a cartridge in the chamber, the pistol will fire 16 rounds without reloading. Later modification reduced its weight and its firing capacity to 14 rounds. Its final version which also included an external hammer was adopted as the official side arm of the Belgian Army and other European and Colonial Troops. Over 200,000 were manufactured in Canada for the Chinese Army during World War II.

Negotiations Between John M. Browning and the U. S. Government

It was only after Mr. Browning's machine guns, rifle and pistol had been officially adopted by the United States Government and production had reached its peak that the question of compensation to the inventor came up for consideration between John M. Browning and the United States Government. A Government official opened negotiations with the following statement:

"I am authorized to make you an offer, under the terms of which the Government will have full rights to manufacture your machine guns, machine rifle and the .45 automatic pistol. It is also required that Mr. Browning will give personal supervision to the production of these arms in all factories where orders are placed. This offer, I know, is only a fraction of what you would realize from royalties on orders already booked, and it may not be acceptable. In that event, further negotiations will be necessary."

He then named the offer. Without the slightest hesitation, John M. Browning replied:

"Gentlemen, if that suits Uncle Sam, it's all right with me."

The Secretary of War, upon hearing of the generous terms that Mr. Browning had agreed upon as a settlement, sent him the following letter expressing the Country's gratitude, not only for his contribution in the field of weapon design, but also for his patriotism in accepting such a modest return on the products of his genius:

WAR DEPARTMENT
WASHINGTON
November 13, 1917

My dear Mr. Browning:

I have learned from Major Little of the patriotic and generous attitude taken by you in the negotiations for the use of your patents of light and heavy machine guns in this emergency, and beg leave to express my appreciation of it.

You have performed, as you must realize, a very distinct service to the Country in these inventions, and contributed to the strength and effectiveness of our armies. You have added to that service by the attitude you have taken in the financial arrangements necessary to make your inventions available to the Government.

Cordially yours,
(Signed) NEWTON D. BAKER
Secretary of War

It was given further utility as a military weapon by the addition of a stock-holster which, when quickly attached to the rear face of the grip, permitted the pistol to be fired as a semi-automatic rifle.

The pistol is also known by the names "Browning High Power" and "Browning Model 1935."

It is currently produced and sold by the Browning Arms Company as a sporting and defense pistol.

It is also the standard military side arm of most of the NATO Countries.

No. 81

**John M. Browning
Semi-Automatic Pistol — 9mm Parabellum
F. N.'s First Factory Model**

This model is the first factory prototype of Mr. Browning's original design, No. 80. It was made in the Model Shop at Fabrique Nationale and was one of the actual models tested by the French Government. The trials were highly successful and Mr. Browning received a congratulatory letter from the French War Ministry upon their termination.

No. 82

**Current Production Model
Browning 9mm Parabellum Automatic Pistol**

No. 83

**Current Production Model
Browning .380 Caliber Automatic Pistol**

No. 84

**Current Production Model
Browning .25 Caliber Automatic Pistol**

Jonathan Browning
Father of John M. Browning
1805 - 1875

Jonathan Browning was born in Tennessee and while still a young boy moved to the mountains of Kentucky at the time when the fame of the Kentucky rifle was widespread. It was in this environment that he learned the art of gunmaking. Establishing his own shop while yet in his teens, Jonathan Browning designed and forged by hand his first repeating rifle as early as 1831.

From Kentucky, he moved westward and established a gun shop in Nauvoo, Illinois. Later he moved his shop to Kanesville, Iowa, near Council Bluffs where he located for two years.

Dated September 19, 1849, the humorously worded advertisement, on display, appeared in the *Frontier Guardian*, published in Kanesville.

No. 85

Jonathan Browning
"Slide" Repeating Rifle

It was here that he produced two repeating rifles. One of the new rifles was a "slide" repeater, **No. 85**, which had features of considerable ingenuity and merit, notably a five-shot magazine consisting of a rectangular bar of iron with holes to accommodate the hand loads, the bar sliding through an aperture at the breech from right to left and being manually operated. This permitted the advantage of being loaded in advance so that the magazine could be put into the rifle and moved quickly into firing position for five comparatively fast shots.

It was possible also for the shooter to carry several extra loaded magazines which could be readily slipped into the rifle as required. The proximity of the forefinger to the hammer permitted cocking without taking the rifle from the shoulder. This added to the speed with which the rifle could be fired as compared with the ordinary muzzle loader.

Loss of pressure was prevented and velocity was increased by making a positive gas-tight connection between the slide magazine and the barrel. It was accomplished by means of a lever located on the right-hand side of the gun, and operated by the thumb which forced the slide against the barrel as each load moved into line with the bore.

Comments by
Gun Authority and Author

In commenting about John M. Browning, Captain Paul A. Curtis, well-known gun authority and author, wrote the following in 1931:

"It is difficult to find words to accurately describe John Browning's achievements. To say that he was a great gun designer is inadequate; to say that he was the Edison of the modern firearms industry does not quite cover the case either, for he was even greater than that. There are, and were, many great men working along the same lines as Edison, including Steinmetz, Westinghouse, Marconi and others too numerous to mention — but Browning was unique. He stood alone, and there never was in his time or before, one whose genius along those lines could remotely compare with his."

The War Department's
Final Tribute

John M. Browning passed away on November 26, 1926, while busily engaged at work at the FN factory in Belgium. He had made this last trip to Belgium to be present when production commenced on his last invention — the Browning Superposed Shotgun.

The War Department, as a final tribute to the man who had served the Armed Forces so well, assigned a military escort to meet the ship, drape the colors, and stand guard until all formalities were completed.

The following is an excerpt from a long eulogy delivered by the Honorable Dwight F. Davis, Secretary of War, upon the occasion of the inventor's death:

"It is a fact to be recorded that no design of Mr. Browning's has ever proved a failure, nor has any model been discontinued. The War Department through its agency, the Ordnance Department of the Army, will be greatly handicapped in its future development work on automatic firearms as a result of the loss of Mr. Browning's services. It is not thought that any other individual has contributed so much to the national security of this country as Mr. Browning in the development of our machines guns and our automatic weapons to a state of military efficiency surpassing that of all nations."

This rifle was a great improvement over guns of that day and age. To this designer goes credit for the craftsmanship necessary to forge by hand such an arm with the few crude tools available in a frontier country.

No. 86
Jonathan Browning
Cylinder Repeating Rifle

The other gun was a repeater having a cylinder holding six shots, **No. 86.** The powder and ball were loaded into the cylinder and a cap placed on each nipple. The rifle was cocked by drawing back the hammer which also revolved the cylinder — the same principle as the single action revolver.

The two repeating rifles which were produced in Kanesville gave the Pioneer people greater protection from Indian invasion and massacre than the slow single shot which had been their only rifle. These rifles became famous throughout the West for their reliability, but were never patented.

When Jonathan Browning had accumulated sufficient funds to move on, he and his family again left their home. Being a reliable and resourceful man, he was chosen to captain a wagon train westward and, despite the hazards of travel in those days, he brought his company safely into the Mormon settlement now known as the State of Utah. Here he kept to his trade and opened a gunshop in Ogden in 1851.

Today's Sporting Arms
by
BROWNING

Automatic-5 shotguns
12 - 16 - 20 gauge and 3" Magnum

Double Automatic shotguns
12 gauge in 3 weights

Superposed shotguns
12 - 20 - 28 - .410 gauge

.22 Automatic rifles
.22 long rifle - .22 short

9mm
caliber

.380
caliber

.25 caliber

Automatic pistols

Browning Arms Co., St. Louis, Mo. and Ogden, Utah

Chapter Two

A Synopsis
of the
Browning Family
and Arms Company

JONATHAN BROWNING
Founder of the Browning gun business

JOHN M. BROWNING
First President Browning Arms Co. and the greatest firearms inventor of history

M. S. BROWNING
First Vice-President of Browning Arms Co.

Three Generations of Gunmaking

Jonathan Browning, moving westward from Kentucky, where he had learned the trade of gunsmith, set up a shop in Council Bluffs, Iowa, in the thirties. For a few years he repaired and made guns, many of original design, for the pioneers of the Gold Rush. In 1851 he captained a wagon train across the plains, and located permanently in Ogden, Utah.

John M. Browning worked with his father until his death, and thereafter carried on the business with the help of his younger brother,

Matthew. An outline of the results of his activities is given in these pages.

V. A. Browning, one of the sons of John M., and for a number of years his technical assistant, has for the past ten years lived in Belgium, in charge of factory interests of the Browning Arms Company. To him has been entrusted the installation of equipment and production is under his active supervision. Browning experience of three generations goes into the manufacture of Browning Superposed and Browning Automatic Shotguns.

M. A. BROWNING

JOHN BROWNING

V. A. BROWNING

Page Two

In 1931 the Browning Arms Company catalog featured the following information included here on pages 36-40 about John M. and his family, you will find it as informative as I.

THE LATEST INVENTION
OF THE
WORLD'S GREATEST GUN DESIGNER

THE inventions of John M. Browning constitute the principal output of four of the largest arms factories in the world. All arms manufacturers know him as the dominant figure in the industry during a period of half a century. A Secretary of War of the United States called him the "Greatest Gun Wizard of the Modern Age." Eight arms of John M. Browning's invention were used by the United States and allied armies during the World War. Seven arms of his invention have been adopted by the United States Government. These include the "45" automatic pistol, machine rifle, machine guns of various models and calibers for ground, air, tank, etc., and a 37 m.m. automatic cannon.

The Vickers-Armstrong Company of England, one of the largest plants in the world, has recently been licensed under the patents of John M. Browning to manufacture Browning machine guns, machine rifles and the automatic cannon, 37 m.m., one of the latest Browning military arms. This arm, like most Browning military weapons, was developed at the express request of the Ordnance Board, and it has won the highest praise from experts who have witnessed its performances at the Aberdeen Prov-

Medal presented to John M. Browning, by the King of Belgium, when he received the Order of Leopold.

ing Ground. Firing a high explosive projectile at the rate of 150 per minute, and a velocity of 3000 ft. per second, it is considered one of the best means of defense against aircraft.

The machine gun designed by John M. Browning, tested in 1916 before the United States Ordnance Board and allied officers, was pronounced the "Finest Machine Gun in the World."

The .45-caliber automatic pistol, adopted by the United States Government in 1911, has the distinction of being the only small arm to complete an official government test with a perfect score. Six thousand rounds were fired, in the course of which the pistol was subjected to rust and sand tests, with under and overcharged cartridges, and there was not even a misfire.

Numerous foreign governments have adopted one or more arms made in accordance with John M. Browning's patents—pistols, machine guns, machine rifles. Many police forces in various countries are armed with pistols of his design.

In the late nineties, John M. Browning developed the first automatic pistol of practicable size—a .32-caliber pocket model. This pistol established a record which will probably stand for

Page Three

In 1931 the Browning Superposed Catalog featured the above.

all time among commercial arms: in a comparatively few years one million were made by the Belgian factory, in one caliber, without a change of any kind. Upon the completion of the millionth, the King of Belgium conferred the Order of Leopold on Mr. Browning. This pistol fixed the trend of modern automatic pistol development, and has been copied wherever automatic pistols are made. Pistols now made under license from John M. Browning include .22, .25, .32, .380, .38, and .45 calibers.

About 1900 Mr. Browning invented the first Automatic Shotgun, and under his personal supervision the arm was brought out in Belgium. No sporting arm, before or since, has won such an immediate and world-wide popularity. It is known wherever shotguns are used, including the United States, as the Genuine Browning Automatic Shotgun.

The illustrations on Page 5 give proof of the amazing versatility of the inventor. It was Mr. Browning's practice, in the United States, to permit manufacturers to use their own names on arms made under license from him. For that rea-

son several million men have used arms of his invention without being aware of it: they have called their arms Winchester, Colt, Remington, Stevens, etc.

In foreign countries the case is different. From the beginning, the numerous sporting and military arms manufactured by the Belgian factory have borne the inventor's name, and that name in consequence is much more widely known abroad than in the United States.

The name Browning, as a sign of dependable design and superior quality, is now well-known among American sportsmen by reason of the Browning Automatic Shotgun 12-gauge and 16-gauge. Since 1923, the Browning Arms Company has imported from the Belgian plant and distributed in the United States so many Genuine Browning Automatics that there are few sportsmen who are not acquainted with that arm.

The foregoing brief summary of John M. Browning's activities is given as an introduction to the Browning Superposed Shotgun. The master gunmaker and the largest small-arms factory in the world have cooperated to produce an arm which will heighten the world-wide fame of both.

The Products of John M. Browning's Genius

Those who are not familiar with the life and work of John M. Browning will perhaps be surprised to learn that many of their old favorite arms are the results of his inventive genius. His inventions were not confined to the products of his own shop, but were—and in many instances still are—manufactured under royalty contracts by leading American factories. The guns shown on this page are all inventions of John M. Browning—quite likely you will find your favorite among them.

ONE HUNDREDTH ANNIVERSARY
OF THE FIRST
INVENTION OF THE BROWNING FAMILY

⌄

JONATHAN BROWNING was born in Tennessee in 1805, and while a boy moved to Kentucky. That was in the days when the fame of the Kentucky Rifle was almost fabulous, and it was in that environment that he learned gunmaking. While still in his teens, he set up his own shop. By several stages he joined and followed the pioneer movement westward, settling permanently in Ogden, Utah, in 1852. Here John M. Browning was born, and, taught by his father, he too became a gunmaker. Browning arms, famous throughout the world, come down in direct succession from the celebrated Kentucky Rifle.

as required. The proximity of the forefinger to the hammer, which could be cocked without taking the gun down from the shoulder, also added to its rapidity of fire as compared with the ordinary muzzle loader.

Loss of pressure was prevented and velocity was increased through making a gas-tight connection between the slide magazine and the barrel. This is not found even in the revolvers of today. It was accomplished by means of a lever located on the right hand side of the gun, the operation of which by the thumb forced the slide against the barrel as each load moved into line with the barrel. All in all, the weapon was a great im-

Original repeating rifle developed by Jonathan Browning in 1831.

Browning Gun No. 1—Notice the horizontal sliding magazine, the principle used in the modern Machine Gun.

It was in 1831 that Jonathan Browning designed and forged by hand his first repeating rifle. Simplicity of construction is paramount even in the gun a century old. Note, for instance, that the trigger guard also serves as the main spring which operates the hammer. This idea of using one part in a gun to take the place of several parts can be traced through the many arms later invented by his son.

Browning efficiency is also very noticeable in the old gun. The gun was designed to handle slide magazines carrying six powder and ball charges. Not only did the pioneer have six shots available for firing without going through the slow process of muzzle loading, but it was the practice for him to carry several extra loaded magazines which could be readily slipped into the gun

provement over guns of that day and age, and credit must be given for the craftsmanship necessary to forge out such a gun with the few crude tools available in a frontier country.

Browning achievement of the highest type of mechanical perfection and performance as represented by the new BROWNING SUPERPOSED has been obtained only through experience accumulated over three generations of gunmaking plus the skill of the master Belgian gunsmiths for centuries renowned for their handiwork.

It is fitting, therefore, that the presentation of the BROWNING SUPERPOSED should occur on the One Hundredth Anniversary of the first Browning Gun.

A SYNOPSIS OF B.A.C.

To help commemorate the 100 anniversary of the founding of Browning, the company put together the following historical time line. This will give you a better idea of the major events that helped shape the Browning Arms Corporation.

January 23, 1855
Birth of John Moses Browning.

October, 1869
John Assembled a single shot rifle out of spare parts for his brother's birthday.

Spring, 1878
John Browning begins work on his first single shot rifle.

April, 1879
John Moses Browning marries Rachel Teresa Child.

May 12, 1879
The application on the single shot rifle was filed.

October 7, 1879
U.S. Patent No. 220,271 was granted to the single shot rifle.

1880
With the aid of his brothers, John Browning established his arms factory.

March 20, 1882
Patent application was filed on a bolt action repeating rifle with a tubular magazine.

July 25, 1882
U.S. patent No. 261,667 was granted to the bolt action repeater.

September 13, 1882
Patent filed on lever action, exposed hammer, tubular magazine repeating rifle.

Spring, 1883
Mr. T.G. Bennett, Vice-President and General Manager of Winchester Repeating Arms Company comes to Ogden, Utah Territory, and forms an alliance that is to last nineteen years and change the course of firearms development. As part of the transaction, the single shot is sold to Winchester, and Mr. Bennett is assured of first rights on a new repeater. The single shot becomes the Winchester Model 1885.

May 26, 1884
Patent filed on lever action repeating rifle that employed sliding vertical locks.

October, 1884
Patent No. 306, 577 was granted on the new repeater, and John, together with his brother Matt, traveled to New Haven to deliver what was to become the famous Winchester Model 1886.

February 16, 1886
Patent No. 336,287 was granted on a lever action repeating shotgun. Known as the Winchester Model 1887, it was the first successful repeating shotgun.

March 28, 1887
John leaves for Georgia to spend two years as a Mormon Missionary.

December 13, 1887
Patent was filed on a 22 caliber pump action repeating rifle. It has been called "the most popular 22 caliber pump action rifle ever made. Patent No.385, 238 was granted on June 26, 1888.

Fall of 1889
Began development of the first models that were designed to employ the expanding gases behind the bullet to operate the action.

January 6, 1890
John filed his first patent dealing with gas operation.

June 30, 1890
Patent application was filed on a pump action repeating shotgun. Marketed as the Winchester Model 1893. A later take-down version was known as the Winchester Model 1897.

August 3, 1891
Patents filed on two separate automatic gas operated guns.

November 7, 1892
Filed first patents on the Colt Model 1895 Automatic Machine Gun. Earned the name "Browning Peacemaker" during the Spanish-American War.

January 19, 1894
Filed patent on what would become the Winchester Model 1894, the first repeating-action sporting rifle to handle smokeless powder cartridges. This rifle is ascribed by many to be the most popular high powered rifle ever built.

November 19, 1894
Patent was filed on a lever action repeating rifle with a non-detachable box magazine designed for jacketed sharp nosed bullets. Marketed as the Winchester Model 1895.

September 14, 1895
Filed patent application on first semi-automatic pistol.

October 31, 1896
Three basic pistol patents were filed that concerned a blow back action, a locked-recoil system with a turning lock, and a locked recoil system with a pivoting lock.

July 17, 1897
A contract between Browning and Fabrique Nationale was signed which authorized the Belgium firm to manufacture a blowback operated 32 caliber semi-automatic pistol for all markets outside the United States. Production commenced in 1899.

February 17, 1899
Application for patent was filed on a single shot 22 caliber plinking rifle known as the Winchester Model 1900.

February 1900

Colt placed a Browning-designed 38 caliber recoil operated semi-automatic pistol on the market. It was the first semi-automatic pistol in the U.S.

February 8, 1900

The first four patents were filed on the revolutionary autoloading shotgun. It would be manufactured by Fabrique Nationale in 1903 and by Remington Arms Company in 1905.

October 16, 1900

The first successful auto-loading high power rifle received patent No. 659, 786. U.S. manufacturing and sales rights were granted to Remington Arms Company, and the first appeared in 1906 as the Model 8.

July 16, 1901

Browning submitted a blowback operated 32 caliber semi-automatic pistol to Colt, who immediately accepted it. The marketing agreement stipulated that the pistol would be priced low enough to compete with the revolvers of the period.

January, 1902

In a disagreement about the pubic acceptability of the autoloading shotgun, John Browning severed his nineteen year relationship with T.G. Bennett of Winchester,

1902

An appointment was made to show the new shotgun to Mr. Marcellus Hartley, President of the Remington Arms Co. This meeting was cancelled by Mr. Hartley's untimely death that afternoon.

February, 1902

With his autoloading shotgun tucked under his arm, John Browning embarked on his first ocean voyage. He would offer the new shotgun to Fabrique Nationale.

March 24, 1902

A contract was signed granting F.N. exclusive world rights, excluding the U.S., to manufacture and sell the autoloading shotgun.

July 10, 1903

Patent application was filed on a pump action shotgun that would become the Stevens Model 520.

Summer, 1903

At the request of F.N., Browning developed a 9mm military semi-automatic pistol.

1904

In the face of restrictive tariffs, F.N. agreed to cede to Remington the rights to manufacture and sell the autoloading shotgun in the U.S.

June 21, 1909

The application for a patent on a 25 caliber semi-automatic pistol was filed. It has been manufactured and sold by both F.N. and Colt. It was part of the Browning Arms Co. line from 1955 to 1969.

February 17, 1910

Patents were filed on a 45 caliber semi-automatic pistol known as the Model 1911.

November 26, 1913

Filed patent on a pump shotgun that would be marketed as the Remington Model 17. It was John M. Browning's last repeater type shotgun.

January 6, 1914

Patents were granted and production began on a semi-automatic 22 caliber rifle. Remington also produced this rifle as the Model 24.

February 27, 1917

First public demonstration on the Browning 30 caliber Heavy Machine Gun at Congress Heights, Washington, D.C.

July 17, 1917

Began work on a 50 caliber water cooled machine gun. Completed too late for World War 1, this weapon played a prominent role in World War 2 and Korea.

August 1, 1917

Application for patent filed on the Browning Automatic Rifle. The B.A.R. first saw combat in 1918.

July 26, 1919

Patent application filed on a 22 pump action rifle that would be produced exclusively by F.N.

Early 1921

John M. Browning began work on his 37mm Aircraft Cannon.

October 15, 1923

The first two patents were filed on the Superposed over and under shotgun.

June 28, 1923

Patent application was filed on a 9mm short recoil locked breech exposed hammer semi-automatic pistol. This was Mr. Browning's last pistol development and would later develop into the High Power.

November 26, 1926

John Moses Browning died of heart failure at Liege, Belgium. The great gun maker had laid down his tools.

September, 1927

J.M. & M.S. Browning Company was incorporated in Utah with the Browning Arms Company as a subsidiary.

November 14, 1927

The Browning Arms Company was incorporated and set up business at 719 First Security Bank Building, Ogden, Utah.

1928

The Superposed was introduced into the U.S. as part of the Browning Arms Company's line.

1930

St. Louis distribution center and sales organization established at 1132 Spruce St. Ogden remained headquarters location, directing all activities.

1940 to 1942

After the German occupation put a stop to Belgian production, Remington made an American made A-5 for Browning. This was their Model 11 with the magazine cut off, which was not part of the Remington version. U.S. entry into the war ended this production.

1945 to 1949

Remington resumed making the A-5 for Browning until they discontinued production of their Model 11 to introduce their Model 11-18.

1949

12 gauge Superposed reintroduced to the U.S.

1951

The J.M. & M.S. Browning Company liquidated and the Browning Arms Company became an importer with wholesale functions.

1954

The Double Automatic 12 gauge shotgun, the 9mm High Power, the 380, and 25 Semi-Automatic pistols now being imported.

January 1, 1955

A newly created Browning Industries accepted the import functions previously held by J.M. & M.S. Browning Company. The Browning Arms Company became the parent company.

1956

The 22 Automatic designed by John M. in 1914 was now being imported.

1958

Browning Arms Of Canada created, 70% owned by Browning and 30% owned by F.N. The A-5 20 gauge was also introduced.

1959

The Safari rifle introduced.

1962 to 1963

Browning acquired Silaflex and Gordon Plastics, makers of bows, rods, and vaulting poles.

1962

The Nomad, Challanger, and Medalist 22 pistols introduced; archery, fishing rods, ski poles and vaulting poles added to the line.

1964

Headquarters relocated to Route 1, Organ, Utah.

1965

The T-Bolt 22 rifle introduced. A line of leather goods including belts, holsters and flexible gun cases also cataloged. Browning started working with Miroku of Japan. Entered into the sailboat business with Newport Boats of California and Virginia.

1966

Archery accessories added to the line.

1967

The Browning Automatic centerfire rifle added to the line.

1968

St. Louis operation relocated in Mountain Green Warehouse, and the parts and service was moved to Arnold, Mo. The Barth Leather Co. and the Caldwell Lace Company in Auburn, Ky. acquired; also, hunting clothes added to catalog.

1969

Acquired Harwill, Inc., manufacturers of Fiberglass outboard/inboard motorboats as well as small aluminum boats and canoes. Knives were added to the catalog.

1970

Lever action rifle and Medalist International 22's added to the line.

1971

The BT-99, BDA 380, and the BLR centerfire rifles added to the line.

1972

BSS Double barrel shotgun added.

1973

The 12 gauge Citori and Liege over and under shotguns, the BSS 20 gauge, and the B-78 single shot rifle introduced.

1974

The B-2000 12 gauge automatic shotgun, the Citori 20 gauge, and Trap and Skeet models introduced. Also, the Harwill Boat Co. liquidated.

1975

The Citori 20 gauge skeet and the B-2000 20 gauge introduced.

1976

The 22 Challanger 2, BT-99 Competition, B-78 in 45/70 and 7mm Remington Magnum, BLR 358, and Citori extra barrels added. The Auto-5 production moved to Japan and the 16 gauge was discontinued. The Newport Boat Company liquidated.

1977

Superposed in Grade 1, Pigeon, Diana, Midas discontinued, and the P-Series introduced. The BAR and BPR 22's, the BPS, Jonathan Browning Mountain rifle, the BBR bolt action centerfire rifle, the B-2000 Trap and Skeet with high post rib, the BDA pistol in 38 Super, 9mm, and 45 Auto introduced. Ninety percent of the Browning Arms Company outstanding stock purchased by F.N. and Miroku of Japan.

1978

Browning enters the company's Centennial year. To commemorate this event, five limited Centennial editions are prepared. They include a Superposed Continental shotgun and rifle/shotgun combination, a Centennial Edition of the Mountain Rifle, a replica of the Winchester Model 1892, a chromed version of the 9mm High Power, and a special set of folding knives.

Chapter Three

General Information,
Limited Editions,
Gun Cases, and
Collector's Knives

GENERAL INFORMATION

This is our catch-all section that has information of a general interest which does not deal with one gun but with several. The items discussed here are some of the most important in this book. Please read them carefully, for you will probably want to refer to them often.

I have also used this to save many of you a phone call for, as you will see, there is a lot of information contained here that you may have looked for in the past or may have alluded you altogether.

REPAIRS

The company's policy on repairs and a detailed list of prices for common repair and restoration are published in the Service Price List, which may be obtained from either of these two addresses:

Customer Information Manager
Browning F.A. Company
Route 1
Morgan, Utah 84050

or

Browning Service Department
Route 4, Box 624-B
Tenbrook Road
Arnold, Mo 63010
314-287-6800

Some things to remember about Browning's repair policy:
1. One of the Browning Authorized Service Centers may be able to do the work and maybe faster, since the transportation distance will often be shorter and since Arnold is usually behind in their work. You may get a list of these centers from the Customer Information Department, Browning Arms Company, Route 1, Morgan Ut 84050, 801-876-2711.
2. Repairs are limited to Browning guns only.
3. Browning will not undertake to restore a high grade gun to its original condition with regard to engraving or other special features. Repairs are restricted to parts replacement and mechanical repair.
4. Rebluing of badly pitted guns or their parts may require polishing, for which there may be an extra charge. Browning does not accept any responsibility for the effects of such polishing on markings or engraving.
5. Be sure to ask for an estimate of the cost of repairs before sending your gun to Arnold.
6. Guns should be packed securely in heavy cartons, not in gun cases or original shipping cartons, as they would cause extra effort in returning the same container. Be sure the gun is not loaded.

BROWNING COLLECTOR'S ASSOCIATION

To get information on the Browning Collectors Association contact:

Bobbie Hamit
P.O. Box 526
Aurora, NE 68818

Please be aware that the Secretary of the association changes from time to time.

GRADING OF WOOD

Fabrique Nationale places each piece of "high grade" wood in one of five groups. For your general information, here is how it is done.

Group 1: Grades 2 and 3 walnut was specified for use on Grade II guns such as the 22 Semi Auto rifles Grade II.

Group 2: Grades 4 and 5 walnut was specified for use in the B-78 Single Shot rifles, Pointer Grade Superposed, Citori Grade II and the Medallion Grade rifles.

Group 3: Grades 6 and 7 extra-fancy walnut was specified for use in the Grade III.22 Semi Auto rifles, Citori Grade V and VI, Grade III BAR rifles, and the P1 and P2 Grade Superposed.

Group 4: Top quality select extra-fancy walnut was specified for use in Diana and Midas Grade Superposed, Olympian Grade rifles, Grade IV BAR rifles, P3 and P4 Superposed, and the Waterfowl Series.

Group 5: This was specially selected wood ordered for Exhibition pieces or those given to a special person. This is not an official group, but when you look at as many Brownings as I do, you now and then know that a certain piece was held back to be used on only those guns with which F.N. wanted to do something special.

If you have a different model than the ones listed above, you can pretty well determine about where your gun should be. This is just a guide for you to go by.

MASTER ENGRAVERS

Felix Funken was the first master engraver employed at Fabrique Nationale's Liege manufacturing facilities. In 1926, he established a school for F.N. to help develop good engravers. He also rebuilt the shop after the devastations of World War II and trained young engravers to follow in his beautiful style; this was done quite successfully. At his retirement, he was honored with the title of Chief Engraver, a tremendous honor bestowed only on a few people.

Since then, the school has been discontinued and all new engravers come from The Liege Armorer's School in Liege, Belgium. Additional training by Andre Watrin and Jose Baerten, who are both now Chief Engravers, is given them when they are employed by F.N. While there are still some master engravers working a F.N., the in house engraving department was basically shut down in 1987.

Take heart ladies, most of the engravers at F.N. are young women working in the great atmosphere of song birds hanging from cages all over the engraving room and walls painted with wildlife scenes. All you hear are these little birds and the tiny taps of hundreds of little hammers creating beautiful patterns and scenes on some of the world's finest firearms.

Some signed their names with a stamp and some by hand. Many guns were engraved by more than one engraver, so you may see more than one signature on the same gun. This was sometimes done as a matter of economics or to expedite an order. I have personally owned guns with up to four signatures and have heard of as many as five on a single piece. Also, many times only the main panels were done by a master engraver, while the borders or minor background work was done by others.

Don't be surprised by variations from one gun to another. These engravers were and many still are artists working with steel. They are very apt to express their artistic capabilities and do a little something special. You will generally find this more on the Exhibition or Special Order guns as engravers were usuallay paid by the piece on the lower grades.

For those interested in some of the names of the master engravers, they are listed below in alphabetical order. Most of the time, the master engravers would use either their initials or their last name only. As you can see, many of them had the same last name and there you will sometimes find a first initial.

MASTER ENGRAVERS BY NAME

Louis Acampo	L.A.
Claude Baerten	C.B.
Jose Baerten	J.B.
Jean Marie Bague	J.M.B.
Bailey	
Robert R. Baptiste	R.B.
Angelo Bee	A.B.
Rosa Bee	R.B.
Louis Bleus	L.B.
Bodson	
J. Mario Bodson	J.M.BO.
Callebrese	
Gino Cargnel	G.CA.

G. Cockran	G.C.
Rene Coenen	R.C.
Lilly Cortis	L.C.
Andre Crousse	A.C.
Jean Marie De Brues	J.M.D.
Rene Dewil	R.D.
Andre Dierckx	A.D.
Jean Diet	J.D. or J.H.D.
Ramon Du Bois	R.D.B.
Lucien Ernst	L.E.
J.M. Florent	J.M.F.
Felix Funken	F.F.
Louis Goffar	L.G.
W. Jansens	W.J.
Richard Kowalski	R.K.
Lallamand	
Lilly Lambert	L.L.
Charles Legiers	C.L.
Lemaer	L
Jules Lwanczk	J.L.
M. Magis	M.M.
Name Unknown	M.N.
Alfonse Marachal	A.M.
Francoise Marachal	F.M.
George Marachal	G.M.
Peter Marachal	P.M.
S. Missen	S.M.
Pauwels	
Pefido	
Poes	
R. Risak	R.R.
Rompen	R
Charles Servais	C.S.
L. Severn	L.S.
J. Spiegel (Vanderspiegel)	J.S.
R. Towarski	R.T.
Gaston Vandermissen	G.V.
Edmond Vos	E.V.
Louis Vracken	L.V.
Andre Watrin	A.W.

Although you will find their last names spelled out in full, many times these master engravers used only their initials. Angelo Bee used the letter "A" with the picture of a bee. Gaston Vander Missen signed his work several different ways including V Missen, Smissen, Vandersmissen, G, G. Vandersmissen and G.V. Felix Funken sometimes used a double F back-to-back. Other engravers such as J.M. Bodson, Gino Cargnel and several more used three or four initials to help distinguished themselves from others with the same last name.

The list you see above includes husbands and wives as well as fathers and daughters or fathers and sons.

SPECIAL ORDERS

Don't be surprised about what you might find in the way of guns and special features. Browning has always been a company that was willing to make whatever a customer wanted.

You will find special engravings, inlaying, barrel lengths, choke combinations, silver plating, gold plating, nickeling, chroming, blueing, case hardening, stock configurations, woods variations, and caliber variations. If you've got imagination, add whatever you care to the list and there is a chance that it was done.

One special feature cataloged regularly was the production of name plates in either German silver or 10 carat gold. These were generally done in the U.S. and placed between the grip and toe of the stock with initials in what Browning called the style "A" or style "B"; the main difference was only in the style of the initials. They also offered to engrave a person's full name on all models except the Superposed, Grade II or III 22 Automatics, and the bolt action rifles. They used their style "C" which was block letters and "D" which was script. This was done on the side of the Double Automatic receiver above the trigger or on the top of the Auto-5 receiver.

The models that were excluded could also be engraved, but this was done in Belgium and required a little extra time.

Special order features were not restricted to any one model or variation. If Browning and F.N. deemed it safe, they would try to accomplish whatever you wanted. It was expensive and time consuming, but the work was always outstanding and of the highest order.

As you will read in this publication, F.N. and Browning even had a hand in creating many collectors' items. To them, this was business as usual. I have been in the manufacturing business and we never made an item without first making a sample. What would make anyone think that a gun company wouldn't do things the same way?

As an example, Val Browning had about six different colors made up of the Double Auto that he didn't like and had them sold off at a discount to a dealer just to get rid of them. Now they are bringing thousands of dollars. Many of the unique and beautiful Superposed shotguns with special engraving were done as samples when Browning decided that they wanted to change their engraving of the standard patterns. The ones they didn't like were sold at bargain prices.

Don't be surprised at what you'll find. If it's unusual and appealing and you get it at the right price, you've got yourself a bargain.

1975 TO PRESENT SERIAL NUMBERS

This serial number system started in September, 1975. You can get a lot of information from them. They consist of three parts. The first part is numerical and is the actual number applied to that particular gun in that model. The next two characters, which are alphabetical, are the year designations. The last three characters are the model and grade.

Numbers from 1975 start at 1,000 at the beginning of each year. The year of manufacture for all Japanese Browning firearms for the years 1975 to 1992 are as follows:

1975 —RV—	1981 —PZ—	1987 —PR—
1976 —RT—	1982 —PY—	1988 —PP—
1977 —RR—	1983 —PX—	1989 —PN—
1978 —RP—	1984 —PW—	1990 —NM—
1979 —RN—	1985 —PY—	1991 —NZ—
1980 —PM—	1986 —PT—	1992 —NY—

So serial number 123456RR246 on a .22 Auto rifle would be serial number 123456 made in 1977 in a Grade II.

On guns made in the U.S. or Europe, the three digit product code is first, year code second, and the serial number third.

Example: 151RR1000.

On guns made in Japan, the serial number is first, then the year, followed by the product code.

Example: 1000RR151.

Exceptions may be found on special order, Commemorative, or Exhibition grade guns.

DATE CODES MASTER CHART

Unless changed, you may use the chart below to figure out the codes for all future years.

The letter Z stands for 1	The letter T stands for 6
The letter Y stands for 2	The letter R stands for 7
The letter X stands for 3	The letter P stands for 8
The letter W stands for 4	The letter N stands for 9
The letter V stands for 5	The letter M stands for 0

CLARIFYING YEARS INTRODUCED

The year introduced refers to the year that a particular model was first imported into the U.S. Production for other countries may have started previous to or after these dates. In addition, models will often be imported for distribution and never cataloged. Perhaps this is F.N. trying to distribute inventory that is not selling elsewhere or a special order by a group or company.

SALT WOOD

Here is the final story on the cause of salt wood.

First, let me say that this was not a Browning problem but a supplier problem. The wood that was shipped contained salt residue from the drying process. This procedure was tried as early as 1930 by some folks and caused the same problems. Of course, the idea was soon dropped. About 1965, a large wood supplier sent wood not only to Browning for F.N.'s use but also to Bishop, Fajen, Winchester, Ruger and — would you believe — to the U.S. Military for M-14 stocks. This company was drying their walnut using granulated salt, by covering the wood with salt and placing it in quonset huts.

The wood dried so quickly that the workers said they could actually see a steady drip of moisture coming from the wood. Of course, the wood was already cut into the appropiate size planks and no one thought that any salt residue would remain on or in the wood after final shaping, sanding and finishing. Well, they were dead wrong, so wrong in fact that the U.S. government stopped using walnut for the M-14 rifles and went to other types of wood because properly cured wood was so scarce at the time that sufficient supplies were not to be had!

In Browning's case the problem first shows itself in guns made starting in 1966. It pretty well ends on all their guns made after 1976.

Any purchase of a *Superposed* made between the years 1967 and 1973 should be looked at carefully.

Any purchase of a *T-Bolt* made between the years 1967 and 1973 should be looked at carefully.

Any purchase of a *Safari, Medallion* or *Olympian* made between the years 1967 and 1976 should be looked at carefully.

Any purchase of a *Auto-5 2,000,000th Commemorative* should be looked at carefully.

I have also heard of the rare instance where the grips on three High Power pistols were found to have been made with salt wood.

Inspect any place the metal touches the wood. Take out the butt plate screws and look them over very carefully. If you find no rust here, the gun is probably all right. Always look for salt wood right through 1976.

Sometime you can test the wood with silver nitrate. Place a drop or two on a hidden spot on the wood, and if it bubbles you have a problem.

CUSTOM WORK FROM BELGIUM

Custom work from F.N. has always been available to anyone who wanted to take the trouble or expense to get it done. Since the beginning of production on Browning designed guns, Browning and F.N. have promoted their custom work shop facility extensively.

The program going on now is to have any gun they currently make custom fitted, engraved, stocked, internally polished, etc. They will get the gun "in the white" from Japan, Portugal, or wherever and take over from there. Anything you want is yours within reason.

I can personally endorse their work, for it is of the highest quality and is being done for the most part by the same people that worked on the earlier all-Belgium collectors guns.

The person to contact is Mr. Jack Lanham, Browning Arms Company, 901 Yorkshire, Grande

Prairie, TX 75050. His toll free number is 800-527-4713.

CHOKE CODES MASTER CHART

The symbol *** stands for cylinder bore
The symbol **$ stands for skeet choke
The symbol **_ stands for improved cylinder
The symbol ** stands for modified choke
The symbol *_ stands for improved modified
The symbol * stands for full choke

The purpose of using symbols is simple. Barrels are initially bored full choke (*). As orders are received, the chokes are bored and symbols are added to correspond with the new choke. This is also why you will sometimes see overstamping one choke symbol with another or the original choke stamping punched out and/or a new choke stamping added. The new stamping may be heavier or lighter than the original.

STEEL SHOT

If you like your Belgium Browning, don't ever use steel shot. It will, after a few hundred rounds, bulge the barrels slightly. This won't ruin the patterns but will bulge the barrel(s) and severely hurt the value of your firearm. This goes for all Belgium made guns except for the B-80 and the B-2000. You can shoot all the Japanese-made shotguns except the Citoris made between 1972 and 1975. If you open up the chokes on these guns too improved cylinder and improved cylinder the very tightest, you can probably get away with shooting them.

RENAISSANCE PROBLEMS

You've heard the saying that the worst things happen to the nicest people. Well, the worst things often happen to the nicest guns as well.

If you've been in the Browning game long enough, you've seen "rust colored spider webs" appear on Renaissance grade guns from time to time. I used to think that it was the neglect of a previous owner but have found out differently after having this occur on some of mine.

When these guns were finished, F.N. applied a clear coat of baked enamel over the metal of the Renaissance guns. Sometimes this enamel will crack and allow moisture to seep in. Sometimes this can be stopped but not always. A coating of a good quality gun oil or RIG will sometimes help.

You can inquire at Browning and see if they can help you get a piece re-greyed without hurting the engraving.

PROOF AND OTHER MARKS OF INTEREST

One of the most important things you can learn is the importance and meaning of proof marks. Not only can you learn where a certain gun was made but when and if it's black powder or nitro proofed, chamber and barrel length, choke, and many other items of importance. I prefer to use "The Standard Directory Of Proof Marks" by Gerhard Wirnsberger

translated by R.A. Steindler and distributed by the Blacksmith Corporation, Box 424, Southport, CT 06490 when doing my research.

Since our concern is Belgium Brownings, I am including only Belgium proof marks for you to compare with your gun.

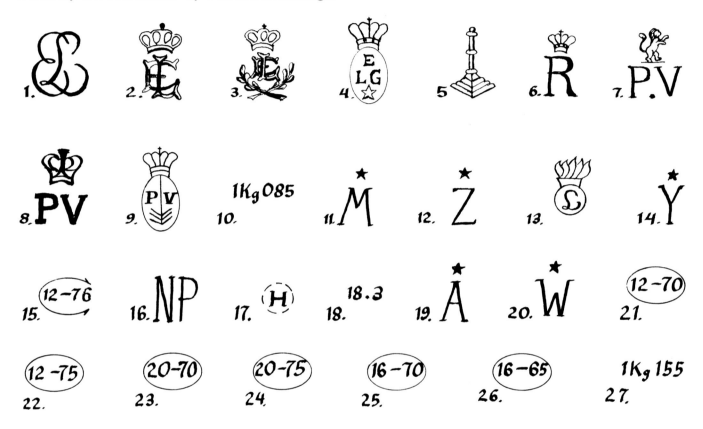

The proof marks shown above mean the following:

1. Provisional Proof
2. Double Proof Provisional Marking
3. Triple Proof Provisional Marking
4. Definitive Proof
5. View Proof
6. Rifled Arms Definitive Proof
7. Nitro Proof
8. Superior Nitro Proof
9. Passed by the Government Proof House. The letters "pv" indicates that the part has been passed by the government proof house. The letter following is that of the inspector.
10. Proof Denoting Various Pressures
11, 12, 14, 19, 20 are all inspectors marks and not proofs at all. You may see other letters but they all are inspector' marks.
13. Definitive Proof
15. 12 gauge with 3" chambers
16. Nitro Proof

17. Japanese Proof
18. On Belgium made shotguns the 18.3 and 18.2 Indicate the choke at a point 22 cm from the chamber and at the muzzle.
21. 12 Gauge with 2 3/4" Chambers
22. 12 Gauge with 3" Chambers
23. 20 Gauge with 2 3/4" Chambers
24. 20 Gauge with 3" Chambers
25. 16 Gauge with 2 3/4" Chambers
26. 16 Gauge with 2 1/2" Chambers
27. Proofs Denoting Various Pressures

You will see many Brownings stamped with the words "Acier Special." This simply means "Special Steel."

The marking "ch b raye" is the Belgian government proof house mark used from July 11, 1893, to February 26, 1930, to identify a shotgun barrel which was wholly choked or partially rifled.

LIMITED EDITIONS OF ORIGINAL BROWNING DESIGNS

Since these models fall under both the rifle and shotgun sections and there is no reason to print it twice, I will include it here in the General Information section.

Browning decided, in 1973, to once again introduce some of John M. Browning's greatest gun designs. These reproductions have proved quite popular and much sought after by folks who can't afford or find an original but still want a taste of the guns of yesteryear. As of 1992 there have been twelve different guns or configurations not including grades.

This series started in 1973 when they decided to produce an updated version of the John M. Browning single shot rifle, which was the Winchester Model 1885. Since then, other models have followed. A complete listing follows:

1973 the Model 78
1978 the Model 92 Carbine
1984 the Model 1895 Rifle
1986 the model 1886 Rifle
1987 the Model 71 Rifle & Carbine
1988 the Model 12 in 20 gauge

1989 the Model 65 Rifle
1990 the Model 12 in 28 guage
1990 the Model 53 Rifle
1991 the Model 52 Rifle
1992 the Model 42
1992 the model 1886 Carbine

This is quite an array of guns that have proven very popular. Hey, you out there in "Browning Land," how about producing a few more Trombones, Double Autos, Safari and Olympian rifles, 25 and 380 autos, and T-Bolts; a whole new generation of shooters would like a taste of them as well, I betcha.

The models listed above will all appear in their own sections.

BROWNING GUN CASES

Probably the second best thing to buying a great gun is buying one in the original box or gun case. In order for you to recognize a proper case for the time period in which your new acquisition was made, I am listing here the various cases and when made.

Since there were no cases offered by Browning prior to 1930 we will start in 1931.

In ordering state gauge of gun and length of barrel, whether 26, 28, 30 or 32-inch.

Model "A" $19.95

Browning Model "A" Case

Neat—Compact—Light—Durable
(genuine cowhide)

Hand-made and covered with genuine cowhide leather, black in color and machine grained to prevent marring. All seams hand-sewed. All edges rounded, giving smooth, neat appearance. Sides and ends of case constructed of ½-inch northern basswood. Top and bottom ¼-inch, 3-ply northern basswood.

All corners of case reinforced inside with steel angles. A flange covered with genuine cowhide leather around inside of case prevents dust and water from getting in. Hand-made, solid-leather handle all hand-sewed. Two mahogany steel snap locks, one on each side of handle and center snap. This insures a tight fitting case at all times, yet the contents are easily and quickly accessible.

Inside of case lined throughout with soft but tough, highest quality dark fabric. Leather straps hold gun and barrel securely in position to prevent rattling and rubbing. Note the snug fitting compartments for gun and barrel; also extra section for cleaning rod, oil can, cloths, etc.

Supplied with brass plate for your name and address.

Model "B" $13.85

Browning Model "B" Case

The Browning model "B" gun case, while less expensive than the Browning model "A", is indeed worthy of your gun. It will afford the same protection and convenience, but is covered and lined with less expensive material.

The Model "B" case is of the same general specifications as the Model "A." The Model "B," however, is covered with black, heavy leatherette, machine-grained to give unusual wearing quality. The inside is lined with dark, heavy fabric. Your gun will fit snugly, will be protected against dust and moisture, yet will be easily accessible. Comparing the Model "B" with any other case similar in price, you will find it the best value for the money.

Cases for two barrels, either model, $3.25 extra.

Cases for special stocks, either model, $3.25 extra.

View of gun case closed. Dust and moisture proof. Opens easily and quickly.

The cases shown above were taken from a 1931 Browning catalog.

Two shotgun cases were available, one for the Auto-5 and one for the Superposed. These were known as "A" and "B" models for the A-5's and the "S" and "SB" models for the Superposed.

The "A" was covered with black textured cowhide and the "B", which was the cheaper case, was covered in black leatherette. The "B" variation also had a less expensive lining.

Both styles were made using a wood frame; they had compartments for the barrel and butt stock, along with an additional compartment for cleaning tools, etc. There was a "Browning" logo plate on the inside and a brass I.D shield on the outside, and the handles were leather covered. The hinges were mahogany steel and the snap latches were lockable.

You had a choice of barrel length for one barrel or, at an additional charge, two barrels. In addition, you could purchase a variation that had an extra compartment for additional parts such as a stock or forearm.

The "A" or leather case was priced at $19.95 and the "B" or leatherette case was $13.95. The "S" for the Superposed was $23.75 and the leatherette was $15.85.

In 1935 an additional option of either black or brown was offered; these were made without much change until 1957. The prices for these gradually increased throughout the years.

In 1939 two additional cases were offered in the leg-o-mutton style. These were cancelled by World War 2.

SHOTGUN and RIFLE LUGGAGE CASES

FOR ALL BROWNING GUNS — Proper protection of a fine gun when not in use is equally as important as reasonable care and treatment during and immediately after shooting. Many methods are recommended but one of the finest is a fixed luggage type gun case. It protects polished surfaces of wood and metal alike from marring or scratching. The rigidity of the case protects against dents or bruising from external forces. The case keeps the gun free from moisture but allows enough circulation to prevent sweating. A luggage type gun case is compact and easily stored and is provided with lock for safety and security from children.

The Browning case was designed to provide every essential qualification of the finest luggage type at a price within the means of every sportsman. The frame is made of solid plywood, covered with the most durable plastic leathercloth obtainable which has many characteristics superior to more costly leather. The tough exterior is waterproof and fireproof and highly resistant to scuffing, oil, gasoline, caustics and acids. The surface is easily cleaned with soap and water. The fitted interior is covered with a soft velvet and space is provided for cleaning equipment or extra shells. All models are fitted with strong stop hinges, statuary bronze hardware and lock and key.

LUGGAGE CASE SPECIFICATIONS

	Model
For AUTOMATIC-5, 12 and 16 gauge. Has compartment for extra barrel	A
For DOUBLE AUTOMATIC. Has compartment for extra barrel	DA
For SUPERPOSED, 12 and 20 gauge, 26½" and 28" barrels	S
For SUPERPOSED, 12 gauge, 30" barrels	ST
For SUPERPOSED with 2 sets of barrels. (All models except Trap)	SX
For SUPERPOSED Trap Models with 2 sets of barrels	SXT
For BROWNING .22 AUTOMATIC RIFLE	R

These cases and descriptions were taken from a 1958 Browning catalog.

1957

At this time two more variations were offered. In addition to the Auto-5 and Superposed cases, a case for the Double Automatic and the 22 Automatic were now in the line. They have come to be known as the "Tolex" cases after the name of the manufacturer.

These were made with plywood frames and covered with simulated leather which was an orange-tan color. The edges were stitched leather. All interiors were covered with royal blue velvet. The cases had compartments like the previous ones and the hinges were all made of brass. The Auto-5 cases had an extra compartment for a second barrel. These three cases were now priced at $35.00 and the 22 Auto case was $20.00.

BROWNING FITTED LUGGAGE CASES

for BROWNING shotguns and rifles

Proper protection of a fine gun when not in use is equally as important as reasonable care and treatment during and immediately after shooting. Many methods are recommended but one of the finest is a fitted luggage type gun case. It protects polished surfaces of wood and metal alike from marring or scratching. The rigidity of the case protects against dents or bruising from external forces. The case keeps the gun free from moisture but allows enough circulation to prevent sweating. A luggage type gun case is compact and easily stored and is provided with lock for safety and security from children.

The precisely fitted Browning luggage case is as rugged and durable as the Browning gun for which it was specifically engineered — designed especially for the sportsman who wishes to give his gun the fine care it deserves.

The solid frame is made of the finest grade, lightweight Virginia plywood. Its cover is of scuff-resistant vinyl, with a handsome crush-grain effect, simulating the finest leather while preserving the added wearability and toughness of vinyl.

The satin finished locks are of solid brass with draw bolts. The stop hinges and glides are purposely extra strong to withstand the knocks and bumps the bottom of any case encounters.

The lining is an extremely tough resilient material providing excellent protection. The lid and all appropriate areas are padded for complete cushioning of the gun. All of the interior has an invisible shield. It is Scotchguard® treated which protects the fabric from oil, water, dirt, and grease and permits easy cleaning.

Since the fabric is non-absorbing, there is less chance for accidental damage to your gun. Spilled liquids remain surfaced and can be gently blotted away with a cloth or tissue. Dry soilage remains on the surface of the fabric and can be whisked away.

These features combined with the waterproof, fireproof exterior which resists oil, gasoline, alcohol, caustics and acids, and is easily cleaned with soap and water, give your gun maximum protection.

FOR AUTOMATIC SHOTGUNS
— old as well as new

Automatic-5 or Double Automatic (Model A). Case includes an extra barrel compartment.

FOR SUPERPOSED SHOTGUNS
— old as well as new

12, 20, 28 or .410 gauge (Model S)
With one extra set of barrels (Model SX)
With two extra sets of barrels (Model SXX)
With 32 inch BROADway barrels (Model ST)
With extra set of BROADway barrels (Model STX)
With two extra sets of BROADway barrels (Model STXX)

FOR .22 AUTOMATIC RIFLES

Model RS is designed to accommodate the Browning .22 Automatic Rifle (.22 LR Model only) either with or without a scope. Careful internal design makes the case suitable for the rifle with the scope mounted on either receiver or barrel. A handy compartment for cartridges is an integral part of the case.

FOR HIGH-POWER RIFLES

Model HR. Accommodates rifles with any scope size mounted and with or without sling. Contains a compartment for cartridges.

Shown here is a page from a 1965 Browning catalog featuring gun cases that were available at that time.

1960

The Tolex cases were now replaced by those made with a vinyl material. One additional case was offered at this time which could hold three barrels and which cost $50.00. These were compartmented with pads to support the various parts of the gun. They were covered with a flannel-like material. Later, this was changed to a heavier fleece fabric. The handles were now being made with plastic that had ivory colored inserts. They were made by a firm called Hartmann, whose name you can find on the snap locks. The cost was still $35.00.

A Broadway trap case was offered in 1962 at $35.00 for the one barrel model or $50.00 for one that held two barrels. Also, in 1963 a three barrel trap case was offered at the same prices as the two barrel, and a Safari rifle case was available at $45.00.

In 1965 the 22 Auto case was changed so that it could accommodate a longer barrel with a scope. Meanwhile prices keep increasing.

In 1969 a BT-99 case was added to the line at $41.50. This was also the cost of the Auto-5 and Superposed single barrel cases. The 22 Auto case was now also $31.50, and the Safari case, which had been changed so that a scoped rifle would fit, was $49.50.

1971

This was the start of the "Airways made" Naugahyde case, which had a plywood frame, brass hinges and locks, and nylon fleece liners. The handles were now covered with a simulated leather that was stitched and the color was tan. Surprisingly, the prices were the same as 1969. Three new variations were added in 1975, the BSS case was added at $42.95, and the BAR and BBR at $49.95.

1977

A BT-99 two barrel case was added in 1977, as well as, a new cover which was a brown mottling on a light background of crushed Naugahyde, the handles were plastic again. In 1978, a case was offered that would accommodate the 34" barreled BPS.

In 1982 European styled leather cases were offered for the shotguns. These were green colored felt lined with compartments and priced at $159.95. Prices for the bolt action rifle was $96.95; the 22 Auto, $74.95; and the A-5, $89.95.

Hope you find your case.

BROWNING KNIVES

I know this is supposed to be a book on firearms, but collectable knives are becoming more and more popular among Browning enthusiasts.

In 1969 Browning had Gil Hibben of Manti, Utah, design three models. These were produced by the Ensign Knife Company of Gunnison, Utah.

Production of these ended in the mid 1970's.

Style 4018F is a folder with a 4'' blade.

Style 4018 is a fixed blade sheath with a 4'' blade.

Style 4518 is a fixed blade sheath knife with a 4 1/2'' blade.

Style 5518 is a fixed blade sheath knife with a 5 1/4'' blade.

All were produced with 440-C stainless steel. Blade thickness was 3/16''.

Since none are serial numbered, you must look at the thickness of the blade. Later, non-collectable knives have a thinner blade. Also, the earlier knives have palm contoured wood grips and heavy scooped pommels. All were shipped in smooth leather sheaths from Mexico. Later knives came in a basketweave designed sheath.

Be careful not to confuse the earlier knives with the later one. Values vary considerably.

GUN CASES FOR BROWNING SUPERPOSED

⌄

BROWNING Superposed Gun Cases are built especially for Browning Superposed Guns. They are designed to afford the greatest convenience and ease for removing or replacing the gun in the case. The quality of leather, strength of construction and all essential requisites necessary for appearance, and protection of the gun, have been carried throughout the building of the Superposed case. The gun fits snugly in the case, yet ample room is provided for such essential equipment as cleaning cloths, cleaning rod, oil can, etc.

When closed it is tight fitting and neat in appearance.

Long life and satisfactory wearing quality are assured by the use of dragon grained genuine cowhide leather.

Superposed Model "S" Cases

Price $23.75

SPECIFICATIONS: Hand-made and covered with genuine cowhide leather. Color—black only. Dragon machine grained leather to prevent marring. All seams hand sewed. Edges rounded giving it a smooth neat appearance. Sides and ends are constructed of northern basswood. Top and bottom constructed of 1/4-inch 3-ply northern basswood.

All corners of case reinforced inside with steel angles. A flange covered with genuine cowhide leather around inside of case prevents dust and water from getting in. Handmade, solid leather handle all hand-sewed. Two mahogany steel snap locks, one on each side of handle and one center snap—this insures a tight fitting case at all times, yet the contents are easily and quickly accessible.

Inside of case lined throughout with soft but

durable, highest quality dark colored fabric. Leather straps hold gun and barrel securely in position to prevent rattling and rubbing. Note the snug fitting compartments for gun and barrel; also extra section for cleaning rod, oil can, cloths, etc.

Supplied with brass plate for your name and address.

Cases for two sets of barrels $4.00 extra. Cases to accommodate special stocks and Beaver-Tail Fore-End $4.00 extra.

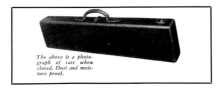

The above is a photograph of case when closed. Dust and moisture proof.

Chapter Four

Over and Under Shotguns

The front cover as it looked in the 1931 Superposed catalog.

THE BROWNING SUPERPOSED

THE overunder represents the highest development of the double gun and the Browning Superposed is the highest development of the overunder type. Designed by John M. Browning and built in the world's greatest firearms factory, by old world craftsmen, to old world standards of craftsmanship. You are now offered, for the first time in firearm's history, an overunder that has been produced at a price which makes it available to almost every sportsman.

BROWNING
ARMS COMPANY

Headquarters and

General Offices

ST. LOUIS, MISSOURI

Ogden, Utah, U. S. A.   Liege, Belgium.

The cover design is a combination photograph and pen drawing of Mr. G. L. Becker,
nationally known trapshooter and holder of numerous titles.

When introduced the Superposed was presented as a quality over and under that was affordable to the American shooter.

JONATHAN BROWNING
Founder of the Browning gun business

JOHN M. BROWNING
First President Browning Arms Co. and the greatest firearms inventor of history

M. S. BROWNING
First Vice-President of Browning Arms Co.

Three Generations of Gunmaking

Jonathan Browning, moving westward from Kentucky, where he had learned the trade of gunsmith, set up a shop in Council Bluffs, Iowa, in the thirties. For a few years he repaired and made guns, many of original design, for the pioneers of the Gold Rush. In 1851 he captained a wagon train across the plains, and located permanently in Ogden, Utah.

John M. Browning worked with his father until his death, and thereafter carried on the business with the help of his younger brother,

Matthew. An outline of the results of his activities is given in these pages.

V. A. Browning, one of the sons of John M., and for a number of years his technical assistant, has for the past ten years lived in Belgium, in charge of factory interests of the Browning Arms Company. To him has been entrusted the installation of equipment and production is under his active supervision. Browning experience of three generations goes into the manufacture of Browning Superposed and Browning Automatic Shotguns.

M. A. BROWNING

JOHN BROWNING

V. A. BROWNING

The Browning Arms Company always used their reputation as a family organization to gain the confidence of the buying public. The pictures you see here are of three generations.

BROWNING SUPERPOSED--*A New Overunder Gun*

OVERUNDER guns, though manufactured for years, are better known in Europe than in America, several factories over there having specialized in hand production of these guns, which have necessarily brought very high prices. The building of a gun, entirely or almost entirely by hand, involves many months of labor by the most skilled artisans, hence the combined production has never run more than a few hundred a year.

Despite their high cost, their merit has long been recognized by discriminating shooters in this country, who have imported them when they could afford it, and wished for them when they could not.

The handmade guns of Europe, however, possessed some serious faults, largely because they were, strictly speaking, based on the principles of the side-by-side guns with which their makers were more familiar. Instead of working out the details from the ground up, they adapted, as far as possible, the principles of the type they were accustomed to building. This naturally brought about mechanical difficulties, in the overcoming of which they were never entirely successful.

Browning Superposed is the first overunder gun offered at a price which is not prohibitive.

SUPERPOSED PREWAR 1931 TO 1938

HISTORY

According to the Browning Arms Company, production of the pre-war Superposed started in 1927, and it appeared on the American market in 1928. Not to dispute what they say, but according to the catalogs and written material I have been able to get, sales didn't start until 1931.

It was the last design of John Browning and was unusual in that it was the first design in many years that was not a pump, automatic, or semi-automatic.

Mr. Browning was an avid shotgun shooter and was in fact one of the members of the famous "Four B's," Utah's premier live bird team and later trap shooting squad. One of the other members of the squad, Gus Becker, suggested to John that he look at designing an over-and-under, for it would be a good alternative to the double barrel. A 1920's diary entry ran as follows:

"J.M. Browning called us together one day around the drafting table in his model-making shop. The table was covered with pencil sketches of details of arms mechanisms. Laid across one end of it were four shotguns of entirely different types, each the latest word in its class. He spoke about them as follows:

" 'The great American Gun Rack is pretty well filled, but there is a conspicuous gap among the shotguns. I have had an eye on that gap for a long time, and now that there are no urgent military jobs on hand, I am going to have a try at filling it. As a matter of fact, I have the gun pretty well worked out in my mind, and I have told the shop to get ready to start on the model at once.' "

He must have seen, when he started the design of this model, that military weapons were not in great demand. Whatever his thinking, this is the most successful over-and-under design in history. The initial introduction of the Superposed in the 1931 catalog reads as follows:

The first patents taken out on this model were on October 15, 1923. Mr. Browning died on November 26, 1926, while supervising the making of the prototype. It was unfinished until his son, Val Browning, designed the trigger mechanism which has proven the most reliable of any over-and-under of any make.

The new gun was endorsed by some of the leading outdoor writer including Capt. Paul A. Curtis, editor of *Field and Stream*. He said,

"I have owned four over-and-unders, and think I might safely say that I have shot or handled every variety of over-and-under of any importance produced during the last generation, and I have yet, regardless of price, to open and close a smoother working one than this inexpensive weapon. It is like rubbing velvet together."

Probably, the most read and knowledgeable shotgun writer during this time was Capt. Charles Askins who wrote in *Outdoor Life*.

As a final word, "the Browning overunder is an attractive gun in appearance, quality and price."

BROWNING SOLVES THE PROBLEM

INASMUCH as John M. Browning had revolutionized most types of small arms, both sporting and military, it was hardly likely that a type as important as the two-barrel shotgun should escape his attention. He long ago realized the superiority of the overunder positioning of barrels, and often discussed the subject in family councils. It would be necessary, he perceived, to design a gun which would retain all the inherent advantages of the type, and which would at the same time be sufficiently simple mechanically to go into large scale production under modern manufacturing conditions. If this result could be attained, the comparatively low price at which the arm could be sold would attract a large number of sportsmen. It could not be a cheap gun; all high grade two-barrel guns require a considerable amount of hand fitting; but it seemed possible to bring an overunder within reach of a great many sportsmen. He, of course, understood the mechanical difficulties involved, but difficulties merely heightened his interest.

His speculations on the subject are now a realized fact in the Browning Superposed. This year we have in the making probably twice as many overunder shotguns as have heretofore issued from all sources. Methods that were almost medieval have been replaced by methods that are thoroughly modern. A well-nigh prohibitive price has been brought down to a comparatively low price. And all this has been achieved merely by applying well-known manufacturing principles; simplified design, expensive but, in the long run, money-saving equipment, a highly trained organization, a large output.

FITTING---CHECKERING *and* FINISH

THE two-barrel gun is the standard sporting gun in Europe, and for generations Liege has been a leading center of manufacture for that type of arm. The essential problems of manufacture are the same in side-by-side and over-under guns, and the size and prestige of the factory wherein Browning Superposed guns are made enable us to select the most skillful mechanics in a highly industrialized community.

Scrutinize the finish; compare it part by part with that of any other gun. The wider your acquaintance with firearms, the more you will appreciate the amount of painstaking handwork which goes into the Browning Superposed.

Follow the lines where wood joins metal—all handwork. Examine the contact of barrels and frames. We wish you could stand beside one of our fitters. An oil lamp is used to smoke each surface as it is being fitted, and, touch by touch with fine files and emery, the points of bearing are brought into perfect contact. A gun is taken apart and put together just as many times as is necessary—possibly 100 times in fitting barrels to standing breech. The adjustment is not considered finished until a thin smear of carbon shows evenly on the entire surface of contacting parts.

Examine the wood, finish and checkering of stock and fore-end; the polish, bluing and engraving of metal. The Browning Superposed is not built to meet a price, it is built to meet exacting tastes.

"Dollar for dollar, this gun is still the most attractive gun of any in appearance and price. You have to look at the English over-and-unders to approach the balance and shootability of this great design."

John's thinking was that the shooter could get on a bird more accurately if he had a single sighting plane rather then two as you do in a double barrel. The Brownings made a big thing of this and devoted an entire page in the introductory catalog explaining his thinking. We can sum this up in the last part of the description:

"When one walks along a narrow ledge overhanging a precipice, one instinctively holds the eyes on the trail. The distinct sighting plane of the Superposed rib is like a narrow ledge, and the deep side lines are precipices on either side. Instinctively the eye clings to that plane."

It concludes with,

"It was the study and correlating of these factors by the master gunmaker which makes the Superposed seem possessed of eyes of its own, with which to pick up and center the flying target."

APPEARANCE WHEN OPEN

The breech is unencumbered by lugs. If the hammers are down, the ejector heads must, of course, protrude, but nothing else is there to mar the smooth chamber openings. The Browning system of locking does not require lugs at this point. The locking bolt is a large, sturdy piece, not expensive to make, and it is hidden from sight. We have, therefore, eliminated both a costly and exacting manufacturing job and unsightly extensions. The smooth chamber openings facilitate loading and the shooter who reloads in the hurry of excitement will not skin his fingers. This is another of the numerous points at which we have at once beautified the arm, increased the ease of operation, and lowered manufacturing costs.

From the 1931 catalog.

This was quite a comparison, a precipice and the rib of a shotgun, but they had their way of saying things in 1931.

It always appeared ironic that the last gun designed by John Browning would be of this type when he spent his whole life designing semi and full automatics. Mr. Browning was a very versatile man that loved all types of guns and prone to none. He was just as capable of designing one type as another.

A LOOK AT THE
BROWNING SUPERPOSED

ｖ

LET US begin with a look at the gun. The beauty of simplicity is axiomatic, and the axiom has striking proof of its verity
in the new Browning. The sides of the frame are smooth, easy to
make and pleasing to the eye. Protuberances are never added to the
sides of a frame for the sake of beauty. They are necessary evils.
Something inside requires room, and the resulting bulges are
rounded and glossed over as well as can be. The same comparison is applicable between the intricate body designs
of early automobiles and present-day streamlines. Those
curiously shaped bodies were difficult to make, were
made in small quantities, entailed much handwork,
and you paid more for them than for their beautiful and simple successors.

The streamlines of the Browning Superposed are analogous
in every way. Furthermore, the
straight lines, apart from reducing
costs and increasing beauty, achieve an
interesting and important purpose which
will be discussed under the subject of "Sighting." This detail is stressed particularly for
those who, for no discoverable reason, are erratic,
who make mysterious misses and harass themselves
with wondering why; and also for men who are ambitious to improve their average in competitive shooting.
This is a fine point which did not "just happen" into the gun,
but which was carefully figured out to conform to well-known
laws of optics.

The name given to this gun derives from the French word "superpose". It means in the past tense "to superpose" or to place one over the other. As you know, the basic language of the Belgian people is French, and John M. spoke it fluently. He must have wanted to give his fancy new invention a fancy new name. Whatever the reason, Superposed, has become synonymous with over-and-under shotguns.

When introduced, the only gauge available was the 12. Although Val Browning redesigned the gun to handle 20 gauge loads when he designed his trigger system, it was not available in this country until 1949. This brings us into the post-war era which will be covered later. Another strange thing is that the gun was never made in 16 gauge which is the second most popular gun in Europe.

ANNOUNCING

OUR NEW SALES POLICY

DIRECT-FROM-BROWNING-TO-YOU

AT NEW REDUCED PRICES

IN KEEPING with the trend of the times, we announce a new sales policy—one which effects a material reduction in cost of distribution and permits a materially lower price to the consumer. This new saving is shown in the prices at which we are able to offer the Browning Superposed, $107.50, delivered to the purchaser. Similar reductions have been made in the Browning "16" Automatic and Browning "12" Automatic, both now being $49.75. Formerly the Browning "16" Automatic was $65.50 and the Browning "12" Automatic was $61.00.

This new policy, we feel, is directly in line with the present trend to give the purchaser the greatest possible value for his money. The change was made after a most careful investigation among our owners and of all trade channels. We found that the tremendous increase in the number of Browning Automatic Shotgun owners year after year was largely due to the good word passed along by users of these guns.

The new sales plan gives a direct contact with the ultimate purchaser, which should be beneficial both to him and to ourselves, and, most important of all considerations, it permits us to offer the purchaser an actual saving of from 20% to 25%.

We hope that this new policy will meet with your approval and support. Again we wish to emphasize that a nation-wide chain of service stations will be maintained and that Browning Superposed and Browning Automatic Shotguns are backed by an ironclad guarantee for quality, workmanship, and material.

Browning direct to you was the 1931 sales technique used to try to boost sales during the worst time of the depression.

GRADES

When introduced in 1931, the Standard, Pigeon, Diana, Midas, and Hand-made were available. In 1936 the Trap model was also introduced. These could be ordered with any barrell, stock dimensions, pad, rib, trigger, etc. you wanted; all these options will be covered in their section.

THE BROWNING SUPERPOSED

I N ALL the world of guncraft there is no arm so ingeniously designed, so carefully and accurately manufactured, so finely finished both within and without, as the new BROWNING SUPERPOSED . . . this is the consensus of discriminating sportsmen and disinterested experts . . . men who know good guns and whose understanding goes beneath the surface. Such men have pronounced this the outstanding work of the greatest arms designer of all time—John M. Browning—the crowning achievement of a lifetime of accomplishment.

Whether your choice be the standard grade at $107.50, or one of the special grades, highly embellished custom jobs costing from $175.00 to $1200.00, the same high standard of material and workmanship prevails in *every* BROWNING SUPERPOSED. So the sportsman of limited means who buys a standard grade need never question its quality . . . it is the finest that knowledge, skill, and unlimited resources can produce. Automatic ejectors and Level Hollow Rib are standard equipment and are therefore supplied without additional cost. Chambered for $2\frac{3}{4}$-inch shells.

EXTRAS: Non-Crossfire Ventilated Rib, $20.00.

This is the Standard Grade shown with Non-Crossfire Ventilated Rib.

STANDARD GRADE
$107.50

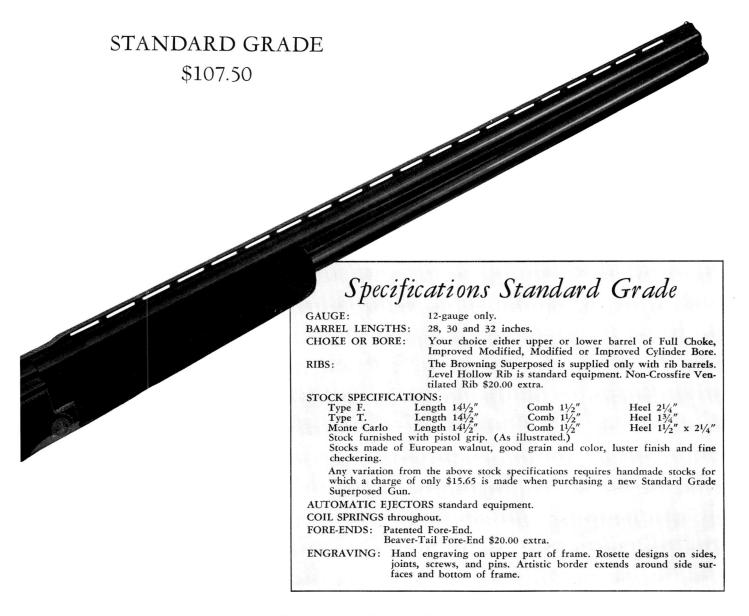

Specifications Standard Grade

GAUGE:	12-gauge only.
BARREL LENGTHS:	28, 30 and 32 inches.
CHOKE OR BORE:	Your choice either upper or lower barrel of Full Choke, Improved Modified, Modified or Improved Cylinder Bore.
RIBS:	The Browning Superposed is supplied only with rib barrels. Level Hollow Rib is standard equipment. Non-Crossfire Ventilated Rib $20.00 extra.

STOCK SPECIFICATIONS:

Type F.	Length 14½"	Comb 1½"	Heel 2¼"
Type T.	Length 14½"	Comb 1½"	Heel 1¾"
Monte Carlo	Length 14½"	Comb 1½"	Heel 1½" x 2¼"

Stock furnished with pistol grip. (As illustrated.)

Stocks made of European walnut, good grain and color, luster finish and fine checkering.

Any variation from the above stock specifications requires handmade stocks for which a charge of only $15.65 is made when purchasing a new Standard Grade Superposed Gun.

AUTOMATIC EJECTORS standard equipment.

COIL SPRINGS throughout.

FORE-ENDS:	Patented Fore-End. Beaver-Tail Fore-End $20.00 extra.
ENGRAVING:	Hand engraving on upper part of frame. Rosette designs on sides, joints, screws, and pins. Artistic border extends around side surfaces and bottom of frame.

General Specifications:

STANDARD GRADE. 12-gauge only; barrels of special fluid compressed steel, 28, 30, or 32 inches. Line engraving bordering joints, rosettes on sides and around screws and pins, add beauty and distinction. Stock and fore-end of selected, dark rich European walnut, hand rubbed and polished, and finely hand checkered. Fore-End slides forward for removing barrels—cannot be dropped or lost. Automatic ejectors. Level Hollow Rib barrel. All external metal blued. Price $107.50. EXTRAS: Ventilated Rib, $20.00.

We are prepared to supply butt stocks to any special specifications, at a cost for standard wood of $15.65 additional, fancy selected curly walnut from $35.00 to $75.00—time required for delivery, about two weeks. We also solicit correspondence from those who appreciate the finest, most elaborate, highly engraved and inlaid guns, as we are prepared to carry out the purchaser's individual ideas to the minutest detail, the cost of such work being limited only by the amount you desire to invest. At the same time, we are in position to give you, on such work, the greatest dollar-for-dollar value.

The Standard Grade was the lowest one offered in 1931. It was more than twice the price of an Auto-5. Notice the double triggers and the fact that you could get a gun made to your specifications for $15.65 additional.

STANDARD GRADE

As first introduced, the Standard grade had only borderline engraving until 1936 when rosettes on the edges of the frame, the trigger guard, around the pins and screws, and on the forearm hanger started to appear. It was very similar to the post-war Grade I except that the wedges of engraving on the sides and bottom were not done.

In the Standard Grade, the wood was about group 1-2 and checkering was about 26 lines per inch. The oil finish was similar to the early post-war Grade I's in that all pores are filled, but the finish is not high polish like the higher grades.

In 1936 it became the Grade 1 and the Lightning was the next highest grade. When introduced, the Standard Grade sold for $107.50, but sales were slow, so in 1934 the price was reduced to $99.50. Things still were slow during the depression, so in 1936 the price was again lowered to $79.80 and remained there until the end of the war.

Although it was the lowest grade offered, it was by no means a shoddy piece. All interior parts were polished, and the fit and finish of the exterior was superb. For $15.65 you could order a gun with a custom stock, and if you wanted better wood, you could spend from $35.00 to $70.00 additional.

LIGHTWEIGHT MODEL

In 1933 the "Lightweight" was introduced, but it lived the short life of only five years, for in 1936 the Lightning grade replaced it.

The Lightweight can immediately be recognized by the very slender forearms and weight of only 6 1/2 lbs. The engraving and all else is identical to the Grade I.

The Lightweight was to the Superposed what the "Browning Special' was to the Auto-5 in that it was a step up without spending any more money. The basic engraving was borderline and rosettes on the edges of the frame, the trigger guard, around the pins and screws, and on the forearm hanger with a wedge of engraving on the sides and bottom. It was very similar to the post-war Grade I guns. Of course, because the invasion of Belgium came soon after the introduction of the grade, to find one like this would be very rare.

LIGHTNING

When introduced in 1938, the Lightning grade had only borderline engraving and sold for the unbelievable price of $79.80 and remained at that price until the war. As introduced rosettes on the edges of the frame, the trigger guard, around the pins and screws, and on the forearm hanger were engraved. It was very similar to the post-war Grade I except the wedge of engraving on the sides and bottom were not done.

In the Lightnings the wood was about group 1-2 and checkering was about 20 lines per inch. The oil finish was similar to the early post-war grade I's in that all pores are filled and the finish is a semi gloss.

All interior parts were polished and the fit and finish of the exterior was perfect. The standard specifications were listed in the catalogs as follows: 26", 28", or 30" barrels with a level matted rib; automatic selective ejectors; and single selective triggers with a special Type "F" stock. These dimensions were length of pull 14 1/8", drop at heel 2 1/2", and drop at comb 1 5/8"

The standard chokes available on the Lightning were coded as C, D and E. "C" was under-barrel modified and over-barrel full, "D" code was under-barrel improved cylinder and over-barrel modified, and "E" was coded skeet and skeet.

SKEET

From the beginning of importation of the Superposed, Browning made available the 12 gauge only Skeet model.

These were always available in Grades 1, Pigeon, Diana, Midas and, although not cataloged, the Exhibition grade. Any Skeet model in Grade 1 is rare and extremely rare in a high grade. All features such as the triggers, ejectors, sights, and engraving were available or the same as the other models.

Barrels were all 26" or 28" and matted with a striped pattern unless special ordered with a solid swamped rib or a ventilated rib that was also matted. Needless to say, they were only skeet choked.

Unlike the later post-war guns, the pre-war Skeet model had no recoil pads as standard and were stocked with the following dimensions: drop at comb 1 1/2", drop at heel 2 1/4, and length of pull 14 1/2". The later stocks have the drop at comb 1 5/8", drop at heel 2 1/2", and length of pull 14 1/8". The "F" style stocks all had pistol grips and checkered like the other models. The forearms are literally the only way to tell them apart from the field guns, in that they are slightly beavertail, not a full beavertail.

TRAP

Also available from the beginning of importation of the Superposed was the 12 gauge only Trap model.

These were always available in Grades 1, Pigeon, Diana, Midas, and, although not cataloged, the Exhibition grade. Any Trap model in Grade 1 is rare and extremely rare in a high grade.

Standard features were automatic ejectors and the twin single trigger; other triggers were also available as an extra cost option.

Barrels were all 30" or 32" with a matted ventilated rib only. The chokes were made only two ways, both full or top-barrel full, and bottom-improved modified.

Unlike the later post-war guns, the pre-war Trap model had no recoil pads as standard and were stocked with the "T" style stock that had the following dimensions, drop at comb 1 1/2", drop at heel 1 3/4, and length of pull 14 1/2". Later, the length of pull was changed to 14 3/8". They all had pistol grips and were checkered like the other models. The forearms were the same as the field models.

PIGEON GRADE

Same dimensional specifications as the Standard Grade. An especially attractive feature is the color finish of the frame, which is a rich gray instead of the usual blue-black. The finish is little known in this country, but of recent years has become very popular for high grade guns on the Continent. It is advantageous in that it does not wear bright with handling, as is the case with bluing, and it affords a fitting background for the fine line engraving. The gray finish throws the finest lines of a design into relief.

The frame, trigger guard and top lever are decorated with a high quality of fine line engraving. Oak leaves are carved in relief on the top curve of the frame, pigeons are engraved on the sides and bottom. Fine line conventional designs and borders surround the birds and cover joints, screws and pins. Stocks are of choice French walnut, of attractive grain and color, finely checkered and brought to a high luster by Browning painstaking methods of polishing and dressing.

All parts of the mechanism are hand polished. The Pigeon Superposed is a high grade gun bearing those touches which you have associated only with arms much higher in price.

PRICE $175.00

Stock Specifications:

Type F.   Length 14½″ Comb 1½″ Heel 2¼″
Type T.   Length 14½″ Comb 1½″ Heel 1¾″
Monte Carlo Length 14½″ Comb 1½″ Heel 1½″ x 2¼″

Automatic Ejectors and Level Hollow Rib—Standard Equipment.

Non-Crossfire Ventilated Rib $20.00 additional.

All above stocks furnished with pistol grip, as illustrated on page 16.

Any variation from these stock specifications requires special handmade stocks for which a charge of only $15.65 is made when purchasing new Pigeon Grade Guns.

The Pigeon Grade has always been one of the most popular through out the years both pre and post war.

PIGEON GRADE

The next grade up was the "Pigeon" grade. The frame, trigger guard, and top lever were decorated with a high quality of fine line engraving. Oak leaves were carved in relief on the top curve of the frame, pigeons were also engraved, appropiately enough, on both sides and bottom of the receiver. Fine line conventional designs and borders surround the birds and cover joints, screws, and pins. Coverage is about 90%. The frame and trigger guard was greyed, and the look of the engraving is very much like the modern Pigeon grade.

The wood is group 2-3 French walnut checkered about 22 line per inch and finished to a high degree.

All internal parts were hand polished, and automatic ejectors and hollow ribs were standard.

When introduced, the Pigeon grade sold for $175.00.

DIANA GRADE

Diana of the Chase might be pictured in such scenes as are engraved on this gun. Deer are shown on one side of the frame, wild boars on the other, with appropriate scenic backgrounds. Oak leaves are hand carved in relief on the curve of the standing breech. The entire decorative scheme is executed by the most skillful engravers, much of the work being microscopically fine. These men are artists, and the animals they picture in steel have life and animation. We believe sportsmen will enjoy this departure from dog and bird subjects. The latter may be had by special order, however, without change in price.

The frame of the Diana Superposed is finished in the rich gray, noted above, in order to make the fine engraving stand out distinctly.

All exterior metal is brought to a mirror-like polish by hand, after which the bluing process imparts a superb luster. This finish is never surpassed, and frequently not equalled, on the highest priced, hand-made, imported arms.

Stocks are those selections of European walnut which are becoming increasingly rare and costly. We have standing orders at numerous points for the superior figures and colors. Nothing is more conducive to pride in a gun than a fine stock, and we keep that fact always in mind—from rough block to finished stock.

PRICE $277.00

All parts of the mechanism are hand polished—firing pins, ejector hammers, latches and trip rods gold plated.

Stock Specifications:

Type F.   Length 14½″   Comb 1½″   Heel 2¼″
Type T.   Length 14½″   Comb 1½″   Heel 1¾″
Monte Carlo Length 14½″   Comb 1½″   Heel 1½″ x 2¼″

Automatic Ejectors and Level Hollow Rib—Standard Equipment. Non-Crossfire Ventilated Rib $20.00 additional.

All above stocks furnished with pistol grip, as illustrated on page 16. Stock to special specifications at no extra charge when purchasing new Diana Grade Superposed gun.

The Diana Grade was offered as a fitted gun at no extra charge, all grade below the Diana incurred these charges.

DIANA GRADE

The third highest grade was the "Diana" grade named after "Diana" of the hunt. This was, however, very different from the post-war Diana that you are probably used to seeing. It featured a 10 point buck and three does on the right and wild boars on the left of the frame. This was all surrounded by hunting scenes. Oak leaves were hand carved on the curve of the standing breech; coverage was virtually 100%.

As an alternative, you could order at no extra charge pointing dogs and birds. The entire action including the trigger guard was finished in a greyed manner, and all interior parts were very highly polished and finished.

The wood is group 3-4 French walnut checkered about 24 line per inch and finished to a high degree. This grade was available with custom stock work at no additional charge.

All internal parts were hand polished, automatic ejectors, and hollow ribs were standard.

When introduced, the Diana Grade sold for $277.00.

MIDAS GRADE

All stocks furnished with pistol grip, as illustrated on page 16.

Stock to special specifications at no extra charge when purchasing new Midas Grade Superposed gun.

Stock Specifications:

Type F.   Length 14½", Comb 1½", Heel 2¼"

Type T.   Length 14½", Comb 1½", Heel 1¾"

Monte Carlo

        Length 14½", Comb 1½", Heel 1½" x 2¼"

Automatic Ejectors and Level Hollow Rib—Standard Equipment.

Non-Crossfire Ventilated Rib $20.00 additional.

PRICE $374.00

The Midas Superposed startles even the connoisseur of fine arms with the richness and artistry of its embellishments. The superintendent of the engraving department was instructed to design and execute the finest possible job of gold inlaying—regardless of time and expense. The artist welcomes such a commission; he likes to escape the exactions of time and cost limitations, and to give his imagination and skill free play. The Midas Superposed is the result of such a commission.

The subject is a gold pigeon with spreading wings in relief, one on each side of frame and one on the bottom. Heavy lines of gold form a conventional foliage and geometric design around the birds, extending to the trigger guard and top lever, and continuing a short distance on the top barrel. It is a superb design superbly executed. The frame is blue, in order to furnish a fitting contrast for the gold. Stocks, checkering, metal polishing and bluing are of the same quality as on the Diana Superposed. All interior parts are hand polished and firing pins, ejector hammers, latches and trip rods are gold plated.

Like all Browning high grades, the Midas is built for use.

Although called a Midas, it is much different from the post war engraving.

MIDAS GRADE

Let the Browning catalog introduce you to this grade.

"The Midas startles even the connoisseur of the fine arms with the richness and artistry of its embellishments. The superintendent of the engraving department was instructed to design and execute the finest possible job of gold inlaying-regardless of time and expense. The artist welcomes such a commission; he likes to escape the exactions of time and cost limitations, and to give his imagination and skill free play. The Midas Superposed is the result of such a commission."

The top of the line in the catalog, other then handmade was the "Midas" grade. This was very different from the Midas you are used to seeing. Engraving was almost "art deco" in looks, featuring a spread-winged pigeon surrounded by a triangle on each side and the bottom. Each corner of the triangle was squared off, and the entire background inside of the triangle was inlaid in gold wire. The balance of the frame was engraved with heavy gold lines inlaid in the form of conventional foliage and geometric design around the birds extending to the trigger guard and top lever and continuing a short distance on the top barrel.

The frame was blued and made a beautiful gun with the gold inlays in contrast.

The entire interior was polished to the highest extremes with the firing pines, ejector hammers, latches, and trip rods gold plated.

The wood is group 5-6 French walnut checkered about 28 line per inch and finished to a high degree. This grade was available with custom stock work at no additional charge.

When introduced the Midas grade sold for $347.00.

OPEN THE BROWNING SUPERPOSED

T HE smooth, even action is the result of design and of infinite pains in fitting. The cocking leverage is unusually powerful and most ingeniously applied. As an illustration, let us use a pair of shears. If the blades are perfectly adjusted, there is a continuous velvety resistance through the entire length of the movement. If the blades do not touch snugly, there is play in the joint. It is better that the contact of the blades be a bit too snug than too loose.

The same is true of the two-barrel gun. Each movable part must bear snugly against its companion surface during the entire movement, and it is better that the contact be a little too tight than too loose. Parts will soon seat themselves with use, if the bearings are tight, but, if they are too loose to start with, they go from bad to worse. It takes a few hundred miles to "limber up" a new automobile.

All parts of the Superposed which operate in the standing breech are hand-fitted and brought to perfect contact by hand stoning.

Browning Superposed Ejectors are strong and sturdy but operate easily and smoothly. See complete description on Page 12.

We could reduce considerably the cost of the Browning Superposed by making it snap open and shut with perfect freedom. Such looseness is a frequent characteristic of cheap guns. If a cheap gun happens to be tight, it is because of high points in bearing surfaces which will soon wear off and leave the joints loose.

But do not think that it is necessary to break the Superposed over the knee. The smooth, even resistance is just enough to give a pleasant feeling of confidence in the fitting. There is nothing jerky in the movement. The leverage is powerful

and ingeniously applied. The hammers are cocked by the opening, and the ejectors are cocked by the closing, thus equalizing the two operations.

Of necessity, there is friction throughout the movements of opening and closing. There is a slight drag at the beginning of the movement of the top lever due to the snug fit of the locking block in the slot of the barrel lug. It would be much easier as a fitting job to make the long gradual slope on the end of the locking block more abrupt, but strength and durability would be sacrificed.

HAND-MADE

If you cared to go to the trouble and had the money during the world's worst depression, you could have anything you wanted on special order. Special order pre-war Superposed are very rare and demand high prices. There was no grade or particular name for these other then what Browning called their "Hand-made" guns. Of course F.N. always produced Exhibition grade examples of their work for Worlds Fairs and such extravaganzas.

STRENGTH

JOHN M. BROWNING not only maintained his position for half a century as the greatest of firearms inventors; he also supervised the laying down of many installations for the manufacture of his arms, and guided the process of manufacture through to the completed product. He became, therefore, the master of two arts, designing and manufacturing. In the designing of an arm, he could look forward to factory operations. And his experience in this respect was not limited to one factory, but extended to several, both in this country and in Europe. Thus, in designing an arm, having the parts of the first model made in his own shop, (he made his earliest models with his own hands) he was able to project his imagination to the equipment that would be required for the manufacture of each part—the tools, jigs, fixtures, etc., and the number of operations.

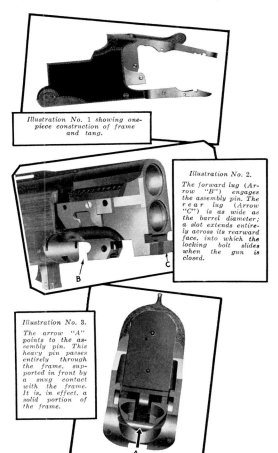

Illustration No. 1 showing one-piece construction of frame and tang.

Illustration No. 2.

The forward lug (Arrow "B") engages the assembly pin. The rear lug (Arrow "C") is as wide as the barrel diameter; a slot extends entirely across its rearward face, into which the locking bolt slides when the gun is closed.

Illustration No. 3.

The arrow "A" points to the assembly pin. This heavy pin passes entirely through the frame, supported in front by a snug contact with the frame. It is, in effect, a solid portion of the frame.

Many ingenious men lack this dual training, and, bending their attention to devising a mechanism that will work successfully, they fail to foresee the difficult and costly factory operations that will be required. The ingenious mind must have a well developed practical side in order to combine successful functioning with simplicity. Mr. Browning's life was a constant refining of the complex into the simple. In that process, scrutinized by the infinite patience of genius, the intricate and unsightly became simple and beautiful.

The frame of the Browning Superposed is a case in point. It is shown in Illustration No. 1 with the mechanism dismounted. The frame and both tangs are cut from a solid block of steel. The lower tang of other two-barrel guns is a separate piece, screwed to the frame, the ends of the two tangs being held by a screw which passes through the stock. The tangs of the Superposed, in one piece with the frame to begin with, and unusually thick, have a heavy binding post slotted into their ends. The detachable tang construction, which the Superposed avoids, necessitates the cutting of a seat in the bottom of the frame, the fitting of the tang into that seat, and the boring and threading of the two holes for the screws which hold the two pieces together. The Superposed construction eliminates the expense of all those operations, and at the same time achieves an incomparable rigidity.

Both barrel lugs enter deep seats in the frame as the gun closes. The locking bolt is thick, (see Illustration No. 3) broad, and hidden from view. With the two-barrel lugs deeply seated in the frame, the assembly pin engaging the forward lug, the fore-end iron bearing against the rounded forward portion of the frame, the heavy locking bolt seated in the slot in the rear lug, the high sides of the frame extending well up the sides of the barrels, and all parts expertly fitted, the Browning Superposed is super-solid.

TRIGGERS

As originally introduced in Europe in 1930, only double triggers were available for a very short time. In 1931 Val Browning designed his double single triggers, which were offered in the U.S. from the beginning of importation until the war. The last of the triggers introduced here were the selective or non-selective single triggers. The selective single triggers have since become known as the most reliable single triggers of any designed for a multi-barrelled gun.

The cost of these ran as follows: The double trigger was standard and there was no extra charge. The single selective, the single non-selective, or the double single trigger were $30.00 extra.

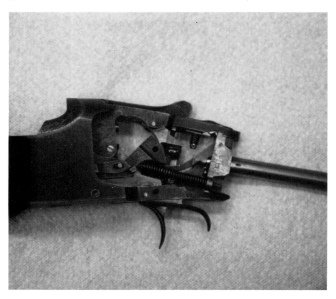

Shown here is a first year production Superposed frame and double trigger mechanism. Notice very little engraving was done on the guns first produced.

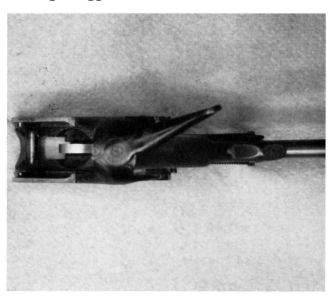

The top view of a first year production gun.

All the above are self explanatory except for the double single trigger or (as they were called when first introduced) "The Twin Single Trigger".

This was really a great invention by Val Browning, and was, in fact, the part of the Superposed he finished because of his father's untimely death. Each worked as an inertia driven single trigger that set the next one. Picture a double trigger shotgun with each trigger capable of firing either the top barrel first, then the bottom barrel, or visa versa; this was the double single trigger. A shooter had, at his option, to pull the front trigger first or the back trigger and utilize either choke, a setup I personally like very much and think much superior to the barrel selector of the later Superposed.

It is a lot quicker to simply place your finger on either the front or rear trigger to shoot the appropriate barrel then it is to move the safety back, move the selector to the right or left (and you never remember which way to move) and then move the safety forward to fire. In fact, I have never successfully used the barrel selector on any of my guns and have just quit trying.

After writing the above I discovered a special six-page brochure that Browing published in 1931 that is quite interesting. The main subject of this brochure is the introduction of these triggers. We will take the space here to duplicate the second page of this important introduction:

1931 CATALOG DOUBLE/SINGLE TRIGGER DESCRIPTION

"1. The Browning Twin-Single trigger is just what the name indicates — two triggers, mounted exactly as in the ordinary two-trigger double gun, but each a single trigger.

"2. The front trigger is set to fire lower-upper and the rear trigger upper-lower, but the purchaser may, if desired, have the triggers mounted to fire in reverse order.

"3. The selectibility of the Browning Twin-Single meets every requirement of trap and field shooting-something that cannot be said of any other trigger mechanism. It combines all the advantages of the selective single trigger and two triggers. It is, in effect, both types in versatile combination.

"4. If an owner, after use, develops an exclusive preference for either trigger — as many well be the case at traps — the superfluous trigger may be removed and the slot filled with a blank.

"5. The Browning Twin-Single is not only selective — it is instantly selective. The user has at his command either trigger position, front or rear, and

1931 Catalog Continued

may instantly select the barrel best adapted to the occasion-with no latch to shift.

"*6. Consider the importance of this instant selectibility in field shooting particularly. Hunters of upland birds usually prefer to have one barrel with a more open choke than the other. With such boring, the ordinary selective single trigger may be set for the open barrel when a bird flushes wild. There is, of course, no time to operate a shift latch, and the open bore merely feathers the bird, or the shot is refused. This is a very serious disadvantage; it has been pointed out by one of the best known authorities on shotguns. But the user of the Browning Twin-Single loses none of the advantages of the two-trigger type; he instantly selects the barrel to suit the flush — and his finger remains on the same trigger for a second quick shot.*

"*7. The Twin-Single offers all the uses of two triggers. It was used by Mr. V.A. Browning in a Browning Superposed at the famous live bird tournament in Monte Carlo this spring (1931). The gun attracted much attention. He lent it for trial to a number of men and said nothing of the single trigger, and they used it as a two trigger gun without knowing the difference. Naturally their interest was greatly intensified when the single-trigger feature was explained. The Twin-Single is a two-trigger system if you want to use it that way. And yet all the advantages of the selective single trigger are present-plus instant selectibility , as contrast with the moving of a shift latch.*

"*8. In the best known single-trigger systems, the trigger changes its position after the first shot — that is to say, after the first pull it does not return to its original position for the second pull. Each trigger of the Twin-Single always occupies the same position for each pull.*

"*9. The exclusive use of coil springs in the Browning Superposed is contnued in the Twin-Single mechanism.*

"*10. Simplicity: There are, by far, fewer parts than in any selective, single-trigger system. The Twin-Single is so simple, in fact, that you will wonder why inventors have made single-trigger mechanisms so complicated. The parts are substantial, their action positive.*

"*11. The Twin-Single is positive as double-proof as two-triggers systems. We learned throughout many experiments how to produce "doubling" and then found a way to prevent it.*

"*12. The Twin-Single was designed by us for the Browning Superposed; it is an integral part of the gun — not an adaptation of an independent system. If you have purchased a Superposed with two triggers and want to change to the Twin-Single, we can mount it for you without cutting or altering the gun in any way. This mounting must be done by us.*"

PRICE $30.00

PERPETUAL GUARANTEE

"Our confidence in the durability of the Browning Twin-Single trigger is such that we offer, without reservation, to furnish without charge any new part that may ever be needed."

BROWNING
ARMS COMPANY

I think you'll agree that the Brownings had a lot of faith in their new design and counted on it to sell many Superposed for them. If you ever run across one, pick it up and examine it for yourself.

The number of different triggers you could order on these pre-war guns is one of the fascinating things about them. Today, you don't see any double trigger guns, for they were discontinued after the first few years.

EJECTORS

Selective ejectors have always been a feature on the Superposed both pre and post war. The description that follows on page 74 from the introductory 1931 catalog does justice to this fine mechanism. You won't find many gunsmiths that have any experience working on them for they are almost infallible and are a credit to the design capabilities of John M. Browning.

AUTOMATIC EJECTORS

STANDARD EQUIPMENT ON ALL GRADES . . Automatic ejectors are often special equipment, supplied at a considerable extra charge, although a gun without them can hardly be called modern. When gloves are worn, or when fingers are cold, the lack of automatic ejectors is a serious handicap.

All parts of the Superposed ejectors are simple and strong, being much larger than ordinarily used.

Note the large area —nearly one-half of the shell head which is gripped by the ejectors. This prevents possibility of failure with a sticking shell due to extractors slipping past shell rim.

Automatic ejectors are standard equipment in the Browning Superposed. Our system is so simple that we are able to incorporate it in the gun at a cost far below the price charged when automatic ejectors are added as special equipment.

There is no comparable ejector system in an overunder gun. The operating mechanism consists simply of ejectors, ejector springs, latches and latch springs and a trip rod for each latch. The movement of closing the gun compresses the ejector springs and latches the ejectors. The last movement of opening the gun trips the latches and permits the ejectors to strike sharply against the ends of the extractors, throwing the shells clear. If only one barrel is fired, only its respective ejector is released.

A particularly ingenious feature of the ejector system is the means of cocking the ejector hammers. A slidable piece, independent of the ejector head which engages the shell, is operated by a small lug on the frame, and the ejector hammers are cocked without pressure against the standing breech. This is obviously more mechanical than a system which makes necessary the bearing of ejector heads against the standing breech in the operation of compressing the ejector springs. The ejector heads are perfectly free and move to and fro without resistance.

The parts are substantial, and the entire operating mechanism is attached snugly to the forearm iron. The ejection is positive, but not unnecessarily violent.

As introduced in the 1931 catalog, the Superposed had automatic selective ejectors as standard on all grades.

BARRELS

Barrels came in only 28", 30", or 32" for the standard guns in each grade, but the Lightweight or Lightning came in 26", 28" or 30". What is interesting is that any choke combination was available for either the top or bottom barrel. So, if you have a gun that is more open choke on the top then the bottom barrels, it doesn't necessarily mean something is wrong or the barrels were marked incorrectly; it could have been ordered that way. The chokes offered were cylinder bore, skeet, improved cylinder, modified, improved modified, and full.

Standard on all guns throughout the pre-war period were the hollow ribs. Ventilated ribs were a $20.00 option.

From the beginning of pre-war production; an extra set of barrels was offered with a second forearm.

Standard sights were an ivory bead front, or you could order anything you wanted, including an ivory center bead.

BARREL MARKINGS

The barrel marking on the left side for the very early guns was as follows:

**BROWNING ARMS COMPANY ST LOUIS MO
12 GAUGE SPECIAL STEEL**

On the right side of the barrels the markings are:

**MADE IN BELGIUM-BROWNING
PATENTS NO 1578638-1578630
OTHER PATENTS APPLIED FOR**

On the later guns the markings on the left side change to:

**BROWNING BROS OGDEN UTAH U.S.A.
12 GAUGE SPECIAL STEEL
L**

On the right side of the barrels the markings are:

**MADE IN BELGIUM-BROWNING
PATENTS NO 1578638-1578630
OTHER PATENTS APPLIED FOR
FABRIQUE NATIONALE D'ARMES
DE GUERRE-HERSTAL**

Around serial number 3,000, the markings were again changed on the left side of the barrel to:

**BROWNING ARMS COMPANY OGDEN UTAH
AND ST LOUIS MO
12 GAUGE SPECIAL STEEL**

On the right side of the barrel you will find:

**MADE IN BELGIUM-BROWNING
PATENTS NO 1578638-1578630
OTHER PATENTS APPLIED FOR**

Also present are the F.N. markings with Belgium proof marks throughout all pre-war production.

PRE-WAR STOCKS

From 1931 to the end of pre-war production, the round knob stock was the standard configuration. The English style straight grip stock was available as a regular order option at an additional charge of $15.65 for Grades I and Pigeon, but included in the price on Diana and Midas grades.

There were three standard stock dimensions which were listed as the Type "F", the Type "T", and the Monte Carlo.

The Type F dimensions were length of pull 14 1/2", drop at heel 2 1/4", drop at comb 1 1/2". The Type T was length of pull 14 1/2", drop at heel 1 3/4", and drop at comb 1 1/2"; and the Monte Carlo style was length of pull 14 1/2", drop at heel 1 1/2"and 2 1/4", and drop at comb 1 1/2".

With the introduction of the Lightning the Type F dimensions were changed to length of pull 14 1/8", drop at heel 2 1/2", and drop at comb 1 5/8" on that model only.

From the beginning of production, oil finish was standard on pre-war guns.

Through out pre-war production custom-made stocks were available. In 1931 a special order stock was $15.65 for a standard grade or from $35.00 to $70.00 for select wood. These special order stocks were actually made in St. Louis, Mo.

Browning ordered a complete shotgun with the wood fitted, but not finished. The blank had enough wood on it that almost any normal custom order could be accommodated. The final shaping, finish, and checkering was done in a timely manner. The above $15.65 might seem like nothing now, but this added $15.65 to a gun that sold for $79.80. Would you believe that when you ordered a special stock, delivery was promised in two weeks?

Some Grade I guns were ordered with special select wood. If you find a Grade I and it has nice wood, that doesn't mean you have a non-original gun. Look for the way it fits and its condition as it relates to the rest of the gun. All the work done on these guns was equal to the best available. Compare what you see to the best.

Any stock dimensions were available in either an "English" straight grip, a half round (most common), or a full pistol grip. Standard was a half pistol grip with what Browning called their Patented Fore-End.

As described in the text, the prewar forearms are non-detachable and have the metal forearm cap. Notice the checkering and solid rib. This fine shotgun was originally purchased in 1931 and is still being used in Virginia every year by the purchaser's son.

All pre-war guns have the non-detachable forearms. As on the butt stocks, they are oil finished and hand checkered starting with 20 lines to the inch on the Grade I and finer as the grades increase. This was discussed under each grade. On the very front of the forearms, you will find a steel piece that surrounds the lower barrel and protects the forearm from splitting.

A beaver tail forearm was offered in 1931 and was pear-shaped in the cross section and nearly flat on the underside. The sides were straight, curving in flush with the frame at the rear end. This option cost $20.00 and up at the time. Browning tried to push this type forearm on the public and advertised that they would replace them on existing guns.

A NEW IDEA IN FORE-ENDS

IT IS characteristic of man that he submits to time-honored inconveniences, and comes to regard them as parts of the great inevitable. The detachable fore-end of two-barrel guns is an example. Generation after generation, men have juggled three parts when mounting or dismounting a two-barrel gun. Fore-Ends have been dropped in dust and in deep duck ponds, and, when lost, have been replaced at considerable expense; but nothing has been done about it.

The fore-end of the Browning Superposed is like the butt stock, in that it can be easily detached if the need arises, but at other times it remains attached to the barrels. In mounting or dismounting the gun, there are only two parts to hold. A handy latch unlocks the fore-end, permitting it to slide three-quarters of an inch forward on the barrels, at which point it permits the barrels to be broken from the frame. It then slips back in place, the latch is snapped down, and the two parts of the gun—never in three pieces—are ready for the case. *This feature is so novel that an unusually broad patent claim was granted on it.*

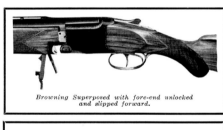

Browning Superposed with fore-end unlocked and slipped forward.

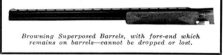

Browning Superposed Barrels, with fore-end which remains on barrels—cannot be dropped or lost.

Fore-Ends of overunders are frequently made in three pieces, the detachable piece with the fore-end iron, and an extension strip above it on each side to keep the hand from contact with the barrels, and to give the necessary grip. This means the expense of a fitting job and an unavoidable joint. The fore-end of the Browning Superposed is in one piece, substantial, handsome, and affording a secure and comfortable grip. The wood is not fraily thin at any point; both ends are reenforced, the front by a metal ring, the rear by its abutment on the fore-end iron and the frame. It lends itself readily to adaptation to the idiosyncrasies of shooters. Beaver-Tails, etc., are furnished to special order. The fore-end, in brief, is an especially attractive feature. It is hand checkered, of course.

THE BEAVER-TAIL FORE-END

Many shotgun users, particularly trapshooters, strongly endorse the Beaver-Tail Fore-End. While our standard fore-end is large and perfectly adapted to the needs of most men, we are nevertheless prepared to furnish a special Beaver-Tail Fore-End when desired.

Our Beaver-Tail is pear shaped in cross section and nearly flat on the under side giving a perfect hand full and is rounded to afford a comfortable grip. Its sides are straight, curving in flush with the frame at the rear end. Shooters have pronounced this the most attractively designed and best shaped Beaver-Tail ever put on any gun.

It is available by special order only on all grades at prices ranging from $20.00 up.

An early pre-war Superposed butt plate.

BUTT PLATES AND PADS

On the very first guns, the butt plates were horn and carved with the muzzles of a Superposed set of barrels in the center. On the top barrels the name Browning is carved in a circular pattern, and on the lower barrels the name Superposed is also in a circular pattern. There is a border all around the edge and encircling the two screws that holds it.

RECOIL PADS
FITTED TO STOCK

Hawkins	$5.00
Jotsam (Hi-Gun, Air Cushion or Anti-Flinch)	5.00
2-Ply Sponge Rubber	6.00
3-Ply Sponge Rubber	6.00
Black Diamond	6.00

Ivory Front and Rear Sights $1.25 for Single Bead—$2.00 for a pair

Five different makes of pads in seven different configurations were available in 1931 as well as the standard buttplate.

Browning marked horn, hard rubber, or plastic butt plates were standard equipment on all guns. On the later guns many were also made with an F.N. butt plate that were either a hard rubber material or horn with 7/8" x 2" scroll oval with the F superimposed over the N in a horizontal pattern of lines, which are 1/16" apart for a 2 3/8" area centered between a smooth top and bottom area.

Pads could be ordered on any model. You could get any contemporary pad made by any manufacturer installed by Browning at their St. Louis service department. The pads that were recommended were the Hawkins, Jotsam (Hi-Gun Air Cushion or Anti-Flinch), Noshoc, D & W, or the Black Diamond. Also available were the 2-ply sponge rubber, 3-ply sponge rubber and Silvers type at $6.00.

PRODUCTION FIGURES

Only 17,000 of these were produced, so they are not that plentiful nor easy to find. Production ended in 1940 when the Germans invaded Belgium.

Recently I have noticed a much greater interest in pre-war models and a subsequent increase in values. The days you could go to a gun show and purchase one for $350.00 Or $400.00 are over. I now see them around $1,000.00 if in 95% or better condition and personally think they're worth every penny.

SERIAL NUMBERS

The serial numbers were placed under the top lever, the flat side of the trigger(s), on both parts of the forearm latch, on the ejectors and the ejector extensions, under the trigger guard, the locking bolt and the steel barrel plates instead of the wood. They also appear on the left side of the lower barrel next to the production mark and on the front forearm on the right front side. On most guns they will be written in pencil on the butt plate. They were also on the barrels and can be seen when the forearm is slide forward to expose them.

1931	1- 2000
1932	2001- 4000
1933	4001- 6000
1934	6001- 8000
1935	8001-10000
1936	10001-12000
1937	12001-14000
1938	14001-17000

Production ceased here because of World War II.

SUPERPOSED POSTWAR

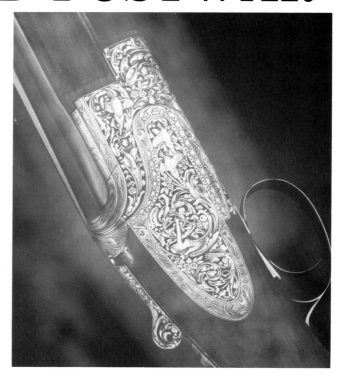

Here is a Jose Baerten engraved Superposed with false side plates produced by Fabrique Nationale on special order. Even as this is written, Browning will accept and Fabrique Nationale will produce anything the customer desires as long as it is safe to shoot.

GENERAL INFORMATION

F.N. and especially Browning were anxious to get the Superposed back into the line after the war. They were so enthusiastic about its return that they started to advertise it almost a full year before many guns became available for distribution. In a 1947 flyer they said, *"Factory tooling-up is now underway for the production of the Browning Overunder Shotgun. We expect to offer the 12 gauge during the first months of 1948. The new Browning 20 gauge will appear in the Fall of 1948."*

The Superposed was not originally intended to be a custom or prestige gun. John Browning designed this model to be made on a production line in order to keep prices down. He was trying to produce a gun that he could sell to a great many shooters, shooters that were then shooting the cheaper doubles being imported into the U.S. from Belgium and elsewhere. His words were,

"My plan is to design a mechanism so simple that it can go into regular quantity production. Of course, the barrels and frames will have to be fitted by hand and some other work will be required, so that it will be a considerable more expensive gun then the automatic shotgun. But I figure that the retail price can certainly be brought below $150.00, the cheaper we can make it the more people we can reach. To obtain these results it will be necessary to lay down an expensive installation, and another fortune will have to be invested in the first lot of guns. In the first lot we will have to put through more guns than the total of all overunders so far made-probably two or three times as many. But that's the only way it can be done. If we started with some chisels and files and fiddle drills, and turned out four guns a year per man, our price would have to be up with the others."

The Superposed is not an easy or economical gun to make as can be seen from data taken from early catalogs.

Twenty-two different types of steel are utilized in the making of every gun, 84 of its individual parts undergo 794 precision machining operations, and 67 of its components receive varied and complicated heat treatment depending upon the function. To go on, 1,490 different gauges and instruments are used in 2,310 separate operations to test and retest both dimension and strength of the various parts. After all this is done, production goes on, as 155 meticulous operations by the most experienced gunsmiths complete the gun. After all of this, assembly and hand fitting are completed to hairline precision. Then all must be polished and repolished and engraved and blued and patterned and function tested. Are you ready to go on? After all of this, the gun is sent to the Liege proof house for government tests. I may not have the procedure in exact order, but you get the idea. There's a whole lot in the production of every gun.

F.N. always maintained the quality of the Superposed and never allowed the name to be applied to anything they produced other than to the best. Other models were imported to take the place of the Superposed that looked similar to the Superposed, but they were never named the Superposed. This top quality commitment was the reason for its success and for its ultimate downfall. Labor costs were just so great that sales dropped to the point that it was no longer economically feasible to keep producing it.

The post-war guns were even better than the pre-war. In time, you will see shotgun collectors comparing postwar Browning over and unders with prewar production from the best European makers. These are truly fine quality guns. Fabrique Nationale production from 1954 until 1966 is outstanding and considered the best quality; they are also the ones that command the highest prices.

One last word about quality: The warrantee was the best ever offered for any gun ever made either custom or factory. It can be summed up as follows:
"THIS BROWNING SUPERPOSED SHOTGUN IS GUARANTEED FOR AS LONG AS YOU OWN IT, AGAINST ANY AND ALL DEFECTS IN MATERIALS OR WORKMANSHIP."

It seems reasonable to say that the best stock makers and engravers worked for F.N. At that time. F.N. was making lots of money, and their attitude about quality was on the right track, for the workers were given the time to do their work properly.

After 1966 demand exceeded production and the quality dropped. This added demand was also the cause of the salt wood problem. In their rush to purchase wood, F.N. requested Browning to find good walnut, The subsequent purchase resulted in buying wood that was dried using salt in the process, and the end result was devastating. You will find many Superposed having salt wood from 1966 through 1973. The presence of salt wood will hurt the value of a gun whether rusting has started or not. You will find many guns that have been redone by Browning, but don't let any dealer tell you that since it was done by them, it's now O.K. The value of any piece changed in any way after it left the F.N. plant is lower then an original — period. Not all guns made in these years have salt wood, but be careful.

As far as the high grades, the guns to buy are those **signed** by the master engravers unless you have enough experience to tell their work without a signature. All the Superposed graded guns were engraved by the masters. You just have to be able to tell the high grade of work for which collectors look from the other.

You will find a list of their names and initials under the General Information section in the front of the book; the initials are how they usually signed their work, Don't turn down a nice piece because it doesn't have the name or initials of an engraver, look at the execution of the cut. These people did a lot of work they didn't sign. In fact, just because a gun has the signature of a master shouldn't make you assume it was entirely done by that person. A lot of work signed by a master wasn't entirely done by that person. Many pieces were initially polished, bordered and started by people in training and then finished by a master who signed it. Remember, many guns were done by a master engraver and not signed at all. If you really get into this, you can tell a person's work by his cut just like a painter's brush strokes.

Putting an apprentice on work to get a piece out was sometimes necessary. As a former manager of a manufacturing facility, I can say it only makes good sense to put the people necessary on an item to get it out quickly.

The apprentice engravers spent most of their time engraving things like borders, backgrounds, line work, scroll, etc. They also learned on the A-5 Grade 1's, the BAR Grade 2's, and similar types of engraving. When they got really good and showed promise, they were put on the better pieces doing the preliminary engraving, the scenes and animals were then done by the masters.

If the high grade orders got slow, the masters were sometimes put on the lower grades. When you have up to 250 engravers working for you at one time, you have to improvise.

Anything that was in reason could be ordered for your Superposed. It was expensive and took a long time to receive, but it was available. Among these options were different triggers, initials, special engraving, special order stock work, pads, sights, ribs, chokes or choke combinations, barrel lengths. How about a 16 gauge? Ever see one? Special order guns are rare and hard to find, but you do see one pop up once in a while.

Information about barrels, triggers, master engravers, grades, stocks and stock finish, the various models, and years produced will be found in detail under their particular section.

GRADES

The classic Superposed 12 gauge as produced immediately after W.W. II. Notice the fully checkered grip and forearm. Also notice the early oil finish, round knob stock, engraving, and high grade of wood for a production gun.

The beginning of Fabrique Nationale's postwar Superposed production was in 1948, but only the Grade 1 or Standard grade was manufactured that year and in very limited numbers. Total production was about 200. In 1949 production was greatly expanded to 2,800, again in Grade I only. As far as we can tell no high grades were made in those two years. 1950 was the beginning of all high grade postwar production.

At that time Browning decided to rename all high grade guns. The Pigeon was now called the Grade 11, the Pointer the Grade 111, the Fighting Cocks the Grade 1V, the Diana the Grade V, and the Midas was now called the Grade V1.

Browning again changed the grade designations in 1959-60 back to Standard, Pigeon, Pointer, Diana, Midas, and Special Order. At the same time the engraving patterns were altered.

All grades from Pigeon up had standard receivers until the introduction of the Lightning in 1955. After this, all were based on the Lightning frame and barrels. Of course, the 12 gauge magnum were always on standard weight frames.

Common to all grades from the Lightning up was gold triggers. Of course each grade had wood increasing in complexity of pattern and denseness of grain. All higher grades, in addition to the receivers and trigger guards were engraved on the forearms hangers, screws, etc.

GRADE I OR
STANDARD GRADE

The Grade 1 is only lightly engraved with a scroll oval on each side of the receiver surrounded by a wedge of scroll on each corner and a border of plain line work. The bottom of the receiver as well as the trigger guard has some light scroll as well, total coverage is about 50%, and the receiver is blued.

The amount of checkering on each grade may vary with the year of production. As an example, the Grade 1 guns in the early stages of post-war production were made with 26 lines per inch checkering; after this it dropped to 20 lines per inch. No matter when the year, the work was always done in an excellent manner.

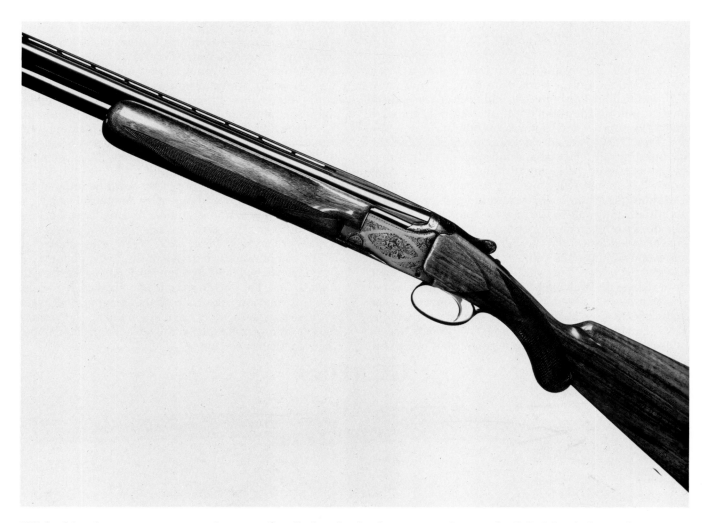

With this picture you can see in more detail the checkering, engraving, and oil finish of the early guns.

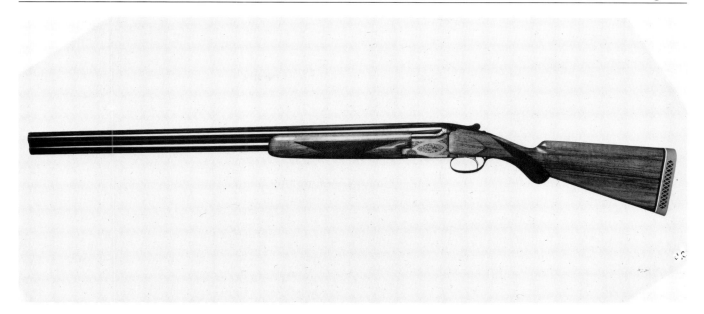

The dream of every aspiring young duck and goose hunter in the 1950's was to down his limit. Perhaps with a Superposed 12 Gauge 3'' Magnum? Twelve Gauge Magnums all came with a recoil pad. The one shown here has the rarer raised matted rib. Most you will find will have a ventilated rib.

LIGHTNING

The Lightning grade was introduced in 1955 in 12 and 20 gauges only. They were almost identical in looks to the Grade I. The basic difference as advertised by Browning is that it weighed 6 oz less.

Like the Grade I, these were only slightly engraved with a light scroll oval on each side of the receiver surrounded by a wedge of scroll on each corner and a border of plain line work. The bottom of the receiver as well as the trigger guard had some light scroll as well, total coverage is about 50%, and the receiver is blued.

Checkering on each grade may vary, but overall this will remain constant and was done in an excellent manner. The checkering on the Lightning grades were 20 lines per inch.

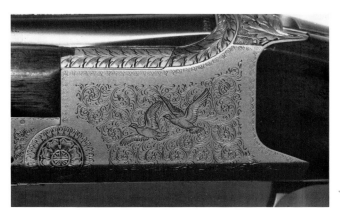

The Pigeon Grade shown above is a good example of this lowest of the high grade Superposed. It is a Superlight.

GRADE II OR PIGEON

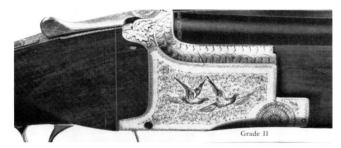

The Grade II or Pointer grade as described in the text.

The Grade 11 was produced from 1950 to 1959, and the Pigeon grade was produced from 1931 until 1949 and from 1960 to 1973.

The right side of the Pigeon Superlight is shown above.

A bottom view of the Pigeon Grade.

The engraving on both sides consist of two pigeons in flight on each side surrounded by light scroll and rosettes. The bottom of the receiver has an oval of flowers and additional scroll. The top has deep cut oak leaves on each side of the top lever, and the entire action is greyed. The top lever and trigger guard are lightly engraved with scroll. Internal parts on this and all other high grades are polished and definitely give you a feeling of a slick, well-made shotgun. The engraving pattern on the Pigeon or Grade II remained pretty well constant over the years.

The checkering on each grade may vary with the year of production, but the quality was always the best. The checkering on the Pigeon grade will run 22 lines per inch, but on the early guns, you may see some as high as 26 lines per inch.

The only barrels offered for this grade after the war were ventilated rib, however, you might find a solid rib gun.

GRADE III OR POINTER

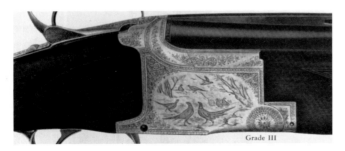

Grade III

The Grade III shows much more detail in execution and coverage.

The Pointer, which was made from 1960 to 1966 and from there on out only from existing parts or special order, is a beautiful gun. It is presently being produced at Browning's Custom Shop. On the later Pointer guns, the right side of the receiver shows a retriever running with a pheasant in his mouth, surrounded by a field scene. The left side also depicts a retriever, but he is now standing in marsh,

also with a duck in his mouth. The bottom of the receiver shows a bird standing by himself. The trigger guard is covered with scroll and shows a pheasant in flight. The entire action is covered with light scroll and rosettes, and the action is greyed.

On the earlier Grade III, which were made from 1950 to 1958 or 1959, the left side has fighting cocks and the right side has pheasants flying and milling around. All this is enclosed in an oval by scroll and border work that is a bit more fine and generous then the later Pointer grade. The balance of the engraving is similar to the Pointer in that there are field scenes and the trigger guard and forearm hangers are engraved similarly.

The amount of checkering on each grade will vary with the year of production, but overall this will remain constant The checkering on this grade is 22 to 24 lines per inch and on early guns as high as 26 lines per inch.

The only barrel offered for this grade was the ventilated rib but a solid rib special order is possible..

FIGHTING COCKS

The Fighting Cocks shows — guess what — fighting cocks. It features rosettes and scroll over the entire action. The receiver is also greyed. The balance of this grade is engraved similar to the Grade III.

The checkering on this grade will vary with the year of production. As late as 1958, the checkering on the Fighting Cocks was 24 lines per inch on the late guns and 26 to an inch on the early one.

Left side of the receiver.

Right side of the receiver.

Bottom of the receiver.

Pointer trigger guard.

The four photos above are from a Pointer Grade done by Master Engraver R. Spinosa.

The only barrel offered for this grade was the ventilated rib.

GRADE IV

A Grade IV, as all higher Grades V and VI has virtually 100% coverage.

The Grade IV was made from 1950 to 1959. The engraving consists of a fox and her young on the left side and bird dogs watching three pheasants fly off on the right. Both these scenes are surrounded by trees and various woods scenes in a panal located on the rear two-thirds of the action. There are also rosettes, oak leaves, and scroll over the entire action, trigger guard, forerm hanger and top lever. Coverage is about 95% and the receiver is greyed.

The checkering on the Grade IV was 24 lines per inch on the late guns and 26 on the early ones.

Left side of receiver.

Right side of receiver.

Bottom of receiver.

Trigger guard.

The four photos above show in detail the fine workmanship of Felix Funken on a Grade IV. Funken was considered by many to be the best Fabrique Nationale engraver and was chosen by them to do many important presentation pieces. Notice part of his signature in the bottom right of the picture on the upper left.

The only barrel offered for this grade was the ventilated rib.

GRADE V OR DIANA

The Grade V, or Diana, showed only slight change during its production as described in the text. Many, including the author, consider it the prettiest of all the production grades.

The Grade V, or Diana, is considered by many collectors the prettiest of all the high grades. It is deeply chiseled in a tasteful manner, not in any way gaudy. The right side features two ducks in flight and two standing in a marsh scene. The left side shows one pheasant flying and four standing in a wooded area. The bottom shows two quail in flight and the trigger guard shows a rabbit standing up. The entire action is covered with scroll, trees, grass, and rosettes; and it features 100% coverage. The action is greyed. It is truly a beautiful gun.

The amount of checkering on each grade may vary with the year of production, but it was always excellent. The checkering on the Diana is 24 lines per inch on the late guns but up to 28 lines per inch prior to 1958.

Left side of receiver.

Right side of receiver.

Bottom of receiver.

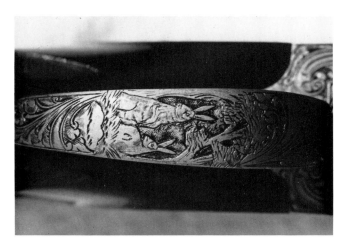

Trigger guard.

A. Marechal was one of Fabrique Nationale's most prolific engravers. You will see this signature on many Superposed guns as are shown on both the left and right sides of this Diana Grade receiver.

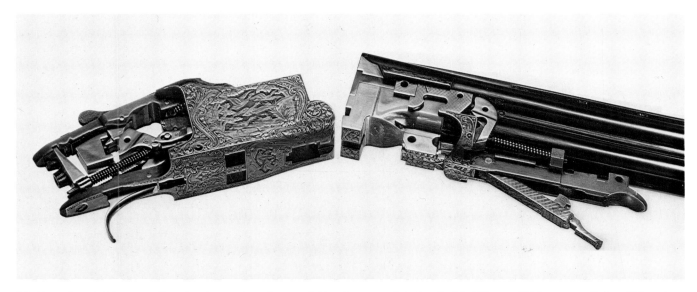

Notice the etching on the ejector extension and the forearm latch of this Diana. This type of detail is often overlooked when someone tries to upgrade a Superposed. Knowing this could be something that can save the knowledgeable collector from making a costly mistake.

GRADE VI OR MIDAS

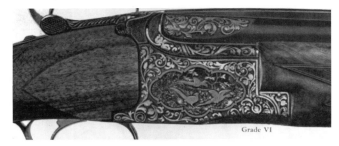

Grade VI

The deep chiseling gold inlays and attention to detail is only highlighted by the internal details of all Midas Grade Superposed.

The Grade V1 or Midas is the only blued high grade. This was done to show off the 18 carat gold inlays on the receiver which consists on the right side of three ducks flying surrounded by gold wire. The left side shows three pheasants in flight, also surrounded by gold. The bottom of the receiver shows a quail in flight, also in gold. All pins, along with ejector rods, ejector hammers, and firing pins, are gold plated.

The entire action and about 2 1/2" of the upper barrel is deeply chiseled and very elaborately engraved with scroll work. The trigger guard has a place left blank for your initials. As described by Browning in their catalogs of the early 60's, the Midas incorporates every refinement known to shotgun making. The receiver is embellished with inlaid game scenes in 18 carat gold sparkling as on jewelers velvet, against a specially blued and deeply carved background. No two scenes are alike. Each gun is the only one of it's kind." The postwar Midas is much different then the pre-war and is the most changed of all the high grades. The pre-war variation is described in that section.

The amount of checkering on the Midas never was reduced or varied as were the lower grades. Only the top artisans that worked for F.N. were permitted to checker this grade. The checkering on the Midas grade will run 28 lines per inch.

More details of the Midas Grade.

The only barrels offered for this grade after the war were ventilated rib.

GRADE VI

In 1957 Browning advertised a new Grade V1 as a grade higher then the Midas. It was designed by Louis Vranken and originally done by a German engraver named "Mueller." Some of these could have been made as early as 1955 and sold in Germany. The patterns were gold inlaid birds on a blued receiver. The catalog states the Grade V1 depicts 18 carat gold inlaid hunting scenes and that no two are exactly alike, each gun only one of its exact kind. Some of these were also engraved at the F.N. plant in Liege.

PRESENTATION SERIES

The "P" series, which is short for Presentation, was first produced in 1977, but some were made as early as 1976. They were introduced to take the place of the Lightning, Pigeon, Diana, and Midas Grades.

Each grade, P-1, P-2, P-3, and P-4 was offered with a higher degree of engraving and grade of wood as described below. The P-4 is the only grade 100% hand engraved, other than early P-1's, P-2's, or P-3's, which will be signed if they are hand-engraved and which were always done in early 1977. A hand engraved P-1, P-2 or P-3, is rare, and very few are known. It is reported that only about 15 P-3's were done. The P-1 and P-2 guns are so rare to find hand engraved that advanced collectors have informed me that they haven't seen any at all over the past 15 years. Remember, any "P" series guns you see hand engraved, other then the P-4's, should have an RR serial number code.

A good thing to look for is options. If a gun has any of the options listed below other then what you would normally look for in an original Superposed, it is likely that it is not hand engraved. Hand engraving was done before these options were offered in catalogs. To the untrained eye, it is difficult to determine whether a gun is etched or not, but I will try to explain this as well as I can.

When checking for hand engraving, look at the scenes and see if they are hand cut. The etching looks flat where there should be a raised cut. To illustrate, if you look at the edges of the cut, they will stand "proud" to the surface. Look at the address stamping on a gun you know is not reblued and you can see around the edges of the letters where the metal was pushed up by the die. Hand cut engraving looks similar. The main difference is that in hand engraving you can see a series of cuts. An engraver doesn't follow his pattern continuously but taps the graver making little cuts. Everywhere the graver was tapped, you will see a separate cut. The better the engraver, the less apparent or distinct these separate cuts will look unless it is done intentionally as part of the pattern.

Etched guns had prepared patterns etched on them and touched up by hand by the engravers. During this period, many guns have no engravers' signatures due to their refusal to sign their work. F.N. was experiencing labor problems with the engravers at that time. It is speculated that the labor problems going on at this time might have contributed to F.N.'s decision to start acid etching a good many of their guns in the first place. Another speculation I heard is that the etching idea is what caused the labor problems. Whatever the case, the etching on the P-1, P-2, and P-3 were not popular and they didn't last; they were discontinued in 1984.

In my opinion, the P-series was an attempt to make the Superposed a strictly special order gun, and was based on the assumption that anybody that couldn't afford a $3,000.00 special order gun would settle for a Japanese Citori. At the time, they were wrong. People who purchase Brownings want the extra quality they've always seen. The values of Pre '76 Superposed have gradually increased until they too are not a run of the mill hunting gun. More and more of them are collector's items as you can see by the dealers that are specializing in them. However, over the years, the American public has accepted the Citori to the point that it is now considered by the general public as "the" Browning over and under.

The P-4's or the early P-1's, P-2's, and P-3's are the grades with 100% hand engraving and are the ones you should keep for investment purposes. If your pocketbook agrees with me, stick to the Pre-76 Superposed, for they are bringing less money mint then many of the "P" Series and are much more collectable at this time.

Common to all the "P" Series as standard were ventilated ribs with engine turned matting, gold plated triggers, chrome plated chambers, and many polished internal parts. Each one could be ordered either as a field, a trap or a skeet gun. All gauges were available including the 12, 20, and 28 gauges, as well as the 410 bore.

You will find a short paragraph about the grade of wood for each gun. Other then the choice of Standard Hunting, Skeet, Trap and Superlight models there is nothing else to say about the American walnut stocks, for they were all custom ordered with the options listed below.

The "P" Series ribs were in several different configurations. The P-1 and P-2 grades had very fine engine turned matting. The P-3 and P-4 guns were hand matted more intricately. Now we will get on to the variations in each grade.

THE P-1'S

In the Presentation series introduced in 1977 the P-1 was the basic configuration offered.

The stocks were made with American walnut with either a high gloss finish or hand rubbed oil finish as an extra cost option. All checkering was 25 lines per inch on about group 2-3 wood. The basic engraving was oak leaf and fine scroll work covering about 99% of the action, trigger guard, top lever and forearm hanger. The following was the engraving variations from which you could choose:

P1A — Ringneck Pheasants - greyed receiver
P1B — Bobwhite Quail - greyed receiver
P1C — English Pointer Dog - greyed receiver
P1D — Black Labrador Retriever - greyed receiver
P1E — Mallard Ducks - greyed receiver
P1F — Canada Geese - greyed receiver
P1G — Ringneck Pheasant in gold - greyed or blued receiver
P1H — Bobwhite Quail in gold - greyed or blued receiver
P1I — English Pointer Dog in gold - greyed or blued receiver
P1J — Black Labrador Retriever in gold - greyed or blued receiver
P1K — Mallards Flying Out of Marsh in gold
P1L — Canada Geese in gold - greyed or blued receiver

Here is an excellent example of a P-1 in the P1K configuration.

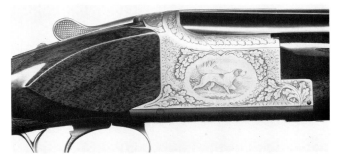

The P-1 in P1C engraving.

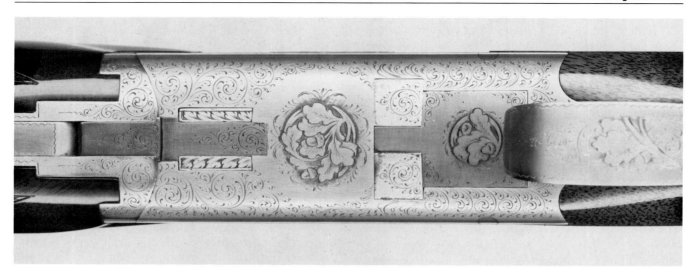

Bottom view of the P-1.

THE P-2'S

The Superposed P-2 as first introduced.

The stocks were all American walnut and finished either with a high gloss finish or hand rubbed oil finish at the same price. All checkering was 25 lines per inch on about group 3 - 4 wood.

The basic engraving was fleur-de-lis scroll covering about all exposed parts of the action, trigger guard, top lever, and forearm hanger. The following was the engraving variations from which you could choose:

P2M — Mallard on right, Ringneck Pheasant on left and a Bobwhite Quail on the bottom — no gold and greyed

P2N — Golden Retriever on right, Canada Geese on left, Mallard Drake on bottom — no gold and greyed

P2O — Mourning Doves on right, Chukar on left, English Setter on bottom — no gold and greyed

P2P — Same as the P3M except gold animals could be had in greyed or blued receiver

P2Q — Same as the P2N except gold animals could be had in greyed or blue receiver

P2R — Same as the P2O except gold animals could be had in greyed or blued receiver

THE P-3'S

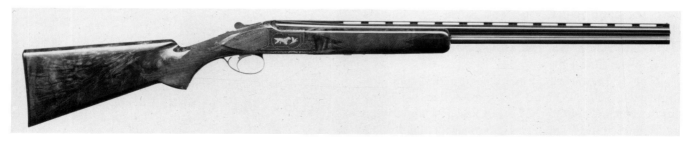

A P-3 with the blue receiver.

The American walnut stocks were finished with either a high gloss finish or hand rubbed oil finish and stained dark at the same price. All checkering was 25 lines per inch on about group 5 or better wood.

The basic engraving was fleur-de-lis and leaf scroll work covering about 99% of the action, trigger guard, top lever, and forearm hanger. The following was the engraving variations from which you could choose in either greyed or blued receiver:

P3S — Pheasants on right, Chukar Partridge on left and Quail on bottom

P3R — Pintail Ducks on right, Mallard Ducks on left and Canada Geese on the bottom

P3U — English Setter and Flushing Pheasant on right, English Pointer and Flushing Quail on left and a Mourning Dove on bottom

THE P-4'S

This is the only grade that was 100% hand engraved throughout production (the P-1, P-2 and P-3 were essentially etched and only highlighted by hand after 1977). The P-4's also had false side plates which allowed the engraver to expand the scenes about 50%; all were originally greyed but later some were blued. Other then better wood as described below and the sideplates, the P-4 was built the same as the other grades with better engraving.

You only had two options to choose from on the P-4's:

P4V — Mallard Ducks on right, Ringneck Pheasants on left, Bobwhite Quail on bottom, and a Retrievers head on the trigger guard.

P4W — The same as the P4V except gold inlaid.

"P" SERIES OPTIONS

If you'll notice, hardly any description at all is given for each grade. That's because each grade was a very basic gun and the purchaser could order more options then F.N. had ever ever advertised in the past. They had been pretty much always available, but you had to get really interested in a special order and inquire. This time, they were actively promoted, with 28 of them either listed or available as a regular option.

They vary from barrels to special order stocks to almost anything you could think of. There was nothing you could order that F.N. wasn't happy to provide as long as you provided the money and it was safe. You could order one or all, whichever you decided and could afford.

ITEM	COST
1. Hand rubbed oil finish	$109.50
2. Checkered butt	109.50
3. Special stock dimensions requiring partial alteration	184.50
4. Special stock requiring completely hand made stock	660.00
5. Tear drop points on checkering	135.00
6. Monte Carlo comb on a trap or any type stock	185.00
7. Sculptured top lever	
8. Deluxe recoil pad	N/C
9. Schnabel forearm	12.75
10. Three piece forearm	
11. Beavertail forearm	
12. Double triggers	
13. Extra barrels	
14. Hand matted vent rib	120.00
15. Hand matte Broadway rib	235.00
16. Ivory bead center and front sights	N/C
17. Engraved initials on the P-2 or P-3 only - with or without gold and in English script or block letters, you could also have your full name or signature	$ 22.00 to 195.00
18. Gold Roman numerals on top of rib designating different barrels	20.00
19. Gold or nickel silver stock inlay with initials	
20. Stock shield of 10 carat gold of nickel silver with initials	$ 77.50 to 90.00
21. Barrels options were 26 1/2" to 32" in solid matted or ventilated rib	
22. Luggage cases	$ 20.95 to 32.95
23. Trap or skeet butt stocks	
24. Straight grip butt stock	
25. Broadway rib	
26. Rounded semi- pistol grip	
27. French walnut	
28. Olympic style trigger	

I can't think of much else anyone would want, can you?

Since everything was left up to the customer, many strange combinations can be found in the "P" series. Everybody that ordered one wanted the unusual and that which was considered rare on the Superposed guns. These should make quite a collectors' group of guns when people finally realize how beautiful and rare they are.

"C" SERIAL NUMBERED ENGRAVING

From mid-1971 to 1976 a series of 100 Superposed "Custom" grade guns were produced with a "C" in the serial number. They are all different, for the engravers were given free reign to do their work. They are very unusual and nice to own.

Some of the variations will have English-style scroll on blued, case hardened, raw steel or greyed receivers; others will have filigree patterns finished as above. In any event you will not see many, if any, with animated hunting scenes or the like. These are European looking guns.

A partial list of these serial numbers are shown below. If you run across an unusually engraved Superposed and it has a "C" in the serial number and it doesn't appear here, it is probably one of these guns. Please send me the number to be included in the next printing.

C-7	C-26	C-77	C-120	C-144	C-88M
C-9	C-32	C-79	C-125	C-145	C-192
C-11	C-33	C-81	C-126	C-146	C-200
C-14	C-34	C-82	C-127	C-152	C-202
C-15	C-39	C-103	C-128	C-156	C-205
C-16	C-43	C-106	C-129	C-157	C-206
C-17	C-49	C-108	C-130	C-168	C-207
C-19	C-55	C-110	C-138	C-177	C-211
C-20	C-64	C-113	C-140	C-178	C-212
C-22	C-71	C-114	C-141	C-184	C-213
C-23	C-73	C-115	C-142	C-185	C-214
C-25	C-76	C-116	C-143	C-186	

The prices for these guns were not as high as the Exhibition or Exposition grade guns, for they are not the same type of engraving that American gun fanciers like. Their quality, however, is excellent, and I can highly recommend that if you want a beautiful gun, one of these could be for you. I have seen some beautiful guns sell for as little as $6,000.00; they would knock you eyes out they were so pretty.

LATE PRODUCTION

In the fall of 1982, about 210 Superposed 410's and 28's were put together from existing parts. There were 200 410's, of which 175 had 28" barrels and 25 had 26 1/2" barrels, and 10 28's that had 28" barrels.

They were all produced in the Superlight configuration with the following features: Rounded Superlight actions, English straight stock, schnabel forearm, high gloss finish, standard Browning inscription, gold single trigger, 3" chambers, choked mod/full, and 100% hand engraved in black and gold Browning boxes with the standard box label. All these guns had the old style serial numbers which will be found in the serial number section at the end of this chapter.

Included in these were five sets of guns; each set would include one gun of each grade. On the 410, the Grade I had a serial number that ended in 1, the Pigeon ended in 2, the Pointer ended in 3, the Diana ended in 4, and the Midas ended in 5. The sets were serial numbered as follows within each set:

410 Gauge	410 Gauge	28 Gauge
26½" Barrels	28" Barrels	28" Barrels
421J83 to 425J83	471J83 to 475J83	3308F84 to 3312F84
432J83 to 435J83	481J83 to 485J83	3313F84 to 3317F84
441J83 to 445J83	491J83 to 495J83	
451J83 to 455J83	501J83 to 505J83	
461J83 to 465J83	511J83 to 515J83	

Five of the 410 sets had 26 1/2" and ten had 28" barrels for a total of fifteen five-gun sets or seventy-five of the two hundred 410 guns. This used up all the short barrels and twenty five of the long barrels. The 28 gauge guns were also made into sets.

The other one hundred and twenty five guns were handled as follows:

    25 Grade I 28" Superlights
     0 Pigeon
    44 Pointer 28" Superlights
    20 Diana 28" Superlights
    34 Midas 28" Superlights
     2 Exhibition style 28" Superlights

The two Exhibition style guns were engraved and signed by Jose Baerten. They were designed like the Midas grade guns with different scenes within the gold ovals. In addition, the backgrounds and scroll work was to be done in more detail than the typical Midas. In addition, a few other options were ordered for these guns, including Exhibition-grade feather crotch walnut, oil finish on butt stock and forearm, checkered butt, and three-piece forearm.

On the right side, the 500J83 has four gold inlaid quail in flight, and on the left side, it has a gold inlaid dog with a pheasant in his mouth. The bottom of the frame has two gold inlaid quail in flight.

The 600J83 has four gold inlaid quail in flight on the right side and a gold inlaid ruffed grouse on the left side. The bottom of the frame has one gold inlaid woodcock.

1983 SERIES

In 1983, the Superposed was offered again in the Lightning and Superlight configurations. Nothing was mentioned about any grades higher then the Standard until 1984, when the original grades were again offered. These were the Pigeon, Pointer, Diana, Midas and custom guns.

They were only available with ventilated ribs in the Lightning and the Superlight 12 or 20 gauges with 2 3/4" chambers or 20 was also offered in the Lightning version with 3" chambers.

The engraving and finish, ejectors, safeties, triggers, receiver-wood contours, and grades of wood were the same as the Pre-75 guns. Also offered were many of the options of the "P" Series guns which were discussed in that section. This series was discontinued in 1988. In 1989 they were still being offered, but only as a custom gun. The original grades were all still available, but only as a suggestion of what to order, it was all special order.

EXHIBITION AND EXPOSITION

The Exhibition and Exposition grades were the top of the line and limited in very small quantities. In 1966, the catalog stated that fewer than 15 would be available that year. Of course, when F.N. had many more engravers and needed to give them work, these special guns became more plentiful. When Louis Vrancken went on his own and started to take commissions, many more of these guns began to show up.

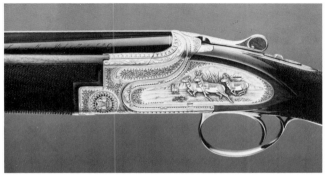

Here is one example of the many Exhibition/Exposition guns produced by F.N. over the years. There are literally hundreds, everyone different.

Each one was especially done as a one-of-a-kind. It is impossible to describe these to you, for they are each different and many engravers were involved in doing them.

The terms, "Exhibition" and "Exposition," were used interchangeably by both F.N. and Browning. Either term will describe the same class of gun.

Most were done by Felix Funken and Louis Vrancken. These gentlemen were the ones F.N. called upon when special work was needed for an exhibition or presentation piece.

At one time I had Vrancken's sample book for several months and got a chance to study it quite carefully. He was truly an artist who spent a lot of time away from F.N.'s plant to work on his own. He privately commissioned a lot of work for collectors and gun fanciers, so there is no telling what you will find done by him. In his book was everything from Diana, the hunting goddess, to unclothed women lounging in all their beauty. If you wanted it, he would do it.

One of the things that Funken, Vrancken and Watrin did so well was to design new patterns and ideas for new grades as well as presentations. The better engravers were often given general parameters to work within and then given a free hand to see what they could produce. The end result was about 99 1/2% rejection, 100% beautiful one-of-a-kind shotguns that had to be sold. If you were in the right place at the right time, you got a bargain, for Browning would want to just get rid of these and they were sold at reasonable low prices.

The only time Exposition grade guns were cataloged were from 1966 to 1970. This is because they were in inventory from previously engraved guns for the above reasons and because F.N. had set up a completely separate department at this time to produce finely engraved guns for sales all over the world. All high-grade guns produced for the U.S. were done in this custom shop, including the wood. Also, at this time, Browning would accept orders for almost any type or amount of engraving desired by the purchaser. Even today, Browning has a salesman whose duty is to see that any custom-made gun a buyer may want will be taken care of in the proper way.

When things got slow in the custom shop, many of the more elaborate pieces you see today were the product of master engravers turned loose to do whatever they wanted. These are the real pieces to buy and are quite expensive. The more advanced Browning Superposed collectors have these, and you bet they're not letting go of them easily or at a modest price. Even at the time they were being built, these pieces were sold as quickly as they could be produced. Between the years of 1970 to 1974, only a total of 100 of these Exhibition or Exposition grade guns were produced, so you can see how rare they are.

The most active time for production of these guns was from 1971 to 1976, from 1985 to 1986, and from 1988 to 1989 because F.N. had 250 engravers working at these times.

The wood is of the finest quality, and only the very best is used. On the Exhibition and Exposition grades, the checkering will run 28 to 32 lines per inch. It is not unusual to find elaborate carving and inlays on this grade.

UPGRADED GUNS

You will not find many guns upgraded after they left Belgium. All the upgrades I have seen were done in a completely different style or pattern than F.N. produced. Learn the standard high grade styles, and you won't make a mistake and purchase an upgrade thinking it is an original gun. If you find anything higher then a Midas, they are all different. Remember, any upgrade will have to be reblued after being engraved, and that will tell you right there that it wasn't done at F.N in Liege.

GRADES AND YEARS PRODUCED

To make it simple for you to look up a grade or style of Superposed and the years it was produced, the following table was put together for you. There have been several of these published in the past, but they were incomplete and misleading. I have therefore revised it. This is not to say I am right and they are wrong; actually, we both could be right or wrong at the same time. What you are getting here is taken out of Browning catalogs, from my own research, and/or price lists. Many times you will find a grade or model listed in one and not the other. You will also find some here I have owned or seen, which will not have appeared in a catalog.

ALL BROWNING POST-WAR GRADE PRODUCTION

	50	55	57	60	66	70	71	72	75	76
STANDARD				X	X	X	X	X	X	X
GRADE I	X	X	O							
LIGHTNING		X	X	X	X	X	X	X	X	
PIGEON				X	X	X	X	X	O	
GRADE II	X	X	X	O						
POINTER				X	O					
*GRADE III	X	X	O							
DIANA				X	X	X	X	X	X	X
GRADE IV	X	X	X	O						
GRADE IV (NEW VERSION)			X	O						
MIDAS				X	X	X	X	X	X	X
GRADE V	X	X								
GRADE VI (MIDAS)	X	X	X	O						
SPECIAL ORDER	X	X		X	X	X	X	X	X	X
EXPOSITION					X	X	O			C
CUSTOM "C" Serial Numbered							X	X	X	X
"P" SERIES										
CONTINENTAL										
BICENTENNIAL										
WATERFOWL										
EXPRESS										

*The Fighting Cock production will also be included.

NAME	77	78	79	80	81	82	84	85	86	87	88	89	90	91	92
STANDARD	O														
GRADE I						P	X	X							
LIGHTNING									X	O	O	O			
PIGEON						P		X	X	C	C	C			
POINTER	P	P	P	P	P	P	X	X	C	C	C				
DIANA	O					P		X	X	C	C	C			
MIDAS	O					P		X	X	C	C	C			
SPECIAL ORDER	O	X	X	X						C	C	C			
EXPOSITION						P		C	C		C	C			
CUSTOM	C														
"P" SER	X	X	X	X	X	X	X	O							
CONTINENTAL		X	X	X	X	X	X	X	X	O	O	O			
BICENTENNIAL	X	O													
WATERFOWL						X	X	X	X	X	X	X	O		
EXPRESS						X	X	X	X	X	X				
B-125												X	X	X	X
B-25												X	X	X	X

X - Listed in catalog and presumed to be available for distribution
O - Dropped from catalog but still available from existing stock
C - From custom shop only
P - Assembled from parts

PRICES

	52	62	63	64	65	69	73	74	75	76	77
STANDARD	261	$ 315									
GRADE I			$ 315	$ 360	$ 375	$ 420					
LIGHTNING		$ 335	$ 335	$ 380	$ 395	$ 435	$ 735	$ 840	$1100	$1100	
PIGEON		$ 475	$ 475	$ 520	$ 550	$ 645	$1095	$1250			
GRADE II	$348										
POINTER		$ 585	$ 585	$ 630	$ 630						
GRADE III	$395										
DIANA		$ 700	$ 700	$ 745	$ 750	$ 855	$1465	$1550	$1950	$1950	
GRADE IV	$520										
MIDAS		$1025	$1025	$1070	$1100	$1200	$1995	$2150	$2650	$2650	
GRADE V	615										
P-1											$2990
P-1 GOLD											$3290
P-2											$3520
P-2 GOLD											$4230
P-3											$5340
P-4											$6050
P-4 GOLD											$6850
SUPERLIGHT						$ 465	$ 785	$ 880	$1170	$1170	

	79	80	
P-1	$3380	$3700	P-1
GOLD	$3740	$4200	P-2
P-2	$3990	$4500	P-2
GOLD	$4790	$5400	
P-3	$6020	$6600	P-P-
P-4	$6840	$7600	P-4
GOLD	$7750	$8600	
CONTINENTAL	$4650	$4650	

MODELS

SUPERPOSED TRAP MODELS — The Superposed Trap model was specifically designed to satisfy the most exacting requirements of balance and handling qualities.

Its skillfully proportioned 30 inch barrels provide the desired steadiness and weight; and the ventilated rib prevents visual interference of heat waves rising along the sight line.

The special trap stock assures added comfort and more consistent alignment of the head; and the long, full semi-beavertail forearm gives just the right amount of additional weight along the forward portion of the gun.

SUPERPOSED SKEET MODELS — The Superposed Skeet model, in either 12 or 20 gauge, possesses those features vital to lightning-fast pointing and shooting — proper weight and balance, a crisp and fast trigger, short over-all length, and single sighting plane. The basic design of the

Superposed minimizes disturbance from the first shot to permit smoother swing and steady alignment for the second target.

These handling qualities make the Superposed eminently suited for this fast sport of skeet and surely account for its widespread popularity on the skeet fields.

Skeet models may be chosen with either 26½ inch or 28 inch barrels. Bores are Browning's special Skeet & Skeet.

SUPERPOSED MAGNUM 12 — The Browning Superposed Magnum 12 was designed to fill the specialized needs of the hunter who wants extra long range and penetrating power.

The gun is chambered for the 3 inch, 12 gauge cartridge which contains a greater weight of shot and up to the equivalent of 4¼ drams of powder. This model features 30 inch barrels with either ventilated or raised rib.

The barrels can be bored to any choke combination desired, although either Modified and Full or Full and Full are ordinarily preferred.

All Magnum models are fitted with the finest type recoil pad.

This is truly a versatile gun since it will also shoot any 2¾ inch cartridge from the lightest to the highest velocity with equal pattern perfection.

SUPERPOSED WITH EXTRA SETS OF BARRELS — All Browning Superposed shotguns in hunting, skeet, or trap models, and in either Standard or Lightning weights may be ordered with two or more sets of barrels fitted to the same receiver.

For example, a shooter may order one set of barrels for duck or goose shooting, even the Magnum if desired; and another set for use in upland hunting or skeet.

Superposed shotguns already in use may also be fitted with one or more extra sets of barrels, even Lightning sets if desired. See your Browning Dealer or write Browning Arms Company for details.

Superposed Specifications

Gauge	Model	Barrel Length	Approximate Weight	Barrel or Rib
12 3" Magnum	Hunting	30"	8 lbs. 4 oz.	Ventilated or Raised Matted
12 Target	Trap	30"	8 lbs. 2 oz.	Ventilated
12 Lightning	Hunting or Skeet	28"	7 lbs. 2 oz.	Ventilated
12 Standard	Hunting or Skeet	28"	7 lbs. 12 oz.	Ventilated or Raised Matted
12 Lightning	Hunting or Skeet	26½"	7 lbs.	Ventilated
12 Standard	Hunting or Skeet	26½"	7 lbs. 8 oz.	Ventilated or Raised Matted
20 Lightning	Hunting or Skeet	28"	6 lbs. 2 oz.	Ventilated
20 Standard	Hunting or Skeet	28"	6 lbs. 12 ozs.	Ventilated or Raised Matted
20 Lightning	Hunting or Skeet	26½"	6 lbs.	Ventilated
20 Standard	Hunting or Skeet	26½"	6 lbs. 8 oz.	Ventilated or Raised Matted

CHOKE — On all models any combination of Full — Improved Modified — Modified — Improved Cylinder — Skeet — Cylinder.

CHAMBERING — All 12 gauge models accept shells up to and including 2¾ inches in all factory loads. The Magnum 12 accepts shells up to and including the 12 gauge 3 inch Magnum. All current 20 gauge models accept shells up to and including the 20 gauge 3 inch Magnum.

STOCK AND FOREARM — Finest select walnut — hand-rubbed finish — hand-checkered. Grade I fine 26 line checkering; Grades II through VI correspondingly more intricate patterns with finer checkering tools.

	Hunting and Skeet	Trap
Stock — Length of Pull	14¼"	14⅜"
Drop at Comb	1⅝"	1½"
Drop at Heel	2½"	1⅞"

Forearm — Hunting and Skeet — Full grip contour.

Trap — Semi-beavertail.

RECEIVER—

Grade I: Blued steel with hand-engraved graceful scroll and rosette designs.

Grades II-V: Steel in silver gray tone with hand-engraved game scenes ascending with grade.

Grade VI: Blued steel with appropriate hand-engraved background and hand-engraved gold inlaid pheasants and ducks on 12 gauge — smaller game birds on the 20 gauge.

TRIGGER — Gold plated all models. Fast, crisp, positive — Doubling impossible.

SAFETY — Manual combined in thumb piece with selector mechanism.

SIGHTS — Medium raised bead; on trap models ivory front sight.

RIB — Raised matted or ventilated on Grade I; ventilated on Grade II - VI and all Lightning models Grade I - VI.

EXTRA SETS OF BARRELS — Any two specifications listed above of the same gauge in any combination of chokes desired. A choice of hunting or skeet or trap stock. Any combination which includes a Magnum 12 set of barrels will be supplied with hunting stock and recoil pad unless otherwise specified.

Here is a page from the 1958 Catalog showing the Trap, Skeet, and Magnum models with the specifications and detail of each.

THE SUPERLIGHT

In 1967, the Superlight configuration was introduced. Only 12 gauge was available in that year, but the 20 gauge was also available in 1969.

As originally cataloged, it was only made in Grade 1, but in 1971 all grades were being produced. Some Superlights in the higher grades are quite rare, especially the Pointer grade. The engraving was the standard Pigeon, Diana, and Midas, as well as the non-standard Exhibition. Be sure you know what you're doing before purchasing one for big money. Some of these guns are being made up from standard frame guns. This is fine as long as they're not represented as original. Grade 1 28-gauge guns are rare.

It is quite difficult to discuss gauges for this model, for only the 12 and 20 were ever cataloged. All were made in all grades, but there is no way of finding out how many. Only the owners will ever know, for Browning cannot tell you — they may not know themselves.

The Superlight model had a tapered solid matted rib until 1972 when it was fitted with a 1/4'' vent rib. The Superlights you see with ribs and forearms out of sequence are guns that overlap as the changes were being made in these two variations. This is why you see guns that sometimes don't make sense when you look at a catalog and compare them to a gun you might have. You'll find them produced with a solid matted rib, tapered slender forearm and then changed to a vent rib with a schnabel forearm. Then again, you'll find a vent rib gun with a tapered forearm and vice-versa. The barrels were generally 26 1/2'' long, but could be ordered 28''. The 28'' would be a very rare find.

The bottom of the frame was rounded, and other parts were also lightened.

The stock dimensions for the Superlight straight grip guns were as follows: length of pull 14 1/4'', drop at comb from 1 5/8'', and drop at heel from 2 1/2''.

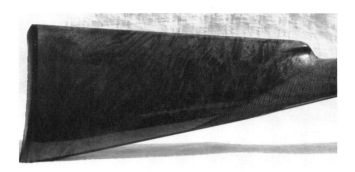

An example of a Diana Grade Superlight butt stock with straight grip.

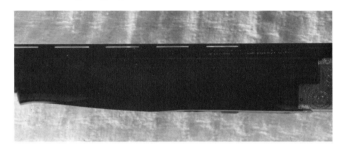

The Schnobel forearm on the Superlight gave a very European look to this Model.

The straight grip Superlight has a long tang extending well beyond the rear of the trigger guard.

This variation was discontinued in 1975 with all the other Superposed. It was reintroduced as the Continental, but you can read about that in the proper section.

THE TRAP MODELS

The classic Superposed trap model was destined to win many championships. Notice the square knob, full forearm, and trap style recoil pad.

These were first introduced during the pre-war series and continued into the post-war era. When reintroduced in 1952, only the Standard frame guns were made, but these were discontinued in 1959.

In 1959 several changes were made including the introduction of the flat knob stock and the Lightning Trap with 30'' barrels and a 5/16'' ventilated rib. it could be purchased in all grades.

The Broadway was introduced in 1961 in all grades and discontinued in 1975. It featured a 5/8" ventilated rib that was grooved only down the center; the outer edges were matted. Sights were the same throughout production. They were a metal bead in the center and an ivory front bead.

The Broadway was designed to appeal to the live bird shooter as well as a quick doubles gun. The rib was supposed to dissipate heat at a greater rate so that there would be a minimum amount of heat wave distortion. It was available in the Lightning, Pigeon, Diana, Midas, and Exhibition grades.

When the gun was originally introduced, you could only get 32" barrels. In 1962 it was offered with extra sets of 12 or 20 gauge barrels and in 26 1/2", 28", 30", or 32" barrels.

You can spot a Broadway Trap a mile away, for the stock was the largest of any model Superposed ever made. The dimensions varied as follows: length of pull 14 3/8", drop at comb 1 3/8", 1 7/16" or 1 1/2", and drop at heel 1 5/8", 1 3/4" or 1 7/8". All Broadway Traps were flat knob. None were round knob, though you might find a special order somewhere.

The main difference in the stocks on the Broadway and the earlier trap guns were the flat knob stock and wider forearm. This forearm was wider, like a beavertail with finger grooves on each side. They make for a heavier gun with the balance more towards the barrels. All these models had "Browning"-marked contoured ventilated rubber recoil pads.

The stock dimensions for the Hydro Coil Trap guns were length of pull 14 3/8", drop at comb 1 3/8", and drop at heel from 1 3/4".

The Lightning Trap was discontinued in 1975. I have seen many of these with an extra set of skeet barrels in 12 and 20 gauge, or with both for a three barrel set.

ST-100 TRAP

The ST-100 Trap variation was introduced in 1979 and discontinued in 1981. It was an innovative new style trap gun with adjustable point of impact barrels. This new style was advertised as a device that enabled the shooter to adjust the barrels so that he or she could adapt the gun to his or her particular shooting technique. Also, as a shooter progressed through various handicap distances, the point of impact could be changed.

This was accomplished by sliding what Browning called "a special impact adjustment device" up or down the barrels. When the indexing collar is slid to the rear, the approximate point of impact of the under barrel is 16 inches above the aiming point at 40 yards with the over barrel dead on. When slid all the way forward, both barrels will impact approximately 4 inches above the aiming point at 40 yards. There are 5 different points of adjustment.

All barrels were 30" long with the floating Broadway 5/8" to 1/2" rib with front and center ivory beads. The 5/8" was offered in 1979, and the 1/2" for the last 2 years of production.

All triggers were full contoured, mechanical, and gold plated.

The stocks were French walnut with a full pistol grip, beavertail forearm, 20 lines per inch checkering, a high gloss finish and a trap-style contoured ventilated recoil pad. The stock dimensions were length of pull 14 3/8", drop at comb 1 7/16", and drop at heel 1 5/8".

The receivers were all blued and engraved in the same manner as the Grade 1 Superposed with "ST-100 engraved within the oval on both sides of the receiver.

THE SKEET GUNS

Skeet guns have been available in all grades almost since the Superposed was first made. The standard configuration was the same as the hunting guns until the stocks were changed in 1969. Browning never offered a separate skeet model with skeet wood until that year. The earlier guns that you see choked skeet without a center bead are field guns. If you see a center bead and its original on one of these early guns, it was a special order.

When reintroduced in 1952, the raised hollow matted or ventilated ribs were available. In 1959 to 1960 only the vent rib was listed as a regular item but matted ribs were still available until 1971 when they were cancelled altogether. I believe that if you requested it, you could still get a solid rib after this date, and some probably were made. The only barrels offered through this model's production were either 26 1/2" or 28", in all four gauges.

The 12 gauge guns all had 5/16" ribs, and the 410 bore, 28 and 20 gauges guns came with a 1/4" rib.

After 1968 the regular skeet gun was cataloged. You could still get a field gun with the proper chokes, but this was really the model they wanted to sell to the shooters at that time. The main difference in this model and the earlier ones were stock dimensions and the skeet style forearm. This forearm is wide like a beavertail with finger grooves on each side. They make for a heavier gun with the balance more towards the barrels. All these models have "Browning" marked ventilated rubber recoil pads.

There were so many changes to the dimensions and so many guns fooled around with by skeet shooters at the time (I know, I was one of them) that you need to know each one for each gauge before and after the flat knob introduction. They were as follows:

The standard stock dimensions on the 410 bore, the 28 and the 20 gauge guns were as follows before the flat knob stock introduction: length of pull 14 1/4", drop at comb 1 1/2", and drop at heel 2 3/8". On the 12 gauge they were as follows: length of pull 14 1/4", drop at comb 1 5/8", and drop at heel 2 1/2".

The standard stock dimensions on the 410 bore and on the 28 and 20 gauge guns were as follows after the flat knob stock introduction: length of pull 14 3/8", drop at comb 1 1/2", and drop at heel 2". For the 12 gauge guns they were as follows after the introduction of the flat knob stock: length of pull 14 3/8", drop at comb 1 1/2", and drop at heel from 2".

The stock dimensions for the Hydro Coil Skeet and Field stocks were length of pull 14", drop at comb from 1 7/16", and drop at heel from 2 1/8". The length of pull, drop, or cast on these stocks were adjustable on request for a maximum drop of 1 1/2" x 2 1/2".

Skeet gun gauge combination came in several different ways over the years. As they were initially introduced, you had to purchase two guns to have both a 20 and a 12. In 1958 to 1959, you could purchase combination sets. A 12 gauge gun could be ordered with additional sets of 12 or 20 gauge barrels. A 20 gauge gun could be ordered with additional sets of 20 or 28 gauge and 410 bore barrels. A 28 gauge or 410 bore gun could be ordered with extra sets of barrels in either gauge.

In 1972 the all gauge skeet set was offered in all grades; therefore, barrel restrictions were lifted. You could now order small gauge barrels for the 12 gauge frame. This still continues today.

THE EXPRESS RIFLE

The Express rifle was produced in many calibers for overseas sales but only in 270 Winchester and 30/06 for the U.S.

As introduced and cataloged in 1981, they were available in .270 Winchester and .30/06 only. Before the Express rifles were introduced that year as a regular production model, about four or five were made on special order; one was a .30/06, and the rest were various European cartridges. At the time, as available in Europe, they were made in 9.3 X 74R and 7 X 65, though others were probably available.

Frames were the Superlight style but with a reinforced action that was necessary to withstand the high pressures of centerfire rifle ammunition. Barrels were 24" with one-in-ten twist and made of a special vanadium steel using the cold forging process. The Express rifles had no ribs, but were fitted with a ramp front sight with gold bead. The rear sight is a flip up adjustable for windage only.

The standard stock configuration was the Superlight style as originally introduced. The dimensions were length of pull 14 1/4", drop at comb 1 11/16", and drop at heel 2 1/2".

The main problem was getting the accuracy that Browning wanted, so instead of pricing themselves out of the market, they lowered their accuracy standards. Don't expect more than a three to four inch group at 100 yards with one of these. That was probably quite adequate for the type of hunting for which it is intended, but it is not what Americans are used to seeing. Double rifles, like double shotguns, are great for quick shots, but for long range shooting they will never be the same or equal to a good bolt action or the BAR automatic.

If you're a whitetail hunter in the east and generally hunt in dense woods, the romance and fascination of using a good double rifle can't be beat.

They were cataloged until 1986, but absent from the 1987 catalog, though some models could still be ordered. All production was given to the "Browning Custom Gun Shop" in 1987. Since Express Rifles and the Continentals were along the same lines and combined after going to the custom shop, it would be simpler to also combine their descriptions in a separate section; please refer to it immediately after the Continental section below.

CONTINENTAL

First introduced in 1978, this is the same gun as the Express Rifle except in a two barrel set. It was made in .30/06 only with an extra set of 20 gauge barrels, 26 1/2" chocked modified, and full with 3" chambers.

The Continental shotgun barrels had ventilated engine turned ribs 1/4" wide. The rifle barrels were fitted with a ramp front sight with gold bead, and the rear sight was a folding leaf adjustable for windage only.

The standard stock dimensions on the Continental sets are for the shotgun barrels' length of pull 14¼", drop at comb 1½", and drop at heel 2⁷/₃₂; for the rifle barrels the dimensions are length of pull 14¼", drop at comb 1¹¹/₁₆", and drop at heel 2½".

All were sent with a Browning case. I have noticed lately that this model is appreciating in value.

EXPRESS AND CONTINENTAL POST-1986 DESCRIPTION & PRODUCTION

As of 1988, these models were available in 9.3 x 74R with or without an extra set of 20 gauge barrels, 7 x 65R, 30-06 with or without 20 gauge barrels, 270 Winchester, 9.3 x 62, and 375 H & H Magnum.

There are several things common to each model that do not need to be repeated for each one. Checkering is 20 lines per inch as standard on the Express models and 25 lines per inch on the Express Special. The forearms are all of Tulip style. These are very similar to the Superlight style and very maneuverable and light weight. An oil finish is common to all guns unless a high gloss is ordered. All rear sights are the folding type adjustable for windage only; the front sights will be discussed separately. All safeties are non-automatic, meaning they do not go on safety when the weapon is open, a feature that makes a lot of sense when you're trying to make a quick third shot. I do not believe the type of triggers are the best for a two barrel gun. They were single selective, which doesn't make a lot of sense; if the first cartridge fails, you have to go through the gyrations of flipping the safety back and forth to reset it for the other barrel. There is some consolation, however: they were gold plated.

We will now get a rundown of each gun offered during this time.

The CCS25 in 9.3 X 74R and 7 X 65R had a barrel length of 25 9/16" with 4 groove rifling. 1/4 ribs were standard and the front sight was a silver bead on a ramp. The stock was pistol grip with a length of pull 14 3/8", drop at comb 1 5/16", drop at heel 1 1/2", and cast off of 3/16" to 1/4". The weight was 7 lbs., 8 oz. and the total length 43". The actions were either blued or greyed, a choice that depended on the purchaser's selection or on the engraving ordered.

The CCS25 Continental in 30-06 had a barrel length of 24" with 4 groove rifling. The front sight was a ramp with a gold bead. The stock was the English straight grip with a length of pull 14 1/4", drop at comb 1 11/16", drop at heel 2 1/2", and cast off of 3/16" to 1/4". The weight was 6 lbs., 14 oz., which is quite light and not recommended for the shooter sensitive to recoil. Length was 41 1/4" and actions were blued. There was also another model called the CCS25 Continental 20 Gauge, which was the same in all respects except it had an extra set of shotgun barrels, which were 26" long in the purchaser's choice of chokes.

The CCS25 Continental in 270 Winchester had a barrel length of 24" with 4 groove rifling. The front sight was a ramp with a gold bead. The stock was the English straight grip with a length of pull 14 3/8", drop at comb 1 11/16", drop at heel 2 1/2", and cast off of 3/16" to 1/4". The weight was 7 lbs., 10 oz.; length was 43"; and actions were either blued or old silver.

The CCS25 Continental in 9.3 X 62 had a barrel length of 25 9/16" with 6 groove rifling. The 1/4 ribs were standard and the front sight had a gold bead on a ramp,

The stock was the English straight grip with a length of pull 14 3/8", drop at comb 1 11/16", drop at heel 2 1/2", and cast off of 3/16" to 1/4". The weight was 7 lbs., 10 oz.; length was 43"; and actions were either blued or old silver.

The CCS225 in 9.3 X 74R had a barrel length of 23 5/8" with 4 groove rifling. Standard were 1/4 ribs, and the front sight had a luminescent red bead on a ramp. The stock was pistol grip with a length of pull 14 1/4", drop at comb 1 5/16", drop at heel 2 1/2", and cast off of 1/16". The weight was 7 lbs., 8 oz.; length was 41 5/16"; and the actions were either blued or greyed, depending on the purchaser or the engraving ordered. There was also another model called the CCS225 Continental 20 Gauge, which was the same in all respects except it had an extra set of shotgun barrels, which were 26" long in the purchaser's choice of chokes.

The CCS25 in 375 H & H Magnum was a special order only gun that had a barrel length of 24" or 26" with 4 groove rifling. Standard were 1/4 ribs, and the front sight had a ramp with a silver bead. The stock was a pistol grip with a length of pull 14 1/4", drop at comb 1 5/16", drop at heel 2 1/2", and cast off of 1/16". The weight was 9 lbs., 8 oz.; length was 40 3/4"; and actions were either blued or old silver, depending on the engraving ordered.

It should be added that whatever you wanted in the way of engraving, grade of wood, extra barrels, etc. was up to you and your pocket book.

CLASSIC & GOLD CLASSIC

This Gold Classic was introduced in 1984.

These were introduced in 1984 and featured a hand engraved upland setting of bird dogs, pheasants and quail, and a bust of John M. Browning across the bottom third of the receiver sides. The entire surface of both models has hand engraved fleur-de-lis patterns. The receiver is greyed as is the trigger guard, forearm hanger, top lever, and bottom tang. Also, across the sides of the receiver are the words "BROWNING GOLD CLASSIC" or "BROWNING CLASSIC". In addition to the engraving, the gold classic featured John M. Browning's bust. All the dogs and birds and also the text were inlaid using 18 carat gold. There was a total of 183 of the Gold Classic made, not the 500 Browning had hoped to sell. We do not know, at this time, how many Classics were produced.

The walnut used was very densely grained and highly figured. The stocks all had schnabel forearms and straight grip stocks checkered 24 lines per inch, surrounded by a carved border and finished in a high gloss. The grade of wood on the Classic was about Group 3, and Group 5 for the Gold Classic.

They were all made in 20 gauge and all featured 26" barrels choked improved and modified. All were hand engraved and featured the engraver's name. Although advertised in 1984, delivery for these did not begin until 1986, and they were dropped from the prices list in 1988.

WATERFOWL SERIES

These were first produced in 1981 in the Mallard, 1982 in the Pintail, and 1983 in the Black Duck; all were discontinued in 1984, but reintroduced in 1985 and then again cancelled in 1988. Originally, Browning was going to also have a Canvasback and a Canadian Goose variation, but the three previous editions didn't sell well and the idea was dropped.

MALLARDS

The hand engraving is really beautiful in this series. The entire receiver, trigger guard, forearm hanger, and top lever is 100% covered with fleur-de-lis style scroll. On the left side are two mallards taking off, one with wings up and the other with wings down. On the right side are two mallards with wings set to land on a pond. If that's not enough, there are two more mallards on the bottom of the receiver in flight and another inlay of a mallard's head on the trigger guard. also on the bottom are the words "American Mallard," its scientific name, and the number of the gun in the series. All the birds are surrounded by realistic marsh scenes and gold ovals on each side. The birds and other work are all 24 carat gold; and the receiver, top lever, trigger guard and forearm hangers are all greyed with gold plated triggers and the engraver's signature. These are outstanding guns.

The stocks were not left to chance, either. To start off with they are group 5 or better wood. Each is checkered 24 lines per inch and cut with a scroll pattern into the round knob grip. They are oil finished and have checkered butts.

All were shipped in a black walnut presentation case with full length brass hinge, latches, corner guards and double locks; the lining is red velvet.

PINTAIL

(Above) The Pintail was second in the Waterfowl Series of Superposed.

In 1982 the Pintail model came out. It was the same exact gun as the Mallard series with the exception of the birds. On the left side is a drake and a hen flying over marsh, one with wings straight out and the other with wings up; on the right side there are two more flying full speed over a marsh. The bottom has a pintail getting up from the water and another with wings down and flying. The trigger guard has the head of a drake; also on the bottom are the words "American Pintail," its scientific name, and the number of the gun in the series. All the other engraving is the same as the Mallard.

(Below) A close-up of a pair of the Pintail engraved Superposed.

BLACK DUCK

In 1983, Browning introduced the last of the Waterfowl series, the Black Duck.

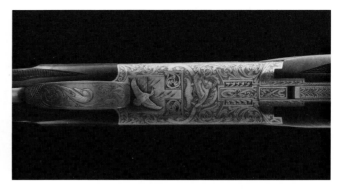

The bottom of each model in the Waterfowl series was engraved with the serial numbers. Here is number 3 of 500 Black Ducks made.

In 1983 the Black Duck model came out. It was the same exact gun as the Mallard series with the exception of the birds. On the left side there is a black duck drake and a hen lifting off the water; on the right side there are two more drakes landing on the marsh. The bottom has a drake with cupped wings and another with wings down and flying. The trigger guard has the head of a drake; also on the bottom are the words "Black Duck," its scientific name, and the number of the gun in the series. All the other engraving is the same as the Mallard.

They were limited to a total of 500 for each model. All made were 28" modified and full with ventilated rib barrels in 12 gauge.

Prices were as follows: in 1981, $7,000.00; in 1982, $7,700.00; and in 1983, a cool $8,000.00. This may be the reason that they were not as successful as Browning would have liked.

BICENTENNIAL MODEL

These were made to celebrate the bicentennial of this country's founding.

Fifty-three were made all together, one for each state in the sequence that it joined the Union and one for the District Of Columbia. There were also two extras made at this time; one was made for The Smithsonian Institution and the other was placed in F.N.'s collection in Liege. It was displayed in 1976 and 1977 by the Belgian Government to help celebrate the Bicentennial. Places shown were the Smithsonian Institution and the N.R.A. national convention in Salt Lake City, Utah.

The receivers had sideplates and were configured in the Superlight style with the corners rounded off the underside. They were all 12 gauge with 28" vent rib barrels and choked full/full.

The straight stocks had about group 5 walnut and all forearms were the Superlight schnabel style. The checkering was truly outstanding, done the same way as the Diana grade.

The engraving was designed by the great artisan, Louis Vrancken; anything Vrancken did was done well.

As mentioned earlier, the engraving was designed to commemorate each states entering the Union; therefore, they were numbered in that sequence. The right side of the receiver shows this; i.e. the 36th State has a frontiersman and wild turkey all gold inlaid. On the left side the legend says, "Nevada 1864," along with the American eagle superimposed over the American flag, all inlaid in gold. The engraving was inlaid with various colors of gold, including a very nice gold border all the way around the engraving.

All were delivered in 1976 or 1977.

B25

The B25 Superposed is being built today exactly like the original models were, all Belgium. Here is a B25 in Diana and Midas grades. They are every ounce a "Browning Superposed."

The B25 is 100% Belgian made and parts. It is known in Europe as the B25, Browning is calling it "The Original Superposed" or "The Belgian

Superposed in this country." It takes several months to get one of these, for they are all custom made and none are held in inventory. The prices in 1992 are Pigeon, $4,050,00; Pointer, $4,900.00; Diana, $5,200.00; and the Midas, $7,200.00.

On pages 101 through 104 are examples of the gun makers skill available from Fabrique Nationale on the B25. This is the quality of work being done at the Engravers Cooperative of Herstal, Belgium even today.

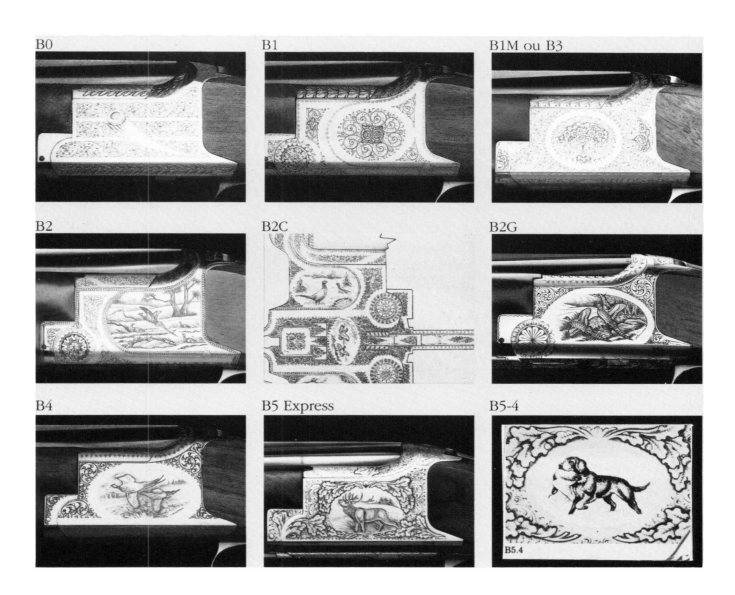

D4G   D5   D5G

D6-1   D6-3   E1

F1   I1   M1

M2   USA Grade 1   USA P1

USA P2   P2 Express   USA P3

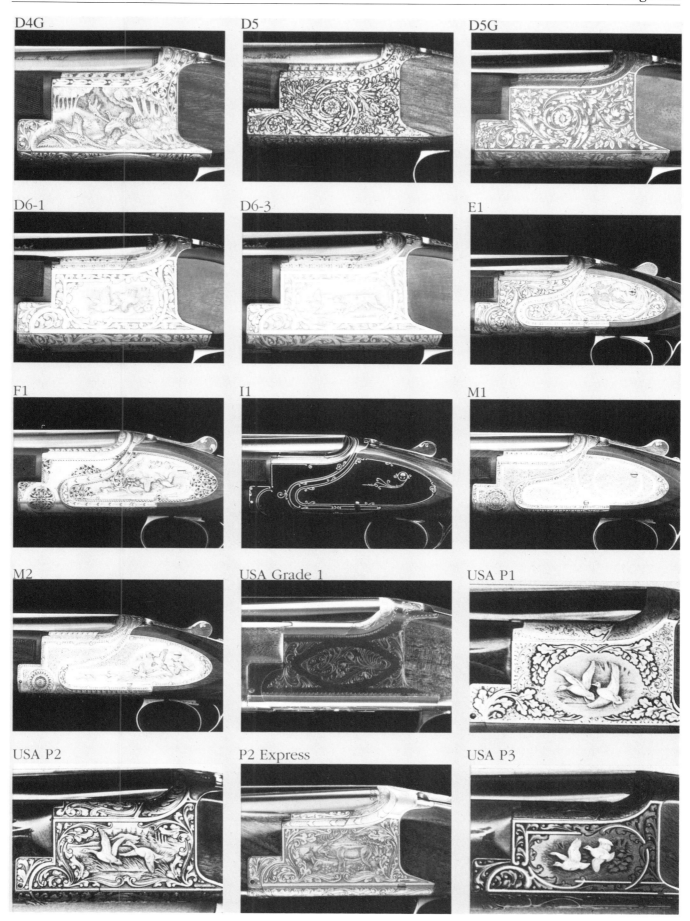

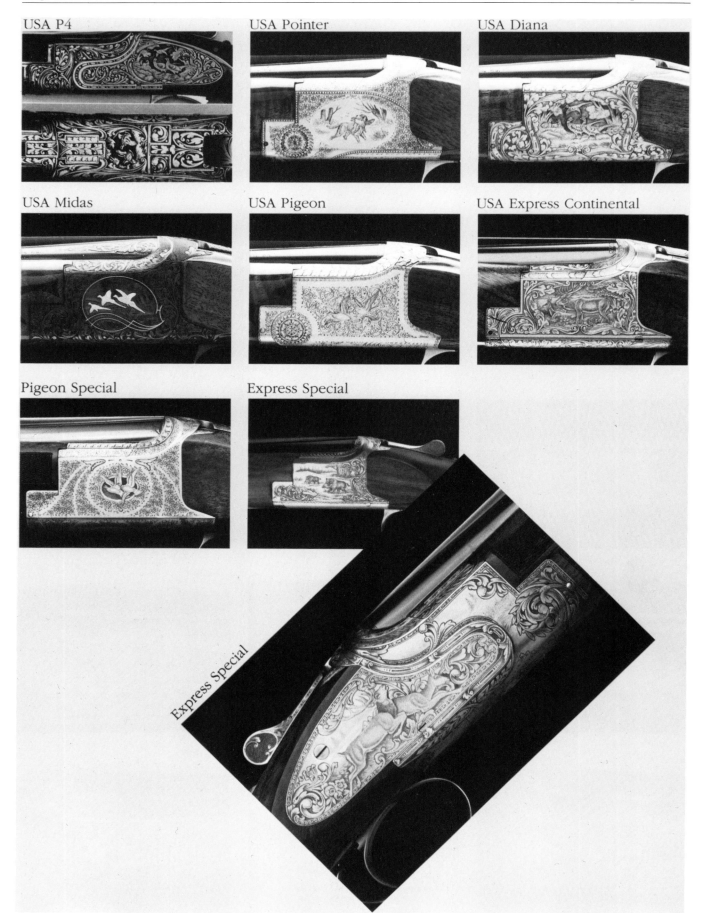

USA P4

USA Pointer

USA Diana

USA Midas

USA Pigeon

USA Express Continental

Pigeon Special

Express Special

Express Special

The standard features are single selective trigger, automatic selective ejectors, vent rib, and non-detachable forearm. Browning has also advertised that any style or amount of engraving can be ordered. In addition, you can order the following:

1. Custom fitted stock with various grades of wood.
2. Checkering and carving.
3. Internal parts polished.
4. Custom chokes.
5. Special ribs or triggers.
6. Hand rubbed oil finish.
7. Checkered butt.
8. Special stock dimensions.
9. Tear drop points on checkering.
10. Monte Carlo comb on a trap or any type stock.
11. Sculptured top lever.
12. Deluxe recoil pad.
13. Schnabel forearm.
14. Three piece forearm.
15. Beavertail forearm.
16. Double triggers.
17. Extra barrels.
18. Hand matted vent rib.
19. Ivory bead center and front sights.
20. Engraved initials on the P-2 or P-3 only - with or without gold and in English script or block letters, you could also have your full name or signature.
21. Gold Roman numerals on top of rib designating different barrels.
22. Gold or nickel silver stock inlay with initials.
23. Stock shield of 10 carat gold of nickel silver with initials.
24. Barrels options of 26 1/2" to 32" in solid matted or ventilated rib.
25. Luggage cases.
26. Trap or skeet butt stocks.
27. Straight grip butt stock.
28. Broadway rib.
29. Rounded semi-pistol grip.
30. French walnut.
31. Olympic style trigger.
32. Special order barrels without Invector or 30".

There are so many variations in several models that I am including the following table so you can see if a B25 you're anticipating purchasing is correct.

	SPECIAL GAME 13	SPECIAL GAME 24	SPORTING 205	SPORTING 206	TRAP 2	TRAP 6	SPEC SKEET 105	DUCK HUNT	SPE PIGEON
GAUGE	12	20	12	12	12	12	12	12	12
CHAMBER	2¾"	2¾"	2¾"	2¾"	2¾"	2¾	"2¾"	3"	2¾"
CHOKE(L)	1-2	2	1	2	3	3	SK	4	4
CHOKE(U)	3-4	4	3	4	4	4	SK	4	4
RIB	¼"	¼"	½"	½"	$5/_8$"	½"	½"	$5/_{16}$"	½"
STOCK	G/A	A	P	P	P	P	P	P	P
LENGTH	14$^3/_8$"	14$^3/_8$"	14¼"	14¼"	14$^3/_8$"	14$^3/_8$"	14¼"	14$^1/_{16}$"	14$^3/_8$"
DROP/COMB	1½"	$^{17}/_{16}$"	$^{19}/_{16}$"	$^{19}/_{16}$"	$^{17}/_{16}$"	$^{17}/_{16}$"	$^{19}/_{16}$"	1½"	$^{17}/_{16}$"
DROP/HEEL	$^{25}/_{16}$"	2$^5/_{16}$"	2½"	2½"	1$^5/_8$"	1$^5/_8$"	2½"	2½"	1¾"
FOREARM	T	T	T	T	Q	Q	Q	Tr	Q
C'ERRING	25	25	25	25	25	25	25	25	25
TRIGGER	US	US	US	US	US	US	US	US	US
ACTION	B/GR	B/GR	B/GR	B/GR	B/GR	B/GR	B/GR	B	GR
WOOD	H	H	H	H	H	H	H	H	H

NOTES

1. Improved Cylinder	G. Swan Neck	T. Tulip	NA. Non-Auto	B. Blued
2. Modified	A. Straight	Q. Semi Beavertail	US. SS Trig	Gr. Greyed
3. Imp. Modified	P. Pistol	Tr.Traditional	Sk. Skeet	H. Oiled
4. Full				

FRAMES

The original design was for a 12 gauge gun only, but after Mr. Browning's death, it was redesigned by Val Browning to handle the 20 gauge shells. This was done at the same time he designed the triggers. You will find this information in the pre-war section.

There were only three frames ever made: the 12 gauge, the 410 bore, 28 gauge and 20 gauge (which were the same), and the Superlight. The smaller gauge frame is a scaled version of the 12 gauge, but the Superlight is machined down on the bottom to round it off and reduce the weight. Other than cosmetics, there are no other apparent changes throughout production.

TRIGGERS

Sad to say, after the war and until the "P" series was introduced, F.N. actively promoted only the the single selective trigger. Double triggers could be ordered, but this was rare and very time consuming to obtain. Triggers were all gold plated except for some Superlight models.

The .410's all have mechanical triggers, but the 28's, 20's and 12's were all of the concussion type. Mechanical triggers work mechanically (makes sense), but concussion triggers require the recoil from the previous shot to reset themselves for firing of the second barrel. If you purchased a two or three barrel small gauge set, it will come with mechanical triggers. You can test this by checking to see that the gun is unloaded and pulling the trigger; it should fire the second barrel without any recoil to set the trigger.

Browning extensively promoted their selective safety, saying that you could instantly select either barrel by moving the safety left or right. This was not totally true and was much more time consuming and required a lot more practice then they led you to believe. Can't you just see yourself pulling the trigger on an incoming bird and experiencing a misfire? You have to push the safety back, slide it to the opposite side and then take it off safety again. All the while, you're begging your target, "Please don't go away," while you're going through all these gyrations. The pre-war double-single or double triggers sure made a lot more sense and would have sold well if they had been offered.

All in all, the triggers were a very reliable setup. They were designed by the son of John M., Mr. Val Browning, right after his father's death. Mr. Browning never got to finish the design of the Superposed, so it was left up to Val to finish it. They are probably the best triggers ever designed for any double or over-and-under. They have proven themselves by working without flaw during many thousands of rounds of competition and for many more thousands of times under hardship in the hunting fields all over the world.

STOCKS, STOCK FINISH, LONG AND SHORT TANGS

Stocks were of standard dimension, or you could order about anything you desired in all of the different grades. Always look for at least 14 1/4" length of pull. The Trap guns had 14 3/8" length of pull. Sometimes a stock is cut, and then a butt plate is put back on the gun; this hurts the value severely. There were some special order guns with length of pull greater or shorter than standard, but finding one is unusual. Longer is no problem, but shorter will hurt the value at least 20%. All stocks are serial numbered with the receiver. You will usually find this number under the trigger guard or under the top tang.

The standard stock dimensions on the 410 bore, the 28 and 20 gauge hunting, and skeet guns were as follows before the flat knob stock introduction: length of pull 14 1/4", drop at comb 1 1/2", and drop at heel 2 3/8".

The standard stock dimensions on the 12 gauge hunting and skeet guns were as follows before the introduction of the flat knob: length of pull 14 1/4", drop at comb 1 5/8", and drop at heel 2 1/2".

The standard stock dimensions on the 410 bore, the 28 and 20 gauge, and the skeet guns were as follows after the flat knob stock introduction: length of pull 14 3/8", drop at comb 1 1/2", and drop at heel 2".

The standard stock dimensions on the 410 bore and on the 28 and 20 gauge hunting guns were as follows after the flat knob stock introduction: length of pull 14 1/4", drop at comb 1 1/2", and drop at heel 2 3/8".

The standard stock dimensions on the 12 gauge hunting guns were as follows after the introduction of the flat knob: length of pull 14 1/4", drop at comb 1 5/8", and drop at heel 2 1/2".

The stock dimensions for the 12 gauge Skeet guns were as follows after the introduction of the flat knob stock: length of pull 14 3/8", drop at comb 1 1/2", and drop at heel from 2".

The standard stock dimensions on the Continental sets and the Express rifles with the shotgun barrels are length of pull 14 1/4", drop at comb 1 1/2", and drop at heel 2 7/32. With the rifle barrels, the dimensions are length of pull 14 1/4", drop at comb 1 11/16", and drop at heel 2 1/2".

The 1985-1986 Superposed stock dimensions for all variations were length of pull 14 1/4", drop at comb 1 11/16", and drop at heel 2 1/2".

The "P" Series gun's stock dimensions were all made to order.

The stock dimensions for the Trap guns varied as follows: length of pull 14 3/8", drop at comb 1 3/8" or 1 7/16" or 1 1/2", and drop at heel from 1 5/8" or 1 3/4" or 1 7/8".

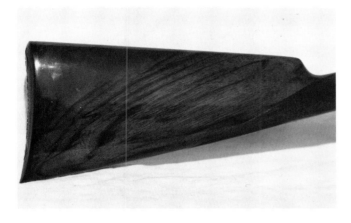

The picture above is an excellent example of the Superlight configuration. This is from a Pigeon in 20 gauge.

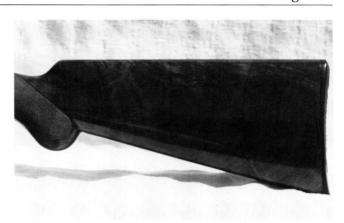

Many examples of the round knob semi-pistol grip can be seen throughout this book. Here is an example close up from an early Diana. The wood on this gun is typical of the high grade materials used on all Brownings.

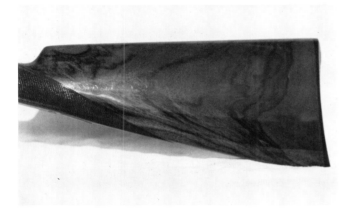

Here is the opposite side of the Superlight 20. Please notice the pattern and extent of the checkering done on these straight stocked guns.

Here is an example of the later flat knob full pistol grip as described in the text.

The stock dimensions for the Superlight straight grip guns were as follows: length of pull 14 1/4", drop at comb from 1 5/8", and drop at heel from 2 1/2".

The stock dimensions for the Hydro Coil Skeet and Field stocks were length of pull 14", drop at comb from 1 7/16", and drop at heel from 2 1/8".

The length of pull, drop, or cast on these stocks was adjustable on request to a maximum drop of 1 1/2" x 2 1/2".

The stock dimensions for the Hydro Coil Trap guns were length of pull 14 3/8", drop at comb 1 3/8", and drop at heel from 1 3/4".

Round knob stocks were made from 1931-1970 on all field guns; they then changed to the later flat knob. You will still find guns made after 1971 with a round knob butt stock. Trap guns made after 1959 were made with the new flat knob, and Skeet guns were made with the round knob until 1968, but many will be found with the flat knob starting in 1964.

On field guns the stocks appear in several different configurations. Until 1966 they are all round knob, long tang. From 1967-1970, field guns are round knob, short tang. From there, production runs flat knob, long tang. There are a few guns which are flat knob, short tang after 1971. These are also transition guns. These changes sometimes took years to complete.

Here is an example of an early round knob, notice the fullness of the checkering and that it covers the entire grip area.

You will find round knob Superposed stocks any time after they were discontinued. F.N., like any other manufacturer, had many parts on hand when changes were announced, and they would use them as needed. While looking over different guns, you will see various combinations of features. Learn your guns so you can see what's right almost at a glance. Always remember, the flawless workmanship of these guns can help in determining originality. Collectors like the round knob, long tang guns best, but many will accept the flat knob, long tang as well. Generally, collectors do not like the short tang guns and many of them have changed these guns to long tang models; be aware of these.

Here is an example of the long tang configuration as described in the text.

As described in the text, the beaver tail forearm first appeared in 1965. You can also see an example of the beavertail forearm on page 110.

Beaver tail forearms were available after 1958 but became standard on trap and skeet guns after 1965. Don't confuse a field style skeet with a full skeet gun. Skeet guns have 3/16" less drop, a beaver tail forearm, and a center bead. Field guns choked skeet don't have these features. All forearm hangers and forearms were serial numbered with the receivers; this number will be found stamped on the side of the hanger.

On multi-barrelled sets made prior to 1976, be aware that each set of barrels had its own undetachable forearm and each barrel was serial numbered to the receiver and bore the usual Browning markings. Browning shotguns with additional non-Browning barrels are not regarded by collectors as desirable.

Stocks were finished in lacquer until the mid 60's when the finish was changed to polyurethane. This type of finish will never develop the beautiful satin look that lacquer guns have. One of the things a collector enjoys seeing is that patina. Oil finish was available on special order any time during the production period.

Checkering and carving on all grades are of very high quality. All are hand cut and very precise. The further you go back in years, the more profuse the checkering on Grade 1 guns. As the years went by, the checkering got a little slimmer — but not much. You really have to look at a lot of guns to see the difference, but the difference is there nevertheless.

The amount of checkering on each grade may vary with the year of production, but overall this will remain constant and done in an excellent manner. The checkering on the Grade I, Standard, and the Lightning grades are 20 lines per inch; on the Pigeon the checkering will run 24 lines per inch; on the Fighting Cocks 24 lines per inch; on the Diana 28 lines per inch; and on the Midas, Exhibition and Exposition grades, the checkering will run 28 lines per inch and may be even finer on some guns.

SALT WOOD

After 1966, the salt wood problem arises. It pretty well ends after 1973. Any purchase of a Superposed made between these years should be made very carefully. Inspect any place the metal touches the wood. Take out the butt plate screws and look them over very carefully. If you find no rust here, the gun is probably all right. Always look for salt wood right through 1976. Sometime you can test the wood with silver nitrate. Place a drop or two on a hidden spot on the wood; if it bubbles, you have a problem.

BUTT PLATES AND PADS

All post-war production except as noted under each model was shipped with the elaborately done F.N or Browning marked black plastic or horn butt plates. Rubber recoil pads could be ordered on any model at any time and were standard on the 12 gauge 3" magnums throughout their production. Also, from 1965 until the end of 1975 production, all Skeet and Trap models were shipped with a Browning pad unless otherwise requested. The Broadway and Lightning pads were the contoured ventilated type, and the others were the hunting type.

Up until 1958, when the Browning marked pad came along, if you ordered a recoil pad from St. Louis, they would install a Pachmayr "Whiteline" pad. Any style or make of pad could be ordered and often was. If a gun was ordered with a special pad directly from F.N., they would first produce it with a regular butt plate and then it would be fitted with a pad in St. Louis at the Browning repair and warrantee shop. This enabled them to purchase whatever pad was popular in this country at the time.

The first "Browning" marked Pachmayr manufactured pads were installed on the Superposed trap guns and the field style 3" magnums starting about 1958. The flat back competition Skeet Superposed pads were first installed in 1966. There are Skeet and Trap models made after these dates that have butt plates, but they were special ordered. They would be a rare find but wouldn't really create any great increase in value.

I would be cautious when purchasing a Superposed that had even a Browning pad installed. Make sure the gun is of at least standard dimensions, 14 1/4" or 14 3/8", and looked original. This is not to say that if it is longer or shorter it's not correct; just be suspicious. Remember, guns that are cut short suffer lower values of at least 20%.

HYDRO-COIL STOCKS

HYDRO-COIL STOCK — The 12 gauge Superposed is also available with the new Hydro-Coil stock and matching forearm which its manufacturer represents will reduce normal recoil by about 85%. The unit is similar to an automatic shock absorber in principal, using an internal pneumatic cylinder to absorb kick. This stock is made of a new synthetic called Cycolac which is extremely strong and which closely duplicates wood in weight and feel. It has been finished to resemble walnut in appearance. Hydro-Coil is offered in both Trap and Field/Skeet models at an extra charge and may be ordered on new guns or fit to guns now in service.

Hydro-Coil Stocks are not looked upon favorably by collectors. They were not looked upon with much favor in 1965 either, for they were only offered that year and dropped.

These stocks were available for 12 gauge guns only and were supposed to reduce recoil by 85%. They were not called stocks but units. These units had shock absorbers inside them similar to an automobile's shock absorbers. They were made from a material called Cycolac and were colored to resemble wood. It is an interesting variation and an attempt by Browning to offer the American shooter something different.

BARRELS

INTRODUCTION OF GAUGES

Originally, the Superposed was made only in the 12 gauge with 2 3/4" chambers, but in 1952 the 3" magnum was offered.

Although originally designed in the late 20's by Val Browning, it was 1949 before the 20 gauge was introduced into the American market. They were all chambered for the 2 3/4" loads until 1957 when all 20's were bored for the 3" shell; this still continues today. It was made with a down-sized frame and other components. Unlike other manufacturers that advertise a 20 gauge gun built on a 12 gauge frame, Browning Superposed are truly light weight guns built in proportion to the gauge and type of hunting for which the 20 gauge is suitable. I do not know if any 20 gauge guns were made for overseas sales prior to this year. There were not any 20 gauge Superposed sent here prior to the war.

In 1960 the introduction of the 28 gauge and 410 bore was a major event in this country, for it opened the market for skeet shooters who had been demanding a small gauge gun for several years. With the high quality ammunition available today, these two gauges are also being used quite extensively for hunting as well. They make great sport when hunting over pen raised birds. I have even killed ducks with my 410. The only true way to enjoy the fine handling qualities of these small gauges is to buy only the ones made on this frame. When you purchase a four barrel set, 12-20-28-410, it is built to accommodate the 12 gauge; therefore, it is much heavier. Of course, 99% of the folks using a four barrel set are skeet shooters who don't care about quick handling.

All triggers on the 410 are mechanical because the recoil on the standard triggers will not reliably reset to the second barrel. If you own a 28 gauge gun and have a 410 bore set of barrels made for it, get the triggers redone. By the time you do all that you might as well buy an original 410; I would.

BARREL MARKINGS
From 1949 through 1958 they are marked as follows:

On the left side of the barrel:
BROWNING ARMS COMPANY ST. LOUIS, MO
MADE IN BELGIUM

On the right side of the barrel are the words:
SPECIAL STEEL-(gauge) GA-SHELLS 2 3/4"
PATENTS NO 2203378-223386

From 1959 through 1968 they are marked as follows:
On the left side of barrel you will find:
BROWNING ARMS COMPANY ST LOUIS MO
& MONTREAL P.Q.
MADE IN BELGIUM

On the right side:
SPECIAL STEEL-(gauge) GA-SHELLS 2 3/4"
PATENTS NO 2203378-223386

From 1969 to the end of production they are marked as follows:
On the left side of barrel are the words:
BROWNING ARMS COMPANY MORGAN UTAH
& MONTREAL, P.Q.
MADE IN BELGIUM

On the right side of barrel:
SPECIAL STEEL-(gauge) GA-SHELLS 2 3/4"
PATENTS NO 2203378-223386

RIBS

From 1948 through 1959, raised hollow matted ribs were offered as an option the same as ventilated. You had to request one or the other, but if you didn't, you were sent the vent. In 1959 to 1960, only the vent rib was listed as a regular item, but raised hollow matted ribs were still available and advertised as such. This continued until 1971 when they were cancelled altogether. I believe that if you requested it, you could still get a solid rib after this date, but I don't know for sure. After the war, no raised hollow matted ribs were available on grades higher then the Lightning or Grade 1.

The ribs were not the same width for each gauge or model. The variations were as follows:

The regular 12 gauge hunting and skeet guns including the 3" magnums came with a 5/16" wide ventilated rib.

The hollow raised matted ribs for the 12 gauge was 5/16" and for the 20 gauge 1/4" wide.

The 410 bore, 28 and 20 gauges hunting and skeet guns came with a 1/4" ventilated rib, I have not heard of or seen a hollow raised matted rib on either one of these gauges, but you know Browning!

When introduced in 1968, the Superlight model had a tapered solid matted rib only. In 1972 a 1/4" ventilated rib started to show up. When examining this model, you will find solid ribs with 1972 and later dates and ventilated ribs with dates earlier than 1972.

The "P" Series ribs were in two configurations. The P-1 and P-2 grades had very fine engine turned matting, and the P-3 and P-4 guns had hand matting, which was more intricate. However, you could order any type rib your little heart desired, so don't be surprised to find something out of the ordinary. Just look for originality.

The Express rifles had no ribs, but were fitted with a ramp front sight with gold bead; the rear sight is a flip up sight which is adjustable for windage.

The Continental shotgun barrels had ventilated engine turned ribs 1/4" wide. The rifle barrels were fitted with a ramp front sight with a gold bead. On the rear is a folding leaf sight which is adjustable for windage only.

SUPERPOSED TRAP MODELS

Browning Superposed Trap models have been designed to satisfy the most exacting requirements in handling qualities and performance. Two distinct models are available, each with characteristics which offer the shooter selectivity according to personal preference and physical requisites. The major differences pertain to weight and sighting plane. Each possesses a natural balance, with just the right amount of forward weight to assure a smooth steady swing and uninterrupted follow-through.

Stock and forearm dimensions are the same on either model. The special trap stock with full pistol grip affords good control of the gun and assists consistent face alignment. The contoured trap recoil pad aids identical gun positioning with each shot and added comfort over a long shoot. The long semi-beavertail forearm places the hands in the same horizontal plane for easier, more natural pointing and adds that desired extra forward weight for steadiness. Front and center ivory sights further support fine pointing. Any combination of chokes is available; Full and Full, Improved-Modified and Full, or Modified and Full are generally recommended.

Either model is available with one or more extra sets of barrels of the same gauge or in 20 gauge, complete with luggage type fitted gun case. The BROADway rib is available only in 12 gauge, 30 or 32 inches in length. However, by special factory order, the BROADway rib will be made in 12 gauge, 28 or 26½ inch lengths at slightly higher prices.

The description above was taken from the 1965 Browning catalog.

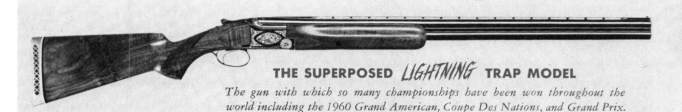

THE SUPERPOSED *LIGHTNING* TRAP MODEL

The gun with which so many championships have been won throughout the world including the 1960 Grand American, Coupe Des Nations, and Grand Prix.

The Lightning model carries carefully proportioned 30-inch barrels and a $\frac{5}{16}$-inch wide full ventilated rib. Being fairly lightweight and extremely compact, it is a fast gun, preferred equally as much by the live-bird shooter as the Trap specialist. It also appeals to those who weary after extensive shooting when using a heavier gun. In Doubles, where a little extra speed is favored, the Lightning will always receive acclaim as a tough competitor.

THE SUPERPOSED **BROAD**way **TRAP MODEL**

After two years of competition in the hands of over 4,000 trap shooters we are now certain beyond doubt that this BROADway Trap Model has features that assure better scores.

The actual width of this new rib is ⅝ inches. This unusual sighting plane quickly aligns eye to target and, without effort, facilitates holding a true bearing on the target during flight. The grooves on either side of the line of sight flatten and break up reflection to further enhance visual sharpness. The slightly diagonal transverse cuts afford natural freedom for the eye to focus dead center during the tracking and firing process. The slightest *cant* is immediately apparent to the shooter.

The perfectly flat sighting plane commences at the rear of the receiver and is actually longer than that provided on most trap guns of any type; still the BROADway's over-all length is shorter. Thus you have the length where it should be; the desirable minimal distance between eye and start of sight line and compactness in over-all length which means better control over the movement of the gun — with less effort.

A side view of the BROADway Trap Model shows the patented ventilated rib from a different angle and more clearly illustrates the ventilating principle which provides over three times the normal circulating area by which to dissipate barrel heat. Shoot as fast as you wish on hot humid or frosty days without the usual heat wave distortion between eye and target.

The target guns were also different, the Broadway Trap model had a 5/8" ventilated rib. Please remember that these barrels were available in 26 1/2", 28", 30", and 32" lengths. You may find a Broadway Trap with one of these short barrels, so don't automatically believe they've been cut off. Also, it's not cataloged as far as I can see, but you could order a Skeet model with a 1/2" ventilated rib.

BARREL LENGTHS & CHOKES

As first introduced after the war, the barrel lengths available for the Standard grade 20 gauge were 26 1/2" and 28", while the 12 gauge were 26 1/2", 28" and 30"; they remained that way until discontinued.

In 1955 the new Lightning grades were introduced were in 20 gauge with 26 1/2" and 28". The 12 gauge was also introduced with 26 1/2" and 28", the Lightning Trap with 30" barrels and the 12 gauge 3" magnum with 30" barrels. In 1973 the 12 gauge 3" magnum was also offered with 28". All these remained as introduced until 1975 when discontinued.

In 1960 the 410 bore and 28 gauge was introduced with 26 1/2" and 28" for all hunting and skeet guns and remained that way until the end of production. In 1961, the 20-28-410 sets also had 26 1/2" or 28" as well as the all gauge skeet sets introduced in 1972.

In 1961, the Broadway Trap as introduced had only 32", but in 1962 you could also order barrels in 26 1/2", 28", 30", and 32" with the Broadway rib.

In 1968, the Superlight 12 gauge with 26 1/2" barrels and the 20 gauge in 1969 with 26 1/2" came along, but I have seen several with 28" barrels.

In 1979 the Continental set was introduced with 26 1/2" shotgun barrels and 24" rifle barrels, and in 1980 the Express rifle was introduced with the same 24" barrel. Longer or shorter barrels could be special ordered at any time.

Since 1952 any combination of chokes on any barrel length could be ordered. These chokes were *** cylinder bore, **$ skeet, **_improved cylinder, ** modified, *_ improved modified, and * full choke.

Some guns, mostly Exhibition grade, were shipped with no choke markings. These were never choked and are probably extra full to full. It is my understanding that if you have the original papers, you can get Browning to choke and mark these barrels without charge.

Sights were ivory bead front with metal center bead on skeet and trap models. Center beads could be ordered on field guns if desired. Special order sights were always available.

Barrels were blued on all grades with the muzzle polished bright.

SUPERPOSED WITH EXTRA SETS OF BARRELS

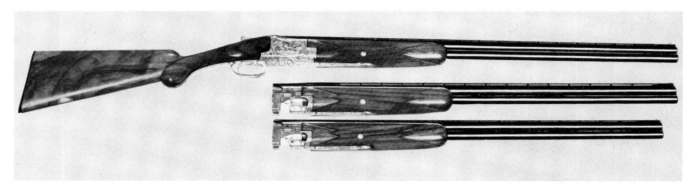

All through production, extra sets of barrels were promoted and advertised.

There was no limit to the number a person could order only the configuration until 1972. A 12 gauge gun could be ordered with additional sets of either 12 or 20 gauge barrels. A 20 gauge gun could be ordered with additional sets of 20 or 28 gauge and 410 bore barrels. A 28 gauge or 410 bore gun could be ordered with extra sets of barrels in either gauge. They did not like to fit barrels that mixed chamber length like a 2 3/4" set of barrels on a 3" magnum gun. You could also order a set of Lightning barrels for a Grade 1 frame.

In 1972 the all-gauge skeet set was offered and the restrictions were lifted for small gauge barrels were being made to fit the 12 gauge frames.

When fitted all barrels were serial numbered to the gun and each had their own forearm. At no time were any barrels made that could interchange with different frames; they were all special fitted.

SUPERTUBES

These were offered from 1965 to 1973. These were pretty popular with the skeet shooters, for they

provided the extra weight needed by many to maintain the proper follow through with the smaller gauge guns. Versions of these are still being made today by Briley and many others. If you decide to purchase these to use be sure to buy them with the understanding that they must fit or can be made to fit your gun. Browning advertised that all must be fitted, and they would not ship them without doing so.

They were only made to work in 12 gauge guns. Ejectors operated selectively; a pair was provided with each set of tubes. All were 16 1/2" long, so they didn't go all the way down the barrels. This meant that the original choke in the gun would still provide the patterns for which they were originally intended, or so Browning said.

These tubes were available two ways — either a pair of your choice or a full set. The pairs were shipped in a padded vinyl case with matching ejectors, tap-out and cleaning rod. The entire set of three gauges were shipped in a luggage case, with a pair of ejectors for each gauge, a tap-out and cleaning rod with a cleaning brush and loop, a pin punch, and a can of gun oil.

SERIAL NUMBERS

The serial numbers were placed under the top lever, on both parts of the forearm latch, on the long part of the ejectors, under the trigger guard on long tang guns or under the top tang or butt plate on short tang guns. On most guns they will be written in pencil on the butt plate. They were also on the barrels and can be seen when the forearm is slide forward to expose them.

From 1931 to 1962, all serial numbers were numeric, and you cannot tell anything from the serial numbers other then the year of production. You also cannot tell from the serial number what grade a gun is until 1976.

Starting in 1976, the product codes came along and this enables us to decipher not only the grade but also the gauge. From 1963 to 1976 all Superposed were marked as follows:

12 Gauge "S"	28 Gauge "F"
20 Gauge "V"	410 Bore "J"

These letters will be found immediately in front of the numerals that designate the date of assembly. From 1964 to 1976 the serial numbers began with number 0001 each January.

12 GAUGE
SERIAL NUMBERS

1948	17001-17200	1964	----S4
1949	17201-20000	1965	----S5
1950	20001-21000	1966	----S6
1951	21001-27000	1967	----S7
1952	27001-33000	1968	----S8
1953	33001-37000	1969	---S69
1954	37001-43000	1970	---S70
1955	43001-48000	1971	---S71
1956	48001-54000	1972	---S72
1957	54001-59000	1973	---S73
1958	59001-68500	1974	---S74
1959	68501-76500	1975	---S75
1960	76501-86500	1976	---S76
1961	86501-96500	1977	--RR--
1962	96501-99999	1978	--RP--
and	1- 6500	1979	--RN--
1963		1980	--PM--

First number this year was 6556S3. You may find some guns with S2 as part of the number

1981	--PZ--
1982	--PY--
1983	--PX--
1984	--PW--

Remember, these are European made guns in all series and grades. The serial numbers consist of the product code first followed by the year code and then the actual number of the gun produced. After 1976 you can tell exactly the year, grade, and gauge of the gun from the serial number.

20 GAUGE
SERIAL NUMBERS

The 20 gauge was introduced into the American market in 1949. No pre-war 20's were imported. They have their own set of serial numbers as does every gauge. They run approximately as follows.

1949	1- 1700	1967	----V7
1950	1701- 2800	1968	----V8
1951	2801- 3200	1969	---V69
1952	3201- 5300	1970	---V70
1953	5301- 6700	1971	---V71
1954	6701- 8400	1972	---V72
1955	8401- 9400	1973	---V73
1956	9401-10500	1974	---V74
1957	10501-11500	1975	---V75
1958	11501-14180	1976	---V76
1959	14181-17060	1977	--RR--
1960	17061-20640	1978	--RP--
1961	20641-23820	1979	--RN--
1962	23821-27300	1980	--PM--

You may find some guns with S2 as part of the number

| 1981 | --PZ-- |
| 1982 | --PY-- |

1963	----V3	1983	--PX--
1964	----V4	1984	--PW--
1965	----V5	1985	--PY--
1966	----V6	1986	--PT--

Remember, these are European made guns in all series and grades. The serial numbers consist of the product code first followed by the year code and then the actual number of the gun produced. After 1976 you can tell exactly the year, grade, and gauge of the gun from the serial number.

28 GAUGE AND
410 BORE SERIAL NUMBERS

The 410 and 28 gauges were introduced in the American market in 1960. Browning will not release the exact numbers produced the first three years, 1960-1962. However, if you take total production for the 410 and the 28 from 1960-1962, you can approximate the year the gun was produced. Some of the 1962 guns have a "J" as part of the serial number, designating a 410 gun.

For the years 1960-1962:

	28 GAUGE	410 BORE
1960	1-165	1-186
1961	166-330	187-332
1962	331-495	333-558

For the years 1963-1976:

	28 GAUGE	410 GAUGE
1963	---F3	---J3
1964	---F4	---J4
1965	---F5	---J5
1966	---F6	---J6
1967	---F7	---J7
1968	---F8	---J8
1969	---F69	---J69
1970	---F70	---J70
1971	---F71	---J71
1972	---F72	---J72
1973	---F73	---J73
1974	---F74	---J74
1975	---F75	---J75
1976	---F76	---J76

The following serial numbers are from the guns imported in 1983:

1983   —-F83   415J83 to 614J83

For year codes please refer to the General Information section in the front of this book.

PRODUCT CODES FROM 1976

Product codes are included in the serial numbers of all Superposed shotguns from 1976 to present. The product code is the first three digits in the serial number followed by the date code and then the actual number of the gun produced. The entire set of numbers — the product code, the date code and the number of the gun produced — is considered the serial number You can find more information about this and how to tell where a gun was made in the General Information section in the front of this book.

The code will not only tell you the gauge but also the model and grade as the gun left the factory. Remember, this code pertains to guns produced after 1975, not on any previously made Superposed. The only information you can get from the serial numbers on guns produced prior to 1976 is the gauge and the year of production on some guns made after 1961 and all those made after 1963.

12 GAUGE

GRADE	LIGHTNING	DIANA	MIDAS	EXHIBITION/EXPOSITION
Magnum	153	553	653	753
Lightning	213	513	613	713
Skeet	203	583	683	783
Trap	243	543	643	743
Broadway Trap	293	593	693	793
Superlight	203	503	603	703

20 GAUGE

	STANDARD	DIANA	MIDAS	EXHIBITION/EXPOSITION
Lightning	233	533	633	733
Skeet	2C3	5C3	6C3	7C3
Superlight	223	523	623	723

28 GAUGE

	STANDARD	DIANA	MIDAS	EXHIBITION/EXPOSITION
Lightning	173	573	673	773
Skeet	1E3	5E3	6E3	7E3
Superlight	123	523	623	723

410 BORE

	STANDARD	DIANA	MIDAS	EXHIBITION/EXPOSITION
Lightning	183	583	683	783
Skeet	1F3	5F3	6F3	7F3

ALL GAUGE

	STANDARD	DIANA	MIDAS	EXHIBITION/EXPOSITION
Skeet	1A4	5A4	6A4	7A4
Continental Set	177			

PRODUCT WARNING

I have inserted this twice because of its importance. It's no fun to have a gun go off unexpectedly, not to mention the chance of a serious accident.

In the later part of 1986-87, Browning published a warning about the Superposed triggers. This warning is for Belgium made guns only that have a single trigger. Perform the following exercise to see if you have one of these defective Superposed:

1. Point the weapon in a safe direction
2. Make sure it is unloaded. Perform steps A and B.

A. Move the selector-safety to one side and then fully forward to the off-safe fire position.
B. With the selector-safety fully forward, attempt to move the selector-safety either straight to the left or right.

Warning: If your selector-safety can be moved to the left or right while in the off safe(fire) position, you are urged to have your gun promptly modified by an authorized Browning service center or by Browning's Arnold service department.

B-125 SUPERPOSED
GENERAL INFORMATION

First introduced in 1988, this over/under is made in 12 or 20 gauge only and is still being made as of 1992. The various parts are made outside of Belgium in Japan; they are, however, decorated and assembled in Belgium at F.N.'s Custom Gun Shop in Herstal. It is a great buy in comparison to the Superposed for those on a budget. All the features of the 100% Belgium Superposed guns are on the B-125 without the full cost.

All B-125 models are finished and assembled in Belgium from parts manufactured by outside sources.

FEATURES AND OPTIONS

The standard features are single selective trigger, automatic selective ejectors, vent rib and non-detachable forearm. Browning is advertising three types of engraving which can be ordered, and these are covered after the list of options.

1. Custom fitted stock with various grades of wood
2. Checkering and carving
3. Internal parts polished
4. Custom chokes
5. Special ribs or triggers
6. Hand rubbed oil finish
7. Checkered butt
8. Special stock dimensions
9. Tear drop points on checkering
10. Monte Carlo comb on a trap or any type stock
11. Sculptured top lever
12. Deluxe recoil pad
13. Schnabel forearm
14. Three piece forearm
15. Beavertail forearm
16. Double triggers
17. Extra barrels
18. Hand matted vent rib
19. Ivory bead center and front sights
20. Engraved initials with or without gold and in English script or block letters; you could also have your full name or signature
21. Gold Roman numerals on top of rib designating different barrels
22. Gold or nickel silver stock inlay with initials
23. Stock shield of 10 carat gold or nickel silver with initials
24. Barrels options were 26 1/2" to 32" in solid matted or ventilated rib
25. Luggage cases
26. Trap or skeet butt stocks
27. Straight grip butt stock
28. Broadway rib
29. Rounded semi-pistol grip
30. French walnut
31. Olympic style trigger
32. Special order barrels without Invector or 30"

ENGRAVING

To keep cost low, Browning designed three different styles of engraving "A", "B", and "C"; the total cost is from $2,400.00 to $3,010.00. You can order other styles, but these are the most economical.

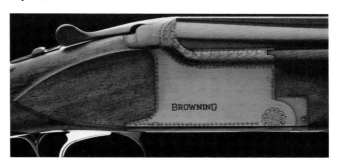

B-125 Grade A engraving.

"A"—This features only border engraving of acanthus leaves around the edges of the receiver reminiscent of the old Superlights; the entire gun is blued quite nicely.

B-125 Grade B engraving.

"B"—This grade has about 60% cover of ducks rising from the marsh, partridges, and a dog's head. The entire receiver and trigger guard is greyed. The wood is a medium grade about group 2-3, and the triggers are gold plated.

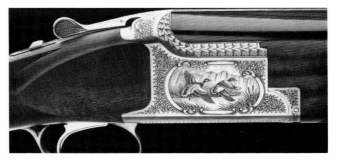

B-125 Grade C engraving.

"C"—This is the highest, having about 90% engraving, also featuring acanthus leaves on the barrel and fences, framed ducks rising from a marsh, and pheasants, all of which are in much more detail on the receiver. The entire receiver and trigger guard is greyed. The wood is of a higher grade, about group 4 with a little bit better job of oil finishing than the other two lower grades, and triggers are also gold plated.

STOCKS

The wood for each grade is noted above. In addition, all are oil finished and checkering is 20 lines per inch except the Grade C, which is 25 lines per inch. Stock dimensions on the Special Game are 12 gauge length of pull 14 1/4", drop at comb 1 1/2",

and drop at heel 2 9/32". On the 20 gauge the dimensions are length of pull 14 1/4", drop at comb 1 9/16", and drop at heel 2 3/8". The Sporting models are length of pull 14 1/4", drop at comb 1 1/2", and drop at heel 2 2/5". There are three different stock configurations or styles:

1. The English straight stock and Tulip forearm in top quality walnut for the Special Game 20 bore.
2. Swan neck stock in top quality walnut for the Special game 12 bore, This gun can also be supplied with a half pistol grip or round knob, both have the Tulip forearm.
3. Pistol grip stock in top quality walnut for the 12 bore Sporting gun with the Tulip forearm.

I am including the following table so you can see if a B125 you're anticipating purchasing is correct.

	HUNTING 12	SUPERLIGHT 12	SUPERLIGHT 20	SPORTING 12	TRAP F1
CHAMBER	2 3/4"	2 3/4"	2 3/4"	2 3/4"	2 3/4"
BBL LENGTH	28"	28"	26"	30"	30"
CHOKE(L)	4-1	4-1	4-1	4-1	3
CHOKE(U)	4-1	4-1	4-1	4-1	4
RIB	1/4"	1/4"	1/4"	1/4"	1/2"
STOCK	P	A	A	P	P
LENGTH	14 3/8"	14 3/8"	14 1/4"	14 3/8"	14 1/16"
DROP/COMB	1 1/2"	1 1/2"	1 1/2"	1 1/2"	1 3/8"
DROP/HEEL	2 5/16"	2 5 /16"	2 5/16"	2 5/16"	1 3/4"
FOREARM	T	T	T	T	Q
C'ERRING	20 TO 25*	20 TO 25*	20 TO 25*	20 TO 25*	10
TRIGGER	US	US	US	US	US
ACTION	B/GR*	B/GR*	B/GR*	B/GR*	B
WOOD	VB	VB	VB	VB	H

NOTES

1. Improved Cylinder	G. Swan Neck	T. Tulip	NA. Non-Auto	B. Blued
2. Modified	A. Straight	Q. Semi Beavertail	US. SS Trig	Gr.Greyed
3. Imp. Modified	P. Pistol	Tr.Traditional	Sk. Skeet	H. Oiled
4. Full	VB. Gloss			

* 20 L.P.I. Grades A & B 25 on C

* B on Grade A and Old Silver on B & C

BARRELS & CHOKES

The barrels offered for the Special Game model are 12 gauge, 28" long with ventilated rib, and Improved Cylinder/Improved Modified or Modified/Full choke combinations. Also available for the 12 gauge were 27 1/2" barrels with Invector chokes. The 20 gauge barrels were 26" long with ventilated rib and Improved Cylinder/Modified, Improved Cylinder/Improved Modified or Modified/Full choke combinations.

The barrels offered for the Sporting Game model are 12 gauge, 28" long with ventilated rib, and Improved Cylinder/Improved Modified choke combinations; or you could get the Invector chokes.

I believe if you want a Belgium over/under to

hunt with and don't want to spend the money on a new Superposed, this is the gun for you, but only if it is purchased in its basic configurations. If you start to fancy it up, you might as well purchase a B-25

Barrel markings are as follows on the left side:
BROWNING ARMS COMPANY
MORGAN,UTAH & MONTREAL P.Q.

After the above marking, you will also find the word "INVECTOR" if it has these or the proper choke code if it does not.

On the right side of the barrel will be the words:
SPECIAL STEEL 12 GA. 2 3/4"

The year codes can be found in the General Information section in the front of this book.

B27
GENERAL INFORMATION

Since this gun was never imported by Browning to sell in the U.S., I will not cover it in detail. The only thing that needs to be said is as follows:

Do not confuse these with the original Superposed. They were designed and produced to sell at a much lower price than the original gun. I have had many phone calls from folks wanting to know whether to buy them as a real Superposed. They are not and never meant to be. As cataloged by F.N., they were never called a Superposed and are in fact listed as a model 27, not a model FSC B25, which is the original Superposed.

These were made in 1980 to 1981 by F.N. to celebrate the one thousandth anniversary of the founding of Liege, Belgium. Some of these were brought over by servicemen returning from Europe; the price in the PX was $1,500.00. These are a much higher grade than the B27's that were being offered at $579.00 to $679.00 for the Grade 1 and 2's by some dealers in this country. These guns are about on the same level as the Citori.

One thing that fools people are the boxes, which were the same as those used for the Superposed. Don't allow a box to fool you also.

SERIAL NUMBERS

For serial number information please refer to the General Information section in the front of this book.

LIEGE SHOTGUN

The Liege 12 gauge was brought into this country from 1973 to 1975. It is essentially an economy minded Superposed known in Europe as the B26. They were all made in Belgium by F.N. but only lived a short life in the U.S., for they were replaced by the Citori after only three years.

The Superposed was getting so expensve that Browning thought it could be replaced by the Liege and recapture the lower end of the better gun market. They were designed to be less expensive than the Superposed and are still being made and offered in other parts of the world through F.N.'s catalog.

Many people have been fooled into believing this model was a Superposed by unknowing or unscrupulous dealers and paid Superposed prices; please do not be one of these people. As an instant check until you can spot them right away, always remember that the forearm latch rotates on the Liege and drops down on the Superposed. This will be a very quick way for a new collector to determine what he is being shown.

FEATURES

All frames were engraved slightly with very light scroll in the center of each side surrounded by a zigzag border. All were blued.

Browning only cataloged this model in 12 gauge, but during the years 1973 to 1975, there were a few 20 guages imported. They are hard to find.

The Liege had many excellent features, one of which was a mechanical single trigger. This type of trigger is an excellent feature on a two barreled gun. If the first shot fails, the triggers automatically set for the next barrel. This is not true with concussion triggers; they utilize the recoil to reset and if you have a bad shell in the first chamber, you will probably lose the opportunity to get off the other barrel. On the original Superposed all triggers for the 12 and 20 gauges were concussion. You may read further about those triggers in the Superposed section, All triggers on the Liege were blued.

Automatic selective ejectors were standard on all guns as were manual safeties. These safeties also selected the first barrel to shoot as well as reset the triggers in case of a misfire on the first barrel. They are marked with a red dot when ready to fire and with a "U" or "O" that lets you know which barrel will fire first.

The barrels available were 26 1/2" and 28" with 2 3/4" chambers or 30" with 3" chambers. No other barrels were offered. All barrels had matted ventilated ribs and nickel silver sight beads. The chokes available for the 26 1/2" and 28" were improved cylinder/modified, full/modified, or full/full; and the chokes for the 30" barrels were modified/full or full/full.

Barrels were marked on the left side,
FABRIQUE NATIONALE HERSTAL CHROME
MADE IN BELGIUM

The "CHROME" means a high chrome content in the steel
On the right side of the barrels will appear
SPECIAL STEEL 12 GA. SHELLS 2 3/4"
PATENT PENDING

Stocks were all French walnut with a full pistol grip. The wood was about group 2 with a high gloss finish, and all were checkered 22 lines per inch. The stock dimensions were length of pull 14 1/4", drop at comb 1 5/8", and drop at heel 2 1/2". All 2 3/4" chambered guns had the F.N. black plastic butt plates, and the 3" guns had a rubber pad.

The field style forearms were finished and checkered the same as the butt stocks, and unlike the original Superosed, they were readily detachable from the barrels. As mentioned previously, the forearm detachs by rotating the lever.

Overall, I would say that these are nice shotguns that can give a shooter many hours of enjoyment. Don't forget they were made by the same folks that built the Superposed.

Sales in 1973 were 2,800; in 1974, 4,000; and in 1975, 3,200 — for a total of 10,000. In 1973 they retailed for $429.50, in 1974 they sold for $497.50, and in 1975 there was no price listed in the retail sheet.

SERIAL NUMBERS

Each year the serial numbers began with 0001. For serial numbers on European market guns after 1976 refer to the General Information section.

	12 GAUGE	20 GAUGE
1973	73J—	73K—
1974	74J—	74K—
1975	75J—	75K—

GRAND LIEGE OR THE B26
GENERAL INFORMATION

Cataloged in 1980 the Grand Liege has many of the same features as the earlier Liege but with some refinements. We will cover these in detail.

All receivers were engraved with fine scroll covering about 60% of the receiver on the top, bottom and both sides. The scroll surrounds two pheasants on the left side, two quail on the right, and two ruffed grouse flying on the bottom. The trigger guards, forearm hangers and other parts are also scroll engraved to match. All receivers were silver greyed.

The gun featured a mechanical single trigger. This type of trigger is an excellent feature on a two barrel gun for it allows you to shoot the second barrel in a hurry if there is a misfire in the first. If the first shot fails, the triggers automatically set for the next barrel. All triggers on the Grand Liege were gold plated.

The barrels available were 28" and 30" with 2 3/4" chambers only; no other barrels were offered. All barrels had 5/16" matted ventilated ribs and German nickel silver sight beads. The chokes available for the 28" barrels were modified/full only. The 30" barrels could be purchased in modified/full or full/full.

The barrels were marked on the left side:
BROWNING ARMS COMPANY MORGAN, UTAH & MONTREAL P.Q.   CHROME MADE IN BELGIUM

On the right side were the words:
GRANDE LIEGE   PATENT PENDING SPECIAL STEEL 12 GA. SHELLS 2 3/4"

Automatic selective ejectors were standard on all guns as were manual safeties. These safeties also selected the first barrel to shoot as well as reset the triggers in case of a misfire on the first barrel.

Stocks were all French walnut with a full pistol grip; the wood was about group 3 to 4 with a high gloss finish. All were checkered 22 lines per inch. The stock dimensions were length of pull 14 1/4", drop at comb 1 5/8", and drop at heel 2 1/2". All guns had the F.N. black plastic butt plates.

The schnabel forearms were finished and checkered the same as the butt stocks, and, unlike the original Superposed, they were readily detachable from the barrels. As mentioned previously, the forearm detaches by rotating the lever.

All serial numbers were of the new type that can be found in the General Information section in the front of this book.

THE CITORI OVER AND UNDER

INTRODUCTION OF THIS MODEL

The 12 gauge Citori was introduced in 1973, and the 20 gauge in 1974. Four years later in 1978, the 28 gauge and the 410 bore came along. To finish out the gauges, the 16 was brought out in 1987 but cancelled in 1990.

This has been an important model for Browning. It has turned out to be one of the most popular shotguns in this country and perhaps the world. More skeet and trap shooters have started to use this shotgun since the introduction of the 28 gauge and 410 bore, and this has resulted in increased sales.

Sporting clays and the expanding number of shooters in this sport have used the Citori for years and now have specially produced models for their purposes.

Many of you purchasing this book are only interested in the Belgium guns, as I am myself. However, the new generation of shooters would not have the pleasure of shooting a Browning designed over and under if it weren't for the Citori, for it is a simplified and more economical variation of the original Superposed. I remember when I was 25 years old and an enthusiastic skeet shooter. That's about all I had, enthusiasm. I found a two-barrel Pigeon Skeet set, and it took two weeks' wages and about a third of my gun collection to buy it. Can you imagine how many hunters and target shooters are in the same boat today? even though this model does not meet with our idea of a collector's gun, neither did the original Superposed when it was being made. The Citori model is serving the American shooter today as the Superposed did prior to 1976, as a great gun the average shooter can afford.

By far, the greatest number of these are purchased by hunters. The Citori has been stiff competition for the Winchester 101 and the Ruger over/under as well as all of the imports in its price range. As of this date, there have been over twenty different models produced, and four times that many when you include gauge, grade, and other variations.

The explanations of the various grades, gauges, and features will be broken down into their respective categories. Some of this might be redundant as you read each section. You will find out as you reference this information in the future that you will only want to read the section you're interested in at the time. You will not have to pick bits and pieces out of several sections. Each section will cover all the information available at the time of printing.

THE HUNTING MODEL AND THE GRADE I

The Citori Hunting grade was introduced in 1973. Originally, it was available in 12 gauge only. The 20 gauge came along in 1974, the 28 gauge and 410 bore in 1978, and the 16 gauge in 1987. All were blued until 1980 when they were blued and engraved slightly. The engraving consisted of the same style as the Superposed Grade I guns. This was very light scroll on both sides, on the trigger guard, and on the bottom of the receiver covering about 30% of the surfaces.

FEATURES

They featured a gold plated single selective trigger, barrel selector incorporated in the manual thumb safety, automatic selective ejectors, a select walnut stock, and the German silver front sight bead set on a matted vent rib.

As of 1992 the Hunting model is still available as above with few changes other than additional gauges, grade variations, and Invector chokes which have been available only in the 12 and 20 gauges since 1987. The variations available can be reviewed throughout this section.

BARRELS AND CHOKES

As introduced the barrels were 26" and 28" with 2¾" in modified/full or improved cylinder/modified, or 30" barrels with 3" chambers and either modified/full or full/full chokes.

Later, all hunting models were manufactured with 3" chambers for the 12 and 20 gauges or the 410 bore; the 28 gauge guns had 2¾" chambers. Some years Browning offered only 3" chambers in the 12 and 20 gauges hunting guns and 2¾" chambers in the skeet and trap guns, so don't take it for granted that all Citoris have only 3" chambers. Carefully look at the barrel markings before loading 3" sheels. They also offered 3" or 3½" chambers in the hunting guns and 2½" chambers only in the 410 skeet guns. In 1989 the 12 gauges were introduced with 28" or 30" barrels and 3½" chambers; these all had Invector Plus chokes.

MARKINGS

On the left side of the barrel are the words:
BROWNING ARMS COMPANY MORGAN, UTAH & MONTREAL P.Q. (serial number)

On the right side of the barrel you will find:
SPECIAL STEEL (gauge) **GA SHELLS-2¾"** (3")- (choke)-(barrel length)

On the bottom of the frame is the word:
BROWNING

On the trigger guard is the Browning logo.

STOCKS

The full pistol grip stocks were French walnut, checkering was 18 lines per inch, and all were fitted with a Browning pad. The forearm was a slenderized beaver tail checkered the same as the butt stock. All wood was about group 2 finished in the standard Browning high gloss or a satin oil finish depending on the model and time of manufacture. Dimensions were length of pull 14¼", drop at comb 1⅝", and drop at heel 2½".

THE GRADE II

The Grade II was introduced in 1978 in 12, 20, 28 gauges, and 410 bore. This grade variation was available in the Hunting and Sporter models as well as in the skeet and trap configurations.

The hand engraving consisted of Canada geese and ringneck pheasant scenes surrounded by large circles of scroll. All actions were greyed and all triggers were gold plated.

Barrels had vent ribs and were available in all the standard lengths and chokes.

Stocks were of American walnut with a high gloss finish in a group 2-3 class and checkered 20 lines per inch.

All other features available or standard on the hunting models were also available on the Grade II's until they were discontinued in 1983.

THE GRADE III

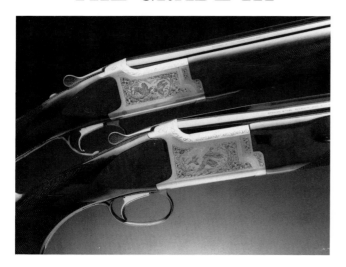

The Grade III is one of the most popular variations in the Citori model.

The Grade III was introduced in 1985 in the Hunting and Superlight models and in 1988 in the Lightning models. The skeet and trap configurations have also been avaiable since it was first introduced.

The 12 gauge engraving is different then the other four gauges. The receiver has about 80% coverage featuring a pair of ringneck pheasants emerging from a thicket and two mallards decoying with set wings. The 16, 20, 28 gauges and 410 bore guns have quail and grouse in the same style as the 12 gauge with about the same amount of coverage. All Grade III guns have greyed satin receivers and all triggers were gold plated. Please note that the scrolls were not hand engraved, but etched.

The wood appears to be about a group 2-3 grade with high gloss finish and checkering of 20 lines per inch.

As of 1992 the Grade III is still being offered in all the above models and gauges except the 16, which was discontinued in 1990. All other features found on the standard Hunting model will also be found on this grade.

THE GRADE V

The Grade V was also introduced in 1978 in 12, 20, 28 gauges and 410 bore.

It had a satin steel greyed receiver and trigger guard with a gold plated trigger. The engraving consisted of hand done mallard ducks and ringneck pheasant scenes. They were surrounded by fairly tight scroll work, which was almost 100% coverage. Please be aware that the scrolls are not 100% hand engraving, but etching instead.

The stocks were about group 4-5 American walnut with pronounced figure. They were checkered 22 lines per inch, and the finish was high gloss.

When introduced, the Hunting and Sporter models and the skeet and trap configurations were available. The Sporter was discontinued in 1982 and the others in 1984, which was also the end of Grade V production.

All other features found on the standard Hunting model will also be found on this grade.

THE GRADE VI

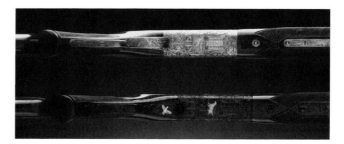

A bottom view of the Citori Grade VI.

The 1983 introduction of the Grade VI was in 12, 20, 28 gauges and 410 bore. It was subsequently made in 16 gauge starting in 1987.

Models available were the Hunting model from 1983 and the Lightning from 1987; the skeet and trap configurations have also been available since 1983. As of 1992 all the above models, configurations, and gauges are still available except the 16, which was discontinued in 1990.

The engraving consisted of ringneck pheasants and mallard ducks on the sides. The bottom had a setter on point and the trigger guard had a quail. Engraving is virtually 100% coverage, and the birds and dog were gold plated as were the triggers. You also had a choice of either a blued or greyed receiver. The scroll work is not actually hand engraving, but etching instead.

The wood was of about group 4-5 high gloss finished and featured 22 lines per inch checkering. All the other features found on the Hunting model will also be found on this grade.

CLASSIC AND GOLD CLASSIC

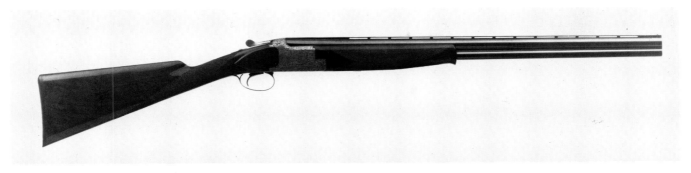

The Classic and Gold Classic models were part of a group of guns featuring a newly developed etching and gold plating process developed in Europe to reduce the high cost of hand engraving.

These were introduced in 1984 and featured a hand engraved upland setting of bird dogs, pheasants, and quail with a bust of John M. Browning across the bottom third of the receiver sides. Also across the sides of the receiver are the words "BROWNING CLASSIC." The receiver is greyed as is the trigger guard, forearm hanger, top lever, and bottom tang. There were a total of 313 made, not 5000 as Browning hoped to sell.

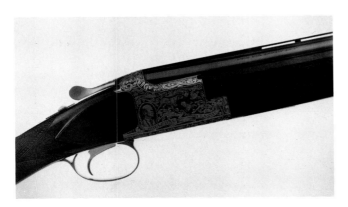

The Classic was introduced in 1984.

The Gold Classic was introduced in 1984 but didn't appear in the Browning catalogs until 1985.

The walnut used was very dense grained and highly figured. The stocks all had schnabel forearms and straight grip stocks, checkered 24 lines per inch surrounded by a carved border, and finished in a high gloss.

They were all made in 20 gauge and all featured 26" barrels choked improved and modified All were hand engraved and featured the engraver's name. Delivery for these did not begin until 1986, and they were not cataloged in 1987.

The Gold Classic has the same engraving and features as the Classic except for grade of wood and gold plated panels over the bust of John Browning, the pointing dogs, the birds, and the words "BROWNING GOLD CLASSIC." There was originally a total of 500 that were to be made.

INVECTOR AND INVECTOR PLUS CHOKES

This outstanding choke system is probably the best offered by the firearms industry today. It was first introduced in 1983 for the 12 gauge, in 1985 for the 20, in 1987 for the 16, and in 1988 for the 10 magnum. Browning experienced such a positive acceptance and sales of the Invector System that they stopped producing fixed choke barrels in the Hunting model 12 and 20 and have only offered the Invector System for the 10 and 16 gauges, never fixed chokes. The Invector System is literally invisible unless you look down the barrel. This makes for a very pleasant and acceptable look. The Invector Plus, however, is visible for about 3/8" and is used mainly by target shooters.

You can use either lead or steel shot with the same tubes. The resulting patterns are different

The Invector system has become so popular that they have become the choke system by which all others are judged. The ones shown here are the Extra Full Special "Turkey" Tubes.

because steel does not deform like lead and the patterns are much tighter. The chokes offered are:

10 GA	12 GA	16 GA	20 GA
Imp/Cyl	Cylinder	Cylinder	Cylinder
Modified	Skeet	Skeet	Skeet
Full	Imp Cyl	Imp Cyl	Imp Cyl
	Modified	Modified	Modified
	Imp Modified	Full	Imp Modified
	Full		Full
	Extra Full		

Each choke is marked for use with either lead or steel shot. The above chart does not mean that you can get the above patterns with both lead or steel.

The Invector Plus system utilizes a 2 1/4" long tube which protrudes beyond the muzzle slightly. Its less rapid constriction improves pattern density.

INTRODUCTION AND CONFIGURATION OF VARIOUS MODELS
THE SIDEPLATE 20

The Sideplate 20 was introduced in 1981 in 20 gauge only. The engraving featured etched game scenes including doves, ruffed grouse, quail and a dog on point. The trigger guard and lower tang were decorated with floral motifs and the head of a quail, receivers featured a greyed satin finish. All this is surrounded by floral motifs and goldplated triggers.

Barrels were only offered in 26" or 28" in improved cylinder and modified or modified and full chokes.

Wood was about group 4-5 with an oil finish and checkered 22 lines per inch. This model was discontinued in 1984.

CITORI TRAP MODEL

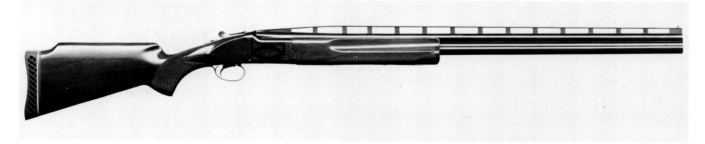

The Citori Trap model with high post rib, beavertail forearm and rubber ventilated recoil pad.

The Citori trap was introduced in 1974 to compete with other manufacturers offering shotguns suitable for shooting trap doubles. As of 1992 it is still being produced.

The engraving in the trap configuration, as well as the grade of wood, is the same as you will find on the other models.

In 1978 grades I, II and, V were introduced.

Grades II and V were both discontinued in 1983 when grades III and VI came along. As of 1992 grades I, III, and VI are still available.

The barrels were only chambered for 2 3/4" shell. Chokes available were full/full, improved modified/full, or modified/full. From 1974 until 1976, only 30" barrels were available. In 1976, 30",32", and 34" barrels came along in the same chokes as the 30" guns, and in 1985 the 34" barrels were discontinued. As of 1992, 30" and 32" barrels are the only ones still being made.

Since the beginning of production, either 11/32" or 13/32" ribs have been made depending on the year of manufacture. All are fully matted and all have a center bead and front sight supplied either ivory colored or metal.

As first introduced until 1982, only fixed chokes were made. In 1983 the Invector Choke system or fixed chokes were the choice of the purchaser. In 1986 only Invectors were made until 1992, when the Super Invector came along.

The Monte Carlo stock configuration was different, measuring length of pull 14 3/8", drop at comb 1 1/2", drop at Monte Carlo 1 1/2", and drop at heel 2". As of 1987, a conventional stock without the Monte Carlo comb became available. Drop at comb was 1 7/16". Since

its initial introduction, the Monte Carlo comb was changed to 1 3/8". All were shipped with a trap-style recoil pad as standard.

The forearms were all full beaver tail.

When it was first introduced, the only trigger offered was the standard you find on the Hunting model. In 1986 the new width Olympic style triggers became available. All Citori trap triggers are gold plated.

TRAP COMBO MODEL

In 1978 a Trap Combo model appears consisting of two sets of barrels, one single and one double. The single barrel was available 34" in full, improved modified, or modified chokes only. The over and under barrels were available 32" long only in full/full, improved modified/full, or modified/full; this was available in Grade I only. The combo model was discontinued in 1984.

CITORI PLUS MODEL

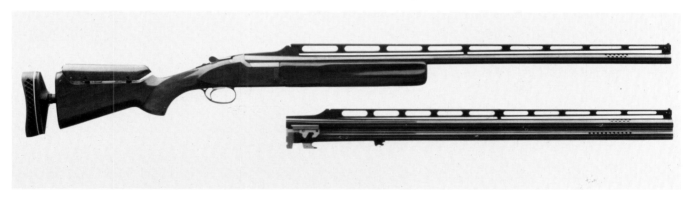

The Citori Plus variation was introduced in 1990, a favorite among trap shooters.

In 1990 Browning introduced the Citori Plus model in grade I only. They featured an adjustable vent rib, fully adjustable stock, back bored barrels,

and the Invector Plus choke system. All other features of this model are the same as other trap models.

THE CITORI SKEET MODEL

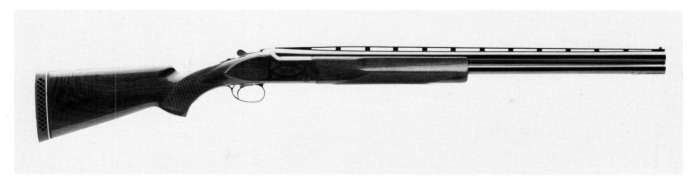

The Citori Skeet has a beavertail forearm and recoil pad as standard.

In 1974 the Citori skeet model was introduced. It was identical to the Hunting model except for the stock and barrel. The 20 gauge was introduced in 1976, the 28 gauge and 410 bore in 1978.

**GRADES AND
YEARS INTRODUCED**

The engraving as well as the grade of wood in the skeet configuration is the same as you will find on the other models and could be purchased from the beginning of production.

In 1978 Grades I, II and V were introduced. Grades II and V were both discontinued in 1983 when Grades III and VI came along. As of 1992 Grades I, III, and VI are still available.

BARRELS, RIBS AND CHOKES

From the beginning of production, the only barrels offered were either 26'' or 28'' with 2 3/4'' chambers. The 410 bore was made only with 2 1/2'' chambers.

The serrated vent rib was 5/16'' wide, later changed to 11/32''. All skeet guns have a center bead.

Fixed chokes were offered until 1987; Invector chokes were first offered in 1983 and still available today. The Invector Plus chokes were first offered in 1992. Neither Invector nor Invector Plus has ever been offered in the 28 gauge nor in the 410 bore.

The barrel markings on the left side are as follows:
BROWNING ARMS COMPANY MORGAN, UTAH & MONTREAL P.Q. MADE IN JAPAN (Serial number)

On the right side of the barrels are the words:
SPECIAL STEEL (Gauge)-2 3/4''-
(Choke)-(Barrel length)

STOCKS

Skeet stock configuration was length of pull 14 3/8'', drop at comb 1 1/2'', and drop at heel 2''. The grade of wood is consistent with the grade of the engraving. All skeet guns were made with Browning recoil pads.

SKEET COMBO SETS

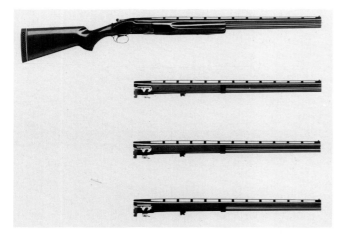

The Citori all gauge skeet set has interchangeable barrels in 410, 28, 20, and 12 gauges.

In 1979 the 12 and 20 gauge combo became available in Grade 1 only. In 1982 the all-gauge skeet set became available and in 1983 the three barrel set was offered in 20 and 28 gauges and in 410 bore.

Barrels could be ordered in 26'' or 28'' length. The radiused receiver was used along with weighted barrels, and one forearm was used for all barrels.

It was available in Grade I only until 1985 when the Grade III and VI were offered. The scroll work on all these guns are etching with the figures done by hand. You can find these grades described under their headings.

A fitted luggage case was included in all multi barrel sets.

THE SPORTER MODEL

This model was introduced in 1978 in 12, 20, 28 gauges, and in the 410 bore. They all had a straight grip stock schnabel forearm and an oil finish. Barrels were 26'' only. Grades offered were I and V. All wood and other features were commensurate with the grade ordered.

It was replaced by the Superlight in 1983.

THE SUPERLIGHT MODEL

The Superlight was introduced in 1982 in the 12 and 20 gauges. This was followed up by the 28 gauge and the 410 bore in 1983 and the 16 gauge in 1988. The 16 was discontinued in 1990.

All had 2 3/4'' chambers except for the 410, which was 3''. It was available in Grade I only until 1984 when the Grades III and VI came out. Only 26'' or 28'' barrels were offered in improved cylinder/modified or modified/full, for this model was meant to be an upland gun only.

Wood was commensurate with the grade ordered. All had an English straight stock and schnabel forearm finished in high gloss.

THE UPLAND SPECIAL MODEL

The Upland Special was introduced in 1984. It featured 24'' barrels in 12 or 20 gauge with Invector chokes only; it was offered in Grade 1 only.

The English style straight grip, high gloss finished stock was shorter then usual. The purpose of this was to allow a faster first shot as well as a ready made gun for women and children. The dimensions were length of pull 14'', drop at comb 1 5/8'', and drop at heel 2 1/2''. All forearms were the schnabel type and the butt stocks all had recoil pads.

All other features of the basic Hunting guns are the same for the Upland special. As of 1992 this model is still being made in the configurations described above.

THE LIGHTNING AND GRAN LIGHTNING MODELS

In 1988 Browning introduced the Lightning model in the 12, 16, 20, and 28 gauges, and in the 410 bore. This model has always been made in Grades I, III, and VI with gold plated triggers.

The barrels are back-bored with Invector chokes only in the 20, 16, and 12 gauges. You can order either improved/modified or modified/full chokes in the 28 gauge or the 410 bore.

Chambers available were 2 3/4'',3'' or 3 1/2'' in the 12 gauge, 2 3/4'' in the 16, 3'' in the 20, 2 3/4'' in the 28, and 3'' in the 410.

The stock is a half pistol grip round knob with slim forearm and a high gloss finish. The configura-tion for the 12 and 16 gauges were length of pull 14 1/4'', drop at comb 1 5/8'', and drop at heel 2 1/2''. In the 20, 28 and 410, the stock measurements are length of pull 14 1/4'', drop at comb 1 1/2'', and drop at heel 2 3/8''.

The Gran Lightning is basically the same model with higher grade wood. The 16 gauge was discon-tinued in 1990.

The Gran Lightning

THE SPORTING CLAYS MODELS

The popularity of Sporting Clays has exploded. Browning recognized this in 1989 and introduced the GTI Sporting Clays.

In 1989 Browning introduced the Sporting Clay Citoris. There are three basic models — the GTI, the Special Sporting, and the Lightning Sporting. They are described as follows:

The GTI's have a 13mm rib, which is slightly higher then a conventional Hunting model; the bar-rels are 28'' or 30'' and have ventilated side ribs. Chambers are all 2 3/4'', and Invector chokes are the only ones offered. All guns have front and center ivory sights.

The stock is full pistol grip with grooved semi-beaver tail forearm, and the finish is satin. They all come with a black trap style recoil pad.

Stock dimensions are length of pull adjustable from 14 1/8'' to 14 7/16'', drop at comb 1 3/8'', and drop at heel 2 1/4''.

The triggers are really unusual in that they are adjustable for length of pull and can be used with three different trigger shoes which are provided. The safety is non-automatic, a feature which makes a lot of sense for a target gun where you don't get any se-cond chances.

The blued receiver has decorative red lettering which says ''BROWNING GTI''.

THE SPECIAL SPORTING MODEL

The Special Sporting has a tapered high post rib and solid side ribs; the barrel lengths available are 28'', 30'', or 32'' only, All chambers are 2 3/4'' with improved cylinder/modified chokes only. There is also a two barrel set, which consists of 28'' and 30'' barrels.

The stock is a flat knob with palm swell and a lightning style forearm with a high gloss finish. The dimensions are length of pull 14'' to 14 5/16'', drop at comb 1 1/2'', and drop at heel 2''. All come with the trap style pad.

The trigger is the same as the GTI model, and like the GTI, the safety is non-automatic.

The blued receiver has decorative gold lettering that says ''SPECIAL SPORTING CLAYS EDITION''.

THE LIGHTNING SPORTING MODEL

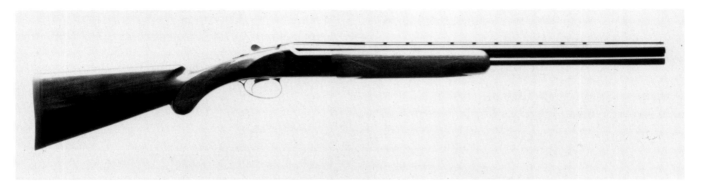

The Micro Citori Lightning 20 gauge.

The Lightning Sporting has either a high or low rib, 30" barrels, and solid side ribs. The 2 3/4" chambers are the only ones available with modified/improved cylinder chokes only.

All stocks are round knob with a lightning forearm. Dimensions are length of pull 14 1/8" to 14 7/8", drop at comb 1 1/2", and drop at heel 2". All have trap style recoil pads and are finished in the Browning high gloss.

The trigger is the same as the GTI model, and the safety is manual.

All receivers are blued with gold lettering that says, "LIGHTNING SPORTING CLAYS EDITION."

There are so many variations in the Citori that it would be easier for you to see the basic information as presented below.

STOCK DIMENSIONS

	12 and 16 Hunting and Superlight	12 and 20 Upland Special	20, 28 and .410 Hunting and Superlight
Length of Pull	14¼"	14"	14¼"
Drop at Comb	1⁵/₈"	1⁵/₈"	1½"
Drop at Heel	2³/₈"	2½"	2³/₈"

Gauge	Model	Chamber*	Barrel Length	Chokes Available	Grades Available
12	Hunting	3"	30"	M-F, Invector	I, III, VI
12	Hunting	3"	28"	M-F, Invector	I, III, VI
12	Hunting	3"	26"	IC-M, Invector	I, III, VI
12	Superlight	2 3/4"	28"	Invector	I, III, VI
12	Superlight	2 3/4"	26"	Invector	I, III, VI
12	Upland Spc.	2 3/4"	24"	Invector	I
16	Hunting	2 3/4"	28"	Invector	I, III, VI
20	Hunting	3"	28"	M-F, Invector	I, III, VI
20	Hunting	3"	26"	IC-M, Invector	I, III, VI
20	Superlight	2 3/4"	28"	M-F, Invector	I, III, VI
20	Superlight	2 3/4"	26"	IC-M, Invector	I, III, VI
20	Upland Spc.	2 3/4"	24"	Invector	I
28	Hunting	2 3/4"	28"	M-F, IC-M	I, III, VI
28	Hunting	2 3/4"	26"	M-F, IC-M	I, III, VI
28	Superlight	2 3/4"	28"	M-F	I, III, VI
28	Superlight	2 3/4"	26"	IC-M	I, III, VI
410	Hunting	3"	28"	M-F, IC-M	I, III, VI
410	Hunting	3"	26"	M-F, IC-M	I, III, VI
410	Superlight	3"	28"	M-F	I, III, VI
410	Superlight	3"	26"	IC-M	I, III, VI

F - Full, M - Modified, IC - Improved Cylinder, Invector. Full and Modified Choke installed; Improved Cylinder and wrench included. Improved Modified, Skeet and Cylinder choke tubes and VI, 12 and 20 gauge available with invector only.

CITORI SKEET AND CITORI TRAP SPECIFICATIONS

Gauge	Model	Chamber	Length	Chokes	Available
CITORI TRAP					
12	Conv. or M.C.	2 3/4"	32"	Invector	I, III, VI
12	Conv. or M.C.	2 3/4"	30"	Invector	I, III, VI
CITORI SKEET					
12	Standard	2 3/4"	28"	S-S, Invector	I, III, VI
12	Standard	2 3/4"	26"	S-S, Invector	I, III, VI
20	Standard	2 3/4"	28"	S-S, Invector	I, III, VI
20	Standard	2 3/4"	26"	S-S, Invector	I, III, VI
28	Standard	2 3/4"	28"	S-S	I, III, VI
28	Standard	2 3/4"	26"	S-S	I, III, VI
410	Standard	2 3/4"	28"	S-S	I, III, VI
410	Standard	2 3/4"	26"	S-S	I, III, VI

SKEET SETS

20,28,410	3 Gauge Set	2 3/4"	28"	S-S	I, III, VI
12,20,28,410	4 Gauge Set	2 3/4"	28"	S-S	I, III, VI
12,20,28,410	4 Gauge Set	2 3/4"	26"	S-S	I, III, VI

F-Full, M-Modified, S-Skeet, Invector-Invector Choke System -Invector Trap models.

Full, Improved Modified, Modified, and wrench included. Skeet models: Skeet and Skeet tubes only, wrench included. All other choke tube sizes are available as accessories.

SERIAL NUMBERS

The letters "N" and "H" stand for the model. Each year began with 0001. For the yearly codes please refer to the General Information section at the front of this book.

Serial number from 1973 - 1976 are as follows:

	20 Gauge	12 Gauge
1973	Not Made	—H37
1974	—N47	—H47
1975	—N57	—H57
1976	—N67	—H67

The model code for the standard 20 is 163. The Superlight 20 and the Upland 20 codes are 123. The 12 gauge code is 143.

Chapter Five

Semi-Auto
Shotguns

The cover from the 1931 catalog in which Browning introduces its new "Direct-to-you" sales policy.

Speed, Power, Safety

THE BROWNING AUTOMATIC SHOT-GUN cannot be fired except by a deliberate and intentional pull on the trigger—the sear adjustment being such as to prevent jarring the gun off under any circumstances. Holding the trigger back will not result in repeat shots—it is necessary to pull the trigger once for each shot fired. But aiming the gun and pulling the trigger constitute all that the shooter must do—the details of ejecting the empty case, reloading and cocking the gun are all automatic.

Barrel and breech-bolt are locked together until the shot charge has left the muzzle—no power is lost through gas escaping from the breech, as in the "blow-back" type of arms.

BROWNING AUTOMATIC SHOTGUNS, therefore, shoot quite as far, quite as accurately, and with as great force and penetration as any other type of arm using corresponding loads. Any factory loads regularly supplied, from the lightest trap to the heaviest field load, will function the Browning perfectly.

A simple, positive safety lock is provided in the forward part of trigger guard by the use of which the gun may be safely carried cocked and locked—and its position may be known by either sight or feel. When the last shot has been fired, the breech remains open—your signal that the magazine is empty.

Lifetime Guarantee

All Genuine Browning Automatic Shotguns are guaranteed for both quality of workmanship and materials for the life of the gun. Any defect attributable to the fault of materials or workmanship will be adjusted by us to the satisfaction of the owner.

All shotguns are made in accordance with the best manufacturing standards, of materials carefully selected for the various parts, by workmen of skill and experience, and to designs that provide a high safety factor.

Genuine Browning Automatic Shotguns are all made to one standard as far as affects their shooting performance; the only difference between grades 1, 2, 3 and 4 is an increasing excellence in the hand finishing and polishing of parts, and in the engraving of the metal and the selection of the wood. The shooting characteristics remain identical in all cases—the highest standard of performance that can be obtained in arms manufacture.

BROWNING ARMS COMPANY

Reprinted from 1931 Browning catalog.

THE BROWNING
AUTOMA

STANDARD GRADE NO. 1

16-GAUGE

Every part is of f i n e s t workmanship, the pieces being carefully hand finished after machining. Special process gives a rich blue-black finish to special high strength steel barrels. Full choke 28 or 30 inches. Modified choke, 26 or 28 inches, cylinder bore 26 inches. Full choke 28 inches without rib furnished unless otherwise specified. Matted receiver. European walnut stock and forearm all hand-checkered. Stock half pistol grip, length 14¼ inches, drop at heel 2¼ inches, at comb 1¾ inches. Chambered for shells up to 2 9/16 inches, weight about 6¾ pounds. Price, direct-to-you, delivered anywhere in the United States, $49.75.

$49⁷⁵

T I C

STANDARD GRADE NO. 1

12-GAUGE The extremely
light weight of the Browning "12" is secured by a combination of high grade materials, unusual simplicity in design and the finest skilled workmanship that has characterized the manufacture of all genuine Browning arms. At no time has strength been sacrificed to weight. In fact, the barrels of all genuine Browning guns carry the stamp of approval of the Belgian government test which requires that they withstand the stress from loads more than double those used in actual shooting. Added to the advantage of weight, you have all of the other Browning features which have caused the American public, as well as purchasers of the world's finest guns in every part of the globe, to give it their unqualified approval.

The Browning 12-gauge is of the same general description as the 16-gauge except barrels are full choke 28, 30, or 32 inches. Modified choke 28 inches and cylinder bore in 26 or 28 inches. Full choke 30 inches without rib furnished unless otherwise specified. European walnut stock and forearm all hand-checkered. Stock half pistol grip, length 14½ inches, drop at heel 2¼ inches, at comb 1¾ inches. Chambered for shells up to 2¾ inches, weight about 8 pounds. Price, direct-to-you, $49.75, delivered anywhere in the United States.

Standard Grade, No. 1, either gauge, without rib	$49.75
Extra barrel, either gauge, without rib	21.35
Raised matted hollow rib, either gauge, additional	8.85
Ventilated rib, additional	13.85

Reprinted from 1931 Browning catalog.

STANDARD SPECIFICATIONS
Browning Automatic Shotguns
To Avoid Error in Your Order—Check Specifications You Want

12-GAUGE

Check Here — Price

☐ Grade 1—32 inch Full Choke—Without Rib.......$ 49.75
☐ Grade 1—32 inch Full Choke—Ribbed 58.60
☐ Grade 1—30 inch Full Choke—Without Rib........ 49.75
☐ Grade 1—30 inch Full Choke—Ribbed 58.60
☐ Grade 1—28 inch Full Choke—Without Rib........ 49.75
☐ Grade 1—28 inch Full Choke—Ribbed 58.60
☐ Grade 1—28 inch Modified Choke—Without Rib 49.75
☐ Grade 1—28 inch Modified Choke—Ribbed 58.60
☐ Grade 1—30 inch Modified Choke—Without Rib 49.75
☐ Grade 1—30 inch Modified Choke—Ribbed 58.60
☐ Grade 1—28 inch Cylinder—Without Rib 49.75
☐ Grade 1—28 inch Cylinder—Ribbed 58.60
☐ Grade 1—26 inch Cylinder—Without Rib 49.75
☐ Grade 1—26 inch Cylinder—Ribbed 58.60

☐ Grade 2—32 inch Full Choke—Without Rib........ 64.75
☐ Grade 2—32 inch Full Choke—Ribbed 73.60
☐ Grade 2—30 inch Full Choke—Without Rib........ 64.75
☐ Grade 2—30 inch Full Choke— Ribbed 73.60
☐ Grade 2—28 inch Modified Choke—Without Rib 64.75
☐ Grade 2—28 inch Modified Choke—Ribbed 73.60
☐ Grade 2—28 inch Cylinder—Without Rib 64.75
☐ Grade 2—28 inch Cylinder—Ribbed 73.60

☐ Grade 3—32 inch Full Choke—Without Rib........ 175.50
☐ Grade 3—32 inch Full Choke—Ribbed 184.35
☐ Grade 3—30 inch Full Choke—Without Rib........ 175.50
☐ Grade 3—30 inch Full Choke—Ribbed 184.35
☐ Grade 3—28 inch Modified Choke—Without Rib 175.50
☐ Grade 3—28 inch Modified Choke—Ribbed 184.35
☐ Grade 3—28 inch Cylinder—Without Rib 175.50
☐ Grade 3—28 inch Cylinder—Ribbed 184.35

☐ Grade 4—32 inch Full Choke—Without Rib........ 277.00
☐ Grade 4—32 inch Full Choke—Ribbed 285.85
☐ Grade 4—30 inch Full Choke—Without Rib........ 277.00
☐ Grade 4—30 inch Full Choke—Ribbed 285.85
☐ Grade 4—28 inch Modified Choke—Without Rib 277.00
☐ Grade 4—28 inch Modified Choke—Ribbed 285.85
☐ Grade 4—28 inch Cylinder—Without Rib 277.00
☐ Grade 4—28 inch Cylinder—Ribbed 285.85

Guns with extra barrel

Grade 1—Without Rib
☐ 30 inch Full and 28 inch Cylinder..................... 71.10
☐ 30 inch Full and 28 inch Modified..................... 71.10
☐ 28 inch Modified and 28 inch Cylinder.............. 71.10

Grade 1—Ribbed
☐ 30 inch Full and 28 inch Cylinder..................... 88.80
☐ 30 inch Full and 28 inch Modified..................... 88.80
☐ 28 inch Modified and 28 inch Cylinder.............. 88.80

Grade 2—Without Rib
☐ 30 inch Full and 28 inch Cylinder..................... 86.10
☐ 30 inch Full and 28 inch Modified..................... 86.10
☐ 28 inch Modified and 28 inch Cylinder.............. 86.10

Grade 2—Ribbed
☐ 30 inch Full and 28 inch Cylinder..................... 103.80
☐ 30 inch Full and 28 inch Modified..................... 103.80
☐ 28 inch Modified and 28 inch Cylinder.............. 103.80

Grade 3—Without Rib
☐ 30 inch Full and 28 inch Cylinder..................... 214.35
☐ 30 inch Full and 28 inch Modified..................... 214.35
☐ 28 inch Modified and 28 inch Cylinder.............. 214.35

Grade 3—Ribbed
☐ 30 inch Full and 28 inch Cylinder..................... 232.05
☐ 30 inch Full and 28 inch Modified..................... 232.05
☐ 28 inch Modified and 28 inch Cylinder.............. 232.05

Grade 4—Without Rib
☐ 30 inch Full and 28 inch Cylinder..................... 328.25
☐ 30 inch Full and 28 inch Modified..................... 328.25
☐ 28 inch Modified and 28 inch Cylinder.............. 328.25

Grade 4—Ribbed
☐ 30 inch Full and 28 inch Cylinder..................... 345.95
☐ 30 inch Full and 28 inch Modified..................... 345.95
☐ 28 inch Modified and 28 inch Cylinder.............. 345.95

16-GAUGE

Check Here — Price

☐ Grade 1—30 inch Full Choke—Without Rib.......$ 49.75
☐ Grade 1—30 inch Full Choke—Ribbed 58.60
☐ Grade 1—28 inch Full Choke—Without Rib........ 49.75
☐ Grade 1—28 inch Full Choke—Ribbed 58.60
☐ Grade 1—26 inch Modified Choke—Without Rib 49.75
☐ Grade 1—26 inch Modified Choke—Ribbed 58.60
☐ Grade 1—28 inch Modified Choke—Without Rib 49.75
☐ Grade 1—28 inch Modified Choke—Ribbed 58.60
☐ Grade 1—26 inch Cylinder—Without Rib 49.75
☐ Grade 1—26 inch Cylinder—Ribbed 58.60
☐ Grade 1—28 inch Cylinder—Without Rib 49.75
☐ Grade 1—28 inch Cylinder—Ribbed 58.60

☐ Grade 2—30 inch Full Choke—Without Rib........ 64.75
☐ Grade 2—30 inch Full Choke—Ribbed 73.60
☐ Grade 2—28 inch Full Choke—Without Rib........ 64.75
☐ Grade 2—28 inch Full Choke—Ribbed 73.60
☐ Grade 2—26 inch Modified Choke—Without Rib 64.75
☐ Grade 2—26 inch Modified Choke—Ribbed 73.60
☐ Grade 2—26 inch Cylinder—Without Rib 64.75
☐ Grade 2—26 inch Cylinder—Ribbed 73.60

☐ Grade 3—30 inch Full Choke—Without Rib........ 175.50
☐ Grade 3—30 inch Full Choke—Ribbed 184.35
☐ Grade 3—28 inch Full Choke—Without Rib........ 175.50
☐ Grade 3—28 inch Full Choke—Ribbed 184.35
☐ Grade 3—26 inch Modified Choke—Without Rib 175.50
☐ Grade 3—26 inch Cylinder—Without Rib 175.50
☐ Grade 3—26 inch Cylinder—Ribbed 184.35

☐ Grade 4—30 inch Full Choke—Without Rib........ 277.00
☐ Grade 4—30 inch Full Choke—Ribbed 285.85
☐ Grade 4—28 inch Full Choke—Without Rib........ 277.00
☐ Grade 4—28 inch Full Choke—Ribbed 285.85
☐ Grade 4—26 inch Modified Choke—Without Rib 277.00
☐ Grade 4—26 inch Modified Choke—Ribbed 285.85
☐ Grade 4—26 inch Cylinder—Without Rib 277.00
☐ Grade 4—26 inch Cylinder—Ribbed 285.85

Guns with Extra Barrel

Grade 1—Without Rib
☐ 28 inch Full and 26 inch Cylinder..................... 71.10
☐ 28 inch Full and 26 inch Modified..................... 71.10
☐ 26 inch Modified and 26 inch Cylinder.............. 71.10

Grade 1—Ribbed
☐ 28 inch Full and 26 inch Cylinder..................... 88.80
☐ 28 inch Full and 26 inch Modified..................... 88.80
☐ 26 inch Modified and 26 inch Cylinder.............. 88.80

Grade 2—Without Rib
☐ 28 inch Full and 26 inch Cylinder..................... 86.10
☐ 28 inch Full and 26 inch Modified..................... 86.10
☐ 26 inch Modified and 26 inch Cylinder.............. 86.10

Grade 2—Ribbed
☐ 28 inch Full and 26 inch Cylinder..................... 103.80
☐ 28 inch Full and 26 inch Modified..................... 103.80
☐ 26 inch Modified and 26 inch Cylinder.............. 103.80

Grade 3—Without Rib
☐ 28 inch Full and 26 inch Cylinder..................... 214.35
☐ 28 inch Full and 26 inch Modified..................... 214.35
☐ 26 inch Modified and 26 inch Cylinder.............. 214.35

Grade 3—Ribbed
☐ 28 inch Full and 26 inch Cylinder..................... 232.05
☐ 28 inch Full and 26 inch Modified..................... 232.05
☐ 26 inch Modified and 26 inch Cylinder.............. 232.05

Grade 4—Without Rib
☐ 28 inch Full and 26 inch Cylinder..................... 328.25
☐ 28 inch Full and 26 inch Modified..................... 328.25
☐ 26 inch Modified and 26 inch Cylinder.............. 328.25

Grade 4—Ribbed
☐ 28 inch Full and 26 inch Cylinder..................... 345.95
☐ 28 inch Full and 26 inch Modified..................... 345.95
☐ 26 inch Modified and 26 inch Cylinder.............. 345.95

Ventilated Ribs furnished from stock in following lengths only: **12-Gauge** 28, 30, and 32 inch full choke; 28 inch modified and cylinder bore; **16-Gauge** 28 and 30 inch full choke; 26 and 28 inch modified and 26 inch cylinder bore. Additional charge Ventilated Rib, $13.85. Add to cost of Gun or Barrel. Choke................Barrel Length.............

BROWNING GUN CASES

Browning Gun Cases built especially for your gun are made in two Grades. Grade "A"—$19.95.................
Grade "B"—$13.85............. Check (X) Grade Desired. Cases for two barrels, or cases for special stocks, either model $3.25 extra.

Include amount for gun case in your remittance.

BROWNING ARMS COMPANY, St. Louis, Mo.

Reprinted from 1931 Browning catalog.

AUTO-5 PRE-WAR

HISTORY OF THE EARLY GUNS

The Auto-5 was one of two guns produced by Fabrique Nationale for the original Browning Company. It was designed by John M. Browning in 1900.

Since 1883, under an agreement between the Browning brothers and T.G. Bennett of Winchester, the Browning brothers had been designing many new models on a regular basis and selling the patent rights to the Winchester Repeating Arms Company. However, on the Auto-5, the Brownings decided not to sell the patent rights, but instead to option for royalties on each gun produced. Winchester Bennett, head of Winchester, told Mr. Browning that he would not go along with paying royalties, for among other things, they did not think an automatic shotgun would appeal to the American sportsman. Needless to say, Winchester regretted this decision for many years to come.

John M. decided to go to Remington with his new gun, but upon arriving, he ran into a major tragedy. The President of Remington, Mr. Marcellus Hartley, died while Mr. Browning was in the waiting room to meet him. To say the least, the Brownings were very disappointed in the outcome of this meeting. They knew that Remington was hurting for new designs, since almost everything they had was from the black powder era and unsuitable for the new smokeless powders. If Mr. Hartley had not died, the whole series of events probably would have changed for Remington and Browning. In years to come, Remington would make the new shotgun in several versions, but more about this later.

The Brownings decided to go to Belgium where they had previous dealings. John knew the complexity of the new automatic required many parts and a great deal of labor. In Belgium, labor was cheaper and the skill of the workers was just as competent as in the U.S.

Fabrique Nationale of Liege, Belgium, was approached with the idea of manufacturing the new design in February of 1902. This, of course, was on a royalty basis. They enthusiastically jumped at the opportunity to work with the then-famous Browning brothers, for they saw a good future in the design. In addition, F.N. liked the idea of producing the gun and saw an excellent and reliable automatic. On March 24, 1902, they agreed to Browning's terms. Fabrique Nationale and the Brownings were no strangers to each other, for they had been working together on a 32 Automatic pistol which had broken all F.N. sales records for the past two years.

To show his good faith and confidence in the success of the Auto-5, John committed himself to an initial order of 10,000 guns. They were stamped with the name "The Browning Automatic Arms Company"; it was a non-existent firm and these are the only guns that bear that name. We do not know why Mr. Browning made up the name instead of using the legitimate name he and his brothers were using at the time. In order to distribute these first 10,000 guns in the quickest way possible, Mr. Browning decided to sell many of them through the jobbing firm of Schoverling, Daly and Gales of New York City, a very large sporting goods dealer at that time.

I realize the above description of these events are brief. They have been covered in detail in the publication "John M. Browning, American Gun Maker" by John Browning and Curt Gentry available from the Browning Company. This book covers Mr. Browning's relationship with Winchester in detail. It would take an entire chapter to cover it here.

THE FIRST 10,000

Serial number 1 was shipped to this country on September 17, 1903, but full production wasn't started until 1904. This first shipment was the beginning of millions shipped all over the world. They were so enthusiastically accepted by the American public that all were sold in just one year. Some people had to wait as long as two years to receive shipment of their new semiauto — so much for Winchester thinking the public would not accept a semi-automatic shotgun.

This shipment was completed in 1905. According to F.N., a total of 60,717 Auto-5's were sold by Browning from 1903 until July, 1913. According to Val Browning, son of John M., the total was 13,000. There is a big discrepancy here, and no one can get the exact figures. Whatever the truth, this is the best anyone has been able to come up with at this point and probably in the future. I have based my serial numbers on Mr. Browning's recollections, for they are the ones accepted by the Browning Arms Collectors Association and many collectors.

The following 18 pages are from the May, 1929 catalog produced by Fabrique Nationale in Leige for the Browning Arms Company to distribute in this country. At the time, this was the only gun being sold by B.A.C. and you can see the extent to which this fine shotgun was being promoted. The catalog is being reprinted here because it is extremely rare and will give Browning collectors some insight into pre-war sales.

INTRODUCTION

« A machine is called automatic when its working is due to the action of inanimate agents, the human intervention being brought down to a minimum : to start or stop the machine, to supervise it in order to avoid any accidental stoppage. » (Captain Cordier : « Les armes automatiques ».)

By applying this definition to arms, it appears that, to reduce the work of the shooter, it is necessary to do away with the operations of loading, extraction, ejection and pulling of the trigger.

An arm is to be called automatic when it gives a continuous fire as long as the shooter keeps his finger on the trigger, such as the machine guns.

An arm will be called semi-automatic or firing after the shot-by-shot system when it is necessary to pull the trigger as often as it is desired to fire : this is the case with automatic pistols.

The famous inventor John Browning has imagined to apply these principles to the sporting arms. He has created a gun after the shot-by-shot system, with bolted breech and long recoil of the barrel, the part of the shooter being limited to the following movements : to provide the magazine with cartridges, to load by cocking ; the firing causes the opening of the breech, the extraction and ejection of the cartridge ; the recoil of the breech results in the tension of a return spring, the release of which causes the return of the breech forward, the introduction of the following cartridge and the closing of the mechanism. It is easy to realize the advantages resulting from such a system by the suppression of all useless movements : great rapidity of shooting, considerable diminution of fatigue, easiness of keeping a steady aim, increased accuracy. These advantages are no longer denied by anybody. The diminution of the recoil makes shooting less enervating, less fatiguing, and this important result is obtained with the Browning shotgun. Indeed, the reaction due to the pressure of the powder gases is absorbed for the greatest part by the springs of the mechanism to perform the movements of ejection and loading. The shock given to the shoulder is consequently very weak and this makes the gun certainly very attractive.

Every shooter wishes, first of all, to possess a gun with accurate and far-reaching shooting, a gun with an ideal line of sight. These advantages are peculiar to the *single barrel*. The Browning shotgun, owing to its single barrel, enables, indeed, to take one's aim direct without it being necessary to rectify the firing, as is the case with a gun with barrels fitted side by

side, the axes of which cannot be parallel. In addition to this, it enables the shooter to find the game clearly and quickly and, for this reason, it is a favourite with the hunters. Another advantage of the single barrel is the excellence of shooting due to a better transmission to the barrel of the vibratory movements when the cartridge explodes. On the other hand, the barrel of the Browning shotgun is made of very resistant steel, which insures a long life to the barrel as well as a first-class shooting.

A five-shot gun meets the requirements of a great portion of the clientele and becomes a necessity in certain kinds of shooting, more particularly as regards ducks and migratory birds. Little by little the Browning shotgun has won the favour of the sportsmen, and, since the last years, its vogue is extra-ordinary in many countries of the world.

The successes obtained with the Browning gun are at present innumerable :

Pigeon Shooting :
Grand Prix of Monte Carlo 1921 ;   Grand Prix of Spa 1923.

Clay Birl Shooting :
World Series Record at the Paris   Championship of Belgium 1927 ;
Olympiads 1924 ;   World's Championship of 1928 in
Gold Medal of the   All Japan   Paris.
Competition in 1924 ;

In the United States, Mr. G. L. Becker has won the famous « Globe Trophy » for the third time with his Browning gun, which has already fired more than 60.000 cartridges and has never been false to him during any match.

These shooting matches show the surprising qualities of this arm, of which more than 200.000 have been supplied by the F. N. Works at Herstal.

J. M. BROWNING.

— 6 —

— 7 —

DESCRIPTION
of the Browning Automatic Gun

The Browning automatic gun has a very simple mechanism and presents numerous advantages over the sporting guns generally used. Indeed, it places 5 cartridges at the shooter's disposal and besides it has but one barrel and one trigger.

It is needless to dwell any further on the advantage of the five cartridges; we would only say, in order to answer certain objections, that, when the hunter wishes to use another grade of shot, he can, by a very simple movement, stop the mechanism from going out of the magazine and insert in the mechanism the shot which he desires; the operation is neither longer nor more complicated than with a hammerless shotgun.

The single barrel can be made mechanically perfect, so that it is possible to obtain a perfectly straight boring and the whole variety of bores with a view to get patterns which it would be practically impossible to obtain with other barrels. In this respect, it is well known that the Browning gun, owing to the careful manufacture of its barrel, has an effective range which is absolutely superior. The thickness of the walls, especially at the chamber, constitutes a first-class security against accidents due to bursts of barrels which are too light or imperfectly centred. In addition to this, aiming with the single barrel is much more rapid and correct.

It is also to be remembered that with the Browning gun the barrel can be changed instantly, since all our barrels are interchangeable. Consequently, the sportsman can possess with one mechanism the whole series of guns he may want according to the effects he desires.

The one trigger system also presents numerous advantages. It will suffice to remember how many laborious researches were necessitated for the realization of this trigger in sporting guns of all kinds, which practical realization has not always answered expectation. In the Browning gun, the single trigger is quite naturally realized and presents a security of working which is absolutely irreproachable.

The various parts of the Browning automatic gun are most carefully made. The materials used are controlled with the same care as those intended for the manufacture of military arms. The machinery, constantly kept up to date, enables to make parts of a finish above reproach and of practically perfect interchangeability. The heat treatment of the parts is executed and controlled by means of the most modern and improved apparatus.

The F. N. manufactures automatic guns in cal. 12 and 16. The usual lengths of the barrels are 26, 28 and 30 inches; however, any other length can be had on application. All possible borings can be realized, including the rifled choke bore barrel for firing with bullets. The standard types are the cylinder barrel, the half choke barrel (0,3 to 0,4 mm), and the full choke barrel (0,8 to 1,0 mm).

Each gun is subjected to the various tests for strength which, according to the Belgian laws, are made in the Government Proof House of Liege, and besides it is submitted at the F. N. to severe tests for pattern and correct working with cartridges taken at random among the various kinds of ammunition found on the market, this in order to insure the proper working of the arm with any usual cartridge whatever.

The stock is of good quality walnut wood; the standard types embrace the usual lengths in three styles: straight stock, pistol stock and pistol stock with cheek piece. Any other style can be had by the clientele on special application.

The exterior finish of the arm is carefully attended to and is submitted to a rigorous inspection which has made the reputation of the F. N. owing to the quality of its products.

Several types de luxe are realized in ordinary engraving, English engraving, shooting scene engraving and inlay. These engravings give the gun a really peculiar stamp, owing to which it can be classed among the arms of value of the finest collections.

At the request of numerous customers, a type for pigeon shooting has been created, which has made it possible for the automatic gun to win a special reputation among clay bird and live pigeon shooters.

Mr. Marcel Lafite, the winner in 1921 of the famous Grand Prix of Monte-Carlo. — Mr. Lafite was a member of the French Olympic Team in 1924. — He gained the Grand Prix of Blankenberghe in 1924 and numerous other distinctions in pigeon shooting competitions.

Some of the medals won with the Browning shotgun by Mr. Takahashi, the best clay bird shooter in Japan.

— 10 —

Mr. Louis d'Heur, of Herstal, got the first place of the Belgian team at the Paris Olympic Games in 1924 and established the WORLD SERIES RECORD by breaking 103 clay birds uninterruptedly. He won the Championship of Belgium in 1927 and the WORLD CHAMPIONSHIP in 1928 for Clay Bird Shooting.

— 9 —

Mr. Gus. L. Becker, of Ogden, Utah, U. S. A., won :
The Globe Trophy at Hayden Lake (Idaho).
The Handicap Championship for the United States in
1921 ; his score reached 95 % on 700 targets shot from
22 yards.
The Utah State Championship in 1918.
The Utah State Handicap Championship in 1918.
The Montana State Handicap Championship in 1918.
The Olympic Club double championship
at San Francisco.

— 12 —

Mr. Indoni, the youngest member of a shooting club of
Rome, uses a Browning shotgun.

— 11 —

Result of a wild-duck shooting on the Corean Coast,
obtained by Messrs. Macda, J. Horita and I. Kimura.

The famous « Globe Trophy », in gold and diamond, won
for the third time by Mr. G. L. Becker.
This trophy is the historical emblem of the Sportsmen's Association of
the Northwest, which was contested for 25 years in the United States.

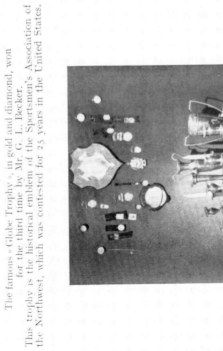

Some two score of trophies, representing winnings all over the U. S. A.,
from Travers Island, New York, to San Francisco.

Mr. Robert Leemans, the winner in 1928 of the
BROWNING CHALLENGE CUP.
The shooting speed record is held by Mr. Marcel Lafite with 80 clay
birds out of 100 in 147 seconds (2nd June 1926).
Tir National, Brussels.

— 16 —

The Browning shotgun is used everywhere.
Photo communicated by Messrs. Schroeder Frères, Liège.

— 15 —

TO OPERATE
the Browning Shotgun

1. To open the action.

Place the gun in the left hand, and, with the right hand, pull back the operating slide completely. (Fig. 1.)

Fig. 1.

2. To load the gun.

The loading is effected by introducing one cartridge into the barrel and four into the magazine. — The first cartridge is dropped into the opening produced by the opening operation of the action (Fig. 2). Then, with the middle finger of the *left hand*, press on the button which is located on the right side of the

Fig. 2.

— 17 —

receiver (Fig. 3). The breech bolt, being free, goes forward again and pushes the cartridge into the barrel chamber. — The gun is thus ready for firing one shot. — To fill the magazine, turn the gun upside down in the left hand, so that the lower face comes above, press the button with the left thumb and drop the four cartridges with the right hand into the magazine, pressing down the carrier (Fig. 4).

The magazine can also be completed in the same manner when partly empty.

It is advisable to load the gun with safety set.

Fig. 3.

3. To put at safe.

The gun is put at safe by pushing rearward the sliding part which projects on the front face of the trigger plate. The safety

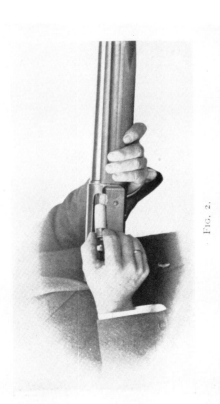

Fig. 4.

— 18 —

Fig. 5

is allowed to be moved backward by pressing up the safety stop with the fore finger, in order to disengage same, then by pulling the safety rearward.

To set at « Fire », it suffices to push the safety forward from the inside of the trigger plate and it is not necessary to act upon the safety stop. Fig. 5 shows the action in the firing position.

Fig. 6 shows action put at safe.

Fig. 6.

4. To fire.

Fig. 7 shows incorrect position.
Fig. 8 shows correct position.

5. To use the magazine stop.

When it is desired to hold back the cartridges in the magazine and use the gun as a single loader, it suffices to draw backward, with the thumb and the forefinger, the magazine stop lever located on the left of the forward end of the receiver.

In the position shown in Fig. 9 the magazine stop allows the cartridges to be thrown from the magazine after each shot.

Fig. 7.

Fig. 8.

In the position of the Fig. 10, the magazine stop prevents cartridges from leaving the magazine.

Owing to the magazine stop, the shooter can change the cartridge and drop into the barrel a different cartridge from those which are in the magazine.

Fig. 9.

Important Remark: It is impossible to introduce cartridges into the magazine so long as this is locked by the magazine stop (Fig. 10). To introduce cartridges it is necessary to place the magazine stop in the position shown in Fig. 9. — If, inadvertently, it was tried to insert a cartridge into the magazine when locked, it would then be necessary to take down the stop in order to draw out the cartridge.

6. To unload the gun.

To remove the cartridge which is in the barrel, whilst there are still other cartridges in the magazine, operate the magazine stop (Fig. 10) and draw the breech bolt backward as for the opening of the action. The cartridge which was in the barrel will be ejected.

and, with the fore-finger of the right hand, keep the carrier as far as it will go inwards (see Fig. 11). At this moment, discontinue acting upon the button and, with the left hand, draw the breech bolt backward, the first cartridge in the magazine will then go out. (See Fig. 12.) Repeat this operation as many¹ times as there are cartridges in the magazine.

The gun can also be unloaded by leaving the stop in the position shown in Fig. 9 and drawing the breech bolt backward with the right hand. In this manner, the cartridge which is in the barrel will be ejected, and the following cartridge in the magazine will be brought in the barrel. — Repeat this operation until the action is empty. — When operating in this manner, it is to be recommended to put the gun at safe in order to give every guarantee of security to the shooter.

Fig. 11.

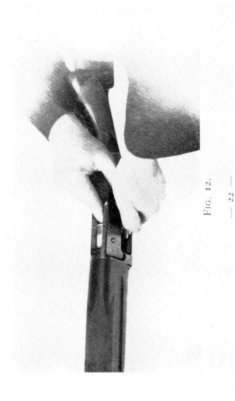

Fig. 10.

7. To empty the magazine.

The cartridge being taken out of the barrel, let the breech bolt spring forward by pressing the button (Fig. 3), and disengage the magazine stop by placing it in the position shown in Fig. 9. Then turn the gun over, as described for the loading of magazine, press the button with the thumb of the left hand

Fig. 12.

2. To dismount action. (*See schema of the working.*)

First remove magazine cap, barrel and front stock, as shown above, then remove the stock by loosening tang-screw ; a slight blow on the rear will allow the easy disengagement of the stock by hand.

Unscrew trigger plate screws and check-screws (Nos. 55 and 56) and withdraw complete trigger guard downward.

By means of a screw-driver, take carrier spring out of the follower on which it is pivoted. Loosen check screws and screws of carrier No. 39 and remove same.

This dismounting allows to clean the arm thoroughly and is sufficient for usual cases. However, should it be desired to take down the action completely, then proceed as follows :

Drive out pin holding wood plug at the end of the tube which extends the receiver at rear, and take care to hold this plug to prevent it from snapping away. Then let action spring slide out softly and remove it from its housing. Let the breech bolt slide until locking block latch pin is in front of the holes in receiver. Drive out pin from right to left. Remove locking block latch with spring, and swing the link so as to release operating slide which can be removed rearward. The breech bolt complete will go out easily through the front part of receiver. Remove firing pin stop pin from left to right, withdraw firing pin and push out the locking block upward. No explanation is necessary for dismounting the other parts remaining on the receiver.

3. To put action together.

Assemble breech bolt. Put operating slide through ejection opening of receiver and draw it back home into the slot which prolongs this opening. Introduce breech bolt into receiver. Push operating slide into breech bolt, swinging the link. Place locking block latch with spring and pin. Fit action spring in its tube, leaning it on link, and fix it by means of the pin which holds the wood plug in receiver tube ; fit carrier with spring. Place trigger plate, assemble stock and barrel.

TO DISMOUNT
the Browning Automatic Gun

1. To remove barrel and front stock.

To dismount the barrel in order to clean it, take hold of barrel with the left hand (Fig. 13), lean stock on the leg and press barrel downward to overcome the pressure of recoil spring. With the right hand, unscrew magazine cap. Barrel and front stock can then be easily removed. (See Fig. 14.)

To assemble, proceed in a reverse manner However, make sure that shoulder of front stock

Fig. 14.

Fig. 13.

fits properly in the corresponding recess in receiver and that no play exists between receiver and front stock after the magazine cap has been screwed up.

If, the barrel being removed, the breech bolt has been completely drawn backward, be careful not to let it snap forward in its closing position before the barrel is assembled, otherwise the operating slide would force back the front part of the receiver, which might be injurious to the proper working of the gun.

THE WORKING
of the Browning Automatic Gun

Before passing on to the detailed description of the working of the gun, some complementary explanations are necessary.

The receiver 1 contains the mechanism and protects it from any deterioration. On the right side is the opening for the loading and ejection of the cartridges.

The barrel 64 fixed to the barrel extension 68 leans by its guide through the friction ring against the recoil spring 69. The barrel extension bears the ejector 69.

The magazine 5 contains the magazine spring 7 which by means of its follower tends to push the cartridges towards the outlet of the magazine.

The locking mechanism is composed of the breech bolt 9, the operating slide 20, the locking block 10, the link 11, the firing pin 13, two extractors 15 and 18 and the locking block latch 21. The locking block, under the action of the link, can perform an oscillating movement resulting from a device consisting of a circular projection on the block and a corresponding groove in the bolt. The locking block link acts under the pressure of the action spring 24.

The trigger mechanism is composed of the trigger plate 41, the trigger 43, the hammer 46, the main spring 50, the safety 42a with its stop and the safety sear 52 with its spring. The hammer bears a roll which facilitates the sliding on the spring. The hooking forms of the hammer for the trigger are of such a kind that the hammer cannot escape, whatever the position of the trigger may be at the moment of the cocking. If the hammer escaped, the shotgun would work as a machine gun. The purpose of the safety sear is to prevent the trigger from working before the mechanism is completely closed.

Working. (See schematic plates.)

Fig. I shows the gun at the moment when the hammer 46 strikes the firing pin 13.

Barrel and breecht bolt are fixed together by the locking block 10, the head of which enters a slot of the barrel extension 68.

Under the pressure of the gases, the breech bolt recoils and draws the barrel with it. As long as the recoil takes place, the mechanism remains completely closed. The movable mechanism, when recoiling, cocks the hammer and hooks it to the trigger, at the same time compressing the recoil spring 61 and the action spring 24.

Under the action of these two springs, the whole mechanism

has a tendency to come forward again. After a motion of a few millimetres, the carrier driver 35 hooks the operating slide 20; the latter holds back the link 11 which, acting upon the locking block, swings it in its circular groove, sets the barrel extension free and holds back the breech bolt. The bolt is thus held in place, maintaining the fired shell by means of the extractors. The barrel and barrel extension, under the action of the spring 64, continue their return forward, as they are no longer held back by the locking block. At the moment when the ejector comes into contact with the rim of the cartridge, it pushes the cartridge towards the right to free it from the left-hand extractor, then throws it out through the ejection opening by swinging it around the right-hand extractor. The barrel and barrel extension resume their first position.

During all these movements, the carrier 34 is held down by the carrier latch 32.

As long as the gun is closed, the first of the cartridges in the magazine projects a little from its opening and leans on the front part of the locking block latch 21. When the movable mechanism recoils, the cartridge comes out further up to the cartridge stop 28. At the moment when the barrel comes again in its place and ejects the empty shell, it unlatches the cartridge stop, and the cartridge in the magazine, being pushed by the magazine spring 7, slides on the carrier 34. On passing on the carrier, the rim of the cartridge presses back the latch 32 and releases the carrier, which, under the pressure of its spring, swings upward and brings the new cartridge in front of the breech bolt. Owing to the swinging movement of the carrier, the carrier driver 35 gets down, the operating slide 20 and the breech bolt with its corresponding parts become free and, pushed by the action spring by means of the link, go forward, introducing the new cartridge into the barrel, and close the mechanism by assembling the barrel extension rigidly to the breech bolt.

During the return movement of the breech bolt, the locking block is kept down by the locking block latch. When the breech bolt comes again into touch with the barrel, the front end of the link 11 presses on the latch 21 and releases the locking block which, swinging in its groove, enters the slot in the barrel extension.

The last shell being ejected, the mechanism remains open, since no further cartridge releases the carrier by swinging the latch 32; the carrier remains downward, holding back the breech bolt as described above. To close the action, it suffices to press upon the button on the right side of the receiver.

CARE
of the Browning Automatic Shotgun

As required with any other fire arms, the barrel of the Browning shotgun should be well cleaned and oiled after use, in order to avoid rust and corrosion.

The action of the Browning shotgun requires but very little attention and it is seldom necessary to dismount it for cleaning, all parts liable to get spoiled being easily accessible with a rag or a brush.

Very little oil is needed, but this must be good gun oil. — Slightly oil the rubbing surfaces and avoid any excess of oil in the action, where residues of unburnt powder sometimes penetrate, which might be injurious to the proper working.

The recoil spring and the outside of the magazine tube are to be oiled properly in order to assist the recoil of the barrel. This recoil can be controlled by using more or less oil. If the recoil is too heavy, put less oil and, if necessary, use the regulating ring. If the recoil is too weak (defective ejection), remove the regulating ring and oil the recoil spring more liberally.

Manufacture of parts for arms.

Use of Regulating Ring

(See explanatory plate.)

It has been shown above that, when the recoil takes place, the barrel guide leans by means of a friction ring on the recoil spring.

The friction ring consists of a first split bronze ring enclosed in a second split ring which acts as a spring and brings the friction ring against the magazine. This friction ring is intended to control the movements when the recoil or return takes place, so as to avoid too sharp thrusts.

The two extreme sides of the friction ring are made conical. — The inside of the barrel guide is also conical, so that, when the barrel leans on the friction ring, it tends to close same and thus increases the braking power of the ring proportionally to the violence of the recoil.

In order to further increase the friction of the ring, a regulating ring is used to that effect. This ring is made of steel, flat on one of its faces and bevelled on the other.

If, on the side which is opposite to that of the barrel guide, we place against the friction ring the bevelled part of the regulating ring (see Fig. 1), when the recoil takes place, the friction ring will be pressed between two cones which are both tending to close it. Consequently, this device will further increase the friction. The same effect will take place as the barrel moves forward under the pressure of the spring.

The regulating ring is used with high pressure cartridges. The proper working of the gun depends upon the judicious use of this ring. Same is not to be used with standard loads. In this case, it should be placed between the recoil spring and the receiver, the cone being against the receiver (see Fig. 2). In that position, the regulating ring serves only as a washer.

To give an instance of the ballistic results of the automatic gun, we beg to reproduce below report of the Test Office annexed to the Firearms Proof House of Liege concerning tests made with a 12 ga. gun and a 16 ga. gun.

ROYAUME DE BELGIQUE
ANNEXE AU
BUREAU D'ESSAIS
Banc d'Épreuves des Armes à Feu
A LIÈGE

ESSAIS DE TIR

effectués le 25 mai 1928
à la demande de la *Fabrique Nationale*
d'Armes de Guerre à Herstal.

Marques et N°   60069
Calibre 16   Longueur des chambres   65 millimètres
Système automatique *Browning*

FUSIL
à 2 coups

Longueur du canon   70 centimètres

REFORAGE   Tube : à la bouche   — 15,9 —
           entre 15 et 30 cm de la tranche de culasse 16,9 —

Douille — Calibre 16   Longueur   65 millimètres
Type : *Liège*   Amorçage *central*
POUDRE   Poids   1,90 gramme
1 disque en liège de 3 millimètres
1 bourre feutre gras graissée n° 60 de 12 m.
1 disque en liège de 3 millimètres

BOURRAGE

PLOMBS n° 6   Poids total   28 grammes
Grms : Diamètre moyen   2,60 — Nombre 266
Fermeture   1 disque en liège de 3 millimètres.

Mesure du groupement à 35 mètres (trente-cinq).
Point visé : *Centre*.

Nombre d'atteintes dans		Canon gauche		Canon droit	
Cercle de		35 cm	75 cm	35 cm	75 cm
TIR N°	1	55	209		
	2	34	180		
	3	50	207		
	4	45	194		
	5	41	206		
MOYENNES		45	199		
• dans cercle de 75 c/m			74,8 %		

LIÈGE, le 26 mai 1928.
Le Directeur du Banc d'Épreuve,
Commissaire de Gouvernement chargé de la haute surveillance des Armes dans le Royaume.

Les feuilles de tir ne sont annexées au présent procès-verbal.

— 30 —

AMMUNITION
for the Browning Automatic Gun

The Browning gun does not require any special cartridge and its construction allows a great variation in this respect; a good cartridge must work the gun irreproachably. It is, however, in the interest of the shooter to employ cartridges regularly loaded. In this respect, we recommend the use of cartridges placed on the market by powder factories, because the charges, which are regularly weighed, are more uniform, or cartridges loaded by careful gunsmiths.

The 12 gauge barrels are all with 70 mm chamber: they take the 2 1/2" cartridge and the 2 3/4" cartridge equally well. The total length of the loaded and crimped cartridge must neither be inferior to 57 mm nor exceed 65 mm to insure proper working of the gun.

The 16 gauge barrels are all with 65 mm chamber. The length of the cartridge must be at least 57 mm and at the utmost 60 mm. These are usual sizes.

CARTRIDGES

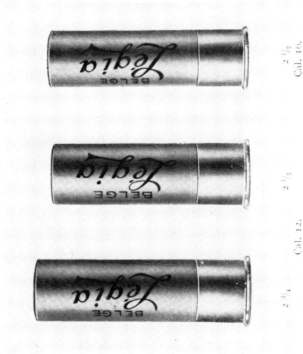

2 3/4"   2 1/2"   2 1/2"
Cal. 12.   Cal. 16.

— 29 —

COMPONENT PARTS
of the Browning Automatic Gun

Nos

1. Receiver
2. Action spring tube.
3. Pin for carrier spring (front).
4. Pin for carrier spring (rear).
5. Magazine tube.
6. Magazine spring follower.
7. Magazine spring.
8. Magazine spring retainer.
9. Breech bolt.
10. Locking block.
11. Locking block link.
12. Pin for 11.
13. Firing pin.
14. Firing pin stop pin.
15. Left hand extractor.
16. Spring for 15.
17. Extractor pins.
18. Right hand extractor.
19. Spring for 18.
20. Operating slide.
21. Locking block latch.
22. Spring for 21.
23. Pin for 21.
24. Action spring.
25. Action spring follower.
26. Action spring plug.
27. Pin for 26.
28. Cartridge stop.
29. Cartridge stop spring.
30. Screws for nº 28 and 32.
31. Carrier latch button.
32. Carrier latch spring.
33. Carrier latch.
34. Carrier driver.
35. Carrier.
36. Spring for 35.
37. Follower for 30.
38. Pin for 35.
39. Carrier screw.
40. Carrier spring.
41. Trigger plate.
42a. Safety.
42b. Safety stop.
42c. Safety stop spring.
42d. Safety stop pin.

Nos

42e. Safety stop spring follower.
43. Trigger.
44. Trigger pin.
45. Trigger spring.
46. Hammer.
47. Hammer roll.
48. Hammer roll pin.
49. Hammer pin.
50. Main spring.
51. Main spring screw.
52. Safety sear.
53. Safety sear spring.
53a. Safety sear spring follower.
54. Safety sear pin.
55. Trigger plate screw (front).
56. Trigger plate screw (rear).
57. Stock.
57b. Pistol grip stock.
58. Butt plate.
59. Butt plate screws.
60. Tang screw.
60p. Tang screw for pistol grip stock.
61. Recoil spring.
61a. Regulating ring.
62. Friction ring.
63. Friction ring spring.
64. Barrel.
66/67. Sight with base.
68. Barrel extension.
69. Ejector.
70. Rivet for 69.
71. Front stock.
71a. Screwed bush for 71b.
71b. Magazine cap stop pin.
71c. Spring for 71b.
72. Magazine cap.
73/5. Sling swivel (upper).
74/5. Sling swivel (under).
76. Stop washer.
77. Rivet for swivels.
78. Magazine stop.
79. Magazine stop spring.
80. Magazine stop spring screw.
82. Check screw.

— 32 —

The barrel of the 12 ga. gun is a 28" barrel with 0,9 mm choke.
The barrel of the 16 ga. gun is a 28" barrel with 1,0 mm choke.

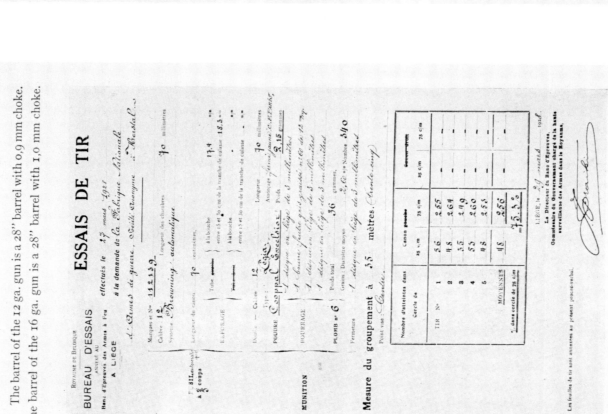

— 31 —

Plate relating to the use of the regulating ring

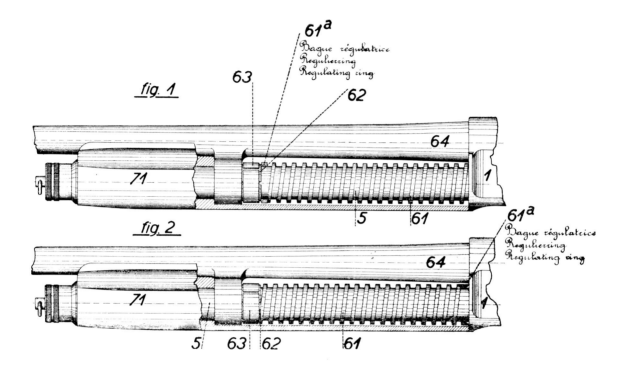

Table of the component parts of the Browning shotgun

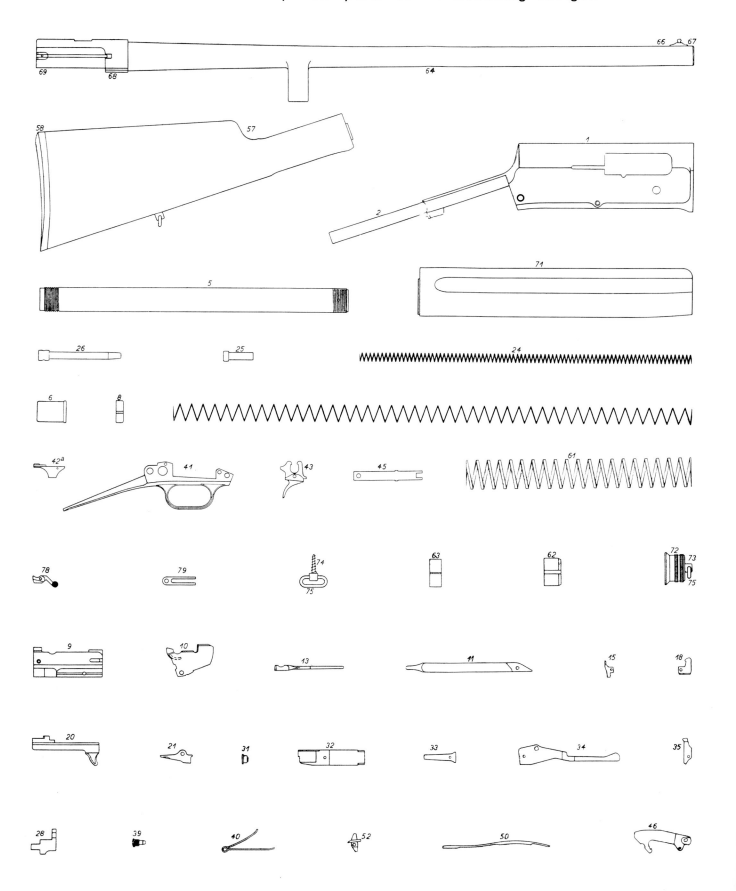

Fig. I.

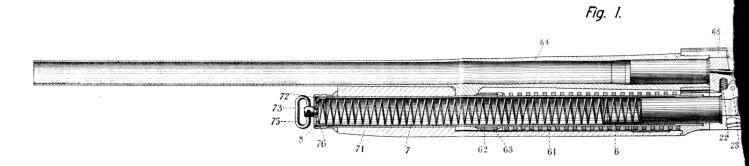

Fig. II.

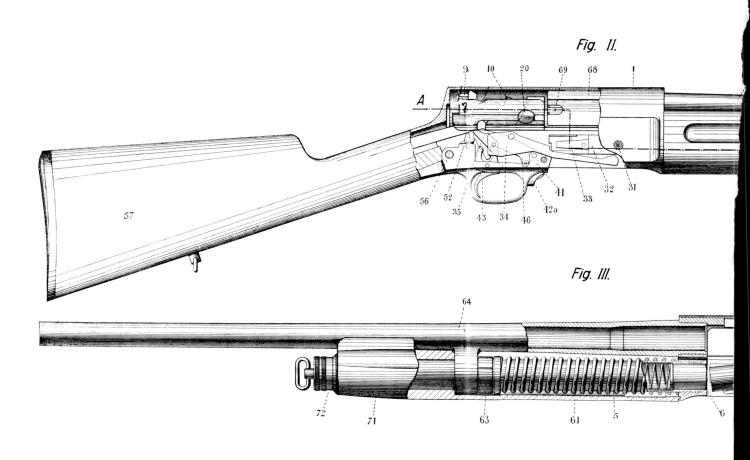

Fig. III.

Section A B seen from under

Magazine open	Magazine closed

Fig. IV.

Fig. V.

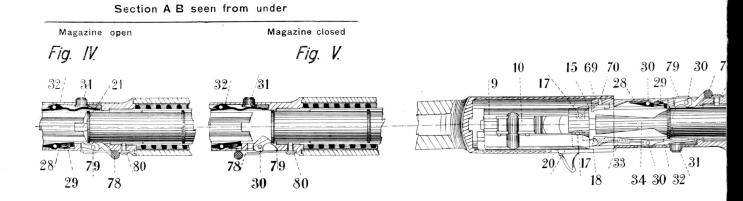

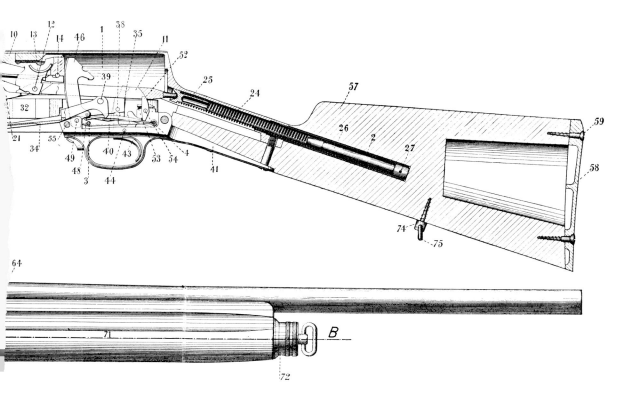

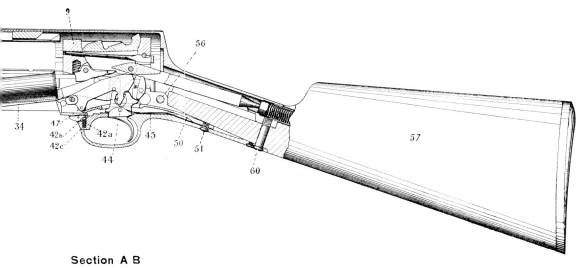

Section A B

Fig. VI.

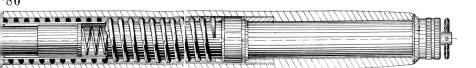

VARIATIONS

The Brownings distributed a pamphlet in 1903 which was printed to announce this new and innovative shotgun, I have used this in part to describe the new gun.

You essentially had four choices: the "Regular," the "Trap," the "Two Shot," and the "Messenger". The Regular model, otherwise known as the No. 1, was described as follows in the 1903 pamphlet:

"12 Gauge, Takedown, 28 inch Cockerill Steel Barrel, English Walnut Stock, Matted Receiver, Rubber Butt, 5 shots, Weight about 7 3/4 pounds."

The Trap model or the No. 2 was described as follows:

"12 Gauge, Takedown, 28 inch Cockerill Steel Barrel, Selected English Walnut Stock, Checkered Grip and Fore-End, Matted Receiver, Rubber Butt, 5 shots, Weight about 7 3/4 pounds."

The Messenger model or the No. 0 was described as follows:

"12 Gauge, Takedown, 20 inch Cockerill Steel Barrel, Cylinder Bore, English Walnut Stock, Matted Receiver, 5 shots, Weight about 7 1/2 pounds."

So when you consider all the options, there was actually six variations. They were the 5 shot Standard and Trap with 28" barrels, the Messenger with a 20" cylinder bore barrel, the Messenger with deluxe checkered wood with 20" barrels, and the two shot Standard or Trap with 28" barrels, which we will discuss below.

I don't imagine the Messenger was ordered very often with checkering, for it was advertised as follows:

"For express messengers and guards, for bank or home protection, street disturbances, etc., no small arm is so effective as this gun loaded with buckshot." How's that for bluntness!

As noted above, the Two Shot Browning Automatic was also introduced. It seems silly today to offer a two shot auto, but not at that time. Obviously, Browning was catering to the Double barrel shooters and to folks who were conservationists. The best way for you to see this is to let you read the description of the new gun for yourself:

"The Browning Automatic Shotgun is also made in all grades to take only two cartridges, one in the barrel and one in the magazine; the appearance and the price being the same as in the regular five-shot guns.

"This arm has all the improvements found in the most modern double guns-single trigger, automatic ejector, hammerless, and, in addition, has the great advantage of reduced recoil. It is also single barrel, requires no hand protector as the hand need never come in contact with the hot barrel, when one shot has been fired it is always ready for the second shot even when the shooter is in the act of loading.

"It's many points of superiority make it the most efficient and desirable two-shot gun. The price is but little more than is charged for fitting a double gun with a single trigger."

What does the above sound like to you? Do you notice how many references are made to the advantages the Browning were trying to point out over a double barrel: the single trigger, one sighting plane, cost versus a double, no burnt hands, auto ejector, hammerless and less recoil? When you think about this, it is quite obvious they were trying to expand their market and maybe they were not 100% sure of the acceptance of this new "Automatic" by the public.

In 1905 the options available were many when you consider this was an initial order and everybody was in a hurry to start shipping. This is how they were described and priced in the pamphlet.

EXTRAS

Checkered grip and fore-end, extra . . . . $ 4.50
Selected English walnut, extra 9.00
Selected English walnut, checkered grip and fore-end, extra 13.50
Plain English walnut pistol grip, checkered grip and fore-end, to order, extra 9.00
Making stock different drop or length, to order, extra 9.00
Full length cover, heavy canvas, sling and handle combined, breech and muzzle, reinforced with leather, leather bound 1.25
Full length cover, soft boarded russet leather, sling and handle combined 2.25
Stiff mutton leg case, heavy brown canvas, brass trimmings, leather reinforcements, sling strap and handle, special shape for Browning Automatic Take-down Shotgun 2.50
Stiff Mutton Leg case, orange leather with rod compartments inside hasp lock, sling, name plate, brass trimmings, special shape for Browning Take-Down Shotgun 4.50

None of the accessories you see listed were from Belgium. I would venture to say they were all stock items from the Browning Brothers inventory, and they were pushing these for additional sales. The additional features on the guns were from Belgium.

FRAME AND BARREL MARKINGS

These markings will continue until the formation of The Browning Arms Company in 1927.

Frame markings are as follows:

On the left side on the top of the frame:
FABRIQUE NATIONALE D'ARMES DE GUERRE
HERSTAL BELGIQUE
BROWNING'S PATENT DEPOSE
Later guns will also have:
FABRIQUE NATIONALE SA D'ARMES
DE GUERRE HERSTAL BELGIQUE
BROWNING'S PATENT DEPOSE

On the right side of the frame just below the ejection port, you will find some of the same proofs and inspector's marks as are noted for the barrels, especially the number 4 *(See page 50)*.

You will find proof marks on the left side of the barrel directly in front of the receiver, on the breech bolt, and on the barrel extension as shown on page 50.

Some, but not all, of the inspector's marks you may find are the letters M,A,W,Y,Z,D,L; there are others. These inspector's marks will have a star above them. You will also find various numbers. These numbers appear at random and verify that an inspection was performed.

From 1903 through the first 10,000 guns you will find markings as follows:

On the top of the barrel:

BROWNING AUTOMATIC ARMS CO.,
OGDEN, UTAH U.S.A.
(Choke)(Gauge)GA SPECIAL STEEL

Please note that the choke marking is spelled out and no code was used at this time.

On the right side of barrel:

MADE IN BELGIUM
BROWNING PATENT

On the left side of the trigger guard assembly are the words:

PATENTED SEPT 30 1902
JUNE 16 1903

On the right side of the trigger guard assembly you will find:

PATENTED OCT.9 1900
DEC.17 1901

The early guns were serial numbered on the barrel ring, the frame, and the forearm, as well as the last four digits on minor parts. Barrels were fitted and made only for one specific gun, so it was necessary to keep these parts together.

CHOKE DESIGNATIONS

From 1903 to 1926 Full, Modified, Improved cylinder, etc. was ahead of the legend "Special Steel".

STOCKS

A good beginning for the description of the stocks can be taken out of the pamphlet. The following appears under standard dimensions:

"We have adopted a standard of dimensions for the Browning Automatic Shotgun which experience and modern practice have demonstrated to be best suited for shooters and shooting generally.

"It is made in 12 gauge only, with 28 inch barrels, full choke, modified choke, or cylinder bore, and is chambered for any length cartridge up to 2 3/4 inches. Unless otherwise specified, full choke will be

sent. The weight is about 7 3/4 lbs. The stock has a drop of 2 1/2 inches at the heel and 1 3/4 inches at the comb, and is furnished in two lengths 14 and 14 1/2 inches. Unless otherwise specified the longer one will be sent.

"As a straight grip is evidently the favorite for the best guns, we have adopted that style. The front stock is so formed that it gives the best possible grip whether the shooter's arm is fully or partially extended, and is arranged for protecting the hand from the barrel. The stocks are all English walnut with fine durable oil finish, only an occasional rubbing with an oily cloth being required to keep them looking as well as new."

The English style straight grip stock was standard but the half pistol grip or round knob was available and shipped only when specified. I have seen some of the first 10,000 with a round knob stock, but they are quite rare.

For the first 10,000 guns, the butt plates were either a hard rubber material or horn with 7/8" x 2" scroll oval with the F superimposed over the N in a horizontal pattern of lines which are 1/16" apart for a 2 3/8" area centered between a smooth top and bottom area. On the inside of these early butt plates you will find six concave holes. I have no idea about their purpose.

There were no additional grades nor was any engraving available on these first 10,000.

If you are a traditional Browning collector who only looks for the post war guns, don't walk through a gun show and pass up the pre-wars that are not mint. Even though you may not want to purchase it, looking at these early rare guns is interesting and educational.

You may do like me when a collector had more then he wanted and brought a mint pre-war to my gun shop. My partner showed it to me and I turned it down immediately. It looked like all the blue was gone and it had turned brown. I didn't want a gun with most of the blue gone. After I left, I started to think about the gun and decided to give it one more look, for the reputation of the owner didn't match my first impression of the gun. Upon looking at it again I noticed the markings were perfect, the checkering was perfect, the condition of the wood was perfect, the face of the breech bolt was shinney and showed no brass marks. Why should the blue be so dull and brownish colored? This didn't make sense, so I found a hidden place on the metal and went over it very lightly with gun oil and 0000 steel wool. VOILA! the brown I was looking at was dried oil that a very considerate previous owner had put on his gun to keep it from rusting. After removal of this residue, the blue was all there and I had a mint gun. What is the moral of this story? Don't get in a hurry at a show and miss opportunities to buy rare and very collectable Brownings, the condition may be better than you first thought.

OTHER MANUFACTURERS

Because of restrictive tariffs, F.N. allowed Browning to enter into an agreement with Remington to produce guns under their name in 1904 as the Remington Auto Loading Gun. Later, in 1911, the name was changed to the Remington Model 11 which had several refinements or changes. Remington didn't have any good designs to reliably handle the new smokeless powders, so an agreement was made for production based on royalties between Browning and Marcellues Hartley Dodge, the grandson of the former president of the company. It was initially made in 12 gauge only to handle all loads, but in 1931 it was changed so it could be made in 20 and 16 as well.

Savage also made this gun starting in 1907 as the model 1907 until 1930. Other manufacturers made the Auto-5 under various model numbers as well. We are not concerned here with them other than to let you know they were made. Do not confuse these with the Belgium manufactured guns that we are concerned with here.

The Wild Mule

▼

THERE is, in every loaded shotgun, a WILD MULE—*and he kicks!* The heavier the load, the harder he kicks, and there is no known way of preventing his kicking. But in the Browning Automatic we have put spring buffers on that mule's heels, and put him to work reloading the gun—thus absorbing the blow so effectually that you can shoot your Browning Automatic day after day without the slightest discomfort—and with a complete absence of the black-and-blue shoulder and arm that is so often associated with the shotgun. The device which accomplishes this end is quite properly called

THE SHOCK ABSORBER . . . and it does all that the name implies. It is composed of just three simple parts, and their adjustment for light or heavy loads to meet every form of shooting is as simple as lacing a shoe.

The modern automobile is built with shock absorbers . . . they give greater riding comfort, and by preventing strains and blows, prolong the life of the car and reduce repair bills. So does the shock absorber on the Browning Automatic; it adds to your shooting comfort—it prevents needless shock and wear to the mechanism—it saves working parts, prevents breakage, saves frequent trips to the repair shop.

In five minutes you can thoroughly familiarize yourself with the simple adjustment of the Browning Shock Absorber, and its intelligent use will repay you with a lifetime of good shooting service and comfort. Complete details of the shock absorber and the simple method of adjustment are given on page twenty-nine.

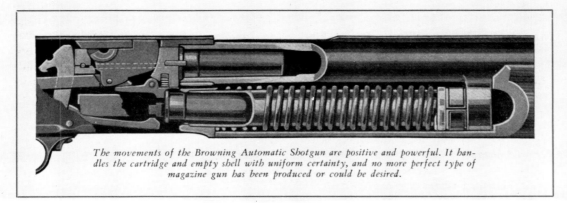

The movements of the Browning Automatic Shotgun are positive and powerful. It handles the cartridge and empty shell with uniform certainty, and no more perfect type of magazine gun has been produced or could be desired.

A segment from the 1931 Browning catalog.

AFTER THE FIRST 10,000

"The genuine Browning Automatic is a gun you will proudly show and gladly use. It's reliable action, light weight, perfect balance, plus the cushioned recoil will add additional pleasure and comfort to your hunting in the marsh or in the field."

This was taken from a 1931 ad on the A-5 that Browning placed in the sporting journals. It was the "Cadillac" of autos when this was published and pretty well stayed that way for almost half a century. There may have been dozens of others produced by other manufacturers but when you had a Browning, you had the gun you always wanted. A boy's dream became a man's reality when he could finally afford an A-5. From the beginning, the Browning Arms Company solicited your business on the basis of quality, engraving, hand checkering, and their personal commitment to satisfy you on any purchase.

The quote in the first paragraph also appeared in the first catalog ever published by the new Browning Arms Company, which was established on November 14, 1927. The address was 719 First Security Bank Building, Ogden, Utah. Previously, the company was known as the J.M. & M.S. Browning Company which was owned by John and Matt. Matt died in 1923 and was succeeded by his son, Marriner. Val and Marriner formed the corporation for the purpose of selling the Auto-5 and the new Superposed which was patented in that same year. Their goals were to sell only these two models under their company name.

Although the corporate headquarters were in Utah, the warehouse was located in St. Louis at 1132 Spruce St., and the company advertised this as their headquarters and corporate offices. All repairs were also done at this location.

This catalog advertised heavily that now you could purchase a Browning directly from Browning. It also consisted of a list of "Service Stations" in 44 states. Obviously, Val and Marriner were not only trying to establish repair centers but also a dealer network. This is what you read when opening the cover:

"In keeping with the trend of the times, we announce, on our hundredth anniversary, a new sales policy. We are doing this to materially reduce the cost of distribution and to lower the ultimate price to the consumer. As you will see by referring to our new prices, the Browning "16" and the Browning "12" are now quoted in No. 1 grade at $49.75. Formerly the Browning "16" was $65.50 and the Browning 12-gauge, $61.00. Similar reductions have been made on Grades 2, 3, and 4 and on extra barrels and cases.

"In announcing this policy we wish to emphasize that the Browning Automatic remains the same high-grade arm as before. Actually, there are several added refinements which have increased our cost of manufacture. There has been no cost-cutting in design nor in the selection of material, nor sacrifice of a single detail in the careful hand-fitting of parts which have characterized the Browning in the past.

"This new policy, we feel, is directly in line with the present trend to give the purchaser the greatest possible value for his money. The change was made after a most careful investigation among our owners and all trade channels. We found that the tremendous increase in the number of Browning owners year after year was largely due to the good word passed along by Browning users.

"It seemed to us, therefore, that our own interests would be best served and that the ultimate purchaser was actually entitled to buy direct from us at a saving of 20 to 25 percent.

"We hope that this new policy will meet with your approval and support. Again, we wish to emphasize that Browning service through a nation-wide chain of service stations will be maintained and that Browning guns are backed by an iron-clad guarantee for quality, workmanship and material."

I have quoted the above to bring out a couple of points and questions. Was Browning having a hard time during the depression in getting dealers to commit to inventorying their guns? Or was Browning trying to maximize sales by lowering prices during those hard times and at the same time cutting out the middle man? Probably, a combination of both.

Since the company was incorporated in 1927 and the catalog was not printed until 1930 and distributed until 1931, it is quite possible that they were taking this time to set up 258 service stations in 203 cities in 44 states. Also, it is probable that they were building a future network of gun shops and hardware stores to inventory and sell their products. Soon after this, in 1933, the "Browning Network" of exclusive dealers started in almost every town in America.

Whatever the case, it is interesting to know a little bit about the history of the company as well as the configuration of their products. A lot more is revealed in "The History Of Browning Guns from 1831," which I have reprinted with the permission of Mr. Val Browning, who has just had his 94th birthday.

The network was comprised of the best gun shops and hardware stores in each location. Browning closely controlled both prices and how their merchandise was displayed. You only got to be a dealer if you would sell at the retail prices they published and maintained the level of sales they thought proper. This was great for the dealer but not for the consumer who wanted a bargain. In effect, Browning obliterated the concept of competition. Of course, this didn't last forever with the mass merchandising concepts initiated in the 1970's.

GRADES

You will find each grade described with the information needed to identify it. The standard stock dimensions, configuration, barrels available, and options will be described under the appropriate section, for they were common to each grade and need not be repeated for each one.

In 1931 and earlier, the Auto-5 could be ordered in grades I, II, III, and IV, each grade having more ornate engraving and nicer wood and finish. In 1940, grades II, III, and IV were discontinued. These early high grade guns are indeed rare and desirable. The Special Grade was also changed to the Grade I and continued after the war until 1975.

GRADE I

The standard Grade I was the plain Jane. It had a plain non-matted barrel which could be purchased with various chokes as noted below. The receiver had no engraving. The stock was about group 1-2, round knob with a horn or hard rubber butt plate, and it was checkered about 20 line per inch. The price in 1931 was $49.75.

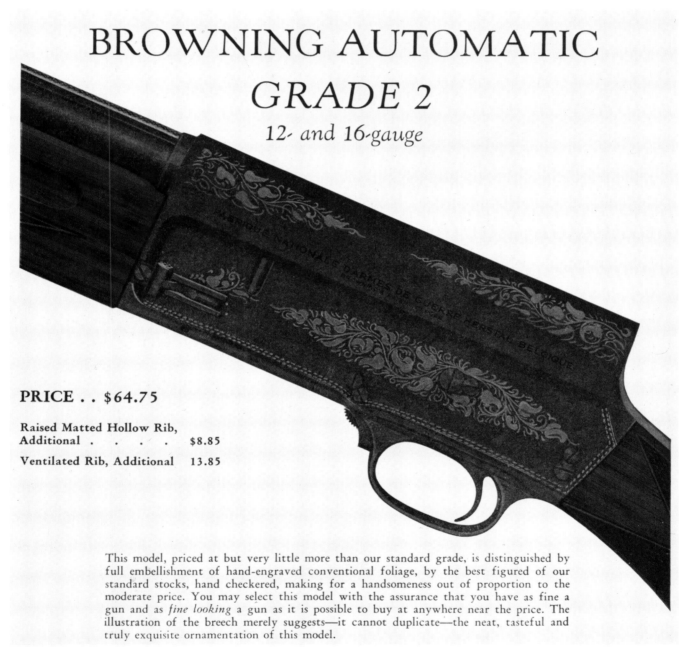

BROWNING AUTOMATIC

GRADE 2

12- and 16-gauge

PRICE . . $64.75

Raised Matted Hollow Rib,
Additional $8.85

Ventilated Rib, Additional   13.85

This model, priced at but very little more than our standard grade, is distinguished by full embellishment of hand-engraved conventional foliage, by the best figured of our standard stocks, hand checkered, making for a handsomeness out of proportion to the moderate price. You may select this model with the assurance that you have as fine a gun and as *fine looking* a gun as it is possible to buy at anywhere near the price. The illustration of the breech merely suggests—it cannot duplicate—the neat, tasteful and truly exquisite ornamentation of this model.

The Grade II Pre-War was very similar to the post-war guns.

GRADE II

The Grade II is actually very similar to the Grade I post-war guns. As described in the 1931 catalog, it was only a little more expensive at $64.75. The engraving was conventional foliage, and the checkered wood was about group 2-3, checkered 20 lines per inch.

BROWNING AUTOMATIC
GRADE 3
12- and 16-gauge

PRICE . $175.50

Raised Matted Hollow Rib,
Additional $8.85

Ventilated Rib, Additional   13.85

In this model, every metal surface is hand polished, and blued by a painstaking process, with the result that the eye is instantly struck by the mirror-like smoothness and satin-like sheen. Even the inner working parts, which are hidden from view, are hand polished. Stocks are of choicest European Walnut, the incomparable grain and luster of which is a particular delight to gun lovers. The illustration merely suggests the embellishment— hand-engraved hunting scenes, birds, dogs, etc., which a sportsman enjoys tracing and retracing when sitting down to rest or during a slow hour in a marsh.

This illustration, and the others that follow, shows the variety available to the American shooter at the time.

GRADE III

Now you're getting into the really rare ones. The engraving sets this grade apart from the others as soon as you look at it. On the top left side of the receiver were four pheasants and a tree line, all surrounded by a very nice game scene. The left side of the receiver was a pheasant sitting, another in flight, and two setters on point. The entire surface below the F.N. logo was covered with an upland game scene. On the right side of the receiver were four

ducks and two more dogs as on the left side.

The receivers were all hand polished and rust blued to a satin-like sheen. All the internal parts were hand polished. The wood was about group 3-4 European walnut with checkering about 24 lines per inch. The wood finish was flawless, for there was not a pore unfilled. The stock dimensions were to your order at no extra charge. This was not a cheap gun at $175.50 in 1931.

BROWNING AUTOMATIC
GRADE 4
12- and 16-gauge

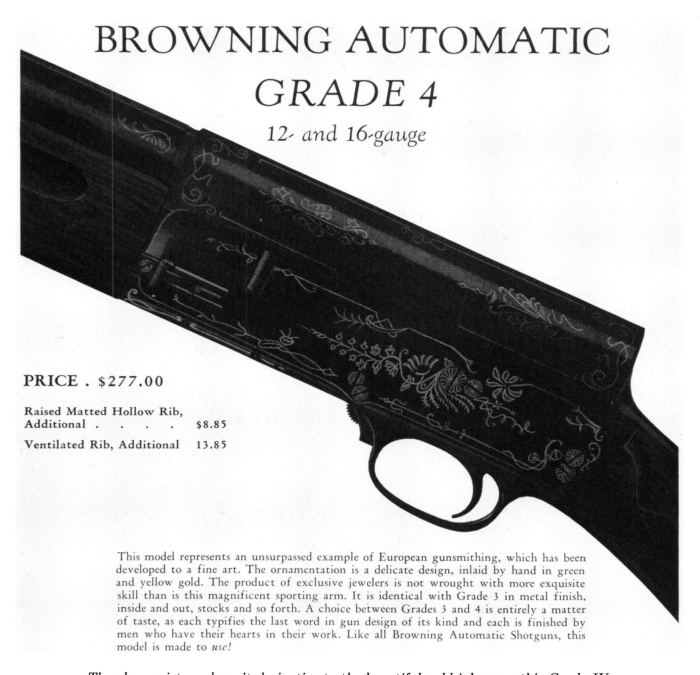

PRICE . $277.00

Raised Matted Hollow Rib,
Additional $8.85

Ventilated Rib, Additional 13.85

This model represents an unsurpassed example of European gunsmithing, which has been developed to a fine art. The ornamentation is a delicate design, inlaid by hand in green and yellow gold. The product of exclusive jewelers is not wrought with more exquisite skill than is this magnificent sporting arm. It is identical with Grade 3 in metal finish, inside and out, stocks and so forth. A choice between Grades 3 and 4 is entirely a matter of taste, as each typifies the last word in gun design of its kind and each is finished by men who have their hearts in their work. Like all Browning Automatic Shotguns, this model is made to *use!*

The above picture doesn't do justice to the beautiful gold inlays on this Grade IV.

GRADE IV

We'll let the catalog describe this one,

"This model represents an unsurpassed example of European gunsmithing, which has been developed to a fine art. The ornamentation is a delicate design, inlaid by hand in green and yellow gold. The product of exclusive jewelers is not wrought with more exquisite skill then is this magnificent sporting arm.

"It is identical with Grade 3 in metal finish, inside and out, stocks and so forth. A choice between Grades 3 and 4 is entirely a matter of taste, as each typifies the last word in gun design of it's kind and each is finished by men who have their hearts in their work. Like all Browning Automatic Shotguns, this model is made to use!"

Quite a description, but it still doesn't fully describe the engraving which was a mixture of lines, leaves, flowers and swirls all gold inlaid. Everything was gold inlaid including both sides of the receiver, the top, and the trigger guard as well as the screws. The receivers were all hand polished and rust blued to a satin like sheen, and all the internal parts were hand polished.

The wood was the best obtainable at the time and carved with a tear drop at the wrist. The checkering was about 24 lines per inch. The wood finish was flawless, for there was not a pore unfilled. The stock dimensions were to your order at no extra charge. This certainly was not a cheap gun at $277.00 in the middle of the depression.

PRICE CHANGES

By 1936 there were grade and price changes. The Grade I was the same gun, but the price was reduced to $45.50, a reduction of $4.25. Back in 1936, this was equal to about a day of work for the average person making $0.25 to $0.50 an hour.

The Grade II was now called the "Browning Special." It had the same engraving with either a ventilated rib at $59.60 or the raised matted hollow rib at $53.50. This was a reduction in the price of $11.25 with a vent rib as compared to the 1931 gun. The engraving on this gun is the same gun as on the post war guns and contributed greatly to the demise of the Grade I.

The Grade III was the same gun, but the price was $148.50 — a reduction of $27.00 — and the Grade IV was $235.25, which was reduced by $41.75.

In addition, the prices of the barrels were also reduced to $19.85 without a rib. There was an additional charge of $8.00 for the matted but the ventilated rib now cost $0.25 more.

Overall, I would say that the depression was hurting sales and forced the reduction in prices drastically, quality was always high.

Until the end of the war only minor changes were made to the line and its prices. Browning introduced cold blue, Browning oil, and powder solvent, but this was minor in comparison to the introduction of one of the company's best sellers which did more to popularize the Auto-5 then any other model, "The Sweet 16."

SWEET 16 INTRODUCTION

The Sweet 16, as originally introduced in 1936, was essentially the same gun as cancelled in 1976, the major changes being only the speed load feature, cross bolt safety, markings on the frame and barrel, chamber length, flat knob stock, frame pins and cancellation of hollow matted barrels.

Originally, these were not marked "Sweet 16," but they can be separated by the gold trigger and the engraving. The Standard 16 didn't have a gold trigger throughout production. The "Sweet 16" engraving on the left side of the frame started to show up about 1953. As you can see by the serial number charts, the numbers were mixed together until 1953 when they were separated. After this they were designated by the codes "R" for the Standard and "S" for the Sweet 16.

To include the differences in this and the Standard 16, I think it fitting that this little gun,

which was extremely popular for 40 years, should have the catalog introduction included.

THE BROWNING "SWEET 16" GAUGE

Special Lightweight Automatic Shotgun about 6 3/4 pounds

"The 'Sweet 16' has been produced to meet the demand of skeet and field shooters who want a lighter weight, finely finished gun-outstanding and attractive-at a moderate price.

"All seven exclusive Browning features in the regular weight guns are in this gun, plus the additional distinctive features of lighter weight, gold plated trigger, safety and safety latch; special conventional foliage design, hand engraving and neat narrower raised matted hollow and ventilated rib have striped matting on barrels."

Sweet 16
   without rib but with striped matting . . $65.75
Sweet 16
   with raised matted hollow rib 69.75
Sweet 16
   with ventilated rib 75.85

Extra barrel without rib
   but with striped matting on barrel 24.60
Extra for raised
   hollow matted rib 8.00
Extra for ventilated rib 14.10

STANDARD SPECIFICATIONS — 5- and 3-Shot "Sweet 16" gauge Barrel lengths, Full choke, 28 inches, Modified choke 26 or 28 inches. Improved cylinder, 26 or 28", Matted receiver. Good quality walnut stock and forearm, all hand-finished and hand-checkered. Specially prepared steel barrel and action parts. Stock specifications: Half pistol grip, length 14 1/4", drop at comb 1 5/8", drop at heel 2 1/2", Chambered for shells up to 2 9/16 inches. Weight about 6 3/4 pounds without rib. Raised matted hollow and ventilated rib guns weigh slightly more.

Only 268 "Browning Service Stations" could hang this sign during the pre-war era.

About the Browning 16-Gauge

▼

FOR many years the 16-gauge Browning Automatic Shotgun was the only automatic made in smaller than 12-gauge. At the present time it is the only 16-gauge automatic on the market. Its popularity has stood the test of time and use; it has today perhaps a wider following than any other one gun and size, and with the improvements in ammunition due to the development of modern progressive burning powders, it is today a more powerful load than the "12" of a few years ago.

There are good reasons for this immense popularity of the Browning "16." Its weight—about 6¾ pounds—makes it comfortable to carry and fast to swing on the birds—a feature which has invariably resulted in making good shots out of mediocre ones, and experts out of good shots.

Upland birds of all kinds seem to become increasingly hard to hit each season—this due to the fact that, while modern game conservation laws are really resulting in an increase in most localities, the number of hunters is also increasing, and the birds are very wild and fast.

Some of the very best bird shooting occurs in close cover, where the rule is a quick shot or no bird. A heavy, slow swinging gun is not the thing for this work; the light, fast handling arm which gets off an accurately placed shot before the bird has disappeared into the brush is indicated. For such work the Browning "16" is in a class by itself. It gives you the first shot with split-second precision, gives you a sporting chance at doubles, and in the case of a miss or a cripple, repeat shots are available in minimum time.

The hunter who carries a Browning "16" knows nothing of the wearying fatigue familiar to those using heavy guns. Consider the number of times in a day's hunt that you raise and lower your gun—shifting it from arm to arm, or shoulder to shoulder, lifting it over fences or raising it to shoot. If you have been wearing yourself out with a heavy, clumsy gun, toting an extra pound or more uphill and down dale—treat yourself to a Browning "16" and learn "what a whale of a difference" a few ounces make.

The Browning "16" is the lightest automatic built which will shoot the 1⅛ ounce shot load—the most popular and efficient load on the market today. The Browning "16" is but slightly heavier than any 20-gauge automatic now on the market! Yet ask any experienced hunter if there is any comparison for efficiency between the "16" and the "20."

You can now buy the Browning "16" at the same price as the "12." Formerly it was necessary to sell the 16-gauge Browning at a considerably higher price than that of the "12." Now, due to world-wide acceptance of this famous arm, and in part also to our new "direct-from-Browning-to-you" policy, we have been able to reduce the price to $49.75—the same as the new reduced price of the Browning "12." There is a definite need for the 12-gauge for certain classes of shooting—but whether you own a Browning "12" or one of some other make, your gun case will be incomplete until you have a Browning "16" also. And if you can afford but one gun, you will find that the Browning "16" covers *all* your shooting requirements in a very thorough and satisfactory manner.

Browning discusses the 16 Gauge.

THREE SHOT MODELS

The three shot autos were introduced in 1934 as a reaction to the new waterfowl three shot rules. These were serial numbered with the five shot so the total production cannot be known at this time.

The only difference in the 3 shot and the 5 shot was as advertised: "a more compact magazine, with shorter forearm."

You will notice that these were marked "Browning Three Shot" on the forearms. They were in every way the same as the five shot and could be ordered with any option. The three shot was discontinued in 1938 but was still available as a special order gun until the war ended production.

It would be appropriate here to say that in 1936, they also introduced "The Browning Adaptor," which was patented by them and sold for $0.15. It was merely a piece of hardwood and what we call today a magazine "plug." Obviously, Browning learned the U.S. Game And Fish Department would accept this plug and the 3 shot was discontinued.

SKEET GUNS

In 1938 a skeet gun was introduced in both 12 and 16 gauges. The barrel length was either 26" or 28" and could be ordered with or without ribs. Select wood and both models were also offered. The stock measured length of pull 14 1/4", drop at heel 1 5/8", and drop at comb 2 1/2", all else was the same.

SAFETY

All the pre-war guns had the safety located on the forward part of the trigger guard. This was an excellent feature that allowed you to put the safety on when your finger was outside of the trigger guard and away from the trigger. When hunting you simply pushed your trigger finger forward to release the safety and then back to fire the round. Why this is not liked by the modern day shooter I don't understand.

MAGAZINE CUTOUT

The Magazine cutout is how the magazine cut off was described before the war. These were originally designed to allow the shooter to load a different type of cartridge without having to unload the entire magazine. It also allows you to unload just one round to climb fences or whatever. The cut off has always been one of the main features of the Auto-5, and Browning has continued to feature it on the later post-war shotguns.

FRAME AND BARREL MARKINGS

Frame markings are as follows:

On the left side on the top of the frame are the words:

BROWNING ARMS COMPANY ST LOUIS MO

Also on the left side of the frame under the above marking will be:

BROWNING
TRADE (Bust of J.M.B. in a circle) **MARK**

On the right side of the frame just below the ejection port, you will find some of the same proofs as are noted for the barrels, especially the proof *(See proof number 4 on page 50)*.

The serial numbers will all be on the bottom front of the frame in front of the loading port.

There were three barrel markings used on the pre-war guns and two after the first 10,000 guns. The last one carries over to post-war production as you will see.

Please do not look for the barrel markings and years manufactured to be 100% in line with the years as noted below. First of all, the serial number tables are not taken from actual production records but from sales records and the recollections of Val Browning. Second, as a normal course of manufacturing, receivers and other parts including barrels are polished before any serial numbers are applied; therefore, you will find variations that are out of the proper sequence. You may have a serial numbered and blued receiver lie around for years before being assembled. This would result in an earlier receiver being shipped with a later barrel or the other way around.

F.N. would make parts in batches, and when the supplies ran low, they would make more. If there were several in the bottom of the parts bin and they happened to get covered up with 1,000 more, you put the ones on the bottom out of sequence and "WOW" you have a piece that throws things out of sequence.

There are many markings found on the barrels. The most important and obvious are described below. It is also important that you are aware of the various proof and inspector's marks.

You will find the proof marks number 1, 4, 5, 7, 8, 9, 10, 13, 15, 16, 21, 22, 23, 24, 25, 26, 27, 28, 29, and others *(See proof marks on page 50.)* on the left side of the barrel directly in front of the receiver, on the right side of the receiver directly under the ejection port, and on the barrel extension as noted below.

Some, but not all, of the inspector's marks you may find are the letters M,A,W,Y,Z,D,L; there are others. These inspector's marks will have a star above them. You will also find various numbers. These numbers appear at random and verify that an inspection was performed.

The main difference collectors look for in the markings are as follows:

After the first 10,000 guns the next were marked:
BROWNING BROS. OGDEN, UTAH U.S.A.
(Choke)(Gauge)**GA SPECIAL STEEL**

Please note that the choke marking is spelled out, and no code was used at this time.

On the right side of barrel are the words,
**MADE IN BELGIUM
BROWNING PATENT**

From 1927 to the end of the war they are marked as follows:
On the left side of the barrel (if matted or rib) and on the top if not were the words,
**BROWNING ARMS COMPANY OGDEN, UTAH U.S.A.
(Choke)(Gauge)GA SPECIAL STEEL**

Please note that the choke marking is spelled out on the early guns in this time period. The choke codes were not used until about 1927.
On the right side of barrel you will find
MADE IN BELGIUM

CHOKE DESIGNATIONS

From 1903 to 1926 Full, Modified, Improved cylinder, etc. was ahead of the legend "Special Steel" or in front of the gauge designation.

Sometime between 1926 and 1927 the now used and often misunderstood symbols appeared in use. These codes were,

*** Cylinder bore	*** Modified
**$ Skeet	*-Improved Modified
**- Improved cylinder	* Full

The standard chokes available and the barrel lengths are described below. Remember, you could special order variations not shown below, so do not turn down a barrel that does not appear below, for it could be rare. Determine the originality by realizing that the code stamps were not available to anyone else other than Browning. If you see a choke designation that is not "Browning,", you'll be able to tell immediately.

12 GAUGE	16 GAUGE
28", 30", 32" Full Choke	28", 30" Full
28" Modified	26", 28" Modified
28" Improved Cylinder	26", 28" Improved Cylinder
26", 28" Cylinder Bore	26" Cylinder

BARREL RIBS AND LENGTHS

Browning advertised extra barrels as an option. Their main selling point was that with an extra barrel, you could make one gun into two or three, depending on how many barrels you purchased. All barrels on pre-war guns must be fitted to the receiver by a competent gunsmith. They were not interchangeable like the post-war A-5's.

The cost, which varied only about $3.00 to $4.00 higher or lower, and their availability ran as follows:
The Grade I 12 or 16 gauge
Plain $21.35
Raised Matted Hollow Rib 30.20
Ventilated Rib 35.20

The Grade II 12 or 16 gauge
Plain $21.35
Raised Matted Hollow Rib 30.20
Ventilated Rib 35.20
The Browning Special prices were the same as the Grade II.

The Grade III 12 or 16 gauge
Plain $38.85
Raised Matted Hollow Rib 47.70
Ventilated Rib 52.70

The Grade IV 12 or 16 gauge
Plain $51.25
Raised Matted Hollow Rib 60.10
Ventilated Rib 65.10

There were four types of barrels available: plain without a rib and not matted, plain without a rib and matted, matted hollow rib, and a matted ventilated rib. You will not find the plain not matted listed in early catalogs, but this was available.

The raised matted rib was hollow thus lighter weight. Over half the guns sold by Browning were shipped with these ribs and are today the most common found. They were brazed to the barrel and not machined as one part. Please do not get these confused with the later "Recessed Rib" that were made for the Double Automatics. The Double Auto's ribs have a channel that is visible. The ribs we are discussing here look solid but aren't. This was their main selling point. Browning advertised it as "scientifically designed to permit the eye to pick it up as an extension of the receiver and follow its entire length to the front sight."

The ventilated rib was brazed to the barrel the same as the hollow rib above. They were similar to today's vent ribs except the intertices were closer together, which made them stronger then many you see today. All were matted.

Barrel lengths available through most of the pre-war Belgium production were the same as advertised in the 1935 catalog:

12 GAUGE	16 GAUGE
28", 30", 32" Full Choke	28", 30" Full
28" Modified	26", 28" Modified
28" Improved Cylinder	26", 28" Improved Cylinder
26", 28" Cylinder Bore	26" Cylinder
20" Messenger Barrel	

However, you could order about anything you wanted within reason including 20", 24", 26", 28", 30", 32", or 34". In other word, if you were willing to wait, you could buy a 34" Cylinder bore for those high flying quail or a 20" full for the low flying geese. If you wanted it and had the money, it was available.

QUALITY

Browning has always been known for quality. It has been the basis upon which the company has always done business and is the secret to its success.

From day one they have always stressed this as can be seen by their original 1931 guarantee:

"Browning Automatic Shotguns are guaranteed to be constructed of the best grade of materials, and are subjected to numerous tests and inspections. Long experience in manufacturing arms of high quality has enabled us to procure the materials best suited to the various parts.

"Browning barrels will not burst, unless an obstruction of some sort is in the barrel at the time of firing. In such cases a ring will always be found partially or entirely encircling the barrel. This swelling may be either above or below the bursting point.

Where improper charges of smokeless powder are used, the barrel may burst either on the bottom, the top of the side, or the portion above the bursting point may be blown entirely off. The receiver and the parts contained therein may give way due to excessive pressures developed by improperly loaded shells. We do not hold ourselves responsible for bursts due to these causes."

The pre-war and post-war guns are all of the highest quality and workmanship. You really can't find many defects until you get into the 1974 to 1975 guns, which have a little less engraving, the borders are gone, and the wood fit is not as exact, this was at the tail end of F.N. production when they were being pushed to produce military arms. Many of these A-5s were probably parts clean-up. However, that still leaves about 2,000,000 to choose from.

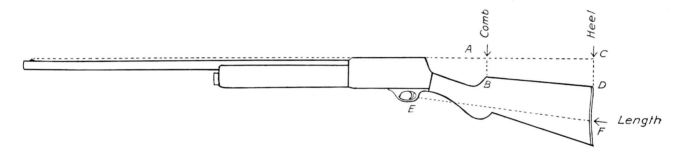

When purchasing a Browning Auto-5 in 1931 special stock dimensions were available. This was common practice in its day. Personal attention by most gun manufacturers today, unfortunately, is a thing of the past.

STOCKS

From 1911 to the end of pre-war production, the round knob stock was the standard configuration. The English style straight grip stock was available as a regular order option at an additional charge for Grades I and II but was included in the price on Grades III and IV.

The standard stock dimensions were length of pull 14 1/4", drop at heel 2 1/4", and drop at comb 1 3/4". All Auto-5's were hand checkered from the beginning of production. The oil finish was standard all the way to W.W.II and continued on afterwards.

Throughout prewar production, custom made stocks were available. In 1935 a special order stock was $15.65 for a standard grade or $35.00 for select wood. These special order stocks were actually made in St. Louis, Mo. Browning ordered a complete shotgun with the wood fitted but not finished. The blank had enough wood on it that almost any normal custom order could be accommodated. The final shaping, finish, and checkering was done in a timely manner. The above $15.65 might seem like nothing now, but this added $15.65 to a gun that sold for $49.75 and at times even a bit less.

This brings us to an interesting point that might save a few phone calls. Some Grade I guns were

ordered with special select wood. If you find a Grade I and it has nice wood, that doesn't mean you have a non-original gun. Look for the way it fits and its condition as it relates to the rest of the gun. All the work done on these guns was equal to the best available. Compare what you see to the best.

There was only one type of forearm that could be had on all Auto-5's besides the two and three shot guns that are discussed in their sections. If you wanted carving or special checkering, it was available.

BUTT PLATES AND PADS

Browning marked horn, hard rubber or plastic butt plates were standard equipment on all guns. Many were also made with an F.N. butt plate that were either a hard rubber material or horn with 7/8" x 2" scroll oval with the F superimposed over the N in a horizontal pattern of lines which are 1/16" apart for a 2 3/8" area centered between a smooth top and bottom area.

Pads could be ordered on any model. You could get any contemporary pad made by any manufacturer installed by Browning at their St. Louis service department. The pads that were recommended were the Hawkins, Jotsam (Hi-Gun or Anti-Flinch), 2-ply sponge rubber, 3-ply sponge rubber, all at $5.00, or the Silvers type and Black Diamond at $6.00.

NUMBERS

The early barrels were serial numbered on the barrel ring, the frame, the forearm, and minor parts were also numbered. The small parts like screws were numbered with the last four digits. The barrels were fitted and made only for one specific gun, so it was necessary to keep these parts together. Additional information about these may be found under the serial number section. There were some shipped without all the parts numbered, so don't be surprised to find one.

SERIAL NUMBERS

I have had many calls about the accuracy of these serial numbers and the dates of manufacture.

What I have used here comes from a memorandum written to the Browning staff by Val Browning, son of John M. Browning, written when he was President of the Browning Arms Company in 1964. This is an estimate by Mr. Browning of Auto-5 production prior to World War 2 when it was halted by the war. These estimates do not compare well with other records which will also follow.

Fabrique Nationale shows a total of 45,327 made in 12 gauge and 15,390 in 16 gauge made for export to the Browning Arms Company before July, 1913. Mr. Browning's estimate is a total of 13,000 made prior to 1925. This accounts for the discrepancy in the serial numbers, but neither I nor anyone else will ever find out, for if the records are still in existance, it would just about be impossible to get to them anyway, so there is no way you will ever find out exactly when any early Auto-5's were made. To a very serious collector this may be important, but to the 99.5% of us that just love Brownings, does it really matter if your early gun was made in 1918 or 1920? If it does, I'm afraid you can't find out this information.

There are also a couple of more things that aid in confusing us.

For the fiscal years from 1903/04 to 1924/25, production of the 12 and 16 gauges serial numbers were recorded together.

For the fiscal years from 1925/26 to 1946/47, detailed figures by gauge for F.N. and Browning were kept separately.

So, as you can see, this can get complicated. I have had people call me up and say that their serial number shows production in 1933 and their dad told them he purchased the gun in 1932; how could I be wrong. Essentially, I told the man the same as I have already said above, "But who really cares sir; what's the real difference!" If you are looking for exact dates, you won't find them here or any place else. No one knows and probably no one ever will, but you at least now have an idea of when your gun was made.

One more "exception" — even today Browning and F.N. are making exceptions to their serial numbering system. These can be either in Exhibition, Special Order, or Commemorative guns.

The best information I can get from Browning or the B.C.A. is contradictory to say the least. That's because, no matter what anybody tries to say, the records were not kept on an orderly fashion, since the war destroyed any order in which they were kept. F.N. has no interest in spending a great deal of money in getting it straightened out, and they will not release the records anyway, for they do not believe that is good business policy. PERIOD!

NUMBERS PRODUCED

The following is the production list of 12 gauge gun from July, 1913 to the end of the war plus a year. The three tables that follow are from M. Claude Gaier, who is Chef Du Service des Affaires Culturelles of Fabrique National Herstal.

| | SALES THROUGH F.N. | | SALES THROUGH BROWNING | | F.N. & BROWNING | |
	PRODUCED	TOTAL	PRODUCED	TOTAL	PRODUCED	TOTAL
Before July, 1913						45,327
1913-14					2,435	47,762
1918-19					370	48,132
1919-20					3,056	51,188
1920-21					1,246	52,434
1921-22					4,588	57,022
1922-23					4,311	61,333
1923-24					4,560	65,893
1924-25					8,439	79,332
1925-26		62,019		20,804	3,497	82,829
1926-27	6,988	69,007	5,794	26,598	12,782	95,605
1927-28	9,848	78,855	13,461	40,059	23,309	118,914
1928-29	7,662	86,517	14,951	55,010	22,613	141,527
1929-30	8,902	95,419	16,189	71,199	25,088	166,618
1930-31	4,648	100,067	3,532	74,731	8,180	174,798
1931-32	1,550	101,617	2,512	77,243	4,092	178,890

	SALES THROUGH F.N.		SALES THROUGH BROWNING		F.N. & BROWNING	
	PRODUCED	TOTAL	PRODUCED	TOTAL	PRODUCED	TOTAL
1932-33	1,122	102,739	651	77,894	1,773	180,663
1933-34	964	103,703	1	77,895	965	181,628
1934-35	1,842	105,545	5,540	83,435	7,432	189,060
1935-36	1,776	107,321	27	83,692	1,753	190,813
1936-37	1,845	109,166	2,713	86,405	4,758	195,571
1937-38	2,184	111,350	5,165	91,570	7,349	202,920
1938-39	1,954	113,304	7,148	98,718	9,107	212,037
7-1-39 to 12-31-39	479	113,783	4,527	103,245	5,006	217,043
1-1-40 to 5-10-40	4,617		Total F.N. & Browning		4,617	221,660
Req 40-44	1,915				1,915	223,575
1944-45	1,546	121,861			1,546	225,121

In trying to decipher the information, I noticed many mathematical mistakes but we were within 510 guns by the end of the war, so all is pretty close. Whether you want to take the above figures as correct or if you want to take Val Browning's recollections as correct is left up to you.

16 GAUGE PRODUCTION RECORDS

F.N. also provided the following production records which we will give here, but please do not compare this to the serial numbers and get confused. These are not serial numbers, only guns produced and shipped all over the world including the U.S.

	SALES THROUGH F.N.		SALES THROUGH BROWNING		F.N. & BROWNING	
	PRODUCED	TOTAL	PRODUCED	TOTAL	PRODUCED	TOTAL
Before July, 1913						15,390
1913-14					2,807	18,197
1918-19					496	18,693
1919-20					21	20,914
1920-21					1,439	22,353
1921-22					1,408	23,761
1922-23					2,484	26,245
1923-24					5,668	31,913
1924-25					6,991	38,904
1925-26	32,202	32,202	14,455	14,455	7,753	46,657
1926-27	2,937	35,139	3,356	17,811	6,293	52,950
1927-28	3,225	38,364	3,381	21,192	6,606	59,556
1928-29	2,932	41,296	6,098	27,290	9,030	68,586
1929-30	3,767	45,063	9,584	36,874	13,351	81,937
1930-31	3,047	48,110	5,405	42,279	8,452	90,389
1931-32	949	49,059	1,846	44,125	2,795	93,184
1932-33	552	49,611	753	44,878	1,305	94,489
1933-34	538	50,149	1	44,879	539	95,028
1934-35	782	50,931	2,860	47,739	3,642	98,670
1935-36	751	51,682	2,044	49,783	2,795	101,465
1936-37	837	52,519	3,170	52,953	4,007	105,472
1937-38	997	53,516	6,879	59,832	7,876	113,348
1938-39	793	54,309	7,004	66,836	7,797	121,145
From 7-1-30 to 12-31-39	227	54,536	2,245	69,081	2,472	123,617
From 1-1-40 to 5-10-40	159	54,695	-	69,081	159	123,776
Requisition 1940-44	332	55,027			332	124,108
1944-45	845	55,872	-	69,081	845	124,953

So, a total of 124,953 Auto-5's were made in 16 gauge according to the production records.

TOTAL FOR ALL PRE-WAR PRODUCTION

The production figures presented here may or may not be correct. During the production of these guns, like all others, many were produced for police or military departments and will have the same or special serial number. The serial numbers at the end of this chapter will not necessarily coincide with the production figures.

Also notice that there were over 3.000 guns produced during the war. The common belief about no production during the war will lead you to believe that only a very few were assembled, but to me, 3,000 guns are enough for us to take them into account when discussing Auto-5 production.

	12 GAUGE	16 GAUGE	TOTAL PREWAR PRODUCTION
Before July, 1913	45,327	15,390	60,717
1913-14	47,762	18,197	65,959
1918-19	48,132	18,693	66,825
1919-20	51,188	20,914	72,102
1920-21	52,434	22,353	74,787
1921-22	57,022	23,761	80,784
1922-23	61,333	26,245	87,578
1923-24	65,893	31,913	97,806
1924-25	79,332	38,904	118,236
1925-26	82,829	46,657	129,486
1926-27	95,605	52,950	148,555
1927-28	118,914	59,556	178,470
1928-29	141,527	68,586	210,113
1929-30	166,618	81,937	248,555
1930-31	174,798	90,389	265,187
1931-32	178,890	93,184	272,074
1932-33	180,663	94,489	275,152
1933-34	181,628	95,028	276,656
1934-35	189,060	98,670	287,730
1935-36	190,813	101,465	292,278
1936-37	195,571	105,472	301,043
1937-38	202,920	113,348	316,268
1938-39	212,037	121,145	333,182
7-1-39 to 12-31-39	217,043	123,617	340,660
1-1-40 to 5-10-40	221,660	123,776	345,436
Req 40-44	223,575	124,108	347,683
1944-45	225,121	124,953	350,074

12 GAUGE SERIAL NUMBERS

What follows are the serial numbers as reported by Val Browning to his staff in 1964 when he was the President of the Browning Arms Company. His estimate matches the serial numbers listing below. I realize that Mr. Browning's estimate is 11,957 more then the production given by F.N., but there is no way of knowing who is right and who is wrong. In filling military or police contracts, F.N. would sometimes produce several guns the same number! How are you going to keep up with serial numbers by the year? Mr. Browning's estimate may have included Remington production.

From 1903 to the end of the war and even until 1953, all serial numbers were numerical. Fabrique Nationale produced Auto-5's for Browning in this country as well as for sales to other parts of the world.

The early guns were numbered on the barrel ring, on the frame, and on the forearm,,as well as having the last four digits on many minor parts. Barrels were fitted and made only for one specific gun, so it was necessary to keep these parts together.

1903-1924	Up to 13000	1932	121001-135000
1925	13001- 28000	1933	135001-159000
1926	28001- 43000	1934	159001-173000
1927	43001- 58000	1935	173001-179000
1928	58001- 79000	1936	179001-191000
1929	79001- 93000	1937	191001-205000
1930	93001-107000	1938	205001-222000
1931	107001-121000	1939	222001-229000

There were approximately 3,000 assembled during the war.

16 GAUGE SERIAL NUMBERS

The first 16 gauge was shipped by F.N.to the U.S. on August 17, 1909. Browning will not give out any information, and these are taken from old sales records and notes from Mr. Val Browning. The standard weight was made from 1909 until discontinued in 1968, the Sweet 16 Belgium from 1936 - 1976.

Please note that many guns were shipped to countries that designated their own serial numbers, which may cause numbers produced not to coincide with serial numbers as listed in this section. Also, good accurate records were not released by Browning during the entire production run. Here are how the serial numbers run from 1923 to the end of the war:

Standard 16

1909-1923	Up to 13000	1935	91001- 95000
1926	13001-22000	Standard and Sweet	
1927	22001-31000	16's are mixed	
1928	31001-39000	together until 1953	
	and	1936	95001-104000
	128000-128500	1937	104001-113000
1929	39001- 48000	1938	113001-122000
1930	48001- 57000	1939	122001-128000
1931	57001- 64000	Production ceased for	
1932	64001- 73000	eight years because	
1933	73001- 82000	of the German	
1934	82001- 91000	occupation	

AUTO-5 POST WAR

GENERAL INFORMATION

A basic history of the Auto-5 in this country has been given in the previous section. I am, therefore. going to cover only the basic configuration changes and models of the post-war guns.

Other than the years from 1947 to 1951 when it was made by Remington and known as "The American Browning" and the years 1976 to 1992 when it was made in Japan, all post war Auto-5's were made by Fabrique Nationale in Liege Belgium.

In 1975, F.N. found the increased labor costs in Belgium too high and moved production of this and several other models to the Miroku Company in Japan. Since so little has happened with the Japanese guns, I have not separated them from the Belgium production. The configuration on the guns are basically the same, with only the markings and the overall look different.

The Auto-5 is a versatile gun that will handle all loads, from the lightest to 3" magnums with equal reliability. Over 3,000,000 have been made; therefore, they speak for themselves.

MODELS

There were 12 post-war models produced. These were:

The Hunting model has always been made
Skeet, made from 1963 to 1983
Trap, made from 1959-1960 to 1970
Buck Special, made from 1963 to 1987
Light Buck Special, 1987 to 1992
Magnum Buck Special, made from 1987 to 1992
Standard 12, made from 1905 to 1968
Light 12, made from 1952 to 1992
Standard 16, made from 1909 to 1968
Sweet 16, made from 1936 to 1975 and
    1987 to 1992
Magnum 20, made from 1958 to 1992
Light 20, from 1958 to 1992.*

So you don't get confused, let me list these as they were produced and cataloged.

Hunting Model was made as the Standard and Light 12, Standard and Sweet 16, Light 20, and 3" Magnum 12 and 20.

*1992 is the writing of this book and those marked 1992 will probably continue to be made until a later date.

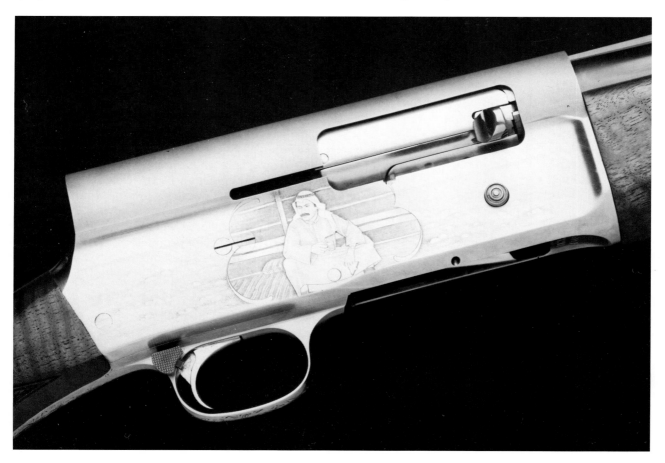

It might take someone like an oil shiek who can afford it, but today, as during the pre-war era, Fabrique Nationale will make anything the shooter desires.

The Skeet Model was made as the Light 12, the Sweet 16, and the Light 20.

The Trap Model was made as the Standard and Light 12.

The Buck Special was made as the Standard and Light 12, the Standard and Sweet 16, the Light 20, the 3" Magnum 12, and the Magnum 20.

Although most deer hunters purchased the Auto-5 with a shot barrel and later purchased a "Buck Special" barrel separately, many Buck Specials were sold for deer hunting exclusively.

The Light Buck Special was made as the Light 12 and the Light 20.

The Magnum Buck Special was made as the Magnum 12 and the Magnum 20.

The above will give you an idea of how you could purchase a certain model during various years. You could put a Buck barrel on any gun and make it a Buck Special if you put sling swivels and the proper barrel on it. You could make a Hunting model into a Skeet model if you changed the barrel and stock. The only differences in these models were the barrels and stocks. The frames used were the same within each gauge and model.

The classic post-war Auto-5, this one an original 12 gauge 3" magnum with 32" barrel.

GRADES

Prior to the war there were eleven grades made at one time or another. These were the Regular, Trap, Messenger, Two Shot, Three Shot, Grades I, II, III, IV, Sweet 16, and the Browning Special. After the war, Browning chose not to offer several engraved grades.

After the start up by F.N. of commercial produc-tion in 1952, the Auto-5 was made in the Sweet 16, Standard 16, Light 12, and the Standard 12. After the production of 20,000 guns by Remington in five years, I cannot understand why the 20 gauge wasn't continued. Maybe F.N. was not set up for this gauge and Browning was anxious to get started. Who knows?

The Grade I's that were produced after the war were actually the pre-war Browning Special or Grade II. No other grades were offered from 1952 to 1992 unless it was special ordered or some type of commemorative model.

On the left side the engraving consisted of light zig-zag scroll all around the edges with a bust of John M. in the center. This bust was highlighted by the name BROWNING just above the bust. All this was surrounded on both sides and underneath with light foliage and scroll designs. This extended about 2 1/2"

on each side, but gradually decreased, starting in 1971. The right side had the same type of pattern but no bust or logo, and it was about 4 1/2" long. The top of the receivers had wedges of engraving about 2" long on both sides and on the back and front.

As production went on, you could see the engraving getting slightly skimpy. The zig-zags surrounding both sides of the frame got a little larger, the wedges of engraving got a little shorter, and the corners that formerly had little bits of engraving disappeared.

When comparing the very early pre-war from configuration to the post-war, many differences are apparent.

FRAMES

Except for commemorative or special orders, all frames are rust blued until 1959 to 1960. After this, they were hot dipped blued.

TRIGGERS

All triggers on the Standard 12 and 16, the Magnum 12 and 20 were blued until 1979, and they

were then gold plated. The Sweet 16, Light 12 and 20 gauge triggers in all models were all gold plated throughout production. No trigger options were ever offered.

SAFETIES

There have been only two safeties in three variations made for this model.

This early frame shows the finer engraving of the early guns.

All the pre-war guns had the safety located on the forward part of the trigger guard. This was an excellent feature that allowed you to put the safety on when your finger was outside of the trigger guard and away from the trigger. This safety will also be found on some of the post war guns made in the late forties.

The next safety was the cross bolt, which came in two versions. Browning made these for right handed shooters, but they could be ordered in a left handed version as an option.

FRAMES
SCREWS VERSUS PINS

The frames on the early post-war guns had several changes made that are important to collectors.

All throughout production, only screws were used, but in 1961 to 1962, hollow pins were substituted. Advanced collectors of this model prefer guns prior to this change. This is not to say that pins are the kiss of death. It just means that if you want the most sought after, you stay with the pre-61 to 62 guns or those that came out earlier.

Browning knew that the new speed load feature would be a hit with the shooters and featured it in all their early post-war catalogs.

SPEED LOAD

Browning didn't coin this term until the late 1950's, but this was an important change. It was originally introduced in the Double Automatic and was so popular with the public that it was incorporated in the Auto-5. Both hunters and collectors look at the those with this feature as more desirable than the ones without it. Many

earlier guns were converted by gunsmiths and by Browning to have this special feature, so you may find an earlier gun with it.

As introduced in 1954, the gun was described in the catalogs as follows:

"NEW, EXCLUSIVE — No other gun will load as fast, except the Browning Double Automatic, from shooting position to reload to shooting position — five shells in six seconds. Loading is equally convenient for right or left hand, and easy even with gloves. While retaining one hand at the grip, with the gun held in position ready to snap to the shoulder, all shells are fed in quick succession into the magazine loading opening. If the gun is empty, the first shell is automatically delivered to the chamber and the others, as loaded, remain in proper position in the magazine. The latch button is no longer necessary and is only provided on the Automatic-5 in case the shooter wishes to close the breech without loading the cartridge into the chamber. Even when speed is not such an essential factor, the ease with which loading is accomplished is a constant source of pleasure to the automatic shooter. This advanced design is found only on Browning automatic shotguns."

The magazine cut off was a feature not on any other semi-auto shotgun of U.S. or Belgium make.

STOCKS

Until 1966, the English style straight grip stock was available as a regular order option. But unless you specified the straight stock, you were shipped the round-knob half-pistol grip style.

This is the more desirable round knob stock configuration. Also please notice the checkering that crosses itself just behind the lower tang on this early gun.

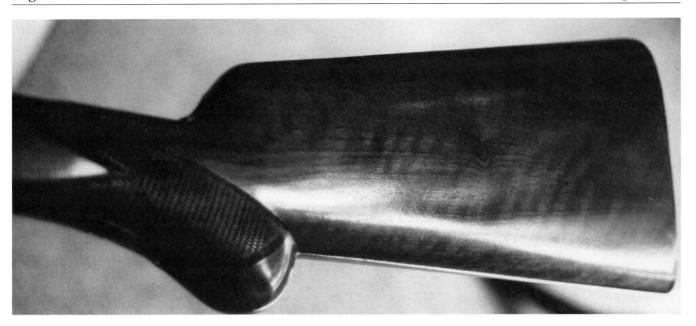

The early oil finish as shown on this buttstock is very apparent.

In 1967, the flat knob or full pistol grip became the standard configuration. However, some guns were produced in 1966 with flat knobs, and round knob guns were assembled until the end of production, probably to utilize spare parts. Round knob stocks were reintroduced as standard in 1987.

The forearm shown here is from a 1958 twelve gauge.

There was only one type of forearm made for each model. Of course, if you wanted a specially checkered and/or carved forearm, it was available.

The 12 gauge Standard and Light forearms are different from the Magnum 12. The Sweet 16 and Standard 16 are the same and the Light 20 and Magnum 20 forearms are different from each other. None of the gauges will fit one another.

All Auto-5's were hand checkered from the beginning of production. Oil finish was standard up until the mid 1960's when they began using a high gloss polyurethane finish. An oil finished gun could be ordered after the mid 60's and quite a few were.

Custom fitted stocks were available throughout Belgium production.

STOCK DIMENSIONS
HUNTING, TRAP & SKEET MODELS

There were four different types of stocks made, but in reality only three different measurements. This description will also include the Trap and Skeet models, for the only difference for these are the stocks and barrels, which are covered in that section. The Hunting and Skeet dimensions were length of pull 14¼", drop at comb 1⅝", and drop at heel 2½". These were all shipped with butt plates.

The Trap dimensions were length of pull 14³/₈", drop at comb 1³/₈", and drop at heel 1³/₄". These were also shipped with but plates.

The 3" magnum Hunting gun dimensions were length of pull 14", drop at comb 1⁵/₈", and drop at heel 2½". These were all shipped with rubber recoil pads marked "Browning."

BUTT PLATES AND PADS

Browning marked horn, hard rubber, or plastic butt plates were standard equipment on all guns except the 12 gauge 3" magnum, which had pads.

Pads could be ordered on any model. You could get a Pachmayr "White Line" or other contemporary pad made by any manufacturer installed by Browning at their St. Louis service department and later in Ogden, Utah. If a pad was ordered on an original gun, it was first produced by F.N. with a butt plate and sent to the U.S., where it was then fitted with whatever pad the customer ordered.

Browning marked Pachmayr manufactured pads were first available in 1958 and were used unless another make was specified in the order. I would indeed be skeptical about the guns I saw with a pad, even those with "Browning" marked pads, for they were rarely ordered.

BARREL CONFIGURATIONS

The barrels available were many and changed throughout production. After the war only the basic barrel configurations were offered in Plain unmatted, plain matted, raised hollow matted, and ventilated. Over the years there were several special barrels that are covered as follows:

SPECIAL BARRELS

The first special barrels offered were the Skeet with a Cutts Compensator in 26" only. In 1962 to 1963 a 28" barrel was also offered. These remained in the line until they were cancelled in 1970. After 1970, the Cutts Compensator was discontinued and the skeet choke barrel was used on the Skeet Model. Many collectors do not know how to tell whether a barrel with this device was original. However, if you look on the coller that attaches it to the barrel, you will see the Allen screw on it. Browning's replaced the slotted screw Cutts supplied with an Allen screw. The barrel was cut to any length and could have any choke marking, so do not automatically assume a Cutts with a choke marking is not original.

Next came the Trap, which was advertised, but I don't believe there was any difference between it and the hunting barrel chambered for 2³/₄" shells. They were only offered in 30" full with a ventilated

rib. These remained in the line until they were cancelled in 1970, they did have a center bead.

The third special barrel introduced was the Buck Special in 1963. Although not cataloged this year, it was available as a special order item for several years prior.

As originally offered in the catalog, it was listed as follows:

Light 12 23½" 7 lbs.	Plain barrel with special sights
Standard 12 23½" 7 lbs. 10 oz. 12" mag. 12 23½" 8 lbs. 4 oz.	Rear adjustable for windage and elevation. Gold bead front sight on contoured Stand 16 23 ramp. Special choked and bored for rifled slug and buckshot loads. Carrying sling and swivel attachments also available.
Sweet 16 23½" 6 lbs. 6 oz. ½" 7 lbs. Light 20 23½" 6 lbs 2 oz.	

The 23½" barrels were only made as a regular order item in the 23½" length in 1963. After this initial offering, they all have 24" barrels.

The Buck Special 20 magnum barrel was introduced in 1968.

The Standard 16 Buck Special was cancelled in 1969, Standard 12 in 1971, Sweet 16 in 1975. In 1991 Browning again offered these barrels in 12, 16, and 20 gauges.

The most common Belgium Buck Special barrels are the 12 gauges in 2³/₄" as well as 3"; and the rare ones for you collectors are the 20's, followed up closely by the 16's.

RIBS AND LENGTHS

Hollow matted rib barrels were discontinued in 1962 to 1963. The Buck barrel, other than special order, was not available until about 1963 in 23 1/2" and 24" in 1964. Plain barrels were also discontinued in 1975, for there are no Japanese made guns originally shipped with plain barrels other than a parts cleanup which is covered under another section.

Barrel lengths available through most of the Belgium production were 24", 26", 28", 30", 32", and 34". However, you could order about anything you wanted within reason.

The various barrels, gauges, lengths, configurations, chokes available were as follows subject to the above notes:

BARRELS AND CHOKES

	32"	30"	28"	28"	28"	26"	Imp	26"	24"	26" Buck
Plain Bar.	Full	Full	Full	Mod	Sk	Mod	Cyl	Sk	Cyl	Special
3" Magnum 12	X	X	X	X					X	X
Standard 12	X	X	X	X	X		X	X	X	X
Light 12		X	X	X	X		X	X	X	X
Standard 16		X	X	X			X		X	X
Sweet 16			X	X		X	X		X	X
Light 16			X	X	X	X	X	X	X	X
Ventilated Rib Bar.										
3" Mag 12	X	X	X	X						
Standard 12		X	X	X	X		X	X	X	
Light 12		X	X	X	X		X	X	X	
Standard 16			X	X						
Sweet 16			X	X		X	X		X	
Light 20			X	X	X	X	X	X	X	

NOTE: Any choke may be obtained in any standard barrel length on a special order, even though it is not listed above. The only exception is the full choke in a 26" barrel. Such a special order does entail a slight additional charge for reboring.

When it comes to finding an unusual barrel, need I say more? Unusual barrels are rare and command premium prices.

CHOKES

All post-war guns are marked with the standard choke codes. These are as follows:

Chokes available were *** Cylinder bore, **$ Skeet, **- Improved cylinder, *** Modified, *- Improved Modified, and * Full.

Cutts Compensators and Polychoke were also available. The Polychokes were put on these barrels by either F.N. or at Browning's St. Louis repair department. When a Polychoke or Cutt Compensator was ordered, any barrel at hand would be used. As an example, if someone ordered a 28" barrel, then the plant would take a cylinder bore 26" and cut it to length so that the end result was 28" long. But if the repair shop had an over supply of 30" full choke barrels, they would cut them to the proper length and used it. The end result was factory fitted Polychoke or Cutt Compensator barrels with all types of choke markings. So, unlike other make of guns, the only way you can tell if a Polychoke barrel is original is by unscrewing the choke collar all the way off and looking at the body of the choke. If, at 12 o'clock or very close you see the number 9, the choke work was done in St. Louis. If you see the number 11, the work was done by F.N.

This is great for the Polychoke barrels, but how do you tell if a Cutt Compensator was original? Well, this is not as cut and dried as the Polychoke situation, but there is a way to tell if it's not original. On the Cutts, a ring is soldered to the front of the barrel and the main body of the choking device is screwed to this ring. Cutts supplied a regular slotted screw to lock the choke to the ring. Browning did not use this screw but replaced it with an Allen head screw instead. This is not a great way to tell but it's the only way, for there were no markings of any kind placed on the Cutts choked guns as there were on the Polychoke guns. I was told that there are a great many more of these around then collectors think, so they are not as rare coming from the factory as was once thought. In my never ending quest to inform my readers, I must tell you that barrels with these choking devices are not looked upon with great favor by collectors, but they are an honest variation. In fact, 264 straight at skeet will attest to my liking the Cutt with a spreader tube pretty well and so did a lot of other skeet shooters, some of whom shot a lot better then I did.

BARREL NUMBERS

I have opened many a new Auto-5 and checked the serial numbers to discover that they did not match. After about 1951 to 1952, the barrel no longer needed fitting and were universal, so numbers were no longer needed on the barrel and only match infrequently. However, there is an exception to each rule, for Mr. Val Browning said that he recalls that early guns were shipped with matching numbers.

Since barrel numbers rarely match receiver serial numbers, you cannot tell from this if a barrel is original. Some barrels don't even have any numbers at all. As long as your barrel address is correct for the year of production and condition and the color matches the receiver and stock, you're probably okay.

BARREL AND FRAME MARKINGS

There are three barrel markings on the post-war Belgium guns. The first one listed was carried over from pre-war production. This does not include the Remington markings.

Nothing is ever 100%, and that certainly goes for Browning markings. First of all, the serial number tables are not taken from actual production records but from sales records and the recollections of Val Browning. Second, as a normal course of manufacturing, receivers and other parts including barrels are polished before any marking including the serial number is applied; therefore, you will find variations that are out of the proper sequence. You may have a serial numbered and blued receiver lie around for years before being assembled. This would result in an earlier receiver being shipped with a later barrel. This can also work the other way around.

There are many markings found on the barrels of this model, the most important and obvious of which are described below. It is also important that you are aware of the various proof and inspector's marks.

You will find the proof mark numbers 1, 4, 5, 7, 8, 9, 10, 13, 15, 16, 21, 22, 23, 24, 25, 26, 27, 28, 29, and others *(See proof marks on page 50.)* on the left side of the barrel directly in front of the receiver, on the right side of the receiver directly under the ejection port, and on the barrel extension as noted.

Some, but not all, of the inspector's marks you may find are the letters M,A,W,Y,Z,D,L and others. These will have a star above them. You will also find various numbers which appear at random and verify that an inspection was performed.

The main difference collectors look for in the markings are as follows:

From 1927 to 1950 they are marked on the left side of the barrel if they are matted or have a rib and on the top if not with the words:

BROWNING ARMS COMPANY OGDEN, UTAH U.S.A.
(Choke code) (Gauge) **GA SPECIAL STEEL**

On the right side of barrel are the words:
MADE IN BELGIUM

On the right side of the frame just below the ejection port, you will find some of the same proofs as are noted for the barrels, especially the proof *(See proof mark 4 on page 50.)*

From 1951 through 1958 they are marked on the left side of the barrel if they are matted or have a rib and on the top or left side if not with the words:
BROWNING ARMS COMPANY ST. LOUIS, MO

(Choke code) **SPECIAL STEEL**-(Gauge)
GA SHELLS-2 3/4"(3" if applicable)

On the right side of the barrel are the words:
MADE IN BELGIUM

On the right side of the frame just below the ejection port you will find some of the same proofs as are noted for the barrels, especially the proof 4 *(See proof mark 4 on page 50.)*

From 1959 through 1968 they are marked on the left side of barrel:
BROWNING ARMS COMPANY ST LOUIS MO & MONTREAL P.Q.

(Choke Code) **SPECIAL STEEL**-(Gauge)
GA SHELLS-2 3/4"(3" if applicable)

On the right side you will find
MADE IN BELGIUM

About 1962 to 1963 the MADE IN BElGIUM moved from the right to the left side under the main address line.

On barrel extension,
You will find various inspectors marks *(See proof marks 5 and 7 on page 50.)*

From 1969 through 1975 they are marked on the left side of the barrel with the words:
BROWNING ARMS COMPANY MORGAN UTAH & MONTREAL, P.Q.

On the right side of barrel are the words:
BROWNING AUTO-5

(Choke)-**SPECIAL STEEL**-(Gauge)
GA SHELLS-2 3/4"(3" if applicable)

BROWNING PATENT

There are no barrel extension marks and the extensions are no longer machined but are smooth

From 1976 to date they are marked on the left side of barrel:
BROWNING ARMS COMPANY MORGAN UTAH & MONTREAL, P.Q.

MADE IN JAPAN

On the right side of barrel:
BROWNING AUTO-5
(Choke)-**SPECIAL STEEL** (Gauge)
GA SHELLS-2 3/4"(3" if applicable)-(Barrel length)

BROWNING PATENTS

OTHER MARKINGS

On early Auto-5's most barrels and even screws were serial numbered with the last three or four numerals, and you may find this on special order or Exhibition grade guns.

The marking "Acier Special" on the barrels simply means "Special Steel."

INTRODUCTION OF THE GAUGES

The standard 12 gauge was made throughout production but was cancelled in all except the 3" magnum, which wasn't introduced until 1958. The Light 12 was certainly the most popular of all the gauges.

The 16 was introduced in 1909 in the Standard model and in 1936 as the Sweet 16. As you can see from the serial numbers, the Standard was discontinued in 1969 and the Sweet 16 in 1975, which was the end of Belgium production. In 1987, the Japanese Sweet 16 was introduced but discontinued in 1992.

The 20 gauge was introduced in 1958, and the 20 gauge magnum, in 1968.

NUMBERS PRODUCED

This is a continuation of the pre-war 12 gauge data. It is a list sent to Reid Betz, Executive Director of the Browning Collector's Association, by M. Claude Gaier, who is Chef Du Service des Affaires Culturelles of Fabrique National Herstal. These figures, according to M. Gaier, are taken from the actual production records of F.N the U.S. and elsewhere.

YEAR	PRODUCED FOR F.N. PRODUCED	TOTAL	PRODUCED FOR BROWNING PRODUCED	TOTAL	F.N. & BROWNNG PRODUCED	TOTAL
1945-46	1,845	123,706	1,160	104,405	2,505	227,626
1946-47	1,979	125,685	11,021	115,426	13,000	253,626

From this point until 1972, which is the last year available, the figures are only available merged together.

	F.N. & BROWNING	
YEAR	PRODUCED	TOTAL
1947-48	12,946	266,572
1948-49	9,899	276,471
1949-50	25,075	301,546
1950-51	26,992	328,538
1951-52	35,464	364,002
1952-53	40,144	404,146
1953-54	64,029	468,175
1954-55	50,938	519,113
6-30-56	52,206	571,319
6-30-57	61,518	632,837
6-30-58	63,148	695,985
6-30-59	59,214	755,199
6-30-60	50,016	805,215
12-31-60	35,252	840,467
1961	59,054	899,521
1962	56,048	955,569
1963	69,602	1,020,171
1964	72,453	1,092,262

	F.N. & BROWNING	
YEAR	PRODUCED	TOTAL
1965	88,083	1,180,345
1966	83,363	1,263,708
1967	84,411	1,348,119
1968	82,036	1,430,155
1969	90,078	1,520,233
1970	81,647	1,603,769
1971	75,812	1,679,581
1972	65,650	1,745,231

Once again, I found a lot of mathematical errors in their addition. The ending serial number for each year is incorrect by F.N.'s figures. I chose to take the actual figures given for each year and add these myself. In the very end, I came up with no descrepancy at all.

The following is a list of shipments that F.N. provided the Browning Company in 1964. We have been fortunate in getting some insight in the shipments of the 16 gauge guns from 1946 to 1958. If you have any guns made during this time, it may give you some idea in the production for those years. However, this list is contradicted by another that follows.

16 GAUGE SHIPMENTS FROM 1946 TO 1958

YEAR	U.S.	ELSEWHERE
1946	8,000	5,200
1948	8,100	700
1949	7,600	1,300
1950	9,900	1,200
1951	12,600	3,200
1952	15,600	100
1953 - Standard 16	11,000	2,600
1953 - Sweet 16	16,400	
1954 - Standard 16	8,700	9,300
1954 - Sweet 16	16,400	5,100
1955 - Standard 16	8,700	11,900
1955 - Sweet 16	16,400	600
1956 - Standard 16	8,700	19,300
1956 - Sweet 16	16,500	4,500
1957 - Standard 16	5,000	26,000
1957 - Sweet 16	20,500	6,500
Through 10-1-58		
1958 - Standard 16	1,500	7,100
1958 - Sweet 16	1,000	0,000
Through 10-1-58		
1958 - Sweet 16	5,000	5,000
Standard 16	5,500	3,500
Totals	203,100	123,100

In 1987, F.N. dug into their production records and sent the numbers of guns produced for the 16 gauge. This does not coincide with the above, which was also provided by them in 1964, but since these are available, I will include them here.

The only post-war production that was kept separate (at least that we have at this time) are the years from 1945 to 1947. The rest is together.

YEAR	PRODUCED FOR F.N.		PRODUCED FOR BROWNING		F.N. & BROWNING	
	PRODUCED	TOTAL	PRODUCED	TOTAL	PRODUCED	TOTAL
1945-46	491	56,363	-	69,081	491	125,444
1946-47	740	57,103	10,645	79,726	11,385	136,829
1947-48					6,302	143,131
1948-49					8,617	151,748
1949-50					11,689	163,437
1950-51					16,561	179,998
1951-52					15,420	195,418
1952-53					18,836	214,254
1953-54					28,938	243,192
1954-55					29,960	273,152
6-30-56					19,639	292,791
6-30-57					39,111	331,902
6-30-58					23,208	355,110
6-30-59					17,366	372,472
6-30-60					21,831	394,307
12-31-60					10,232	404,539
1961					20,229	424,768
1962					18,241	443,009
1963					17,711	460,720
1964					20,898	481,518
1965					17,261	498,779

	PRODUCED FOR F.N.		PRODUCED FOR BROWNING		F.N. & BROWNING	
	PRODUCED	TOTAL	PRODUCED	TOTAL	PRODUCED	TOTAL
1966					18,004	516,783
1967					13,468	531,251
1968					11,533	541,784
1969					10,472	552,256
1970					8,423	560,679
1971					7,034	567,713
1972					4,666	572,379

In 1987, F.N. also dug into their production records and sent the numbers of guns produced for the 20 gauge.

	F.N. & BROWNING	
YEAR	PRODUCED	TOTAL
6-30-58	1	1
6-30-59	4,694	14,695
6-30-60	24,973	39,368
12-31-60	3,908	43,276
1961	8,180	51,456
1962	7,469	58,925
1963	12,030	70,955
1964	11,600	82,555
1965	11,465	94,020
1966	11,489	105,509
1967	22,881	128,390
1968	23,565	151,955
1969	18,482	170,437
1970	18,912	189,349
1971	12,429	201,778
1972	13,829	215,607

TOTALS
FOR ALL GAUGES

A little bit of explanation of the data that follows. The 12, 16 and 20 gauge columns are self explanatory, but the "additional production" column needs explanation.

On the actual hand written data sheet I received, the guns were broken down by gauge and where shipped for some years and not for others. In addition, gauges and for whom produced were mixed together some years and not for others. Also, with the introduction of the 12 gauge magnum, all were mixed together with the other guns and gauges. This threw the numbers off even more. I knew that in order to account for the 12 magnum production which was lumped together with the other gauges, I would have to stay with F.N.'s records. So, the years 1958 and later will have the 12 magnum production and other guns not accounted for by F.N. under this column.

	12 GAUGE	16 GAUGE	20 GAUGE	ADDITIONAL	
YEAR	PRODUCED	PRODUCED	PRODUCED	PRODUCTION	TOTAL
1945					350,074
1945-46	5,510	491			356,075
1946-47	13,000	11,385			380,460
1947-48	12,946	6,302		6,530	406,238
1948-49	9,899	8,617		5,000	429,754
1949-50	25,075	11,689			466,518
1950-51	26,992	16,561			510,071
1951-52	35,464	15,420			560,955
1952-53	40,144	18,836			619,935
1953-54	64,029	28,938			712,902
1954-55	50,938	29,960			793,800
6-30-56	52,206	19,639			865,645
6-30-57	61,518	39,111			966,274
6-30-58	63,148	23,208	1		1,052,631
6-30-59	59,214	17,366	4,694	24,686	1,158,591
6-30-60	50,016	21,831	24,973	24,294	1,279,705
12-31-60	35,252	10,232	3,908	3,988	1,333,085
1961	59,054	20,229	8,180	8,180	1,428,728
1962	56,048	18,241	7,469	7,469	1,517,955
1963	69,602	17,711	12,030	7,030	1,624,328
1964	72,453	20,898	11,600	11,600	1,740,879
1965	88,083	17,261	11,465	6,465	1,864,153
1966	83,363	18,004	11,489	16,389	1,993,398

	12 GAUGE PRODUCED	16 GAUGE PRODUCED	20 GAUGE PRODUCED	ADDITIONAL PRODUCTION	TOTAL
1967	84,411	13,468	22,881	22,881	2,137,039
1968	82,036	11,533	23,565	23,565	2,277,738
1969	90,078	10,472	18,482	18,482	2,415,252
1970	81,647	8,423	18,912	18,912	2,543,146
1971	75,812	7,034	12,429	12,429	2,650,850
1972	65,650	4,666	13,829	13,829	2,748,824
1973				69,834	2,858,387
1974				39,729	2,885,362
1975				26,975	2,912,337
1976				22,855	2,935,192
1977				7,344	2,942,536
1978				3,702	2,946,238
1979				3,703	2,949,941
1980				4,542	2,954,483
1981				16,831	2,971,314
1982				17,396	2,988,710
1983				17,540	3,006,250

BROWNING

Instructions for Browning Automatic-5 Shotgun

DEALER — DO NOT REMOVE FROM GUN — VERY IMPORTANT

Absolutely necessary that customer receive the enclosed instructions for proper operation and care of the Automatic-5 Shotgun.

BROWNING ARMS CO.

1706 Washington Avenue, St. Louis 3
Missouri, U.S.A.

8340 Mountain Sights Avenue, Montreal 9
Quebec, Canada

Made In Belgium

Not only the Auto-5 but all postwar Belgium made Brownings were shipped with an instruction booklet and guarantee in the above envelope which was black with gold printing.

The following ten pages show the Auto 5 instruction manual and warranty card shipped with each postwar Auto 5. Please notice on page two the "Printed in Belgium" which will show the collector a correct instruction manual.

SAVE THIS BOOKLET

BROWNING

on Operation and Care of

Browning® Automatic-5 Shotgun

12, 16 and 20 gauge

VERY IMPORTANT

These instructions should be carefully noted

BROWNING ARMS CO.
1706 WASHINGTON AVENUE, ST. LOUIS, MISSOURI, U.S.A.
8350 MOUNTAIN SIGHTS AVENUE, MONTREAL, 9, QUEBEC, CANADA

BROWNING®

We are proud that you have chosen a Browning. In its manufacture we have endeavored to incorporate the very finest in materials and craftsmanship, and with just reasonable care this gun should provide you with many years of pleasure and dependable service. If, by any chance, you have any observations to make regarding its performance or appearance, we hope you will write us immediately; your Browning must be flawless.

We would also like to know more about you as a Browning owner and would be grateful if you could take but a moment to complete and return the registration card found on the inside back cover.

Thank you.   BROWNING ARMS COMPANY.

BROWNING® NEW GUN OWNER'S RECORD

Browning Automatic-5 Shotgun   LTWT ☐   Gauge .... Serial No. ....
                                STD ☐

Date   Purchase   Purchased
Purchased .... Price .... From ....

IMPORTANT: Please fill out and mail the Registration Card at the back of this booklet.

Printed in Belgium

ASSEMBLY

In conventional gun terminology, the position and movement of gun parts are described as they occur with the gun horizontal and in normal firing position; i.e., the muzzle is forward or front; butt stock is rearward or rear; trigger is downward or underneath; the rib is upward or on top.

1. CLEAN ANTI-RUST COMPOUND FROM BARRELS. Remove with any quality gun oil.

2. Pull rearward on operating handle and draw breech bolt rearward where it will remain locked back. Rest butt end of stock firmly on any convenient surface. With the left hand, pull rearward on the forearm to counteract the forward thrust of the recoil spring around the magazine tube. With the right hand unscrew the magazine cap. Slide wooden forearm forward off the magazine tube. DO NOT SQUEEZE HARD ON THE OPEN REAR END OF THE FOREARM; THIS IS THE MOST FREQUENT CAUSE OF SPLITTING THE WOOD.

3. The Automatic is delivered with the magazine adaptor in the magazine which limits the gun to three shots in accordance with Federal law governing the shooting of migratory birds. If you do not want your gun to be so limited, merely take out the plug, the end of which you will see in the exposed end of the magazine tube. The gun will then be a 5 shot Automatic.

If at some future time you wish to limit your gun to three shots again, take the adaptor and pass the shaft through the hole in the magazine spring retainer which is the exposed end

— 3 —

Proper assembly and disassembly for all Auto-5 Post-War models.

of the magazine tube. With this shaft projecting into the magazine, press or lightly tap the head of the adaptor to force the magazine spring retainer downward until the head of the plug is on a level with the end of the magazine tube if it is not already so. Then proceed with assembly as below.

4. Place barrel guide ring around the magazine tube and force the barrel rearward against the resistance of the recoil spring while guiding the barrel extension into the receiver. Note the guides on the barrel extension which must be placed in the receiver slots.

5. With the left hand maintaining rearward pressure against the barrel to the point where the front end of the barrel extension is even with or slightly inside of the front end of the receiver, replace the forend over the magazine tube and screw cap on tightly. BE CERTAIN THE CAP IS SCREWED COMPLETELY DOWN FORCING THE REAR END OF THE FOREND INTO FIRM CONTACT WITH THE FRONT END OF THE RECEIVER. The semicircular wood ridge at the rear of the forearm should fit into the matching groove in the front of the receiver.

DISASSEMBLY

CHECK YOUR GUN CAREFULLY TO BE CERTAIN THE CHAMBER AND MAGAZINE CONTAIN NO SHELLS. Draw breech bolt rearward at which position it will remain. With the left hand apply rearward pressure to the barrel, then unscrew the magazine cap with the right hand. While maintaining rearward pressure on the barrel remove the forearm from the magazine tube.

— 4 —

While continuing to hold the barrel firmly, gradually release pressure and slide barrel directly forward off the magazine tube.

DO NOT SUDDENLY RELEASE PRESSURE AGAINST THE BARREL. If this is done, the strong recoil spring may throw the barrel off the gun.

After the barrel has been removed from your gun, do not slam the breech block by pressing the button. When the barrel is present on the gun, the breech block stops against the barrel extension. If the breech block is slammed with the barrel removed, the operating handle will be driven against the front edge of the receiver ejection opening.

For convenience in casing and carrying the dismantled gun, return the forend to its position on the magazine tube and screw on the magazine cap. You will then have two neat units. One is the barrel; the other is the action with forend and stock.

INSTRUCTIONS FOR OPERATION

THE FOLLOWING INSTRUCTIONS ARE NOT FOR THE 3" MAGNUM 12 GAUGE AUTOMATIC — SPECIAL INSTRUCTIONS ARE PROVIDED FOR THIS MODEL.

Adjustment of Recoil of Absorbing Mechanism (Shock Absorber).

This mechanism is extremely simple yet it must be given some attention. Proper management will reduce recoil to a minimum. This in turn contributes to pleasant shooting and prolongs the life of your gun by protecting the mechanism against excessive shock.

The adjustments described on the following pages are of two general types. One

— 5 —

	HEAVY LOADS		LIGHT LOADS	
	Drams Powder	Ounces Shot	Drams Powder	Ounces Shot
12 Gauge	3 1/4	1 1/4	2 3/4	1 1/8 Shot
	3 3/4	1 1/4 Shot	3	1 Shot
	4	1 1/2 Shot	3	1 1/8
	3 3/4	1 Slug	3 1/4	1 1/8
	3 3/4	Buck Shot		
16 Gauge	3	1 1/8 Shot	2 1/2	1
	3 1/4	1 1/8 Shot	2 3/4	1 1/8
	3 1/2	1 1/4 Shot		
	3	7/8 Slug		
	3	Buck Shot		
20 Gauge	2 3/4	1 Shot	2 1/4	7/8
	3	1 1/8 Shot	2 1/2	1
	2 3/4	5/8 Slug		
	2 3/4	Buck Shot		

This page shows the heavy and light loads the Auto-5 was designed to use.

for heavy loads, one for light loads.

It should be noted that the weight of the shooter and the manner in which he holds his gun may require some variance from the above chart of loads. For example, a light weight individual may find that his gun will function better for him if adjusted for light loads while shooting a 3 1/4 × 1 1/4, 12 gauge shell.

— 6 —

This mechanism is recoil operated, and this means essentially that the operations of loading and ejection are automatically carried out by utilizing the forces delivered to the mechanism when the shell is fired. The shock absorber merely regulates the mechanism; for instance, your gun may fail to eject if you fire a light load with the shock absorber set as on page 8 « For Heavy Loads ». On the other hand, if you fire a heavy load when your shock absorber is set for light loads the gun kicks you unnecessarily hard; the mechanism of the gun itself receives unnecessarily severe shock.

FOR PLEASANT SHOOTING, READ THESE SIMPLE INSTRUCTIONS

Component Parts of Shock Absorber

Parts which participate in the recoil absorbing mechanism are as follows (See Illustrations « A » and « B »):

1. Barrel Guide Ring
2. Bronze Friction Piece
3. Friction Ring
4. Magazine Tube
5. Recoil Spring

For Heavy Loads

The component parts are assembled on the gun as follows (See Illustration « A »):

— 7 —

HEAVY LOADS

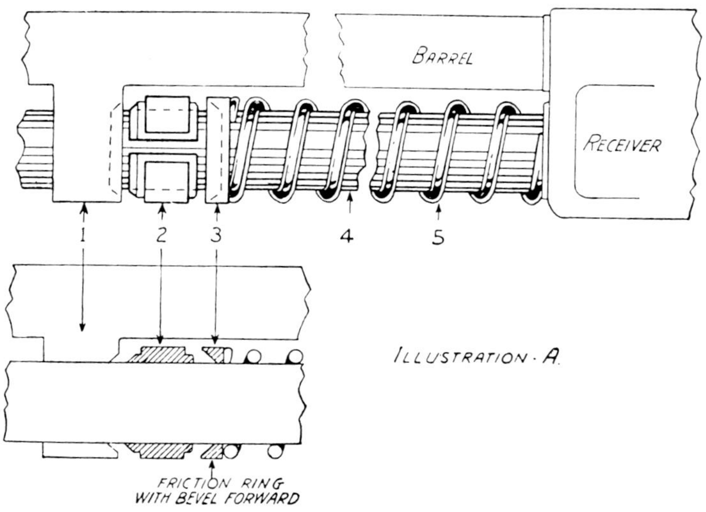

ILLUSTRATION · A.

FRICTION RING WITH BEVEL FORWARD

— 8 —

One of the most common problems new shooters of the Auto-5 run across is improper re-assembly of the friction rings.

The long recoil spring (Part. No. 5) is first placed on the magazine tube (Part. No. 4) and is, therefore, in direct contact with the receiver.

The friction ring (Part. No. 3) is then slipped over the magazine tube with its beveled surface <u>forward</u>. The flat surface of this ring is, therefore, to the rear and rests on the top of the recoil spring.

The bronze friction piece (Part. No. 2) is then slipped over the magazine tube with its beveled surface forward. <u>Gun should never be fired without bronze friction piece in place.</u>

When the barrel is assembled to the gun, the beveled surface at the rear of the barrel guide ring (Part. No. 1) then fits over the forward beveled surface of the bronze friction piece.

For Light Loads

The single difference from the arrangement given for heavy loads is a change in the position of the friction ring. For light loads this friction ring is taken off and placed at the extreme rear end of the magazine tube, between the rear end of the recoil spring and the receiver with the beveled edge turned towards the receiver. See Illustration « B ».

— 9 —

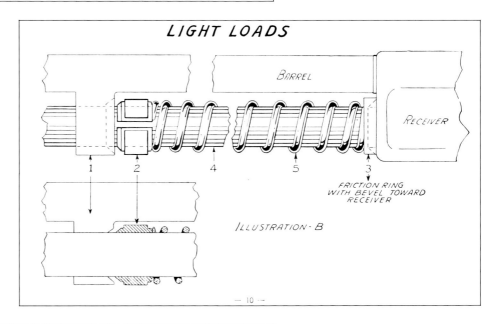

ILLUSTRATION-B

— 10 —

NEVER UNDER ANY CIRCUMSTANCES remove the bronze friction piece from its position rearward of the barrel guide ring. If the gun is fired with either the friction ring or the recoil spring in direct contact with the barrel guide ring, the rear surface of the barrel guide ring will be deformed. Removal of the bronze friction piece permits an excess of recoil. You are getting much unnecessary « kick » and are pounding the mechanism of your gun severely.

Compensator devices of various type may reduce the force of recoil of a given load. You will note, however, that the mechanism must receive a certain amount of force, if it is to operate automatically. The addition of any sort of weight to a barrel will have somewhat the same effect. When such factors as these are introduced, care must be given to suitable adjustment of the shock absorbing mechanism. It is desirable to utilize the setting for heavy loads as long as the mechanism functions properly. When resistance to recoil is too great to permit proper ejection, then the light load setting should be used.

Oil On The Magazine Tube

Whether the friction ring is set for heavy loads or light loads, the amount and kind of oil on the magazine tube will, by varying the amount of friction, have an effect upon the amount of recoil. In general, the more oil that is put on the magazine tube (or bronze friction piece), the easier this friction piece will slide on the tube; hence, a greater degree of recoil will be obtained.

— 11 —

Example of the Use of Oil: if you are firing a light load and the gun still fails to eject, the addition of oil to the magazine tube in the region of the bronze friction piece will sufficiently increase recoil to a point satisfactory for good ejection.

Oil which congeals in cold weather or deposits gummy residue may reduce recoil to the point where the gun will fail to eject. Use a high quality lubricant. Occasionally clean the magazine tube and relubricate. If temperatures of ten to thirty degrees below freezing (20° F - 2° F) are likely to be encoutered, it is best to utilize an oil which maintains its fluidity in such temperatures. Browning Gun Oil is particularly well suited for this purpose.

At all times there should be a film of oil on the magazine tube excepting when 12 gauge, 2 3/4" Magnum loads are being used. With this load it is desirable to wipe the magazine tube practically dry. Function will not be affected and you will find these heavy loads much more comfortable to shoot.

Should your gun at any time commence to give ejection trouble, one or more of the following is usually the cause:

1. Insufficient oil on the magazine tube, rust, gum, or hardened grease, any of which may interfere with normal operation of the recoil spring and friction pieces.

2. The recoil absorbing mechanism is set for the improper load.

3. A slight swelling of the forearm (sometimes quite unavoidable under conditions of excessive exposure to moisture) may cause sufficient resistance to the barrel to affect normal

— 12 —

Proper oiling of the Auto-5 assures more reliable functioning.

This is the manual's description of the new speed load feature.

operation. If a side of the barrel shows signs that it is rubbing against the forearm, the application of a fine piece of emery cloth to the offending portion of the inside of the forearm will quickly rectify the problem.

LOADING
®
(Browning Patented and Exclusive Quick Loading Feature)

This Browning shotgun is equipped with the new, improved loading system. Its design will enable you to load faster and easier. It is no longer necessary to press the button on the right side of the receiver during the loading process, and the same procedure is used in loading the first shell into the chamber as in loading the remaining shells into the magazine.

If the mechanism is not already open, pull rearward on the operating handle until the breech block locks back. The gun is now ready to load.

Hold the gun with either right or left hand at the grip or forearm as you prefer or are accustomed. With the opposite hand, merely introduce the front end of the shell into the under side of the receiver and thrust completely forward as if loading the magazine—then release the pressure of your thumb. The shell is immediately and automatically driven rearward, tripping the feed mechanism, and delivered instantly into the chamber without further manipulation. The first shell is now ready for firing and appropriate safety precautions should be

— 13 —

taken. To load the magazine, continue the same procedure slipping shells past the carrier into the magazine until the latter is full. (Without the magazine plug, the magazine will hold 4 shells, 2 shells if the plug has been inserted.) Be sure to insert each shell clear in the magazine before releasing.

The simplified and faster loading system is equally convenient for right-or left-hand shooters. The instant delivery of the first shell to the chamber in one simple operation eliminates entirely the conventional process of dropping the first shell into the open receiver port and then pressing the button on the right side of the receiver to close the action and drive the shell into the chamber. The button which is still present on the right face of the receiver is only provided to close the action of the gun if and when desired.

Whenever the breech block is closed, shells may be loaded into the magazine even though the latter is only partially empty.

CAUTION

During loading, always have the barrel pointed skyward or in a safe direction. As with any automatic firearm, it is necessary to keep your hand away from the breech block port to avoid being struck by the breech when the mechanism closes.

— 14 —

BREECH REMAINS OPEN

The breech of the gun remains open after the last shot has been fired. It is thus unusually convenient and fast to reload because of this new, quick loading feature.

YOU CAN NEVER BE CERTAIN THAT YOUR GUN IS UNLOADED UNLESS THE BREECH IS OPEN. Even then handle your gun with caution — for safety and good manners.

SAFETY

This improved cross bolt safety has an enlarged head on the right side designed to be conspicuous when « On Safe »; hence, a shooter is not likely to lose a shot through failure to notice that his safety is on. The safety may be moved to « Fire » position with unusual speed and convenience.

To move « On Safe », press the small head to the right. To move « On Fire » press the large head to the left.

MAGAZINE CUT OFF

The magazine cut-off is located at the front end of the left side of the receiver. This cut-off has the purpose of locking the shells in the magazine so that they will not feed into the chamber. This permits one quickly to change the load in the chamber of the gun without

— 15 —

going to the trouble of unloading the whole magazine. In this way a duck load can quickly be thrown out and a goose load inserted if the emergency arises.

To operate the magazine cut-off, merely pull it back. This will lock the shells in the magazine. Push the cutt-off forward when you desire to release the shells in the magazine so that they will feed automatically as the gun is fired.

With the magazine cutoff in operation, the chamber empty, and the breechblock locked in the rearward position, a shell may be instantly delivered from the magazine to the chamber by merely pushing the magazine cutoff forward.

OILING

Ordinary good judgment will indicate that the metal parts of the gun should receive a light film of oil after the gun has been exposed to weather or handling.

Occasionally, a small drop of oil may be placed on breech block and barrel extension guides, etc., to relieve the effects of friction. DO NOT POUR LARGE QUANTITIES OF OIL INTO THE ACTION. A large excess of oil will run back into the wood of the stock and cause softening of the wood with consequent loosening of the stock.

PRECAUTIONS

1. DON'T PUT A 20 GAUGE SHELL IN A 12 GAUGE GUN — if you value your gun and yourself.

— 16 —

Unless you carefully examine every shell you put in your gun, don't even permit 20 and 12 gauge shells in the same room — let alone in the same pocket. Then, EXAMINE EVERY SHELL YOU PUT IN YOUR GUN.

The most certain way to bulge or rupture even the finest barrel is to drop a 20 gauge shell into a 12 gauge chamber. The 20 gauge shell, unfortunately, will not fall clear through the barrel. Its rim is caught by the front of a 12 gauge chamber; accordingly, your gun will misfire. Under conditions of carelessness made lethal by haste, a 12 gauge shell can be loaded behind the 20; and you could not deliberately have created a more serious hazard to your gun and yourself.

2. BEWARE OF BARREL OBSTRUCTIONS — for you gun and yourself. Mud, snow, a forgotten cleaning rag, and a wide variety of objects may find their way into your barrel. If takes only one such obstruction to ruin (swell or rupture) the finest of barrels.

Be careful how you carry your gun. Do not permit the muzzle to dip into mud, snow, or water. Do not thrust it through a thicket with a possibility of ramming a twig down the barrel, etc.

Check your barrel for obstructions before you assemble your gun.

3. DO NOT TAKE YOUR GUN APART. This is a specialized, finely fitted mechanism; and you may mar it for life by an attempt to remove the inner mechanism.

It is unnecessary, and may do damage to the inner mechanism, to take a gun apart

— 17 —

annually for routine cleaning and oiling. Of course, untoward eventualities (such as dropping gun in water) require appropriate attention.

AMMUNITION

All Browning 12, 16 and 20 gauge Automatics are chambered to accept and shoot all standard factory 2 3/4'' shotgun shells, of the appropriate gauge, including 2 3/4'' Magnum shells.

The size and gauge shell your Automatic will safety accept is stamped on the left side of the barrel just above the forearm. (See special instruction book for 3'' Magnum 12 gauge Automatics.)

CHOKE MARKINGS

The gauge and choke of your barrel are indicated by clearly defined marks stamped in the upper rear surface of the barrel. The code for the choke markings is as follows:

Full Choke	*
Improved Modified	* —
Modified	**
Improved Cylinder	** —
Skeet Boring	**$
Cylinder	***

— 18 —

Two or more Guns in One — By Use of Extra Barrels

The same gun can be made suitable for multiple shooting conditions merely by changing from one barrel to another of different choke, length, and rib. On all Browning® Automatics, barrels of the same gauge* are completely interchangeable and no special fitting is required. Thus by merely buying another barrel, you have acquired the utility of another gun at a fraction of the cost of a new gun; a duck gun becomes a skeet gun or a fine upland game gun by the mere addition of an extra barrel.

WHEN ORDERING AN EXTRA BARREL

Be sure to furnish us the gauge, model (Lightweight, Standard) and serial number of gun, the choke, whether full, modified, improved cylinder, skeet, or cylinder and barrel length, whether 26, 28, 30, or 32 inch. Barrels are manufactured without a rib, with a raised hollow matted rib, and a ventilated rib. Please specify when ordering.

PLEASE NOTE: Complete barrel interchangeability without fitting has only been possible in recent years. If your gun was purchased prior to 1950, you should secure the services of a competent gunsmith or our Service Department for the fitting of the extra barrel.

* (3'' Magnum 12 Gauge barrels will not fit or work in a regular 12 Gauge action designed for 2-3/4'' shells and vice versa because the feeding and ejection mechanisms are different.)

— 19 —

BARREL SPECIFICATIONS AVAILABLE

	32" Full	30" Full	28" Full	28" Mod.	28" Skeet	26" Mod.	26" Imp. Cyl.	26" Skeet	26" Cyl.	24" Buck * Special
Plain Barrel										
3'' Magnum 12	X	X	X	X						X
Standard 12	X	X	X	X			X	X	X	X
Light 12		X	X	X	X		X	X	X	X
Standard 16		X	X	X			X		X	X
Sweet 16			X	X		X	X		X	X
Light 20			X	X	X	X	X	X	X	X
Hollow Matted Rib Barrel										
Standard 12		X	X	X	X		X	X	X	
Light 12		X	X	X	X		X	X	X	
Standard 16			X	X						
Sweet 16			X	X			X		X	
Ventilated Rib Barrel										
3'' Magnum 12	X	X	X	X						
Standard 12		X	X	X	X		X	X	X	
Light 12		X	X	X	X		X	X	X	
Standard 16			X	X						
Sweet 16			X	X		X	X		X	
Light 20			X	X	X	X	X	X	X	

* Equipped with fully adjustable rifle type sights.

— 20 —

SIGHT ADJUSTMENT FOR THE BUCK SPECIAL

The Buck Special is equipped with a precision rear sight which is screw adjustable for both horizontal and vertical correction.

1. To move the point of impact to the right, simply loosen the coin slotted screw, located on the right side of the sight, by turning in a counterclockwise direction and tighten the screw on the left side by turning in a clockwise direction. This causes the rear sight to move to the right. To move the point of impact to the left, simply reverse this procedure.

2. Vertical adjustment of the sight is controlled by the two screws located on top and forward of the sight. To raise the point of impact, loosen the forward screw, then tighten the rear screw until the sight has been raised the necessary amount. Conversely, to lower the impact, loosen the rear screw and tighten the forward screw. After either correction the loosened screw should be tightened in turn to lock the adjustment in place.

— 21 —

CLEANING SUGGESTIONS

The correct procedure for cleaning your shotgun is as follows:

BE CERTAIN YOUR SHOTGUN IS UNLOADED

1. Dismount barrel so that it can be cleaned from the breech end.

2. Using a shotgun rod with tip and patch large enough for snug fit in bore, insert rod and patch in breech end of barrel and run back and forth through bore several times.

3. Inspect bore from both ends for leading by looking through bore toward light. Leading will appear as dull longitudinal streaks and is usually more predominant in the constriction area of the choke and just forward of the chamber.

4. A normal amount of leading can be expected with today's high velocity loads and improved gas seal wads but this is not serious. If or when leading should become heavy, it can be removed with a brass bore brush. Dip the brush in Nitro-Solvent and scrub bore until leading is removed. To prevent brass bristles from breaking off, the brush should be pushed completely through bore before being withdrawn.

5. After leading has been removed, the bore should be wiped dry and then a slightly oiled patch run through it for preservation.

— 22 —

6. If the gun has been exposed to much dust, dirt, mud or water, the principal working parts should be wiped clean and lubricated with a light film of oil. Browning Gun Oil is recommended.

7. The magazine tube on the Automatic-5 should be wiped clean of all dirt and grit and then lubricated lightly with an oiled patch. The friction pieces should be assembled according to the loads to be used as covered previously.

8. Reassemble barrel and wipe all exposed metal surfaces with an oiled cloth making sure to wipe gun clean of all finger marks where moisture will accumulate.

9. The wood surfaces can also be wiped with Browning Gun Oil or they can be polished with any quality furniture wax.

SERIAL NUMBER. The serial number for your Automatic-5 Shotgun is found on the underside of the receiver, just forward of the loading port.

— 23 —

BROWNING® ALL-WEATHER GUN OIL

Browning Gun Oil assures dependable gun operation under all weather conditions. Its high viscosity guards against bare metal exposure even at extremely high temperatures without gumming and yet permits jam-free performance in weather as low as 30 below zero. Browning Gun Oil cleans, lubricates, protects bluing and polishes and protects your stock. Suitable for use on all hunting and fishing equipment.

Browning used the owner's manuals supplied with each gun sold to inform the public of new products.

— 24 —

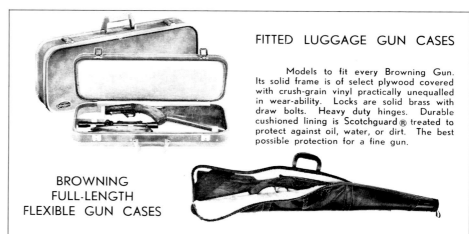

FITTED LUGGAGE GUN CASES

Models to fit every Browning Gun. Its solid frame is of select plywood covered with crush-grain vinyl practically unequalled in wear-ability. Locks are solid brass with draw bolts. Heavy duty hinges. Durable cushioned lining is Scotchguard® treated to protect against oil, water, or dirt. The best possible protection for a fine gun.

BROWNING FULL-LENGTH FLEXIBLE GUN CASES

Sizes for all shotguns, rifles, and scoped rifles. Exterior of waterproof, extremely tough heavy gauge vinyl. Deep, soft pile lining is silicone treated and nonabsorbent. Thick Tufflex® inner padding. Heavy duty zipper with moisture-proofed zipper track. Double handles with steel cores for extra strength.

— 25 —

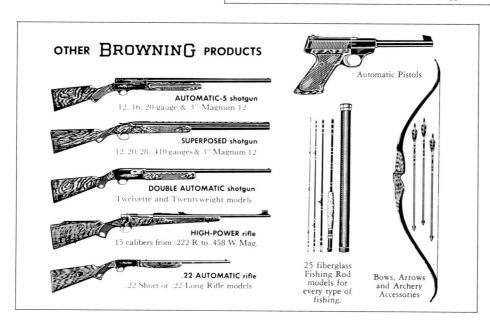

OTHER BROWNING PRODUCTS

AUTOMATIC-5 shotgun
12, 16, 20 gauge & 3" Magnum 12

SUPERPOSED shotgun
12, 20, 28, .410 gauges & 3" Magnum 12

DOUBLE AUTOMATIC shotgun
Twelvette and Twentyweight models

HIGH-POWER rifle
15 calibers from .222 R to .458 W Mag.

.22 AUTOMATIC rifle
.22 Short or .22 Long Rifle models

Automatic Pistols

25 fiberglass Fishing Rod models for every type of fishing.

Bows, Arrows and Archery Accessories

→ → → **PLEASE TEAR OFF** ← ← ←

BROWNING REGISTRATION CARD

Your Name	Serial Number ....
Address	Gauge ....
City & State	Price ....
Dealer Purchased From	Date Purchased ....
City in which Purchased	Your Approximate Age ....

Your reasons for selecting a Browning (check one or more)

☐ I have used Browning Guns before   ☐ Saw an Advertisement

☐ Recommended by another Browning owner   ☐ Saw descriptive literature

☐ Recommended by my Dealer   ☐ I now own ( ) Browning Guns

What magazines do you read regularly (List in order of preference)

1. ....   3. ....

2. ....   4. ....

What is the primary hunting or target sport for which you intend to use your new Browning?

Any comments you wish to make

....

....

....

....

An original warranty card as supplied with all new Browning firearms.

Postage Will be Paid by Addressee

No Postage Stamp Necessary If Mailed in the United States

BUSINESS REPLY CARD
FIRST CLASS PERMIT No. 60   OGDEN, UTAH

BROWNING ARMS Co.

719 First Security Bank Bldg.

Ogden, Utah

OF SPECIAL INTEREST
AND
COLLECTABLE A-5'S

The most collectable Auto-5's are the ones produced in the mid to late 50's. These are the ones with screws attaching the magazine cutoff instead of pins and with the speed load feature. The checkering goes all the way down to the bottom of the grip and crosses at the bottom. You'll find a lot of fine workmanship in these guns for a production item.

Guns with the forward sliding safety are not considered the most desirable unless they are a high grade. A lot of these guns have hollow matted rib barrels. These are not as collectable as vent rib guns.

If you're looking for the most collectable guns, look for the ones that are round knob or straight stocked with the speed load feature, cross bolt safety, vent rib, and hopefully screws instead of pins. Of course, condition is of the utmost importance when collecting any Browning.

Remember, serial numbers are stamped on guns after they are polished and before they are blued or assembled. This means that although every effort is taken to produce these in sequence, sometimes a receiver is not finished and assembled for a period of time. This could put the actual shipping date long after the actual production date.

When the Belgium manufactured guns were made, they were treated with the same care as the Superposed. You'll find great finish, workmanship, fit, and checkering on all produced.

After you study mint to new in the box guns at various shows or, if you're lucky, at a private collection, you'll be able to tell right from wrong. Be careful when purchasing any used Auto-5. Split forearms are sometimes found even on those that look almost new.

TOTAL PRODUCTION

Total production for this model in Belgium was 2,790,724. Regular production of the Auto-5 ended in 1975. After this, it has been steadily made in Japan. This figure was supplied by F.N.

OLD PRICES

I have the following information about prices: 1952, $139.45 1954, $118.25; 1957, $147.95; 1962, $154.50; 1963, $159.75;1964, $174.75;1965, $179.75; 1967, $174.95; 1969, $199.75; 1970, $204.50; 1971, $216.50; 1972, $266.50;1973, $314.50; 1974, $289.50; 1975, $369.50 (quite a jump) and 1975, $399.95.

REMINGTON PRODUCTION —
THE AMERICAN AUTO-5

Browning advertised these as "The American Browning," and they were, for they were made for

Browning distribution by The Remington Arms Company.

Fabrique Nationale, because of legal requirements to produce Belgium military weapons and to supply N.A.T.O. with arms after World War Two, could not make enough sporting guns to meet Browning's demand. So, from 1946 until 1952, the Remington Arms Company produced many of the Auto-5's during that time. Fabrique Nationale did produce a few but not enough to speak of or to really matter in this study of the Auto-5.

These guns were essentially the same as the Remington Model 11 with the magazine cut off added. They are not the guns for which Browning collectors look, since they are not of equal value nor are they very much in demand. You can immediately recognize them by the skimpy engraving and the almost sandblasted look of the receivers. Therefore, I have made little effort to research or describe them here. You will find below total production and serial numbers so you can identify them youself.

Markings are as follows. On the left side of the frame are the words:

BROWNING
TRADE (Portrait of J.M.B.) MARK

The serial number is on the bottom directly below the "**TRADE MARK**"

On the left side of the barrel you will see:
BROWNING ARMS COMPANY ST LOUIS MO
(Choke)SPECIAL STEEL-(Gauge)
GAUGE-SHELLS 2 3/4"

The choke designations are the normal codes.

Immediately in front of the receiver is a encircled "BP"

There are no markings on the right side of the barrel.

You will run across many of these, and some people will tell you that these are Brownings. They are not, however, Fabrique Nationale manufactured and are not worth nearly as much as a Belgium made Auto-5.

There was a total of about 90,000 Remington manufactured guns supplied to Browning. The total production by gauge is as follows:

GAUGE	PRODUCTION	MARKED
12	45,000	B
16	25,000	A or X
20	20,000	C

Production figures and total production are necessarily estimates because they were derived from incomplete sales records analyzed by Browning. Remember, neither Browning nor Fabrique Nationale will release any records until a model has been discontinued and sometimes not even then.

The Remington production serial numbers run along with the Remington Model 11 production, so you will see higher numbers then you see listed as total production. Above you will see a column titled "MARKED." These are the code letters Remington put into the serial numbers to determine which guns were made for Browning.

AUTO-5 CLASSIC AND GOLD CLASSIC

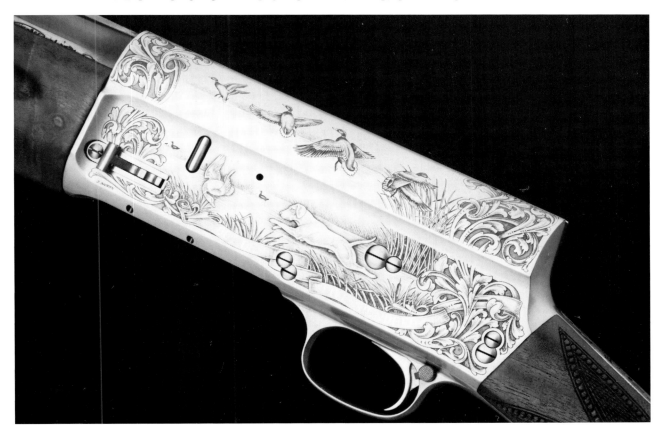

The Auto 5 Classic and Gold Classic is the first in the Classic series that consisted of the Auto 5, Superposed, and High Power models.

The Auto-5 Classic.

This was the first Classic or Gold Classics in the series. They were introduced in 1984 and discontinued in 1988.

The receivers are about 95% covered with ducks landing in a marsh and a bust of John M. Browning on the right side. On the left side there is a Labrador retriever going after a duck. The top of the receiver featured four flying ducks on the top right and fleur-de-las scroll on the top left. The words "BROWNING CLASSIC" are engraved on both sides of the receiver. The engraving is done by hand and all are signed.

The Auto-5 Gold Classic.

On the Gold Classic you will see only the bust of John Browning. The ducks and Labrador retriever on each side and the words "BROWNING GOLD CLASSIC" on each side were inlaid with 18 carat gold. The Classic was stocked with group 2-3 wood. The receivers and trigger guards were grey finished.

The triggers were also gold plated.

These were stocked in high grade walnut of about group 5 with 24 line per inch checkering and a carved border as was the Classic.

Total production was 5000 Classics and 500 Gold Classics as far as we know.

2,000,000 COMMEMORATIVE

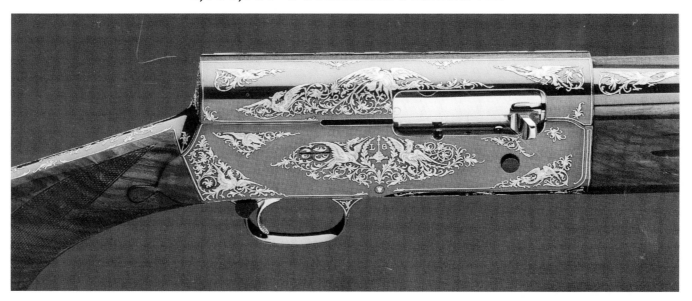

Placed in the hands of Browning's very best Belgian craftsmen, this firearm was prepared for presentation to the President of the United States.

Now it can be Yours.

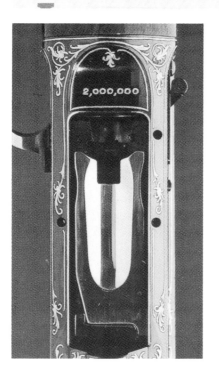

Here are some ad photos of the Two Millionth Auto-5 produced, by Browning, for presentation in 1970 to President Richard M. Nixon. The engraving was inspired by an early exposition model A-5 by Browning's Master Engraver Felix Funken in 1930. Because of his resignation, this beautiful firearm laid in the Browning vault for 15 years. It was auctioned at the 8th Annual SHOT SHOW in Houston, Texas with all proceeds earmarked for NSSF. Bids started in excess of $20,000.

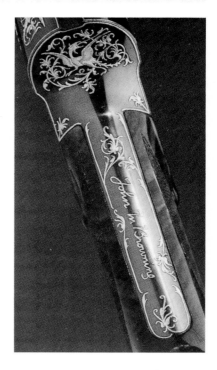

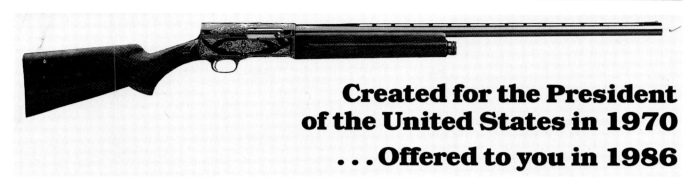

Created for the President of the United States in 1970 ...Offered to you in 1986

The actual 2,000,000 Auto-5 was shipped from F.N. to the U.S. on June 26, 1970, and was valued at the modest prices of $8,350.00. As you can see from the pictures, the engraving and wood is almost indescribable.

The inlaid designs and patterns of the 2,000,000 Auto-5 were done by F.N.'s master engraver, Andre Watrin, whose signature is engraved on the forward portion of the trigger guard. All gold inlay was executed by Master Engraver Jose Baerten and G. Vandermissen. The design features were very much like a early exposition model by Master Engraver Felix Funken in 1930.

The top tang has the same type inlays as the sides with the signature of John M. Browning. Also on the full pistol grip is the gold shield which says:
MANUFACTURED BY BROWNING
ARMS COMPANY
6-6-70
INVENTED BY
JOHN M. BROWNING
OCTOBER 9, 1900

Originally, it was to be presented to President Nixon by Senator Bennett, who would then give it to the Smithsonian for permanent residency with the John M. Browning memorial. Ultimately, the presentation was never made, so the gun lay in the Browning vaults for fifteen years while they detemined what to do with it. In 1985, Browning gave it to the National Shooting Sports Foundation for display and auction at the Eight Annual Shot Show in Houston, Texas. To give you an idea of what it sold for, the only bids accepted were those above $20,000.00.

There were actually two guns made like we have discussed here. The other is serial numbered 2,000,000X and is in the F.N. museum in Herstal.

Now let's discuss the guns that were made for general distribution. These were produced to commemorate the 2,000,000 Auto-5 produced in Belgium. Production began in 1970 and shipments began in September/October of that year.

Announced to Browning dealers directly in the fall of 1970, these were the first commemorative guns produced by F.N.. The 2,000,000th Auto-5 shipped to President Nixon was the gun used to commemorate the event and to begin Browning's Special Edition Series of 2,500 guns.

As mentioned above, the basis for the engraving pattern came from a gun originally engraved by Felix Funken for the Liege International Fair in 1930. From this, the 2,000,000th Commemorative engraving was taken and then offered to F.N. There were three different patterns by Louis Vrancken and J. Watrin from which the final engraving was decided. The serial numbers of these guns were 2,000,000, 2,000,000-X and 2,000,000-X1. The 2,000,000X was the gun used as the basis of this commemorative.

As the production ran, they had the standard Auto-5 engraving plus additional engraving consisting of the Browning logo, the serial number, a John M. Browning's profile, and his signature. All the engraving was gold filled. Blueing was of the very finest polish and finished in a blue black color, which you will find is a little darker then production Auto-5's.

Serial numbers ran from 2,000,000-0001 through 2,000,000-2500 for a total of 2,500 guns. Because of the insistence of a few collectors who wanted certain serial numbers, there were three to four produced with duplicate serial numbers but with an "X" added. This would make the total about 2,503 to 2,504.

All barrels were 28" with a modified choke and a Midas style vent rib. In addition all had a metal bead front sight and ivory center bead.

Stocks were of high grade walnut running from nice to beautiful. The finish is the very finest and like that only done on the best F.N. produced guns. Be particular when choosing one of these. The figure of wood varied and I have seen some with salt wood.

All guns came with a black leatherette case with gold velour interior. The usual booklet for the Auto-5 was included along with a special publication about John M. Browning and the Auto-5. The gun was shipped in a separate box from the case, but most of the time you'll find the box missing. The box is nice to have but doesn't affect the value very much.

Earlier in the year, Browning dealers had been advised earlier about this gun, so many were sold to collectors before shipment even began. However, after initial sales, they were slow to move as seen by the fact that it took until 1974 to get rid of all of them.

Prices ran from $570.00 in 1971-72 to $675.00 in 1973 to $700.00 in 1974 when the last were sold out.

SERIAL NUMBERS

I have had many calls about the accuracy of these serial numbers and the dates of manufacture.

What I have used here comes from a memorandum written to the Browning staff by Val Browning, son of John M. Browning, when he was President of the Browning Arms Company in 1964. This is an estimate by Mr. Browning of Auto-5 production prior to World War 2 and afterwards These estimates do not compare well with other records.

After the war the records were kept in various ways; this is as follows:

For the fiscal year 1925/26 to 1946/47, detailed figures by gauge for F.N. and Browning were kept separately.

For the fiscal year 1947/48 to June 30, 1957 figures for both companies are distinct and separate.

From June 30, 1958 to 1972, detailed figures for all gauges were again kept together, but the figures for F.N. And Browning were kept separately.

From 1973 to 1980, total production for all gauges and companies were kept together.

From 1981 to 1983, sales figures are per year only. After this all production figures are confidential.

One more "exception" — even today Browning and F.N. are making exceptions to their serial numbering system. These can be either in Exhibition, Special Order or Commemorative guns.

From 1903 to 1953 all serial numbers were numerical. Fabrique Nationale produced Auto-5's for Browning in this country as well as for other parts of the world.

Since F.N. will not disclose exact dates of manufacture on guns they still sell, what you see in this publication is taken from Browning's sales records and the recollections of Val Browning. This by necessity is an approximation.

In the beginning of this chapter, I noted that about 60,717 Auto-5's were manufactured by F.N. for export to Browning. Out of respect to Val Browning, I will accept his word as to the true figure. His estimate matches the serial numbers listing below. If you want to extrapolate the first 60,717 guns produced between the years 1903 and 1924 go right ahead. I'll stick with him.

12 GAUGE SERIAL NUMBERS

Other than parts assembled of about 3,000 guns by the Germans during World War II, there was no production of the Auto-5 during the war. When production began again by Remington in 1946, the serial numbers ran like this:

1946	229000-237000	1949	270001-285000
1947	237001-249000	1950	285001-315000
1948	249001-270000	1951	315001-346000

You will see Auto-5's made by Remington with serial numbers different than shown above for the years 1946 - 1951. These will be coded for each gauge. There are no records, so this is mostly conjecture and might have run like this with Remington Model 11's mixed in:

1946	B0001-B7500	1949	B22501-B30000
1947	B7501-B15000	1950	B30000-B37500
1948	B15001-B22500	1951	B37501-B45000

Please refer to the Remington section for more information about Remington serial numbers. In 1952 F.N. began producing the Auto-5 again.

| 1952 | 346001-387000 | 1953 | 387001-438000 |

In the following serial numbers the letters "G", "H", "L", "M", and "V" stand for the model.

From 1946 - 1953 both light and standard weight frames were produced. There is no way of telling from the serial number which frame is which, but you can certainly tell from the configuration of the gun. From 1954 - 1955 the serial numbers were as follows:

	Standard weight	Light weight
1954	H1-H39000	L1-L42000
1955	H39001-H83000	L42001-L83000

From 1956 - 1958 the serial numbers ran like this:

	Standard weight	Light weight
1956	H83001-H99000	L83001-L99000
and	M1-M22000	G1-G23000
1957	M22001-M85000	G23001-G85000
1958	M85001-M99000	G85001-G99000

From 1958 until the end of Belgium production, the year of manufacture is designated by either the first or the first and second numeral appearing before the alpha character in the number. Each year the serial numbers began with the number 0001. Serial numbers from 1958 - 1976 are as follows:

	Standard weight	Light weight	Magnum
1958	8M—	8G—	8V—
1959	9M—	9G—	9V—
1960	0M—	0G—	0V—
1961	1M—	1G—	1V—
1962	2M—	2G—	2V—
1963	3M—	3G—	3V—
1964	4M—	4G—	4V—
1965	5M—	5G—	5V—
1966	6M—	6G—	6V—
1967	7M—	7G—	7V—
1968	8M— or 68M	8G—	8V— or 68V
1969	69M—	69G—	69V—

	Standard weight	Light weight	Magnum
1970	Discontinued	70G—	70V—
1971		71G—	71V—
1972		72G—	72V—
1973		73G—	73V—
1974		74G—	74V—
1975		75G—	75V—
1976		76G—	76V—

1968 will have the same code as 1958, but you will be able to tell the year of manufacture by the butt stock: round knob in 1958 and flat knob in 1968. There are also other differences that you will recognize as you become more familiar with the guns themselves.

Several guns were brought in from Europe in the mid 1960's. Their serial numbers look like this:

SAC	5
2090	60

"SAC" stands for the type of gun which is Superlight Chromed, "5" stands for the engraving, "2090" is the actual serial number, and "60" stands for the year of production.

For years produced after 1976, please refer to the General Information section in the front of this book.

THE AUTO-5 16 GAUGE

The Sweet 16 was made throughout post-war Belgium production. However, the Standard 16 was discontinued in 1968. The Sweet 16 was again introduced in 1987 and discontinued in 1990.

The Remington Arms Company produced this model from 1947 - 1951 with the letter "A" or "X" as part of the designation. About 45,000 were produced. F.N. then took up production again until 1976. The letters "S", "R", and "A" stand for the model.

Please note that many guns were shipped to countries that designated their own type serial numbers, a practice which may cause numbers produced not to coincide with serial numbers as listed in the 16 gauge section. Also, good accurate records were not maintained by Browning during the entire production run. Here are how the serial numbers run from 1923 - 1976:

16 GAUGE
SERIAL NUMBERS

	Standard 16	Sweet 16
1947	X1000 - X13700	
1948	X13701 - X22600	
1949	X22601 - X31500	
1950	X31501 - X42500	
1951	X42501 - X58300	
1952	X58301 - X74000	
1953	X74001 - X99000	
and	R0001 - R1400	S0001 - S2500
1954	R1401 - R19400	S2501 - S24000

	Standard 16	Sweet 16
1955	R19401 - R40000	S24001 - S41000
1956	R40001 - R68000	S41001 - S62000
1957	R68001 - R99000	S62001 - S99000
and		A0001 - A1000
1958	T1400 - T1000	A1001 - A10000
and	8R10001 - 8R20000	8S10000 - 8S20000

From 1959 to 1976 each year the serial numbers began with 0001.

1959	9R—	9S—
1960	0R—	0S—
1961	1R—	1S—
1962	2R—	2S—
1963	3R—	3S—
1964	4R—	4S—
1965	5R—	5S—
1966	6R—	6S—
1967	7R—	7S—
1968	8R— or 68R	8S— or 68S
1969	Discontinued	69S—
1970		70S—
1971		71S—
1972		72S—
1973		73S—
1974		74S—
1975		75S—
1976		76S—

1968 will have the same code as 1958, but you will be able to tell the year by the butt stock: round knob in 1958 and flat knob in 1968. There are also other differences that you will recognize as you become familiar with the guns themselves.

For year codes on Japanese made Sweet 16's, refer to the General Information section at the front of this publication.

THE AUTO-5 20 GAUGE

Remington Arms Company produced the first 20 gauges for this country from 1947 - 1951. Serial numbers had a "C" in them. About 20,000 were produced.

The first F.N. produced 20's for this country were made in 1958. The 20 gauge magnum was first introduced in 1967. There are no round knob 20 gauge magnums that I've ever seen. You find one and you indeed have a rare gun. The letters "Z" and "X" in the serial numbers stand for the model. Each year began with serial number 0001.

20 GAUGE
SERIAL NUMBERS

Serial numbers for the years 1946 - 1976 are as follows:

	Remington 20's		
1946	C0001-C3333	1949	C10000-C13333
1947	C3334-C6666	1950	C13334-C16666
1948	C6667-C9999	1951	C16667-C20000

BELGIUM 20 GAUGE SERIAL NUMBERS
*Light 20

1958	8Z—	1965	5Z—	1971	71Z—
1959	9Z—	1966	6Z—	1972	72Z—
1960	0Z—	1967	7Z—	1973	73Z—
1961	1Z—	1968	8Z—	1974	74Z—
1962	2Z—	1969	9Z—	1975	75Z—
1963	3Z—	1969	69Z—	1976	76Z—
1964	4Z—	1970	70Z—		

Magnum 20

1967	7X—	1971	71X—	1974	74X—
1968	8X—	1972	72X—	1975	75X—
1969	69X—	1973	73X—	1976	76X—
1970	70X—				

	Light 12	Mag 12	Sweet 16	Light 20	Mag 20
1975	2101	1501	2201	2301	1601
After 1975	211	151	221	231	161

1968 will have the same code as 1958 but you will be able to tell the year of manufacture by the butt stock: round knob in 1958 and flat knob in 1968. There are also other differences that you will recognize as you become more familiar with the guns themselves. Round knob 20's are hard to find (in mint condition).

For serial year codes after 1976 please refer to the General Information section in the front of this book.

The product codes for the Auto-5's are as follows:

*You will find Light 20's sometimes with a "X" in the serial number. See the Light 20 table to find the year of production.

The Browning Double Automatic has many features which contribute to better shooting. It is entirely new in operating principle and design; and incorporates into one gun the superior characteristics of the 12 gauge shotgun with those most desirable in smaller gauge bores.

The Double Automatic also meets the needs of the large number of sportsmen who, in view of present day bag limits, believe that two shots are enough. In design careful thought was given to the requirements of today's gunners. It possesses unparalleled soft cushioned recoil — with balance and handling qualities comparable to those of the finest two-barrel shotguns. Thus the Double Automatic, while conserving most of the advantages of the more costly double gun, combines them with the advantages and inherent economy of an automatic to give a fine two-shot gun for a price within the reach of the average sportsman.

The Browning Double Automatic is made only in 12 gauge because its advanced principles of operation permit such a remarkable reduction in the weight of the parts that it is not necessary to reduce the barrel bore to attain the weight and balance of the smaller gauges. The lighter 12 gauge loads (1 ounce or $1\frac{1}{8}$ ounces of shot) give the same number of pellets, the same range, and the same killing power as 20 and 16 gauge loads. The kick on the shoulder isn't any greater either, being directly proportional to the weight of the shot going forward and the weight of the gun. Thus since all the desired qualities of the smaller gauges can be reproduced in the Double Automatic in 12 gauge, why have anything but a 12 gauge — especially since these characteristics are attained in 12 gauge with a comparatively shorter shot string, meaning the pellets are less strung out along their trajectory. In addition, the capacity to shoot the heavier 12 gauge loads is retained.

Accordingly, the Double Automatic is offered in three distinctive 12 gauge models permitting a choice of a 12 gauge weight, or one with the weight and feel of either a 16 or 20 gauge.

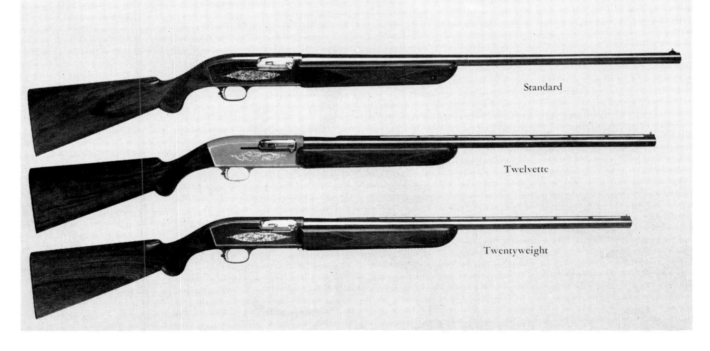

This page featuring the Double Automatic is from a 1958 Browning catalog.

THE DOUBLE AUTOMATIC

GENERAL INFORMATION

This model was originally designed by Val A. Browning, John M. Browning's son, as a response to a request by F.N. for a lightweight version of the Auto-5 for the European market. Many European sportsmen thought the Auto-5 an unsporting shotgun because of its magazine capacity; therefore, this gun was designed to fire only two shots.

Although sold in Europe from 1952, they were not sent in great numbers to the U.S. until 1954. The Double Auto was made in 12 gauge only and discontinued in 1971.

Not many of these were produced, since the American public just didn't go for the two shot limit when game laws allowed three shots for both upland and waterfowl shooting. It is a very enjoyable gun to shoot and I have always liked it. The two shot feature probably just saves you money on the typical dove field. If you used this shotgun for what it was intended, you would appreciate its reliability and good looks, it's very reliable and a great skeet gun.

The main selling point for this model was the weight and handling versus a regular 12 gauge shotgun. Browning advertised that it could shoot and load just as quickly as a three shot gun without having to take the gun down from your shoulder for reloading, this was true.

This was the reason the speed load feature was put into the Auto-5: Browning shooters demanded it when they saw how great it was in this model. Since weights are so important to the Double Auto, we will list them here: The Standard Model guns weighed about 7 1/2 lbs, the Twelvette weighed about 6 3/4 to 7 lbs, and the Twentyweight was six lbs.

MODELS

As first made in 1954, the three models were the Standard, the Twelvette and the Twentyweight.

Each model could be ordered in certain configurations, which will be detailed below.

The Standard model was introduced in 1954 and discontinued in 1959. All had blue steel receivers. They were advertised as the gun to buy for those who shoot 2 3/4" magnum loads or trap and skeet because the extra weight of about 3/4 to 1 lb helped to reduce the recoil.

This model was available in the Hunting, Skeet or Trap variations. The Hunting variation is described here, but the Skeet and Trap variations will be discussed in their sections.

All Standard receivers were scroll engraved similar to the Auto-5 shotguns. The edges of the receivers were outlined with a zig-zag pattern enclosing a wedge of engraving about 4" long on the left side. On the right side there is also a wedge of engraving about as long and continuing below the ejection port to the front of the receiver. The trigger guards are also engraved slightly. All in all, this was tastefully done and brought the gun above the ordinary for a standard grade shotgun. Standard models were not marked; the only way to tell is the fact that they are all steel.

As originally made only 26", 28", and 30" barrels were available. All three lengths could be ordered with ventilated or recessed ribs. Plain matted or plain unmatted barrels were also available. There were also some shipped with solid rib barrels, but they are hard to find and are probably special order. Buck Special barrels were offered from 1962 to 1965, but were available from existing stock afterwoods.

The 26" barrels were available in cylinder, improved cylinder, skeet, and modified. The 28" barrels were available in skeet, modified, or full, and the 30" barrels in full choke only, whether a hunting or trap barrel.

Barrels, stocks, triggers, safeties, etc. will be discussed in their sections.

TWELVETTE

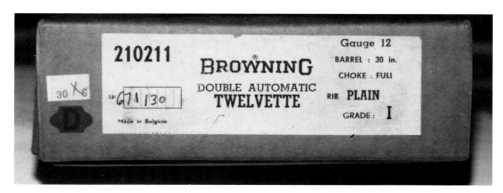

A box label from a 1967 Twlevette. These are hard to find. Guns in their original boxes are a real collectors item.

The Twelvette was introduced in 1954 along with the other two models. Unlike the Standard, this model had its name engraved in script on the left side of the loading port; this, however, was not true on the early guns. On them, there were no markings at all on the receivers. The makeup of the receiver will be covered in its section along with stocks, barrel ribs, safeties, etc.

The engraving is very similar to the Standard model. The edges of the receivers were outlined with a zig-zag pattern enclosing a wedge of engraving about 4" long on the left side. On the right side there is also a wedge of engraving about as long, and continuing below the loading port to the front of the receiver. The trigger guards are also engraved very similar to the Auto-5 trigger guards. Almost, not all engraving is gold filled, some guns were not.

The variations available for the Twelvette grade were the hunting, skeet, and trap guns. The trap and skeet guns will be covered in their sections.

This Twentyweight clearly shows the unusual safety featured on all Double Autos.

From the beginning of production, the Hunting variation could be ordered with plain unmatted, plain matted, or with a ventilated rib are in 26", 28", or 30" barrel lengths.

The 26" barrels were available in cylinder, improved cylinder, skeet, and modified. The 28" barrels were available in skeet, modified, or full; and the 30" barrels in full choke only whether for a hunting or trap barrel.

The variations in stocks, barrel ribs, satefies, etc. will be discussed in their sections.

TWENTYWEIGHT

The Twentyweight was introduced in 1954. The name "TWENTYWEIGHT" is engraved in script on the left side of the receiver on the later guns. On the early guns, there will be no marking on the receiver at all.

The engraving is very similar to the Standard model. The edges of the receivers were outlined with a zig-zag pattern enclosing a wedge of engraving about 4" long on the left side. On the right side there is also a wedge of engraving about half as long but continuing above the loading port to the front of the receiver. The trigger guards are also engraved very similar to the Auto-5 trigger guards. Most, not all guns have gold filled engraving.

The variations available for the Twentyweight were the hunting and skeet guns. The skeet guns will be covered in their sections.

From the beginning of production, the Hunting variation could be ordered with 26 1/2" plain matted or ventilated rib barrels only. These were available in cylinder, improved cylinder, skeet, modified, and full chokes.

RECEIVERS AND COLORS

The speed load feature was a necessary selling point with the Double Automatics two shot limit.

When first introduced, the actions could be bought in either blued steel or the greyed variations of hiduminium, an aluminum alloy intended for the aircraft business which was quite strong. I have never had a receiver crack or give trouble in any way but there are some that have. Twelvette and Twentyweight receivers were made using hiduminium, and the Standard model was always steel.

The hiduminium receivers for the Twelvette came in many colors. After 1956 the colors made were Satin Gray, Jet or Dragon Black, Forest Green, and Autumn Brown.

A few additional colors were made for the Twelvette: Maroon Red, Royal and Light Blue, Light Brown, several shades of Green, and Gold. The last colors listed were samples ordered by Val Browning which were turned down by the Browning staff and ended up being sold to dealers as a close out. They are very rare with probably less then 6 of each made. All colors were discontinued in 1959 to 1960, except the Dragon Black with Gold.

The Twentyweight only came in Jet Black with Gold and brown.

Please call if you find a Twentyweight in Twelvette colors, for I am sure if someone wanted it, Browning would make it. In fact, I wouldn't have any doubt about samples being made in more colors than listed above, but as of this date these are all the ones that have been found. The regular filler for the engraving on these guns was always gold. If you remove this gold foil you will see the original aluminum color beneath; therefore, if it has flaked off, you will have what appears to be a gun with silver in the engraving.

Many times these were displayed in store windows. The results were not good, for the side facing the sun would become discolored. This in no way harms the shootability of the gun, only the overall appearance.

The Standard steel receiver was discontinued in 1959 to 1960. It was the only steel receiver model made for the Double Automatic. This gun was originally intended to be made in hiduminium only, but it was changed for the American market. The thinking was that it would be more acceptable here if the receivers were steel. This just wasn't true, and it was dropped more then ten years prior to the other models.

BARRELS

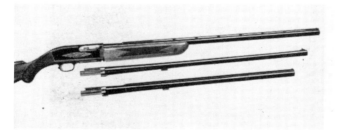

Barrels are interchangeable on the Double Auto. (Some early guns cannot accept barrels without fitting.)

The Double Auto was only chambered for the 2 3/4" shells. Magnum loads could be fired, but this was recommended for the Standard guns only since the others were too light for most people to stand the recoil. Browning recommended that guns be returned to them for fitting of additional barrels but many barrels were purchased and changed by owners. If numbers do not match the serial numbers, don't be dismayed; just make sure the barrel is correct for the model.

BARREL MARKINGS

From 1952 through 1958 they are marked as follows:

On the left side of the barrel,
BROWNING ARMS COMPANY ST. LOUIS, MO
(Choke code) **SPECIAL STEEL-12 GA SHELLS**-2 3/4"
(See proof mark numbers four and seven on page 50.)

On the right side of the barrel,
BROWNING PATENTS
MADE IN BELGIUM

On barrel extension you will find various inspectors marks and proof marks 7 and 5. *(See page 50.)*

From 1959 through 1968 they are marked as follows:

On the left side of barrel,
BROWNING ARMS COMPANY ST LOUIS MO
& MONTREAL P.Q.
MADE IN BELGIUM

On the right side are the words,
(Choke Code) **SPECIAL STEEL-12 GA SHELLS**-2 3/4"
BROWNING PATENTS

About 1962 to 1963 the **MADE IN BELGIUM** moved from the right to the left side under the main address line.

From about 1969 to the end of production they are marked as follows:

On the left side of barrel are the words,
BROWNING ARMS COMPANY MORGAN UTAH
& MONTREAL, P.Q.
MADE IN BELGIUM

On the right side of barrel you will find
(Choke code)-**SPECIAL STEEL-12 GA SHELLS**-2 3/4"
BROWNINGS PATENT

There are no barrel extension marks on the late barrels.

All Double Auto choke markings were codes as follows:

       *** Cylinder
       **$ skeet
       **-improved cylinder
       ** modified
       *- improved modified
       * full

Buck Special barrels are known and are very rare, for they were only offered for four years as noted in the Standard model section. They were 24" long and were designed for shooting either slugs or buckshot loads. They had open sights; the rear was adjustable for both windage and elevation, and the front was a gold bead on a ramp. They are desirable collectors' items for Double Automatic fans.

Skeet model — with compensator

From an early catalog, Browning offers the Skeet Model with the Cutts Compensator.

Original Polychoke, automatic choke, and Cutts Compensator barrels are rare as well. You can tell if Browning or F.N. installed the polychoke, for there will be a 9 or 11 stamped on the adaptor ring of the choking device. The Cutt Compensator barrels will have an Allen screw instead of a slotted screw to retain it. You will note that the improved modified barrel marking is not included in the 1964 catalog, there are many in circulation. More about this on page 176.

There were almost as many barrel variations available for this gun as the Auto-5. When first introduced these were the recessed rib, plain matted plain unmatted, and ventilated rib barrels.

The recessed ribs weren't made as long as the others and were discontinued sometime in 1959. They were always available for replacement and still are even as I write this. The only way you'll get one from Browning, however, is to send in your old one. It would be nice to exchange an old worn out plain barrel for one of these, wouldn't it?

You can readily recognize these for, they had a deep groove milled down the center of the rib to lighten it. Browning liked to advertise this groove as an aid for better shooting; they said the eye could follow the channel to the target. Another feature they noted was that this rib was good for beginning shooters since it was supposed to force your eye down the channel. The "Recessed Rib" was available for the Standard and Twelvette models only.

Plain unmatted barrels were discontinued sometime around 1959 to 1960, but plain matted and the 1/4" ventilated matted ribs were made from the beginning to the end of production in 1971.

The sights were all gold bead, but ivory and center beads could be ordered.

Something that might interest you and clear up a misnomer by some people: Browning never sold any

barrels for this model other than steel. During the development of the gun a few alloy barrels were made and even anodized the same color as the receiver; there is a green one in the Browning Museum in Ogden. During development stages it was found that to safely make the barrels, they would have to be of a larger diameter, and this detracted from the overall look of the gun. Browning said they never sold any of these to the public.

STOCKS AND BUTT PLATES

All stocks were French walnut of about group 1-2 grade. Almost all were round knob; there were some flat knob or full pistol grip guns made towards the end of production.

The checkering was all 20 lines per inch unless special ordered, but this would be very rare indeed.

Lacquer finish was used on all guns until the mid 60's when the polyurethane finish was introduced. You will notice these early Double Autos have developed a very appealing patina that the later ones will never have.

Dimensions for the hunting and skeet guns were length of pull 14 1/4", drop at comb 1 5/8", and drop at heel 2 1/2".

The forearms were changed very little. On the early guns they were more slender then the later ones which were rounder. All were hand checkered 20 lines per inch and had metal rivet heads exposed at the rear.

All guns were shipped with either horn or plastic butt plates unless special ordered with a recoil pad. Horn was used in the beginning of production, and plastic later.

Double Automatic Specifications

Twentyweight

(12 gauge but lighter than most 20 gauge shotguns)

Model	Barrel Length	Approximate Weight	Barrel or Rib	Chokes
Hunting or Skeet	26½"	6 lbs. 6 lbs. 1 oz.	Plain Matted Barrel } Ventilated }	Full, Modified, Imp. Cylinder, Skeet, Cylinder

Twelvette

(12 gauge but lighter than most 16 gauge shotguns)

Trap	30"	7 lbs. 2 oz.	Ventilated	Full
Hunting	30"	7 lbs. 7 lbs. 4 oz. 7 lbs. 2 oz.	Plain Barrel } Recess Rib } Ventilated }	Full
Hunting or Skeet	28"	6 lbs. 14 oz. 7 lbs. 2 oz. 7 lbs.	Plain Barrel } Recess Rib } Ventilated }	Full Modified Skeet
Hunting or Skeet	26"	6 lbs. 12 oz. 7 lbs. 6 lbs. 14 oz.	Plain Barrel } Recess Rib } Ventilated }	Modified, Imp. Cylinder, Skeet, Cylinder

Standard

(12 gauge but lighter than most 12 gauge shotguns)

Trap	30"	7 lbs. 12 oz.	Ventilated	Full
Hunting	30"	7 lbs. 10 oz. 7 lbs. 14 oz. 7 lbs. 12 oz.	Plain Barrel } Recess Rib } Ventilated }	Full
Hunting or Skeet	28"	7 lbs. 8 oz. 7 lbs. 12 oz. 7 lbs. 10 oz.	Plain Barrel } Recess Rib } Ventilated }	Full Modified Skeet
Hunting or Skeet	26"	7 lbs. 6 oz. 7 lbs. 10 oz. 7 lbs. 8 oz.	Plain Barrel } Recess Rib } Ventilated }	Modified, Imp. Cylinder, Skeet, Cylinder

CHAMBERING — For all 2¾ inch factory loads including 2¾ inch Magnum.

STOCK AND FOREARM — Select French walnut. Finely hand-checkered. Stock, full pistol grip. Forearm, gracefully slender with sufficient length and grip for every shooter.

RECEIVERS — All models delicately hand-engraved on both sides of receiver and trigger guard.

Standard Model — Blued Steel.

Twelvette Model — Special lightweight alloy in a choice of four durable colors:

Velvet Gray and Silver
Dragon Black and Gold
Forest Green and Silver
Autumn Brown and Silver

Twentyweight — Special lightweight alloy, Jet Black and Gold.

TRIGGER — Crisp as a double gun — positive — gold plated on Twelvette and Twentyweight models. Doubling impossible.

SAFETY — New and convenient principle equally convenient for right or left hand and absolutely positive.

SIGHT — Medium bead raised for quick orientation.

RIB — Choice of:
New recess rib with recessed sighting line, sturdy and light weight, and black in any kind of light.

New ventilated — a low silhouette six post rib, ¼ inch wide.

A variety of features for barrels, receiver colors, and ribs were available, as shown in the 1964 catalog.

Pads could be ordered on any model. You could get a Pachmayr "White Line" or other contemporary pad made by any manufacturer installed by Browning at their St. Louis service department and later in Ogden, Utah. If a pad was ordered on an original gun, it was first produced by F.N. with a butt plate and sent to the U.S. where it was then fitted with whatever pad the customer ordered.

Browning marked Pachmayr manufactured pads where first available in 1958 and were used unless another make was specified in the order. I would indeed be skeptical about any guns I saw with a pad, even those with "Browning" marked pads, for they were rarely ordered.

TRAP GUNS

Trap guns could be ordered in the Standard model until discontinued or in the Twelvette until the end of production.

The only barrels available were 30" full with a ventilated rib or earlier with a recessed rib. There were also some recessed rib barrels made with an extra wide groove; these were either special order or a sample, they are rare.

The stocks were all round knob with 20 lines to the inch checkering. The basic dimensions were length of pull 14 3/8", drop at comb 1 3/8", and drop at heel 1 3/4". All were shipped with horn or black plastic butt plates or could be ordered with rubber pads, this is described above.

All other features of the regular guns are the same for the Trap variation.

SKEET GUNS

The Skeet variation could be ordered in all three models. When these were made, choking devices were very popular for shooting skeet, and Browning heavily advertised them for sale. You could order any length barrel with these devices, so nothing is standard. When someone ordered a barrel with one of the choking devices, Browning gunsmiths would pick out any barrel that could be cut to the length specified on the work order. These barrels, therefore, can have any choke marking from *** to *.

The original skeet choked barrels for the Standard model came in 26" and 28". They could be ordered with a ventilated or recessed rib and in plain matted or unmatted configuration.

The Twentyweight version came in 26 1/2" length and were either plain matted or ventilated rib.

The Twelvette came in 26" and 28". They could be ordered with a ventilated or recessed rib and in plain matted or unmatted configuration.

The stocks were all round knob with 20 lines to the inch checkering. The dimensions were length of pull 14 1/4", drop at comb 1 5/8", and drop at heel 2 1/2". All were shipped with horn or black plastic butt plates or could be special ordered with a rubber recoil pad as is explained in the butt plate section.

The skeet guns were the same as the standard production guns in all other features.

TRIGGERS

All triggers were gold plated on the Twentyweight and Twelvette models and blued on the Standard. They remained constant through out production. There were no special order trigger configurations.

SAFETIES

NEW CONVENIENT SAFER SAFETY — For Left or Right-Hand Shooters Equally — The new safer safety has been placed on the rear of the trigger guard where the second finger of either hand can quickly control its function; thus for a quick shot, the safety may be flipped "off safe" with the trigger finger in firing position.

In this ingenious new trigger mechanism, putting the gun "on safe" is equivalent positively to locking the hammer of the gun. It is a safer safety.

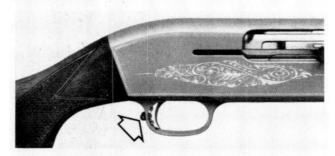

As an additional safeguard, other mechanical features prevent the gun from firing, unless the action is completely closed, and positively prevent doubling.

Browning advertised the Double Automatic safeties as convenient for both left and right handed shooters.

These had a very unique safety for it was mounted on the back of the trigger guard. They slide up and down — up to fire and down for safe. Browning advertised these as convenient for both left and right handed shooters, and they were. There were some made with cross bolt safeties, but these are very rare.

NUMBERS PRODUCED

After 19 years only a total of 67,487 were produced, hardly what you would call a big success. People in the U.S. just didn't like the two shot feature, for they felt it was a handicap, Browning should have made this model to handle three shots and they would have had a proven automatic.

PRICES

These prices are for the Twelvette with ventilated rib; the Twentyweight was only a few dollars more.

Year	Price	Year	Price
1962	$169.00	1965	$194.75
1963	$169.00	1969	$244.50
1964	$184.00		

SERIAL NUMBERS

Browning estimates that 3,600 guns per year were made from 1952 to 1959, this is the data in the serial number book. After it's printing, I received information which sheds new light on the actual truth. The following is the result of research done by dedicated Browning collectors, I believe this is pretty close, for in the research I spoke to many people that had these, and the barrel addresses coincided with the years I am showing. If these numbers are off any at all, it is probably by not over one year. Remember, the "A" for the hiduminium receiver or "C" for the steel receiver will appear as part of the serial number.

	"A" or "C"		"A" or "C"
1952	0001-3600	1956	14401-18000
1953	3601-7200	1957	18001-21600
1954	7201-10800	1958	21601-25200
1955	10801-14400	1959	25201-28800

After 1959 we can pinpoint the actual year of manufacture, because of the beginning of Browning's code system incorporated in the serial numbers. From 1960 through 1971, each year began with serial number 0001.

The model code for guns with a hiduminium receiver is "A" and guns with a steel receiver is "C"; these can be found directly above the serial number which is located under the forearm latch. The serial numbers ran as follows:

HIDUMINIUM RECEIVERS		STEEL RECEIVERS	
1960	A--	1960	C--
1961	1A--	1961	1C--
1962	2A--	1962	2C--
1963	3A--	1963	3C--
1964	4A--	1964	4C--
1965	5A--	1965	5C--
1966	6A--	1966	6C--
1967	7A--	1967	7C--
1968	8A--	1968	8C--
1969	69A--	1969	69C--
1970	70A--	1970	70C--
1971	71A--	1971	71C--

Homer Tyler says that he has seen only one Double Automatic without a code letter missing, serial number 1039 which should have been preceeded by an "A". I have not seen one with a "68" in the serial numbers but there probably are several around.

B-2000

GENERAL INFORMATION

Although shipments began in 1974, the official introduction of the B-2000 was 1974 for the 12 gauge and 1975 for the 20. The B-2000 was the first attempt by Browning to make a gas operated automatic shotgun; the only other automatics made were the Double Auto and the Auto-5. Things didn't work out well.

This model didn't sell well, probably because of manufacturing and minor design problems which should have been ironed out before release to the public. Needless to say that gun folks are like a bunch of hens; when one has a problem with a gun they all hear about it. By the time the engineers solved the problems, the gun had such a bad reputation, people shied away from it. It is a shame that this innovative gas operated gun didn't work out, for it was a true Browning original.

Browning extensively advertised that it could shoot either a 2 3/4" light load or a 3" magnum if you changed the barrels. This was only true on the field gun. Shooting different loads does not apply to the Trap model.

The B-2000's parts were manufacturing in Belgium and the finishing and assembly was done in Portugal where most of the expense of manufacturing was located. Although this shotgun was discontinued in 1979, parts assembly continued until 1983, and many were sold up to that time.

MODELS

There were only four models made for the B-2000 starting with its introduction. The features of the Hunting model are discussed in the text and the variations for the others are discussed in their sections.

SKEET

The Skeet model was introduced in 1974 and made throughout production. All features and introduction of gauges were the same as the Hunting model except for the stock and barrels.

The butt stock's dimensions were length of pull 14", drop at comb 1 1/2" and drop at heel 2 1/2"; they were all finished in a high gloss and supplied with the Browning marked ventilated recoil pad; the forearms were all beavertail.

The barrels were all 26" long and had ventilated ribs with skeet chokes. All had center beads and the front sights were ivory and all were chambered 2¾".

TRAP

The Trap model was introduced in 1974 and made throughout production. All features and gauge introductions were the same as the Hunting model except for the stock and barrels.

The butt stock's dimensions were length of pull 14 3/8", drop at comb 1 3/8" and drop at heel 2 1/8". They were all finished in a high gloss and supplied with the Browning marked ventilated recoil pad.

The barrels were either 30" or 32" long and had ventilated ribs with either full, improved modified, or modified chokes. The 12 gauge only had the high post floating rib, which was higher then the normal one found on other models; also, they were not soldered to the post and would stretch or contract with different temperatures and not warp. All had center beads and the front sights were ivory and all were chambered 2¾".

BUCK SPECIAL

The Buck Special was offered starting in 1976 and continuing until the end of production. It was the same as the Hunting model except for the following:

The 12 gauge had either 2 3/4" or 3" chambers, and the 20 had only 2 3/4"; all barrels were 24" long. The rear sight was fully adjustable for windage and elevation, and the front sight was a ramp front with gold bead.

All other features of this were the same as the Hunting model.

FRAMES

Basically, there were two frames made, the 12 and the 20 gauges. They were both 100% steel and were alike except that the 20 was proportionately smaller.

All were lightly scroll engraved similar to the Double Automatic. On the right side there is a wedge of engraving about 4" long in an oval shape, but each end comes to a point. On the left side there is about 2" of engraving located behind the loading port and a little wedge ahead of it. The trigger guard is also slightly engraved. On the left bottom side of the frame the words "BROWNING 2000" are impressed. All receivers were lustre polish, as Browning likes to call it, and blued.

One of the main features of the B-2000 is the quick loading port that allowed a shooter to load the chamber by just inserting the shell into the side of the receiver. The mechanism would automatically cycle, and you were ready to load another into the magazine. They were set up to load only one shell in the magazine, and one would be exposed through the loading port.

You could also unload by lifting out the exposed shell and then pressing the cartridge stop to unload the magazine. You then unloaded the chamber. This made for a safe and simple way to unload the gun.

BARRELS

When introduced in 1974, they came with either plain or ventilated rib barrels; the plain 12 gauge barrel was discontinued in 1978. Although 2¾" and

3'' barrels could be used on the same receiver, you could not shoot 2 3/4'' loads in the 3'' chambered barrels.

As introduced, the barrels available were 26'', 28'', or 30'' for 2 3/4'' loads with a choice of cylinder, improved cylnder, modified or full chokes. The 28'', 30'' or 32'' barrels for the 3'' magnum shells were available in full or modified chokes only. All barrels including the plain had matted surfaces and German nickel silver sights. The skeet, trap and Buck Special barrels will be discussed under those models.

Only ventilated rib barrels were made for the 20 gauge. In the 26'' barrel length with 2 3/4'' chambers, you could get cylinder, improved cylinder, modified and full chokes. In the 2 3/4'' chamber length for the 28'' barrels, you could get only full or modified. There were 3'' barrels as well. For the 26'' barrel length improved cylinder, modified and full was available. In the 28'' barrel length only full and modified were available. The skeet and Buck Special barrels for the 20 gauge will be discussed under those models.

In 1976 the whole barrel make up was changed where you could get only certain chokes for certain barrel lengths in the different chamber lengths.

For the 12 gauge with 2 3/4'' chambers the 26'' barrels did not change. The 28'' was available with full and modified chokes and the 30'' only with the full choke. The 3'' magnum 28'' barrels remained the same, but the 32'' could only be bought in full; the 20 gauge barrels did not change.

The barrel marking were as follows on the left side:

BROWNING ARMS COMPANY MORGAN, UTAH & MONTREAL P.Q. MADE IN BELGIUM

On the right side were the words:
SPECIAL STEEL (Gauge)GA SHELLS 2 3/4'' (OR 3'')(Choke)

The usual proof markings are also present.
The later guns were marked on the left side of barrel:

BROWNING ARMS COMPANY MORGAN UTAH & MONTREAL P.Q. ASSEMBLED IN PORTUGAL

On the right side were the words:
SPECIAL STEEL
(Gauge)GA SHELLS 2 3/4''(OR 3'')(Choke)

STOCKS

All stocks were French walnut of about group 1-2 grade with a high gloss finish, full pistol grip, and full forearm. The Dimensions for the Hunting model were length of pull 14 1/4'', drop at comb 1 5/8'' and drop at heel 2 1/2''; all models had the Browning marked black plastic butt plates except the skeet and trap guns.

PRICES/SALES/MODEL CODES

The prices given are for the 12 gauge ventilated rib model. In 1974 the retail price was $299.50; in 1975, $369.50; in 1976, $374.95; in 1978, $369.95. When discontinued in 1979, the retail price was $479.00.

Total sales in this country were 95,000 in 12 gauge and 20,000 in 20 gauge. There were also some additional sales in Canada amounting to 12,000 guns.

Here are serial numbers from 1973 - 1976: The letters ''D'' and ''C'' stand for the gauge. Each year began with 0001.

YEAR	20 GAUGE	12 GAUGE
1973	not made	—C37
1974	not made	—C47
1975	—D57	—C57
1976	—D67	—C67

For year codes after 1976, refer to the General Information section in the front of the book.

The following are the product codes for each model:

631 - Standard 20	611 - Standard 12
661 - Magnum 20	651 - Magnum 12

A standard 20 gauge made in 1977 would look like this: 631RR—.

B-80
GENERAL INFORMATION

In 1981, after the problems with the B-2000, Browning introduced the Italian-designed and partly made B-80, a much superior shotgun to the B-2000 that was discontinued in 1989 in lieu of the A-500. The B-80 is actually a Beretta A303 and was partly made by Browning when they were selling this model. If you will notice, the barrels say ''Assembled in Portugal,'' and on the other side, the word ''Italy'' is stamped. This was done because Beretta was making the barrels and some parts, while F.N. was making other parts and finishing them in Portugal. According to Browning, the location that has increased the value of the product the most is the location in which the product is noted as being made.

About this time, the public wanted gas-operated guns, and Browning didn't have anything on the market that could perform like the Remington 1100 and other semi autos that could handle a variety of shells. They were losing sales and the Beretta design was a quality shotgun that was readily available.

This versatile little shotgun could handle 2 3/4'' light loads or 3'' magnums by only changing the barrel, The Remington 1100 couldn't do that, so the Browning was an instant hit with those that wanted to spend a few extra bucks for Browning quality finish and fit.

Let me emphasize that a gun fitted with a 3'' barrel would not handle 2 3/4'' shells safely. You had to have both barrels to shoot each type shell. The 2 3/4'' barrel, however, will handle 2 3/4'' magnums.

The B-80 was originally introduced in 12 and 20 gauge only. The Standard (later the Hunting), the Magnum, and Buck Special models were available at the time of introduction.

SUPERLIGHT

When introduced in 1982, the Superlight model came in 12 gauge only and had a new alloy frame. The weight was 6 lbs, 8 oz., and they were all blued with no engraving. This variation was discontinued in 1984.

Barrels were all 2 3/4'' and came in the following lengths: 26'' choked improved cylinder and skeet, 28'' full and modified, or 30'' in full only.

The stocks, ribs and all other features of the Hunting model are the same for the short lived Superlight.

UPLAND SPECIAL

In 1986, the alloy frame Upland Special in 12 and 20 gauges came along to replace the Superlight. It was truly an upland gun. It featured a straight stock and 2 3/4'' Invector choked barrels in 22'' length only.

Stock dimensions are a bit different. They were length of pull 14 1/4'', drop at comb 1 1/2'', and drop at heel 2 1/2''. It only weighs 5 lbs 7 oz and will shoot 2 3/4'' loads.

In 1988, the B-80 Plus Upland Special was introduced, which was the same gun as the regular model except you got 3'' chambers.

The forearms, butt plates, ribs and all other features of the Hunting model are the same for the Upland Special.

HUNTING FRAMES AND ACTION

When first introduced, this frame had no other name other than B-80, but when the Superlight was introduced, it was given the name ''Hunting'' to differentiate it from the others. This essentially was an all steel* gas operated shotgun with some interesting innovations. As Browning advertised it, the gas system had 10 seals that fed the gas to the operating system and spread the recoil out over a longer period of time. In addition, any excess gas not needed for the operation of the action was vented through a valve through the forearm. This effectively reduced the recoil from a shove to a gentler push.

The parts of the action and operating system that come in contact with the gases were all stainless steel, and the receivers were all blued with no engraving. The triggers were gold plated.

*In 1984 the Superlight and in 1985 the Hunting receivers were offered in alloy only. This continued until 1988 when the B-80 Plus was introduced with an all-steel receiver, again for the Hunting model only.

BARRELS

All barrels were interchangeable within the same gauge. You could shoot 2 3/4'' standard or magnum loads in a 2 3/4'' chambered barrel. The receiver, however, would accept a 3'' chambered barrel, and would handle these loads as well as the lighter and shorter loads.

Barrel markings were as follows on the left side:

BROWNING ARMS COMPANY
MORGAN, UTAH & MONTREAL P.Q.
MADE IN PORTUGAL BY F.N. HERSTAL

On the right side of the barrel you will find
SPECIAL STEEL (12 or 20) **GA SHELLS**
2 3/4'' or 3'' (Choke marking)
PATENT PB ITALY-3420140.

On the Invector guns is the word ''INVECTOR'' instead of the choke marking.

The ''PB'' is enclosed in double circles (Pietro Baretta).

The barrels that were available when it was introduced were the 3'' chambered 12 gauge in 30'' or 32'' choked full only, 28'' choked full or modified. The 2 3/4'' barrels were 30'' choked full only, 28'' choked full or modified, 26'' choked improved cylinder, cylinder, or skeet. The 3'' or 2 3/4'' Buck Special barrel 22'' long was also made.

The 20 gauge was as follows for 3'' chambers: 28'' barrels choked full or modified, 26'' choked full, modified, improved cylinder, or cylinder. The Buck Special barrels came in 3'' or 2 3/4'' chambers; they were 22'' long only.

In 1982, the 2 3/4'' 26'' cylinder bore was cancelled in both gauges, so these are rare. In 1984, the barrels could be ordered with either the Invector System or fixed chokes, but in 1985 and thereafter only the Invector system could be ordered. One more thing: In 1988 only 3'' chambered barrels were offered.

All barrels had chrome plated bores and ventilated ribs except for the Buck Special. This barrel had a rear sight adjustable for windage and elevation. The front sight was on a ramp and had a gold bead. The Buck Special barrel continued as a non-Invector barrel until the end of production.

STOCKS

The French walnut, full pistol grip stocks were group 2 grade, high gloss finished, and fitted with a black Browning marked solid recoil pad. The checkering was 18 lines per inch, and stock dimensions were length of pull 14 1/4", drop at comb 1 5/8", and drop at heel 2 1/2".

SERIAL NUMBERS AND MODEL CODES

For year codes please refer to the General Information section in the front of the book.

The model codes are 411 and 421 for the 12 gauges, and 431 and 471 for the 20's.

The A-500R is the latest in recoil operated firearms technology. As you can see from this photo, some were built with the full pistol grip stock as well as the semi-pistol grip with the round knob feature.

A-500R

In 1987 Browning brought out the Belgium made A-500R semi-auto in 12 gauge only. Since 1988, however, they have been made in Belgium and assembled and finished in Portugal as have so many other Browning models.

This shows Browning's leadership in the gun industry by coming out with a versatile gun to handle all shells. There has been only one grade made for the A500R or G.

FRAMES

This shotgun is really unique for a Browning in that it has the short recoil operating system employing a four lug bolt design. This means that the barrel travels about 1/2" to the rear. At that point, the barrel stops and the bolt begins its rear wood movement and rotates unlocking its four lugs and ejecting the spent shell. Browning claims that this system enables the shooter to use any and all shells from one ounce light loads to heavy 3" magnums one after the other and all will work perfectly.

Frame marking are located on the left and right side along the bottom

500R---------------------------------------BROWNING

OTHER FEATURES

These guns also have the convenient magazine cut off like the Auto-5, enabling the shooter to use a different type of shell without emptying the magazine. The safety is cross bolt either right or left handed. The capacity is four 2 3/4" or three 3" shells, and all triggers are gold colored.

BARRELS

Only matted ventilated rib barrels with Invector chokes have been available. Three are provided with each gun. In addition, all are made with a gold bead front sight.

Barrel lengths are 26", 28" or 30". In 1991 a 24" Buck Special barrel became available with adjustable rear and ramp front sights. You can special order improved modified, skeet or cylinder bore chokes if you desire. Browning has advised its customers that steel shot of all kinds can be used.

On the barrels on the left side are the words:

BROWNING ARMS COMPANY
MORGAN, UTAH MONTREAL P.Q.
MADE IN BELGIUM
ASSEMBLED IN PORTUGAL

Guns made prior to 1988 are marked "**MADE IN BELGIUM**"

On the right side of the barrel is written
SPECIAL STEEL(Gauge) **GA SHELLS**
2 3/4" AND 3" INVECTOR

There is also a logo on the trigger guard. Serial numbers are on the front of the receiver and on the barrels under the forearm. There are also several proof marks.

STOCKS

Specifications are length of pull 14 1/4", drop at comb 1 1/2", and drop at heel 2 1/2". All have ventilated rubber recoil pads marked "BROWNING" as standard as well as semi-pistol grip stocks. The wood used is about group 2 grade walnut finished in Browning's high gloss finish. Checkering is 18 lines per inch.

SERIAL NUMBERS

For dates of manufacture please refer to the General Information section in the front of this book.

Warning

Browning has recalled some of the A-500R's because of parts breakage in the trigger assembly. Only guns without the letter "H" stamped on the trigger assembly are faulty. If you have an A-500 without this letter "H" stamping, call Browning at 800-322-4626 for repairs. Missouri resident can call 314-287-6800 collect.

The A-500G will handle all types of loads under difficult shooting conditions. This one features the round knob stock.

THE A-500G

Introduced in 1990, the A-500G has always been made in Belgium and assembled and finished in Portugal. They have been made in 12 gauge only. These are part of the gun industry coming out with a versatile gun to handle all shells; several other manufacturers are also making this type shotgun.

MODELS — SPORTING CLAYS

Two models have been made for this model — the Hunting and the Sporting Clays.

The Hunting model is described throughout this section, all features pertaining to it also pertain to the Sporting Clays except the following.

The finish is a phosphatation process plus a semi-gloss varnish that results in a little flatter finish than the regular high gloss polish of the Hunting model. The receivers are marked on the side of the frame "Sporting Clays" and the sights are ivory both front and center.

FRAME

The A-500G works on a new gas valve system. It meters just enough gas to operate the action, and it employs a four lug bolt design. This means that the barrel travels about 1/2" to the rear. At that point, the barrel stops and the bolt begins its rear wood movement and rotates unlocking its four lugs and ejecting the spent shell. Browning claims that this system enables the shooter to use any and all shells, from one ounce light loads to heavy 3" magnums one after the other and all will work perfectly.

Frame marking are located at the left and right side along the bottom

500G ---BROWNING

OTHER FEATURES

These guns also have the convenient magazine cut off like the Auto-5 which enables the shooter to use a different type shell without emptying the magazine. The safety is cross bolt either right or left handed. The capacity is four 2 3/4" or three 3" shells, and all triggers are gold colored.

BARRELS

Only matted ventilated rib barrels with Invector chokes have been available. Three are provided with each gun. Also, gold bead sights are provided.

Barrel lengths are 26", 28" or 30". In 1991 a 24" Buck Special barrel became available with adjustable rear and ramp front sights. You can special order improved modified, skeet or cylinder bore chokes if you desire. Browning has announced that steel shot of all kinds can be used.

Markings on the barrels on the left side are:

BROWNING ARMS COMPANY
MORGAN, UTAH MONTREAL P.Q.
MADE IN BELGIUM
ASSEMBLED IN PORTUGAL

Guns made prior to 1988 are marked "**MADE IN BELGIUM.**"

On the right side of the barrel are the words:

SPECIAL STEEL(Gauge) GA SHELLS
2 3/4" AND 3" INVECTOR

There is also a logo on the trigger guard. Serial numbers are on the front of the receiver and on the barrels under the forearm; there are also several proof marks.

STOCKS

The stock is of select walnut of about group 2 grade. Specifications are length of pull 14¼", drop at comb 1½", and drop at heel 2½". All have rubber ventilated recoil pads marked "BROWNING" as standard as well as semi-pistol grip stocks. These are finished in Browning's high gloss, and checkering is 18 lines per inch.

SERIAL NUMBERS

For dates of manufacture please refer to the General Information section in the front of this book.

Warning

Browning has recalled some of the A-500G's because of parts breakage in the trigger assembly. Only guns without the letter "H" stamped on the trigger assembly are faulty. If you have an A-500 without this letter "H" stamping, call Browning at 800-322-4626 for repairs. Missouri resident can call 314-287-6800 collect.

Chapter Six

Double Barrel
Shotguns

BSS DOUBLE BARREL

GENERAL INFORMATION

The 12 gauge BSS boxlock was introduced in June, 1971, and the 20 gauge in 1972. This fine little double was discontinued as of 1987.

It took a lot of daring to bring out a double barrel in this day and age. Everyone who didn't shoot a pump or auto was shooting an over and under. Browning took the chance of producing a double barrel when they are today considered by the mass of hunters an antiquated shotgun. Of course, the more sophisticated shooter knows this is not true. In any case, like everything else, we don't appreciate something until it's no longer available.

During its production some parts of this gun were made in Korea to cut down on the costs, but this didn't help. As sales fell, the cost went up and the price of this gun was just too high. In the year that it was discontinued, you couldn't hardly give one away.

As an example let me give you several prices over the years. In 1979 the retail price for a BSS Sporter grade II was $735.00, in 1980 it was $825.00, in 1981 it was $975.00, in 1982 it was $1,285.00, and in 1983 it was $1,275.00. In just three years the price went up 75%.

Now that these have been discontinued, they are fetching higher and higher prices. I can understand this, for any decent double will command a good price.

Just before they were discontinued and immediately after, I had sold several for as low as $400.00 new in the box. Now, in 1992, they are bringing $800.00 to $850.00 in the boxlocks and two and a half times that much in the sidelock version. This shows what can happen to a high quality Browning when its discontinued even if it is made in Japan.

Beginning in 1983 a sidelock 12 gauge version was introduced with the 20 gauge following in 1984. These have many special features found only in expensive quality shotguns. Some of these have a Purdey locking bolt, selective ejectors, and a genuine bar action. We will be discussing the boxlock followed by the sidelock version.

The BSS Sporter made a fine bird gun for the Double Barrel shooter. Both the BSS Boxlock and Sidelock versions are fast increasing in value.

BOXLOCK

GRADE AND MODEL INTRODUCTION

This gun was made only in what was later called the Standard grade until 1978 when the Grade 2 was introduced. The Grade 2 was discontinued in 1985. Also introduced in 1978 in both grades were two models, the Sporter and the Standard.

GRADE 1

The Grade 1 was only lightly engraved on each side with a scroll oval that comes to a point on each end; there is also some rosette engraving surrounding the hinge pin. All this is surrounded by a border of plain line work. The bottom of the receiver as well as the trigger guard has some light scroll. Total coverage for this hand engraving is about 50%, and the receiver is blued.

The French walnut stock was checkered 20 lines per inch when it was introduced, but it was changed to 18 lines per inch in 1978 and remained so until the end of production. The stocks were high gloss finished for the Standard model and a semi-gloss for the Sporter, they were all shipped with the ''Browning'' black plastic butt plate.

GRADE 2

The Grade 2 has much more embellishment including medium scroll covering about 40% to 50% of the action. The scroll surrounds a mallard duck in flight on the left side, a ringneck pheasant in flight on the right, and a brace of pointers on the bottom. The engraving on the trigger guard also consists of medium scroll surrounding a bobwhite quail. This is all hand engraved and the receivers were greyed, trigger guards, top levers, and forearm latches are blued.

The group 3 French walnut stock was checkered 20 lines per inch with a high gloss finish for the Standard model and a semi-gloss for the Sporter.

SPORTER

As introduced in 1978, the Sporter differs from the Standard only in the stock, the long tang trigger guard, and the barrels which were made 26" or 28" long for either gauge. The checkering, engraving and other features for each grade were the same as the Standard model

All had straight grip butt stocks, semi beavertail forearms, and a semi-gloss finish. The Sporter dimensions were the same as the Standard model for each gauge and they had black plastic butt plates marked "Browning."

FRAMES

This was a true boxlock, scalloped frame, top lever break open shotgun with an all steel receiver. They were all blued until 1978 when the Grade 2 came along. They feature bushed firing pins which are only found on the better European doubles. Browning went all out to have a quality double and this is reflected in the increase in value since they were discontinued.

Bushed firing pins, as found on the BSS, is a quality feature not normally found on lower priced doubles.

Since their introduction, all were made with selective automatic ejectors; selective ejectors only eject the shells fired and lift for hand removal all those that are not fired.

The chromed plated triggers were first non-selective and mechanical. They fired the right barrel first, followed by the left.

In 1978 some major changes were made in the triggers. Besides now being gold plated, they were made single selective and capable of firing either barrel the shooter desired.

Here is an example of the double trigger BSS prototype. About 10-25 were made in 1971.

According to Browning 10 to 25 guns were made in 1971 with double triggers, they were all 12 gauge since this was the initial year of introduction. They were sent here by the manufacture as a prototype and later sold thru their normal business channels. These are virtually unknown among Browning collectors and will one day be very collectible. As you can see in the accompanying picture, the trigger guard is the same size as the early single trigger guards and the triggers take up the entire inside of it.

The barrel selector, for the single trigger guns, was located in the trigger guard. To fire the right barrel first, you shifted the barrel selector to the right, and to the left to fire the left barrel first. The gold plated trigger was short lived on this model, for it was discontinued in 1981 for just a "golden colored" trigger as Browning liked to call it.

BARRELS/MARKINGS
SERIAL NUMBERS

When introduced, barrels were 26" long with improved cylinder/modified and modified/full choke combinations or 28" long with modified/full chokes; the more open barrel was always on the right side. In 1975 the 30" barrel was introduced for the 12 gauge only. These were choked modified/full or full/full and made until 1987.

All had, as introduced, a solid matted rib with German nickel silver bead front sights and 2 3/4" chambers for the 12 gauge and 3" for the 20. In 1975, when the 30" barrels were introduced for the 12 gauge, 3" chambers came along and all 2 3/4" chambers were discontinued.

The markings on the barrels for guns made and assembled in Japan are as follows:

On the left side of the barrel:
BROWNING ARMS COMPANY
MORGAN, UTAH & MONTREAL P.Q.
MADE IN JAPAN

On the right side of the barrels:
B-S/S = SPECIAL STEEL (Gauge) **GA.**
SHELLS 2 3/4" (or 3" if applicable)

On the water table you will find proof mark 17. *(See page 50)*

You will also find the serial numbers on the frame, barrels and forearm.

On the guns first assembled in Korea with Japanese parts you will find the following markings:

On the left barrel:
BROWNING ARMS COMPANY
MORGAN, UTAH & MONTREAL P.Q.
MADE IN JAPAN AND ASSEMBLED IN KOREA

On the right barrel:
B-S/S = SPECIAL STEEL (Gauge) **GA.**
SHELLS 2 3/4" and 3"

On the later guns assembled in Korea the left barrel is marked:
BROWNING ARMS COMPANY
MORGAN, UTAH & MONTREAL P.Q.
MADE IN KOREA WITH JAPANESE
COMPONENTS

On the right barrel are the words,
B-S/S = SPECIAL STEEL (Gauge) **GA.**
SHELLS 2 3/4" and 3"

On the water table you will find proof mark 17 *(See page 50)*.

You will also find the serial numbers on the frame, barrels, and forearm.

STOCKS

All were made with group 2 walnut with a full pistol grip and beavertail forearm. The checkering was 18 to 20 lines per inch and the finish was a high gloss. All combs were fluted and they had a black plastic butt plate marked "Browning." Stock dimensions for the 12 gauge was length of pull 14 1/4", drop at comb 1 5/8", and drop at heel 2 1/2". The 20 gauge's dimensions were length of pull 14 1/4", drop at comb 1 1/2", and drop at heel 2 3/8".

SAFETIES

The safeties were automatic. This means that they would engage every time the lever was operated. I do not like this at all for you always have enough time to put a safety on, but sometimes don't have time to take one off. Automatic safeties are pretty well standard on all double guns.

SIDELOCKS

The sidelock was introduced in 1983 as a 12 gauge and as a 20 the following year; unfortunately, they were discontinued in 1987. The reason was price. When they were introduced, the retail price was $1,500.00 but when discontinued they had jumped to $2,000.00.

These are true sidelocks, not boxlocks with false side plates. Of all the different types of sidelocks produced, this is what is known as a bar action which is a good strong design. Of course, a boxlock gun is stronger in the wrist area because very little wood is cut away to accommodate the action. A sidelock has the mechanism mounted to the sideplates and the wood must be cut away. You therefore, have a weaker stock in a critical area. You must be very careful when purchasing any sidelock and examine the wood for cracks or outright breakage.

The internal mechanism of this model is excellent, displaying a high quality of workmanship and care in polishing and assembly. You will have no complaints with the speed nor the reliability of the action. In fact, the long cocking levers make the action rather easy to open after firing.

All through production they had double triggers, selective ejectors, and automatic safeties only. The forward trigger fired the right barrel, and the rear, the left barrel.

One very nice feature often found only on higher priced European guns is the cocking indicator located on the sideplates. You can tell by feel if a barrel is cocked.

The sideplates, receiver, forearm bracket, trigger guard, top lever, safety, and long tang trigger guard are engraved with medium scroll and rosette patterns; these are finished in grey.

BARRELS

When first introduced the 12 gauge was offered with 26" improved cylinder/modified or 28" modified/full barrels. Both had 2 3/4" chambers. In 1985, the improved cylinder/modified barrels were discontinued and you could get the 26" barrels in modified/full only. This was again changed back to the original chokes in the last year of production, 1987.

The 20 gauge barrels were originally offered in 26'' improved cylinder/modified and 28'' modified/full. Both had 2 3/4'' chambers. These were available until the end of production.

Barrel markings are the same as on the boxlock guns.

STOCKS

Stocks were group 3-4 French walnut with straight English grip checkering 24 lines per inch, and they all had a checkered butt. The forearms were all splinter in the tradition of a true upland game gun. The plunger type forearm release is easy to work, yet will not allow the forearm to come loose at an inopportune time.

All shipped had a safety sear and automatic ejectors.

Guns sold were 714 in the 12 gauge and 451 in the 20, this totals 1,165. This is quite a rare gun, and I believe will become collectible as soon as folks start to realize this.

SERIAL NUMBERS AND PRODUCT CODES

In the serial numbers that follow, you will note the letters "A" and "B"; these stand for the gauge. Each year the numbers began with 0001. For serial numbers after 1976, please refer to the General Information section in the front of this book.

The following are the serial numbers from 1971 to 1976:

YEAR	20 GAUGE	12 GAUGE
1971	NOT MADE	—-A71
1972	—-B72	—-A72
1973	—-B37	—-A37
1974	—-B47	—-A47
1975	—-B57	—-A57
1976	—-B67	—-A67

Please don't be surprised to find the year codes reversed; B73 might look like B37 or vice versa.

The model code are as follows:

Hunter 20	368	Sporter 12	358
Hunter 12	158	Sidelock 12	918
Sporter 20	126		

Chapter Seven

Pump
Shotguns

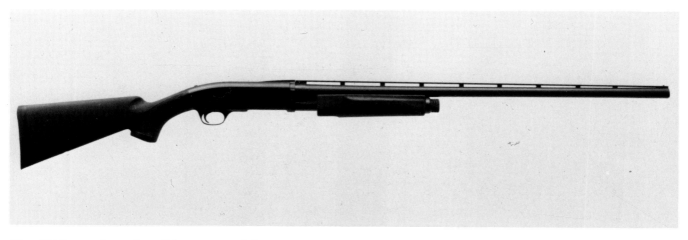

The BPS was introduced in 1977 and has been made in three gauges and several configurations.

THE BPS

GENERAL INFORMATION

Since its 12 gauge introduction in 1977 and availability in 20 gauge since 1982, this has been a very popular shotgun. It has many desirable features including bottom ejection, double action bars, top tang safety, a magazine cutoff with five shot capacity, and one of the slickest actions I have ever seen on a pump shotgun. In fact, with the double action operating bars, its smoothness and dependability rivals the great Winchester Model 12. It was originally available only in the Hunting, Buck Special, and Trap models.

With the advent of steel shot, Browning has done an outstanding job in producing products that will handle these difficult loads successfully. One of these is the introduction of the 10 gauge magnum. Shell capacity is four rip snorters, and only Invector chokes are available in full through improved cylinder. The improved cylinder is for hunting quail! Chambers are 3 1/2'', and needless to say a recoil pad is standard. This little cannon weighs 9 lbs., 8 oz. with its 30'' barrel. I've been poking fun at this gauge, but in all honesty I can't think of anything better for the goose or duck hunter now that lead shot is no longer legal and the I.C. choke does quite well on mid-range geese.

Also, because of the steel shot situation, the BPS 12 gauge with 3 1/2'' chambers was brought out in 1989. It is built on the 10 gauge frame, can handle all length 12 gauge shells interchangeably, and has a back bored barrel with Invector chokes. It comes in a hunting or stalker configuration with either 28'' or 30'' barrels.

The BPS has turned out to be a great shotgun for everyone including left handers from the upland to the wetland bird hunter. It has proven extremely reliable and functional over the years.

HUNTING MODEL

This was the basic model with no engraving and high polished blue. Otherwise known as the Field Model, this was originally made in 12 gauge only; the 20 came along in 1982.

BUCK SPECIAL

The Buck Special is the same gun as the Hunting model except it has a 24'' barrel with adjustable rear and ramp front sights. It was originally introduced in 12 gauge in 1977 and 20 gauge in 1983.

TRAP MODEL

Like the Buck Special the Trap was identical to the Hunting model except for some minor differences. It was introduced in 1977 and discontinued in 1984. All barrels were 30'' and chambered for 2 3/4'' only. They had ivory center and front beads with the floating rib.

Stock dimensions were length of pull 14 3/8'', drop at comb 1 3/8'', and drop at heel 2 1/8''. The Monte Carlo stock dimensions were length of pull 14 3/8'', drop at comb 1 3/8'', and drop at heel 1 3/8''. They all have the trap contoured ventilated recoil pad with a high gloss finish.

UPLAND SPECIAL

The Upland Special is a handy little gun for most bird hunters.

In 1984 Browning introduced the Upland Special in 12 and 20 gauges. They all had straight grip stocks with 22'' barrels and Invector chokes.

Stock dimensions were length of pull 14'', drop at comb 1 1/2'', and drop at heel 2 1/2''. The purpose of the shorter stock was to allow the shooter to mount the gun quickly for a faster first shot. All other features standard on the Hunting model were also standard on the Upland Special.

YOUTH MODEL

In 1986 the Youth model came out in 20 gauge only. This little gun had a 22'' Invector barrel and weighed only 6 lbs., 11 oz.

Stock dimensions were length of pull 13 1/4'', drop at comb 1 1/2'', and drop at heel 2 1/2'' with a Browning marked ventilated pad. All models featured a high gloss finish and hand checkering 18

lines per inch with about group 2 select walnut. All other features were the same as the Hunting Model.

STALKER

Browning introduced the 12 gauge 3'' chambered Stalker in 1987 and the 10 gauge with 24'' Invector or Buck Special barrels in 1989. Also in 1989, the 3 1/2'' 12 gauge with 24'' Buck Special barrels or 28'' or 30'' Invector Plus barrels were introduced. At first, it could be ordered only with a 28'' Invector barrel, but in 1990 it was available with either 22'' or 26'' Invector choked barrels.

It has a non-glare painted finished stock, which was changed to a graphite type material in 1988. The metal also had a dull black non-glare finish.

Stock dimensions were length of pull 14 1/4'', drop at comb 1 1/2'', and drop at heel 2 1/2''.

PIGEON GRADE

In true tradition, Browning came out with the BPS Pigeon Grade in 1992.

In 1992 this grade came out in 12 gauge only. It was the same as the Hunting model except with a group 3 grade of wood. "Pigeon Grade,"

"Browning BPS," and the Browning logo are all stamped and gold filled on the side of the receiver.

GAME GUNS

In 1992, Browning introduced both Game Guns in two configurations. The upper gun is the Turkey Special, the lower the Deer Special.

Also introduced in 1992 are the Game Guns in two configurations: the Deer Special and the Turkey Special.

The entire receiver, magazine, and barrel were redesigned so there was a minimum of play and the best accuracy obtainable, Browning was advertising groups as good as 1 3/4'' at 100 yards. The receivers are drilled and tapped for scope mounts that are supplied with the gun. In addition, the rear sight is adjustable for windage and elevation, and the ramp front sight has a gold bead.

The stocks are length of pull 13 7/8'', drop at comb 1 3/4'', and drop at heel 1 3/4'' with a satin finish. All have sling swivel studs and a Browning marked rubber recoil pad.

The Deer Special has a 5'' rifled Invector style choke tube that screws into the heavy 20 1/2'' barrel.

The Turkey Special is the same as the Deer Special except it has a full choke tube.

FRAMES

This was basically a 12 gauge hammerless, bottom ejecting and loading, five-shot pump gun with double action bars. All were highly polished and blued with no engraving until the Stalker model was introduced in 1987 and the Pigeon in 1992.

In 1982 the 20 gauge was introduced with a scaled down frame proportional to the smaller shell. It was identical to the 12 but didn't have the magazine cut off feature. In 1988 the 10 gauge magnum came on board with a massive frame that can handle the 10 gauge 3 1/2'' magnum loads; this is the same frame used for the 3 1/2'' 12 gauge variation.

One great feature is the same magazine cut off that Browning has been putting the Auto-5 for many years. It is a great plus that allows you to load a different type shell than in the magazine if the occasion calls for it. It is also a great feature for the trap shooter that has to load one shell at a time; the shell carrier stays up when the cut off is on and allows the shooter to load directly into the chamber. In fact, it's the only pump shotgun with such a cut off.

TRIGGERS

Triggers were blue until 1986 when they were gold colored.

STOCKS

All, except where noted, had group 1-2 walnut with full pistol grip stocks, long semi-beavertail forearm and solid rubber pads. Stock dimensions were length of pull 14 1/4", drop at comb 1 1/2", and drop at heel 2 1/2".

Checkering was 18 lines per inch when first introduced but changed to 20 lines per inch in 1976 on both the butt stock and forearm. In 1980 the checkering was changed back to 18 lines per inch. The finish was the Browning high gloss.

The 12 gauge stocks all had the "Browning" marked rubber recoil pads, the 20 gauges had a black plastic butt plate marked "Browning" and the 10 gauges had "Browning" marked ventilated recoil pads.

BARRELS & CHOKES

As first introduced all barrels were vent rib and chambered for 3" shells in the Hunting models and 2 3/4" in the target models. In 1989, the 3 1/2" 12 gauge Hunting model was brought out.

Barrel marking are as follows:
On the left side are the words:

BROWNING ARMS COMPANY
MORGAN, UTAH & MONTREAL P.Q.
MADE IN JAPAN

On the right side of the barrel you will find:
INVECTOR BPS SPECIAL STEEL (Gauge) **GA 2 3/4" AND 3"**-(Bbl length)

If it didn't have Invectors, then it had the choke code, and if it wasn't 3", it wouldn't have the 3" marking.

Barrel lengths were 26", 28", 30", and 32"; all had German nickel silver front sights, except the 24" Buck, Deer, and Turkey Specials, which had adjustable sights.

The chokes available were 26" improved cylinder or modified; 28" modified or full; 30" full, improved modified, or modified; and 32" full or improved modified. The 32" barrels were discontinued in 1976 and brought back in 1979. Also in 1977, all the barrels could be purchased in full, modified, or improved cylinder, but when the 32" barrels were reintroduced, the original chokes and barrel lengths came back.

As noted above only fixed chokes could be ordered until 1938 when the Invector chokes became available for the 12 gauge and in 1985 for the 20. At this time fixed chokes were discontinued for both gauges. In 1989 when the 12 gauge 3 1/2" was introduced, it was made with the Invector Plus system.

Browning has never made a plain barrel for this model. Only vent ribs have been available other then the deer and turkey guns with adjustable sights.

The 20 gauge barrels were 26" improved cylinder or modified and 28" modified or full; in 1983 a 24" Buck Special barrel came out for the 20 gauge.

As introduced, the 10 gauge barrels were all 30" long with the Invector chokes. Improved cylinder, modified, and full choke tubes were all supplied with this gun. In 1990 Browning started to make a 28" barrel for this gauge with the Invector chokes.

MAGAZINES

As introduced all magazines would hold five shots, in 1985 this was reduced to four shots in all gauges for the 2 3/4" shells and three for the 3".

SERIAL NUMBERS AND CODES

For yearly codes refer to the General Information section in the front of this book.

The model code for the 12 gauge Hunter is 152 and for the 20 gauge Hunter is 162. These are also valid for the Upland Specials.

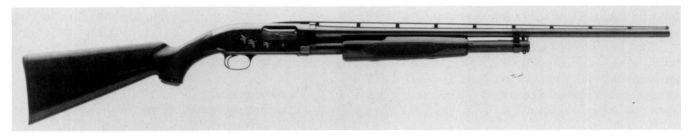

Here is the Model 12 in 28 gauge. The upper example is a Grade I and the lower a Grade V. So far, the engraving for all gauges introduced look the same.

MODEL 12 PUMP SHOTGUN

The Model 12 Winchester is one of the greatest firearm inventions of the Twentieth Century, it is the pump shotgun by which all others are judged. Hunters and collectors seek out the Model 12 in any form and in any condition to use and collect. The Browning Model 12 was originally made in 20 gauge like the Model 1912, and it is only fitting that it was re-introduced in the same gauge.

Although John M. Browning is not credited with the design of the Model 12 — it was designed by Thomas Johnson of Winchester — it is generally believed that many of his ideas were incorporated into the final design. Since Mr. Browning and Mr. Johnson worked many years in the Winchester plant together and cooperated with each other, Johnson learned a lot from him. In addition, many Winchester Model 97 features (an invention of J.M.B.) will be found on the Model 12. There is no doubt Mr. Browning had a great deal of influence and who knows how much input into this great little pump.

Ever since its demise in 1964 because of rising production costs, the Model 12 has been in great demand, not only by collectors, but also by hunters. This undoubtedly contributed to Browning's decision to reproduce this and the Model 42 as well.

When Browning introduced their version of the Model 12 in 1988 in 20 gauge only, it was the sixth in the series of reintroductions. As promised at that time, they have since come out in 1990 with the 28 gauge, which was the eighth in the series, and in 1992 with the Model 42, which is the eleventh. As of June 1992, Browning has said the Model 42 will be the last of this series.

Other than the trigger assembly, it is a replica of the original Winchester Model 12. The trigger was changed internally to improve safety.

GRADE 1

The Grade 1 is close to the same configuration as the Winchester Deluxe Field. They have no engraving and are plainly finished with a high polish blue.

The walnut is group 2 finished semi-gloss and has checkering 20 lines to the inch. The forearm is of the long style configuration, also checkered 20 lines per inch. The butt stock has a semi pistol grip with a metal grip cap and fluted comb.

GRADE V

The Grade V is the same configuration as the Grade 1 except for the finish. The engraving is a duplication of the pattern Winchester called their Grade V pattern. The right side displays a marsh scene with four greenheads skimming the cattails. The left side shows two setters flushing a ruffed grouse. These guns are not hand engraved nor are they gold inlaid; instead they are etched and gold plated.

The wood is grade 5 Walnut and has 22 lines per inch checkering on the butt stock and forearm. The configuration is the same as the Grade 1, except it has a high gloss finish and some of the most beautiful wood I have ever seen on a Browning. I have a Grade V 20 that is absolutely incredible. The wood looks like marble and is 100% figure from butt to trigger guard.

FRAME

This is exactly the same frame as the original Model 12 except the trigger and sear mechanisms were changed for safety purposes. All are made from forged and machined steel. This is basically a hammerless, pump action, takedown, double extractor action with a single action bar.

All were blued including triggers, and the receivers were grooved to accept the rib extension.

BARRELS

All barrels were 26" long with 2 3/4" chambers and were choked modified only. The ventilated high post floating ribs with grooved sighting plane were different from the original but only in the shape of the posts and the matting. They all had center and front silver beads.

MAGAZINE

The magazines are the same as the original and will hold 5 2¾" shells. A plug is furnished.

STOCKS

Although you could order full or straight English style butt stocks on the original Winchester version, the Brownings are all semi pistol grip. They also have a metal grip cap, fluted comb, and black plastic butt plate marked "Browning." The guns I have seen really have nice wood, All wood isn't the same, so if you have a choice, look over several of them to pick out the best one. The stock dimensions have a length of pull 14", drop at comb 2 1/2", and drop at heel 1 1/2"; these are skeet dimensions that you may find a bit high for hunting purposes.

The forearms are all the long type as used on the original deluxe skeet guns. They extend behind the forearm slide about 3" to give the shooter a very comfortable forearm to grasp.

SERIAL NUMBERS AND PRODUCT CODES

For serial numbers please refer to the General Information section in the front of this book.

The product codes are as follows:

	GRADE 1	GRADE V
20 Gauge	832	932
28 Gauge	872	972

The Model 42 in Grade I, upper and Grade V, lower.

MODEL 42

Although not a design of John M.Browning's, the Winchester Model 42 does have some of the features of the Winchester Model 97, which was one of his designs. Browning has advertised that 12,000 of these will be made, 6,000 in Grade 1 and 6,000 in Grade 5.

If you've ever hunted with one of these, you'll welcome its return even for a short period of time.

This is one of the slickest pumps ever designed, and in combination with the 3" 410 shell it is a real game getter on running rabbits or plantation style bird hunting. That's not to say that it won't do well on wild birds; it's just hunting wild birds with a 410 is best left up to the accomplished shot gunner.

There were over 160,000 of these made prior to 1964 by Winchester. This will add about 7.5% more to the total number of Winchesters ever made. Experts agree that there were many given away over the years by Mr. John Olin and other Winchester executives for promotional purposes, so there is no real way to tell how many were actually made, although the number would not run over 164,000.

GRADE 1

The Grade 1 is hardly a Grade 1 or field model as Winchester would have called it. These are really deluxe grade guns that will add to anyone's gun cabinet. The only difference is these and the Grade 5 is the final finish, the grade of wood, and checkering. All the metal is blued with no engraving.

The group 2-3 stocks are finished semi-gloss and checkered 20 lines per inch in a plain pattern covering both sides of the forearm and the pistol grip.

All else is described in their sections.

GRADE 5

This is the same gun as described under the Grade 1 except it is etched engraved, has better wood, and possesses a more deluxe finish.

The etching consists of medium scrolls covering about 50% of the front and back sides of the receiver. In between this is a woods scene on the left side showing 2 pointers watching a single quail flying away. On the right side is about the same amount of scroll but also extending along the bottom. There are also four ducks flying over a marsh.

The dogs, quail and ducks are all gold plated, not inlaid. On the original Winchester Grade 5 guns these were inlaid.

The wood is about group 5 with a high gloss finish and checkered 22 lines per inch. There are two diamonds left uncheckered on both sides of the forearm and one on the bottom. In addition, there are two diamonds that are checkered on the bottom. The pistol grip is checkered the same as the Grade 1 except it is 22 lines per inch.

All other features will be described in their sections.

FRAME

This is exactly the same frame as the original Model 42 except the trigger and sear mechanisms were changed for safety purposes. All are made from forged and machined steel. They are basically a hammerless, pump action, takedown, double extractor action with a single action bar.

All were blued including triggers; the receivers were grooved to accept the rib extension.

BARRELS

All barrels were 26'' long with 3'' chambers and were full choked only. The ventilated high pose floating ribs with grooved sighting plane were different from the original but only in the shape of the posts and the matting. They all had center and front silver beads.

The barrels are marked on the left side:
BROWNING MODEL 42 410 3''
SHELLS ONLY FULL.

On the right side they are marked:
BROWNING ARMS COMPANY
MORGAN, UTAH & MONTREAL P.Q.
MADE IN JAPAN

MAGAZINE

The magazines are the same as the original and will hold six 2 1/2'' or five 3'' shells, and a plug is furnished.

STOCKS

Although you could order half or straight English style butt stocks on the original Winchester version, these are all pistol grip. They also have a metal grip cap, fluted comb, and black plastic butt plate marked "Browning." The guns I have seen have nice wood; in fact, one Grade 5 I looked at had one of the prettiest pieces of wood I've ever seen. These aren't all this good, so if you have a choice, look over several to pick out the best one. The stock dimensions are length of pull 14'', drop at comb 2 1/2'' and drop at heal 1 1/2''. These are skeet dimensions that you may find a bit high for hunting purposes.

The forearms are all the long type used on the original deluxe skeet guns. They extend behind the forearm slide about 3'' to give the shooter a very comfortable forearm to grasp.

SERIAL NUMBERS AND PRODUCT CODES

For serial numbers please refer to the General Information section in the front of this book.

Chapter Eight

Single Barrel
Shotguns

BT-99 TRAP

GENERAL SPECIFICATIONS

The BT-99 was introduced to this country in 1970 and was still being made as of 1992. Browning did import some of these as early as 1969, they have always been made in Japan.

GRADES

When introduced, only the basic Grade 1 was made. It was lightly scroll engraved on the edges and on both sides of the receiver. On the top and bottom, the trigger guard was also engraved. The style was similar to the Auto-5 engraving featured for so many years. The coverage was about 25%.

The barrels, ribs, stocks and other features will be described in their sections.

PIGEON GRADE

The Pigeon grade was introduced in 1978 and discontinued in 1985. Although there were several later models, it was the only model that was engraved.

The hand engraving consisted of close to 100% deeply cut fleur-de-las scrolls, vines and leaves covering the entire action. On the left side, it surrounded two pigeons in flight, and on the right side, one pigeon in flight. On the bottom it is 100% scroll. The trigger guard and the sides of the barrel that join the action were also engraved in like manner. The entire action and triggers guard were greyed.

The wood was about group 3 French walnut checkered 22 lines per inch with a high gloss urethane finish. The stock dimensions were length of pull 14 3/8", drop at comb 1 7/16", and drop at heel 1 5/8" for the conventional stock; and a length of pull 14 3/8", drop at comb 1 3/8", and drop at heel 2" for the Monte Carlo. All were furnished with a trap-style ventilated recoil pad marked "Browning."

The barrels, ribs, stocks and other features will be described in their sections.

RECEIVERS AND TRIGGERS

It is essentially a single barrel, trap style, top lever break open shotgun. All receivers in Grade 1 are blued steel with light scroll on each side.

Other than the Pigeon grade the only finish on the frames for these throughout production was a high luster blue. The overall quality of the Grade 1 BT-99 over the years has been excellent.

On the bottom of the frame is the word
"BROWNING"

They were all machined steel, not investment castings like so many guns are that we see today. This is one of the strengths of this model and a feature that trap shooters like very much.

The triggers were extra wide and gold plated until 1987 when they were just gold colored, not plated. A selective ejector was standard and there were no safeties.

BARRELS, RIBS AND CHOKES

As it was introduced in 1970, you could order either 32" or 34" barrels with 2 3/4" chambers. The chokes available were modified, improved modified or full. In 1977 the two barrel set came along, and you could order different lengths and/or chokes.

All barrels featured the high post floating rib except for the adjustable ribs that were introduced later. It was attached to the posts so that as the barrel heated up, the rib would be able to move back and forth and not warp. All were built high so that when you pointed it you didn't have to hide the bird to lead it properly. All were matted, were 11/32" wide, and had ivory center and front sights.

The barrel markings were as follows:
On the left side of the barrel —
BROWNING ARMS COMPANY
MORGAN, UTAH & MONTREAL P.Q.
MADE IN JAPAN

On the right side of the barrel —
INVECTOR BT-99 SPECIAL STEEL
12 GA 2 3/4" (BARREL LENGTH)

Also on the barrels on the bottom side are the proofs 16, 17, and 18. *(See page 50)*

Starting in 1984 the 32" barrels were made with either the original chokes or the new Invector. The 34" barrels could now be bought with the improved, modified or full fixed chokes or the Invector. Each Invector gun was shipped with modified, improved modified, and full choke tubes.

In 1986 the fixed chokes were discontinued for both barrel lengths, but in 1987 you could order either the fixed choke or the Invector system again. As of 1992 there have been no other changes made in the barrels or chokes.

STOCKS

The stocks and forearms were of group 2 French walnut. From 1970 until 1977 when the Monte Carlo stock was introduced, all were the conventional trap configuration. After this, the Monte Carlo was considered standard and the conventional trap was available as a no cost option, but later they were offered either way as a standard variation. I might add that at this time the name was changed to BT-99 Competition for those that had a Monte Carlo stock. This only lasted one or two years and the name was dropped.

The stock dimensions were length of pull 14 3/8", drop at comb 1 7/16", and drop at heel 1 5/8" for the conventional stock and a length of pull 14 3/8", drop at comb 1 3/8", and drop at heel 2" for the Monte Carlo. All were furnished with a trap style ventilated recoil pad marked "Browning" and with the high gloss finish.

Checkering was 20 lines per inch until the Pigeon grade was introduced in 1978. At that time the Grade 1 checkering was changed to 18 lines per inch and the Pigeon was 22 lines per inch. All were fitted with the beavertail forearm and the finish was the standard Browning high gloss with no special orders available.

BT-99 PLUS

GENERAL INFORMATION

The BT-99 Plus was introduced in 1989 and was the first real change in this gun other then the Pigeon grade since it's introduction in 1970. It wouldn't be the last, however, for several more would come about in the next two years. We will describe the difference between it and the basic BT-99, but we will not go over the features that are the same. You can get that information from the BT-99 section.

This model featured the recoil reducer system. Since I've never taken one apart, I really can't explain the way it works, but essentially it is mounted in the butt stock and divides the recoil from each shot into two less noticeable pushes that are less apparent.

The way it looks reminds me of a try gun. A try gun has a stock that is fully adjustable for length of pull, drop at comb, drop at heel, pitch and cast. It is what gunsmiths use to find the dimensions that are proper for a particular person. This model might not have all the adjustments of a try gun, but it comes real close. The adjustments available are drop at comb and drop at heel, cast off and on, length of pull, and the pitch of the butt pad. They are French walnut checkered 18 lines per inch and finished in the Browning high gloss. All have the contoured trap "Browning" ventilated recoil pad.

The fully adjustable rib was introduced with the BT-99 Plus. The basic concept of this new idea is an adjustable point of impact from 3" to 12" above the point of aim at 40 yards in 1/2" increments. This allows you to see the bird at any distance you are shooting.

The barrels are back bored and have the Invector Plus choke tubes as standard. Back bored simply means that the forcing cone in the barrels are longer and constricts the shot column to conform to the size of the bore slower, therefore distorting less shot. You can see the details of the Invector choking system in its section. When introduced in 1989, only 34" barrels were available, but in 1990 the 32" started to be made. These were still available as of 1992.

BT-99 RECOILLESS

This model was short lived, for it was only made in 1989. It was a completely different design than the BT-99 The entire action is different, for it utilizes a bolt-type mechanism. The barrel, inner bolt, and receiver are driven forward when the trigger is pulled, thereby reducing the recoil.

This gun came in two variations — the Regular and the Short. The Regular had an adjustable length of pull from 14" to 14 3/4", drop at comb from 1 3/8" to 1 3/4", drop at Monte Carlo from 1 1/8" to 2 1/4", drop at heel from 1 1/2" to 2 1/4", and a 30" barrel.

The Short version has a length of pull from 13" to 13 3/4", drop at comb from 1 3/8" to 1 3/4", drop at Monte Carlo from 1 1/8" to 2 1/4", drop at heel from 1 1/2" to 2 2/3", and a 27" barrel.

The variations in the length of pull and drop at heel is achieved by using the "Customizer" interchangeable recoil pads that slip on and off. Four different ones were supplied with each gun.

The barrels were all back bored and used the Invector Plus chokes. All other features of the BT-99 Plus are the same other than as noted above.

MICRO BT-99 PLUS

Introduced in 1991, this is the same gun as the BT-99 Plus and has all the same features, it is made with 28", 30", 32" and 34" barrels. The overall gun is scaled down for smaller shooters.

SERIAL NUMBERS

1971	71D-----	1974	74D-----
1972	72D-----	1975	75D-----
1973	73D-----	1976	76D-----

The letter "D" in the serial number refers to the model. Each year the serial numbers began with 0001. For date codes after 1976, refer to the General Information section.

Chapter Nine

The Invector
and
Invector-Plus
Chokes

THE INVECTOR AND INVECTOR-PLUS CHOKES

In 1983 Browning introduced the Invector Choke System. This was further refined in 1989 as the Invector-Plus. It has become quite popular among hunters and target shooters and is quite durable. This is the most successful of all the screw-in chokes promoted by anyone. People are even calling other makers' chokes "Invectors" when they have nothing to do with Browning's product. It is becoming a generic term used to describe this type choke.

They are also good looking. Unless you look down the barrel you don't realize there's a screw-in choke present. Browning has started installing these on all 10, 12, 16, and 20 gauge models except the Model 12; they are even using them in the B25 made for European sales.

I patterned a BPS 12 gauge quite extensively and was impressed with the patterns when using both lead and steel shot of various sizes. These loads shot consistently with the choke markings, and the patterns were well dispersed. Most can be used with steel shot with which I bagged many a Texas goose. Make sure you clean and lubricate the threads before inserting the choke, or they may get stuck to such an extent that only a gunsmith will be able to get it out. Below, you will find an 800 number to call to make sure your gun will handle steel shot.

Originally Invector chokes were only offered as an option in the 12 gauge Citori hunting and target guns as well as the Browning Pump Shotguns and the BT99 Trap guns. Later they were designed for the 20 gauge in 1985, the 16 gauge in 1987, and the 10 gauge in 1988.

In 1989 the Extra Full Special Tube came out in 12 gauge to fit in barrels made for the original Invector. They do, however, extend beyond the muzzle of the barrel. These are 2 1/4" long and give better long range patterns for trap, deer, or turkey hunters. If you have an original Invector barrel and want a longer range gun, these are for you. While you won't have a back bored barrel, you don't have to spend extra money for a completely new one. In 1991, they also came out for the 10 gauge.

The Invector-Plus system was also introduced in 1989. They have tubes that are 2 1/4", which makes them longer; they cannot be used in barrels threaded for the original Invector system. These are designed for the back bored series of barrels as described under each model in this book. This provides the shot column a gentler constriction thereby distorting it less; the results are better patterns with fewer flyers. As is the case for the original, they do not protrude beyoned the end of the barrel.

Not all Invector guns are suitable for steel shot. You can find out by calling Browning at 800-333-3288 to see if your gun is OK.

Since it can get quite complicated, I have created the following chart for you to use to distinguish which choke you have in your gun without your having to take it out.

The following table is for lead only.

MARKS	**	1	11	111	1111	11111	NONE
10 GAUGE	XF	F	M	IC			
12 PLUS	XF	F	IM	M	IC	S	C
12	XF	F	IM	M	IC	S	C
16		F	M	IC	S	C	
20		F	M	IC	S	C	

CODES ARE XF⁵EXTRA FULL, F⁵FULL, IM⁵IMPROVED MODIFIED, M⁵MODIFIED, S⁵SKEET, IC⁵IMPROVED CYLINDER, C⁵CYLINDER.

1. The above codes simply designate the approximate patterns you may expect.

2. Do not use the "XF" or the "F" tubes with steel shot. The "XF" tube has a nurled rim and no rim code.

3. The 12 Plus chokes are for use in the back bored barrels only.

The following is for steel shot only:

MARKS	**	1	11	111	1111	11111	NONE
10 GAUGE			F	M			
12 PLUS			F	F	M	IC	C
12			F	F	M	IC	IC
16				F	M	IC	IC
20		F		IM	M	M	IC

CODES ARE XF⁵EXTRA FULL, F⁵FULL, IM⁵IMPROVED MODIFIED, M⁵MODIFIED, S⁵SKEET, IC⁵IMPROVED CYLINDER, C⁵CYLINDER.

1. The above codes simply designate the approximate patterns you may expect.

2. Do not use the "XF" or the "F" tubes with steel shot. The "XF" tube has a nurled rim and no rim code.

3. The 12 Plus chokes are for use in the back bored barrels only.

Chapter Ten

Bolt Action
Rifles

BROWNING® HIGH-POWER
Bolt Action Rifles

In designing its new High-Power Bolt Action Rifle, Browning chose to retain the renowned Mauser-type action which has become the standard for bolt actions in practically every nation of the world since its introduction.

In the Browning models, every refinement is incorporated into these actions; then fine steel, choice walnut and the painstaking skill of master craftsmen have been added to give you Browning's concept of shooting excellence. The Browning rifle receives its strength and functional precision from sound engineering, its accuracy from careful design, meticulous hand-fitting and thorough testing.

Through every step of its development, the Browning standards of quality and performance were patiently tested and, as always, sound utility was foremost in design considerations. Its classic beauty stems from basic things — good lines, highly polished steel richly blued, select walnut carefully finished and hand-checkered. It's the kind of gun that grows in value with tough use; the scars of many hunts will only emphasize its inherent quality. We know you will be proud to own one.

BARRELS — Browning's barrels are made in specific weights and contours in order that outside diameters more suitably correspond to bore diameters and the ballistic requirements of the caliber. Thus each caliber displays a profile entirely appropriate to its cartridge and combines minimum weight and handsome lines with fine accuracy. One barrel is for the .222 caliber; another is for the .22/250, .243, and .308; another for calibers .264 Magnum, .270, .284 and .30/06; and still another for all other Magnum calibers. In addition, a heavy barrel model is also offered in calibers .222, .22/250, and .243. These heavy barrel models are drilled and tapped for target scope mount bases. Every barrel is individually machined from forged, specially heat treated billets of chrome vanadium steel, rather than rod stock, to assure maximum strength and resistance against wear and erosion. The precision boring procedure provides a perfectly concentric mirror-like bore; exterior surfaces are highly polished and richly blued to a lustrous durable finish.

STOCK — The stock is made from select walnut in Monte Carlo design with cheek piece and is carefully dimensioned to be ideally suited for either telescopic or open sights. Each rifle is individually hand-bedded for added accuracy and also utilizes the steel recoil lug for even recoil distribution as well as to safely absorb the shock of the heaviest ammunition. To accentuate the beauty of the fine walnut, each stock is skillfully hand-checkered and hand-finished to a tough, polished texture. Recoil pads are standard equipment on all Magnum calibers from 7mm through the .458.

Here is the opening page of the Safari rifle section as it was in the 1964 Browning catalog.

7mmR Magnum Safari Grade High-Power Rifle

SIGHTS — Both the front and the rear open sights have been scientifically mounted to give a sighting plane corresponding to that for a telescope without need of removal when the latter is used.

The front sight is a gold bead on hooded ramp. The ramp is knurled to flatten light reflection.

The rear sight is entirely new and uniquely adaptable to the needs of the shooter. It is of an exclusive folding leaf design and is dovetailed to a separate base. Either the sight or base can be easily removed or replaced as desired. When the base is removed, two small flush screws leave the barrel profile intact, thus barrel rigidity is unaffected and there is no dovetail slot to fill or refinishing required. Fine, clear calibrations are provided for both horizontal and vertical adjustment. The adjusting screws are coin slotted for convenience in making sighting corrections in the field or on the range. Settings are positive and highly resistant to rough treatment. The sight folds neatly out of the way when a scope is mounted or when the rifle is not in use.

SAFETY — The safety is the silent, sliding type, positioned on the right side of the receiver at the stock line for quick and easy manipulation with the thumb from its normal position while firing. It is a 3-position safety, moving completely forward for "Off" and rearward for "On." Because of its design and location, this safety is highly impervious to accidental movement. When in the "On" position, both the trigger and bolt are locked. A red plastic dot recessed in the stock signals the "Off" position. Its central position locks the trigger but permits the opening of the bolt for removal of a chambered cartridge.

TRIGGER — The trigger mechanism is individually adjusted at the factory to assure every desirable feature of good trigger pull — so smooth, short and crisp, in fact, that the veteran marksman should be wholly pleased. The weight of pull holds closely to three pounds. The trigger is grooved for more positive release. The trigger guard is attractively engraved.

ACTION — The Browning actions are machined from solid bars of laboratory tested, forged steel expertly heat treated to perform their function with wide safety margin.

The action used for longer cartridges (.270, .30-06 and the heavy Magnum calibers) is of a more conventional Mauser design. The highly polished, one-piece bolt contains the strong three lug locking system and features a streamlined bolt sleeve. The new Browning short action models utilize a smooth, strong action of modified Mauser design. This action has the short, fast bolt throw which is in accord with the newer short cartridges, both in varmint and hunting calibers. This shorter one-piece bolt provides two relatively massive locking lugs at the forward end as well as utilizing the bolt handle in conjunction with a machined recess in the receiver to provide an additional element of safety. A pleasingly contoured polished bolt sleeve finishes off the appearance of this handsome, compact action.

All Browning receivers are drilled and tapped to accept telescopic mounts and in addition the receivers of heavy barreled varmint rifles are drilled and tapped for receiver sights.

The smooth operation of the bolt as it glides rearward or forward on the mating grooves of the receiver certifies to the precision with which this important mechanism has been fitted. A compact bolt stop positioned on the left side of the receiver adds the finishing touch to the flowing lines of these actions.

FLOOR PLATE — The floor plate is hinged to permit the quick, safe removal of unfired cartridges. The release latch, positioned just forward of the trigger guard, is specifically designed to safeguard against accidental release. The integral magazine contains a twin-row feed guide to supplement smooth loading. Magazines are adjusted to caliber to give close tolerance for each cartridge. The floor plate matches the trigger guard in rich, hand engraving.

ACCURACY — Every Browning rifle is carefully test fired, first with proof loads to attest its strength, then for demanding accuracy. Each rifle is then zeroed in at 200 yards with one bullet weight and type (the .458 Magnum is zeroed in at 100 yards since it is normally used at closer range). It is realized that many variables, including the specific bullet and load, and the sight picture to which the owner is accustomed, will quite possibly necessitate re-sighting the rifle. The 200 yard zero, however, is a final confirmation of our accuracy standards as well as a convenience to the owner in making final adjustments, which at the most will be minor.

SPECIAL MODELS — For those who desire the very finest in a High-Power rifle, Browning offers in all calibers special Medallion and Olympian grades which bear the flawless skill of the master gunmaker. No detail has been neglected in making these models superlative in appearance and function.

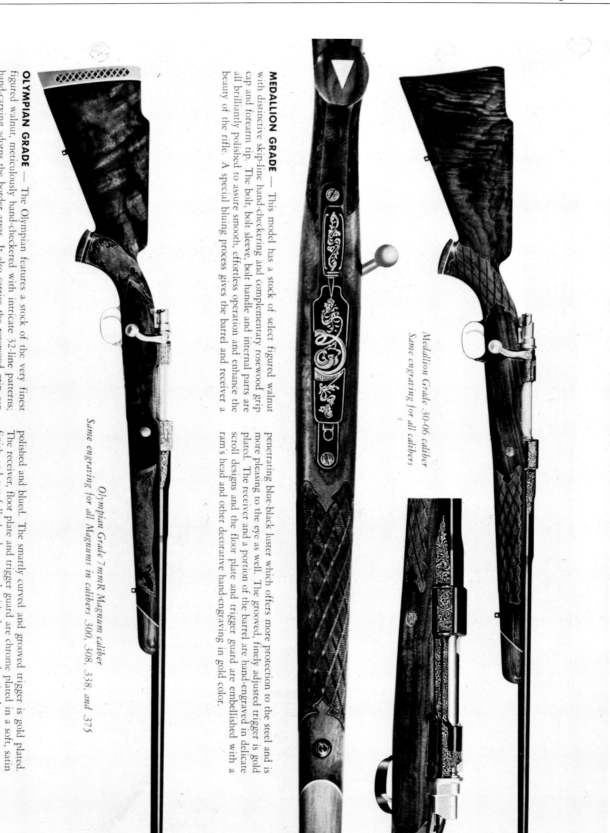

MEDALLION GRADE — This model has a stock of select figured walnut with distinctive skip-line hand-checkering and complementary rosewood grip cap and forearm tip. The bolt, bolt sleeve, bolt handle and internal parts are all brilliantly polished to assure smooth, effortless operation and enhance the beauty of the rifle. A special bluing process gives the barrel and receiver a penetrating blue-black luster which offers more protection to the steel and is more pleasing to the eye as well. The grooved, finely adjusted trigger is gold plated. The receiver and a portion of the barrel are hand-engraved in delicate scroll designs and the floor plate and trigger guard are embellished with a ram's head and other decorative hand-engraving in gold color.

Medallion Grade .30-06 caliber
Same engraving for all calibers

OLYMPIAN GRADE — The Olympian features a stock of the very finest figured walnut, meticulously hand-checkered with intricate 32-line patterns; hand-carving adorns the border areas. It also carries the rosewood grip cap and forearm tip. On the face of the grip cap is fitted an 18-carat gold, diamond shaped initial medallion. All internal parts, bolt and bolt sleeve are polished to a brilliant finish with the extractor damascened for added beauty. The barrel is hand-engraved forward of the receiver and magnificently polished and blued. The smartly curved and grooved trigger is gold plated. The receiver, floor plate and trigger guard are chrome plated in a soft, satin finish and tastefully hand-engraved with deep-carved animal scenes appropriate to the specific caliber.

Both the Medallion and Olympian grades come without
open sights on all calibers except the .458 Magnum.

Olympian Grade 7mmR Magnum caliber
Same engraving for all Magnums in calibers .300, .308, .338, and .375

The early Browning catalogs emphasized that higher grades were available right off the shelf for the hunter or shooter that wanted something special.

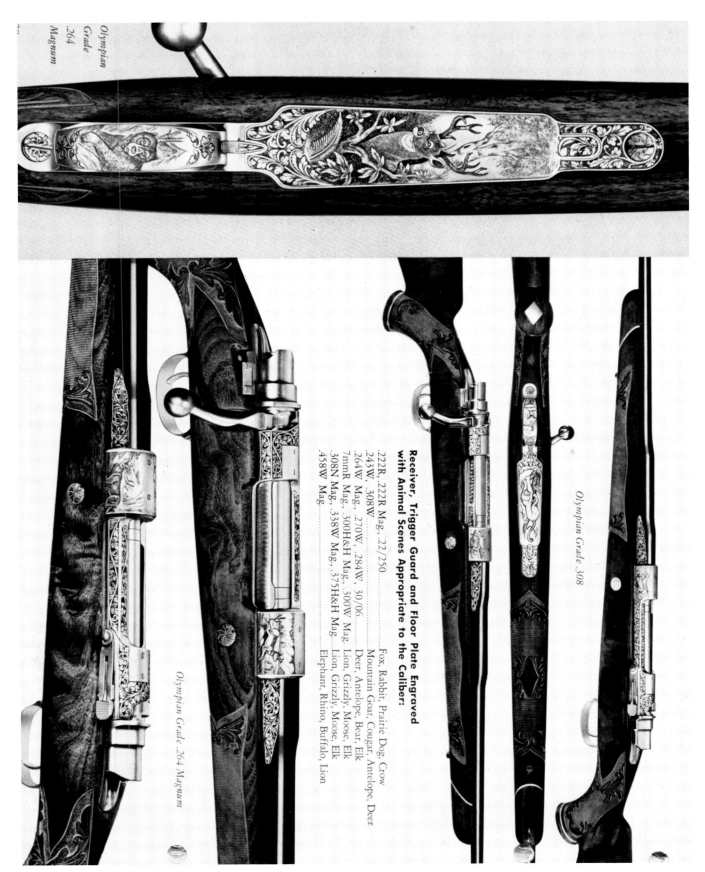

Receiver, Trigger Guard and Floor Plate Engraved with Animal Scenes Appropriate to the Caliber:

.222R, .222R Mag., .22/250 .... Fox, Rabbit, Prairie Dog, Crow
.243W, .308W .... Mountain Goat, Cougar, Antelope, Deer
.264W Mag., .270W, .284W, 30/06 .... Deer, Antelope, Bear, Elk
7mmR Mag., .300H&H Mag., .300W Mag. ..... Lion, Grizzly, Moose, Elk
.308N Mag., .338W Mag., .375H&H Mag. ..... Lion, Grizzly, Moose, Elk
.458W Mag. .... Elephant, Rhino, Buffalo, Lion

Olympian Grade .264 Magnum

Olympian Grade .264 Magnum

Olympian Grade .308

GENERAL NOTES AND HISTORY

In 1959, one of the greatest and most popular massed produced rifles ever made by any company was introduced, the Safari, made by Fabrique Nationale (F.N.) and marketed by Browning. If Browning's attempt in only introducing the Safari in 1959, without the Medallion and Olympian variations, was a test for the acceptability of this fine rifle by the public, it was not necessary. From the very beginning, it was the number one and without question the finest quality bolt action rifle ever made for the general public, and it remains so to this day. It may not have some of the action refinements of the Winchester Pre-64 Model 70's or the ostentatious look of the German Weatherby but it had all the refinements of a custom rifle and one of the overall finest and strongest actions ever made, the Mauser 98, sporterized. These fine rifles are superior not only to all those made until 1975, its discontinuation, but to all made since! This is a lot of bragging, but I'm ready to back up my words with facts; just look at one or all of them.

1. **Shootability** — Out of the box they compare with any and all factory and most of the best custom rifles ever made. They are accurate, all were sighted in and tested for accuracy standards that were within the tightest in the industry. They all have excellent balance and are proportioned for each chambering. There was no less then four different size actions used and a fifth configuration. No other manufacturer offered a series of actions for various chambering in high powered rifles at the time, more of this in the action section. They handle well and have positive extraction and feed. All the grades from the Safari right on up have polished actions and are extremely well suited for that quick second or third shot.

The open sights were well thought out and very usable in case of scope loss. Many manufacturers at the time were not putting open sights on their rifles or were only supplying the shooters with a cheap folding sight that had to be removed in order to get a scope mounted properly. I have been on big game hunts with folks that had scope problems and no open sight to back them up. It's not a good feeling to have spent several thousand dollars on a hunt and end up with a useless rifle and a ruined hunt.

The safeties are state of the art for hunting. They are positive, quiet, positioned properly and allow the chamber to be unloaded safely. The floorplate drops down for easy unloading of the magazine and at the same time is designed so that it is difficult to open accidentally. The weight of each rifle is proportioned to the chambering for which it was made. Each varmint cartridge came in both pencil and heavyweight barrels and each cartridge right on up from the 222 Remington to the 458 Winchester had

the appropriate barrel weight, properly proportioned stock and features that were correct to handle the recoil and fulfill the task for which it was designed.

The bolt action rifles made by all other American manufacturers at the time don't have many of the refinements of the Safari. Most will not shoot as well out of the box as the Safari will; you have to tune them up, Safaris come tuned up from F.N.. All Safaris were sighted in at 200 yards and checked for accuracy, whereas most of the others were just proofed for pressure.

The above are just a few features that you got when purchasing a Browning. Browning has never been the cheapest gun, in fact, they have always charged a little bit more but they provided the hunters of this country with a lot more. When purchasing a Browning, the shooters in America always expected a little bit extra hand work, a little bit better finish, hand checkering not machine cut, a little bit of hand engraving and the little extras that weren't provided on other manufacturers rifles.

2. **Versatility** — They were made, on a regular basis, in all calibers popular at that time. Some of the cartridges for which these rifles were chambered have since become vary popular, this includes, at that time, the wildcat 22/250 which is now the 22/250 Remington. In addition, you could order one in any caliber you wanted with three different barrel sizes and two different barrel lengths at a reasonable price. If you ever tried to order a special rifle from Winchester, Savage or Weatherby in an unlisted caliber, you had to wait forever, if they would do it for you at all. The others were the mass producer, and F.N. was the quality gun maker, one at a time. Not only were they made in more calibers then any other rifle, but they were made correctly for each one. Over the period of their production, these fine guns were made using five different and distinct actions. The Sako L461 was ideal for the smaller 222 Remington type cartridges, the F.N. small ring and Sako L579 for the 308 Winchester size, and the F.N. large ring or F.N. Supreme large ring for all others including the 458 Winchester Magnum and other belted magnums. If Browning didn't make it, 99 1/2% of the buyers didn't need it, and the other 1/2% only thought they did.

You could roam the hills all day long varmint hunting with the little 222 Remington which weighed in at six pounds 2 ounces or track down dangerous game in Africa or elsewhere with the 458 Winchester Magnum which weighed eight pounds four ounces. From 1959 through 1976 it was produced in no less than twenty-seven different cartridge and barrel weight configurations to suit almost any shooter. One of the most popular big game hunters and once game control officer in Africa, Peter Hathaway Capstick, almost exclusively hunted with the F.N. action in 375 H & H Magnum. His life was on the line almost every day and he let it ride on this fine action. He speaks of it in several of his fine books and goes into detail about why he chose it over all others in several of them. Others may have a feature or two that brings it out of the ordinary, like the Pre-64 Model 70, but none have the all around versatility, strength and reliability that the F.N. does.

3. **Appearance** — The Safari appeared to be a custom rifle when you first saw it on the gun store rack. It had all the features of one, excellent metal polishing and deep blue, fine hand checkering, well filled stock finish, great open sights, a little bit of engraving, extremely smooth action, proportioned action and barrel weights, etc.

In 1963, I remember walking into Dean's Firearms in Atlanta, Georgia, wanting to buy a rifle. Being a typical gun bug, I didn't care what caliber it was, just as long as it was macho and a magnum. "I was a big reader of the gun pulp magazines and fell for most of the editorializing, which was really advertising in disguise." I asked to see one of the Brownings that were on the rack behind the counter because they caught my eye. The pulp mags didn't write about Brownings all that much, I guess Browning didn't have to go to the extremes to sell their wares like the other gun companies did, but they stood out on the shelf in comparison to the others. It had the features not found on the other factory produced guns, but I couldn't stand the $175.00 price tag and ended up buying a Model 70 Winchester for $129.95. In thinking back, everything I didn't like about the Model 70 and what I really wanted was a standard feature on the Safari: the grade of wood, shape and finish of the stock and profuse checkering, the great polishing of the metal, just enough engraving to bring it out of the ordinary and the general appearance that showed hand workmanship. The Browning Safari was truly a deluxe grade rifle and well worth the $46.00 difference. I realize that now, not then.

Medallion and Olympian, need I say more! I don't know of any other mass produced rifles made in or outside of the U.S. that has the beautiful, changing and wonderfully executed engraving and stock work that is present on these rifles. How many factory engraved production rifles have you ever seen? If you find one, the engraving is not in the same league with these rifles. Also, you can buy an Olympian today for less then 1/2 the cost of an engraved Pre-64 Winchester Model 70 and little more then any other engraved rifle. All three grades, the Safari, Medallion and Olynpian, were the finest factory produced rifles from 1959 to 1976 and have not been duplicated since.

4. **Collecting** — The most collectible rifle today is the Winchester Model 70 Pre-64. There were 581,471 of these produced; that's a bunch of guns, many more then the total production of the Safari, Medallion and Olympian grades combined. With the help of Fiore Passaro, who has researched the Safari guns thoroughly, we have estimated that only a total of approximately 66,000 were made with the F.N. actions, 6,000 with the Sako L461 action, and 16,000 using the Sako L579 action. That's only a total of 88,000 ever made. These guns were scarce when discontinued and even more so today. Have you been to a gun show lately and looked for one of them? How many have you seen? Fiore recently told me that he went to a 2,400 table Houston, Texas show, and saw from three to four collectible Safaris in common calibers. I produce almost 30 shows a year in Georgia and actively look for them. In the past year, I haven't seen more then 25 Safaris that were collectible, and they were priced higher and higher each month. These guns are gaining in collector's interest quickly, therefore, in value.

Look at things in 1993: the Browning Safari 30/06 is now $750.00 in 99% condition and the Winchester is about the same or now maybe even slightly less. The Safaris are keeping up with the Winchesters in value and are even getting ahead. You have to limit the Pre-64 guns to Pre-57 production to find decent workmanship and finish in the Winchesters. The Browning Safari's workmanship was excellent throughout its production. The only thing you must look out for in the Browning rifles are the magnum guns with a short extractor and salt wood. These are just as good a gun to hunt with as the long extractor guns but collectors actively look for the earlier ones, we will go into this and salt wood later. Most of the Model 70's worth more in the standard grades are the odd ball calibers and the large magnums. When you speak of the Model 70 Supergrades you have to compare them to the Medallions where most Model 70 chamberings are 50% to 100% higher in value. But when you compare the Supergrades to the Olympians the Olympians are only slightly higher and with no comparison in the overall rifles themselves. I write here in generalities, you start comparing each chambering and one will be higher priced on the Model 70 and one on the Browning. My point is that the Brownings are creeping up in value and surpassing the Pre-64 Winchester Model 70, the most collectible modern American made rifles in history.

Please let me clarify that I am only picking on the Model 70 in order to compare the Brownings with them. Unquestionably, the Winchester was a fine rifle and is extremely collectible, I own a few myself. I believe that the Browning rifles deserve to be compared to the most collected rifles and am doing so. I also believe that the Browning rifles are today a better investment then most and will continue to increase in value at a greater pace then most other collector grade guns in the future.

The increase in popularity that the Safaris are gaining is a darn good reason you better get as familiar with them as possible. As they go up in value and the rarer calibers increase in price, you will find more and more people trying to pass off redone or bogus guns on the public. It has gotten so bad with the Winchesters that some barrels, boxes and other parts are even being made from scratch. When it pays to put $2,000 or $3,000 in a gun and sell it for four or five times as much, there will be folks out there willing to take the risk and there are also collectors out there willing or too anxious to buy a rare piece and make a mistake. Remember, if they could make it from 1959 to 1976, they can make it today. Brownings have not reached the value level that would justify all out fakery just yet but when they do you will start to see common calibers like the 30/06's being redone into rare calibers. Right now, if you were to take a $750.00 30/06 and rebarrel it into a $2,000.00 220 Swift you would be way ahead. I haven't seen this sort of thing yet and hope I never do but you must be on the look out for it. Nothing kills a new collectors spirit and enthusiasm like diving into collecting, spending a lot of money, and finding out later that he was taken advantage of by some unscrupulous dealer. I hope this never happens in the world of Browning collecting like it has in others and I certainly hope it never happens to you.

Mr. David Banducci, who has been a Safari, Medallion, and Olympian collector for many years recently wrote in the Browning Collector Association's newsletter the following which should give you an idea of how folks look at the quality and collecting of these rifles:

"Belgium Browning Bolt Action Rifles became a fascination to me about twelve years ago. The first one I ever saw was at a gun show in Sacramento, California. It quickly became evident to me that I would have to buy one to see if it would shoot as good as it looked. I was not disappointed. The 243 heavy barreled gun would consistently group one inch at 100 yards from a bench. From that point on I knew one would never be enough." The longer time goes on, the fewer Safaris you will find available."

As if the Safari wasn't enough, in 1961, Browning brought out the great Medallion and Olympian Grades. There's not another company, that ever came close to cataloging, on any basis, guns of this quality. Winchester would advertise special engraving, grade of wood and stock carving but failed to offer these features as a stock item. Other U.S. manufacturers also failed to offer any off the shelf high grades as well. Year after year, sportsmen had the opportunity to own factory produced custom rifles. You can purchase approximately 20 different calibers in six different engraving patterns by over 75 to 100 master engravers and only stick with the standard factory configurations. If you start looking for the unusual and odd, you'll not only have a ball looking, but you'll make many friends along the way and have works of art to show off. We will go into each grade in their own sections.

Even though we will be discussing long and short extractors under that section it seems correct to mention them here in the introduction of this section of the book.

There is a lot of interest, not only with collectors but also by hunters in rifles made only with the long extractors. These are the guns that everyone wants. When you call a dealer, don't inquire about a standard caliber gun and then ask if it has a long extractor. All standard calibers were made with long extractors; only the F.N. Supreme actions in the magnum calibers were short extractor guns.

I really don't see a tremendous difference in the short extractor guns as far as general usage is concerned, so if you can save money and purchase a short extractor gun, why not? Unless you're collecting, a short extractor gun could fill the bill for your use. Another reason that the knowledgeable collectors like the long extractor guns is that the earlier guns had oil finished wood; they were a little nicer then the later guns. Some of the most knowledgeable Safari collectors limit their magnum rifles in their collections to 1965 and earlier; these are the guys really in the know. We will have more discussion on the long and short extractors in the extractor section.

Please note: The basic features of these rifles discussed in the text includes the Olympians and Medallions; if I just mention the Safari, I am also referring to the other grades unless different in their sections.

GENERAL INFORMATION FOR ALL GRADES

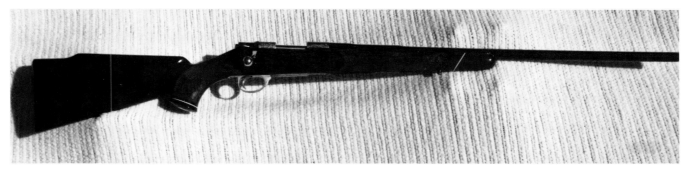

Here is a good example of an Olympian in 222 Remington Magnum. Please note there are no recoil lugs on any short action rifles.

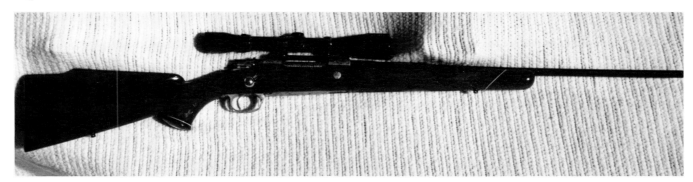

This is the same 308 Winchester Olympian pictured with the non-factory gold inlaid scope bases. This is the medium action with one recoil lug.

F.N. ACTIONS

The F.N. action was the main stay for this model and is respected to this day as the bolt action by which all others are judged. Many of these actions are sought after for restocking or embellishment into a custom rifle. I have seen several Safaris restocked and customized. Why someone would want to do this is beyond me, for they could start with a F.N. action and have it custom barreled and stocked for a lot less money and not ruin a great and hard-to-find rifle like the Browning Safari. F.N. produced a great many rifles for themselves and other companies beside Browning so the actions are not ultra rare, you can find a list of these companies on page 279.

As noted above, they were the same as the basic F.N. action being produced at the time for sales all over the world. It was based on the venerable Mauser 98 military rifle that the Germans fought two world wars with and supplied to almost every country all over the world from Chile to China. It was a proven action and has been the basis for tens of thousands of custom rifles put together by hobbyists and some of the best gunsmiths around like Griffin & Howe.

Many companies have made minor changes to the triggers, safeties, etc., but no one has been able to better it. Of course, the Mauser 98 has been refined and sporterized, but it really hasn't been improved upon very much other then for use by sportsmen. You just can't go wrong with one of these and the Safari rifle is proof. All three grades used these actions, as well as the Sako actions, which will be described later.

The three locking lug all-steel actions were blued in the Safari and Medallion grades but greyed on the Olympians. The round top receiver rings were drilled and tapped for scope mounts, whether they had iron sights or not, they were also drilled for a receiver sight from 1963 to 1964. I mentioned that the Medallion and Olympian grades had polished actions. Don't think for one moment the Safari was lacking in smoothness, for this simply is not so.

All had the streamlined bolt sleeve and long extractors (see page 242), they were polished bright on all three grades. The extractors themselves were also polished bright but polished and damascened on the Olympians.

The changing of the safety from the bolt shroud to the right of the top tang allowed a more streamlined and up to date bolt shroud to be designed. It also kept dirt out of the action and allowed the shooter to tell at a glance or touch if the rifle was cocked and ready to fire. More important then dirt is moisture getting into the bolt and then freezing, oil can also freeze but there hasn't been a bolt shroud designed that will ever prevent this from happening. It's not a good feeling to pull the trigger on the trophy of a lifetime and just hear a click. Browning tried to prevent this sort of thing by enclosing the inside of the bolt as much as possible.

By three locking lugs I mean two up front and a safety lug on the rear of the bolt that fits into a safety notch when closed. This notch is machined into the bottom of the action in front of the trigger assembly just below the rear receiver ring. The front receiver ring is threaded the same as the earlier Mauser 98 which is 14 T.P.I and the diameter is 1.100". All the tang screw threads are 1/4" by 22 T.P.I. The shape, length and configuration of the tangs did not change through out production, they are the same as all other F.N produced actions. There was basically no changes to these actions other then those noted in the bolt and extractor sections on page 242.

The early production bolt handles were flat on the under side and checkered, but the later ones were not. Although the Medallion and Olympian grades received special polishing you will still find the Safari bolts have the same quality and ease of operation of the higher grades.

The bolt stop was also redesigned from the original military style. A serrated spring bar was mounted on a pin that when pushed would extract the bolt stop and allow the bolt to be removed. This was not only efficient and safe but also enhanced the general sleekness and lines of the gun, all were polished bright.

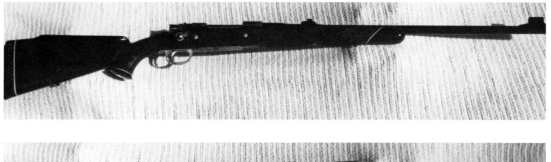
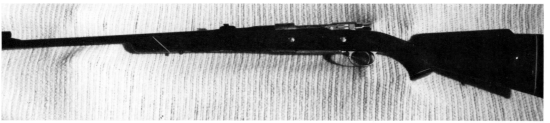

This powerhouse 458 Winchester Magnum features two recoil lugs. F.N. found two lugs necessary in these big magnums after experiencing cracked stocks on some early guns. You can find more information on this in the text.

As originally produced from 1959 until 1964, when the Sako L461 (small action) and the Sako L579 (medium action) came along and used for the small and medium cartridges, F.N. used their small ring action for the 243 Winchester and 308 Winchester rifles. These are hard to find since production was so short and early. Many are now in collector's hands and will be there for quite a while. The balance of the calibers were on the standard large ring unless otherwise described under the Sako section which follows.

F.N. FLOOR PLATES AND MAGAZINES

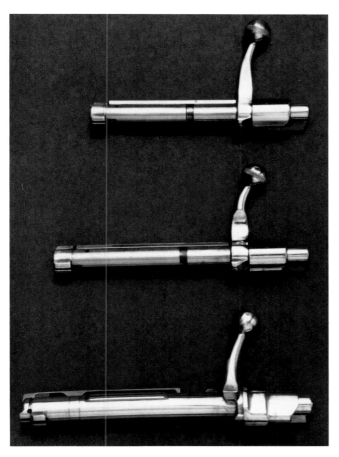 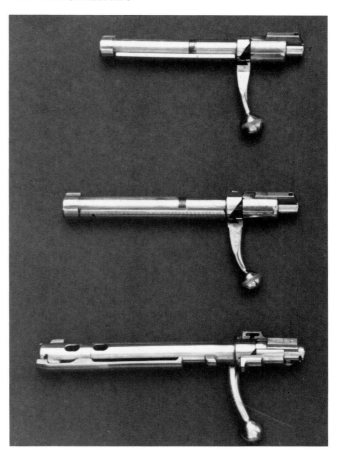

The three bolts pictured here on the left are from top to bottom for the short, medium and long action guns. On the right are the same bolts bottom view. Of course, the long action in the magnum calibers also had the short extractor which you will read about in the main text.

The hinged floor plates dropped down for easy unloading and was made of aluminum and anodized dark blue, the engraving was gold filled. The release latch was directly in front of the trigger guard on the outside so that an anxious shooter would not push it open with his trigger finger. Cartridge feed was adjusted for each individual caliber to assure a slick feed. Magazine capacity varied with each cartridge. This was as follows:

CARTRIDGE	MAGAZINE CAPACITY
243 Winchester	6
270 Winchester	6
284 Winchester	4
30/06 Springfield	6
308 Winchester	5
264 Winchester Magnum	4
7mm Remington Magnum	4
300 H & H Magnum	4
300 Winchester Magnum	4
308 Norma Magnum	4
338 Winchester Magnum	4
375 H & H Magnum	4
458 Winchester Magnum	4

The hinged floor plate allowed the shooter to unload the rifle without having to run each cartridge through the chamber. The best way to do this was to point the muzzle in a safe direction and open the action and withdraw the loaded round from the chamber, then open the floorplate and allow each cartridge to drop into your hand. When closing, be sure to push the floorplate closed with your thumb close to the latch. The floorplate and latch is fitted very snug, I have seen them come open at inopportune times. This will not to happen if you visually look at the latch to make sure it's secure. Further descriptions of the standard engraving will be found under the Safari section.

F.N. SAFETIES

The original safeties on the Mauser 98 military and sporting guns were located on the bolt shroud; they were not acceptable for a rifle meant to be used with a scope and were too noisy. The safeties on the F.N. actions were positioned on the right side of the top tang. They were serrated and blued on the Safari and Medallion but greyed on the Olympian. When in the rear position, the safety was on and the bolt could not be opened, but when the safety was forward and the red dot showed, it was off and the bolt could be operated. They were quiet and positive, which is important when hunting big game that might spook as the result of the slightest metallic sound. The safety also has a middle position that allowed the bolt to be opened when the safety was on. This facilitated unloading the magazine when on safe, but I wouldn't recommend this. The best thing to do is to open the floor plate and allow the cartridges to drop out the bottom after you unload the chamber.

F.N. TRIGGERS

The grooved gold plated triggers were all adjusted at the factory for a three pound pull that would remain constant. All were fully adjustable for weight of pull, creep and backlash. The triggers on these rifles left nothing to be desired and were accepted by the American shooters with enthusiasm. Rarely will you find a trigger replaced with another make, for they had all the advantages that most custom trigger manufacturers offered at that time. When shipped from F.N., they were properly adjusted for hunting conditions, if you don't like the trigger, I would not recommend you try to adjust one yourself; get a competent gunsmith to do it instead.

F.N. EXTRACTORS

The biggest difference to collectors on the early and late actions are the long and short extractors. The only cartridges or rifles affected by this change were magnums produced after 1967. All extractors were polished bright except the Olympian's which were damascened.

Long or claw extractors were like those found on the original Mauser 98's or the Pre-64 Winchester Model 70's. The short extractors were found on the

"FN Supreme" actions and were also like those found on the Remington Model 700 series and other late model rifles.

One of the reasons F.N. went to the short extractor was it just seemed the thing to do at the time. The gun writers were all saying that the short extractor required less of the receiver ring to be cut away and therefore it was safer and stronger. They didn't mention it was cheaper to make and not as reliable as the long extractor. The long claw extractor actually grabbed the cartridge rim and therefore guided it into the chamber. Upon extraction, the wider claw would have more cartridge rim to pull on so in the case of some problem with a bad case or hot load you had more of a chance of extracting the cartridge. When operating the action under dangerous or unusual conditions, it is a bit more secure to have the cartridge guided into the chamber rather then simply pushed out of the magazine with the bolt and then merely pushed into the chamber under no control whatsoever. What if you only pushed the bolt partially forward and stopped? People do all kind of crazy things when nervous and in the middle of a bad situation when hunting. The cartridge could fall out and you would have to start the process all over again if you had another cartridge in the magazine. What if you were holding the rifle sideways or upside down for some reason and it got jammed in the chamber when only half way in?

You may not think this is too important sitting in your easy chair reading this book but big game hunters think it is when a seven ton elephant comes charging down on them or a Brown bear about ten feet tall steps out right in front of the path they're on and there's no place to go or you're in the middle of the hunt of your life in Alaska and all of a sudden you have a useless rifle in your spike camp because of a stuck case. But let's get down to the good old boy on his annual deer hunt. Wouldn't he rather have a more positive feeding action for that follow up shot after sitting in a deer stand all day? I realize this is pure speculation, but if you were a big game guide in Alaska hunting Kodiak or a White Hunter in Africa guiding clients whose lives depended on you, what would you want?

You read these wonderful books by Capstick and Ruark about split seconds between you and death, and you want everything going for you that you possibly can. Besides, all you Nebraska prairie dog hunters might think about this when going after those ferocious little things with your 222 Remington Magnum; you might get attacked. Better get you a Safari in 375 Winchester Magnum in a pre-68 model with a long extractor just to be safe.

There are trends in rifles just like trends in clothes, automobile, etc. Just because it's new doesn't mean it's better. I have personally never heard of any problems with the short extractor guns but some folks just don't collect them and I would advise any new collector to do the same.

F.N. FRAME MARKINGS

The frame markings varied with the years and were as follows:

From 1959 to 1968 on the bolt handle underneath where it is welded to the bolt body you will find the serial number. The proof number 13 shown on page 50 will be on the right side of the handle. You will find various proof marks on the left side of the receiver ring, these are assembly, inspection marks and proof marks. F.N. did not put the serial numbers on these earlier actions.

From 1969 to 1975 the serial number appeared on the left side of the frame on the receiver bridge about half way down. On the Olympian you will find the serial numbers on the right rear receiver ring just above the wood line and sometimes on the tang. Proof, assembly and inspection marks numbers 6, 12, 7 and 4 all on page 50 will also appear.

You will also find markings such as the red dot for the safety.

CALIBERS FOR THE
F.N. ACTIONS

As originally introduced in 1959, the standard calibers that were available on the large ring actions were 264 Winchester Magnum, 270 Winchester, 7mm Remington Magnum, 30/06 Springfield, 300 H & H Magnum, 308 Norma Magnum, 338 Winchester Magnum, 375 H & H Magnum, and the 458 Winchester Magnum. There were many unusual and special order chamberings and we will get into them later.

In 1960, the 243 Winchester and the 308 Winchester were also introduced but only on the small ring action. These two cartridges only were made on this action until 1964 when the Sako medium length or L579 action was introduced in the Browning line. The guns produced using the early small ring F.N. actions are hard to find since production was so short and early. They all have that special early look with an oil finish that has started to develop the patina that collectors like to see. However, like everything else when it comes to collecting Brownings, there are exceptions to the rule. There were a few 243 Winchester and 308 Winchester rifles produced on the large ring F.N. actions, but they are even rarer. Many are now in collector's hands and will be there for quite a while. They are a desirable variation of which you should be aware.

The balance of the calibers were on the standard large ring action unless otherwise described under the Sako section. These were the 222 Remington, 222

Remington Magnum and 22/250 Remington. A full breakdown of the calibers made on the large ring actions are:

STANDARD CALIBERS
243 Winchester
264 Winchester Magnum
270 Winchester
7MM Remington Magnum
284 Winchester
308 Winchester
30/06 Springfield
308 Norma Magnum
300 H & H, Magnum
300 Winchester Magnum
338 Winchester Magnum
375 H & H Magnum
458 Winchester Magnum

SPECIAL ORDER OR EUROPEAN

220 Swift	7.65 x 53
244 Remington	8 x 57
257 Roberts	8 x 60
7mm Mauser	9.3 x 62
25/06 Remington	9.3 x 64
300 Savage	10.75 x 68
6.5 x 57	404 Jeffries
7 x 64	425 Wesley Richards
250/3000	9.5 x 57

SAKO ACTIONS

When you look over the bulk of the factory produced guns in unusual or small cartridges, you simply see out of proportion actions like the Winchester Model 70 in 22 Hornet. While this is a great little classic in Supergrade configuration and one which I like very much, you just can't justify a 1.403" length case in an action perfectly capable of handling the 458 Winchester Magnum. I guess F.N. and Browning couldn't either, so they contracted with Sako to supply them with barreled actions that were specifically designed for the smaller cartridges, they ended up with one of the best bolt action rifles ever produced. Until 1964, when F.N. started to use the Sako actions, the 243 Winchester and 308 Winchester guns were mostly built on the F.N. small ring actions. After this, they were built on the Sako L579 action along with several other cartridges discussed later. The use of these small actions also made it possible for Browning to expands it's product line into the 22 centerfire cartridges.

Sako had nothing to do with the stocking, engraving, or finish of these rifles, they only manufactured the actions and barrels to F.N.'s specifications. Stock inletting of the barreled action, blueing, sight fitting, engraving, and all other aspects of the manufacture of the guns were 100% F.N. Sako was one of the few manufacturers that could stand up to F.N.'s standards. These were the smoothest little actions ever produced for the smaller calibers.

Fiore Passaro has done some extensive research with the help of some Browning employees and has estimated that only about 6,000 L461 action guns and about 16,000 L579 action guns were ever produced.

The serial numbers for these actions were kept separate from the F.N. produced actions, so it is possible to estimate the total production of each. You divide the L461 by both the calibers it was chambered for, and you come up with only an average of about 3,000 for each cartridge. From what we have seen in the market, there were more 222 Remingtons Magnums made than 222 Remingtons, and that makes the latter even rarer. Maybe even as rare as 1,500 or so. I would also like to point out that both of the L461 calibers were also made with the heavy barrel, which was much more popular then the pencil barreled variation, so a pencil barreled Safari, Medallion, or Olympian rifle with this action is a rare gun indeed and will fetch a good price.

The L579 was made in four calibers, so only about 4,000 were made on average for each of these calibers. When you consider that the 243 Winchester and the 22/250 Remington calibers were made with a heavy barrel, you can see again the rarity of these calibers with a pencil barrel. The pencil barrel configuration is the one the collectors look for more than any other in these smaller calibers. The 284 Winchester was not a popular caliber at the time, so these are also quite rare to begin with and even rarer in the L579 action. In fact, Fiore has some excellent information about the 284 Winchester that estimates total 284's sales ran as low as only 348 guns from 1964 to 1978 but I believe the true figures are a bit higher. This will be covered in detail in the all calibers both standard and special order section.

This has nothing to do with the Sako actions but I would like to point out the following. It's not known by most Browning collectors that when Sako was building barreled actions for Fabrique Nationale, they were receiving actions from F.N. for their Finnish made rifles. You will find many Sakos built during this time with the large ring F.N. action, this was done until the Sako L-61 action came into existence.

These were the basic L461 and L579 actions. The L461 was used for the small cartridges such as the 222 Remington and the L579 was used for the medium cartridges such as the 308 Winchester. Fabrique Nationale specified exactly how they wanted the barrels contoured, but the action configuration other than the shape of the top of both the rear and front receiver rings was all Sako.

The three locking lug all-steel receivers were blued in the Safari and Medallion grades and greyed on the Olympians. All bolts, bolt sleeves and extractors were polished bright on all three grades. By three

locking lugs I mean two up front and a safety lug on the rear of the bolt. All were drilled and tapped for scope mounts, whether the rifle had iron sights or not. These are the smoothest actions ever mass produced and one of the most attractive features of this action even today. You will find these actions have the same quality and ease of operation of the finest custom rifles ever made.

None have ever been drilled for receiver sights. I wouldn't doubt that there is one out there, but it would be an earlier action finished and assembled at a later year. Always expect the unexpected when collecting Brownings.

The blued bolt stop was a small button mounted on a pin, when pushed it would retract the bolt stop and allow the bolt to be removed, the button itself was polished bright. This was not only efficient but also out of the way so there was no chance of it snagging on a branch or piece of clothing.

SAKO FLOORPLATES AND MAGAZINES

The hinged floor plates dropped down for easy unloading. The release latch was directly in front of the trigger guard on the outside so there was no chance of an accidental opening and loss of the cartridges at an inopportune moment in the field. Cartridge feed was adjusted for each individual caliber to assure a slick feed, magazine capacity varied with each cartridge. This was as follows:

CARTRIDGE	MAGAZINE CAPACITY
222 Remington	7
222 Remington Magnum	7
22/250 Remington	7
243 Winchester	6
284 Winchester	4
308 Winchester	5

The hinged floor plate allowed the shooter to unload the rifle without having to run each cartridge through the chamber. When closing, be sure to push the floorplate closed with your thumb close to the latch. The floorplate and latch is fitted very snug and I have seen them come open at inopportune times. This will not happen if you visually look at the latch to make sure it's secure.

The gold filled floor plate engraving pattern on the Sako action guns was different then the F.N. but generally are of the same quality and type. You can see the difference in the picture which shows long and short action floor plate engraving.

SAKO SAFETIES

The blued safeties on the Sako actions were positioned on the right side of the top tang. When in the rear position, the safety was on and the bolt could not be opened, but when the safety was forward and the red dot showed, it was off and the bolt could be operated. They were quiet, which is important when hunting big game that might spook as the result of the slightest metallic sound. The safety also has a middle position that allowed the bolt to be opened when the safety was on. This facilitated unloading the magazine with the safety on, but I wouldn't recommend this. The best thing to do is to open the floor plate and allow the cartridges to drop out the bottom after you unload the chamber. In May of 1993, I went on an Ontario black bear hunt and saw the importance of a completely silent safety. One of my fellow hunters said he was thirty yards away and about twenty feet up a tree from a feeding bear. He covered his bolt with a gloved hand and very slowly took the rifle off safety. Even with this precaution the bear immediately looked up directly at him. A black bear's hearing compared to a whitetail deer is far greater. By the way, he waited until the bear started feeding again and got his trophy, a silent safety is important.

SAKO TRIGGERS

The grooved triggers were all adjusted at the factory for a three pound pull that would remain constant. All were grooved, gold plated and fully adjustable for weight of pull, creep and backlash. The triggers on these rifles left nothing to be desired. When shipped from F.N., they were properly

adjusted for hunting conditions at three pounds, if you don't like the trigger, I would not recommend you try to adjust one yourself; get a competent gunsmith to do it instead.

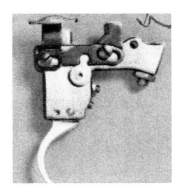

Pictured here is the Sako #4 trigger variation. These were the triggers used by F.N. on all short and medium action rifles. They are excellent triggers that require little care and are probably one of the best ever supplied on a mass produced rifle.

SAKO EXTRACTORS AND BOLT GUIDE

The Sako actions used the same short style extractors from beginning to the end of their use by F.N., they were positive and reliable and extract and feed very smoothly. All were polished bright except for the Olympian grade which were polished and damascened.

This has little to do with the extractors but behind them was a solid steel bar that was utilized as a bolt guide. They were fastened to the bolt by a blued ring. This is one of the reasons that these actions are so easy to operate, the bolts don't bind.

SAKO ACTION CALIBERS

There were basically only two actions supplied by Sako to build the Safari, Medallion and Olympian rifles, the L-461 short action and the L-579 medium action. These Sako actions were not only used by F.N. but also Marlin, Beretta, Harrington and Richardson and Colt. Custom rifles makers Winslow and Bill Wiseman have also used these or other actions by Sako. The two shown here are the L-461 or short action on the left and the L-579 on the right. The only differences from the actions Sako used for their own production were the absence of the integral tapered dovetail for scope mounting. All Browning guns with Sako actions have the round top receiver.

The Sako barreled actions came in the following cartridges:

L461 ACTION
222 Remington
222 Remington Magnum

L579 ACTION
22/250 Remington
243 Winchester
284 Winchester
308 Winchester

The 22/250 was the first introduction of a wildcat cartridge by a major firearms manufacturer and it caused quite a stir in the gun magazines. As a result, this excellent cartridge became a factory round soon after Browning's introduction of this gun. As mentioned previously, this was quite a step for a gun company at the time and contributed to the uniqueness of these rifles.

SAKO ACTION FRAME MARKINGS AND PROOF MARKS

Since all guns made or partially made in Liege must go through the Liege proof house the Sako actions will have the same proof marks as described for the F.N. actions. Most will have only the lion standing upright with "PV" under it.

The action markings varied with the years and were as follows:

From 1964 to 1968 underneath the bolt handle where it is welded to the bolt, you will find the serial number. On the top of the bolt handle is the proof number 13 as shown on page 50. On the left side of the front receiver ring you will also see the same proof mark and on the right front receiver ring just above the wood line you will see the serial number as well.

From 1969 to 1975 the serial number appeared on the left side of the frame on the receiver bridge about half-way down. On the Olympian you will also find the serial numbers on the right rear receiver ring just above the wood line or sometimes on the tang.

You can find additional markings later in this chapter in the barrel section.

BARREL CONFIGURATIONS FOR ALL ACTIONS

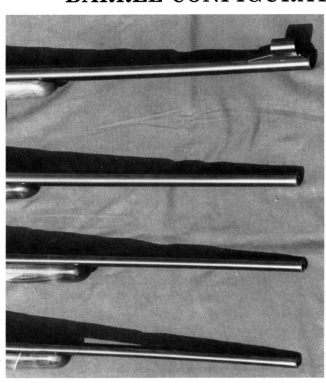

Here we have the four basic barrel configurations for all Safari, Medallion and Olympian grade rifles. The top is the 24 inch magnum barrel. Second from the top is the 24 inch heavy barrel as you will find on the varmint rifles. The third from the top is the 22 inch standard barrel with no sights and the bottom barrel is the 22 inch pencil barrel for the medium and short action rifles. The pencil barrel were supplied to F.N. by Sako and are the same as Sako used in their rifles only tapered differently.

All the barrels were very high lustre polished and blued, there were four different weights found on the Safari rifles. They are known as the pencil or light weight 22", the medium weight 22" or 24", and the heavy weight 24".

I will make a little note by each one so you can quickly see if a gun is hard to get and make a quick intelligent decision whether to pursue any purchase considerations. If there is no note, it means that they are not as hard to come across.

22" PENCIL OR LIGHT WEIGHT BARRELS
222 Remington (rarer than the 222 Magnum)
222 Remington Magnum (hard to find)
22/250 Remington (hard to find)
243 Winchester (rarer in the F.N. action then the Sako and even rarer in the F.N. large ring)
308 Winchester (rarer in the F.N. action then the Sako and even rarer in the F.N. large ring)

22" MEDIUM WEIGHT
244 Remington (very, very rare)
257 Roberts (very rare)
250/3000 Savage (very rare)
25/06 Remington (very, very rare)
264 Winchester Magnum (most common 264)
270 Winchester (not rare but desirable)
7mm Mauser (very, very rare)
284 Winchester (rare)
300 Savage (very, very rare)
30/06 Springfield (most common)

24" MEDIUM WEIGHT
220 Swift (very, very rare)
243 Winchester (very rare)

264 Winchester Magnum (hard to find only about
   1,000 were made)
7mm Remington Magnum (fairly common)
300 H & H Magnum (desirable but not uncommon)
308 Norma Magnum (hard to find)
300 Winchester Magnum (desirable but not
   uncommon)
338 Winchester Magnum (hard to find because of
   demand)
375 Winchester Magnum (hard to find because of
   demand)
458 Winchester Magnum (desirable but not uncommon and not worth as much as the 375's)

REMEMBER: look for the long extractor
magnums.

24" HEAVY BARREL

222 Remington (desirable and not common)
222 Remington Magnum (desirable and not common)
22/250 Remington (desirable and not common)
243 Winchester (hard to find)
25/06 (very,very rare)

26" MEDIUM WEIGHT

The 264 Winchester Magnum and others were
made but not produced extensively. You might run
across one, but it would be very rare indeed. While
we're on the subject of the 264 Winchester Magnum,
let me bring out the point that this was the only
caliber produced in two different barrel lengths and
experimented with in a third length. I am not forget-
ting about the heavy 24" barrels, but we won't count
them since they are also of the varmint configuration.

The notes I made next to each caliber were not
meant to make you believe that any you find in a
caliber marked "hard to find" are to be snatched up
immediately. They may also be common with a different barrel length or weight. Also, they are not
nearly as rare as the ones marked "rare." As time
goes by and more collectors come about they are all
going to be hard to find.

Do not be surprised to find a cartridge in a barrel length or weight not listed, but I believe all are
covered. If you have a caliber not listed in a certain
barrel configuration, please get in touch and let me
know about it. I would also like to know the grade,
date of manufacture and the barrel configuration.

Remember, from the beginning to the end of production, Browning would accept special custom
orders as long as they deemed the rifle safe to shoot.

I have not included the metric cartridges here for
I do not know the barrel lengths. While these are a
great find for the average collector and something
unusual, these rifles are not worth what an American
chambered rifle in a rare caliber would be. Let's just
say a 7.65x55 would not bring the kind of money a
25/06 would bring. But a large bore cartridge like a
404 Jeffreys would bring more money. In fact, I
would say that any large bore metric cartridge would
be very desirable. Don't buy anything unusual and
pay a lot of money anticipating what it would be
worth to someone else, purchase it on the basis of
what it would be worth to you.

While we're on the subject of cartridges, let me
pass on to you the barrel twists for all the common
cartridges for you bench shooters and reloaders.

CARTRIDGE	TWIST
222 Remington	14"
Heavy Barrel	14"
222 Remington Magnum	14"
Heavy Barrel	14"
22/250 Remington	14"
Heavy Barrel	14"
243 Winchester	10"
Heavy Barrel	10"
270 Winchester	10"
284 Winchester	10"
30/06	10"
308 Winchester	12"
7mm Remington Magnum	10"
300 Winchester Magnum	10"
308 Norma Magnum	12"
338 Winchester Magnum	12"
375 H & H Magnum	14"
458 Winchester Magnum	16½"

COMPLETE ACTION & BARREL SERIAL NUMBERS & OTHER MARKINGS

We have already covered the F.N. and Sako action markings in their sections, these are the barrel
markings for both actions. I have also included the
action markings so that you will not have to look in
three places to find all the information you need. This
can be rather confusing since the serial numbers moved around throughout production. The following is
a guide.

FROM 1959 TO 1968

On the bolt handle where it's welded to the bolt,
you will find the serial number as well as proof
number 13 as shown on page 50. On the left side of
the front receiver ring, you will find the same proof
marks.

On the left side of barrel under or adjacent to the
rear sight on the F.N action rifles are the words:
**BROWNING ARMS COMPANY
ST LOUIS MO & MONTREAL P.Q.**

The barrel address as stamped on all rifles produced during the 1959 to 1968 period.

On the left side of the barrel immediately in front of the receiver ring you will find proof number 13 as shown on page 50 as well as several other proof and assembly marks.

On the right side of the barrel under or adjacent to the rear sight are the words:

CALIBER (caliber) ONLY
MADE IN BELGIUM

These few pictures of caliber marking are far from a complete showing of all the calibers produced. These will suffice to show you the typical manner in which they were marked including the Liege proof markings.

The serial number did not appear on the frame but only on the barrels on the right side about 1/2'' in front of the receiver ring.

On the Sako actions for these years you will find the same proof marks as on the F.N. action rifles. The serial number and proof will also appear on the bolt. In addition, you will find the Finnish pressure proof.

The barrel markings for the Sako rifles on the left side are:

BROWNING ARMS COMPANY

You will also find the same proof marks as on the F.N. action barrels.

On the right side of the barrel you will find:
CALIBER (caliber) ONLY (serial number here)
MADE IN FINLAND

The Gun Control Act of 1968 changed things a little bit.

1969 TO 1975 MARKINGS

The serial number appeared on the left side of the action on the receiver bridge about half way down. You will also find the serial number on the right side of the rear receiver ring on some rifles but not in both places. This will appear just above the wood line. The serial number and proof will also appear on the bolt.

On the left side of the barrel immediately in front of the receiver you will find the proof marks numbers 6,12,7 and 4 as they appear on page 50.

For the F.N. action rifles you will find on the left side of the barrel about four inches from the receiver ring the following marking:

BROWNING ARMS COMPANY

Here is the "BROWNING ARMS COMPANY" stamping used between the years 1959 to 1968.

On the right side of the barrel four inches in front of the receiver ring are the markings:

CALIBER (Caliber) ONLY (serial number here)
MADE IN BELGIUM *and the proof number 9 on page 50.*

All guns produced in Liege required proofing and proof marks. Here are a couple of examples of them. You can get complete drawings of the many proof marks used on page 50.

The action markings for the Sako actions are the serial number on the left side of the frame on the receiver bridge about half way down. On the Olympian you will find the serial number on the right rear receiver ring just above the wood line and sometimes on the tang. The words "Made In Finland" will also appear.

The barrel markings for the Sako rifles on the left side are:

BROWNING ARMS COMPANY

On the right side of the barrel you will find:

CALIBER (Caliber) ONLY
MADE IN FINLAND

SIGHTS FOR BOTH ACTIONS

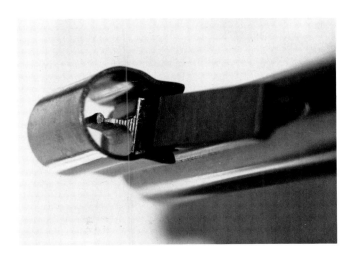

There were several front sights used, pictured here is the variation with the short ramp. Please note the gold bead as seen from the rear of the sight.

The front sight base was screwed onto the barrel and consisted of a gold bead mounted on a knurled ramp. There were three front sights used and all were provided with a hood. There are only minor differences in the three front sights and not important to this discussion.

Left and right side views of the early rear sight used from 1959 through 1963.

After 1963 until the end of production, the flip up rear sight was used on all rifles supplied with open sights.

The rear sights are a different matter for collectors look for the first variation.

There were two types of rear sights used. The early ones appeared from 1959 to 1963. They were a machined steel base with a separate sight dovetailed into it. The base was screwed on to the barrel, not dovetailed. The sight itself was detailed in white and was adjustable for both windage and elevation. These adjustments were coin slotted for use in the field if needed.

The later ones which were used from 1964 to the end of production were also a machined steel base with a separate folding leaf sight dovetailed into it. The base was screwed on to the barrel, not dovetailed. The folding leaf sight itself was detailed in white and adjustable for both windage and elevation. These adjustments were coin slotted for use in the field if needed. You can see the difference in the photos.

Browning emphasized the fact that you didn't have to remove the sight to mount a scope. When these rifles were being made, sight positioning was a problem, for gun manufacturers were slow to recognize the importance that scopes had taken. The fact that hunters were having a hard time in keeping their iron sights intact and getting scopes put on with mounts that weren't a mile high and uncomfortable to use was a problem that Browning recognized before other manufacturers did. The Winchester Model 70 is an example of a gun that had rear sights completely incompatible for use with a scope; many of these were removed and subsequently lost. I can't think of a worse feeling then to be in hunting camp a good days ride from the closest gun shop and end up with a damaged scope. At least, if you had iron sights you could still hunt. This is just another example why the extra $46.00 it cost to purchase a Browning Safari over a Winchester Model 70 in 1962 would have been worth it. In fact, if you consider the extra cost of purchasing special sights or scope bases it wasn't even a matter of $46.00 extra dollars any more.

Pencil barreled 243 Winchester rifles are found with sights only when they were special ordered. Browning specifically announced in the catalog that this cartridge could be ordered with or without barrel sights; they did not do this with any other caliber. All Safari grade medium weight barrels, both 22" or 24", were made with sights unless the rifle was special ordered without them. The heavy weight barrels were made without any sights and were drilled for target scope bases.

The above paragraph looked so complicated that I've prepared the following table that should clarify things nicely.

SIGHT TABLE

	22" PENCIL	22" MEDIUM	24"	24" HEAVY
222 Remington	S			N
222 Remington Magnum	S			N
22/250 Remington	S			N
243 Winchester	O			N
257 Roberts		X		
250/3000 Savage		X		
25/06 Remington		X		
270 Winchester		X		
7mm Mauser		X		
284 Winchester		X		
30/06 Springfield		X		
308 Winchester		X		
264 Winchester Magnum		X	X	
7mm Remington Magnum			X	
300 H & H Magnum			X	
300 Winchester Magnum			X	
308 Norma Magnum			X	
338 Winchester Magnum			X	
375 H & H Magnum			X	
488 Winchester Magnum			X	

X-Normally had iron sights
S-Iron sight when special ordered
O-Iron sights optional
N-No iron sights available

All Medallion and Olympian rifles came without sights unless special ordered with them, except the 458 Winchester Magnums, which were shipped with sights unless special ordered without them.

STOCKS

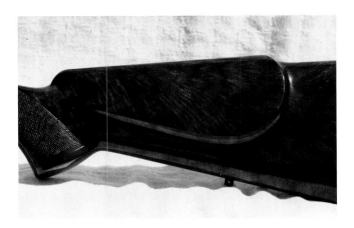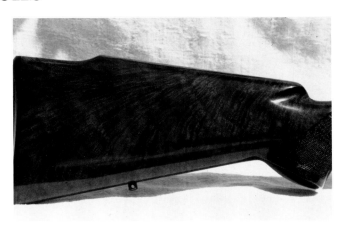

The wood pictured here is not typical of Safari grade rifles but can be found from time to time. This is from a 243 Winchester rifle. Many people will say that this was Olympian wood mistakenly used on a Safari, I believe it was simply a piece that was used to either expedite an order or there was a fault in the blank we cannot now see. In any case, it's one fine piece of wood that will increase the value of this Safari by at least 25% to 40%.

The stocks featured a full pistol grip with a Monte Carlo comb and cheek piece. The stocks were hand bedded and so well executed and the finish was so refined that most folks thought they were custom made or of special order when they first saw them. The dimensions were not changed throughout production and were length of pull 13 5/8", drop at comb 1 5/8", drop at Monte Carlo 1 5/8", and drop at heel 2 3/8", they were specially proportioned for use by the average(?) person with either iron sights or a scope.

All Olympian grade wood was at least as nice and of the quality of this butt stock of a 338 Magnum rifle. Please note the carved, checked grip cap with white line spacer and ventilated Browning pad.

The wood on all three grades is outstanding. I have never seen any of them with anything other then very acceptable to exceptional wood for the grade. In fact, F.N. produced many Safaris with Medallion or Olympian grade wood or Medallions with Olympian grade wood. Please do not take this to mean that the Safaris I've observed had Olympian style carving, checkering, grip cap or forearm tip just that the grade of wood was of Olympian standards. This was probably because they didn't deem a piece of wood 100% acceptable for a high grade rifle and knew any Safari buyer would flip out over the rifle. Also, the rifles might have been ordered with better wood or the lower grade wood was not available at the time of assembly, and production just couldn't be held up.

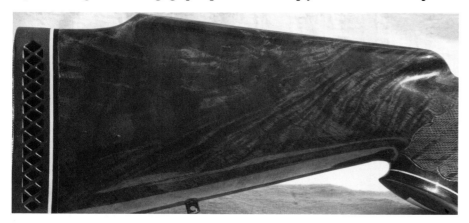

Another fantastic piece of wood used on a Medallion 375 H & H Magnum rifle. As you can see, the ventilated pad was used on magnums as standard.

Wood was purchased a carload (or whatever) at a time and then graded by F.N. Better grades of wood were not purchased separately other than for a special rifle. All cost the same and the better wood was separated from the other in the grading process.

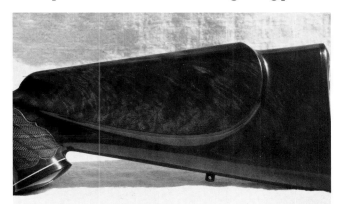

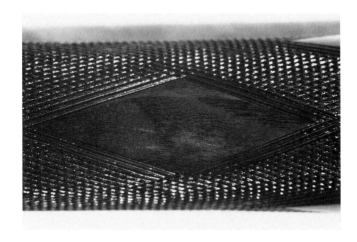

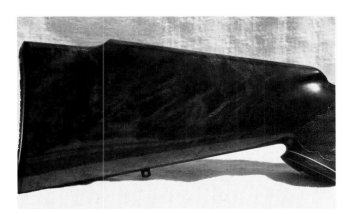

It must take the trained eye of the Belgium stock maker to see the difference in a piece of wood suitable for an Olympian and a piece suitable for a Medallion. This 284 Winchester Medallion grade is as nice as any piece of wood ever used on a production rifle. Please note the skip line checkering pattern, grip cap, and Monte Carlo comb.

All Safaris were hand checkered 20 lines per inch with a single border on the sides and top and a double border on the bottom of the pattern adjacent to the bottom of the pistol grip.

The Medallion was either 20 or 22 lines per inch skip line pattern as you can see in the illustration. I don't really know many lines per inch for they are too difficult to count exactly.

The Olympian was quite another matter for it was quite lavishly carved and had outstanding 32 lines to the inch checkering. It takes quite a piece of wood to handle checkering this fine not to mention the skill of the stock maker. It's hard to find a gunsmith that would be willing to tackle a checkering job 32 lines to the inch but there are some out there.

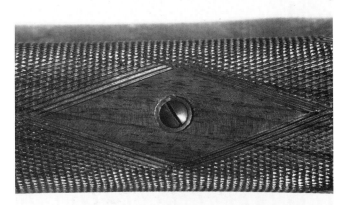

Here are two variations of the early uncheckered diamond in the center of the forearm on the F.N. Mauser action Safaris. The forearm without the screw is from a standard caliber and the one with the screw is from a magnum. Only Safaris produced from 1959 until 1965 will have this diamond. However, all Sako action Safari grade rifles had this feature until the end of production.

After 1965 all Safari and Medallion rifles were made without the diamond checkering pattern as shown here. This particular rifle is a Medallion grade in 375 H & H Magnum with the forearm screw.

The quality and the amount of checkering didn't vary from the beginning to the end of production. However, on the Safari forearms, the stocks made for the F.N. actions from 1959 to 1965 have a diamond uncheckered in the center. After this year, the forearms are fully checkered. The forearms for the Sako rifles had the diamond through out production. You can see examples of this in the photos.

All original factory stocks were marked in the barrel channel with the serial number that should match the action and/or, if applicable, the bolt and barrel. On the salt wood guns that were returned to Browning for restocking, the serial numbers on the new stocks will not be in the barrel channel as they were on the original; instead they were placed on the butt under the buttplate or pad. The workmen at Browning in St. Louis placed it here so they could see which stock was which as the finish dried, the stocks hung from a wire. Browning did an outstanding and costly job in trying to solve the salt wood problem. The St. Louis made stocks they made to replace the salt wood stocks are of excellent workmanship. They are entirely acceptable for the purpose for which they were originally made. Browning was inundated with so much work on restocking guns that some of it was done by Art Isaacson of Arnold, Missouri who was later to go to work for Browning but again is now on his own.

However, Browning collectors shy away from any restocked gun because they are not as they came from Belgium. Besides, if the rifle was restocked, it was also reblued and that of course hurts the value considerably.

The workmanship on every Safari was of the same standard as the higher grades, so you must look at the fit and finish to make sure all is original and proper. In judging a stock for originality be careful for there are some folks who have remarking dies that can pass for original and can replace a stock and apply new numbers. If you will look at a gun and examine the numbers, you will notice they are not perfectly in line and straight. It would be a small matter to take individual dies and stamp each number one at a time to match the receiver number. I can't see anyone at this time absorbing the cost of a completely new stock to recondition a Safari, but as they increase in value, it could become financially rewarding and you must be able to recognize such bogus work. Besides, you sure don't want to purchase a $3,500.00 Olympian with a replaced stock and find out later it's not original.

There were three basic ways the recoil lugs were engraved and installed. The top picture shows a Safari in 308 Winchester with only one lug. The second picture shows a Medallion grade with two lugs, this is a 338 Winchester Magnum. The bottom picture shows an Olympian with two lugs in 338 Winchester Magnum. The small chamberings with no recoil lugs are not shown.

The 222 Remington and 222 Remington Magnum never had a recoil lug inletted in the stock, but all the others did. The medium actions like the 243 Winchester and 308 Winchester had one recoil lug but not always. The longer F.N. actions like the 270 Winchester and 30/06 had only one and sometimes two depending on the date of assembly. The long magnum actions like the 300 Winchester Magnum, 338 Winchester Magnum, and 458

Winchester Magnums only had one lug at the very beginning of production, but this changed about 1960 when Browning had to start repairing the large magnums with split stocks.

All wood was finished in oil until about 1967 when the high gloss finish came along. If I can criticize these fine rifles at all, it would be the changes made to them in that year, stock finish, and short extractors in the magnum calibers. Browning was catering to the tastes of American shooters, everything was going high gloss and all the other makers such as Remington, Sako, Winchester, and Weatherby were screaming the advantages of the short extractor. As mentioned previously, the pulp gun magazine writers were editorializing extensively about the durability of the new finish and influenced the tastes of many sportsmen.

While the high gloss finish looks great on the store shelf, it didn't hold up as well in the field. You can take an oil finished stock and raise a dent or touch up a scratch, but you need to know what you're really doing with a urethane finished gun to refinish or touch it up properly. One of the best restorers in the business says that True-Oil, if used properly, will touch up one of these later guns and do a good job.

Not only did the urethane finished rifles lack the durability of the oil finished guns when they were made, but this finish will sometimes come off in spots, especially on the edges of many rifles. This cannot be readily helped and is not the fault of the previous owners. The urethane finish is very sensitive to any water spots and it will come off if the rifle gets and stays wet. In looking at this a little closer, if the rifle gets damp from storage, will the urethane finish come off? Let's look at this even closer and ask if a salt wood gun attracts moisture, will this moisture attack the urethane finish as well as the metal and cause the peeling of the finish around the edges where you generally find the problem? If the previous statement is correct, can you inspect the finish of the later guns, and if it is peeling, use this a another guide to finding salt wood? I believe so.

The oil finish applied to the early guns has a beautiful sheen but does not have the shine to the extent of the urethane finished guns; it is much more subdued. You will be able to tell the difference after looking at a few guns.

When you think you've found a rare caliber look over the finish of the rifle's wood. If it was originally produced for sale outside this country, it will have a well filled, but almost completely flat, finish. European and South American shooters prefer a flat finish and F.N. catered to their tastes just like they did to the tastes of the U.S. market. You can also tell the guns originally shipped to other countries by the barrel markings, which will be different. Many of the Safari rifles were brought here by servicemen who purchased them in a PX. This is also the reason you see these in a European chambering or a flatter looking metal finish. These rifles are desirable but do not bring exorbitant prices like the rifles made for the U.S. in rare calibers.

All three grades in all calibers were made with sling swivel eyelets that would accept quick detachable swivels, no swivels were provided unless special ordered with the rifle.

SALT WOOD

Salt wood was a big problem with these rifles in all three grades from 1967 until the end of production.

Look over very carefully any gun produced after 1966. The first sign of salt wood will generally show up around the recoil lugs, but don't neglect to look at the butt plate screws, the edges of the magazine well, and the edge of the barrel immediately under the wood line. Pull the barrel away from the wood and expose the metal slightly; you can generally tell from this quick inspection. If you see any rust at all, ask the seller to allow you to pull off the butt plate screws and check them out. If there is salt wood present, they'll be rusty where they were in contact with the wood. Please also refer to the previous section about the urethane finish and additional problems that salt wood may cause.

I am advising you not to purchase any gun if you can't thoroughly inspect it for salt wood, and that includes the butt plate screws if needed. It's no fun to lay down $3,000.00 or more for an Olympian and later find out it's got salt wood. Guns made in 1969 and 1970 are the worst years, you will find many more guns with salt wood then without.

It had been difficult for many years to obtain the quantity and quality of walnut needed by F.N. from its European sources. In 1966 or earlier, F.N.'s wood inventory was low and they asked Browning's help in securing some American walnut, especially the beautiful California Claro that was used to a great extent. A large quantity was ordered from a supplier that sent wood not only to Browning for F.N.'s use, but also to Bishop, Fajen, Winchester, Ruger and — would you believe — to the U.S. Military for M-14 stocks. The supplier was drying their walnut using granulated salt. The wood was covered with salt and placed in quonset huts. The wood dried so quickly that one of the workers told me he could actually see a steady drip of water coming from the wood. The wood was cut into the appropriate size planks and no one thought that any salt residue would remain on or in the wood after final shaping, sanding, and finishing. Well, they were dead wrong, so wrong in fact that the U.S. government stopped using walnut for the M-14 rifles and went to other types of wood or fiberglass because properly cured wood was so scarce at the time that sufficient supplies were not to be had!

The salt impregnated in the wood will absorb moisture, and any place it touches metal, you will find rust sooner or later, there is nothing you can do about it. Even coating the surface of the wood with finish will not stop the rusting; the wood must be replaced.

Over the course of collecting and dealing in these guns, I have heard enough sad stories about this problem to fill another book. The fact that someone tells you that he has owned a gun for many years and it hasn't rusted doesn't mean it is not a salt wood gun. I had folks tell me that they have meticulously cared for their guns, wiping them down at regular intervals, and inspecting them every few weeks or so, only to find one day the beginning of the salt wood problem arising and rust appearing. The rusting process can start at any time after lying dormant for many years.

This is not the first time someone has tried to cure out walnut with some sort of salt process and will probably not be the last.

As mentioned in the Post war Superposed section, sometime you can test the wood with silver nitrate. Place a drop or two on a hidden spot on the wood; if it bubbles, you have a problem. I would strongly recommend this upon purchase of any expensive rifle. Remember, the salt wood problem can lay dormant for many years and start giving trouble without warning. If this happens, the seller cannot be blamed and you may suffer a loss in value in that particular piece.

At one time Browning would replace the wood free of charge for the original owner with the original warrantee card, but you will have to talk with them about any work at this late date.

BUTTLATES AND PADS

All standard rifles were shipped with black plastic butt plates marked "Browning" unless they were special ordered with a pad. In any case, even if a standard caliber rifle was originally ordered with a pad the value would still be hurt unless it was new in the box and the label was stamped "RECOIL PAD". The standard pads were made by Pachmyer and also marked "Browning." You could order any kind of pad you wanted factory installed, but I have never seen any other then like those noted above.

Here is an example of the ventilated pad used by F.N. and Browning for the rifles made in magnum calibers and all special requests by customers for pads on rifles either ordered originally with a pad or returned later for one. In addition to the ventilated pad, Browning used the black plastic recoil plate on all standard caliber guns. Please see text for exact dates of manufacture of these Browning marked pads.

When these special orders were received, the pad was installed by Browning at their Arnold, Missouri, repair department, not by F.N., so the end label on a box may or may not be labeled "RECOIL PAD." I have seen them both ways.

All magnum rifles came standard with a "Browning" marked recoil pad except for the 264 Winchester Magnums which will be discussed in the next paragraph. I am sure some were special ordered without a pad, but I have never seen one with just a butt plate.

When the 264 Winchester magnum guns were first introduced, they had a 24" barrel and no recoil pad. Soon after introduction, Browning was receiving so many complaints about the recoil that they installed pads on the remaining stock of guns in inventory. You, therefore, will find some of these with and some without pads, and they will both be original. When the 22" barrel was introduced, they were also made with or without a recoil pad, so you can find these original with a butt plate or a pad. The

best thing to do is measure the length, look at the workmanship, and determine if the pad is original. I would prefer a 264 with a butt plate for my collection rather then a pad, that way there would be no question as to originality.

ALL CALIBERS — BOTH STANDARD & SPECIAL ORDER

Almost any caliber could be special ordered and some were. This is what created so many unusual guns today and why I receive so many phone calls from folks wanting to know why they have a Safari in an unlisted cartridge or configuration.

In addition, many servicemen brought back rifles they purchased from the PX or elsewhere. These were manufactured in European metric or other unusual calibers that are, in this country, very unusual and rare. F.N. not only made these rifles for this country, but for distribution all over the world. The European guns you will most often find will have the flatter oil finish and blue so liked by European hunters, who do not like the typical high gloss finish that was shipped here.

On the F.N. action the cartridges that were produced were:

STANDARD	SPECIAL ORDER	OR	PX PURCHASE
243 Winchester	220 Swift		7.65 X 53
264 Winchester Magnum	244 Remington		8 X 57
270 Winchester	257 Roberts		8 X 60
7MM Remington Magnum	7mm Mauser		9.3 X 62
284 Winchester	25/06 Remington		9.3 X 64
308 Winchester	300 Savage		10.75 X 68
30/06 Springfield	6.5 X 57		404 Jeffries
308 Norma Magnum	7 X 64		425 Wesley Richards
300 H & H, Magnum	250/3000		9.5 X 57
300 Winchester Magnum			
338 Winchester Magnum			
375 H & H Magnum			
458 Winchester Magnum			

Of course, the listing you see above is not completely honest. You see a lot of odd balls listed above, but they are not really rare. They may be rare in this country but not worldwide. The list above may not be complete, for other special orders, I am sure, were made through several distributors. If you go to Europe and visit a local gun shop you may find a Safari, Medallion or Olympian style rifle in a Metric chambering, make a deal and ship it back for you have a U.S. collectors gun. Also, any Olympian you may find probably has different engraving, that indeed would be a nice addition to an Olympian collection.

As an estimate only, since neither Browning nor F.N. will release the information at this time, there were about 100 to 150 Safaris made in 257 Roberts, about 9 in 25/06 Remington, and about 100 to 150 in the 7MM Mauser cartridges. Approximately 350 in 284 Winchester were produced in the Safari Grade, along with 23 Olympians and about 20 Medallions.

One of the rare bits of information we were able to get on annual production shows the total sales of the 284 Winchester. These ran as follows:

1965	1
1966	156
1967	59
1968	60
1969	14
1970	21
1971	14

From 1964 to 1973 a total of 332 were sold
From 1974 to 1978 a total of 16 were sold

So, if this information, which is direct from Browning, is anywhere correct, a total of only 348 of the 284 Winchester guns were ever made.

In comparing the 348 estimate with the information above, there is a large discrepancy. While the information given by Browning may be partially correct, we must take into account the number of guns seen at shows and listed in the trade journals. There are certainly more then 348 guns made in 284 Winchester, but we don't exactly know how many, so let's just say anywhere from 348 to 1,000. The end result in all this is that it is not the exact number produced that will deem what the value is but collector demand.

Below, you will also find the 264 Winchester Magnum information given to us by Browning. According to them, the total number of rifles produced in that caliber in both barrel lengths was 787. This also doesn't seem correct, for there are too many of these around also. The 264 production according to Browning's estimate is as follows:

264 Winchester Magnum

1964	108
1965	192
1966	187
1967	156
Additional Production	144
1964-1967 Total	787

Do not be surprised to hear about or find a rifle made in any unusual cartridge. Browning would accept special orders throughout the entire production of these rifles.

DATES OF MANUFACTURE FOR EACH CARTRIDGE

	59	60	61	62	63	64	65	66	67	68	69	70	71	72	73	74	75*
222 REMINGTON					X	X	X	X	X	X	X	X	X	X	X	X	X
222 REMINGTON MAG					X	X	X	X	X	X	X	X	X	X	X	X	X
22/250 REMINGTON					X	X	X	X	X	X	X	X	X	X	X	X	X
220 SWIFT$										X							
243 WINCHESTER		X	X	X	X	X	X	X	X	X	X	X	X	X	X	X	X
25/06 REMINGTON-										X							
257 ROBERTS-										X							
6MM REMINGTON►													X				
264 WINCHESTER MAG	X	X	X	X	X	X	X										
284 WINCHESTER						X	X	X	X	X	X	X	X	X	X		
7 MM MAUSER-										X							
7MM REMINGTON MAG						X	X	X	X	X	X	X	X	X	X	X	X
270 WINCHESTER	X	X	X	X	X	X	X	X	X	X	X	X	X	X	X	X	X
308 WINCHESTER		X	X	X	X	X	X	X	X	X	X	X	X	X	X	X	X
30/06 SPRINGFIELD	X	X	X	X	X	X	X	X	X	X	X	X	X	X	X	X	X
300 H & H MAG						X	X	X	X	X	X	X	X	X	X		
308 NORMA MAG						X	X	X	X	X	X	X	X	X	X	X	X
300 WINCHESTER MAG						X	X	X	X	X	X	X	X	X	X	X	X
338 WINCHESTER MAG			X	X	X	X	X	X	X	X	X	X	X	X	X	X	X
375 H & H MAG			X	X	X	X	X	X	X	X	X	X	X	X	X	X	X
458 WINCHESTER MAG	X	X	X	X	X	X	X	X	X	X	X	X	X	X	X	X	X

*Not cataloged but available from inventory as late as 1978.

I have not listed the years of production of the metric calibers, for they were not made for the U.S.
►6MM Remington — there was only one produced as far as I am able to determine.
$I have seen only one 220 Swift.
-The 25/06, 257 Roberts, and 7mm Mauser produced in 1968 was an order of from 100 to 150 in the 257 Roberts and the 7mm Mauser and about 9 for the 25/06 from the Hollywood Gun Shop in Los Angeles, Ca.

SAFARI GRADE

The Safari grade was the hunter's rifle. Many are being used today from the prairie dog towns of Nebraska to the game control stations on the African Veldt; they are strong accurate and dependable. The Safari is the professional hunter's choice; on my guided hunts I have seen many a guide preferring them over all other makes. The dependability of the F.N. action is legendary all over the world and is in great demand. The basic action was derived from the Mauser 98 and only refined to give it a better adjustable trigger, a safety and bolt handle that was useable with a scope, a hinged floorplate, drilled for scope bases, and a nicer streamlined looking bolt sleeve ejector and bolt release. Last but certainly not least, they were slightly engraved to take them out of the ordinary and give them that "Browning" touch for which the company is famous. The lockup, feed, extraction, ejection, and basic concept are exactly the same as the original that was used by the Germans to fight two world wars and shipped all over the world to supply armies from Mexico to China. What other action can compare to it? Need I say more about dependability or function?

SAFARI ACTIONS AND BARRELS

All were highly polished and lustre blued, the bolts and extractors were polished bright. The finish on the Safari rifles must be compared to custom rifles instead of other factory produced standard grades. Every gun was hand polished and fitted as only the workmen at F.N. in Belgium were allowed to do. Notice I said allowed and not can. Fortunately, F.N. and Browning have always taken a special interest in producing only the best, and this was achieved by spending a little extra time and money on the Safari rifles then other manufacturers spent on their models. I have never seen one with other then perfect workmanship. This is what really brings these rifles out of the ordinary. When you compare them today, as I did in 1963, with other makes, they stand out as the best mass produced rifles ever made. The quality of post-war F.N. guns are as good if not better then pre-war and even pre-1900 workmanship of other companies. Nothing was left to chance in their production nor was a gun ever considered finished unless it was properly done. Pick one up and you will find the checkering, inlaying, fit, and finish absolutely the best.

SAFARI TRIGGER GUARDS AND FLOOR PLATES

This is the engraving you will find on the floor plates of the medium and short action Safari grade rifles in all calibers.

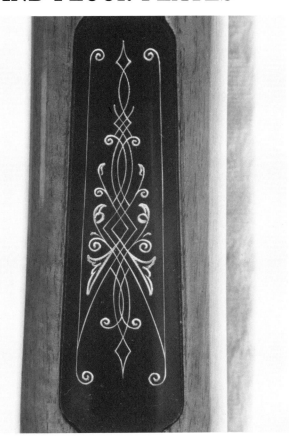

As you can see, the floor plate engraving for the F.N. long action models was different from the short and medium action rifles.

The dark blue anodized trigger guards and floor plates were very lightly engraved with a light broad scroll that was gold filled, just enough to let you know this wasn't a run of the mill rifle. There was one pattern for the short and medium actions and another for the long actions, this can be seen in the photographs. When a Safari was on a gun shop rack and mixed with the other manufacturers' guns, it was the first one you noticed. Not only did the engraving catch your eye, but the higher grade of finish in the wood and metal stood out. Even though the novice engravers at F.N. did the work on the Safaris, the workmanship was always good. You will not find second rate engraving on any gun from the beginning to the end of production.

Additional information on the trigger guards and floorplates will be found in their sections.

SAFARI STOCKS

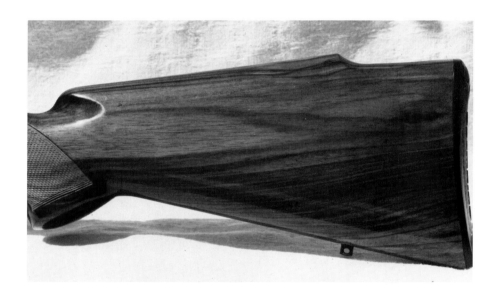

A typical Safari grade rifle butt stock. Even though this was the lowest grade rifle produced for the American market, F.N. still made every effort to give the buyer a little bit more in the way of quality.

The wood on the Safari grade was generally about group 2. I have never seen any of them with other than very acceptable to exceptional wood for a standard grade rifle. Look at the picture which shows an outstanding stock found on a Safari I located in California. A good grade of wood was necessary to accept the checkering that this grade had. If they used a grade of wood that wasn't dense enough, then the checkering wouldn't be acceptable. In fact, F.N. produced many Safaris with Medallion or Olympian wood, you can see an example of this in the photos. This was probably because they didn't deem a piece of wood 100% acceptable for a high grade rifle and chose to use it on this Safari. In any case, there were some that were ordered with a better grade of wood by the customer. All were plain hand checkered 20 lines to the inch with no flaws. The amount of checkering from the beginning to the end of production didn't vary very much other then the forearms which will be discussed later. Browning and F.N. always felt that it was better to maintain quality then to save a couple of dollars and cheapen the look of their product and the end result was very collectible guns today.

The Safari grade was made without grip or forearm caps, though some had these made of rosewood through special order. They all came with eyelets only but detachable sling swivels could be special ordered.

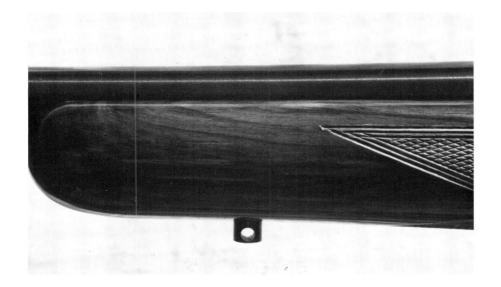

The Safari grade had no forearm tip. Here is an example of the way your rifle should look. You can also see the presence of the front sling swivel bases on this example.

As I have said previously about wood, there have been many Safaris and Medallions with upgraded wood. Do not shy away from any original looking rifle, for it could very easily have been special ordered or the wood used through necessity; look for originality. All three grades had the serial numbers stamped in the barrel channel. If in doubt about the originality of the wood, take the rifle apart and make sure the numbers match. You can also simply tell by the workmanship. Rarely will you find a replaced stock that is fitted and finished to the level of the original. There are some gunsmiths here that can do this sort of work, but they are few. You must especially be aware of the replacement of stocks on the salt wood guns. Many of these were returned to Browning for replacement and are quite acceptable, but they are not original and will never have the collector's value of the 100% factory original guns. When a rifle was returned to Browning for wood replacement, the new stock had the numbers stamped under the butt plate or pad and not in the barrel channel. They were stamped in this way to facilitate finding the stock while it was hanging from the wire and drying. So, you can tell a replaced stock by where the numbers were stamped. Of course, if the gun was restocked, it was also probably reblued and no one can do this without leaving some evidence of their work. In addition, restocked guns will have a different look about them from the finish to the checkering. You have to look at a few original guns to start telling the difference.

All standard calibers rifles and some early 264 Winchester Magnums were shipped with black plastic butt plates marked "Browning" unless special ordered with a ventilated pad that had the same marking.

All magnum rifles except the early 264 Winchester Magnums came standard with a Pachmyer-made "Browning" marked recoil pad unless special ordered without one. I have never seen a magnum made without a rubber pad other then that noted above. Also, to find a pad with any other makers name and installed by Browning or F.N. would not be original.

SAFARI CALIBERS

Safaris were made in all calibers as described under the caliber section, I will not list them here so as not to be redundant; in addition many were made as one-of-a-kind special order. During the entire reign of production, custom calibers were always available and even made on a production basis for certain gun shops at times. Browning was the first company to make a production rifle in the 22/250 which was a "wildcat caliber,". When they first appeared on the market, only reloaders could shoot them, for the cartridges were not factory made. I grant you that it was only a short time for Remington to introduce "their" 22/250 Remington, but it was Browning that really paved the way for this great little caliber that is still popular today and is probably the most used centerfire 22 caliber cartridge in the U.S.. Browning didn't only produce this and the standard calibers like other manufacturers, but also made such calibers as the then-unpopular 257 Roberts; the 243 Winchester almost killed it. They were also made in other wildcats such as the 25/06, which was later legitimized by Remington. Few people realized that not only were Browning and F.N. producing a higher quality and out of the ordinary rifles as a matter or course, but they were willing to make whatever the customer wanted if it were safe. If you will refer to the section "YEARS OF PRODUCTION FOR EACH CARTRIDGE," you will see a rundown of when each was made.

MEDALLION ENGRAVING, STOCKS AND PARTICULARS

The floor plate engraving on the Medallion rifles didn't vary much throughout production. Any variation you may see was mostly the result of the engravers work. On the left is a floor plate from a medium or short action, the floor plate on the right is from an F.N. long action rifle.

The Medallion was scroll engraved over 75% of it's action surface. Here is a closeup of the broad scroll engraving as was done on this grade. The engraving was the same for all three actions.

Both the Medallion and Olympian grades had white line spacers and rosewood tips. Please notice the checkering and where it appears in relation to the forearm tip.

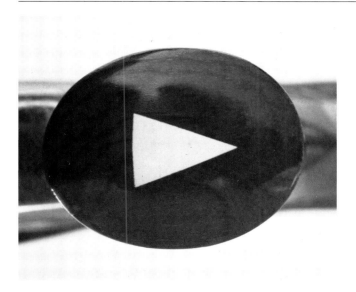

The Medallion grade had not only rosewood grip caps but also inserts. This example is from a Medallion grade in 338 Winchester made about 1965. Please note the difference in the insert as it appears here and the example shown in the Olympian section.

The Medallion grade was designed for a shooter that wanted more then a Safari but just couldn't justify or afford to drag an Olympian through the woods, and I couldn't blame him or her.

The wood was group 4 and finished just as nicely as the Olympians. They all had a high grade rosewood forearm tip and grip cap that had an ivory colored insert; the skip line checkering was about 20 to 22 lines per inch if you can count it. Notice this is the same as the Safari checkering lines per inch but looks a lot fancier because of the skip line pattern. This was highly popular at the time and played up as a special feature on many of the custom rifles being pumped up by the gun magazines at the time.

They were offered in the same calibers, barrel weights, and configurations as the Safari grade, I am not aware at this time of any special caliber orders.

No barrel sights were provided on any cartridges other then the 458 Winchester Magnum unless special ordered. I have not seen any other caliber with this special order feature although there may be some.

The metal was highly polished and given a lustrous blue, the bolt, bolt sleeve and bolt shroud were not blued. This polishing also included all internal parts and the bolt handle, bolt, bolt sleeve, action rails, and locking bolts. The polishing made for an extremely smooth operating action and definitely upgraded the rifle above the ordinary. All triggers were grooved and gold plated.

Unlike the Olympian, the engraving was the same for all cartridges. It consisted of light scroll covering about 75% of the action and extended about three inches beyond the front receiver ring. The floor plate engraving featured a ram's head surrounded by broad scroll. The floor plate engraving was not always gold filled but as a regular course of production was supposed to be. This work was generally done by the student engravers and always executed well. You will find, once in a while, a Medallion done by a master but this would be unusual and a real find for the advanced collector.

I do not know the actual production of the Medallions, but I don't believe it was very high, for you don't see many of them at shows or in collections, perhaps about 5,000 to 6,600 pieces. However, it must have been high enough for Browning to keep them in the line for over fifteen years. With a total production of approximately 88,000 guns in all three grades and in so many calibers the production for each one must be very limited, this is a rare and very collectible variation. Later, we will go into a more detailed discussion of total numbers produced.

Although they don't compare even remotely with the beauty of the Olympians, they are nice for the person wanting a special rifle to shoot or to collect. As collectors realize the rarity of these guns, they are sure to increase in value.

OLYMPIAN ENGRAVING, STOCKS AND PARTICULARS

I've seen good and I've seen great engraving on these rifles but never poor. If you're a fine rifle buff or a collector of fine engraved guns, the Olympians are the Brownings for you. It is not possible, in my opinion, to find a modern made production rifle that even comes close to the Olympian grade's quality and uniqueness.

Most of the rifles done by the master engravers are signed, usually on the right side of the receiver ring. I have seen many signed there and on the floor plate and other places as well. Get a good glass and look over the gun; you will probably find a signature somewhere. It was the option of the engraver whether to sign a piece or not, and many times they didn't. This work was done on a piece rate basis, and the more they turned out the more they earned. While production was high, in their haste to get to the next piece, sometimes they did not sign it.

Many times, you will find two and up to four different signatures on the same rifle. I had a 30/06 once that sported four signatures by three different master engravers! F.N. must have either been in a heck of a hurry to get it out or it was a parts cleanup gun. The signatures were on the left and right side of the receiver ring on the trigger guard and the floor plate. I wish I could clean up some more of those kind of parts.

Look over the list of master engravers in the front of this book, any gun found signed by one of these men or women is a quality piece and very collectable. That the gun was not signed does not mean it was not done by a master. All the Olympians were done by a master class engraver and not by an apprentice. Signatures are sought after by many collectors because it adds something to the piece and makes it more desirable. Some collectors make a study of the engraving and can tell you who did the gun without a signature present. These fellows are really into the engraving and are knowledgeable. It

pays to do this for guns engraved by the more respected engravers, Vrancken, Baerten and others, bring higher prices. When you spot an unsigned or signed rifle by one of these people and you know it will bring a better price then the average Olympian you may have a bargain. I just finished a very nice custom rifle with comparable coverage as the Olympian and the engraving alone cost $3,100.00. This shows you the great value of these Brownings. If you ever anticipate building a custom rifle and having it engraved, forget it, purchase an Olympian at an established value and save money.

Each caliber is engraved with appropriate game scenes and animals that correspond with the typical use of the cartridge; coverage is about 95%. Keep in mind that all these animals are surrounded by trees, grass and other types of foliage. Every square inch of these rifles is adorned with either animal scenes or medium to tight fleur-de-lis scroll including the screws and pins. All five engraving patterns featured scroll on each side of the upper side of the barrel extending from about 2 1/4" to 3" inches beyond the front receiver ring. This will vary slightly with each piece for they were all hand done.

The variations are as follows:

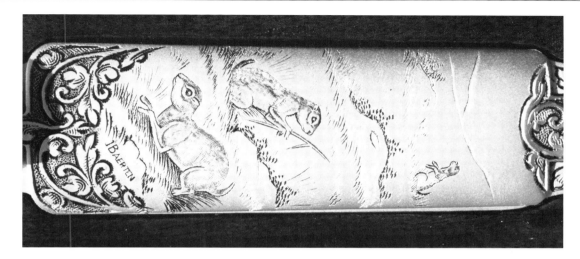

The 222 Remington Magnum (pictured on page 264 and here) engraved by Jose Baerten, a very prolific engraver who you will see much of in this book. Although his scroll work is not as smooth as most of his other work, he does a better job on animals.

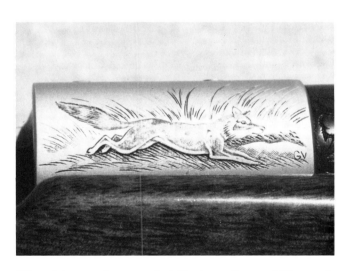

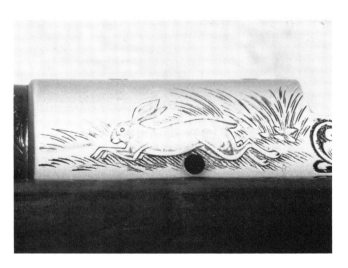

The pictures above and at the top of page 266 are of an Olympian 222 Remington receiver engraved by Gaston Vander Missen, note the GV on the right front receiver ring under the nose and forward of the fox's nose. The background and surrounding foliage is a bit sparser on this receiver. The engravers at F.N. were paid by the amount of work they turned out and a few cuts less on each piece soon paid off for the engraver in more work turned out. On the same 222 Remington is a floor plate and trigger guard done by Rene Dewil. You will see many Olympians with two or more engraver's names on the same rifles.

Vandermissen, 22/250 Remington

Another Vandermissen Mountain Lion

Vandermissen, 22/250 Remington

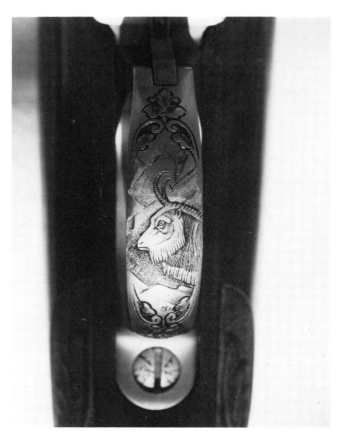

Another good example of Olympian engraving.

These pictures show a 22/250 Remington Olympian with the receiver and trigger guard engraved by Rene Dewil and the floor plate engraved by Gasten Vander Missen. Please notice that Ms. Dewill must have gotten up on the wrong side of the bed the day she engraved this little rifle. Beside the fact that this 22/250 has the wrong engraving, the running antelope and feeding deer are on opposite sides from where they were supposed to be engraved. You will sometimes find differences like these on some Olympians, things like this make fine collector's rifles.

The 222 Remington, 222 Remington Magnum and 22/250 Remington had a beautiful fox on the right side and a rabbit on the left of the front receiver ring; there also were prairie dog scenes on the floor plate and a crow on the trigger guard. This was really a great looking little rifle that had many game scenes with trees and other foliage. The smaller size of the action and the fine engraving made it look like a fine custom gun.

The picture below and the two at the top of page 268 are from a 308 Winchester Olympian which was 100% engraved by Gaston Vander Missen. Please note the non-factory engraved and gold inlaid scope base pictured here. You will find much of his work on Olympians as well as other Browning high grade guns.

See page 267 for description of two photos above.

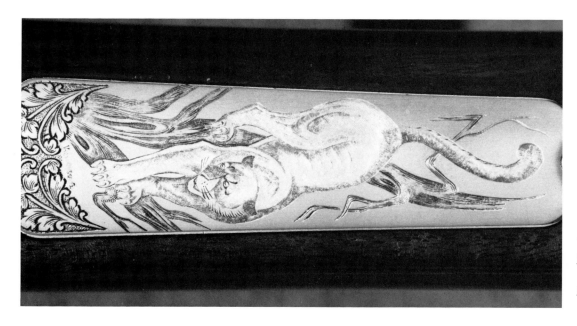

This is a detailed picture of the 308 Winchester floorplate engraved by Vander Missen.

The 243 Winchester, 284 Winchester and 308 Winchester were adorned with a mountain goat on the trigger guard, a cougar on the floor plate, a running antelope on the left side, and a feeding deer on the right side of the front receiver ring. This was another good looking rifle with many game scenes: mountains, hills, trees, leaves, prairies, and other foliage which depicted the animals in their natural habitat.

The fifth Olympian we have chosen to show is pictured above and shows a 30/06 with three engravers work featured. The receiver was done by R (Richard) Kiwalski. While the cut in the scroll is far from perfect, you will note that it is much better then we have previously shown. Please note that this is true for the entire rifle. These engravers must not have been in a hurry when they worked on this gun, the result is better engraving. You will also notice that there is a bit more shading on the bugling elk. Every Olympian is different in both sytle and execution and as a collector you must determine what is to your liking. The floor plate was done by Louis Acampo (LA). You can see his name just above where the scroll work appears below the deer. Can you find it? The trigger guard is engraved by L Severn (LS).

The 264 Winchester, 270 Winchester, and 30/06 had a standing deer on the floor plate, a running antelope on the right side and a bugling elk on the left side of the front receiver ring. It also featured a bear on the trigger guard. The detail that you see on the animals is incredible. Even the very small antelope on the front receiver ring was perfect in every way. The floor plate was really exceptional and had some of the nicest foliage patterns of the series. There were also some great game scenes of mountains, hills, trees, leaves, prairies and other foliage surrounding the figures on the balance of the gun. You could look high and low and not find better engraving even on the best custom rifles.

Jose Baerten engraved this 338 Winchester Magnum Olympian pictured above. His signature appears on the right receiver ring below the elk's neck and on the floor plate just above the scroll and below the bear's left foot. This and other magnums are hard to find so collectors put a greater value on this style engraving as well as the calibers on which it appears.

The 7mm Remington Magnum, 300 H & H Magnum, 300 Winchester Magnum, 308 Norma Magnum, 338 Winchester Magnum, and 375 H & H Magnum featured a mountain lion's head on the trigger guard, a standing grizzly bear on the floor plate, a moose on the right side and an elk on the left side of the front receiver ring. The lions and bears look as if they are about to jump off the floor plate and trigger guard to bite a big hunk out of you. The floor plate was really exceptional and the second nicest in the series; it had some of the greatest backgrounds of mountains and other typical grizzly country on any engraved rifle. There were also great scenes of mountains, hills, trees, leaves and other foliage surrounding the figures on the balance of the gun.

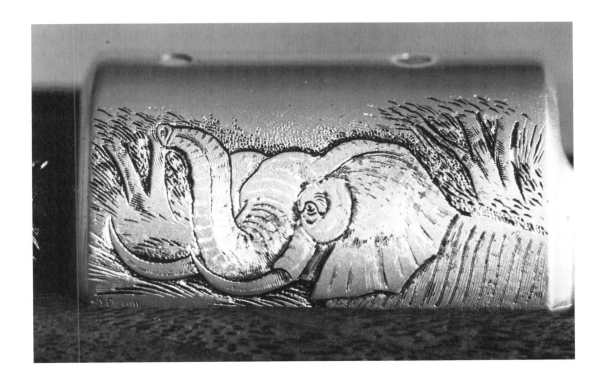

Pictured on page 271 and above are examples of a 458 Winchester Magnum Olympian grade rifle engraved by two different engravers. The trigger guard was done by Jose Baerten as evidenced by the JB initials, the receiver and floorplate was done by Rene Dewil. These are pictured in magnificent detail to show the quality of the workmanship on these rifles. You would be hard pressed to find better engraving on any factory or custom rifle short of some of the most expensive guns being built for $20,000.00 and better.

This is additional detail of 458 Winchester trigger guard engraved by Jose Baerten and floorplate by Rene Dewil.

The 458 Winchester Magnum was the only caliber that had its own engraving. You will very appropriately find an elephant on the left side of the receiver, a rhino on the right side of the receiver, a cape buffalos on the floor plate, and an African lion on the trigger guard. When you look at these rifles, they almost make you run out to mortgage your home and leave immediately on safari. The floor plate was really exceptional and had some of the nicest game scene patterns of the series. There were also some great game scenes of hills, trees, leaves and other foliage surrounding the figures on the balance of the gun.

The photos shown above picture another 458 Winchester Magnum Olympian engraved by the same engravers, Baerten on the trigger guard and floor plate and Dewil on the receiver. These are presented here to show the differences that can occur in the engraving even done by the same engravers, compare this with the other engraving already described. When purchasing an Olympian, as in rifles manufactured by other makers, purchase only those engraved to your liking.

Many times you will find engraving on calibers not corresponding with the patterns as described above. Don't let that stop you from looking over the piece as a potential buy; just remember to check out the serial numbers. There are exceptions to the serial numbers where you might find a Safari number on an Olympian but this is a rare occurrence, more discussion about this in the serial number section. You have to look for originality and the fine points. Almost never will you find an upgraded rifle done 100% properly. Look over the stock and carving, the grip cap and insert, the barrel on a Safari originally had sights but very few Olympians did other then the 458 Winchester Magnum. There is a lot of unusual or out of order engraved Olympians for which you should look.

As I have said many times, Browning has always been there to please, and if you wanted a 222 Remington elephant gun with 458 Winchester Magnum engraving, by golly you got it. Also, there were some factory errors; a certain caliber barrel could have mistakenly been screwed on a receiver with an incorrect game scene. These are very rare and make for great collectibles. You must look out for this sort of oddball if you're an Olympian collector.

OLYMPIAN RECEIVER, FLOOR PLATE, TRIGGER GUARD FINISH

As you can see, the jeweling on the Olympian grade bolts were meticulously done. Every part of each Olympian was polished to perfection.

The receivers, floor plates, and triggers guards were coin finished in a soft satin. The bolt, bolt handle, bolt lugs, action rails and bolt sleeves were all polished to a high luster and the triggers were grooved and gold plated. The extractors on the long extractor guns were damascened and all internal parts were polished. The actions on this grade were extremely smooth to operate and will compare with any custom or special order rifle made.

OLYMPIAN SIGHTS AND SERIAL NUMBER PLACEMENT

No open sights were provided on any caliber other then on the 458 Winchester magnum, unless it was special ordered, I have never seen a special order but there is probably some out there. An unusual feature for which you might look is the serial numbers' placement. On Olympian receivers, they are sometimes on the right rear of the receiver or on the rear tang. This was done so that the engraving would not cover the number.

OLYMPIAN STOCKS

Olympian stocks were group 5 or higher figured walnut checkered 32 lines per inch with intricate fleur-de-lis carving around the borders. All had rosewood grip caps and forearm tips with an 18 carat gold diamond shaped shield on the grip cap. Swivel eyelets, no swivels, were provided on all guns along with the "Browning" marked vent recoil pads on all magnums. Except for the early 264 Winchester magnums, the plastic "Browning" butt plates were on all the standard rifles. You could order a Browning pad on the standard rifles if desired. It's hard to tell if it's original but in general look for the proper length of pull and workmanship. In any case, a pad on a standard rifle hurts value whether original or not.

OLYMPIAN RINGS AND BASES

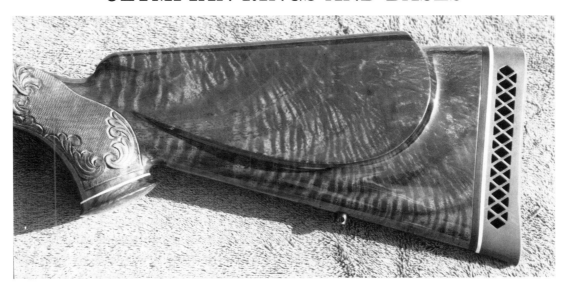

All Olympians featured exceptional wood, carving and checkering as only the Belgium artisans can produce. The stock shown here is from a 338 Winchester Magnum, please note the original Browning ventilated recoil pad and fantastic wood.

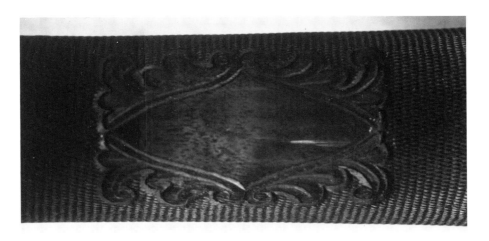

The Olympian grade stocks were all made with the forearm carved as shown here. This is standard for all rifles made with the F.N. Mauser or the Sako actions. The forearm shown without the screw is a 222 Remington and the one with the screw is from a 458 Winchester Magnum.

The Olympian grade had not only rosewood grip caps but also inserts. This example is from an Olympian grade in 222 Remington Magnum. Please note the difference in the insert as it appears here and the example shown in the Medallion section.

Redfield especially made for Browning twenty-five sets of rings and bases which were shipped to Belgium and engraved to coincide with the Olympian engraving. These were all in one order and shipped together. Browning sold these on the general market and there is no way to know where they went. It would indeed be a rare find to have one of these sets. The engraving matched the scroll found on the receiver and the balance of the rifle.

The Olympian grade had white line spacers and rosewood tips. You can also see the presence of the front sling swivel bases on this example.

CAUTION

If you find an unusual or rare high grade gun and the serial number codes don't match the serial number table, be careful. You could be purchasing a rare caliber that has been upgraded. Since the value of Olympians at this time in a common caliber is not as much as making up a custom rifle from scratch you will not find too much of this. But if you are looking at a 7mm Mauser or some such rarity and it's engraved, you are looking at a gun that could be valued 50% to 100% higher then the ordinary. In the future, when the rarity of even the standard calibers are known, the demand will increase and values will rise to the extent that faking them will be profitable; the serious collector must be extremely knowledgeable and cautious. Over the course of researching these guns some rifles were run across that had Olympians made in the 1970's with a Safari "L" in the serial numbers. One of these guns was new in the box and all looked 100% original, don't turn down a good buy when you're sure the rifle is correct.

There are some Belgium engravers in this country that are engraving and producing not only Olympian rifles, but also Renaissance grade handguns even today. I am of the belief that if it didn't leave the F.N. plant as you see it, then the gun is not original. I don't care if an engraver was once a master at F.N. and he does the work; it's not original. Most all other experienced collectors believe the same as I do. Remember, if it's engraved, then it must be greyed and reblued, and no one can reblue a gun so the experienced collector can't tell. The only thing that hurts you is when you find something rare and desirable and get in too much of a hurry without studying the piece properly. I know; I've done it myself. Learn from my mistakes.

PRICES

I will not give every year, for this is not important. What is important is that you see the general gist of the price increases. Each year, except for the first and last, I will give only prices for the standard calibers. Magnums were generally from $5.00 more in the earlier years to $20.00 more in the later ones.

In 1959 prices were $164.50 for the standard calibers, $169.50 for the magnums, and $174.50 for the 458. These were priced at $295.00 for the Medallion and $495.00 for the Olympians.

YEAR	SAFARI	MEDALLION	OLYMPIAN
1962	$175.00	$295.00	$495.00
1963	180.00	298.00	525.00
1964	185.00	298.00	525.00
1965	190.00	298.00	525.00
1969	227.50	354.50	594.50
1973	375.00	575.00	975.00

In 1974 the prices were $425.00 for the standard calibers, $440.00 for the magnums. The prices were $700.00 for the Medallion and $1200.00 for the Olympian. The Olympian engraving alone would cost you about $2,500.00 today.

SERIAL NUMBERS & PRODUCTION FIGURES

From 1959 to mid 1962, all serial numbers were numeric, so there is no way at this time to tell the year or number of rifles produced. However, from mid 1962 to 1975, which is the last year of cataloged production, the year of manufacture appears as part of the serial number. As you can see in the serial number tables, the grades and type of action also are coded so you can see if an Olympian left the factory as an Olympian or something else. However, we've spotted three Olympians, one new in the box, with L70, L71 and L73 serial number codes, which were the codes for the Safari grade so don't be surprised to find one. Since F.N. would occasionally take a Safari serial numbered action and build an Olympian with it you have to be able to distinguish an original from an upgrade. If you have an original Olympian with a Safari serial number you have something a little bit special. We get back here to knowing your rifles so that you can tell an original from an upgrade.

After 1969, the serial number codes changed again to "Y" for the short actions, "L" for the long actions and "Z" for the medium actions. So, you will begin to see guns manufactured during this time period with codes different from those previous.

All three grades ran together, so it is not possible to tell how many of each were made. But, if the sales of about 88,000 guns in 15 years is any indication, I would say that the high grades are indeed rare. Is it reasonable to figure five per cent of the total were Medallion and Olympians? This figure is probably high but would only total about 4,400 guns total. If you broke this down to 1/2 each grade, then a total of about 2,200 of each were made or about 150 a year. I realize this is pure speculation, but even if I'm wrong by 100%, the sales would still only total about 4,400 of each grade or about 300 per year. If you own an Olympian or Medallion, you own a rare gun.

Some serial numbers are reversed with the alpha character, so don't be confused when looking at a rifle; just look at the serial number table. The serial numbers ran concurrently, so it's possible to determine the approximate year a rifle was made after mid 1962.

In a conversation with Fiore Passaro of Houston, Texas, who is one of the leading Safari collectors and has gathered much needed data about them, he has estimated that about 66,000 guns were built on the F.N actions, 6,000 on the Sako L461, and about 16,000 on the Sako L579 action. He has determined that the Sako actions have their own set of serial numbers and therefore he has been able to break down total production for each action. The serial numbers on the L461 action that he has been able to find have reached 5,536Y5, and for the L579 they have reached 16,830Z75. He cannot find any L461 actions with serial numbers showing production after 1965. We know that the 222 Remington and Magnum was not a good seller, in discussing this with him, we have come to the conclusion that a large number of these were made during the first year of their production and sold over a period of time, right up to 1975 or even later if still in inventory.

The following table which was compiled by him is presented here to show about how many of these guns he believes were produced. Remember, from 1959 to mid-1962, there were no year codes in the serial numbers, so it is not possible to determine exactly how many were made. However, we can come pretty close by dividing the approximate number by 3 years.

The years of manufacture as broken down by him are as follows:

YEAR	LOWEST NO. FOUND	HIGHEST NO. FOUND	APPROXIMATE NUMBER MADE	GAP
1959	L1	L3889	3,889	
1960	L3890	L7779	3,890	
1961	L7780	L11669	3,890	85
1962	2L11754	2L17380	5,711	34
1963	3L17414	3L22930	5,550	397
1964	4L23327	4L28168	5,238	417
1965	5L28585	5L35085	6,917	74
1966	6L35159	6L38234	3,149	555
1967	7L38789	7X44271	6,037	?
1968	8L43008	8L48848	4,577	397
1969	9L49245	55522L69	6,674	560
1970	56082L70	61020L70	5,498	?
1971	59922L71	62933L71	1,913	416
1972	63349L72	64487L72	1,554	328
1973	64815L73	65626L73	1,139	?
1974	No Numbers found	66685L74	1,059	?

The "L" appears in the serial numbers because that is the actual serial number of the gun located. If you have a Medallion with the letter "X" or an Olympian with the letter "P", it will also fall into these numbers. Please notice that there is only one "X", no "P"'s, and the rest are "L"'s; that's only 1 out of 31 numbers or about 3% of all those noted. This is additional evidence of the scarcity of the Medallion and Olympian rifles. Three percent of 88,000 is only 2,933 guns. Divide this figure by two and you only have 1,467 of each grade, these are scarce guns indeed. I would like to mention that Fiore probably didn't see as many of the Medallion and Olympian rifles because they are less likely to show up at gun shows, they are stashed away in collections. Collectors usually don't part with their guns until they find a better one or liquidate their collection. A safer figure, because not many are brought to gun shows, probably would be five percent for total high grade production which would amount to 4,400 guns.

As you can see, these numbers in some years are quite close, as low as just 34 guns. This is the first time anyone has taken the effort to find out Safari production to the extent Mr. Passaro has, and he should be congratulated for doing this. If you will notice, there are some gaps in the serial numbers from year to year, so it is not possible with the information he has at hand to give exact numbers. These gaps run from as few as 34 guns to as many as 560.

Please notice that several times the serial numbers run lower for a year than the previous year. Were the F.N. serial number people making a mistake by perhaps changing a serial number on an earlier gun, we do not yet have enough information to make a fairly decent judgement or was this done on purpose? We need more serial numbers to come to any further conclusions. If you will notice the highest number for 1967 was 44271 and the lowest number for 1968 was 43008; also notice this phenomenon also appears in 1970-1971 where the 1970 ending number is 61020 and the beginning number for 1971 is 59922.

There is much to be learned about these guns, so if you have a Safari rifle and would like to help in solving the total production and configuration question, please send the serial number along with the grade, type of bolt handle, forearm checkering style, front sight ramp style, rear sight type, serial number placement and markings on the receiver and barrel to my address at the front of this book. This information will be forwarded on to him for further evaluation.

Remember, the more we know about these fine guns, the more valuable they become to the collecting world and yourself. Also, if you would like to contact him about exchanging information and starting a group of Safari, Medallion, and Olympian rifle collectors, please feel free. His address and phone number is Fiore Passaro, 187 Evanston St., Houston, Texas 77015, 713-458-6557.

F.N. & SAKO SERIAL NUMBERS
FOR THE SAFARI, MEDALLION & OLYMPIANS

	62	63	64	65	66	67	68	69
F.N. Long Action								
SAFARI	2L-	3L-	4L-	5L-	6L-	7L-	8L-	-L9*
MEDALLION	2X-	3X-	4X-	5X-	6X-	7X-	8X-	-X9*
OLYMPIAN	2P-	3P-	4P-	5P-	6P-	7P-	8P-	-P9*

*Sometime in late 1969 the codes were changed so I am showing them here both ways.

	69	70	71	72	73	74	75
F.N. Long Action*							
Safari	-L69	-L70	-L71	-L72	-L73	-L74	-L75
Medallion	-X69	-X70	-X71	-X72	-X73	-X74	-X75
Olympian	-P69	-P70	-P71	-P72	-P73	-P74	-P75

SAKO	62	63	64	65	66	67	68	69	70	71	72	73	74	75
SAFARI														
L461	2Y-	3Y-	4Y-	5Y-	6Y-	7Y-	8Y-	-Y69*	-Y70	-Y71	-Y72	-Y73	-Y74	-Y75
L579	2Z-	3Z-	4Z-	5Z-	6Z-	7Z-	8Z-	-Z69	-Z70	-Z71	-Z72	-Z73	-Z74	-Z75
MEDALLION														
L461	2A-	3A-	4A-	5A-	6A-	7A-	8A-	-Y69*	-Y70	-Y71	-Y72	-Y73	-Y74	-Y75
L579	2A-	3A-	4A-	5A-	6A-	7A-	8A-	-Z69	-Z70	-Z71	-Z72	-Z73	-Z74	-Z75
OLYMPIAN														
L461	2B-	3B-	4B-	5B-	6B-	7B-	8B-	-Y69*	-Y70	-Y71	-Y72	-Y73	-Y74	-Y75
L579	2B-	3B-	4B-	5B-	6B-	7B-	8B-	-Z69	-Z70	-Z71	-Z72	-Z73	-Z74	-Z75

*The "L" was used on all three grades during these years. You may find a 1969 gun with just the "9" appearing instead of "69".

FABRIQUE NATIONALE DIRECT IMPORTS

You will also find F. N. produced rifles that were being imported about the same time Browning was selling theirs. To the uninformed, it is confusing to see one of these at first, but you can tell the difference when you look at the butt plate, stock finish, and lack of engraving on the floor plate. In addition, the overall finish of these rifles are not up to the level of the Browning imported guns. The early ones had a large "FN" and were not drilled and tapped for a scope on the front receiver ring. Do not confuse these with a Browning Safari that was perhaps made for European sales. They were sold for quite a bit less when new, about the price level of the Remington Model 700 or Winchester Post-64 rifles. Recently, I have seen some at gun shows priced close to the Browning guns but still a few dollars less. This occurs because knowledgeable hunters know they are superior to many of the rifles made today. These folks don't want to spend the extra dollars it costs to get a Safari, but still want the old style classic looking rifle.

When the Safari rifles were being built, Fabrique Nationale was also selling actions as well as barrelled actions to gunsmiths but they were all custom stocked and very different. You will also find some J.C. Higgins, Sear Roebuck, and other guns with this action, but they have no interest here other than for you to be aware that they do exist.

This is the end of the 1959-1975 era of Browning's bolt action rifles. We have much more to learn about them and as we do they will become more and more valuable. In the past five years a standard Safari new in the box has gone from $750.00 retail to over $1,000.00. I would advise any of you who just love Brownings as a great hunting rifle or who want to collect for investment to get busy and start accumulating for they will continue to go higher and sooner or later be out of the average person's budget.

BBR BOLT ACTION RIFLE

The basic BBR rifle as introduced in 1977.

GENERAL INFORMATION

I'm sort of like the fellow that was still driving a 1936 car in 1976. Friends asked him about all the new conveniences. Doesn't he want something new? Why, you can now get A/C, FM radio, power windows and seats, 120 mph, etc. He said, "All that's real nice, but it's just not the sort of thing I'm used to, I need the aesthetics."

The rifles built after 1976 are great guns and will sooner or later carve their notch in the nostalgic minds of the younger shooters when they get older, but not in the minds of the shooters and collectors born in the 1940's and prior.

Competition from other gun companies with new and innovative guns, production costs in Belgium, more lucrative business for F.N. elsewhere — whatever the reasons, the Safaris, Medallions and Olympians are gone, hopefully, not forever.

The BBR, as made in Japan, was an innovative bolt action rifle with many fine features that was introduced in 1977 to replace the Safari, Medallion and Olympian grade F.N. and Sako rifles. Many of the other firearms manufacturers and the pulp gun magazines were pumping up such things as short extractors being better then the long ones, free floating barrels being the only way to go and several other new and so called modern features which you just had to have if you were ever to be a successful hunter. Browning had the BBR built with many of these features. Typical for Browning, however, these features were done in a quality way. As an example, look at a 1964 Winchester Model 70 with it's free floating barrel. There is a barrel channel in the stock big enough to store your lunch. You stood every chance of getting leaves, dirt, sticks and whatever stuck between the barrel and forearm. Browning chose the more innovative way by inletting an aluminum block in the barrel channel to keep the forearms from warping and altering the line of sight. We will get into this and other features in this chapter. The BBR was discontinued in 1984 with the introduction of the A-Bolt which is still being made as of 1992.

The later 1982 BBR configuration.

GRADES

This model was made for much of its eight year life in only one grade. The Standard was originally offered in 1977 and made until 1984 in three variations: First variation, Lightning light barrel and Lightning heavy barrel. For only one year, 1983, the higher grade Limited Edition was also made; we will describe it next. The following descriptions pertain to the First variation. All deviations from these descriptions will be noted in the Lightning and Limited Edition sections.

LIMITED EDITION

BBR Limited Edition

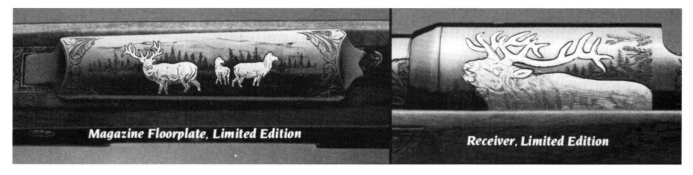

Magazine Floorplate, Limited Edition   *Receiver, Limited Edition*

The Limited Edition variation was introduced in 1983 and cataloged in 1983 and 1984 for the very short run of 1,000 rifles.

They featured hand engraved fleur-de-lis and oak leaf scroll on the front and rear receiver rings, the floor plate, the stock bolt, and even 1 1/2" down each side of the barrel. This scroll is highlighted by a game scene on the floor plate of mountains, trees and three 24 carat gold plated elk. This consists of two cows standing and a Royal bull looking towards you. The left and right sides of the front receiver ring also have gold plated Royal Elk bulls bugling to their heart's content. These are very pretty guns that should please anyone. The barrels were all in 7mm Remington Magnum, blued, 24" barrels and made without sights, and to top off everything, the triggers were gold plated.

The group 5 wood was the same configuration as the Lightning style except for a few changes. The checkering was skip line with a beaded or pearl border carved all the way around. The rosewood forearm tip, grip cap, and the rubber recoil pad were all separated from the stock with brass spacers.

ACTIONS-BOTH LONG AND SHORT

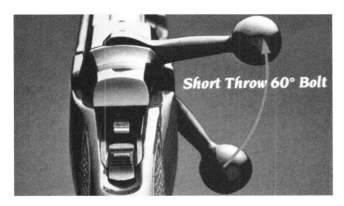

The 60° bolt throw allowed the shooter to mount a scope lower and operate the bolt faster than conventional rifles.

There were two frames and three bolts made for this gun: the Standard, which was made for magnum and standard calibers in the 30/06 length, and the Short, which was made from 1983 to 1984 for the 308

Winchester length cases. All the features for the Standard frame also pertain to the Short frames. These all steel actions were drilled and tapped for scope mounts and high gloss blued with no engraving of any sort.

The cartridges they were designed for were as follows:

STANDARD ACTION	SHORT ACTION
25/06 Remington	22/250 Remington
270 Winchester	243 Winchester
30/06 Springfield	257 Roberts
7mm Remington Magnum	7mm/08 Remington
300 Winchester Magnum	308 Winchester
338 Winchester Magnum	

Please refer to the barrel section in this chapter to see the dates of introduction for each caliber.

The features for this rifle were many, including a 60 degree bolt throw, scissors magazine follower, a separate box magazine that detached from the floor plate, two safety indicators, adjustable trigger, and a few others that will be discussed in the stock and barrel sections.

BOLT

One of the features of this model that Browning played up quite a bit was the short bolt throw of only 60 degrees. This was made possible by the use of nine small locking lugs rather then the earlier Mauser style action which had two. The decrease of 33% in the amount of travel left a 60 degree arc in which the shooter needed to lift the bolt to operate it. You can mount a scope lower and decrease the time it took to cycle the action. The bolt head was also recessed and surrounded the cartridge head for safety purposes, and there was a plunger-type ejector. This was no doubt a rub off of the Weatherby Mark 5 bolt configuration and a very nice feature.

SAFETY

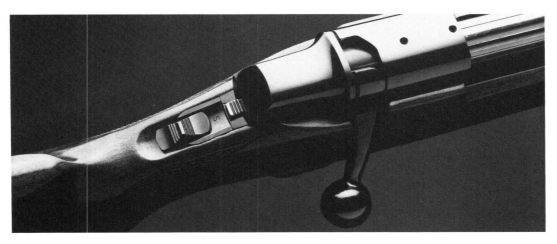

Here is a closeup of the BBR Safety, cocking indicator, bolt, and bolt sleeve.

The safety was located on the top tang and was quiet. This is important when hunting spooky big game. There was also a cocking indicator that extended past the rear of the bolt shroud and allowed the shooter to tell by feel if the gun was cocked.

TRIGGERS

The triggers were fully adjustable from three to six pounds and grooved throughout production. They were gold plated from 1977 to 1978 only, for the balance of production they were blued except for the 1983 Limited Edition.

MAGAZINE

This 1984 catalog picture shows the unique, for 1984, magazine setup for the BBR.

The magazine had a unique scissors spring that Browning introduced for this model. It was actually two metal pieces that are crisscrossed and spring loaded to push the follower up on both ends. Browning claimed a smoother and more uniform loading and feeding of cartridges.

Another feature that was introduced was the detachable magazine that was very similar to the BAR. The floor plate was also hinged for removal of the magazine and the capacity was three rounds in the magnum cartridges and four in the standard. What I like more about this feature then anything else is the hunter has the capability of carry an extra magazine fully loaded. This not only facilitates the carrying of extra cartridges but also speeds up reloading.

FRAME MARKINGS

The only frame markings were on the right receiver ring where the serial number appeared.

BARRELS

The free floated medium weight barrels were all blued with a recessed polished muzzle. There were no iron sights ever offered.

When introduced the 7mm Remington Magnum, 300 Winchester Magnum, 30/06 Springfield, 270 Winchester, and 25/06 Remington were the only calibers. In 1983, the 338 Winchester Magnum was introduced and in 1984, the 308 Winchester, 257 Roberts, 243 Winchester and 22/250 Remington all came along. Please notice that these last calibers were just made one year and the 338 Winchester Magnum only two years. These are rare guns. I have never heard of any orders being accepted by Browning for a special cartridge.

Barrel lengths are as follows:

    24'' STANDARD
    25/06 Remington
    7MM Remington Magnum
    270 Winchester
    300 Winchester Magnum
    30/06 Springfield

    22'' LIGHTWEIGHT
    22/250 Remington
    243 Winchester
    257 Roberts
    7mm/08 Remington
    308 Winchester

    24'' HEAVY
    22/250 Remington
    243 Winchester
    7mm/08 Remington
    308 Winchester

Barrel markings are as follows:
On the left side:
    BROWNING ARMS COMPANY
    MORGAN, UTAH & MONTREAL P.Q.
    MADE IN JAPAN

On the right side are the words:
    BBR CALIBER(Caliber)ONLY

Immediately in front of the receiver ring on the left side of the barrel, you will see "NP" stamped which stands for nitro proofed. You will also find various inspectors and machinists stampings

STOCKS

There were three stocks made for this model: the Standard, Lightning, and Short Lightning.

A pistol grip with Monte Carlo style comb and a flat forearm was the original configuration for the Standard stock model. This was in group 2 grade. They were all made of American walnut finished in the Browning high gloss. Checkering was 18 lines per inch on the grip and forearm with a rosewood grip cap and black plastic butt plate marked "Browning." The magnums had a black rubber recoil pad also marked "Browning" with a white spacer. Flush sling swivel studs were furnished from 1977 to the end of production. The dimensions were length of pull 13 3/8" to 13 5/8", drop at comb 1 5/8", and drop at heel 2 1/8".

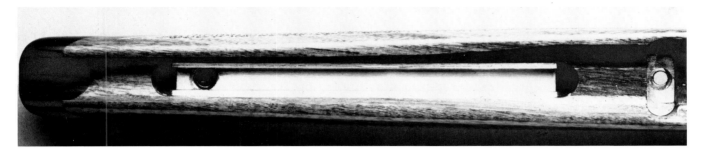

As described in the text, one of the most innovative features of the BBR was the aluminum forearm inlay.

The forearm and how it was made was another new innovation by Browning. Inlaid into the barrel channel was an aluminum piece that was 1/8" thick and 8" long. This piece prevented the forearm from warping and touching the barrel. A shooter was assured of a perpetually free floating barrel. The advantages of this were many including the assurance of a rifle staying sighted in. Also, the space needed to free float the barrel was much less then other makes and you had much less of a chance of getting any debris between the barrel and forearm.

This was a very modern European looking stock that eventually gave way to the more classic looking Lightning that the American shooter likes so much more.

In 1982, the Lightning stock configuration was introduced also in group 2 grade. This new pistol grip stock with Monte Carlo comb and cheek piece had a more classic look than the previous version. The forearms were round and all had a rosewood forearm cap. They were made of American walnut finished in the Browning high gloss, and all had a stock cross bolt. Checkering was 18 lines per inch on the grip and forearm with a rosewood grip cap. The butt plates were made from black plastic, and the magnums had a black hard rubber recoil pad with a white spacer; both were marked "Browning." The dimensions were length of pull 13 3/8", drop at comb 1 5/8", and drop at heel 2 1/8".

The Short Lightning stock was exactly like the above except it was proportioned for the shorter action and there were no magnums therefore no rubber pads.

SERIAL NUMBERS

All year codes for this model can be found in the General Information section in the front of the book.

A-BOLT RIFLE

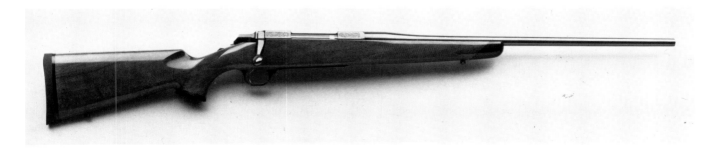

The A-Bolt Medallion was introduced in 1985.

GENERAL INFORMATION

When introduced in 1985, Browning stressed that the advantage of the A-Bolt over all previous models was a reduction in weight. Whatever the reasons, the A-Bolt has turned out to be a quality rifle that has been well accepted by the American hunting public.

As I look over my notes, there are almost twenty variations in grade, caliber, stocks, left or right hand, models and actions over the past seven years. This is no different from the other manufacturers, for it's almost like the gun companies are trying to make something for everybody. There are so many variations and models that we must cover each one individually.

MEDALLION GRADE

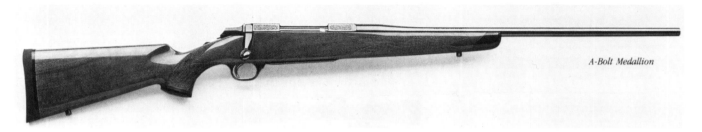

The A-Bolt Medallion proved to be a great rifle for those who wanted something more. This is from the 1987 catalog.

The Medallion grade was introduced in during the first year of production, 1985, and is still being made in 1992. It is quite popular and one of the big sellers in the quality rifle market. It may seem redundant to go over the calibers here and in the barrel section as well. The purpose is to inform you of the dates of introduction, configuration and in which calibers each grade was made.

The calibers for this model are listed in the A-Bolt cartridge section. The short action cartridges have 22" barrels, the long action standard barrels are 24", and the magnums have 26" barrels as of 1992. This variation was made with 24" barrels in the magnum calibers for three years from 1985 to 1987. No iron sights were available until the 375 H & H was introduced in 1988.

From 1985 to 1986, there was no engraving on any A-Bolt until 1987. Thereafter the etched engraving on the Medallion action consisted of medium fleur-de-lis scroll on the action flats only. All blueing was high luster that is quite nice, and the triggers are gold colored.

The full pistol grip stock with fluted comb is group 3 American walnut 20 lines per inch checkering, and all have a rosewood grip cap and forearm tip. The finish is high gloss polyurethane and all stocks have hard rubber butt plates with the name "Browning". The dimensions are length of pull 13 5/8", drop at comb 3/4", and drop at heel 1 1/8".

During the first year of production the Medallions were fitted with Pachmayr sling swivels that were flush mounted. After this initial year, these were changed to the standard detachable sling swivals and studs.

The left hand A-Bolt Medallion has been made in many calibers over the years as described in the text.

A left hand version became available in 1987 in 7mm Remington, 30/06, and 270 Winchester calibers. The 300 Winchester Magnum was also introduced in 1988. In 1990 more was to come in the form of the 25-06 Remington and the 280 Remington, but these

were discontinued the following year. To add confusion to all the above, the 375 H & H Magnum, 338 Winchester Magnum, 25/06 Remington, and the 280 Remington were introduced or brought back in 1992.

All the features of the left hand Medallions are the same as the right hand guns.

HUNTER GRADE

As introduced in 1985, the Hunter grade is made to fill the nitch for the sportsman who needed a working rifle without any of the frills. It's still being made in 1992 and is a great rifle used by many hunters.

There is no engraving or special embellishments of any kind. The blueing was a matte finish from 1985 to 1986 but changed to a high lustre in 1987 and thereafter; all triggers were gold colored.

The calibers for this model are listed in the A-Bolt cartridge section. The short action cartridges have 22'' barrels, the long action standard barrels are 24'', and the magnums have 26'' barrels as of 1992. This variation was made with 24'' barrels in the magnum calibers for three years from 1985 to 1987.

Unlike the Medallion, the Hunter can be ordered with front sights. The front is a ramp with gold bead and hood, and the rear is on a base screwed to the barrel. These are fully adjustable for windage and elevation.

The full pistol grip stock has a fluted comb and is made of American walnut. It is about group 1 checkered 18 lines per inch with a border. In the first two years of production the finish was more of a satin. In 1987 and thereafter, this was changed to a high gloss.

Stock dimensions are length of pull is 13 5/8'', drop at comb 3/4'', and drop at heel 1 1/8''. All are fitted with the Michaels post type stud for sling swivels. During the first two years of production, the Hunter grades in the standard calibers had black plastic butt plates and the magnums a black rubber recoil pad. From 1987 through 1992, all calibers had the rubber pads, and they were all marked "Browning."

BIG HORN SHEEP

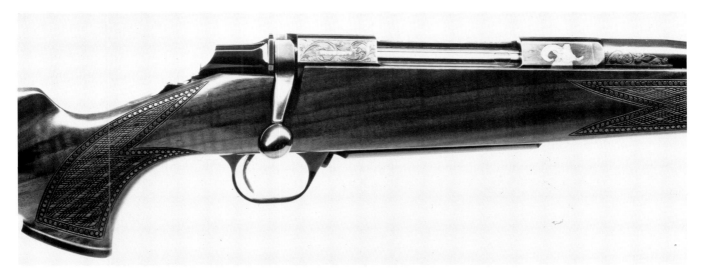

The A-Bolt Big Horn is Browning's answer in providing todays hunter with a quality rifle.

From 1986 to 1989, Browning offered the new Limited Edition series in two variations, the Big Horn Sheep and the Pronghorn. When first advertised, I believed that a whole series of these would be made. As it turned out, only two were made and they are now hard to find. These were special rifles that had features not found in any other A-Bolt. We will discuss both variations made individually.

The first thing you notice when observing the engraving are the Big Horn sheep on the receiver ring and floor plate. On each side of the front receiver ring is the head of a full curl ram surrounded by a broadly engraved background of mountian ridges. The floor plate has two standing rams and one lying down; two of them are looking to their right. They are also surrounded by a mountain range. All the animals are 24

carat gold plated and done very nicely. The etched engraving, which consists of a medium fleur-de-lis scroll, surrounds the sheep on the floorplate and is also on about 90% of the receiver, floor plate, trigger guard, and 1 1/2'' down each side of the barrel. The receivers are all blued and the triggers are gold colored.

The barrels and other parts are highly polished and blued, they were limited to 600 guns in 270 Winchester and all had 22'' barrels with no sights.

The full pistol grip amd high lustre classic style stock was group 4 American walnut with skip line checkering surrounded on all sides by a carved border of beads. The rosewood forearm tip, grip cap, and rubber butt plate had brass spacers between them and the stock. The dimensions were length of pull is 13 5/8'', drop at comb 3/4'', and drop at heel 1 1/8''.

PRONGHORN

The 1987 Pronghorn was originally made in very limited numbers and is a difficult variation to find.

The 1987 Pronghorn edition was limited to 500 guns and featured Pronghorn antelope.

When looking at the engraving on this little rifle you are reminded of the three ways you get to see one of these critters, running about 100 miles per hour, standing no closer then a half mile from you or seeing the sentry they invariably have standing alone. If you've ever been antelope hunting you can relate to what you just read.

On the left side of the front receiver ring there is a single antelope running and on the right there is another standing watch. These are surrounded by a broadly engraved background of prairie. The floor plate has three pronghorn, a yearling walking, and a buck and doe standing, they are surrounded by prairie with a mountain range in the background. All the animals are 24 carat gold plated and done very

nicely. The etched engraving, which consists of a medium fleur-de-lis scroll, surrounds the pronghorns on the floorplate and is also on about 90% of the receiver, floor plate, trigger guard, and 1 1/2" down each side of the barrel. The receivers are all blued and the triggers are gold colored.

The barrels and other parts are highly polished and blued. They were limited to 243 Winchester, and all had 22" barrels with no sights.

The full pistol grip amd high lustre classic style stock were group 4 American walnut with skip line checkering surrounded on all sides by a carved border of pearls or beads. The rosewood forearm tip, grip cap, and rubber butt plate had brass spacers between them and the stock. The dimensions were length of pull 13 5/8", drop at comb 3/4", and drop at heel 1 1/8".

STAINLESS AND CAMO STALKER MODELS

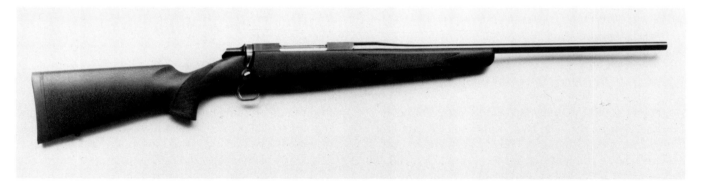

The A-Bolt Stalker

Browning introduced these two rifles in 1987. They are a far cry from what Browning had ever made previously. When you think of the Safari, Medallions, and Olympians of years past and how conservative things were back then, it is hard to believe what the American sportsman likes and what is popular today. Like any other company, Browning must keep up with the times and tastes of their customers.

STAINLESS STALKER

Throughout production the entire gun, other than some minor parts, has been made with stainless steel. I can't think of anything that could damage these rifles short of salt water. All action and barrel configurations are the same as the Hunter model other than no iron sights. The metal has a matte gray finish to cut down the glare.

When first introduced, the full pistol grip and glass bedded stock was painted black with a stipple finish, but in 1988 this was changed to a graphite-fiberglass composite stock. It also has a full pistol grip, rubber recoil pad, and molded checkering. The stock dimensions are length of pull is 13 5/8'', drop at comb 3/4'', and drop at heel 1 1/8''.

In 1987 only the right hand version was made in 270 Winchester, 30/06, and 7mm Remington Magnum; but in 1990 the 375 H & H Magnum, 338 Winchester Magnum, 300 Winchester Magnum, 25/06 Remington, and the 280 Remington were also made. The short action cartridges have 22'' barrels, the long action standard barrels are 24'', and the magnums have 26'' barrels as of 1992. This variation was made with 24'' barrels in the magnum calibers for one year, 1987.

In 1990, the left hand model was introduced in all the long action calibers including the 270 Winchester, 25/06 Remington, 280 Remington, 30/06, 7mm Remington Magnum, 300 Winchester Magnum, 338 Winchester Magnum, and the 375 H & H Magnum.

I don't think there are any left handed shooters that could possibly say they are being ignored by Browning with this array of calibers available. As of 1992, the short action cartridges have 22'' barrels, the long action standard barrels are 24'', and the magnums have 26'' barrels. All other features of the right hand model also pertain to this one.

CAMO STALKER

As introduced in 1987 and discontinued in 1990, the Camo Stalker was basically the Hunter grade with a laminated stock. All other features of the A-Bolt Hunter were the same other than not having an iron sight available.

The layers of wood were painted with black and green paint in various shades. When the stock is carved, a camo effect is created, and the rifle in deep woods or a well constructed blind is camoflaged very effectively. Browning calls this their *"CAMOWOOD"; it was checkered 18 lines per inch with a non glare finish. The full pistol grip and semi-gloss finished stock had dimensions that were length of pull 13 5/8'', drop at comb 3/4'', and drop at heel 1 1/8''. All other features of the Hunter model were consistent with the Camo Stalker.

The all steel barrelled action was matte blued and configured like the Hunter. Originally, it was offered in 270 Winchester, 30/06, and 7mm Remington Magnum. The short action cartridges had 22'' barrels, the long action standard barrels were 24'', and the magnums were 26''. When introduced in the magnum calibers, this variation was made with 24'' for only one year, 1987. Are these the future rarity that the Safari 264 Winchester Magnum was with 24'' barrels?

There were approximately 1,500 A-bolts manufactured with laminated stocks. About 1,152 of these had sights, and about 348 were shipped without sights. This totals 1,670 guns, of which 170 had walnut stocks. This would make the A-Bolt with a laminated stock rare and potentially a collector's item.

You need to notice the descrepency in what is noted above. The text, like the catalogs, says that no iron sights were available, but the statistics say 1,152 were made with them. This is another example of how collectors items are made. Obviously, dealers were requesting this model with iron sights, and as always Browning was there to please. Don't be surprised as to what you'll find and don't rule out any gun until you inspect it thoroughly for originality. You may have a rare variation.

*"CAMOWOOD" is a registered trademark of the Browning Arms Company.

GOLD MEDALLION MODEL

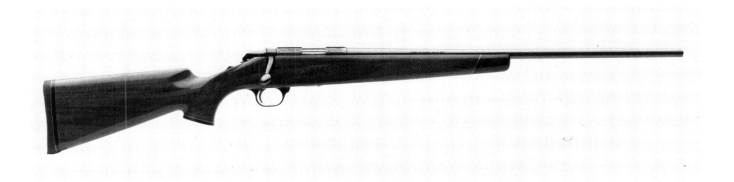

The A-Bolt Gold Medallion was introduced in 1988.

The Gold Medallion was introduced in 1988 and was still being made as of 1992. The original calibers available were 7mm Remington Magnum, 270 Winchester, and the 30/06 as they still were in 1992.

The long action standard barrels are 24" long and the magnums have 26" barrels as of 1992.

All the features of the Medallion are also present for this variation except the finish. All blueing is high lustre and is quite nice. The triggers are gold colored.

The engraving is also like the Medallion with the added touch of having the words "Gold Medallion" engraved and gold filled on the right side of the receiver.

The full pistol grip Monte Carlo stock with fluted comb and cheekpiece is group 4 American walnut with 22 lines per inch checkering and a double border. Other features are a palm swell, rubber butt pad marked "Browning," a rosewood grip cap, and forearm tip. The finish is high gloss polyurethane, and there are brass spacers dividing the grip cap, forearm tip, and rubber pad from the stock The dimensions are length of pull 13 5/8", drop at comb 3/4", and drop at heel 1 1/8".

MICRO MEDALLION MODEL

The A-Bolt Micro Medallion is perfect for the younger shooter.

This little rifle as brought out in 1988 is just the ticket for younger shooters and people of smaller stature. It is also suitable for hunters that want to carry a rifle a great distance or over hill and dale. Mainly, it's smaller in every way including a 20" barrel and short action.

Engraving is the same as the standard medallion model and the magazine capacity is only three rounds.

Calibers available are 243 Winchester, 308 Winchester, 7mm-08 Remington, 257 Roberts, and the 22-250 Remington. In 1989 the 223 Remington chambering came along and in 1990 the 22 Hornet, but the Hornet was discontinued in 1992. As of 1992, there have been no Hornets made because of manufacturing problems, but they will be made as of 1994.

It weighs in at 6 lbs 1 oz, about 10 oz. lighter then the Stalker, a difference which is not that significant. Of course I might change my mind if I had to carry it 10 miles.

The full pistol grip stock with fluted comb is group 3 American walnut 20 lines per inch checkering. All have a rosewood grip cap and forearm tip.

The finish is a high gloss polyurethane, and all stocks have hard rubber butt plates with the name "Browning." The dimensions are length of pull 13 5/16" — which is shorter than the standard stock — drop at comb 3/4", and drop at heel 1 1/8". The standard detachable sling swivels and studs were furnished.

The magazine capacity is a little different for this variation. It will hold only three standard cartridges.

COMPOSITE STALKER

As introduced in 1988, this is the same gun as the Hunter with a matte blued finish and graphite stock. The stock has a full pistol grip, rubber recoil pad and molded checkering. Stock dimensions are length of pull 13 5/8", drop at comb 3/4", and drop at heel 1 1/8".

It was introduced in 30/06, 280 Remington, 270 Winchester, 25/06 Remington, 7mm Remington Magnum, 300 Winchester Magnum, and the 338 Winchester Magnum; and these have not chamged up to 1992. The long action standard barrels are 24", and the magnums have 26" barrels as of 1992.

A-BOLT CARTRIDGES BY VARIATION

(1)BBL LGTH	HUNTER	MEDAL MEDAL	LEFT H MEDAL	GOLD MEDAL	LEFT H STAIN STALK	STAIN STALK	COMP STALK	MICRO MEDAL
LONG ACTION MAGNUMS								
375 H & H 26"(1)		X			X	X		
338 WIN. 26"(1)	X	X	X		X	X	X	
300 WIN. 26"(1)	X	X	X		X	X	X	
7MM REM. 26"(1)	X	X	X	X	X	X	X	
LONG ACTION STANDARD								
25/06 REM 22"	X	X	X		X	X	X	
270 WIN 22"	X	X	X	X	X	X	X	
280 REM 22"	X	X	X		X	X	X	
30/06 22"	X	X	X	X	X	X	X	
SHORT ACTION CALIBERS(2)								
243 WIN 22"	X	X						X
308 WIN 22"	X	X						X
284 WIN 22"	X	X						X
7MM/08 REM 22"	X	X						X
257 ROBERTS 22"	X	X						X
22/250 REM 22"	X	X						X
223 REM 22"	X	X						X
22 HORNET 22"								X
MICRO MEDALLION								
243 WIN 20"								X
308 WIN 20"								X
284 WIN 20"								X
7MM/08 REM 20"								X
257 ROBERTS 20"								X
22/250 REM 20"								X
223 REM 20"								X
22 HORNET 20"								

(1) these were 24" prior to 1988

(2) The 22 Hornet has been cataloged since 1990 but never made because of manufacturing difficulties. Word has it that they will be made in 1994. I hope they will; this is a great little cartridge that anyone can enjoy shooting.

ACTIONS

The actions went through several changes and modifications over the years, and we will cover them all here.

As basically produced, this is an all steel bolt action with many innovative features that makes it quicker, handier, and safer for the hunter to use. Some of these features include a thin bodied fluted bolt with three locking lugs, a 60 degree bolt throw, plunger type ejector, and a receissed bolt head.

BOLT

Instead of the conventional two locking lugs as are used on the Mauser actions, the A-Bolt utilizes three, thereby decreasing bolt travel by 30 degrees.

The earlier BBR had nine smaller lugs that accomplished the same thing, but I suppose three decreases the amount of machine work it takes to get the same results. As you might be aware, Weatherby has been building their Mark V rifles with nine locking lugs for years. This idea is not new but that doesn't take away the convenience and slight increase in speed this feature adds.

The bolt only turns 60 degrees to open and unbreech, facilitating the opening and closing of the action for a quick second shot since it doesn't travel as high. Another good thing about this short bolt throw is the ability to mount a scope lower.

As first introduced, the bolt was smooth and polished. In 1987 this was changed to flutes — also polished though the grooves are blued. It really is a pretty feature, and it does serve to lighten up the rifle a bit.

ACTION LENGTHS AND SAFETY

From 1985 through 1992, there have been three actions: long standard, long magnum, and short for standard cartridges. The long magnum was used for all the magnum loads, the long for all cases in the 30/06 length, and the short for the 308/7mm Mauser length. The safety is mounted on the top tang. It is quiet, which is important since you won't spook game when preparing to take a shot.

The calibers for the long action magnums are 375 H & H, 338 Winchester Magnum, 300 Winchester Magnum, and the 7mm Remington Magnum. The calibers for the long action are 25/06 Remington, 280 Remington, 270 Winchester, and the 30/06. The short actions have been used for many more calibers then the others. These are 243 Winchester, 308 Winchester, 284 Winchester, 7mm/08 Remington, 257 Roberts, 22/250 Remington, 223 Remington, and the 22 Hornet. As far as I know, all are still being made which will come along in 1994.

On the left front receiver bridge flat, the Medallions have the marking "MEDALLION," and on the Gold Medallion, the words "GOLD MEDALLION" are present and gold filled.

From the 1987 catalog.

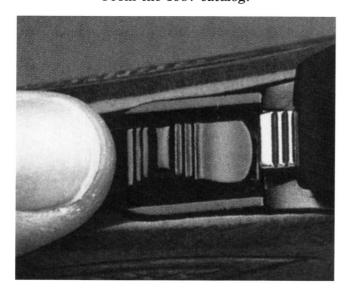

Quick top tang thumb safety. *The A-Bolt's safety is on top of the tang for quick access. A glance downward, or a touch of your thumb, keeps you in touch with the rifle's safety status. Push it forward with your thumb when you're ready to shoot. Also at the rear of the bolt shroud is a serrated cocking indicator. When the rifle is cocked, the indicator*

protrudes from under the bolt shroud. You can tell by sight or touch whether or not the rifle is cocked.

BARRELS

All barrels from introduction through 1992 are the same barrel diameter. However, word is out that in 1993 there will be a heavy varmint introduced.

The long action rifles had 22" barrels in the standard calibers and 24" barrels in the magnums until 1988 when the magnum barrels were changed to 26". Short action rifles have 22" barrels except for the Micro Medallion which has a 20" barrel.

The barrel marking are as follows on the left side:

**BROWNING ARMS COMPANY
MORGAN, UTAH & MONTREAL P.Q.
MADE IN JAPAN**

On the Stainless Steel model the words "STAINLESS STEEL" are in front of the above marking. No other special model has other then standard markings.

On the right barrel are the words:
PAT 4723369 A-BOLT CAL(Caliber) ONLY

STOCKS

The full pistol grip stock has a fluted comb and is made of American walnut. They are from group 1 to group 4 or higher in quality and checkered 18 to 22 lines per inch with or without a border. In the first two years of production, the finish on the Hunter was more of a satin, in 1987 and thereafter, this was changed to a high gloss. The Camo Stalker and other models will vary. These are described in their sections.

The standard stock dimensions are length of pull 13 5/8", drop at comb 3/4", and drop at heel 1 1/8"; and all are fitted with the Michaels post type stud for sling swivels. These will differ for the Micro and Gold Medallion only.

During the first two years of production, the Hunter grades in the standard calibers had black plastic butt plates and the magnums a black rubber recoil pad. From 1987 through 1992, all calibers in all variations had rubber pads that were marked "Browning."

I must make a comment about the graphite stock, I guess, because I am old fashioned.

Even though non-traditional the graphite stock does hold its zero and it is rugged. Although not a graphite stock expert, I am sure Browning is using the best available. I don't know about you, but when I'm sitting on the side of some mountain in Alaska and get tired of looking at the beautiful scenery, I like looking at a beautiful rifle. To me it's part of the hunt. Plastic is not included in my list of beautiful things. I enjoy the checkering, engraving, workmanship, and the figure of the wood — to each his own.

MAGAZINES

One of the best features of the A-Bolt is the magazine: it's detachable from the floorplate. This is the same setup as the BAR and very handy, for it enables you to carry extra ammunition very conveniently in a spare magazine.

The magazine capacity is four in the standard calibers and three for the magnums. In addition, you can have one in the chamber. This does not hold true for the Micro Medallion. Its magazine will hold only three in any caliber.

By the way, I would highly recommend you purchase a spare to carry in case anything goes wrong with the original or it gets lost.

INTRODUCTION OF CALIBERS

In 1985, Browning made this model in 25/06 Remington, 257 Roberts, 270 Winchester, 7mm Remington Magnum, 30/06, 300 Winchester Magnum, 338 Winchester Magnum, 22/250 Remington, 243 Winchester, 7mm/08 Remington, and the 308 Winchester. The following calibers were introduced after 1985.

1987
280 Remington

1988
375 H & H Magnum

1989
223 Remington
284 Winchester

1990
22 Hornet

The only cartridge that has been discontinued during the entire run of the A-Bolt is the 22 Hornet, but it is returning in 1994, so I hear.

For year codes on this model please refer to the General Information section in the front of this book.

A trio of Brownings. John M. Browning designed the Superposed and Auto 5 Models and his grandson, Bruce W. Browning, true to family tradition designed one of the most successful semi-auto sporting rifles ever built, the B.A.R.

Chapter Eleven

Semi-Auto Rifles

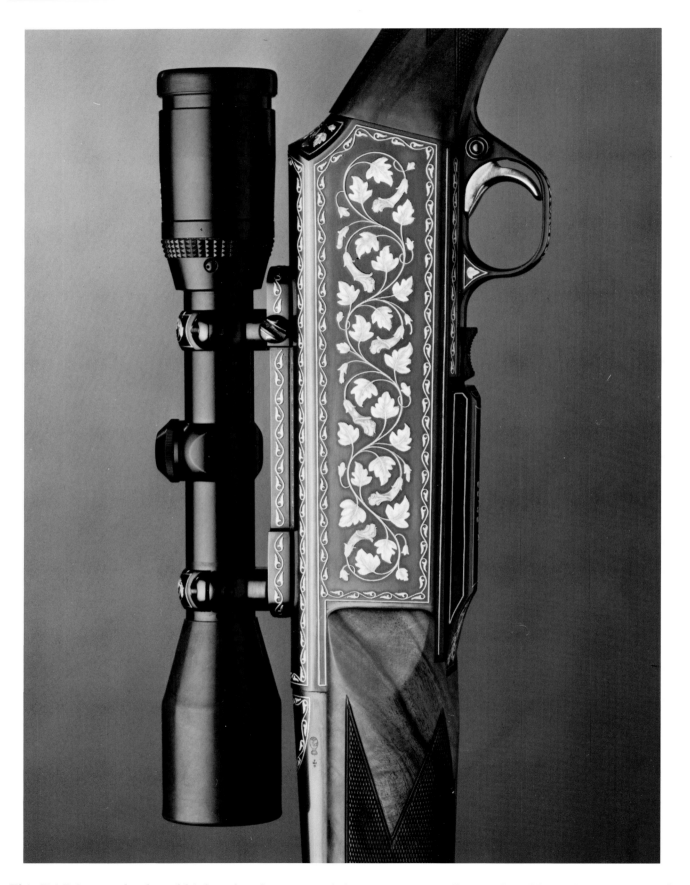

This BAR is completely gold inlayed and was one of the most ornate rifles produced by Fabrique Nationale in this series.

THE BAR HIGH POWERED RIFLE

GENERAL INFORMATION

This very successful and collectable rifle was designed by John M. Browning's grandson, Bruce W. Browning, who had a hand, not only in the successful design of this and the T-Bolt, but also in other models as well, the Browning legacy goes on.

The BAR was introduced to the American public on July 17, 1967. It was an instant success and is still the best selling semi-auto sporting rifle in the world. It has become the one by which all others are judged. One of the main reasons is that it is so accurate. I have sighted in several off the shelf. The first time I ever shot one was off the top of a car at a deer camp and was amazed at the groups attained with factory ammo let alone more accurate reloads.

Although Browning is still making a high quality rifle, collectors favor the ones made and assembled in Belgium. These will be so marked on the barrels. If you refer to the serial numbers, you will also be able to tell the Belgium guns, for all were made prior to 1976. The rifles made with parts from Belgium and assembled and finished in Portugal will be marked as such and will neither bring collectors' prices nor much interest, other than from the hunter. There are many Browning collectors who collect nothing but the BAR for there are many grades and calibers that will keep the most ambitious collector busy for several years.

To save some of you a phone call, let me say that Browning was like every other manufacturer: If they had parts they needed or wanted to use, they would mix them whether they were from Belgium or Portugal. Don't be surprised if you find a standard caliber with a magnum game scene or visa versa. Also, don't automatically turn down a rifle because it has a recoil pad. Some of these were ordered with them, especially the higher grades. I have also seen magnums with plastic butt plates because they were special ordered without a recoil pad.

Remember, serial numbers are stamped on guns after they are polished and before they are blued or assembled. This means that although every effort is taken to produce these in sequence, sometimes a receiver is not finished and assembled for a period of time. This could postpone the actual shipping date long after the production date.

The breaking point on collectable high grade BAR's is 1974 when 100% hand engraved guns only marked "Made In Belgium" began to be replaced by partly etched guns. This, of course, doesn't pertain to Grade I's, since they have no engraving, or Grade II's, because they were all hand engraved. All this will be explained in the high grade sections.

Buy only guns made and assembled in Belgium if you want a collectable. Buy guns assembled in Portugal if you want a shooter, because for all practical purposes they are just as good as the all-Belgium guns.

GRADE I

The BAR is one of the most popular hunting rifles ever produced. This is a Grade 1.

The Grade I was introduced in 1967. It had no engraving and all the receivers were blued. The wood was about group 1-2 walnut and checkered 18 lines per inch. This grade is still being made today.

The descriptions and changes under frames, barrels, magazines, stocks, etc., that follow all pertain to this grade, so please refer to the appropiate sections.

GRADE II

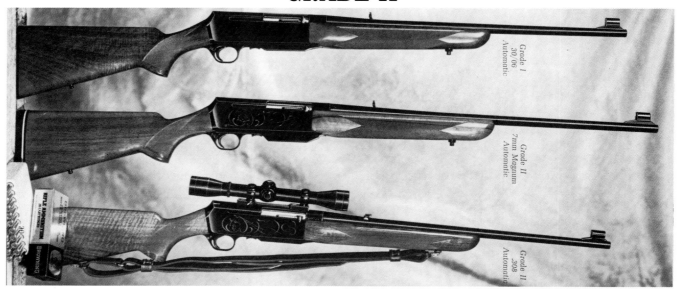

The BAR in Grade I and II promoted as the most reliable semi-autos offered by any gun company. Through years of experience I can also add, they are some of the most accurate.

The Grade II was introduced in 1967 and discontinued in 1975 but reintroduced in 1993 roll engraved not hand engraved like the earlier version.

It had just a touch of light engraving on both sides consisting of broad scrolls and big game heads. There were just two patterns for all calibers, the standard calibers had a deer and antelope head, while the magnums had a grizzly bear and ram head.

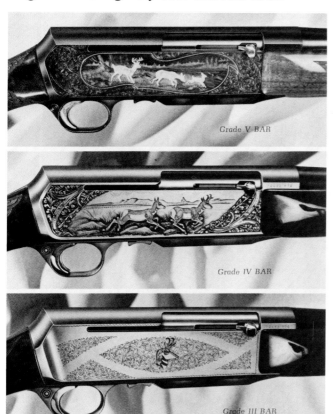

Grade V BAR

Grade IV BAR

Grade III BAR

The stocks were a higher grade, about group 2-3 walnut and checkered close to the same as the Grade I's. They were finished a little nicer. I have seen some really nice wood on a few of these but really nice figured wood is hard to find on a Grade II.

The early Grade II rifles from 1969 to 1970 had blued triggers, and the later ones from 1971 until the end of production for this grade had gold plated triggers.

GRADE III

The hand engraved Grade III was introduced in 1971 and discontinued in 1974

The engraving consisted of about 50% fine fleur-de-lis scroll that surrounded detailed game heads. The standard calibers featured antelope and deer heads, and the magnum calibers had moose and elk heads. All receivers were greyed steel finished and the triggers were gold plated.

In 1979 the Grade III was reintroduced with photo etched scroll and hand engraved game scenes. These were discontinued in 1987. The engraving was the same for all calibers, triggers were gold plated. The scroll covers both sides of the receiver, the trigger guard, and the floor plate. Coverage was about 50% with fine fleur-de-lis patterns surrounding the game scenes. The left side depicted two fighting elk, and the right side had several bighorn rams. The trigger guard and floor plate were also etched with the same type of scrolls. The receivers were finished in a greyed steel color, and the triggers were gold plated. These are not the ones to buy if you are a

The top three grades had hand stoned and fitted parts. The BAR with its large areas lends itself well to engraving.

collector; stick with the 100% hand engraved guns made from 1971 to 1974. Remember, if you see a Grade III with a good price, it probably is an etched gun, so be careful and don't over pay.

The wood on both early and late guns of this grade was of about group 3-4 and finished in Browning's traditional high gloss. The checkering was about 22 lines per inch, and the beaded carving around the edges of the engraving was well done. All standard calibers had a black plastic butt plate and the magnums a black ventilated rubber recoil pad, they were both marked "BROWNING".

GRADE IV

The hand engraved Grade IV was introduced in 1971 and discontinued in 1974. The etched guns were made from 1975 to 1984 when this grade was discontinued altogether.

This was a pretty gun that rivals Belgium's best engraving. The scroll work covered both sides of the receiver, the trigger guard, and the floor plate. Coverage was about 90% on the sides with ribbons and fleur-de-lis patterns surrounding the game scenes of prairies, mountains, trees, and forest. In addition, there were running deer and antelope on the standard calibers and moose and elk on the magnum. All the receivers were greyed. These were all 100% hand engraved, and the triggers were gold plated.

From 1975 to 1984, the scroll work was done using a photo etching process. The animals and scenes were the same as the 100% hand engraved guns. The scenes themselves, however, were still hand engraved, so you have to look at the scroll work closely. Don't buy a gun with etched scroll work for big money; they are not nearly as desirable to the collector as the 100% hand engraved guns.

The wood was high gloss finished and about group 4-5. The checkering was 22 lines to the inch with beaded carving surrounding the checkering around the edges. Also carved were beautiful fleur-de-lis scroll patterns. The standard calibers had a black plastic butt plate and the magnums a black ventilated rubber recoil pad. They were both marked "BROWNING."

GRADE V

The Grade V was introduced in 1971 and discontinued in 1975. When you pick up one of these, the first thought in your mind is, "This is a gun to look at and collect but not to shoot." They are very pretty and equal to the Midas grade Superposed in quality and decoration, but cost and labor problems stopped production of this model. This cancellation was a shame, for they are beautiful.

They had about 98% coverage on each side, while the top and bottom of the receiver had about 60%. Bold and deep fleur-de-lis scroll surrounded game scenes that were enclosed by inlaid gold wire. The game scenes were complete with woods, prairie, and fields; they featured deer and antelope on the standard calibers, elk and moose on the magnums. The animals were inlaid with 18 carat gold as was the gold wire surrounding these scenes. All receivers were blued and the triggers gold plated. The blued receivers contrasting with the gold makes for a really nice looking rifle.

The wood was all select French walnut of group 5 or better and impeccably finished with Browning's high gloss. The checkering was so fine that I had difficulty in counting it, but I will say 28 lines to the inch with beaded carving surrounding the checkering on the edges, it takes a dense piece of walnut to handle checkering this fine. Also deeply carved were beautiful fleur-de-lis scroll patterns. Since only master engravers and stock makers were allowed to work on the Grade V rifles all checkering and border carving was the finest from F.N.. The standard calibers had a black plastic butt plate and the magnums a black ventilated rubber recoil pad. They were both marked "BROWNING."

THE LIMITED EDITION OR BIG GAME SERIES

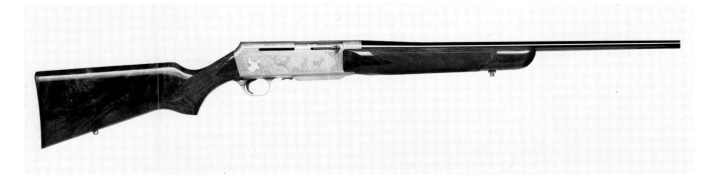

The Big Game series was produced from 1982 to 1989.

From 1982 to 1989, Browning brought out their big game series in 30/06 caliber.

On the left side was the head of a five point buck mule deer in 18 carat gold; in addition, there were three other mule deer standing over a ribbon with the words "[the number in the series] OF SIX HUNDRED." On the right side, the head of an eight point whitetail buck was inlaid in 18 carat gold, another was running, and another pair of deer were standing in a meadow; one was looking and the other ready to run. All of this was surrounded by ribbons and fleur-de-lis scroll and game scenes of fields, trees, and mountains. The top of the receiver had "MULE DEER" engraved on the left side and "WHITE TAIL DEER" on the right. The trigger guard and floor plate also had the same type of scroll engraving.

The entire receiver was finished in a greyed steel finish. Each rifle was signed with the master engraver's name, and all the triggers were gold plated.

The stock was about group 5, with a carved beaded border entirely surrounding the 25 lines per inch hand checkering. It was finished in a high gloss. They had a black plastic butt plate marked "**BROWNING**."

The rifle was cased in black walnut with a velvet lining.

GRADES AND YEARS OF PRODUCTION

	67	68	69	70	71	72	73	74	75	76	77	78	79	80	81	82	83	84
GRADE I	X	X	X	X	X	X	X	X	X	X	X	X	X	X	X	X	X	X
GRADE I MAGNUM		X	X	X	X	X	X	X	X	X	X	X	X	X	X	X	X	X
GRADE II	X	X	X	X	X	X	X	X										
GRADE II MAGNUM		X	X	X	X	X	X	X										
GRADE III HAND ENG					X	X	X	X										
GRADE III ETCHED													X	X	X	X	X	X
GRADE IV HAND ENG					X	X	X	X										
GRADE IV ETCHED									X	X	X	X	X	X	X	X	X	X
GRADE V					X	X	X	X										
BIG GAME(LTD ED)																X	X	X

	85	86	87	88	89	90	91	92
GRADE I	X	X	X	X	X	X	X	X
GRADE I MAGNUM	X	X	X	X	X	X	X	X
GRADE III ETCHED	X	X						
GRADE IV	X	X						
BIG GAME SERIES		X	X	X	X			

FRAMES

Everything we discuss here pertains to all models and variations, unless it is described differently for a certain grade.

From the beginning of production, the frames have always been machined from steel and blued. They were all drilled and tapped for a scope with all triggers blued.

It is a gas operated action that utilizes the force of the expanding gases upon firing to actuate the operating cycle. The gases are directed to a gas piston, which in turn transmits this energy through an inertia piece and double operating bars to the breech bolt, which has a rotary head design. The breech bolt has 7 locking lugs that lock directly into the barrel directly behind the chamber. The bolt face is recessed so it surrounds the base of the cartridge. This amounts to a very safe and reliable locking system that helps in delivering the great accuracy of this gun.

All had cross bolt safeties with an enlarged head that blocked the trigger, no left hand safeties were ever offered by Browning.

The serial number for all Belgium made and assembled rifles appeared on the left side at the top of the frame directly above the slot in front of the ejection port.

MAGAZINES

The detachable box magazine is an excellent feature for quick reloading when an extra is carried in the field.

All BAR's have a separate magazine that detaches from the floor plate. This is a great feature, for it enables you to carry extra ammunition very conveniently in a spare magazine. Capacity is four in the standard calibers and three for the magnums; in addition, you can have one in the chamber.

SIGHTS

Sights in the rear were dovetailed until 1984 when they were screwed on using a base. They were all of the flip up type and fully adjustable for elevation, but they had to be slid within the dovetail for windage until 1984 when they were mounted on a base. These rear sights could be adjusted by loosening a screw. The later ones were marked in white lines denoting the range. The ramp front sight had the same gold metal bead with a hood throughout production; the sight radius was 17 1/2''.

Grades I and II came with barrel sights from their introduction until 1988 when you could choose the Grade 1 without sights. The Grade 11 had sights until it was cancelled. Grades 3, 4, 5 and the Big Game series had no sights unless they were special ordered.

WEIGHTS

The standard calibers weigh in at about 7 lbs. 6 oz., and the magnums 8 lbs., 6 oz.

BARRELS

Barrels were all standard weight, tapered and blued with polished muzzles.

The standard calibers had 22'' barrels and all the magnum barrels were 24'' long. The muzzles were all polished bright.

MARKINGS FOR BELGIUM GUNS

I have included the actual proof marks here for those who want to make sure a barrel is original for a gun.

The markings on the 1967-1968 guns were as follows:

On the left side of the barrel under or adjacent to the rear sight were the words:

**BROWNING ARMS COMPANY
MADE IN BELGIUM**

On the left side of the barrel immediately in front of the receiver you will find proof marks 6, 12, 7, and 4. *(See proof marks on page 50.)*

On the right side of barrel adjacent to the rear sight:

**CALIBER (cal) ONLY
PATENT PENDING**

The barrel markings from 1969 to 1975 for all Belgium guns were as follows:

On the left side of the barrel adjacent to the rear sight:

**BROWNING ARMS COMPANY
MORGAN,UTAH & MONTREAL P.Q.
MADE IN BELGIUM**

On the left side of the barrel immediately in front of the receiver you will find proof mark number 9. *(See proof marks on page 50.)*

On the right side of the barrel under or adjacent to the rear sight:

**BAR CALIBER (cal) ONLY
BROWNING PATENTS**

The early guns assembled in Portugal were marked as follows:

On the left side of the barrel under or adjacent to the rear sight:

**BROWNING ARMS COMPANY
MORGAN UTAH & MONTREAL P.Q.
MADE IN BELGIUM
ASSEMBLED IN PORTUGAL**

To the right of the marking are the proofs 9 and 11. *(See proof marks on page 50.)*

On the right side of the barrel under or adjacent to the rear sight:

**BAR CALIBER (cal) ONLY (or)
CALIBER (cal) ONLY
BROWNING PATENTS**

The late guns assembled in Portugal are marked on the left side of the barrel with the words:

**BROWNING ARMS COMPANY
MORGAN,UTAH & MONTREAL P.Q.
MADE IN BELGIUM BY FABRIQUE NATIONALE
HERSTAL ASSEMBLED IN PORTUGAL**

To the right of the marking are the proofs 9 and 11. *(See proof marks on page 50.)*

On the right side of the barrel they are marked:
BAR CALIBER(cal)ONLY BROWNING PATENT

The following is etched on the top, front, and left side of the action:

**BROWNING
BAR**

On the left side of the frame on the lower front is the serial number.

For those of you who suspect you have a BAR manufactured for sales outside of the U.S., here are the barrel markings taken from a late production rifle, 1990, intended for European sales.

On the left side of the frame etched on the upper front:

**BROWNING
BAR**

On the left side of the frame on the lower front is the serial number.

On the left side of the barrel under or adjacent to the rear sight:

**BROWNING ARMS COMPANY
MORGAN,UTAH & MONTREAL P.Q.
MADE IN BELGIUM
BY FABRIQUE NATIONALE HERSTAL
ASSEMBLED IN PORTUGAL**

On the left side of the barrel immediately in front of the receiver are proof marks 11 and 9. *(See proof marks on page 50.)*

On the right side of the barrel under or adjacent to the rear sight:

**BAR CALIBER (cal) ONLY
BROWNING PATENTS**

The wood is finished in the usual well filled but flat look so well liked by the Europeans. The balance of the gun appears to be the same as those for the U.S.

STOCKS

The French walnut stocks were all full pistol grip and checkered, this varied with the grade, The finish was the traditional Browning high gloss, and there were no grip caps unless special ordered. I have never seen a straight stocked BAR but I wouldn't doubt F.N. making one on special order.

Standard stock dimensions were length of pull 13 5/8", drop at comb 1 5/8", and drop at heel 2". All were shipped with black plastic butt plates marked "BROWNING" in standard calibers and black rubber recoil pads marked "BROWNING" if a magnum. Sling swivels studs were also provided.

Forearms were full, hand checkered and finished like the butt stock. There were no forearm tips unless special ordered.

CARTRIDGES

Original introduction was in 243 Winchester, 308 Winchester, 30/06, and .270 Winchester.

Browning then brought out the magnums in 1968; calibers were 7mm Remington Magnum, 300 Winchester Magnum and 338 Winchester Magnum. All the above cartridges were available until the end of Belgium production, except the .338, which was discontinued in 1975. They are around, but the 338 in Grade I is rarer then the Grade II.

In the later guns, the 280 Remington and the 338 Winchester Magnum were brought back in 1988.

CALIBER YEARS OF PRODUCTION

To make it easier for you to follow the grade and caliber introductions and cancellations, I have put together the following table.

	67	68	69	70	71	72	73	74	75	76	77	78	79	80	81	82	83	84
GRADE I	X	X	X	X	X	X	X	X	X	X	X	X	X	X	X	X	X	X
GRADE I MAGNUM		X	X	X	X	X	X	X	X	X	X	X	X	X	X	X	X	X
GRADE II	X	X	X	X	X	X	X	X										
GRADE II MAGNUM		X	X	X	X	X	X	X										
GRADE III HAND ENG						X	X	X										
GRADE III ETCHED													X	X	X	X	X	X
GRADE IV HAND ENG						X	X	X										
GRADE IV ETCHED									X	X	X	X	X	X	X	X	X	X
GRADE V					X	X	X	X										
BIG GAME (LTD ED)																X	X	X
243 WINCHESTER	X	X	X	X	X	X	X	X	X	X	X	X	X	X	X	X	X	X
270 WINCHESTER	X	X	X	X	X	X	X	X	X	X	X	X	X	X	X	X	X	X
308 WINCHESTER	X	X	X	X	X	X	X	X	X	X	X	X	X	X	X	X	X	X
30/06	X	X	X	X	X	X	X	X	X	X	X	X	X	X	X	X	X	X
7mm REMINGTON MAG		X	X	X	X	X	X	X	X	X	X	X	X	X	X	X	X	X
300 WINCHESTER MAG		X	X	X	X	X	X	X	X	X	X	X	X	X	X	X	X	X
338 WINCHESTER MAG		X	X	X	X	X	X	X	X									

	85	86	87	88	89	90	91	92
GRADE I	X	X	X	X	X	X	X	X
GRADE I MAGNUM	X	X	X	X	X	X	X	X
GRADE III ETCHED	X	X						
GRADE IV	X	X						
BIG GAME SERIES		X	X	X	X			
243 WINCHESTER	X	X	X	X	X	X	X	X
270 WINCHESTER	X	X	X	X	X	X	X	X
280 REMINGTON				X	X	X	X	X
308 WINCHESTER	X	X	X	X	X	X	X	X
30/06	X	X	X	X	X	X	X	X
7mm REMINGTON MAG	X	X	X	X	X	X	X	X
300 WINCHESTER MAG	X	X	X	X	X	X	X	X
338 WINCHESTER MAG				X	X	X	X	X

SERIAL NUMBERS AND CODES

All have the letter "M" in the serial number until 1976 when the new codes started. From 1967-1976 each year began with serial number 0001. Serial numbers from 1967-1976 are as follows.

| 1967 ——M7 | 1969 ——M69 | 1971 ——M71 |
| 1968 ——M8 | 1970 ——M70 | 1972 ——M72 |

| 1973 ——M73 | 1975 ——M75 |
| 1974 ——M74 | 1976 ——M76 |

For yearly codes after 1976 refer to the General Information section in the front of the book.

Model codes for the Grade I is 137, Grade II is 237, Grade III is 337, Grade IV is 437, and Grade V is 537.

F.N. SEMI AUTO

In the 1950's, F.N. offered for sale the much sought-after F.N. Browning Semi-Automatic Rifle.

This model was originally designed for military purposes and adopted by many countries including Canada, Great Britain, Australia, New Zealand, Germany, Belgium, Austria, Israel, Venezuela, Cuba, Peru, and several others.

It was a gas operated, military style rifle that was brought over here for sporting purposes such as hunting and target shooting. The only cartridge it was chambered for was 308 Winchester, and the weight on the standard gun was 8 1/2 lbs. The barrels were 25 1/2'' long and the entire gun was matte finished with a semi-gloss finished walnut stock of strictly utilitarian grade.

The breakdown feature allowed cleaning and repair in the field. This rifle was well accepted by the public, but it cost so much that only a few sportsmen could afford them.

LIGHTNING MODEL

The general characteristics are the same as for the standard model except that the cover, the trigger guard, the action spring tube, and the magazine are made out of aluminum alloy, reducing the weight of the rifle without the magazine to eight pounds.

BASIC FEATURES

It had many outstanding features that more modern military rifles do not have even today. I will list these as the introductory flyer did.

Adjustable Gas Regulator — The amount of gas utilized to actuate the mechanism can be regulated to suit all operating conditions. The regulator exhausts surplus gas out of the system and thus keeps fouling to a minimum.

Closed Action — When firing, the moving parts are completely enclosed and sealed from the outside, making the gun an outstanding performer in mud, dust, or rain.

Stability — Through careful design and the placing of the gas cylinder above the barrel, the center of gravity of the rifle is on a line with the axis of the barrel. This feature eliminates any upward jerk of the rifle due to recoil and permits the shooter to remain on target with ease during a series of fast, successive shots. The stability of the rifle combined with its other characteristics contributes to remarkable accuracy to make excellent scores possible.

Low Line Of Sight — Other rifles designed to locate the center of gravity along the axis of the barrel often necessitate high raised sights. In the F.N. Browning, the sighting line is kept low so that the shooter can maintain maximum concealment, a feature especially beneficial to those individuals in law enforcement work.

Ease Of Manipulation — All manual operations required to operate the rifle, such as cocking, feeding a round in the chamber, replacing the magazine, or putting on the safety are performed with the left hand only, so that the weapon can be kept shouldered with the right hand on the pistol grip.

In addition, a collapsible handle is attached at the balance point to facilitate carrying the rifle in the field.

Field Stripping — The receiver of the F.N. Browning is hinged to the trigger guard butt section of the rifle and can thus be swung open like a shotgun. This gives the easiest possible access to the slide bolt assembly, which need merely be pulled out of the receiver for cleaning.

The firing pin and extractor can be disassembled from the bolt with a cartridge as a tool.

The only other components which require removal or cleaning in the field are the magazine and the gas plug and piston. The magazine is detached through the operation of the magazine latch. The gas plus and piston are easily removed by turning the gas plug one quarter turn with a cartridge as the only aid.

Flash Hider — Each rifle is equipped with an integral flash hider, which not only suppresses a good deal of the revealing flame glow of firing, but also reduces recoil and improves the accuracy of the rifle.

Sights — The sturdy sights allow both windage and elevation correction.

ACCESSORIES

Telescopic Sight Mount — The F.N. Browning rifle is particularly well adapted for the use of a telescopic sight. A special cover is made which incorporates a telescope mount and which may be substituted for the regular rifle cover. Each time the telescope cover is placed on the rifle, it springs in place to maintain an identical setting of the sight.

Bayonet — A special bayonet for use in conjunction with the rifle with flash hider can be easily snapped on the end of the barrel. It has been especially designed to eliminate any detrimental effect when the rifle is fired with a bayonet in place. It is capable of a forward movement relative to the barrel against the action of a spring so that when the rifle recoils, the corresponding recoil of the bayonet is delayed until the bullet has left the barrel.

Magazine Loader — To facilitate loading the 20 round magazine, a magazine loader is available which can be fitted over the mouth of the magazine and used to load it by five round clips.

Sling — For shooting with a sling, an adjustable leather strap can be attached to the sling swivels provided on the rifle.

The F.N. Browning is a good looking rifle that appeals to the military aa well as the civilian shooter.

This information on the FN FAL has been graciously given to us by Rick Cartledge who is a writer for Machine Gun News. This is a little off the beaten track for this book is only supposed to be about sporting guns imported to or made in the U.S. Those of you who like this model will be interested in the following.

The FN FAL stands today as the standard by which all battle rifles are measured. Though available in full auto, it is as a semi automatic battle rifle that the Fusil Automatique Leger (light automatic rifle) really shines. Forged in the .761 x .51 NATO caliber, the weapon is robust, simple and very reliable. The upper receiver is essentially an improved version of the famed FN 49 while the trigger group is pure John Moses Browning. This rugged Herstal, Belgium gun has captured the hearts of soldiers and sportsmen alike because of it's excellent handling and ergonomics.

The rifle cocks from the left side while being held by the pistol grip on the right. It balances well when being carried by the fore grip or the carry handle. The 9 lb 8 oz weapon wields easily with one hand and can be carried smoothly on a dead run while crossing a deep ditch or vaulting a barricade. The 20 round box magazine loads and ejects quickly and holds it's cargo of 2800 fps cartridges reliably at the ready. Armories cut the gun in either the inch or metric pattern and fit it with furniture of wood. plastic or aluminum. Some troops favor the heavy bipod version of the rifle while other prefer the classic configuration.

Armies through out the world have embraced this reliable well made weapon. They have purchased the gun from Fabrique Nationale in Belgium or have manufactured the rifle in their own countries under contract. So successful is the FN FAL that the number of standing armies using it in some form approaches 100. Such is it's reputation that it is said that the second American wave into Panama carried M-14's out of respect for Noriega's FALs. Marine gunners carried the M-14 and the Airborne and Special Forces hefted the legendary Barretts for the same reason in Desert Storm. Though this elder statesman of the battle rifles was born in 1950, it is still held in such esteem that no knowledgeable soldier with an M-16 would face it unreinforecd-even in the hands of a third rate army.

I think you can see the FN FAL is a great gun and the reasons they demand such a high price in todays market.

I want you to also note the trigger group was designed by John Browning. To this day, modern technology has not been able to design a trigger mechanism with more reliability or ease of manufacture.

The following was found on the heavy barrel version of this model:

On the left side of the receiver above the safety is the marking:

".308 MATCH"

On the right side of the receiver:
Fabrique Nationale Herstal (SN)
Made in Belgium Steyr Secaucus N.J.

Chapter Twelve

Single Shot
Rifles

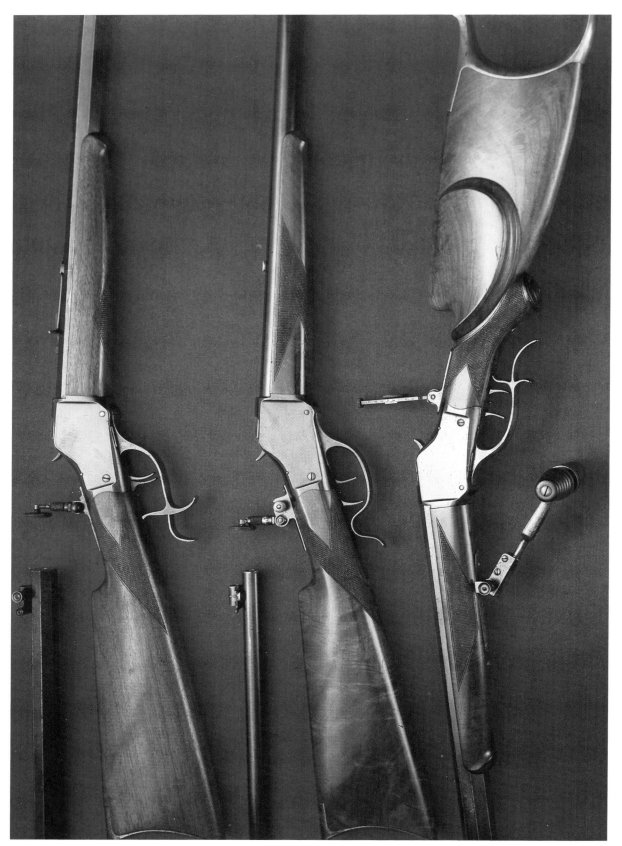

The Model 1885 Winchester was the first of many of John M. Browning's inventions that secured many successful years at the Winchester Repeating Arms Co. At the top is a high-wall No. 3 octagonal barrell with wind gauge, spirit level front sight, and single set triggers. The center example is a very similar rifle with deluxe wood, round barrel, and double set triggers. This is an unusual gun in that it is a .22 Long Rifle. The bottom example has a No. 5 barrel, which was the heaviest made, Schuetzen style butt stock, and palm rest.

THE B-78 HIGH POWERED RIFLE

GENERAL INFORMATION

The B-78 was the first in the series of John M. Browning inventions to be reintroduced. As of 1992, there have been a total of 12 including various configurations and gauges. These guns have been so well accepted by the public that more are to come.

As you have already read, the Winchester Model 1885 was the first patent that John M. sold to Winchester on October 7, 1879. This was the rifle that kicked off the beginning of their long relationship, it's only fitting that the B-78 was used to start another series of fine guns. Originally, they were made from 1885 to 1913 with many different barrel weights, configurations, calibers, butt stock and forearm styles, sights, and butt plates. The list could go on and on, but it has nothing to do with the B-78. I mention this to give you the idea that it was a very versatile and adaptable rifle. Unfortunately, today's labor costs and mass marketing didn't allow Browning to produce these on a custom basis.

The B-78 was produced in Japan starting in 1973 and had been great competition for the Ruger No. 1 Single Shot. In 1985 it was reintroduced as the Model 1885 with some modifications. The final production year for the B-78 was 1982. We will cover the various changes and basic introduction in each section.

The B-78 has become a very collectible gun and is much sought after by some collectors. This brings up a point that Browning gun fanciers must start to see. The Japanese-made Brownings are starting to come into their own as collectibles, and if you're going to anticipate what will increase in value, you need to study the catalogs and purchase the slowest sellers. These are the ones that will be the rarest and that will increase the value and uniqueness of your collection.

FRAMES

This was an all-steel falling block, exposed hammer singleshot. All were blued with no engraving other then the Centennial 78. Only one grade was offered, but within that grade, there were several stock and barrel changes, caliber introductions, and other features that will be discussed.

The triggers on the standard guns were all polished bright and grooved. They were also fully adjustable from 3 to 4 1/2 lbs. This is really nice on a factory gun and the kind of little features that you look for in a quality rifle.

The ejectors are one of the most unique things about the B-78 in that they are adjustable not only for direction, but also for how the distance the shell will be ejected. Other rifles like the Ruger No. 1 will allow you to either eject or extract but not adjust the direction. Depending on whether you are a right or left handed shooter, you can change the direction in which the cartridges are ejected after a shot. This is important when a quick follow up is needed and you don't want to dismount the rifle. Who wants a hot 7mm mag shell in the eyeball? Also the distance that a shell is thrown can be adjusted right down to only extraction for the reloader.

The action has an exposed hammer with a full and half cock notch. Browning has always recommended that all rifles be carried with the hammer on half cock in case of a blow to the hammer. If the gun is carried with the hammer all the way down and resting on the firing pin, a blow to it can fire the chambered cartridge.

BARREL CONFIGURATION/ PRODUCTION FIGURES

As introduced, there was a choice of a medium round and later heavy barrel or a medium octagon barrel 26" long. As you can see by the chart below, the original calibers, 22/250 Remington, 6mm Remington, 25/06 Remington and the 30/06 are the ones that sold the most in both style of barrels. In 1976 the 45/70 was introduced but only with a 24" octagon barrel. In 1976 the 7mm Remington Magnum in either barrel was produced, and in 1977 the 243 Winchester came along in either barrel configuration. In 1979 the round barrel was discontinued for the 30/06. These are all the introductions and calibers made unless someone comes up with a special order of which I am presently unaware.

All calibers were discontinued in 1982. The total production by caliber and barrel type, octagon or round, appears below.

Caliber	Round	Octagon	Total
243 Winchester	280	391	671
22/250	2431	3481	5912
6MM Remington	1280	1911	3191
25/06	1475	3293	4768
30/06	1588	2330	3918
45/70	0	3839*	3839
7MM Remington	635	961	1596
	7689	16207	23896

* Includes 966 Bicentennial Models.

From the above, you can see the rare ones; these are the ones to collect and have the highest value. Things like this aren't taken into consideration in those publications that are supposed to give you proper values. These folks try to cover thousands of different guns from manufacturers all over the world, and they can't do it. They are valueless and you as a Browning collector or dealer must realize this.

There were no iron sights furnished on any gun until 1976 when the 45/70 came along. The front looked like the knife blade sight of the early Winchesters but only in reverse where the high end of the sight faced the shooter. The rear was the full buckhorn with an elevator to adjust elevation. On these 45/70 rifles, the barrels were also drilled and tapped for scope mounts.

From 1973 to 1981, scope bases and 1" rings were furnished with each gun except the 45/70. These were made by Burris and marked on the scope base "BROWNING".

The octagon barrels were unique among modern made rifles and really added a lot to the appeal of the B-78. By the way, these were all tapered octagon and not straight like many of the antique rifles you run across. This was an expensive option that isn't found very often on the original Winchester 1885. All barrels were blued with a polished and recessed muzzle.

On the left side the barrels are marked:

BROWNING ARMS COMPANY
MORGAN,UTAH & MONTREAL P.Q.
MADE IN JAPAN

On the right side they are marked:
BROWNING-78 CALIBER(Cal) only
PATENT NO. 3830000

STOCKS

The full pistol grip and fluted comb butt stocks were made from American walnut and about group 2 grade. All had a full cheek piece, grip cap with an initial medallion, recoil pad marked "Browning", and were high gloss finished.

The checkering was 20 lines per inch throughout production; the dimensions were length of pull 13 1/4", drop at comb 2", and drop at heel 2 3/4".

The forearms were all schnabel and attached by a hanger that was screwed to the front of the action. This allowed the barrel to feel no pressure from the forearm and free float; accuracy was improved over the original Winchester. The finish was high gloss and checkering was 20 lines per inch.

The 45/70 butt stock was also a bit different in that it was a straight grip with a crescent steel butt plate. The checkering was 20 lines per inch and finish was also high gloss, forearms were the same as the other calibers. Stock dimensions were length of pull 13 5/8", drop at comb 1 5/8", and drop at heel 2 1/8".

Another unique feature was the detachable and hidden sling swivels. Browning wanted to maintain the former look of this rifle and provided these so they would not show and change the underside of the gun. One inch loops were provided with the gun and a 1 1/4" loop could be purchased as an option.

SERIAL NUMBERS AND MODEL CODES

The "W" in the serial number stands for the model. Serial numbers from 1973 - 1976 are as follows:
1973 —W73 1974 —W74 1975 —W75 1976 —W76

After 1976 the new serial number codes began. These have the new designation number of 149 for all models except in 1976, Browning's Bicentennial model with the product code, 1776.

For year codes after 1976, refer to the General Information section in the front of this book.

MODEL 1885 RIFLE

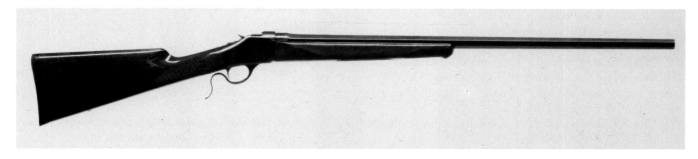

As introduced in 1985 the Model 1885 was essentially an improved Model 78.

GENERAL INFORMATION

The 1885 was introduced in 1985 to replace the B-78, and it is still being made as of 1992. It is basically the same rifle as the B-78 with some minor changes, which were a new trigger assembly, straight stock and a 28'' octagon barrel.

Much of what you will read here is redundent, but it is necessary so you don't have to pick through the B-78 section to read about the 1885.

FRAMES

The pictures below show the Model 1885 breech block, they are from the 1988 catalog.

Strong falling breech-block. *The Model 1885 lever gives you all the strength falling block actions are respected for. Because the breechblock travels in vertical channels milled into the solid steel receiver wall, massive lock-up strength is achieved. The breech-block opens by swinging the lever down. This drops the breechblock, which in turn cocks the hammer and exposes the chamber for loading. As the lever returns, the hammer remains cocked, and the breechblock seals the cartridge in the chamber.*

Adjustable shell deflector. *Dropping the lever extracts the cartridge and ejects it rearward. The cartridge deflector, at the rear of the receiver, allows you to direct the empty cartridge either to the right or the left, or catch it by the base and retain it for easy recovery.*

This was an all steel falling block, exposed hammer single shot. All were blued with no engraving, and there was only one grade offered. Within that grade, there were several caliber introductions and other features that will be discussed.

The trigger sear arrangement on this rifle was completely different from the B-78. The 1885 uses an inertia sear which prevents the hammer from being fully lowered without first pulling the trigger; this was done

for safety purposes. They were also fully adjustable from 3 1/2 to 5 1/2 lbs and all were gold colored.

The ejectors are the same as the B-78 and are one of the most unique features of the rifle. They are adjustable not only for direction but also for how far the shell is ejected. Other rifles, like the Ruger No. 1, will allow you to either eject or extract but not adjust the direction. Depending on whether you are a right or left-handed shooter, you can change the direction in which the cartridges are ejected after a shot. This is important when a quick follow up is needed and you don't want to dismount the rifle. Also the distance that a shell is thrown can be adjusted right down to only extraction for the reloader.

The action has an exposed hammer with a full and half cock notch. Browning has always recommended that all rifles be carried with the hammer on half cock in case of a blow to the hammer. If the gun is carried with the hammer all the way down and resting on the firing pin, a blow to it can fire the chambered cartridge.

The only markings on the frames are the serial numbers and the Browning logo on the lever.

BARRELS

The octagon barrels are now 28'' instead of the B-78's 26'' or 24''.barrels. Also discontinued was the optional round barrel of heavier weight, although the 1885's 7 lbs 12 oz is still plenty to tote around. All octagon barrels have been blued with recessed muzzles only; no changes have been made in configuration since the rifle was first introduced. The octagon barrels were not straight but tapered like many of the antique rifles you run across. This was an expensive option that isn't found very often on the original Winchester 1885.

The original calibers offered in 1985 were 22/250 Remington, 270 Winchester, 7mm Remington Magnum, and 45/70 Government. In 1986 the 223 Remington and the 30/06 were introduced, but they were discontinued in 1987. Things stayed this way until 1989 when these were again being made (and are still being made as of 1992.

On the left side the barrels are marked:
BROWNING ARMS COMPANY
MORGAN,UTAH & MONTREAL P.Q.
MADE IN JAPAN

You will also see proof 16 on these barrels. *(See proof marks on page 50.)*

On the right side they are marked:
BROWNING MODEL 1885 CALIBER(Cal) ONLY

There were no iron sights except for the 47/70; all were drilled and tapped for scope mounts that were not furnished. You could order them from Browning as a special order option; they were made by Burris and marked on the scope base "BROWN-ING." As mentioned above, the 45/70 does have iron sights that are the same as the B-78. The front looked like the knife blade sight of the early Winchesters but only in reverse where the high end of the sight faced the shooter. The rear was the full buckhorn with an elevator to adjust elevation. On these 45/70 rifles, the barrels were also drilled and tapped for scope mounts.

STOCKS

The Straight grip and semi-fluted butt stocks were made from American walnut and about group 2 grade. All had a straight comb without a cheekpiece, recoil pads marked "Browning," and a high gloss finish; some were made in the first year of production with a semi-gloss finish.

The checkering was 20 lines per inch throughout production, and the dimensions were length of pull 13 1/8", drop at comb 1 5/8", and drop at heel 2 1/8".

The forearms were all schnabel and attached by a hanger that was screwed to the front of the action.

This allowed the barrel to feel no pressure from the forearm and free float; accuracy was improved over the original Winchester 1885. The finish was also high gloss* and checkering was also 20 lines per inch. *See note above about finish.

Another unique feature was the detachable and hidden sling swivels. Browning wanted to maintain the former look of this rifle and provided these so that they would not show and change the underside of the gun; 1" loops were provided with the gun and a 1 1/4" loop could be purchased as an option. This changed in 1991 when they were no longer supplied; Browning then started to use the Michaels post type swivel studs without the swivels.

SERIAL NUMBERS

Serial numbers are all of the new type and can be found in the General Information section at the front of this book.

Model code for all calibers is 247.

Specifications — Model 1885

Action — Falling block, high wall single shot lever action.

Barrel — Octagonal, free floating. Recessed muzzle.

Hammer — Exposed, three position.

Sights — Drilled and tapped for scope. Two-piece scope base available as an accessory from Browning. Open sights standard on 45-70 Govt. model.

Stock and Forearm — Select, high grade walnut straight grip stock, Schnabel forearm. High gloss finish. Cut checkering. Recoil pad, standard.

Sling — Post-style sling swivels and loops standard.

Stock Dimension — Length of pull 13 1/8". Drop at comb 1 5/8". Drop at heel 2 1/8".

Calibers	Barrel Length	Sight Radius	Overall Length	Approximate Weight	Rate of Twist (R. Hand)
22-250 Rem.	28"	—	43 1/2"	8 lbs. 13 oz.	1 in 14"
270 Win.	28"	—	43 1/2"	8 lbs. 12 oz.	1 in 10"
7mm Rem. Mag.	28"	—	43 1/2"	8 lbs. 11 oz.	1 in 9 1/2"
45-70 Govt.	28"	21 1/2"	43 1/2"	8 lbs. 14 oz.	1 in 20"

Delivery of Model 1885's scheduled for mid-1988.

The specification table above is also a reproduction from a late 80's catalog.

Chapter Thirteen

Lever Action
Rifles

THE MODEL 81 BLR RIFLE

The BLR as originally introduced by Browning.

GENERAL INFORMATION

The Browning BLR is an interesting gun, which was first produced in 1966 by the Thompson Ramo Woolridge Corporation as a centerfire high powered lever action rifle.

Based on an agreement with Browning, the T. R. W. Company made parts for as many as 750 guns when manufacturing difficulties stopped any further production; only 75 were initially assembled. Later, there was an additional 175 more assembled but not sold to the pubic. Therefore a total of 250 guns were assembled, boxed, and held by T.R.W. in their vaults. Over the years, approximately fifty got out as lunch box specials, but this number is not known for sure.

After manufacturing contract negotiations fell through with T.R.W., Browning and T.R.W. negotiated for Browning to purchase the remaining parts that could be used by them or by F.N. As a point of interest, the T.R.W. manufactured guns cannot be repaired with Belgium parts; they will not fit because the measurements and tolerances are different.

The completed rifles lay in T.R.W.'s vaults until 1988 when the Springfield Armory approached them about purchasing the remaining 200 guns; T.R.W.'s lawyers advised the company, however, that liability was too great, and the decision was made to destroy the rifles. Some of the workers couldn't pass up a free rifle, and while this was being carried out, twenty-five guns disappeared. Now, only a total of 175 were left to be destroyed. The end result of all this is that 50 to 75 ended up in circulation somewhere. In addition to the above, two to three were sent to F.N. to be proofed of which one is a cutaway.

T.R.W. serial numbers started from 6KO1001 to 6k0xxxx. They were stamped only on the barrels and not on the frames. During production a die was broken, so no one really knows how many barrels were actually made, but the figure is probably 700 to 800. This brings up some interesting points. Browning purchased the remaining stock of parts

from T.R.W.; therefore, there may be as many as 500 made in Belgium with "USA" stamped on them. Some of the barrels might have had the markings removed, which is more likely. A third possibility is that Browning kept all or part of the parts, including the barrels, for use as replacement parts. In any case, anybody out there that has a "USA" marked Belgium BLR has a rare gun. This is an interesting variation and very collectable indeed.

Whatever the case may be, this is one of the few high quality lever action guns that have been successful other then the Savage 1899 or 99 and the now discontinued Sako Finnwolf and Winchester Model 88. There are still the Winchester 94 and the Marlins, but they don't handle cartridges like the 7mm Remington Magnum, 270 Winchester, and the 30/06. BLR collectors are popping up all the time, and I can tell by the number of inquiries that they are increasing.

BELGIUM PRODUCTION AND GRADES

The BLR has only been made in a standard grade with no engraving nor embellishment of any kind. Belgium production was from 1971-1974; it has since been made in Japan only.

As mentioned above, these were first introduced in 1971, though some were made in 1970. I have more calls by irate BLR owners about this then I care to recall. Remember, F.N. is like any other manufacturer: they sometimes produce their product ahead of time in anticipation of good sales. They also don't plan changes in models, markings, parts or anything else to occur on some exact date. Yes, BLR collectors, they did start producing this rifle in 1970 and they are marked ——-K70.

While we're at it, let me reiterate that serial numbers are stamped on guns after they are polished and before they are blued or assembled. This means that although every effort is taken to produce these in sequence, sometimes a receiver is not finished and assembled for a period of time. This could place the actual shipping date long after the production date.

ACTIONS

The BLR's action is based on a compound arrangement patented by a former employee of Browning, Carl Lewis. The action enables rapid bolt movement with a short lever stroke. It is also quite smooth and offers a lot of leverage for extraction after firing.

The prototype was made with a one piece bolt that relied on the notches machined on the bottom for lock up. These notches were not strong enough to withstand the pressures exerted by firing high intensity cartridges. Browning engineers designed a two piece bolt with a rotating head and interrupted locking lugs to solve this problem.

The BLR is really an unusual rifle in that it employs a gear drive. The underside of the bolt is driven back and forth by the lever which has matching teeth. This makes for a very smooth action. The leverage developed by this system along with the rotary bolt and seven locking lugs, and a recessed bolt head makes it possible to chamber the rifle to use modern high intensity calibers. The end result is a lever action rifle capable of shooting the type of calibers hunters want today.

Another great feature is the trigger assembly. It drops down with the lever and keeps you from pinching a finger while you are operating it in a hurry. The triggers were gold plated and later gold colored.

The disconnect system prevents firing until the lever and breech are fully closed. If the trigger is pulled and held while working the lever to reload another round, the gun will not fire until the bolt is closed all the way. Another safety feature is the three position hammer which was used from the beginning of production until 1991 on the standard or Short action. It had what Browning calls full cock, half cock, and dropped positions until 1992, when the fold down hammer was introduced on the Short action.

The inertia firing pin will not gain enough force to fire a cartridge from a hammer blow if the hammer is all the way down. This prevents someone from inadvertently dropping the gun and hitting the hammer, resulting in an accidental firing of the gun.

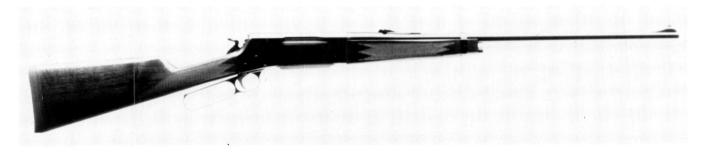

The BLR long action.

In 1991, Browning introduced a second action which they designated the BLR Long. Unlike the previous style, which was specifically sized to handle the 308 Winchester length calibers, the Long action would handle 30/06 length calibers and even magnums. This new action also had the new two position fold down hammer. The fold down hammer enables the shooter to push the hammer spur up and block the hammer from hitting the firing pin. These are also high lustre blued with the top surface serrated and the triggers gold plated. They are drilled for scope mounts, and the trigger assemblies also drop down with the lever. In fact, they are the same actions as the original, only longer.

All actions are all high lustre blued with the top surface serrated and drilled for scope mounts.

The only markings on the frames is a "P" under the forearm on the bottom, and directly in front of the receiver on the right side of barrel is the serial number.

MAGAZINES

The magazine on this rifle is a detachable box which allows the shooter to carry extra ammunition without it rattling around and making noise. The capacity is four rounds for the 308 Winchester length cases except for the 284 Winchester which is three. The Long action will hold five if you insert the magazine in the action when it's open but will normally hold four.

There have been two types of magazines used. The first variation was from 1971 to 1981 and has noticeable finger grooves projecting on each side. The newer type was first used in 1982 and thereafter. It is a better looking magazine and very much resembles the BAR. The magazine adds much to the BLR for it allows this modern lever action to be used with spire point bullets; it was designed for today's hunting conditions and cartridges.

BARRELS

The tapered barrels were all blued with polished and crowned muzzles. Here are the barrel lengths, calibers, dates of introduction and the action lengths used.

SHORT ACTION	BARREL	71	72	73	74	75	76	77	78	79	80	81	82
243 Winchester	20"	X	X	X	X	X	X	X	X	X	X	X	X
308 Winchester	20"	X	X	X	X	X	X	X	X	X	X	X	X
358 Winchester	20"						X	X	X	X	X	X	X
22/250 Remington												X	

SHORT ACTION	BARREL	83	84	85	86	87	88	89	90	91	92
243 Winchester	20"	X	X	X	X	X	X	X	X	X	X
308 Winchester	20"	X	X	X	X	X	X	X	X	X	X
358 Winchester	20"	X	X	X	X	X	X	X	X	X	X
22/250 Remington	20"	X	X	X	X	X	X	X	X	X	X
257 Roberts	20"	X	X	X	X	X	X	X	X	X	X
7MM/08 Remington	20"	X	X	X	X	X	X	X	X	X	X
222 Remington	20"			X	X	X	X	X			
223 Remington	20"			X	X	X	X	X		X	X
284 Winchester								X	X	X	X

LONG ACTION			
270 Winchester	22"	X	X
30/06	22"	X	X
7mm Remington Mag	24"	X	X

Please note that the 222 Remington was made the shortest time of any gun. Do you think we have a potential collector's item here?

All the BLR's were made with iron sights until 1988. From 1988 to 1990, the shooter had a choice of ordering the 22/250 Remington, 243 Winchester, 7mm/08 Remington, and the 308 Winchester with or without iron sights. After 1990 all were made with iron sights as before. Again, do we have some potential collector's items? Some of the above calibers were only made for two years without sights. There couldn't have been that many made.

The front sights were all gold bead on a grooved ramp with a hood until 1982 when the hood was discontinued. The rear sights were low profile square notch that is adjustable for windage and elevation.

For the very early guns that were made by T.R.W., the markings are as follows on the left side of the barrel:

FOR CAL.(Caliber) ONLY
BROWNING ARMS COMPANY
ST LOUIS AND MONTREAL P.Q.

On the right side of the barrel are the words,
MADE IN U.S.A. PATENT PENDING

The barrel markings on the 1970 to 1975 all-Belgium guns were on the left side of barrel adjacent to the rear sight:

BROWNING ARMS COMPANY
MORGAN,UTAH & MONTREAL P.Q.
MADE IN BELGIUM

On the right side of barrel under or adjacent to the rear sight are the words:

BLR CALIBER (cal) ONLY
BROWNING PATENTS

The early guns made in Japan were marked as follows: On the left side of barrel under or adjacent to the rear sight you will find:

BROWNING ARMS COMPANY
MORGAN UTAH & MONTREAL P.Q.
MADE IN JAPAN

On the right side of barrel under or adjacent to the rear sight is written:

BLR CALIBER (cal) ONLY
(or) CALIBER (cal) ONLY
BROWNING PATENTS

The BLR's with the long actions are marked on the left side as follows:

BROWNING ARMS COMPANY
MORGAN UTAH & MONTREAL P.Q.
MADE IN JAPAN

On the right side they are marked:
MODEL 81L BLR CALIBER(Caliber)only

There is also an "NP" near the action that denotes "nitro proofed."

STOCKS

Only straight grip stocks were made from American walnut of group 2 grade with a semi-gloss oil finish until 1979. In 1980, it was changed to a high lustre urethane and has remained such to at least 1992.

The forearms were retained by one barrel band and configured to remind the shooter of the western style carbines of yesteryear. Browning even went to the trouble of giving the rifle a half magazine look. All forearms were finished the same as the butt stocks.

They were all checkered 18 lines per inch and the stock dimensions from 1971 to 1981 were length of pull 13 3/4", drop at comb 1 3/4", and drop at heel 2 3/8". From 1982 until 1984, the dimensions were length of pull 13 3/4", drop at comb 1 5/8", and drop at heel 2 1/8". They were changed again from 1985 through 1992 to length of pull 13 1/2", drop at comb 1 3/4", and drop at heel 2 3/8". The long actions are different still. They were length of pull 13 7/8" drop at comb 2", and drop at heel 2 1/2". I have never seen any other model produced by Browning with so many changes. Maybe people were quickly getting taller or shorter.

There were two kinds of pads. When first introduced, the ventilated black rubber recoil pad was used until 1982. Thereafter the solid black rubber pad was used until at least 1992. They are both marked "BROWNING."

SOME NOTES

All in all, the BLR is a nice lever action rifle for the shooter that likes this type of rifle. Browning has taken every effort to provide a great assortment of calibers and in the meantime has produced a rifle that is adaptable to a scope as well as iron sights.

The ones to collect, of course, are the ones made in Belgium and the few variations as noted above. This limits you to a very few guns, but if you throw in the T.R.W. Guns, which are very hard to find, you don't get to spend a lot of money, but you do get to go to a lot of gun shows searching. How can you have more fun then that?

SERIAL NUMBERS

The "K" in the serial number stands for the model from 1970-1976. Serial numbers begin with 0001 at the beginning of each year.

They run as follows:

1970 ——-K70	1973 ——-K73	1976 ——-K76
1971 ——-K71	1974 ——-K74	
1972 ——-K72	1975 ——-K75	

For year codes after 1976 refer to the General Information section in the front of this book.

The code for these rifles is 127 for the short action and 327 for the long.

B-53 LEVER ACTION

The B-53 was the ninth gun in the series that has revived many of John M. Browning's designs.

The Winchester 53 was the ninth gun in the series of models produced by Winchester. It originally came along in 1924 when Winchester was reorganizing its product line in an effort to streamline production costs. Many of the features of this model had the most popular special order items that shooters were ordering for the original Model 92. The 53 only lasted for nine years, as it was discontinued in 1932, with 24,916 being produced. The original is a scarce gun in comparison to other Winchesters. Today, the 53 is one of the most collectable guns ever made in this country.

The original 53 was available in 218 Bee, 25-20, 32-20 and 44-40. Browning had chosen the 32-20 as the cartridge for this run of 5,000 guns. Perhaps they are planning other calibers in the future.

The original 53 was a basic rifle with straight grip, 22" barrel, six shot magazine, and shotgun style butt plate. The Brownings will have these and other features as described below. The Browning version of the 53 was introduced in 1990 and discontinued in 1991. Even though offered in only one way with no options, it was deluxe enough to satisfy any rifle buff.

FRAME

This was the same frame that was used on the Browning 92 with the exception of the grip. The 53 had a full pistol grip and lever. Every pin and screw was the same as the original Winchester 92. All were blued included the triggers, and the vertical locking bars were polished.

The hammers had three positions: full cock, half cock or safety notch, and all the way down.

BARRELS

The barrels were all 22" long with a 1-in-20 twist for the short 32-20 bullet.

The barrels were marked on the left side:

BROWNING ARMS COMPANY
MORGAN,UTAH & MONTREAL P.Q.
MADE IN JAPAN
BROWNING MODEL 53 CALIBER 32-20 WIN

On the right side the markings were:
BROWNING MODEL 53 CALIBER 32-20 WIN

The rear barrel sights were a copy of the original cloverleaf being adjustable with an elevator for vertical adjustment and by drift within the barrel slot for windage. The front sights were a gold bead on a ramp with hood.

STOCKS

The French walnut butt stock had a full pistol grip, metal grip cap and fluted comb. The finish was high gloss, and they were all checkered 20 lines per inch. Stock dimensions were length of pull 13 1/2", drop at comb 1", and drop at heel 2 1/8".

The butt plates were also like the original Winchester in that they were checkered in the center with a diamond shaped pattern around the screw holes, while the edges were plain.

The forearms were semi-beavertail, finished and checkered like the butt stock, and there was a metal forearm cap just like the Model 53 Winchesters had in the 20's.

MAGAZINES

The 1/2 magazine went the full length of the forearms and were capped at the very end. They held seven cartridges.

PRICES

This deluxe gun sold retail in 1990 and 1991 for $675.00.

SERIAL NUMBERS

For year codes please refer to the General Information section in the front of this book.

MODEL 65

GENERAL INFORMATION

The Winchester 65 was the seventh gun in the series of models produced by Browning. It was introduced in 1989 and discontinued in 1990.

The original 65 came along in 1933 when Winchester again reorganized its product line in an effort to streamline production costs. This rifle was designed to incorporate the features that were the most popular and shooters were ordering. The Winchester version lasted for fourteen years. It was discontinued in 1947 with 5,704 being produced. The original is the scarcest gun of all produced after the turn of the century. It was available in 218 Bee, 25-20, and 32-20. Browning has chosen the 218 Bee has

the cartridge for this run of 5,000 guns, though they may be planning on other calibers in the future.

The original 65 was a basic rifle with straight or pistol grip, 24" barrel for the 218 Bee, six-shot magazine, and shotgun style or crescent butt plate to order. The Brownings had features that were not the same as the basic Winchester, and they are described below.

Today, the 65 is one of the most collectable guns ever made by Winchester.

GRADES

The Model 65 was made in two models; there were 3,500 Grade 1's and 1,500 High Grades.

GRADE 1

Shown above is the Model 65 rifle as presented in the 1990 Browning catalog.

This grade was blued including the triggers and the stocks, were not checkered. All else is described under each section.

The group 1 French walnut stocks were high gloss finished and uncheckered, all other features are described in the basic stock section.

HIGH GRADE

Being the seventh in the Limited Edition series of rifles, the 65 was offered in a higher grade. All descriptions found in the other sections are also true for this grade except as noted here.

The action has etched scroll engraving covering about 50% of the sides of the receiver with a coyote on the left side and a bobcat on the right. The animals are both 24 carat gold plated. The balance of the metal is not engraved nor embellished in any way. The receivers and levers are greyed; the triggers are gold plated, and the hammers and the balance of the gun had a high polish-blue finish.

The stocks were group 3 grade and high gloss finish. Checkering was 20 lines per inch. The semi-beavertail forearms were finished and checkered like the butt stocks.

FRAME

This is the same frame that was used on the Browning 92 with the exception of the grip the 65 has a full pistol grip and lever. Every pin and screw is the same as on the original Winchester 92. All the Grade 1's were blued, and the vertical locking bars were polished.

The hammers have three positions: full cock, half cock, or safety notch, and all the way down.

BARRELS

The barrels were all 24" long with a 1-in-16 twist for the short 218 Bee bullet.

SPECIFICATIONS

Action — Lever action with vertical locks.
Hammer — Exposed, three position.
Caliber — .218 Bee, round nose and hollow point bullets only. No spitzer (pointed) bullets.
Magazine — Tubular, half style loaded through side port.
Magazine Capacity — Six cartridges of .218 Bee.
Trigger — Grade I: blued. High Grade: gold plated.
Sights — Open sights standard. Hooded ramp style front and buckhorn style adjustable rear sight.

The barrels were marked on the left side:
BROWNING ARMS COMPANY
MORGAN, UTAH & MONTREAL P.Q.
MADE IN JAPAN
BROWNING MODEL 65 CAL 218 BEE

On the right side the markings were:
BROWNING MODEL 65 CAL 32-20 WIN

The rear barrel sights were a copy of the original Buckhorn, being adjustable with an elevator for vertical adjustment and by drift within the barrel slot for windage. The front sights were a gold bead on a ramp with hood.

STOCKS

The French walnut butt stock had a full pistol grip and a fluted comb. The finish was high gloss and the stock dimensions were length of pull 13 1/2", drop at comb 1", and drop at heel 2 1/8".

The butt plates were also like the original Winchester in that they were checkered in the center with a diamond shaped pattern around the screw holes; the edges were plain.

Forearms were semi-beavertail, finished like the butt stock, and there was a metal forearm cap just like the old timers had in the 30's and 40's.

MAGAZINES

The 1/2 magazine went the full length of the forearms and were capped at the very end; they held six cartridges. If you will notice, the end of the magazine tube extends almost 1/2" beyond the forearm cap, whereas on the model 53 it did not.

SERIAL NUMBERS

For the year codes please refer to the General Information section in the front of this book.

Stock and Forearm — Both grades: Full pistol grip with semi-beavertail forearm. Select walnut with high gloss finish. High Grade: Cut checkering on stock and forearm.
Metal Finish — Grade I: Deeply blued on all metal surfaces. High Grade: Grayed receiver with engraving and gold plated animals.
Buttplate — Metal, straight style. Stock Dimensions — Length of pull 13 1/2". Drop at comb 1 1/8". Drop at heel 1 3/4".

Models	Caliber	Barrel Length	Sight Radius	Overall Length	Approximate Weight	Rate of Twist (R. Hand)
Grade I	218 Bee	24"	20¼"	41¾"	6 lbs. 12 oz.	1 in 16"
High Grade	218 Bee	24"	20¼"	41¾"	6 lbs. 12 oz.	1 in 16"

The specifications table for the Model 65.

MODEL 71 LEVER ACTION RIFLE

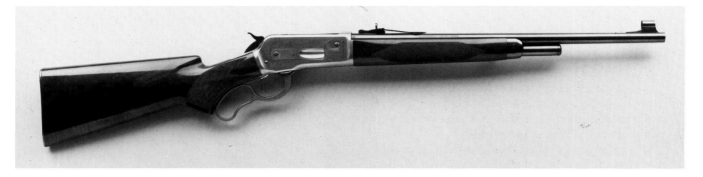

One of the most collectable Winchesters is the Model 71 in 348 Winchester caliber. The revival of this fine Browning design has given today's hunter the opportunity to own one for a fraction of the cost of a Winchester.

GENERAL INFORMATION

The Browning Model 71 was only offered for one year, 1987. It was the fifth in the series of Limited Editions.

The original Winchester 71 was a direct offshoot of the 1886, which was designed by John M. Browning in 1885. Because of the demand for a high powered lever action, Winchester reintroduced the 1886 in 1935 and called it the Model 71. It was made in one form or another right up to 1958 when it was discontinued after a production run of 47,254. The 348 Winchester cartridge was designed specifically for the new gun and proved itself more than adequate for elk and game of equal size, including many a bear.

Today, the Model 71 is a very collectible rifle, especially with the long tang and special bolt peep sight that were made in the first 15,000 guns or so. If you are the type of hunter that doesn't require a scope and wants a lever action rifle with plenty of punch, this is the gun for you.

The basic configuration was 348 Winchester only, 24" barrel, pistol grip with a shotgun buttplate, 1/2 magazine, and forearm cap. There were many variations including two grades, two barrel lengths, long or short tangs and sights, but we will not cover them here.

GRADES

The Model 71 was made in four variations. There were 3,000 Grade 1 rifles and 4,000 carbines; in the High Grade model, there were 3,000 rifles and 3,000 carbines made.

GRADE 1

This grade was plain and blued including the triggers. The group 1 walnut stocks were satin finished and uncheckered. All other features are described in the basic stock section.

HIGH GRADE

Being the fifth in the Limited Edition series of rifles, the 71 was offered in a higher grade. All descriptions found in the other sections are also true for this grade except as noted here.

The action has etched scroll engraving, covering about 60% of the sides of the receiver with a running whitetail on the right side. There is an Imperial bull elk and another elk in the background on the left. These are all surrounded by game scenes, and the animals are all 24 carat gold plated.

The balance of the metal is not engraved nor embellished in any way. The receivers and levers are greyed, the triggers are gold colored, and the hammers and the balance of the gun had a high polish blue finish.

The stocks were group 3 grade and high gloss finished, checkering was 20 line per inch. The classic styled forearms were finished and checkered like the butt stocks.

FRAME

This is the same frame that was used on the Browning 1886 with the exception of the grip; the 71 has a full pistol grip and lever. Every pin and screw is the same as the original Winchester 86 except for some minor changes. All the Grade 1's were blued, and the vertical locking bars were polished.

The hammers have three positions: full cock, half cock or safety notch, and all the way down.

BARRELS

The carbine barrels were all 20" long, and the rifles were 24" with a 1-in-12 twist for the heavy 348 Winchester loads.

The barrels were marked on the left side:
**BROWNING ARMS COMPANY
MORGAN,UTAH & MONTREAL P.Q.
MADE IN JAPAN**

BROWNING MODEL 71 CAL 348 WIN

On the right side the markings were:
BROWNING MODEL 71 CAL 348 WIN

The rear barrel sights were a copy of the original Buckhorn, being adjustable with an elevator for vertical adjustment and by drift within the barrel slot for windage. The front sights were a gold bead on a ramp with hood.

STOCKS

The walnut butt stock had a full pistol grip and a fluted comb. The finish was semi-gloss; and the stock dimensions were length of pull 13 3/8", drop at comb 1 7/8", and drop at heel 2 1/2".

The butt plates were also like the original Winchester in that they were checkered in the center with a diamond shaped pattern around the screw holes, while the edges were plain.

The forearms were the slim classic style found on all the old Winchesters. They are finished like the butt stock and there was a metal forearm cap just like the original 71's.

MAGAZINES

The 1/2 magazine went the full length of the forearm and extended out about 2 1/2". They were capped at the very end and held four cartridges.

SERIAL NUMBERS

For year codes please refer to the General Information section in the front of this book.

MODEL 1886 LEVER ACTION RIFLE

The Model 1886 Browning Rifle in Grade 1.

GENERAL INFORMATION

This is the only gun in the Limited Edition series that has so far been introduced, discontinued and introduced again in another form. As first made in 1986, it was the fourth in the series and was a rifle, but in 1992 it appeared again as the twelfth in the series as a carbine. Among Winchester collectors, the '86 carbine is one of the rarer guns and much sought after in any caliber.

The original Winchester Model 1886 was designed by John M. Browning in 1885. Winchester was getting beat up by Remington and the other companies because they didn't have a repeating rifle to handle the more powerful cartridges sportsmen were then shooting. Their original toggle link actions, the Henry, 1873 and 1876 models were out of date. Who else to go to but John M.; he had already proved himself with the great model 1885 single shot and was ready to get started with a repeater. In fact, Mr. Browning already had the basic design worked out in his mind when Winchester requested him

to get them a working model. The original 1886 in any form is one of the most collectible of all the Winchesters and wasn't discontinued until 1932 after a total production of 159,337.

GRADES AND PRODUCTION

The Browning version of this model was such a collectible gun that right from the beginning, many were shipped and sold in pairs. The Grade I rifles and carbines were limited to 7,000 pieces.

The Grade 2, both rifles and carbines, were limited to 3,000 pieces. They featured an engraved receiver greyed with gold plated animals.

GRADE 1

This grade was plain and blued including the triggers. The group 1 walnut stocks were satin finished and uncheckered. All other features are described in the basic stock section.

HIGH GRADE

Being the fourth in the Limited Edition series of rifles, the 1886 rifle was offered in a higher grade. All descriptions found in the other sections are also accurate for this grade except as noted here.

The action had medium etched scroll engraving covering about 90% of the sides of the receiver with a standing bison on the right side. There were two elk on the left side, the bull bugling and the cow standing within a game scene. The animals were all 24 carat gold plated.

The Model 1886 Browning High Grade Carbine.

On the carbines the etched scroll engraving was very similar to the rifles; the only real difference was the animal scenes. On the right side there were two grizzly bears, one walking and one standing. On the left side there were two whitetail bucks running, surrounded by a game scene covering most of the side. As on the rifles, the animals were all 24 carat gold plated.

The balance of the metal on either model was neither engraved nor embellished in any way. The receivers and levers were greyed, the triggers were gold colored, and the hammers and the balance of the guns had a high polish blue finish.

The French walnut stocks were group three grade and high gloss finished, and the checkering was 20 lines per inch. The classic styled forearms were finished and checkered like the butt stocks. On the rifles the forearms had a metal cap and the carbines were retained by a barrel band.

FRAME

This was the same frame that was used on the original Winchester Model 1886. It was all steel, and every detail was the same as the original Winchester except for some minor changes. The carbines all had saddle rings and all the Grade 1's were blued 100%.

Hammers had three positions: full cock, half cock or safety notch, and all the way down.

BARRELS

Both variations had medium tapered barrels; the rifle barrels were all 26" long, the carbines were 22", and all were chambered for the 45/70 Government cartridge only.

The barrels were marked on the left side:
BROWNING ARMS COMPANY
MORGAN,UTAH & MONTREAL P.Q.
MADE IN JAPAN

.45-70 GOVT.

The right side of the barrels were marked as follows:
BROWNING MODEL 1886 CALIBER 45/70

On the top of the High Grade barrels are the words:

ONE OF THREE THOUSAND

On the the rear barrel sights of the rifle was a copy of the original Buckhorn; the sights were adjustable with an elevator for vertical adjustment and by drift within the barrel slot for windage. The front sights were a gold bead on a ramp with no hood.

On the carbines the rear sights were the old style 42 and 44 adjustable leaf sights like those on the earlier Winchester carbines. The front sights were the plain steel post type.

STOCKS

The French walnut straight grip butt stock had a non-fluted comb. The finish was satin gloss on the Grade 1's as described under the High Grade section. The stock dimensions had a length of pull 12 3/4", drop at comb 2" and drop at heel 2 7/8".

The rifles had crescent style all steel and blued butt plates and the carbines had the modified shotgun style; these were all like the original Winchesters.

The forearms were the classic style found on all the old original Winchester rifles that were standard; they were finished like the butt stock and secured with a forearm cap on the rifles and a barrel band on the carbines.

MAGAZINES

The tubular magazines were all full length on both rifles and carbines. The rifles held eight cartridges, and the carbines, which were retained by a second barrel band, held five.

SERIAL NUMBERS

For year codes please refer to the General Information section in the front of this book.

B-92 LEVER ACTION

The B-92 was the second original Browning design.

The B-92 was the second model produced in this series and was introduced in 1978 as the Centernnial model to help celebrate 100 years of John M. Browning's inventive genius. The Winchester 1892 was one of the most popular guns ever produced with 1,001,324 being made in several different models from 1892 to 1941. These models include the Models 53 and 65, which Browning also reintroduced later. Only World War Two and Winchester's belief that the public wouldn't be interested in this type of gun stopped any post war production. The long run of its production is quite a tribute to the gun and its inventor.

Today, the '92 is one of the most collectable guns ever made in this country — or for that matter, in the world. The Browning didn't have the long run of the original and was discontinued in 1985.

CENTENNIAL

The Centennial variation was used to introduce this model and was made only in 1978. It is exactly like the basic 92 except for two things: a gold plated sling swivel and the center of the frame is engraved on each side with medium scroll covering about 20% of the frame area. They are marked on the left side within an elongated oval with the words:

BROWNING
1878-1978
CENTENNIAL

FRAME

It's a 92. That's the best way to describe this, the second of a series of John Browning designs that are still being introduced in 1992. Every pin and screw is the same as the original gun. All were blued and none engraved other then the Centennial variation. The vertical locking bars are polished and the triggers are gold plated.

Hammers have three positions, as does the original. These are full cock, half cock or safety notch, and all the way down. Originally, they was made in 44 Magnum but the 357 Magnum was introduced in 1979.

BARRELS

This model is not actually a rifle but a carbine, for it has a 20" barrel with a 1-in-38 twist for the 44 magnum and a 1-in-18 3/4 twis for the 357 to accomodate the handgun cartridges.

The barrels are marked on the left side:
BROWNING ARMS COMPANY
MORGAN,UTAH & MONTREAL P.Q.
MADE IN JAPAN

BROWNING MODEL 1892 CALIBER 44 MAG

On the right side the markings are:
BROWNING MODEL 1892 CALIBER 44 MAG

The barrel sights were a copy of the original cloverleaf, the rear being adjustable with an elevator for vertical adjustment and by drift within the barrel slot for windage. The front sights are a steel post just like they're supposed to be.

STOCKS

Like the rest of the gun, the stocks were similar to the original. Winchester didn't use French walnut like Browning, but the butt stock did have a straight grip and the same type of carbine steel butt plate. The forearms were also a duplicate of the original being retained by one barrel band like most other carbines. The finish was high gloss and they were all uncheckered. Stock dimensions were length of pull 12 3/4", drop at comb 2", and drop at heel 2 7/8".

MAGAZINES

The magazines were retained by two barrel bands and went the full length of the barrels less 3/16". They held eleven 44 or 357 cartridges.

PRICES

The Centennial model sold for $219.95 in 1978. The standard gun in 1979 was $249.95.

SERIAL NUMBERS AND MODEL CODES

For year codes please refer to the General Information section in the front of this book. Model code for all calibers is 167.

MODEL 1895 LEVER ACTION RIFLE

The Browning Model 1895 is an excellent hunting rifle today as it was almost 100 years ago. This is a Grade 1.

GENERAL INFORMATION

The 1895 Winchester was another John M. Browning design that took the gun world to a whole new dimension in design and innovation. It was the only lever action designed not only to handle the new high intensity smokeless powder cartridges, but also to handle the spire pointed bullets without any problem. The box magazine meant that all loads and cartridges could now be shot with this gun including the 405 Winchester. Now don't write me and say the 1894 was the first to handle smokeless powder; I'm saying that the 1895 will handle not only smokeless powder but spire point bullets as well.

The original gun, like the Browning version, was chambered for eight different cartridges including the 30/06.

As the Browning catalog of 1984 quotes Theodore Roosevelt, "The Winchester gun with a full load of the new 405 cartridges is my BIG MEDICINE." This may not be exactly what he said, but you get the idea; old Teddy knew how to tell it like it is. Wouldn't it be nice

if Browning brought out a '95 chambered for the 405 with a whole new stock of ammo?

The original Winchester configuration was a 28" round barrel, straight grip stock, blued, rifle butt plate and open sights. The Browning gun is described below.

Introduced and made only in 1984, this was third in the series of original John M. Browning designs being reproduced by Browning.

GRADES

The Model 1895 was made in two grades, the Grade 1 and the High Grade. I do not know, at this time, how many of each were made.

GRADE 1

This grade was plain and blued including the triggers. The group 1 walnut stocks were satin finished and uncheckered; all other features are described in the basic stock section.

HIGH GRADE

The Model 1895 High Grade is a popular collectors item and much sought after by today's Browning Collector.

Being the third in the Limited Edition series of rifles, the 1895 was offered in a higher grade. All descriptions found in the other sections are also true for this grade except as noted here.

The action has medium etched scroll engraving covering about 90% of the sides of the receiver with a walking grizzly bear on the right side and a moose on the left. These are all surrounded by game scenes. The animals are all 24 carat gold plated.

The balance of the metal is not engraved nor embellished in any way. The receivers, box magazines and levers are greyed, the triggers are gold colored, the hammers and the balance of the gun had a high polish blue finish.

The French walnut stocks were group three grade and high gloss finish, and the checkering was 20 lines per inch. The schnabel styled forearms were finished and checkered like the butt stocks.

FRAME

This is the same frame that was used on the original Winchester Model 1895. It is all steel with the later milled receiver. The original Browning design called for a flat receiver, and about 5,000 were produced from 1895 to 1896. The levers are straight and every pin and screw is the same as the original Winchester except for some minor changes. All the Grade 1's were blued 100%.

The High Grade receivers are marked on the right side:

1895 BROWNING
(Gun number) **OF ONE THOUSAND**

They are also marked:
1895 REPLICA

Hammers had three positions, these are full cock, half cock or safety notch, and all the way down.

BARRELS

The rapid taper barrels were all 24" and chambered for the 30/06 cartridge only.

The barrels were marked on the left side:
**BROWNING ARMS COMPANY
MORGAN, UTAH & MONTREAL P.Q.
MADE IN JAPAN**

BROWNING MODEL 1895 CALIBER 30/06

**The right side of the barrels were marked:
BROWNING MODEL 1895 30-06**

The rear barrel sights were a copy of the original Buckhorn being adjustable with an elevator for vertical adjustment and by drift within the barrel slot for windage. The front sights were a gold bead on a ramp with no hood.

STOCKS

The French walnut straight grip butt stock had a non-fluted comb. The finish was semi gloss, and the stock dimensions had a length of pull 12 3/4", drop at comb 2" and drop at heel 2 7/8". Blued butt plates were also like the original Winchester.

The forearms were the schnabel style found on all the old original Winchester rifles that were standard; they are finished like the butt stock and secured by a single screw located on the bottom.

MAGAZINES

The box magazine was the most innovative of all the new features of this revolutionary rifle. Since the cartridges were stacked one above the other instead of one in front of the other, any kind of ammunition could be used including spire point. It held five cartridges which is adequate.

SERIAL NUMBERS AND MODEL CODES

For year codes please refer to the General Information section in the front of this book.

The model designation for the Grade 1 is 187 and Grade 2 is 287.

Chapter Fourteen

The Jonathan Browning Mountain Rifle

THE JONATHAN BROWNING MOUNTAIN RIFLE

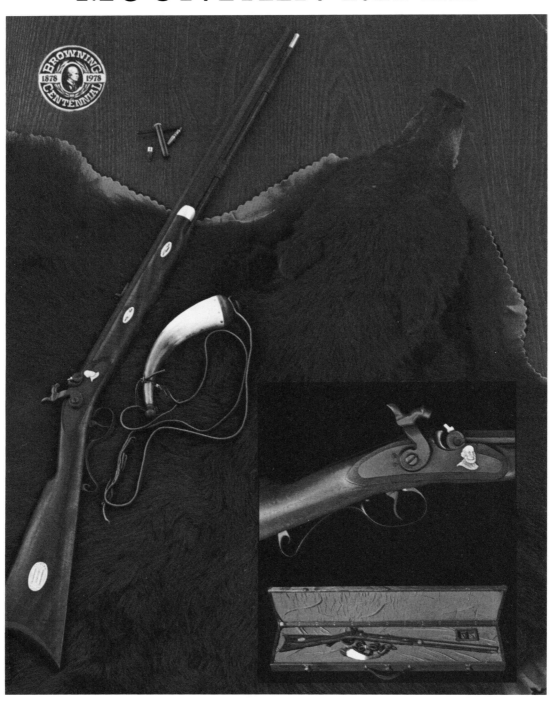

The Centennial version of the Mountain Rifle as cataloged in 1978.

GENERAL INFORMATION

Made from 1977 to 1981, the Mountain Rifle was a quality black powder half stock rifle designed along the lines of the Hawken rifles carried by the frontiersmen from the 1830 to 1850 era. In fact, short of a custom made gun, this was the highest quality gun ever offered by any black powder rifle manufacturer on a production basis.

MODELS

There were two models available; these rifles look entirely different from one another.

The first variation had a browned steel finish on the butt plate, trigger guard, barrel, lock, and ram rod retainers. The barrel wedges, pins and the forearm tip were polished brass.

The second model had a browned barrel and lock; the butt plate, trigger guard, ram rod retainers, barrel wedges, pins, and forearm tip were polished brass.

CENTENNIAL JONATHAN BROWNING MOUNTAIN RIFLE

In 1978, to help celebrate the 100th anniversary of the original Browning Brothers' store and gun shop, the Centennial variation was introduced with a total production of only 1,000 rifles. This is essentially the same gun as described in the sections that follow but with many refinements that will be described.

The entire set consisted of the rifle, nipple wrench, brass cleaning jag, patch remover, and powder horn. The serial numbers started at 1878A-0001 and went to 1878A-1000; they appeared on the powder horn, barrel, and the sterling silver stock medallion. The locks also had a sterling silver bust of Jonathan Browning, and the wedge plates and forearm tip were tinned.

The powder horn also had a leather strap, walnut cap and plug, and a medallion which said:

JONATHAN BROWNING MOUNTAIN RIFLE
1878-1978
"ONE OF ONE THOUSAND"

The serial number was also carved on the powder horn.

The stock was about group 2 grade with an oil finish and a medallion which also had a bust of Jonathan Browning with the inscription:

BROWNING
1878-1978
CENTENNIAL

Barrels were marked on the left side:
BROWNING ARMS COMPANY
MORGAN, UTAH MONTREAL P.Q.
MADE IN U.S.A.

On the right side of the barrel was:
50 CALIBER BLACK POWDER ONLY
PATENTS PENDING

Immediately ahead of the breech plug on the right barrel flat is the serial number:
1878A-XXXX

On the top of the barrel was:
JONATHAN BROWNING MOUNTAIN RIFLE

All this was in an alder wood case with a suede fabric lining that was buckskin colored and wrinkled. The case itself had brass hinges and locks, leather corner guards, and a leather plate with the inscription "Browning."

LOCKS

This was basically a single shot percussion lock with a side hammer. The locks were typical of those used on most black powder rifles.

One of the main features of this model was the single set trigger. I say, "single set," because you can set it for a very light let off. The normal trigger pull is about 4 to 5 lbs, but if you push the trigger forward after cocking the hammer, you will set it for a trigger pull adjustable from 2 oz to 2 lbs. I don't know if you've ever shot a gun with a 2 oz trigger, but don't even think about touching the trigger until you're ready for the shot. Even then, you have to sort of roll your finger on the edge and "boom" you've shot the "X" out — maybe.

The basis of Browning's trigger was a roller bearing sear. Instead of the normal direct contact of the sear to trigger, you have a roller bearing that connects with the trigger and rolls off instead of sliding off.

The unique breech plug was in the shape of a Ram's horn, quite attractive and unusual.

BARRELS

The octagon barrels were 1" across the flats, making for a rather heavy but good looking and accurate rifle; they were all 30" long. All were made the old and traditional way by cutting one groove at a time with a 1-in-56" twist for the 45 caliber, 1-in-62" twist for the 50 caliber, and a 1-in-66" twist for the 54 caliber.

These large bores might make you think they were overdoing it, but remember that the lead bullets didn't expand much, if any, and the velocity wasn't what it is with modern rifles. It takes a big bore to knock down a large animal. Browning recommended no less then the 50 caliber for black bear, deer, or elk, and at least the 54 caliber for larger game like moose.

All rifles had what is known as a hooked breech. The rear of the barrel had a hook, when inserted into the tang. The barrel was secured to the stock on the back end. All the shooter had to do was insert the barrel wedges and the rifle was put together. This is important in a quality rifle, which, as you know, must be cleaned after every shooting session.

The breech plug was a bit different than in conventional guns. Mainly, the plug bears against the bore shoulder when it is screwed all the way down; this eliminates any stress against the barrel.

Sights were a little different then found on the old guns in that they were the adjustable buckhorn type. The adjustment for elevation was the simple turning of a screw, but the whole sight had to be drift punched within its slot for windage.

The ramrods were made from hickory wood with two polished brass ends. One was for a cleaning jag and patch retriever, and the other was plain.

Barrels were marked on the left side:

BROWNING ARMS COMPANY
MORGAN,UTAH MONTREAL P.Q.
MADE IN U.S.A.

On the right side of the barrel were the words:
(Caliber)**CALIBER BLACK POWDER ONLY**
PATENTS PENDING

Immediately ahead of the breech plus is the serial number.

On the top of the barrel was:
JONATHAN BROWNING MOUNTAIN RIFLE

STOCKS

The semi pistol grip half stock was made of American walnut of about group 1 grade with a semi-cheek piece and hand rubbed semi-gloss oil finish.

They had a very thick wrist which was traditional of the old mountain rifles. The steel butt plates were very similar to the Winchester rifle or crescent butt plate with a toe guard extending about 4". All had a forearm cap and barrel escutcheons; and the dimensions were length of pull 13 1/2", drop at comb 2 1/2", and drop at hell 4".

All were shipped with a spare nipple and cleaning jag.

PRICES

In 1978 the cost for this model in both styles and all calibers was $319.50; in 1979, the cost was $373.50; in 1980, the cost was $399.95; and the cost of the Centennial was $650.00.

For year of manufacture codes, please refer to the General Information section in the front of this book.

Chapter Fifteen

22 Rimfire
Rifles

These two pictures show details of the beautiful and unusual engraving that has been done on the Auto 22. This particular rifle was engraved for Val Browning by master engraver Jose Baerten.

AUTO 22 RIFLE

Designed in 1914 the Auto 22 is one of the most famous designs by John Browning. It has been made on a continuous basis since its inception.

GENERAL INFORMATION

This little auto was originally designed by John M. Browning in 1914 but not introduced into this country until 1956. It had never been made by anyone other then Fabrique Nationale or The Remington Arms Company until Japanese production began in 1974.

During W.W. I, John M. Browning obviously meant to have his little 22 and the Auto-5 produced for sale during the 1914-1924 period but F.N. was busy producing guns for the war. War production by Fabrique Nationale and the exorbitant tariffs are the reasons Remington was permitted to make this model as well as the Auto-5. Remington had great success with this gun, and they continued to manufacture it for many years after the patents ran out as the Models 24 which originally sold for $13.85; later, it sold as the Model 241.

Prior to the introduction of this model in the U.S., F. N. produced almost 200,000 of these fine little rifles for export all over the world, These all had either 19" or 19 1/4" barrels in 22 Short or Long Rifle; the receivers were not normally engraved nor grooved for a scope. They are known as the Model "A" as opposed to the gun shipped to this country, which is the Model "B". The earlier model A loads from a portal on the very top or comb of the stock, while the later model B's load from the right side of the stock. These are the ones we will be discussing in this book as the model A's were not brought into this country in sufficient quantities to justify discussion here.

When the early guns were special ordered, any type engraving and checkering was furnished. They were made in the semi pistol grip configuration unless the customer specified differently. There were many different sights used over the course of the production of this model, and we will go over them in a different section.

As mentioned above, you will not find many of the early model A guns in this country unless they was brought back by soldiers who had purchased them in a PX or from another source. I also imagine some were brought back as war trophies immediately after World War II. You will also find other variations of this rifle including some that are not checkered or engraved with wood other then walnut, They were even produced in a solid frame version designated Model "F". All this is nice to know, but you will probably never run across any of these variations.

I want you to be aware that they exist, so you don't lay down big money for what you think is a rare gun when it's just one of 200,000 others made for foreign sales. I was in Argentina last year and hit every gun shop in Buenos Aires. There were Brownings galore on the shelves, but all were of different configuration then you're used to seeing, so this is an idea of the numbers that were made. We are not concerned with these, for they were not imported by Browning for sporting purposes and are rare in the U.S.

The patents were originally granted June 24 and March 20, 1913. These patents were for the take down and locking mechanisms. Later patents were granted on January 6, 1914, for 48 other features which cover a myriad of minor details.

By 1966, F. N. had produced 478,289, of which 249,00 were for the U.S.

Let me close this introduction to one of the most successful of John M.s patents with this quote from the 1958 catalog introducing it:

"The Browning .22 Automatic Rifle is so different from any other on the American market it can rightfully be considered in a class by itself. Appropriate to the cartridge it shoots, characteristics essential to heavy caliber rifles did not influence its design. Ideal proportion, neat slender lines, a compact action, light weight and comfortable balance all contribute to its popularity with amateur and expert alike." I agree.

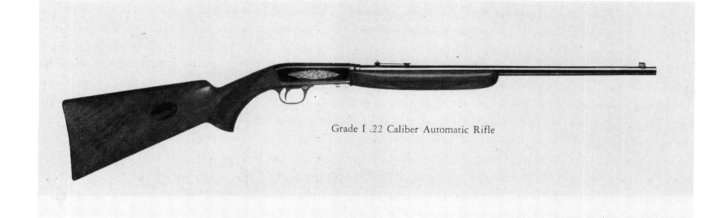

Grade I .22 Caliber Automatic Rifle

BROWNING

.22 AUTOMATIC

different from
any other .22 on
the American
market

The Browning .22 Automatic Rifle is so different from any other on the American market it can rightfully be considered in a class by itself.

Appropriate to the cartridge it shoots, characteristics essential to heavy caliber rifles did not influence its design.

Ideal proportion, neat slender lines, a compact action, light weight and comfortable balance all contribute to its popularity with amateur and expert alike.

The autoloading action permits the requisite speed for small, fast moving targets, and one will enjoy the ease with which the rifle comes to firing position and stays on the target even under rapid fire conditions.

The full size stock with pistol grip and trim semi-beavertail forearm provide the maximum in shooting comfort in the hands of an adult. Light weight, splendid balance, and ease of operation make the rifle equally ideal for the youngster or beginner.

It is a rugged little "plinker" of all steel construction, built for years of dependable service.

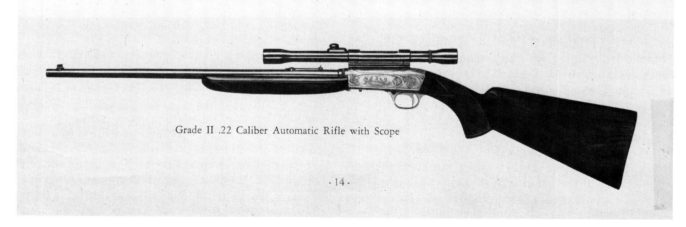

Grade II .22 Caliber Automatic Rifle with Scope

· 14 ·

A page out of the 1958 Browning catalog showing the Auto 22 in Grade I and II.

GRADES

Grades were I, II, III, and the Gallery model. Some special order and presentation guns were made, but they are rare; each will be covered under their section.

GRADE I

The Grade I has been the hunting partner of many a small boy. It's convenience as a plinker is famous.

The Grade I was the most popular. All have blued receivers engraved with a zig-zag pattern on the edges of the receiver and light scroll wedges on each side; the triggers are all blued. There were variations as to the amount and pattern, but these were very slight.

The wood is about group 1 or 2 with 18 lines per inch checkering. The early guns were oil finished and have developed a very nice patina that collectors like so well.

The barrels, markings, cartridges, stock finish and dimensions, etc will be discussed under separate sections, for these were common to all grades.

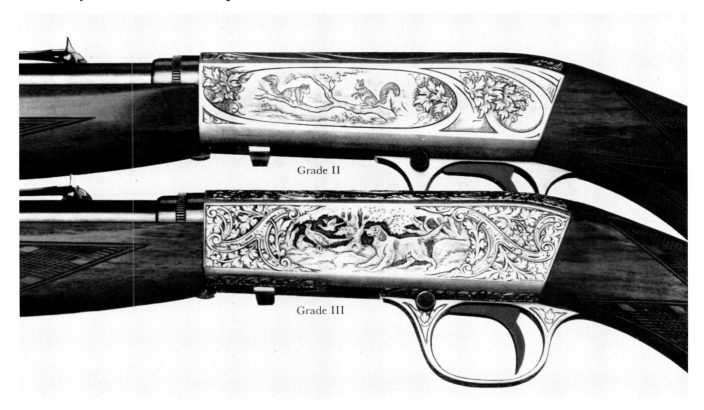

Browning always offered a high grade configuration. This was one of the things that made guns by Browning guns of distinction.

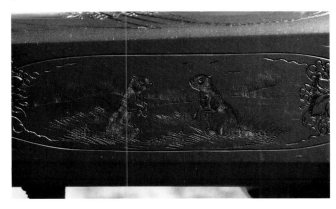

Here is a detailed look at a Grade II receiver left side. This little rifle is marked J.B. for Jose Baerten.

The right side of the Grade II by Baerten.

GRADE II

Here is the top view of the Grade II signed J.B. It's unusual to find any Grade II signed by any engraver much less a master like Jose Baerten.

From 1956 until 1962, the engraving consisted of two prairie dogs on the right side and two squirrels in a tree on the left. in addition, there is a lone duck which is in flight on the top of the receiver. These all had the coin finished.

Not many of the Grade 11's are signed, but if it is, it's usually found on the top of the receiver either on the left or right.

From 1962 until the end of Belgium production, you will find the same engraving pattern but reversed. The engraving consisted of two prairie dogs on the left side and two squirrels in a tree on the right. In addition, the lone duck is still in flight on the top of the receiver. The coverage for this grade is about 50%, and they were mostly greyed finished.

Not many of the late Grade II's are signed, but if it is, it's usually found on the top of the receiver either on the left or right.

From 1962 until the end of Belgium production, you will find the same engraving pattern but reversed. The engraving consisted of two prairie dogs on the left side and two squirrels in a tree on the right. In addition, the lone duck is still in flight on the top of the receiver. The coverage for this grade is about 50%, and they were mostly greyed finished. All triggers were gold plated.

The wood on this Grade II speaks for itself. It is not on a Grade III only because the trained eye of the Fabrique Nationale grader didn't deem it so. What do you think?

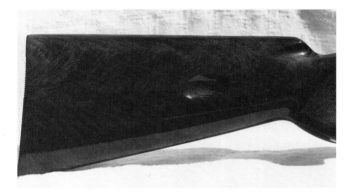

Here is the other side of the Grade II shown. You can see the loading port and pistol grip configuration.

The wood on the Grade II's are about group 3-4, which is much nicer then on the Grade 1. In addition, you will find checkering 22 lines to the inch and finished to perfection.

The barrels, markings, stock finish and dimensions, etc. will be discussed under separate sections, for these were common to all grades.

GRADE III

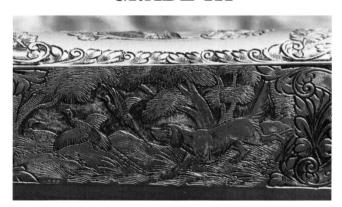

The above Grade III was engraved by master engraver Angelo Bee. Mr. Bee has lived in the U.S. doing the same high grade work for discerning sportsmen.

Here is the right side of the Angelo Bee engraved Grade III.

Top view of the A. Bee engraved Grade III. Mr. Bee signed many of his pieces with an "A" and a picture of a bee.

Originally, this grade had on the right side three ducks being chased by what appears to be a setter in a woods scene. The left side has a dog and three pheasants surrounded by grass and other foliage, and on the top is another setter or spaniel type dog with a rabbit in his mouth and surrounded by oak leaves. The entire action is hand engraved with oak leaves and scroll with about 95% coverage, and all the triggers were gold plated.

In 1963, this grade was also changed slightly. The dog appears to have a duck instead of a rabbit, and the dog hasn't changed just what's in his mouth. As on the Grade II, in the first years of production you will find the coin finish changed about 1965 to the greyed finish. After this change, all the triggers were still gold plated.

There were slight variations to the descriptions given above, but if you see this, don't panic; you'll be able to distinguish between and original and an upgrade after looking over some of these. Just remember, an upgrade must be refinished after engraving. This can be readily detected by looking at the markings, screw holes, screws, general appearance and color. In addition, at the prices for which these guns are sold, it would cost more to upgrade a Grade I then to purchase a Grade III.

I have found that almost all the Grade III's were signed throughout production other then the first two years. Refer to the Master Engravers section in the front to determine who your engraver was.

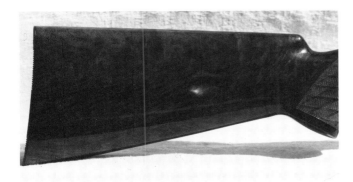

This Grade III wood is truly outstanding. It is 100% figure.

This is the left side of the Grade III buttstock shown. Notice the skip line checkering pattern.

The wood on a Grade III is always group 5 and beautifully checkered in a skip line pattern about 22 lines per inch. The wood is also very highly finished.

The barrels, markings, stock finish and dimensions, etc. will be discussed under separate sections, for these were common to all grades.

FRAMES

This is essentially a blowback, hammerless, bottom ejection rifle with all steel construction. There are double extractors and a takedown feature that is the best. I say the best because it is very easy to adjust and keep tight and it's accurate, yet it is very simple and quick to breakdown. You simply slide the button release forward and push the breech bolt back; at the same time you twist the barrels and the gun is apart. If it ever works loose, you simply adjust the knurled ring a notch and it's tight again.

Taking one apart, which you very rarely have to do, requires no tools at all. After taking the barrels off, you simply slide the trigger guard forward and down. The breech bolt and all else is now exposed and removable. I do not recommend taking one down very often because once adjusted tight and sighted in you have to go through the whole process of retightening and sighting in when you reassemble. This rifle will not bring you pinpoint accuracy because of the takedown feature but it still is accurate to the point that it makes a great utility rifle.

Grooved receivers were never made for the Grades II and III rifles, only the Grade I. Browning offered a scope mount that screwed on the barrel and extended over the action. They did this because the engraving was so extensive on the higher grades that the grooves would have interfered. This is a good tip off if you suspect an upgrade. More will be discussed on the screw holes later.

EASY, SAFE LOADING AND UNLOADING — The location of the magazine tube with the loading port on the right face of the buttstock simplifies loading and supports safe shooting practices. The rifle can always be pointed in the safest direction during loading.

The pictures here are from the Browning catalogs.

Unloading of unfired cartridges is likewise simple and safe. Merely work the breechblock back and forth with the index finger of either hand until all cartridges have been individually ejected.

DOWNWARD EJECTION — All moving parts are contained in the slender receiver which is completely closed on the top and both sides. The bottom of the receiver has the only opening, which is covered by the trigger plate. In the trigger plate is a small aperture through which the empty cartridges are ejected. Thus, any harmful gases or powder grains are always ejected downward, the most harmless direction.

As shown in the basic instructions, the loading and unloading was convenient and simple.

EASY TO DISMOUNT AND CLEAN — The rifle can be completely and quickly dismounted without tools, and owing to the simplicity of its mechanism, it can be cleaned easily and rapidly.

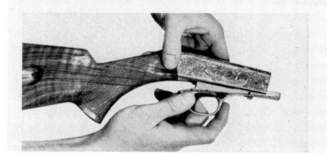

The Auto 22 can be field stripped using no tools.

The safeties were cross bolt located on the front of the trigger guards throughout production. In 1959 to 1960 a left hand safety was cataloged and offered only when a rifle was specifically ordered with one. It is a very convenient gun for either left or right handed shooters because the ejection is straight down and it doesn't send hot little 22 hulls down your shirt.

BARRELS AND VARIATIONS

The two cartridges this rifle was designed to shoot had different barrel lengths. The 22 Short came with a 22 1/4" barrel; a very few were made in the

22 3/8" length. The 22 Long Rifle came with a 19" barrel, but about 100 or so were made in the 19 1/4" length at the beginning of production. Prior to this about 200,000 were made by F.N. with their markings for sale outside the U.S. About 4% of the rifles made with 19 1/4" barrels were 22 Shorts.

All barrels were blued with the muzzle polished bright. Look under the appropriate sections to find placement of serial numbers, sights and scope mounting holes.

The original 1914 markings on the barrels were:
**FABRIQUE NATIONALE
D'ARMES DE GUERRE BELGIUM
- PAT'D JAN 6-1914
"BROWNING ARMES CO"
OGDEN - UTAH**

In addition, you will also find one of the following markings:

**"22 SHORT SMOKELESS"
"22 LONG RIFLE SMOKELESS"
"CALIBER 22 SHORT"
"CALIBER 22 LONG RIFLE"**

You will also find the serial numbers on all major parts on these early guns as well as the Liege proof marks and various inspectors marks. Sometimes you will find a double stamping that simply says BROWNING PATENTS.

Later barrel markings are:
FABRIQUE NATIONALE
D'ARMES DE GUERRE-HERSTAL-BELGIQUE
BROWNING ARMS COMPANY
ST LOUIS MO & MONTREAL PQ
MADE IN BELGIUM

The 1956 to 1958 markings for this country are as follows:
BROWNING ARMS COMPANY
ST LOUIS MO

The next marking which was from 1958 to 1970 for the U.S. was:
BROWNING ARMS COMPANY
ST. LOUIS MO & MONTREAL, P.Q.

The last Belgium marking was:
BROWNING ARMS COMPANY
MORGAN UTAH & MONTREAL P.Q.

You will also find the following markings depending on the date and cartridge:
"BROWNING PATENTS"
"22 SHORT"
"22 LONG RIFLE"

The guns made in Japan will be marked on the left side of the barrel:
BROWNING ARMS COMPANY
MORGAN UTAH & MONTREAL P.Q.
MADE IN JAPAN

On the right side of the barrel you will find:
CALIBER .22 LONG RIFLE
BROWNING PATENTS

The serial numbers, the Liege proof marks, and various inspectors marks will also be found. Do not be surprised to find guns sold directly by Browning that have European markings. Like anyone else, F. N. used parts when they needed them. A slight variation in the marking didn't stop its usage. An awful lot of these guns were purchased by G.I.'s in the PX's and brought back, so you'll also see come of these as well.

Serial numbers are stamped on guns after they are polished and before they are blued or assembled. This means that although every effort is taken to produce these in sequence, sometimes a receiver is not finished and assembled for a period of time. This could put the actual shipping date long after the actual production date. Also, the receiver can be assembled with parts out of sequence, which would mean that a barrel marking would not coincide with the serial number either.

MAGAZINES

All those shipped to this country loaded from the right side of the stock. You simply twisted the magazine release located at the butt and pulled rearward until the outer tube was exposed. After you drop in either 11 Long Rifle or 16 Short cartridges (for the 22 Short version only) nose first and close the magazine tube, the gun is loaded for either bear or squirrels, whichever you're hunting that day.

You may run into earlier guns that loaded from the top. These were never shipped to this country and will not be discussed here other then to say that you use the same procedure.

CARTRIDGES

The 22 Short and 22 Long Rifle versions were both introduced in 1956 and produced throughout Belgium production. The short in Grade I only and the long rifle in all grades. This is not to say that short Grade II and III models were not made; they were and are highly desirable.

The 22 Short version was only about 6% of production and is hard to find but not impossible to do so. They have a 22 1/4" barrel, but a few were made with a 22 3/8" barrel.

The 22 Long Rifle model came with a 19" barrel, but a few in the beginning of production had a 19 1/4" barrel.

I am going over this again because some of the rarities for which collectors look are these cartridge/barrel length combinations.

WOOD

All wood is described in the appropriate sections under grades. There are some slight variations common to each grade that should be noted, for they have varying amounts of collector value.

From the introduction in 1956 until 1963, the butt stock was attached with a bolt through the bottom of the pistol grip, and collectors like these more then the later guns. From 1964 through 1992, the butt stock is attached with a large nut through which the magazine tube fits.

The result of this change was the need for F.N. to decrease the size of the butt stock to 1 5/8' by 4 7/8" from 1 3/4" by 5 3/8".

In about 1965 the high gloss polyurethane finish came along. You will see many of these later guns that have the finish coming off them; this is not because of mishandling or abuse by the previous owner, but just the nature of the finish.

All 22 Automatics brought into this country by Browning were pistol grip configuration and hand checkered in varying degrees as discussed under grades. The stock dimensions were length of pull 13 3/4", drop at comb 1 3/16" and drop at heel 2 5/8".

SIGHTS

ADJUSTABLE REAR SIGHT — The unique disc leaf rear sight has four elevation adjustments for shooting at 50, 75, 100 and 125 yards, any of which can be chosen and locked instantly into place by a mere turn of the dial.

The Auto 22 was originally produced with the excellent and collectable "wheel sight."

I will cover only the variations imported into this country by Browning.

From 1956 until 1960 the desirable 4 step wheel sight was used. This was adjustable from 50 to 125 yards in 25 yard increments. These were not cataloged in 1961, but rifles were being shipped with them, probably parts cleanup.

The wheel sight was very desirable and probably the best Browning ever produced for any rifle. They were discontinued because of the popularity of scopes. They would get in the way and would have to be taken off.

From 1962 to the end of Belgium production, you will find the fold down sights which vary only slightly. They were all dovetailed in the barrels and adjustable for elevation in 3/4" increments at 50'. The windage adjustment was attained by sliding the sight left or right in the dovetail.

The front sights for the first five years were a plain blade. From 1960 until about 1973, you will find either a white or gold bead on the blade; after this you will find a plain blade with gold bead only.

From 1960 to 1963 Browning would honor requests for drilling scope mounting holes. These would have three holes only, for that was the only kind of mounts available at the time. After 1963 there would be either two or three holes, and after 1966 only two holes would be correct. Please look for this when purchasing one of these for investment. Scope mounting holes that are incorrect would hurt the value of the most desirable gun tremendously. Browning never drilled holes in the side of the receivers for a side mount.

POST BELGIUM PRODUCTION

In 1974 about 100 or more engraved receivers were shipped from Belgium to Japan. These were fitted with Japanese barrels and stocks. You will notice

a Belgian engraver's name on the receiver but a "Made in Japan" marking on the barrel. Most of these were engraved by a lady named M. Magis. You will find receivers engraved in Belgium on Japanese guns as late as 1979.

All three grades were made in Japan until 1983 when the Grade II was discontinued; in 1984 the Grade III was also discontinued. In 1987 the Grade VI was introduced. This featured the usual high grade polyurethane checkered wood, blued receiver, and gold plated animals.

The Japanese guns are not highly regarded by collectors. This does not mean that the Japanese made guns are not just as functional or of the quality of the Belgium made guns; they are. As long as they are still being made, collectors will not have a big interest in them. You will find, however, some are collecting the Belgium engraved and Japanese marked guns.

TOTAL PRODUCTION

From what I have been able to find from researching serial numbers, I will give you an approximate figure for each year's production. Remember, neither F. N. nor Browning will give out these facts, so we must go by what we can learn from observing the thousands of Auto 22's I have seen at gun shows.

YEAR	NUMBER PRODUCED		
1956	0001	12,000	12,000
1957	12,001	28,000	16,000
1958	28,001	44,500	16,500
1959	44,501	68,500	24,000
1960	68,500	90,500	22,000
1961	90,500	117,300	26,800
1962	117,301	143,200	25,900
1963	143,201	178,000	34,800
1964	178,001	201,000	23,000
1965	201,001	235,000	34,000
1966	235,001	249,200	14,200
1967	249,201	276,149	26,949
1968	276,150	302,000	25,851
1969	302,001	331,004	29,004
1970	331,005	348,000	16,996
1971	348,001	362,025	14,025
1972	362,026	371,000	8,975
1973	371,001	427,000	56,000

SERIAL NUMBERS AND MODEL CODES

From the beginning of U.S. sales, the serial numbers have moved around to such an extent that I constantly receive calls from people asking me where to look. I hope the following will help you in your quest.

As first introduced until about 1957 or 1958, the serial numbers were located on the front of the receiver, the trigger assembly, and at the top of the butt plate. The locations will vary from the top of the butt plate to the inside and sometimes will not appear on the trigger guards at all.

After 1958, the locations of the serial numbers were changed to the metal magazine stop plate on the butt stock and on the trigger assembly and receiver. The numbers may not appear on all three parts.

From 1960 to 1961 the serial numbers will be found on the bottom of the barrel just in front of the forearm. The serial number again moves to the front of the receiver on all three grades sometimes on the top or the side, and sometimes on the very front where the barrel fits.

From 1956 to mid 1961, the serial numbers were preceded with a "T" for the long rifle model and with an "A" for the 22 Short model. In 1961 the short designation was changed to a "E". Sometimes, probably through error, you will find these reversed.

Serial numbers for these years were:

1956	0001-12000	1958	28001-44500	1960	68501-90500
1957	12001-28000	1959	44501-68500	1961	90501-117300
				or	E—

From 1961 to 1975 each year began with the number 0001 and the serial numbers were as follows:

Year	Long		Short	
1961	1T—	1A OR	1E—	
1962	2T—		2E—	
1963	3T—		3E—	
1964	4T—		4E—	
1965	5T—		5E—	
1966	6T—		6E—	
1967	7T—		7E—	
1968	8T—		8E—	
1969	9T—		9E—	
or	69T—		69E—	
1970	70T—		70E—	
1971	71T—		71E—	
1972	72T—	OR —27T	72E—	OR —27E
1973	73T—	OR —T37	73E—	OR —E37
1974	74T—	OR —47T	74E—	OR —47E

End of Belgium Production

| 1975 | 75T— | OR 57T— | 75E— | OR 57E |

1973 was the last year of 100% Belgium production. Many parts were sent to Japan in 1973, so you will find a lot of these with mixed parts; this also included the boxes.

For yearly codes after 1976, refer to the General Information section in the front of this book.

Production codes before 1975 were Grade I 22 Short, 1406; 22 Long Rifle, 1506; Grade II, 2506; and for the Grade III, 3506.

Model codes from 1976 to date are Grade 1-146, Grade 2-246, Grade 3-346 and the Grade 6-646.

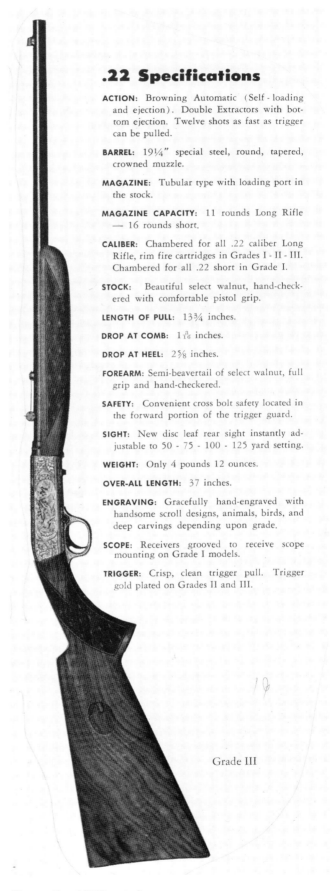

.22 Specifications

ACTION: Browning Automatic (Self-loading and ejection). Double Extractors with bottom ejection. Twelve shots as fast as trigger can be pulled.

BARREL: 19¼" special steel, round, tapered, crowned muzzle.

MAGAZINE: Tubular type with loading port in the stock.

MAGAZINE CAPACITY: 11 rounds Long Rifle — 16 rounds short.

CALIBER: Chambered for all .22 caliber Long Rifle, rim fire cartridges in Grades I - II - III. Chambered for all .22 short in Grade I.

STOCK: Beautiful select walnut, hand-checkered with comfortable pistol grip.

LENGTH OF PULL: 13¾ inches.

DROP AT COMB: 1¹⁄₁₆ inches.

DROP AT HEEL: 2⅝ inches.

FOREARM: Semi-beavertail of select walnut, full grip and hand-checkered.

SAFETY: Convenient cross bolt safety located in the forward portion of the trigger guard.

SIGHT: New disc leaf rear sight instantly adjustable to 50 - 75 - 100 - 125 yard setting.

WEIGHT: Only 4 pounds 12 ounces.

OVER-ALL LENGTH: 37 inches.

ENGRAVING: Gracefully hand-engraved with handsome scroll designs, animals, birds, and deep carvings depending upon grade.

SCOPE: Receivers grooved to receive scope mounting on Grade I models.

TRIGGER: Crisp, clean trigger pull. Trigger gold plated on Grades II and III.

Grade III

From the 1958 catalog.

THE .22 PUMP (TROMBONE)

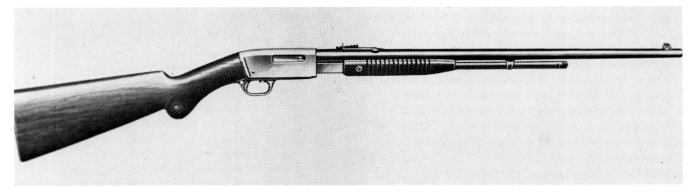

The above picture shows the Trombone as it was produced in the later part of production with rear elevator sights.

GENERAL INFORMATION

This neat little rifle is nicknamed the "Trombone". It was originally patented in 1919, first produced in October, 1922, and discontinued in 1973.

Fabrique Nationale made this rifle for sales in Canada, South America, Europe and just about everywhere in the world except this country. Why, I don't know and can't figure out. If you ever run across one, you won't figure it out either because they are truly a great little gun that would have sold like hot cakes. Browning only brought 3,250 guns into this country in 1970. They will be marked with a 70W as part of the serial number. Since so few were imported, it is one of the rarest guns a Browning collector can get in new condition.

Some were also brought in through servicemen coming back from Europe. The early serial numbers are unobtainable from F.N. Except for some commemorative guns. All of those brought here by Browning were a standard plain grade, they were uncheckered, but the forearms were grooved.

About 150,310 were produced through 1974. There were some high grade guns produced on special order, but beware of non-factory upgrades, for this would indeed be an expensive little gun.

FRAME VARIATIONS

This was basically a takedown, hammerless, all steel action that remained unchanged for the entire 50 years it was produced.

On the first rifles produced, you will find the lower tang finished square. This was the cause of many split stocks. After Browning produced about 20,000, the tangs were changed to round.

The action is just as slick as any pump ever made. The magazine tube slides back and forth only about 1 1/2" when you pump the action, and this only adds to the ease in which it operates.

Most frames up to serial number 70,000 are not grooved for scope mount, while from 1957 to the end of production, most of the receivers are grooved.

This little gun has many other features: it weighs only 4 3/4 to 5 pounds, they were all blued, and it is a takedown. It could be loaded with any combination of 22 Short, 22 Long, and 22 Long Rifle, interchangeably.

The takedown feature was also excellent; it was dissambled by removing the knurled takedown screw. You then lifted the barrel-receiver group off the trigger guard-butt stock group and split the rifle in half for easy packing. This also exposed the inner mechanism for cleaning or maintenance.

BARRELS

Barrels for export other than to the U.S. are marked:

**FABRIQUE NATIONALE
D'ARMES DE GUERRE HERSTAL BELGIQUE
BROWNING'S PATENT DEPOSE**

The barrels on the rifles made for this country are marked:

**BROWNING ARMS COMPANY
MORGAN UTAH & MONTREAL P.Q.
MADE IN BELGIUM**

Other markings are the standard Liege proof marks, serial numbers and inspectors' stamps.

The barrels are 22" long.

SIGHTS

The leaf rear sight is dovetailed directly into the barrels with an elevator to adjust the elevation. Windage can only be adjusted by sliding the sight left or right in the dovetail. Over the years the sights have changed very little. These changes only pertain to the guns made for other countries so we will not cover them here.

The front sight is dovetailed directly into the barrel; it is a gold bead.

MAGAZINE

The magazine will feed and hold interchangeably 15 shorts, 12 long, or 11 long rifle cartridges. It slides back and forth with the forearm and makes for a very slick action. They were all blued.

STOCKS

The wood was about group 1, very plain and oil finished; they were all half pistol round knob. The butt stocks on the standard rifles were not checkered.

The next grade up was produced strictly for sales outside of the U.S. It had wood of about group 3 to 4 and is highly finished with 18 line per inch checkering on both the butt stock and forearm. It is a very handsome rifle that would satisfy the wants of any shooter. If you're lucky enough to ever have an opportunity to purchase one for a reasonable price, you need to make a withdrawel from the saving account, for you may never get another chance.

All had thin steel butt plates up until the last of production when they were changed to black plastic. All the ones I've seen exported to this country had steel butt plates.

The dimensions were length of pull 13 1/2", drop at comb 1 3/4" and drop at heel 2 3/4".

Forearms had 15 grooves and were 1 1/4" in diameter, tapering down to about 3/4" within 2" of the front. They are 6 1/2" long.

SERIAL NUMBERS AND YEARS PRODUCED

This is an approximation based on the total production of 150,310. Please be aware that this is just an estimation and the year your rifle was produced can be different then the year shown.

1922- 1- 3758	1936- 52612- 5636	1960- 97708-101465
1923- 3759- 7516	1937- 56370- 60127	1961-101466-105223
1924- 7517- 11272	1938- 60127- 63885	1962-105224-108891
1925- 11275- 15031	1939- 63885- 67643	1963-108892-112739
1926- 15032- 18790	Production ended here	1964-112780-116497
1927- 18791- 22547	because of W.W. II	1965-116498-120255
1928- 22548- 26305	1952- 67644- 71401	1966-120256-124013
1929- 26306- 30063	1953- 71401- 75159	1967-124014-127771
1930- 30064- 33821	1954- 75159- 78917	1968-127772-131529
1931- 33822- 37579	1955- 78918- 82675	1969-131530-135287
1932- 37580- 41337	1956- 82676- 86433	1970-135288-139045
1933- 41338- 45095	1957- 86434- 90191	1971-139046-142803
1934- 45096- 48853	1958- 90192- 93949	1972-142803-146561
1935- 48854- 52611	1959- 93950- 97707	1973-146562-150310

The late rifles brought into this country by Browning will have serial numbers that look like this:

YEAR   SERIAL NUMBER
1970   70W—-

The "W" was the product code.

THE T-BOLT 22

GENERAL SPECIFICATIONS AND HISTORY

The T-Bolt in Grade II right hand.

This rifle was introduced in 1964, and although discontinued in 1974, it was still being shipped in 1975. It was not known then, but if you ordered a gun after they were discontinued, you could probably have gotten one on special order, for F.N. still had parts.

The original prototype was designed by Jack Donaldson of Suguache, Colorado. Mr. Donaldson was an amateur inventor very interested in firearms design. Although companies like Browning have many models under design in house at all times, they rarely have a gun as innovative as this model brought to them.

The T-Bolt is a very interesting design, for it was the first straight pull rifle built in this country since the pre-1900 Lee Straight Pull Rifle. The Lee Straight Pull was built by Winchester for the U.S.Navy and fired a centerfire cartridge called the 6mm Lee. As a point of interest, the 6mm Lee was also the last 6mm cartridge in almost 60 years before the 243 Winchester came along in the early 1950's. This shows once again that there is rarely anything new, just change.

The four page flyer that follows was made available to all Browning dealers in 1964 as a supplement to their wholesale catalog of the same year. Please notice what they say about this model which is all true, Browning has always been one of the most innovative of all the gun companies in the U.S. starting with the Auto-5 and continuing with the T-Bolt.

NEW BROWNING **T-BOLT** .22 CALIBER REPEATING RIFLE

An entirely new concept in bolt-action design

Featuring Exceptional: Accuracy . . . Dependability . . . Safety . . . Ease of Operation

The Browning T-Bolt .22 caliber repeating rifle is entirely new, entirely original and so unique in operating principle that it will be difficult to fully appreciate its many exclusive features without actually shooting it. One thing is certain; you'll like it.

The T-Bolt combines fine accuracy, maximum safety and an exceptionally strong locking system with an ease of operation that is unmatched by any other bolt action design. It is fast, rugged and dependable and possesses the good balance and handling characteristics so vital to precision shooting.

Its handsome lines verify that appearance too was carefully considered in its design. The slender, compact receiver blends smoothly into the tapered barrel and both are richly polished and blued. The one-piece stock of select walnut has a full pistol grip and well contoured forearm.

This is a rifle that will appeal to the precision shooter as well as the hunter or casual plinker or the father who wants a well made, extremely safe rifle with which to teach a youngster proper gun handling and marksmanship.

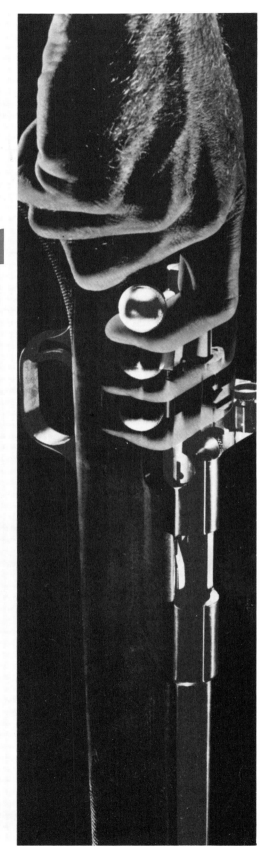

T-Bolt operates with a simple, straight rearward and forward movement.

From the 1964 catalog.

BROWNING'S NEW T-BOLT PRINCIPLE — Unlike conventional bolt-actions, the new Browning T-Bolt operates with a simple, straight rearward and forward movement to complete the ejecting, cocking and loading cycle, *thereby eliminating the necessity of lifting up and pushing down the bolt handle.* This smooth, effortless motion has been achieved by a unique cross-bolt locking system wherein the operating handle is so pivoted that when pulled rearward, the cross-bolt clears the opposing locking recesses in the receiver. The forward motion securely seats the cross-bolt and so precisely orients the breech bolt to the chamber that accuracy is exceptional. The bolt handle serves as a powerful lever that can easily withdraw a deformed or stuck cartridge case and, in unity with double extractors, assures positive ejection of spent cases. The T-Bolt trigger is clean and crisp without creep and not over 4 lbs. in weight of pull. Hammer fall is short and extremely fast which further enhances the accuracy of this little rifle.

The Browning T-Bolt action design is intrinsically so strong there is an extra margin of safety far in excess of that considered adequate for any .22 rimfire cartridge.

6-SHOT REPEATER — The new Browning T-Bolt is clip fed. The clip holds five *Long Rifle* cartridges. By adding a cartridge to the chamber, the rifle has a capacity of six rounds.

T-2 Model

This is from the 1964 catalog.

SINGLE-SHOT CONVERSION — The T-Bolt may be easily converted to a single-shot version through use of a simple two-piece adapter (provided with each rifle).

One piece of the adapter serves as the cartridge loading ramp while the other encloses the underside of the magazine recess when the clip magazine is removed. Installation takes mere seconds while the rifle is fully assembled. On the other hand, reconversion to a repeater is just difficult enough to discourage the not yet qualified young shooter . . . an ideal safety modification when the rifle is being used for training purposes or by young shooters. In its single-shot version, one may use *Short, Long,* or *Long Rifle* cartridges.

ACCURATE SIGHTING SYSTEM — The receiver of the T-Bolt is grooved to accept the receiver sight provided with the rifle as well as Browning's .22 scope and mount, or most other scope mounts designed for a grooved receiver. The receiver sight is fully adjustable, both horizontally and vertically, and is calibrated to aid in the zeroing-in process. Adjustments require no tools. The front sight is a $\frac{1}{16}$" blade type on a raised ramp.

TWO MODELS — The Browning T-Bolt .22 is offered in two models, identical in mechanical operation and varying only in stock and barrel specifications. The more deluxe model, designated *T-2,* features a beautiful select walnut stock, finely checkered and hand lacquered to a brilliant finish. With its straight, tapered 24" barrel, the *T-2* weighs approximately 6 lbs. For the shooter who subjects a .22 to slightly rougher usage or who wants a rugged little trainer, the *T-1* model is ideal. Its stock is uncheckered and has a new oil finish that readily lends itself to the removal of dents or scars without the

PRICES

Model	Code Number	Net Wholesale Dealer Price	Net Wholesale Dealer Margin	Wholesale Less 3% Dealer Price	Wholesale Less 3% Dealer Margin	Wholesale Less 6% Dealer Price	Wholesale Less 6% Dealer Margin	Suggested Retail
T-1	**1106**	$40.87	$13.63	$39.64	$14.86	$38.42	$16.08	$54.50
T-2	**2106**	55.87	18.63	54.19	20.31	52.52	21.98	74.50

Prices include two-piece adapter for single-shot conversion.

Printed in U.S.A.

T-1 Model with Browning 4X .22 Riflescope and two-piece ring-mount

need of refinishing the entire stock. And, should the owner be so inclined, he may supplement the finish with any degree of hand rubbed luxury desired by the application of additional coats of any good linseed oil base, stock finish. The T-1 weighs 5 lbs. 8 oz. and comes with a 22″ barrel.

SAFETY — The manual or thumb safety is conveniently located at the left rear of the receiver where it may be manipulated by either hand. In its up or "on safe" position, both the trigger and the bolt are securely locked. When in its down or "off safe" position, a red warning dot is clearly visible. The safety lever is completely encased within the steel receiver, minimizing its exposure to dirt and rust. In its "on safe" position there is *positive* locking of both the trigger and the bolt. The rifle will not fire until the cross-bolt is locked into position and, when locked, no blow-back of any sort can reach the shooter.

T-BOLT .22 SPECIFICATIONS

ACTION—The exclusive Browning straight-pull-back breech bolt. Double extractors. Side ejection. Easy conversion between magazine repeater or single-shot.

BARREL—Straight taper. Recessed muzzle. Medium heavy. Barrel length—T-1 Model: 22 inches; T-2 Model: 24 inches.

OVERALL LENGTH—T-1 Model: 39¼ inches; T-2 Model: 41¼ inches.

CAPACITY—As a repeater, 6 Long Rifle cartridges; clip holds 5 cartridges. When converted to a single-shot accepts .22 Short, Long or Long Rifle.

STOCK—Select walnut with full pistol grip and molded butt plate. T-1 Model has new oil finish without checkering; T-2 Model possesses fine checkering and highly polished lacquer finish. Length of pull 13½″, drop at comb 1⅛″, drop at heel 3″.

MANUAL SAFETY—Locks both trigger and breech bolt. Red warning dot exposed in "off safe" position.

SIGHTS—Rear: Receiver peep, fully adjustable for horizontal and vertical correction. Fits to grooved receiver and is quickly interchangeable with scope mounting. Front: ⅟₁₆″ blade on raised ramp.

SCOPES—Browning Model 1217 and two-piece ring-mount Model 9417. (Extra)

TRIGGER—Clean and crisp without creep. Maximum pull, 4 pounds.

ADAPTER—Two-piece adapter provided with each rifle. Converts rifle to a single-shot as desired.

WEIGHT—T-1 Model: 5 pounds 8 ounces; T-2 Model: 6 pounds.

GRADES

There were two grades produced in the model, they were very different: the T-1 and the T-2.

Originally conceived as a boy's or beginners rifle, this thinking was quickly changed when Browning and F.N. saw how much it was going to cost to manufacture. This is also the reason they came out with the T-1.

The T-1 was not as popular as Browning would have hoped, for it didn't meet the standards by which shooters judge a Browning. The T-2, however, was a beautiful rifle and quite popular, a man's .22.

None were ever offered factory engraved as a standard feature, and I have never heard of nor seen a factory engraved T-Bolt at any time.

THE T-1 GRADE

The T-1 was a utility rifle introduced in 1964 and discontinued in 1971. It had a group 1 plain uncheckered walnut pistol grip stock with an oil finish. The finish was far below what you would expect from Browning. In fact, its description in the 1965 catalog sounds almost apologetic. The catalog says, "Should the owner be so inclined, he may supplement the finish with any degree of hand rubbed luxury desired by the application of additional coats of any good linseed oil base stock finish." Ever seen any other gun company describe a gun stock in that way? I haven't. It almost sounds as if Browning is telling you to finish the stock yourself.

The balance of the rifle is the same as the T-2 except the barrels are only 22" long.

THE T-2 GRADE

Unlike the T-1, the T-2 had the traditional high gloss finish, more of what you would expect from Browning. The wood had much more figure, which was about group 3, All were hand checkered 18 lines per inch with a glossy polyurethane finish. The checkering didn't vary much from the beginning of production to the end in the first production series.

The grip checkering was changed from three point to two, and the forearm checkering was wrap-around through out production.

The barrels were all 24" long on this grade.

FRAME

The action was a completely new concept for 22 rifles.

A conventional bolt action requires four distinct movements to operate and complete a cycle: up, back, forward, and down. The T-Bolt operates with a simple straight rearward and forward movement to cycle the action. This is much simpler and quicker to operate. In addition, it is one of the strongest ever built for a 22. The cross bolt locking system that works as part of the operating handle provides a positive lockup. When the bolt handle is pulled to the rear, the bolt clears the locking recesses machined into the receiver; when the bolt is pushed forward, the locking bolt reenters the locking recesses. This also aids accuracy, for the bolt realigns itself with the barrel.

The caming action of the bolt also makes it easier to extract a deformed or stuck case, and with the double extractors, smooth operation is almost assured.

All were made of steel, highly polished and blued; only the bolts were left polished bright. They were all grooved for a scope mount and were clip fed. All the early guns had an anodized black aluminum trigger guard, but later production guns have ones made of black plastic.

The action is very safe, for it will absolutely not fire until fully closed.

Another interesting feature of this rifle is that it was made in right and left hand configurations throughout its production run or immediately thereafter. I don't know of any other time Browning catered to the left handed shooter this early, but they sure did this time, and it was really appreciated by southpaws like myself. Left and right hand models were available in both grades.

The T-Bolt in Grade II left hand.

If you could get used to pulling the bolt straight back towards your nose while the gun was still mounted to your shoulder, it was a very fast bolt action rifle, I couldn't get used to it, though; it's just impossible for me to trust anything that close to my face.

All actions on both grades were grooved for scope mounts.

SAFETY

The safety was mounted on the left side of the receiver and could be rotated up for safe or down for fire with your thumb. It was quick to use, quiet and positive.

CLIPS

This was one of the negatives about the T-Bolt. Ever listen to folks looking at a 22 in a gun shop? The first thing they say is, "How many will it hold?" The more it holds, the better the gun, right? Well, that may not be right, but unfortunately that's how the average hunter looks at a 22. Browning should have come out with a 10 or 15 round magazine, and many more of these would have been sold.

Each rifle was supplied with a five round clip that fed 22 Long Rifles only. An extra clip was offered starting in 1969 but I am sure you could have purchased them earlier.

They also came out with an adaptor that plugged up the bottom and top of the receiver. This effectively made it a single shot. The top part of the adaptor acted like a loading ramp and allowed the rifle to feed Short, Long, or Long Rifle cartridges. The bottom part simply closed up the bottom. Browning was aiming at the father/son market, the father with a man-sized gun and the son with a 22 single shot.

BARRELS AND SIGHTS

All T-2 barrels were medium weight, blued and 24" long with recessed muzzles. The T-1 barrels were 22" long, medium weight, blued and also had recessed muzzles. Neither changed throughout production.

This is how the barrels were marked from 1958 to 1970:

BROWNING ARMS COMPANY
ST. LOUIS MO & MONTREAL, P.Q.
MADE IN BELGIUM

The next marking to the end of production was:
BROWNING ARMS COMPANY
MORGAN UTAH & MONTREAL P.Q.

You will also find the following markings:
"BROWNING PATENT"
"22 LONG RIFLE"

Also present will be the Belgium and Liege proofs.

SIGHTS

The rear sight was really unique, for it slid back and forth on the top of the receiver. In this way, you could move it back and forth to the spot that best suited your shooting technique. They were fully adjustable for windage and elevation, and all calibrations were marked in white. The biggest disadvantage in these was the fact that you had to take them off to mount a scope. This also meant that they could get lost easily.

The front sight was a 1/16" blade on a ramp. They were fully blued and never changed throughout production.

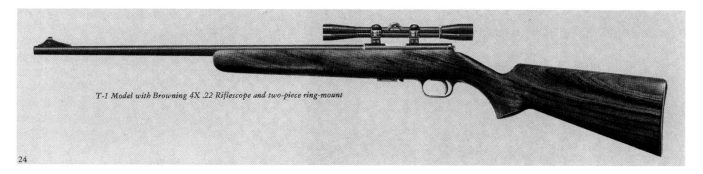

T-1 Model with Browning 4X .22 Riflescope and two-piece ring-mount

24

As this 1966 catalog shows, Browning offered 22 scopes and mounts for the T-Bolt.

WOOD

There really isn't much to say about the wood for this model that wasn't covered under each grade.

All had the black plastic butt plates marked Browning. The dimensions were length of pull 13 1/2", drop at comb 1 15/16" and drop at heel 3".

Salt wood was a problem with this model, so be careful. I always take the butt plate screws out and look them over carefully. Any rust and I become suspicious. You can find a lot more information about salt wood in the Superposed section.

TOTAL PRODUCTION

Total production for the T-1 and the T-2 was about 69,300 guns. Please be aware that the following list is just an estimation by year. According to F.N., the total that they produced was 66,787; the 69,892 figure I come up with includes the parts guns which will be discussed later. The 1965 to 1966 figures are also F.N. supplied.

YEAR	START	END	TOTAL
1965	0001X5	5468X5	5,468
1966	5469X6	24783X6	24,783
1967	24784X7	30034X7	30,034
1968	30035X8	35284X8	35,284
1969	35285X9	40534X69	40,534
1970	40535X70	45784X70	45,784
1971	45185X71	51034X71	51,034
1972	51035X72	56284X72	56,284
1973	56285X73	61534X73	61,534
*1978-1980	61535X	66787X	66,787
1981	66788X	69300X	69,892

*See additional information below.

Some year codes are reversed.

PARTS GUNS

From 1978 to 1981 F.N. assembled about 3,105 more of this model from parts left over from the 1973 to 1974 production.

Total production for these parts guns were 499 for the T-1's and 2,606 for the T-2's.

Every T-2 I've seen assembled from parts had very plain oil finished wood of about group 1. Some of it came from Japan, and it has absolutely no figure whatsoever. They are all hand checkered, however, with 18 lines per inch. This plain wood is probably T-1 wood that was left over from previous production and checkered so that F.N. could sell some T-2's. I had one collector that called to tell me he had one of these later guns with what appeared to be an original high gloss finish. He failed to describe the quality of the wood, so I don't know if it was an original T-2 stock, but in any case it is rare to find a parts gun with an acceptable stock.

The serial numbers on most of these parts guns are all followed by an "X". You cannot tell from the serial numbers which year the rifle was assembled other than the table above.

Collectors are not willing to pay as much for these later guns, so it is important to be able to tell the difference. This sometimes can be done by the serial number. These were applied three different ways:
*(1) 216PM—(2) —X37 or X47-(3) — X- No year code

The easiest way to tell is by the first serial number variation, for none of the earlier guns had the code 216. The second variation serial number is the same as the early T-Bolt, but the wood is plain,

oil finished and checkered, clearly not an early T-2. The third variation doesn't have a number after the "X." This was because the year wasn't marked on a gun until it was polished and assembled. When these were put together, a mistake was made at the plant and they never got coded with the year.

PRICES

Here are the prices for all the years they were made:

YEAR	T-1	T-2
1965	$54.50	$ 74.50
1966	54.50	74.60
1967	57.50	77.50
1968	57.50	77.50
1969	59.50	79.75
1970	62.50	84.50
1971	65.59	88.50
1972	65.50	88.50
1973	72.50	97.50
1974	72.50	114.50

When last sold in 1981 they were $199.95.

SERIAL NUMBERS AND MODEL CODES

When they were first introduced, the serial numbers were placed on the bottom of the barrel in front of the forearm. The only other place they will appear is on the receivers on the right side. This started in 1968 because of the new Federal gun laws.

The serial numbers for the early guns had an "X" proceeding the year of manufacture. This designated the model. During each year from 1965 - 1974, the serial numbers began with 0001.

It is not possible to tell if a rifle is for a left handed shooter or not by just the serial number, nor can you tell which grade a gun is from the serial numbers.

1965 —X5	1970 —X70
1966 —X6	1971 —X71
1967 —X7	1972 —X72
1968 —X8	1973 —X73 or X37
1969 —X69 or X9	1974 —X74 or X47

The model codes for the T-Bolts prior to 1975 were "X". These were then changed to 116 for the T-1 and 216 for the T-2.

When the parts guns were assembled, the boxes were labeled with the product code 21062 for the T-2, so if someone offers you a new in the box gun, be sure to ask about the end label; that will tip you off as to when it was made.

For the yearly codes after 1975, please refer to the General Information section in the front of this book.

THE BPR 22

The BPR Grade II.

GENERAL INFORMATION

The BPR was introduced in 1976 and discontinued in 1984. It was the first pump Browning introduced in this country in any great numbers. Why they chose to introduce this model rather then the tried and true Trombone, I will never know. The Trombone was designed by John M. Browning over 60 years earlier and is described elsewhere.

This was not a boy's 22 but a full sized rifle that had all steel contruction and came in 22 long rifle and 22 magnum models as well. The barrels were medium size as 22's go and the dimensions were full size. It weighed in at 6 lbs 4 oz, about a pound less the many centerfire rifles.

GRADES

This model was introduced in only one grade; when the Grade II came along in 1980 there was only cosmetic differences between them. They were both discontinued as of 1984.

GRADE 1

This was the first grade introduced. It has no engraving and is group 1-2 walnut checkered 18 lines per inch. All triggers were black anodized, and it was made in 22 Long Rifle only. Other features will be described under their sections.

GRADE II

The Grade II was introduced in 1976 in 22 Long Rifle and in 1980 in 22 Magnum, both were discontinued in 1984. This is the better grade that Browning always gave to the public that liked something a little better.

The etched engraving consisted of very light and broad scroll, covering about 25% of the receiver on both sides. On the left side was the head and shoulder of a rabbit and on the right was a squirral lying down on a tree limb. All receivers were greyed and the triggers were black anodized.

It had select grade wood about group 2 and was checkered 18 lines per inch.

All other features will be described under their sections.

FRAMES

It was designed like most other 22 pumps, for the weight of the bolt, slide and other parts held the action closed when the gun was fired. Receivers were all blued unless otherwise noted, and they were hammerless. The slide release mounted inside the trigger guard held the action closed until fired. After the first shot the release did not need to be pressed to operate the slide and load another cartridge.

The takedown feature was also excellent; it dissambled by removing the takedown screw and cocking handle. You then lifted the barrel-receiver group off the trigger guard-butt stock group and split the rifle in half for easy packing. This also exposed the inner mechanism for cleaning or maintenance.

This rifle was made in two versions: the 22 Long Rifle and the magnum. You could not interchange cartridges; the magnum version would shoot the 22 Magnum cartridges only, and the 22 Long Rifle would shoot 22 Long Rifle only. All actions were side ejection and had a cross bolt safety on the rear of the trigger guard. The receivers were grooved for a scope mount as well.

BARRELS

Both the 22 Long Rifle and 22 Magnum barrels were 20 1/4'' long and all had a recessed muzzle.
Barrel markings on the left side were:
BROWNING ARMS COMPANY
MORGAN, UTAH & MONTREAL P.Q.
MADE IN JAPAN

On the right side for the standard chamberings:
BPR CALIBER-22 LONG RIFLE ONLY

On the right side for the magnums:
BPR CALIBER-22 MAGNUM ONLY

SIGHTS

Sights were dovetailed into the barrel and folded down. They were all adjustable for elevation but had to be tapped left or right within the dovetail for windage. All markings were painted white.

The front sights were dovetailed on a serrated ramp and had a gold bead. The sight radius was 16".

MAGAZINES

All had tubular magazines with a loading port under the barrel. They held 15 Long Rifle or 11 22 Magnums only.

The magazine tube latch allowed the shooter to secure it after loading without having to find a notch. It had the capability of locking 360 degrees.

STOCKS

The pistol grip stocks were of French walnut and finished in the traditional Browning high gloss. Both grades were checkered and had the Browning marked black plastic butt plates, dimensions were length of pull 13 3/4", drop at comb 1 1/2" and drop at heel 2 1/4".

PRICES

I do not have the prices as introduced but during some of the other years they cost as follows:

Year	Grade I 22 L.R.	Grade I 22 Magnum	Grade II 22 Magnum
1978	$179.95	$189.95	
1979	199.95	209.95	
1980	209.95	229.95	329.95

SERIAL NUMBERS

For serial numbers please refer to the General Information section at the front of the book.

BLR 22

The BLR 22.

GENERAL INFORMATION

Fabrique Nationale first produced this rifle in 1956, but it wasn't introduced into the U.S. until 1969. It has always been made for the U.S. in Japan by Miroku.

GRADES

They were made in two grades with only cosmetic differences between each of them. They are still being made as of 1992.

GRADE I

This grade has no engraving and a plain walnut non-checkered stock; the wood is about group 1. All other features will be described under their sections.

GRADE II

This is the better grade that Browning always gave to the public that liked something a little better.

The engraving consisted of very light scroll wedges on both sides of the action reminiscent of the Auto-5 engraving. There are four sections on the right side and five on the left in the center and on the corners. All triggers were gold plated until 1981 when they were changed to gold color.

It had select grade wood about group 2 and was checkered 18 lines per inch with a high gloss polyurethane finish.

All other features will be described under their sections.

History repeats itself

Promontory Point, Utah. Site of the completion of the first transcontinental railroad 100 years ago.

Top to bottom: Originals of the Winchester Models 86, 87, 92, 94, 95 — invented by John M. Browning.

the new BL-22 by Browning

TO ORDER just complete the order form with your name and address. Indicate either Grade I or Grade II and mail to the dealer listed below. Do not send orders directly to the Browning Arms Company.

Please Check

Handsome and rugged Grade I — $67.50 ☐
Engraved and checkered Grade II — $84.50 ☐

☐ Charge ☐ Check or Money Order Enclosed

Name ....

Address ....

City .... State .... Zip ....

Send your order to the dealer whose name appears below.

AUTHORIZED **BROWNING**® DEALER

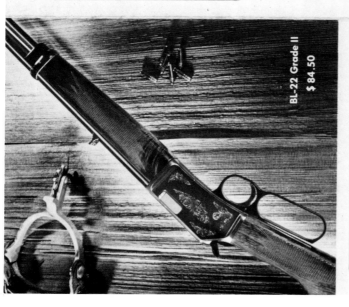

BL-22 Grade II
$ 84.50

BL-22 SPECIFICATIONS

ACTION: Short throw lever. Travels in arc of only 33°, carrying trigger with it thereby preventing finger pinch.

MAGAZINE: Tubular magazine with capacity for 15 Long Rifles, 17 Longs, 22 Shorts *in any combination.*

SAFETY: Unique disconnect system, exposed hammer with half cock position, and inertia firing pin.

ACCURACY: Crisp trigger with no creep, recessed muzzle, precision folding-leaf rear sight.

RECEIVER: Forged and milled, steel receiver; grooved to accept most groove or tip-off mounts or receiver sights.

STOCK & FOREARM: Select walnut, brilliantly finished.

BARREL LENGTH: 20 inches; overall length, 36¾".

WEIGHT: 5 lbs.

GRADE II MODEL: Skillfully hand-engraved and hand-checkered. Gold plated trigger.

BL-22 Grade I: $67.50

Introducing Browning's New .22 Caliber Lever Action Rifle...THE BL-22

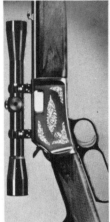

FORGED AND MILLED STEEL RECEIVER — The forged and milled steel receiver is grooved to accept the Browning .22 riflescope and two-piece ring mount as well as most other groove or tip-off type mounts or receiver sights.

BROWNING QUALITY CRAFTSMANSHIP — Select, polished Walnut stocks are carefully fitted to specially processed, richly blued steels. All parts are machine-finished and hand-fitted to function flawlessly. The Grade II model features delicate hand-engraving on the receiver and hand-checkering on the stock. We are confident your judgement of quality will class the BL-22 another "golden spike" milestone in Browning's lever action heritage.

HANDLES ALL .22 LOADS — Designed to feed Long Rifle, Long, and Short .22 caliber ammunition *in any combination* from its tubular magazine without hangup. Magazine capacity is 15 Long Rifles, 17 Longs, or 22 Shorts. The positive magazine latch opens and closes easily from any position.

ACCURACY — This rifle's fine accuracy is enhanced by its clean, crisp trigger with no creep (average pull — 5 pounds) and its recessed muzzle. The precision, folding leaf rear sight is adjustable.

The great levers of the past, invented by John M. Browning in Utah territory between 1882 and 1895, are the forerunners of the new Browning BL-22. Capturing their classic lines and reminiscent of the ruggedness and adventure of the Old West, the new Browning BL-22 offers these exceptional features:

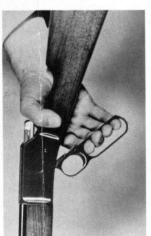

SHORT LEVER THROW — The lever on the BL-22 travels through an arc of only 33 degrees and carries the trigger with it, preventing finger pinch between lever and trigger on the upward swing. One smooth, even flick of the wrist ejects the fired shell, cocks the hammer and feeds a fresh round into the chamber.

SAFETY FEATURES — The BL-22 design incorporates complete safety features: A unique disconnect system prevents firing until the lever and breech are fully closed and pressure is released from and reapplied to the trigger. An inertia firing pin and an exposed hammer with a half cock position are other, well-accepted safeguards.

Browning Arms Company, Route 1, Morgan, Utah 84050

FRAMES

All receivers are forged and milled steel with the internal parts hand fitted and machine finished. All have exposed hammers and inertia firing pins; they can handle Short, Long, or Long Rifle cartridges interchangably.

These rifles are quite safe to use, for Browning has incorporated every feature possible to assure they are safe. The disconnect system prevents firing until the lever and breech are fully closed. If the trigger is pulled and held while working the lever to reload another round, the gun will not fire until the trigger is released, even if the breech is fully closed. Another safety feature is the three position hammer. It has what Browning calls full cock, half cock, and dropped positions. The inertia firing pin will not gain enough force to fire a cartridge from a hammer blow if the hammer is all the way down. This prevents someone from inadvertently dropping the gun and hitting the hammer, resulting in the gun going off accidentally.

Another good feature is the ease of operation. The short throw lever only travels 33 degrees carrying the trigger with it. This prevents someone from accidentally pinching a finger when closing the action.

All actions were grooved to accept scope mounts, which were highly polished and fully blued in both grades, the tops matted to break glare.

BARRELS AND SIGHTS

All barrels were 20" long with a recessed muzzle.

At the time of introduction, the rear sights were folding leaf that was adjustable for both windage and elevation and the markings were highlighted in white. The front sights were a gold bead dovetailed into the barrel. There was no hood.

Barrels were marked on the left side:
BROWNING ARMS COMPANY
MORGAN,UTAH & MONTREAL P.Q.
MADE IN JAPAN

Barrels were marked on the right side:
BLR CALIBER 22 SHORT LONG & LONG RIFLE

In addition, the logo appears on the lever.

MAGAZINE

All had tubular magazines with a loading port under the barrel. You could switch Short, Long, or Long Rifle cartridges interchangeably.

In 1971 a new style magazine latch was introduced to allow the shooter to secure it after loading without having to find a notch. It also had the capability of locking 360 degrees.

STOCKS

The stocks were straight grip finished high gloss, and the forearms were slim and retained by a single barrel band. Butt plates were all Browning marked black plastic. The dimensions were a length of pull 13 1/2", drop at comb 1 5/8" and drop at heel 2 1/4".

SERIAL NUMBERS AND MODEL CODES

All guns imported into the U. S. were made in Japan and marked with a "B" in the serial number, standing for the model.

From 1970 to 1976 serial numbers began with 0001.

Serial numbers from 1979 to 1976 are as follows:

1970	70B—	1972	72B—·	1974	74B—
1971	71B—	1973	73B—	1975	75B—
				1976	76B

Model number for the the BL-22 Grade I is 126 and 226 for the Grade II.

For yearly serial number information please refer to the General Information section in the front of this book. Some early codes were reversed.

THE BAR 22

GENERAL INFORMATION

The BAR 22 was introduced in 1976 and discontinued in 1984. It was the first automatic Browning introduced since the 22 Automatic that was designed by John M. Browning over 60 years prior. "The gun a boy can own and a man can shoot": That's how Browning presented this gun in the catalogs. As direct competition for the tried and accepted 22 Auto, this gun was made to cater to someone that wanted a heavier more man-sized rifle.

This was not a boy's 22 but a full sized rifle that had all steel construction. The barrels were medium size as 22's go, and the dimensions were full size as well. It weighed in at 6 lbs 4 oz, about a pound less the many centerfire rifles.

BROWNING SEMI-AUTOMATIC RIMFIRE 22 RIFLE

If you're like most of us, you probably learned to shoot over the sights of a 22. And because of this, a 22 occupies a special place in your heart. No matter how old you are, you can still have fun with a 22.

Because it's a Browning, you know the BAR-22 is built to last a lifetime. But did you realize the BAR-22 is also built to fit a lifetime? This rifle has a robust weight of six pounds, four ounces and high powered rifle dimensions that contribute to a good steady hold. It has one of the huskiest barrel profiles you can find on a 22 sporter, which helps preserve accuracy. And it has the familiar receiver lines that have identified Browning square shooters since the turn of the century.

A boy can grow up with just about any 22, but a BAR-22 is the one 22 he'll never grow out of.

DEPENDABILITY

When you fire a BAR-22, the same gases that push the bullet out the barrel also push against the brass casing and the face of the bolt. The greater mass of the bolt prevents unlocking before the bullet

15 CARTRIDGE TUBULAR MAGAZINE

The BAR-22 has the kind of capacity you need for rabbit hunting, squirrel shooting or just plain woodlot plinking. Just push the button on the magazine latch, pull out the tube and drop in 15 Long Rifle cartridges. Return the tube (there are no slots and pins to line up as on most 22's), and you're ready for action.

LOCK OPEN BOLT

Draw the breech bolt fully rearward, and pushing the cocking handle inward. This locks the bolt open to facilitate safe handling, loading and cleaning.

SIMPLE TAKEDOWN FOR THOROUGH CLEANING

Just remove the takedown screw and cocking handle, and you can lift the receiver cover off the trigger group to expose the inner mechanism. Your BAR-22 is easy to keep in top working order.

PRECISION SIGHTS

Sight the BAR-22. The folding leaf rear sight adjusts vertically for elevation using

ACCURATE AUTOLOADER

The BAR-22's 20½ inch precision rifled barrel has a recessed muzzle to preserve accuracy over the years. The trigger has a deep contour for sure control. The mid-weight barrel profile, which gives you a heavier barrel than any other 22 sporter, makes a real contribution to accuracy. The stiffness of this barrel greatly minimizes barrel vibration while the bullet is traveling down the barrel. Further, the overall weight of the BAR-22 contributes to holding and aiming stability; there is more inertia than most other 22 rifles, lessening rifle movement before the bullet exits the barrel.

TWO GRADES

Choose your BAR-22 in Grade I with a blued receiver or in Grade II with small game scenes on a grey satin receiver.

BROWNING QUALITY WOOD AND METAL FINISHING

The receiver, barrel and most other exposed metal surfaces are blued. Stock and forearm are seasoned walnut with hand cut checkering to give you a good grip, then sealed and polished with a

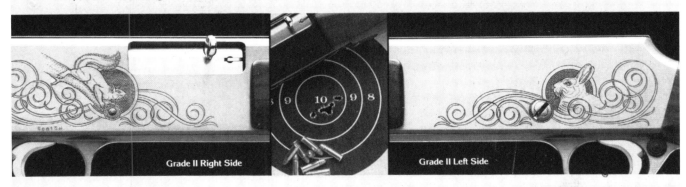

Grade II Right Side   Grade II Left Side

safely leaves the barrel, but enough energy has been applied to the bolt to give it the momentum needed to cycle the action. This blowback operation is one of the most dependable ways to operate a semi-automatic rimfire rifle. It's as dependable as the 22 LR ammunition it gets its power from.

two screws to lock your zero. Each calibration on the sight will move the strike of the bullet approximately 2 inches at 50 yards depending on your ammunition. The gold bead front sight shows up well under all daylight conditions. The rear sight is also designed to fold down when you slide a scope onto the grooved receiver or when you case your BAR-22.

CONVENIENT SAFETY

The Browning BAR-22 gives you a convenient cross bolt safety at the rear of the trigger guard. Both sides are grooved to assist positive shifting. In the off safe position a red warning band is visible.

durable, lasting finish. And the wood to metal fits are tight, to give you a dependable long lasting 22 rifle.

See page 59 for all 22 rifle specifications.

This is from the 1981 catalog.

GRADES

This model was introduced in only one grade. When Grade II came along in 1980, there were only cosmetic differences between them. They were both discontinued as of 1984.

GRADE I

This was the first grade introduced. It has no engraving and group 1-2 walnut checkered 18 lines per inch, all triggers were black anodized. Other features will be described under their sections.

GRADE II

The Grade II was introduced in 1980 and discontinued in 1984. This is the better grade that Browning always gave to the public that liked something a little better.

The etched engraving consisted of very light and broad scroll covering about 25% of the receiver on both sides. On the left side was the head and shoulder of a rabbit, and on the right was a squirral lying down on a tree limb. All receivers were greyed and the triggers were black anodized.

It had select grade wood, about group 2 and was checkered 18 lines per inch.

All other features will be described under their sections.

FRAMES

It was designed on the blowback principle like most other 22 automatics; the receivers were all blued unless otherwise noted. They were hammerless and featured a lock open bolt, which was an excellent feature when the owner cleaned or stored the gun for short periods of time. You pulled the bolt to the rear and pushed the cocking handle in to lock the bolt in the rearwood position. This facilitated cleaning, loading, and handling.

The takedown feature was also excellent; it dissambled by removing the takedown screw and cocking handle. You then lifted the barrel-receiver group off the trigger guard-butt stock group and split the rifle in half for easy packing. This also exposed the inner mechanism for cleaning or maintenance.

This rifle was made to handle 22 Long Rifle cartridges only. The actions were side ejection and had a cross bolt safety on the rear of the trigger guard. The receivers were grooved for a scope mount as well.

BARRELS

All barrels were 22 1/4" long, except in 1981-1982 when they were 20 1/2" long. All had a recessed muzzle. Barrel markings on the left side were:

BROWNING ARMS COMPANY
MORGAN,UTAH & MONTREAL P.Q.
MADE IN JAPAN

On the right side were the words:
BAR-CALIBER .22 LONG RIFLE ONLY

SIGHTS

Sights were dovetailed into the barrel and folded down. They were all adjustable for elevation but had to be tapped left or right within the dovetail for windage. All markings were painted white.

The front sights were dovetailed on a serrated ramp and had a gold bead. The sight radius was 16".

MAGAZINES

All had tubular magazines with a loading port under the barrel. They held 15 Long Rifle cartridges only.

The magazine tube latch allowed the shooter to secure it after loading without having to find a notch; it had the capability of being locked 360 degrees.

STOCKS

The pistol grip stocks were of French walnut and finished in the traditional Browning high gloss. Both grades were checkered and had the Browning marked black plastic butt plates. The dimensions were length of pull 13¾", drop at comb 1½" and drop at heel 2¼".

PRICES

I do not have the prices as introduced, but during some of the other years they cost as follows:

	Grade I	Grade II
1978	$209.95	$309.95
1979	199.95	
1980	179.95	

SERIAL NUMBERS AND MODEL CODES

For serial numbers please refer to the General Information section at the front of the book.

Model code for the BAR 22 was 146 for the Grade I and 246 for the Grade II.

THE A-BOLT 22 BOLT ACTION

GENERAL INFORMATION

This fine little rifle was introduced in 1986 and is still being made as of 1992.

I would say that it is really a man's 22 with its fully proportioned stock that is very similar to the A-bolt centerfire rifle. In fact, many of the parts used on the centerfire A-Bolt are also used on this model. Browning set out to produce an accurate gun on the same format as the Winchester discontinued and now Browning reintroduced Model 52, I think they have been successful. This is a beautiful little .22 that should satisfy anyone who likes a quality gun.

SPECIFICATIONS

Action — Bolt Action.

Bolt System — Short 60° bolt throw.

Barrel — 22" with recessed muzzle.

Safety — Top tang safety, thumb-operated with cocking indicator.

Magazine — Detachable. 22 LR and 22 WMR: 5 shot included. 22 LR: 15 shot available as an accessory.

Trigger — Gold-colored. Screw adjustable. Pre-set at approximately 4 pounds.

Wood and Metal Finish — Grade I Models: High gloss stock with polished blue metal finish. Gold Medallion: Polished blued with engraving on receiver flat and gold-filled inscription "Gold Medallion," high gloss stock.

Sights — Grade I available with or without open sights. Gold Medallion available without sights only. All Models: Grooved for 22 mount and drilled and tapped for 1" scope mounts. Open Sight Models: Ramp front and adjustable folding leaf rear.

Stock — Grade I Models: Cut checkering on select walnut classic style stock with rosewood grip cap and forearm tip. Gold Medallion: Classic style stock of high grade walnut, cut checkered with brass spacers between stock and recoil pad, grip and rosewood grip cap and between the fore-end and rosewood tip.

Stock Dimensions—Length of pull, 13 3/4". Drop at comb, 3/4". Drop at heel, 1 1/2".

Convenient, top tang thumb safety. The safety is located on the top tang. It's easy to see. Easy to feel. Easy to get to. Easy to work. For added safety, a cocking indicator is built into the bolt just under the bolt shroud. This tells you visually or with a touch, whether the rifle is cocked and ready to fire.

Model	Caliber	Barrel Length	Sight Radius	Overall Length	Average Weight
A-Bolt 22 Mag Gr. I w/o sights	22 WMR	22"	—	40 1/4"	5 lbs. 9 oz.
A-Bolt 22 Mag Gr. I w/sights	22 WMR	22"	17 5/8"	40 1/4"	5 lbs. 9 oz.
A-Bolt 22 Gold Medallion[1]	22 Long Rifle	22"	—	40 1/4"	5 lbs. 9 oz.
A-Bolt 22 Grade I	22 Long Rifle	22"	—	40 1/4"	5 lbs. 9 oz.
A-Bolt 22 Gr. I w/sights	22 Long Rifle	22"	17 5/8"	40 1/4"	5 lbs. 9 oz.

[1]No sight models only.

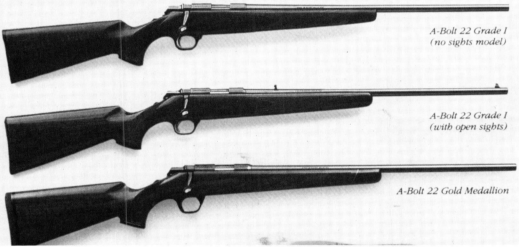

A-Bolt 22 Grade I
(no sights model)

A-Bolt 22 Grade I
(with open sights)

A-Bolt 22 Gold Medallion

A page out of the 1989 catalog shows the various grades and main features of the 22 A-Bolt.

Fast, 60° bolt rotation. The bolt cycles a round with only 60° of bolt rotation. This is more convenient and faster than a conventional 90° bolt lift. The bolt knob is human-engineered to be easily grasped by your fingers. The bolt knob is canted at a 30° angle so it fits naturally as you cycle the bolt. Because the bolt handle has a short lift you won't strike your knuckles on your scope.

GRADE I

When originally introduced in 1986, only the Grade I in 22 Long Rifle was available, it is still available as of 1992. There is no engraving on the Grade I.

The wood has always been pretty on this grade and only got prettier. When introduced they were checkered 18 lines per inch; however, they did not have a forearm tip or grip cap, and all butt plates were plastic. In 1987 the stock was changed to include a rosewood forearm tip and grip cap, and the butt plates are now rubber pads.

All other features will be discussed in their own section.

GOLD MEDALLION GRADE

In 1988 Browning introduced the Gold Medallion in 22 Long Rifle only. It is still being offered in 1992.

The metal finish is excellently polished to a high luster. All actions are engraved on each side with the words "Gold Medallion" gold filled.

It features high grade walnut of about group 2-3 and is checkered 22 lines per inch. An unusual touch are the brass spacers between the rubber butt pad and the stock, the rosewood grip cap and the grip, and the forearm tip and the rosewood forearm. All wood is finished in a high gloss polyurethane.

As of 1990 no gold medallions were available with open sights or in 22 Magnum.

FRAME

Basically, this is an all steel bolt action with many innovative features. The firing pin not only is used as a firing pin but also as a second extractor and ejector. The safety is located on the top tang and is quiet, a feature which means a lot when hunting wary game like squirrels. There is also a cocking indicator that lets you know by touch whether the rifle is cocked and ready for firing. This is a great thing to know when you are sitting in the dark and waiting for dawn and need to find out if you're ready.

The action features only a 60 degree bolt travel, 5 or 15 (Long Rifle only) shot box magazines, and an adjustable gold trigger.

All actions are drilled and tapped for full size scope mounts. As introduced the bolts were plain, but in 1987 Browning started fluting them. They said this was done to make the action smoother.

All actions are blued, the Gold Medallion has some minor acid etched scroll on the front and rear receiver rings with the words "Gold Medallion" gold filled.

STOCKS

Stocks are all full pistol grip and high luster finished. The combs are fluted with rosewood forearm tips and grip caps.

The stock dimensions have a length of pull 13 3/4'', drop at comb 3/4'' and drop at heel 1 1/2''.

BARRELS

The medium weight barrels are 22'' long with recessed polished muzzles; they are all blued.
The barrels are marked on the left side:
**BROWNING ARMS COMPANY
MORGAN, UTAH & MONTREAL P.Q.
MADE IN JAPAN**

On the right side are the words:
A-BOLT 22 CALIBER-22 L.R. ONLY

SIGHTS

Since its introduction in 1986, the Grade I 22 Long Rifle version was available with or without open sights, and as of 1992 this is still true. This is also true for the 22 Magnum as introduced in 1989.

The Gold Medallion has never been offered with open sights as of 1992.

CARTRIDGES

As introduced in 1986, only the 22 Long Rifle was offered, but since 1989 the Grade I has been offered in the 22 Magnum cartridge.

The Gold Medallion, as of 1992, is still available only in 22 Long Rifle.

MAGAZINES

Optional 15 shot magazine available. All A-Bolt 22s come with a 5 shot magazine standard. To increase your firepower, an optional 15 shot magazine is also available for .22 LR models. Inside the magazine, cartridges are staggered for efficient space use. The magazine drops into your free hand with a push on the magazine latch button. Both magazines can be fully disassembled for cleaning.

Since their introduction, only 5 and 15 round staggered magazines have been offered by Browning. They are detachable and can only feed 22 Long Rifle cartridges.

From 1986 to 1987 both were supplied with each rifle, but starting in 1988 only the 5 round came with the rifle and the 15 round became an extra cost option. Only 5 round magazines have been made for the 22 Magnum; they can be dissembled for cleaning.

SERIAL NUMBERS AND MODEL CODES

You can find all serial number codes for the year produced in the General Information section in the front of this book.

The model code for the Grade I is 136 and for the Gold Medallion it is G36.

MODEL 52

The Browning Model 52.

GENERAL INFORMATION

The Model 52 is the tenth gun in the series of reintroductions to be made by Browning. It was designed by Thomas C. Johnson, who, as you will remember, designed the Model 12. He also worked with John Browning on many designs within the Winchester organization.

This is what Philip B. Sharpe, who was one of the most respected gun writers in the country back in the 1950's, had to say about the Winchester Model 52: "In 1919 Winchester brought out their famous target rifle, which made smallbore match history." Later, he said, "The Winchester Model 52 was the absolute pioneer in this target field and it incorporated many novel ideas. The name Winchester 52 means about the finest thing in smallbore rifle shooting." Mr Sharpe was not known to deliver praise when it wasn't due and was famous for telling it like it was. Browning has certainly picked themselves a winner in choosing this great design to reproduce.

ACTION

This was an exact duplication of the Winchester 52C with only some minor changes for safety reasons. The "C" was the fourth in a series of five changes that progressed down to the 52D. These model changes noted various design changes but mostly pertained to the trigger, which was considered the best ever produced when the "C" came out.

It was a bolt action, all steel and blued with a detachable magazine. As of 1992, only one grade has been offered, so none have been engraved.

The triggers are the same as the original 52C; they are all blued. They adjust for pull and overtravel with two screws found just forward of the trigger guard.

The magazine release was on the right side of the stock directly under the bolt. Only five shot magazines were offered. The receivers were all drilled and tapped for scope mounts and a receiver sight.

The safeties were two position and mounted on the right side of the receiver.

All of this made up a beautiful rifle that proves great design and quality can stand the test of time.

On the left side of the receiver the word "BROWNING" is stamped and on the right is the word "SAFE."

BARRELS

These were all 24" long and chambered for 22 Long Rifle only. They are almost pencil size; all were blued and none had sights attached. The barrels were not drilled for a front sight, since Browning recommended a scope or sights from Lyman or you could purchase Burris made rings from Burris directly.

The markings on the barrels are as follows:
On the left side were the words:
BROWNING ARMS COMPANY
MORGAN, UTAH & MONTREAL P.Q.
MADE IN JAPAN

On the right side was written:
BROWNING MODEL 52
CALIBER 22 LONG RIFLE ONLY

STOCKS

This is what sets the gun off more then anything else and takes it out of the ordinary. The Franch walnut is about group 2-3, full pistol grip and 20 lines per inch checkered. The checkering very closely duplicates the original. The metal grip cap and rosewood forearm cap also adds to the stock. On the original Winchester gun, the grip cap was black plastic and had Winchester markings.

The finish is oil like, this closely duplicates the original, when the finish was oil. The butt plates are also like the original Winchester in that they are checkered in the center with a diamond shaped pattern around the screw holes. The edges are plain.

The stock dimensions are length of pull 13 5/8'',

drop at comb 1 3/8'', and drop at heel 2 5/16''.

I guess you can tell that the writer is a big fan of the Winchester Model 52 Deluxe Sporter, this will be a collector's gun in the very near future.

SERIAL NUMBERS

For year codes please refer to the General Information section at the front of this book.

Chapter Sixteen

Semi Automatic
Centerfire Pistols

The following five pages contain the original four page brochure and price list introducing Browning handguns.

MATCHED *Renaissance Engraved*
"THREE PISTOL SET"

Automatic Pistols

From the Hand of John M. Browning

Austerity of thought and conduct, and blunt mechanic fingers carved out these honest pistols.

Techniques difficult for the talented, and impossible for the ordinary, made these Browning pistols the finest of their class:

Design of Simplicity
Steels Matched to the Job
Machining and Hand Work of Perfection

These automatic pistols are made for the thoughtful person who chooses with discrimination; who knows and loves good guns; who takes pride in possessions.

Examine these pistols meticulously. Compare them leisurely for finish and fitting . . . for function through generations . . . for pride of possession . . .

BROWNING
9mm Parabellum
Automatic Pistol
ACTUAL SIZE
(Renaissance Engraved model illustrated on cover)

The Browning 9mm Parabellum is also known as the 9mm Browning Hi-Power. It is the last and perhaps the finest pistol designed by John M. Browning. The pistol was first designed as a military weapon and after meeting the severe requirements of military usage, was adopted by Belgium and other countries as the standard military side arm.

Among all pistols, sporting and military, the Browning 9mm Parabellum is noted for its remarkable accuracy and dependability. The gun's accuracy stems from its exceptionally rigid barrel mounting. The proven dependability evolves from its simplicity of design.

The Browning 9mm Parabellum has the unusually large magazine capacity of 13 cartridges; it is compact, of rugged construction but still light of weight—only two pounds. The full grip, which contains the double-row magazine is positioned to give the pistol excellent balance and pointing qualities.

In outward appearance it resembles former John M. Browning heavy duty automatic pistols; however there are notable improvements.

The front end of the slide is solid and accordingly provides firm mechanical support. Again, to provide superior accuracy additional grooves have been milled into the forward end of the frame effectively preventing side-play between the slide and the frame.

The design of this pistol incorporates a wide variety of safety features into a number of different parts, making it among the safest of modern firearms.

The firing mechanism includes an external hammer. The external hammer is invaluable as a safety measure, making it possible to tell at a glance or touch whether the pistol is cocked. The loaded pistol is perfectly safe to carry with the hammer down, because a blow on the lowered hammer cannot discharge the gun.

The hammer can be cocked with the thumb of the right hand. A half-cock notch is provided to catch the hammer should the thumb slip while cocking the pistol.

The trigger mechanism will not actuate the firing mechanism unless the breech is closed. Likewise, the trigger must be released after each shot before the next cartridge can be fired. Full automatic fire is impossible.

A magazine safety prevents firing when the magazine is removed, even though there is a cartridge in the chamber. This device also renders impossible the discharge of the pistol should the shooter keep the trigger depressed while inserting a loaded magazine.

Renaissance
Engraved Models

The automatic pistols shown on these pages are also available in Renaissance Engraved models, as illustrated on cover.

Hand Engraved
Lustrous Nickel Finish
Trigger Gold Plated
Grips of Nacrolac Pearl

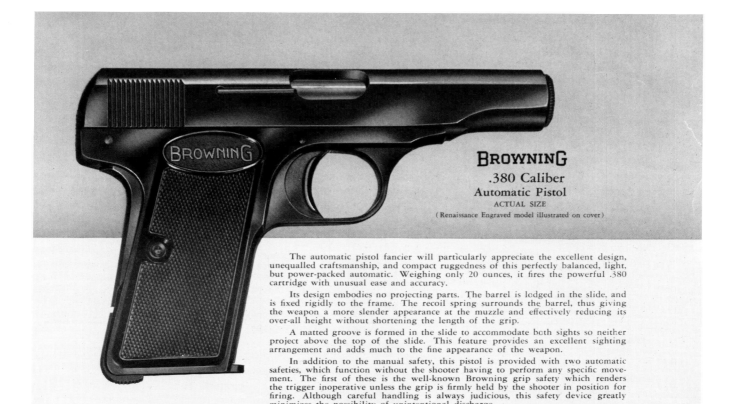

BROWNING
.380 Caliber
Automatic Pistol
ACTUAL SIZE
(Renaissance Engraved model illustrated on cover)

The automatic pistol fancier will particularly appreciate the excellent design, unequalled craftsmanship, and compact ruggedness of this perfectly balanced, light, but power-packed automatic. Weighing only 20 ounces, it fires the powerful .380 cartridge with unusual ease and accuracy.

Its design embodies no projecting parts. The barrel is lodged in the slide, and is fixed rigidly to the frame. The recoil spring surrounds the barrel, thus giving the weapon a more slender appearance at the muzzle and effectively reducing its over-all height without shortening the length of the grip.

A matted groove is formed in the slide to accommodate both sights so neither project above the top of the slide. This feature provides an excellent sighting arrangement and adds much to the fine appearance of the weapon.

In addition to the manual safety, this pistol is provided with two automatic safeties, which function without the shooter having to perform any specific movement. The first of these is the well-known Browning grip safety which renders the trigger inoperative unless the grip is firmly held by the shooter in position for firing. Although careful handling is always judicious, this safety device greatly minimizes the possibility of unintentional discharge.

The Browning magazine safety, as on the other Browning models, locks the entire firing mechanism when the magazine is removed, thus preventing unintentional discharge while the gun is being loaded, even though a cartridge still remains in the chamber.

Although the pistol will operate as rapidly as the trigger can be pulled, a positive disconnector incorporated into the firearm prevents firing until the action is completely and safely closed.

BROWNING
.25 Caliber
Automatic Pistols
ACTUAL SIZE

Standard Model
(Renaissance Engraved model illustrated on cover)

Popular demand instigated the development of these unusually compact .25 caliber automatic pistols. Although much smaller than other Browning automatics, the same basic principles of operation have been adopted. They are of the same sturdy construction and contain the same simplified, dependable action.

For serving the many purposes of its miniature design, they provide the perfect compromise between size and utility. The Standard model weighs only 9 7/10 ounces, the Lightweight only 7¾ ounces, with an over-all length of only 4 inches. Both are remarkably accurate, most adequately powerful for any emergency, and assure the same incomparable regularity of performance common to all Browning automatics.

The .25 caliber Browning carries the manual safety conveniently positioned to the thumb, and has the desirable magazine safety present on larger Browning automatics. When the magazine is removed, even though there is a cartridge in the chamber, the gun cannot be fired. It is not possible to insert the magazine while pressure is being exerted against the trigger.

A cocking indicator projects from the rear face of the pistol when the gun is cocked, thus enabling the user to determine at once, even in darkness, whether the pistol is ready to fire.

Double recoil springs insure consistent and lasting performance.

Lightweight Model

Satin-Silvery Finish
Grips of Nacrolac Pearl
Gold Plated Trigger
Anodized Alloy Frame
Other Surfaces Chrome Plated

54

Specifications

BROWNING AUTOMATIC PISTOLS

PISTOL:	9mm PARABELLUM	.380 CALIBER	Standard .25 CALIBER	Lightweight .25 CALIBER
Caliber	9mm Parabellum	.380 Caliber	.25 Caliber	.25 Caliber
Capacity of Magazine	13 Cartridges	6 Cartridges	6 Cartridges	6 Cartridges
Over-all Length	7¾ inches	6 inches	4 inches	4 inches
Length of Barrel	4 21/32 inches	3 7/16 inches	2 inches	2 inches
Height of Pistol	5 inches	3⅞ inches	2¾ inches	2¾ inches
Width of Pistol	1 13/32 inches	1 inch	¾ inch	¾ inch
No. of Rifling Grooves	6 Grooves	6 Grooves	6 Grooves	6 Grooves
Twist of Rifling	Right Hand	Right Hand	Right Hand	Right Hand
Weight of Pistol (Empty Magazine)	2 Pounds	20 Ounces	9 7/10 Ounces	7¾ Ounces
Grips	Hand-Checkered French Walnut	Checkered Hard Rubber	Checkered Hard Rubber	Nacrolac Pearl
Sights	Fixed Front, Windage Adjustment Rear	Recessed	Recessed	Recessed
CARTRIDGE:				
Weight of Bullet	115 Grains / 124 Grains	95 Grains	50 Grains	50 Grains
Muzzle Velocity	1,150 ft./sec.	970 ft./sec.	820 ft./sec.	820 ft./sec.
Muzzle Energy	365 ft. lbs.	199 ft. lbs.	75 ft. lbs.	75 ft. lbs.
Penetration	10*	5.5*	3*	3*
Name of U.S. Ammunition	9mm Parabellum / 9mm Luger	.380 Caliber Automatic	.25 Caliber Automatic	.25 Caliber Automatic

*Number of ⅞" Pine Boards at 15 ft.

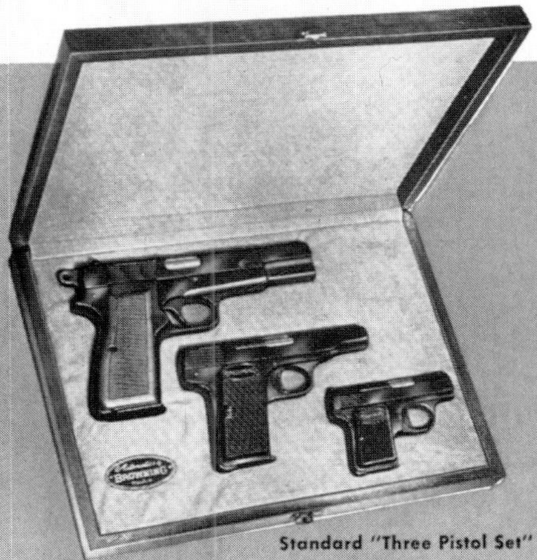

Standard "Three Pistol Set"

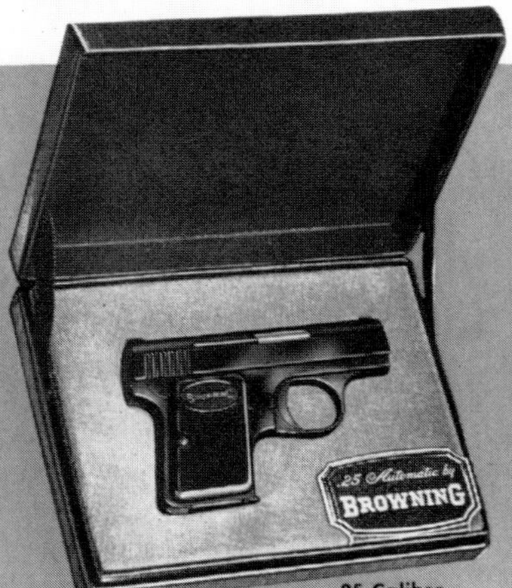

.25 Caliber

Browning Automatic Pistols Are Presented In Handsome Fitted Cases

STANDARD MODELS

Individual Standard Models come in black cases, red velvet-lined, fitted to each pistol.

LIGHTWEIGHT MODEL

Individual Lightweight Models come in black cases, red velvet-lined, fitted to each gun.

ENGRAVED MODELS

The Renaissance Engraved Models come in luxurious blue velvet presentation cases, intended to be permanent companions to the pistols.

CASED SETS

All "Three-Pistol Sets" are recessed in specially designed, beautifully hand-finished Walnut cases with red velvet lining.

BROWNING ARMS CO.

St. Louis 3, Mo.

Made in Belgium

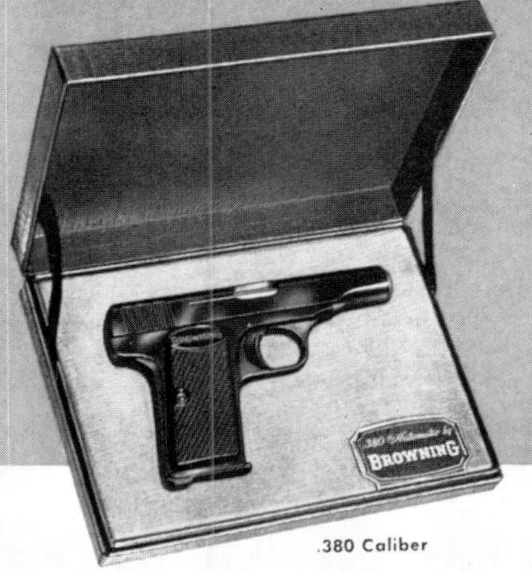

.380 Caliber

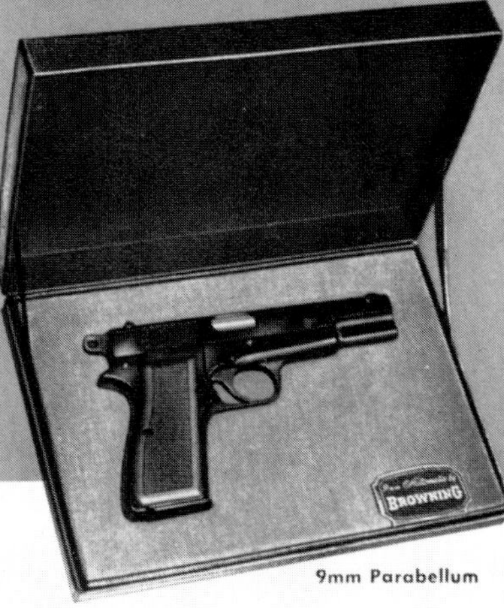

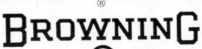

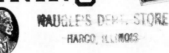

9mm Parabellum

® BROWNING

BROWNING

RETAIL PRICE LIST
Belgian Made Browning Automatic Pistols

MARCH, 1954

Standard Models:

.25 Caliber Browning Automatic..$ 29.95

.380 Caliber Browning Automatic.. 44.50

9mm Parabellum Browning Automatic........................... 74.50

Cased Set—One of Each Pistol................................. 148.95

Individual models come in black cases, red velvet-lined,
fitted to each pistol.

Renaissance Engraved Models:

.25 Caliber Browning Automatic..$ 75.00

.380 Caliber Browning Automatic.. 115.00

9mm Parabellum Browning Automatic........................... 200.00

Cased Set—One of Each Pistol................................. 390.00

The Renaissance Engraved Models come in luxurious blue velvet presentation cases, intended to be permanent companions to the pistols.

All Cased Three-Pistol Sets are recessed in specially designed, beautifully hand-finished Walnut cases with red or blue velvet lining.

Prices Subject to Change Without Notice.

PARTS PRICE LIST

BROWNING AUTOMATIC PISTOLS

9MM PARABELLUM

Part No.	Part	Retail Price	Part No.	Part	Retail Price
2	Barrel	$11.50	30	Magazine Latch	$ 2.00
3	Slide w/Front Sight & Slide Ring	22.00	31	Magazine Latch Spring	.25
7	Rear Sight	1.00	32	Magazine Latch Spring Guide	.50
13	Recoil Spring Guide w/Assembled Guide Cap and Slide, Stop Retaining Ball and Spring	3.00	33	Sear	1.75
			34	Sear Pin	.25
17	Recoil Spring	.25	35	Sear Spring w/Button	.75
18	Firing Pin	1.00	36	Hammer	3.00
19	Firing Pin Spring	.25	37	Hammer Strut Pin	.25
20	Firing Pin Retaining Plate	1.00	38	Hammer Strut w/Assembled Mainspring, Mainspring Support Pin	2.00
21	Extractor	1.50	42	Ejector	1.00
22	Sear Lever	.75	43	Safety w/Assembled Spring Follower, Spring and Pin	3.00
23	Sear Lever Pivot	1.50	47	Right Hand Grip	1.25
24	Slide Stop	3.00	48	Left Hand Grip	1.25
25	Trigger	2.50	49	Grip Screws (2 Parts)	.50
26	Trigger Lever	1.75	50	Complete Magazine	6.50
27	Trigger Pin	.25	55	Magazine Safety	1.00
28	Trigger Spring and Magazine Lever Pins (2 Parts)	.50	56	Magazine Safety Spring	.25
29	Trigger Spring	.50			

.380 CALIBER

Part No.	Part	Retail Price	Part No.	Part	Retail Price
2	Barrel	$ 7.50	20	Slide Ring	$ 1.50
3	Slide	9.00	21	Left Grip Plate	1.25
4	Extractor	1.00	22	Right Grip Plate	1.25
6	Extractor Pin	.25	22A	Grip Plate Threaded Escutcheon	.25
7	Firing Pin	1.00	22B	Grip Plate Escutcheon	.25
8	Firing Pin Spring	.25	23	Grip Plate Screw	.25
9	Firing Pin Spring Guide	.25	24	Complete Magazine	3.50
10	Trigger	2.50	25	Safety	2.00
11	Trigger Pin	.25	26	Safety Spring	.25
12	Connector	2.50	27	Magazine Safety	1.50
13	Sear	2.50	28	Magazine Safety Spring, Extractor Spring (2 parts assembled)	.50
15	Grip Safety	3.00	29	Sear—Magazine Safety—Grip Safety Pins (3 parts assembled)	.50
17	Sear Spring	.75			
18	Magazine Latch	1.50			
19	Recoil Spring	.25			

.25 CALIBER AUTOMATIC

Part No.	Part	Retail Price	Part No.	Part	Retail Price
2	Slide	$ 7.50	17	Sear	$ 1.25
3	Barrel	4.50	18	Sear Pin	.25
4	Recoil Spring Guide	.25	19	Sear Spring	.50
5	Recoil Spring Washer	.25	20	Magazine Safety	.75
6	Recoil Spring Pin	.25	21	Magazine Latch	1.00
7	Inner Recoil Spring	.25	22	Magazine Latch Spring	.50
8	Outer Recoil Spring	.25	23	Magazine Latch Pin	.25
9	Firing Pin	1.00	24	Extractor	1.00
10	Cocking Indicator with Assembled Spring and Bushing	.50	25	Extractor Pin	.25
			26	Extractor Spring	.25
11	Firing Pin Spring	.50	27	Complete Magazine	2.50
13	Connector	1.75	30	Left Grip Plate	.75
14	Trigger	1.25	31	Right Grip Plate	.75
15	Trigger Spring	.25	32	Grip Plate Screw	.25
16	Safety	1.50	33	Grip Plate Threaded Escutcheon	.25

(Subject to change without notice.)

25 AUTOMATIC PISTOL

Shown here is a special order "Baby" 25 Automatic. All non standard engraving is by special order only. This little jewel also has plain ivory grips.

GENERAL INFORMATION

We will go a little further on this then most of the other models since this little gun is of such great historical value in the study of Browning guns.

Patented in 1905 by John M. Browning, the original version of this gun was one of the guns that put F.N. and Liege Belgium back to work. It was first known as the Vest Pocket model.

The introduction and acceptance by the public was nothing short of phenomenal for the period. By 1909, 100,000 were produced, and by 1915, 500,000 were already made. By 1935, F.N. was putting out 40,000 a year, and production reached 1,080,408 by 1940. Since its inception, there have been over 130 variations of this and its successor, the F.N. "BABY".

The result of this production was a complete turn around for the economy of Liege. This city of gun making for so many centuries never had anything of this sort ever happen. John M. was considered the man that saved the city from ruin. Men and women who saw him on the street would stop and curtsey or bow in respect. He was recognized by the authorities as a hero and was given the Medal Of Leopold by the King Of Belgium, as well as receiving other awards. You can read further about this in *The History Of Browning Firearms* from 1831.

The main feature of this little gun was that the recoil spring was aligned by a short stud, which was held by the frame. When the slide is all the way back, both the stud and barrel extend from the front of the slide. As described in the Model 1955 section, this gun has three safeties: the grip safety, the thumb safety, and — later in production — the magazine safety. All this made for a very tiny pistol that could

be concelled very easily. There are no protrusions such as hammers or sights that could catch on a pocket or holster.

The Vest Pocket model was redesigned in 1930 by Dieudonne Saive of F.N.. This new model that is so famous was called the "Baby," since all of these were marked "Baby" on the grips. Production started in 1932, and this model immediately became a very popular little gun. The war stopped production for the civilian market, but by the late 40's F.N. was again producing 43,000 per year.

The guns we will be discussing were first introduced into this country in 1954 in three versions: the Standard, the Lightweight, and the Renaissance.

It may sound amazing now, but the original cost for the blued version was $29.95. This was the Standard weight version.

.25 CALIBER

Popular demand prompted the design of this unusually compact .25 caliber automatic pistol. Although much smaller than other Browning automatics, the same basic principles of operation have been adopted. It is of the same sturdy construction and contains the same simplified, dependable action.

The Standard model is all steel, richly blued. The Lightweight model comes with a highly polished chrome plated slide, lightweight metal alloy frame in a durable satin gray anodized finish, sparkling pearl type grips and gold plated trigger.

PERFECT COMPROMISE — To serve the many purposes of a miniature design, it provides the perfect compromise between size and utility. The Standard model weighs only 9 7/10 ounces, the Lightweight model only 7¾ ounces. Its over-all length is just 4 inches.

The .25 caliber Browning carries the manual safety conveniently positioned to the thumb, and has the desirable magazine safety present on larger Browning automatics. When the magazine is removed, even though there is a cartridge in the chamber, the gun cannot be fired.

This extremely lightweight, compact and adequately powerful little automatic serves many needs. It is ideal for self-protection at home or when traveling; for smaller animals, snakes or intruders while on camping trips; as an auxiliary weapon for law enforcement officers.

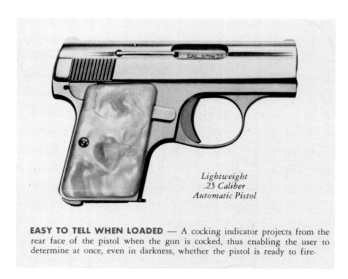

Lightweight .25 Caliber Automatic Pistol

EASY TO TELL WHEN LOADED — A cocking indicator projects from the rear face of the pistol when the gun is cocked, thus enabling the user to determine at once, even in darkness, whether the pistol is ready to fire.

This 1964 catalog illustration and text shows the lightweight model with Nacrolac Pearl grips.

Also introduced in March of 1954 was the Lightweight model, which also sold for the astronomical price of $39.50. It was advertised as having a satin silver finish on a polished alloy frame. The slide and all other parts on the Lightweight model was also chrome plated, and it had grips of "Nacrolac Pearl" and a gold plated trigger.

They are marked on the left side of the slide from 1954 to 1963 as follows:

**BROWNING ARMS COMPANY
ST LOUIS MISSOURI
MADE IN BELGIUM**

Renaissance guns were marked:

**BROWNING ARMS COMPANY
MADE IN BELGIUM**

We have found none of these marked with the Montreal address, probably because of the restrictions in that so-called free country.

Slide marking after 1963 are:

**BROWNING ARMS COMPANY
MADE IN BELGIUM**

Almost all guns shipped into this country are marked "BROWNING" on the grips.

Remember, it is not a true "BABY" model unless it says BABY on the top of the black plastic grips. The 25 Automatic was discontinued in this country because of the 1968 Gun Control And Anti-Honest Citizens Act.

In 1979 the Baby was still being produced by F.N., by this time total production was 493,200 pieces. After 1979, production was by their subsidiary in France "Manufacture d'Armes de Bayonne," (MAB). These guns are not marked, "Made in Belgium." The grips are marked either "Baby" or "Browning." The slide marking consists of only FABRIQUE NATIONALE on the left side. I am including this so that if you see one, you don't get them confused with the earlier guns shipped to this country prior to 1968.

Another late manufactured gun that was produced was the 1985 production of 1,000 Renaissance engraved and chrome plated guns. These have serial numbers beginning with 1/1000 and ending with 1000/1000. Again, do not get these confused with the earlier guns made prior to 1969.

As of 1983, F.N. had just about stopped making this model with a total production of 527,482.

The letter "S" under the serial number indicates the position of the safety lever — up for on and down for off.

Notice on the bottom right of this illustration you can see the letter "S" denoting the position of the safety.

SERIAL NUMBERS

YEAR	MADE	ENDING SERIAL NO.
1931	1096	1096
1932	6548	7644
1933	8489	16133
1934	6041	22174
1935	4652	26826
1936	6670	33496
1937	7032	40528
1938	5428	45956
1939	4178	50134
1940	13	50147
1940-1944	129	50276
	REQUISITION	
1945	0	50276
1946	6999	57275
1947	19736	77011
1948	17221	94232
1949	7362	101594
1950	5375	106969
1951	2578	109547
1952	718	110265
1953	7343	117608
1954	12508	130116
1955	11933	142049
1956	13614	155663
1957	15322	170985
1958	15061	186046
1959	18435	204481
1960	20516	22497
1961	21994	246991
1962	20870	267861
1963	19796	287657
1964	17232	304889
1965	30247	335136
1966	35938	371074
1967	42797	413871

YEAR	MADE	ENDING SERIAL NO.
1968	42588	456459
1969	1957	465416
1970	4106	469522
1971	4183	473705
1972	4260	477965
1973	2562	480527
1974	2879	483406
1975	642	484048
1976	1470	485518
1977	848	486366
1978	6637	493003
1979	2022	495025
1980	7863	502888
1981	2293	505181
1982	11151	516332*
1983	11150	527482*

*Estimate

	Standard	Lightweight
Caliber	25 Caliber	25 Caliber
Capacity of Mag	6	6
Overall Length	4"	4"
Length of Barrel	2"	2"
Height of Pistol	2 3/4"	2 3/4"
Width of Pistol	3/4"	3/4"
No.Rifling Grooves	6	
Twist of Rifling	Right Hand	
Weight(Empty)	9 7/10 oz	9 7/10 oz
Grips	Checkered Hard Rubber	Nacrolac Pearl
Sights	Recessed	Recessed
CARTRIDGE	- 25 A.C.P.	
Weight of Bullet	50 grains	50 grains
Muzzle Velocity	820 ft/sec	820 ft/sec
Muzzle energy	75 lbs.	75 ft. lbs
Penetration	3*	3*
U.S. Ammunition	25 Caliber Automatic	25 Caliber Automatic

*Number of 7/8" pine boards at 15 ft.

MODEL 1955 AUTOMATIC PISTOL

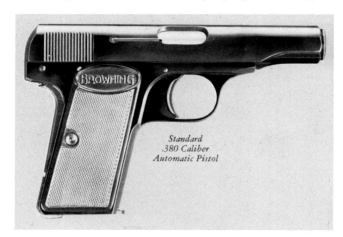

Standard
380 Caliber
Automatic Pistol

GENERAL INFORMATION

This model was first introduced in the U.S. under the Browning name in 1954. It was unfortunately discontinued in 1968 because of the National Gun Control Act. It is a shame that our glorious politicians fall for such nonsense and stop the import of such a nice handgun that had been made by F.N. for over 80 years.

This was originally the Model 10 invented by John Browning in 1910 and sold to Fabrique Nationale to replace the Model 1900, which had sold over 724,450 by that year. It was originally made in 7.65mm (.32 A.C.P.) and 9mm Short from 1912 to about 1922. In 1922 the eight shot 4 1/2 barreled model 1922 was designed; it was later modified into the Model 1955. In its original configuration, it was such a reliable and well made gun that several police departments in Europe adopted it as their official sidearm.

At first, they were offered only in 380 A.C.P., but in 1966 a 32 A.C.P. was also offered. I had one with two barrels, which I believe was a post production addition and not ordered from the factory that way.

This was an excellent gun to have for home protection, since there were three safeties. In addition to the manual safety, there was also a grip and magazine safety. A disconnect prevented discharge unless the breech was fully locked as in the larger frame pistols.

Originally, it had a 3" barrel, but the ones imported for the U.S. had 3 7/16" barrels. The overall length was 6", height 3 7/8", width 1", 6 groove rifling with a right hand twist; the total weight was 20 oz, and the magazine capacity was six rounds.

From 1954 to 1963 the markings are as follows: On the left side of the slide:

**BROWNING ARMS COMPANY
ST LOUIS MO
MADE IN BELGIUM**

From 1963 to the end of production for this country you will find them marked:

**BROWNING ARMS COMPANY
MADE IN BELGIUM**

The proof marks appear under these markings *(See proof mark seven on page 50.)* as well as an inspector's mark, i.e. "E", "P", "N" or other. The only marking on the right side of the slide is the serial number. The serial number will appear on the inside of the slide on the Renaissance. You will also find the serial number located directly under the ejection port. Also, on the right side of the trigger guard, you will find inspector's marks. On the barrels you will find directly over the chamber CAL 9m/m00 as well as proof mark nine *(See proof marks on page 50.)* Also, the serial number will be over the chamber, but hidden by the top of the slide. You will find this number only if you disassemble the gun.

On the left side of the frame, you will see proof mark seven *(See proof marks on page 50.)* and the same inspector's mark as stamped on the left side of the slide.

Throughout all production, the basic pistol came in a full blue finish, fixed sights and black plastic grips with "Browning" on the top of the grips.

RENAISSANCE

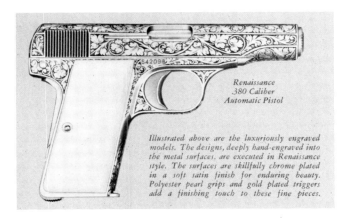

Renaissance
.380 Caliber
Automatic Pistol

Illustrated above are the luxuriously engraved models. The designs, deeply hand-engraved into the metal surfaces, are executed in Renaissance style. The surfaces are skillfully chrome plated in a soft satin finish for enduring beauty. Polyester pearl grips and gold plated triggers add a finishing touch to these fine pieces.

This beautiful Renaissance 380 is from the 1965 catalog.

Introduced in 1954 and discontinued in 1968, the early Renaissance models were nickel plated in a soft luster and later changed to chrome prior to 1966.

Engraving was fantastic, to say the least. All parts were covered with at least 95% engraving. The standard Renaissance style is scroll and leaves in a very appealing style. Triggers, barrels and sights were not engraved. You could also order the Renaissance engraved with greyed finish and checkered walnut grips, this would indeed be a rare find.

The standard grips for the Renaissance were made of Nacrolac pearl, which is a polyester material. All triggers were gold plated.

On Renaissance guns the left side of the slide is marked:

BROWNING ARMS COMPANY
MADE IN BELGIUM

Please note that "St Louis Mo" is not present and should help you in spotting an early fake.

As first introduced in 1954, the Renaissance guns were all shipped in recessed walnut, blue velvet lined presentation cases. Later guns were shipped in black leatherette pouches with red velvet lining. The cased sets came in recessed walnut cases lined with red velvet. Later sets are in leatherette covered cases, also velvet lined.

When purchasing a Renaissance set, 25 Auto, 380 Model 1955, and High Power all cased together, make sure all three guns were made the same year. These, unlike the blued sets, were put together by the factory. If they are not all the same year. There is a very good chance that the set was put together by someone else. Also check for variations to make sure they coincide with each other. The sets to get are the ones with High Powers that have tangent sights, though these are extremely rare. The next best sets are the early ones with nickel finish and then the ones with High Powers that have adjustable sights.

You could also order the Renaissance engraved with greyed finish and checkered walnut grips. I have seen several .32 A.C.P. chambered guns, and one collector has showed me a .320 Auto, probably made for the European market or a police department. It is a rarity in this country. Be careful not to buy one that was originally a 380 but had the barrel replaced to make it a 32 A.C.P.

From 1954 - 1964, poor records were kept as to the year of production. We have been able to obtain the data that follows, but remember, this is approximate until we can get more accurate information from Browning or F.N. We cannot find out the exact date any 1955 was manufactured. I would say from the research we have done that this data probably comes within two years of the correct date.

SERIAL NUMBERS

YEAR	BEGINNING SERIAL NO.	ENDING SERIAL NO.
1954	00001	45455
1955	45456	90912
1956	90912	136367
1957	136368	181823
1958	181824	227279
1959	227280	272735
1960	272735	318191
1961	318192	363647
1962	363648	409103
1963	409104	454559
1964	454560	499999

Better records from 1965 - 1968, the last years of production, are:

1965-500000-598804
1966-598805-603890
1967-603891-619474
1968-619475—-

AUTOMATIC PISTOL SPECIFICATIONS

PISTOL:	.22 CALIBER	9mm PARABELLUM	.380 CALIBER	.25 CALIBER
Capacity of Magazine	10 cartridges	13 cartridges	6 cartridges	6 cartridges
Over-all Length	8⅞ or 11⅛ inches	7¾ inches	6 inches	4 inches
Length of Barrel	4½ or 6¾ inches	4 21/32 inches	3 7/16 inches	2 inches
Height of Pistol	4⅞ inches①	5 inches	3⅞ inches	2¾ inches
Weight of Pistol (Empty)	26 ounces②	2 pounds	20 ounces	9 7/10 ounces④
Sights	③	Fixed Front, Lateral Adjustment Rear	Fixed and Recessed	Fixed
Name of Ammunition	.22 Long Rifle	9mm Parabellum / 9mm Luger	380 Caliber Automatic	.25 Caliber Automatic

GRIPS—*Nomad 22*: Wrap around; checkered; tough, durable Novadur plastic. *Challenger .22*: Select walnut; finely hand-checkered, full wrap around. *Medalist .22*: Special target type. Select walnut. Full wrap around with thumb rest. Scientifically contoured for the most sensitive control while firing. The special target type grips are also available for left handed shooters: *9mm Standard*: Hand-checkered walnut. *9mm Renaissance*: Polyester Pearl. *.380 Standard*: Checkered hard rubber. *.380 Renaissance*: Polyester Pearl. *.25 Standard*: Checkered hard rubber. *.25 Lightweight*: Polyester Pearl. *.25 Renaissance*: Polyester Pearl.

ALL BROWNING PISTOLS COME IN HANDSOME, FITTED CARRYING CASES

① *Nomad and Challenger* 4⅞ inches; *Medalist* 5 3/16 inches.
② *Nomad* 4½" barrel 26 oz.; *Challenger* 4½" barrel 35 oz.; *Medalist* 46 oz. (Variable weights extra). For 6¾" barrels on *Nomad* and *Challenger* add 3 oz.
③ Front — On *Nomad* and *Challenger*: ⅛" wide non-glare blade; On *Medalist*: removable blade. Rear — On *Nomad* and *Challenger*: Stationary, non-glare, screw adjustable for horizontal and vertical. On *Medalist*: Stationary, click adjustable, micrometer target type. Sight radius 9½".
④ *Lightweight* model weighs 7¾ oz.

MODEL 1971 AUTOMATIC PISTOL

This was a redesign of the Model 1955 to conform to the Gun Control Act of 1969. Here is a beautiful special order Model 1971.

GENERAL INFORMATION

This model was made to replace the Model 1955 that was a victim of the 1968 National Gun Control Act.

Some were imported as early as 1969, but the official introduction wasn't until 1971. This was a short lived little gun, for its demise occurred in 1975 when almost the entire line of Browning guns was changed.

It was basically the same gun but with several refinements: a 4 7/16'' barrel, adjustable sights, and thumb rest grips. The only caliber it was ever made in for the U.S. was 380 A.C.P.

The basic specifications were blue only with black plastic grips, overall length 7 1/16'', barrel length 4 7/16'', height 4 11/16'', weight 23 oz, sight radius 6'' and magazine capacity 6 rounds.

The markings are as follows on the left side of the slide:

BROWNING ARMS COMPANY
MORGAN UTAH & MONTREAL P.Q.
MADE IN BELGIUM

You will also find blued guns marked:
BROWNING ARMS COMPANY
MADE IN BELGIUM

The proof mark appears under these markings *(See proof mark seven on page 50.)* as well as an inspector's mark, i.e. "E", "P", "N" or other. The only marking on the right side of the slide is the serial number.

On Renaissance guns the left side of the slide is marked:

BROWNING ARMS COMPANY
MADE IN BELGIUM

The proof mark appears under these markings *(See proof mark seven on page 50.)* as well as an inspector's mark, i.e. "E", "P", "N" or other. The only marking on the right side of the slide is the serial number. The serial number will appear on the inside of the slide on the Renaissance.

The Renaissance variation was not introduced until 1972, one year after the blued version. Like all the engravings, it was excellent. All parts were covered with at least 95% engraving. The standard Renaissance style is scroll and leaves in a very appealing style. Triggers, barrels, and sights were not engraved.

The standard grips for the Renaissance were Nacrolac pearl, which is a polyester material. All triggers were gold plated and they were finished in chrome.

I might add that this variation has never become very popular with Browning collectors. The main reason, I believe, is that the romance of John M. Browning's original design is not there and the size of the Model 1971 takes away a lot of the concealability. In other words, an awful lot of the usefullness of the Model 1955 is gone.

SERIAL NUMBERS
AND MODEL CODES

The "N" designates the model. From 1971 to 1975 each year the serial numbers began with 0001. Serial numbers from 1971 to 1975 are as follows:

1971 71N—	1973 73N—	1975 75N—
1972 72N—	1974 73N—	

The model code was 325.

HIGH POWER PISTOL

This unique Renaissance style High Power has nine separate types of chimera or gargoyles. Engraved in 1950 by Jose Baerten. Please note the internal extractor and ring hammer.

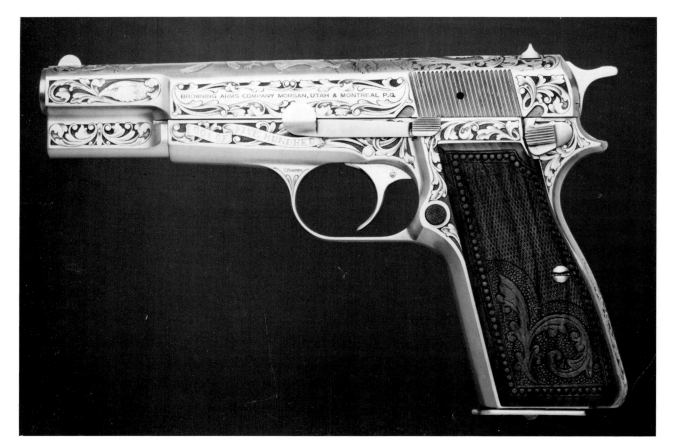

Another special order High Power that illustrates the outstanding work still available from Fabrique Nationale on special order.

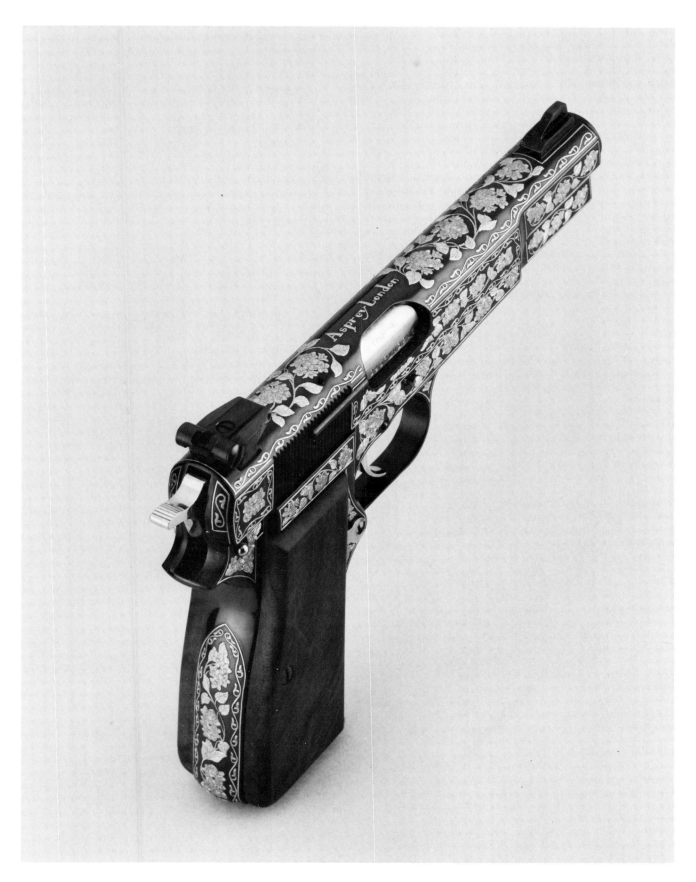

This special order High Power is part of a set, all engraved alike. The set consists of handguns, rifles, and shotguns. All are marked "Asprey London".

GENERAL INFORMATION

Boy, when it comes to sales, this is really a high powered design. It's the result of John M. Browning's desire to always produce the best, and he certainly did it here. Originally, it was designed as the French Model Grand Rendement of 1922 and redesigned in 1923.

After World War I, The French were interested in a 9mm 15 shot pistol and approached F.N. with the idea. Of course, F.N. went to John Browning, he did not think it was necessary to design a handgun with that much capacity. F.N., desiring to obtain a contract with the French Government, asked their designer Diendonne Joseph Saive to come up with something. He designed a magazine and adapted it to the Browning blowback Model 1903. This was then shown to Mr. Browning, who took the magazine to Utah.

In a few days, he and brother Ed, came up with two different designs. They eliminated the toggle link like the one on the 1911 that was expensive to build. Instead, they utilized a cam milled on the bottom of the barrel. Johns son, Val, took these to Colt. With the design of this cam action John Browning essentially had to his credit all basic lockup designs for handguns. The toggle link as in the Colt 45 Auto Model 1911 and the cam action as in the High Power are still the basic designs used in all handguns to this very day.

At this time, Colt was responsible for drawing and submitting all patent requests for the Browning brothers. Colt turned down the opportunity to produce these, so Val took the designs to F.N. This was eventually produced as the Browning Model 1922, which had a total capacity of 16 rounds. This model was also called the "Grand Rendement" and was the last pistol designed by Mr. Browning.

In 1928, after Mr. Browning's death and the patent rights for the 1911 takedown system lapsed, Mr. Saive, who was also the man who redesigned the 25 Auto, redesigned the Grand Rendement into what is presently the High Power. It was originally known as the Model 1928 and then further refined into the Model 1929.

After six more years, it was reintroduced as a new model, the 1935. It had the largest capacity for any handgun at that time, and pretty well has held that distinction ever since.

Variations for the pistols that we are interested in here are many. Those made by F.N. for export to other countries will not be covered here. I can recommend "The Browning. High Power Automatic Pistol" by Blake Stevens for a very comprehensive work on this gun from inception until 1984.

The High Power was introduced into this country in 1954 along with the other Browning designs, the 25 and 380 Autos. At that time, the Browning company was only selling the Superposed and the Auto-5, opening a whole new world for the company. In the years to come, many more rifles, shotguns and handguns have been imported by them.

COMMON CHARACTERISTICS
MARKINGS

Please be aware that finding a High Power that does not correspond with what you read below does not make your gun incorrect. Parts usage was not in the same exact order as produced, and you may find parts out of sequence several years.

I have seen High Powers with the following marking on the left side of the slide:

**FABRIQUE NATIONALE D'ARMES DE GUERRE
HERSTALL   BELGIQUE
BROWNING'S PATENT DEPOSE**

On the right side of the frame the only marking is the serial number. The barrels are marked with the serial number under the slide, 9mmP. and the normal proof marks.

These are guns that were shipped to this country in the beginning of handgun sales in the U.S. and are not marked with the First Variation markings. They have internal extractors. The example shown below is from the author's personal collection.

FIRST VARIATION
MARKINGS

On the left side of the slide were the words:
**BROWNING ARMS COMPANY ST LOUIS MO
MADE IN BELGIUM**

The proof mark appears under these markings *(See proof mark seven on page 50.)* as well as an inspectors mark i.e. "E", "P", "N", or other. The only marking on the right side of the slide is the serial number.

The barrels are also marked with proof marks and CAL 9/mmP along with the serial number, which is hidden. You will find this number only if you disassemble the gun. It will appear over the chamber hidden by the top of the slide.

On the left side of the frame, you will see proof mark number seven *(See proof marks on page 50.)* and the same inspector's mark as stamped on the left side of the slide. The right side of the frame appears the serial number only. You will also find an inspector's mark on the right front side of the trigger guard.

Serial numbers ran from 70,000 to 115,823. These are the most valuable guns in all configurations made at that time.

SECOND VARIATION MARKINGS

This marking change was commenced because in 1953 F.N. started commercial sales of the High Power in Canada. At that time the slide had the following markings on the left side:

BROWNING ARMS COMPANY
ST LOUIS MO & MONTREAL P.Q.
MADE IN BELGIUM

Under the word Montreal you will find proof mark seven *(See proof marks on page 50.)*

The barrels are also marked with proof marks and CAL 9/mmP along with the serial number, which is hidden. You will find this number only if you disassemble the gun. It will appear over the chamber hidden by the top of the slide.

On the left side of the frame, you will see proof mark seven *(See proof marks on page 50.)* and the same inspector's mark as stamped on the left side of the slide. On the right side of the frame appear the serial number only. You will also find an inspector's mark on the right front side of the trigger guard.

THIRD VARIATION MARKINGS

When the Browning Arms Company expanded into Canada in 1958 with F.N. as a partner on a 70-30% basis, the markings were changed as follows: On the left side of the slide you will find:

BROWNING ARMS COMPANY
MORGAN UTAH & MONTREAL P.Q.
MADE IN BELGIUM

The proof marks are now on the inside of the slide.

FOURTH VARIATION MARKINGS

This variation started in 1973 on the left side of the slide:

BROWNING ARMS COMPANY
MORGAN UTAH & MONTREAL P.Q.

On the right side of the slide you will find:
MADE IN BELGIUM
BY FABRIQUE NATIONALE HERSTAL

On the barrel, now exposed, you will find the serial number as well as inspector and proof marks.

FIFTH VARIATION MARKINGS

The last markings as of this date are as follows: On the left side of the slide:

BROWNING ARMS COMPANY
MORGAN UTAH & MONTREAL P.Q.

On the right side:
MADE IN BELGIUM
ASSEMBLED IN PORTUGAL

On the Barrel are the words:
CAL 9mm LUGER
SERIAL NUMBER
Proof mark nine *(See proof marks on page 50.)*
and inspectors marks

On the right side of the frame is the serial number.

On the magazine is:
ITALY CAL 9mm NATO/LUGER

This tells us that Beretta is now making the magazines for the late model High Powers.

PHYSICAL CHARACTERISTICS

The magazine capacity of 13 in the magazine and 14 with one in the chamber has been standard on all models imported into the U.S. In the 30 caliber Luger models shipped to other countries F.N. will supply 20-round magazines on special order. These have not been offered for sale in the U.S.

The overall length is 7 3/4" with a 4 21/32" barrel and a height of 5". The width of all single action models is 1 13/32". The rifling is 6 grooves in a right hand twist, and the weight empty is 2 lbs.

All have been chambered for the 9mm Parabellum cartridge except for 1,800 guns which were shipped here in about 1986 or 1987. This was part of a production run that was not taken by the purchaser after the guns were manufactured. Browning was asked by F.N. if they wanted them, and they accepted these guns only after one customer took the entire shipment. They were never really cataloged or marketed by Browning, so you will not see any advertising or such by them. Also, the High Power in 30 Luger is very popular in Europe, and some were brought back by servicemen. Browning has never cataloged a 30 Luger or any other caliber other then 9mm.

As introduced, the standard models were shipped in black leatherette cases lined in red velvet; these were later changed to pile lined. The cased sets came in recessed leatherette cases lined with red velvet.

I have listed the above because this pertains to all the models that follow unless otherwise noted. I didn't want to reiterate the same things over and over again and bore you with them.

INTERNAL/EXTERNAL EXTRACTORS

As originally imported into the U.S. in 1954, internal extractors and ring hammers were standard.

Starting in 1965 or 1966, right after the beginning of the "T" serial numbers, the external extractor and spur hammer guns started. These were also made without the finger groove on the right side of the slide. The "T" serial number gun with an internal extractor, ring hammer, and finger groove is a desireable variation.

GRIPS

Ivory and Pearl grips were available on special order throughout production but not ordered in large quantities.

TANGENT SIGHTED MODELS

These are the real collectors' items when it comes to High Powers. More collectors look for the tangent sighted guns then any other.

They were classified as military models by F.N. and designated with a TS for tangent sight without a slot or TS-S for the tangent sight with a slot. The product codes for these were 1305M for the plain and 1305SE for the slotted guns, SE standing for Special Edition. The slot is on the rear grip strap to facilitate the placement of a stock.

They were imported into this country from 1965 to 1978, so they will have either "T" serial numbers or the new codes after 1976.

We do know that on March 11, 1965, there was a shipment of 40 TS-S guns shipped to the Brass Rail Gun Shop in Hollywood, California. They were within the serial number range of T150901 to T150950. The same year 460 TS guns were also imported. Also, we know that distribution of the TS-S model did not resume until 1970 when only 6 were imported.

Sales reached a peak in 1968 with 2,447 sold, but they dropped off considerably after the passage of the 1968 Gun Control Act. By 1976 sales had risen to 1,305 guns, and by 1978 sales were about 7,100 TS guns and about 232 TS-S guns. No serial number records were kept of each model. All the TS-S guns were brought over on special order only. Please be careful when purchasing a slotted High Power; there are fakes. Remember, after you machine cut the slot, the gun has to be reblued.

You will find many variations of the slotted models with a tangent sight; don't be duped into buying one unless they have the proper U.S. markings as described above. F.N. produced variations of the High Power for police and military units from many countries. You will find these from time to time, for many were brought in by soldiers returning from overseas duty. This will also account for variations not cataloged or imported by Browning.

Most of these had black plastic grips but some were shipped with the checkered walnut grips. Also, Browning imported about four to five TS-S guns that were nickeled. How about that for your collection?

STANDARD OR POLISHED BLUE MODEL

All through High Power production the high polished blue model has been available. This was nothing more then the standard military gun with a high polish blue. F.N. really had little interest in producing a special sporting model. Military and police orders were going strong and they felt this was not necessary. However, after the Korean War, sales started to slip and they came out with this gun.

The standard model, as introduced in late 1954 to the U.S., had walnut grips checkered 18 line per inch with a high gloss finish. The use of these has continued through 1992. Some early guns were shipped with plastic grips. From 1985 to 1987 you had a choice between walnut or Pachmayr rubber in the adjustable sight version.

The fixed sight variation has been available throughout production. The rear sight is adjustable for windage only and the front is fixed. It sits on a ramp and is 1/8" wide with the rear surface serrated to prevent glare.

Throughout the years these all had fixed sights. A few guns with adjustable sights were imported in the early years, but they were not cataloged until

1971. The TS and TS-S models are covered in a separate section.

NICKEL MODEL

Nickel was introduced in 1980 and discontinued in 1985. Between 1981-1985 there were approximately 11,609 nickel plated High Powers made. All triggers were gold plated, and the grips were checkered walnut.

In 1974 F.N. unexpectedly shipped 100 High Powers in 9mm with nickel finish and Nacrolac grips. This is a real rarity, for they were a one time shipment and will have serial numbers in the 74C13xxx range. I know nothing else about these other than that they were not cataloged.

RENAISSANCE

Introduced in 1954 and discontinued in 1979, the early Renaissance models were nickel plated in a soft luster and later changed to Chrome prior to 1966.

Engraving was fantastic to say the least. All parts were covered with at least 95% engraving. The standard Renaissance style is scroll and leaves in a very appealing style. Hammers, triggers, barrels, and sights were not engraved.

The standard grips for the Renaissance were Nacrolac pearl, which is a polyester material. All triggers were gold plated.

The Renaissance guns were not made with adjustable sights until cataloged in 1975 but some were bought over on special order. One of the rarest is the tangeant slotted model.

On early Renaissance guns the left side of the slide is marked:

**BROWNING ARMS COMPANY
MADE IN BELGIUM**

Please note that St Louis Mo is not present. That should help you in spotting an early fake.

The above marking is followed by the third variation slide markings on later guns.

As first introduced in 1954, the Renaissance guns were all shipped in recessed walnut blue velvet lined presentation cases. Later guns were shipped in black leather pouches with natural lambskin lining. In the last year of production, they were again shipped in walnut presentation cases. The cased sets came in recessed walnut cases lined with red velvet. Later sets are in leatherette covered cases, also velvet lined.

When purchasing a Renaissance set — 25 Auto, 380 Auto, and High Power all cased together — make sure all three guns were made the same year. These, unlike the blued sets, were put together by the factory. If they are not all the same year, there is a very good chance that the set was put together by

someone else. Also check for variations to make sure they coincide with each other. The sets to get are the ones with High Powers with tangent sights; these are extremely rare. The next best sets are the early ones with nickel finish and then the ones with High Powers that have adjustable sights. There were none in 32 Automatic caliber as far as I know. When these were shipped, they came in individual pouches as described above with the presentation case. If you get a complete set as it came from F.N., you should get the pouches along with the case and booklets, etc. You have to be a collector that cuts hairs if the pouches or booklets keep you from purchasing a set, but they are nice to have if they are available. These were made from 1955 to 1968 when the enactment of the infamous 1968 Gun Control Act outlawed the 25 and 380 models.

LOUIS XVI

The Louis XVI style High Power was introduced in 1980 to replace the Renaissance hand engraving.

This model was introduced in 1980 and discontinued in 1983.

The greyed colored surface is covered with about a 95% acid etched leaf scroll design, not nearly what the quality of the Renaissance was. You can see by the short life of this model that public acceptance was not what Browning nor F.N. would have liked.

I cannot recommend this as an investment, for the interest by collectors is nil. Would you believe I have people who purchased these thinking they were Renaissance guns? Learn your stuff before laying down your money.

The grips were walnut checkered 26 lines per inch. Triggers were gold plated, and the gun could be purchased with either fixed or adjustable sights.

This model was shipped in a walnut finished presentation case throughout production.

CLASSIC AND GOLD CLASSIC

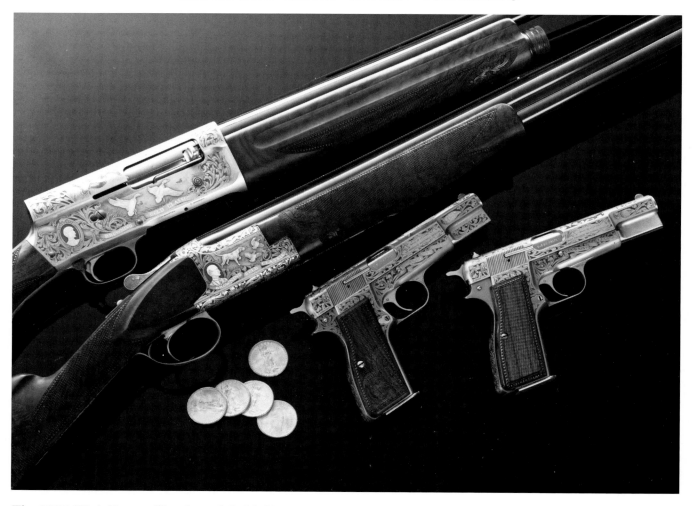

The 1985 High Power Classic and Gold Classic models were part of a three gun set. Here you see the Auto 5 and Superposed in Gold and both variations of the High Power.

These were designed in 1985 to commemorate the 50th anniversary of the genius of John M. Browning and on the 50th year of production for the High Power. Total production was limited to 5,000 of the Classic and 500 of the Gold Classic.

The entire surface of both models have hand engraved fleur-de-lis patterns, all exposed metal backgrounds are greyed. On the top of the slide is a scene of an American bald eagle fighting with a lynx to protect her brood. Also, there is a bust of John Browning. On the left side there is an eagle's head and a banner that says "ONE OF FIVE HUN-DRED" or "ONE OF FIVE THOUSAND." On the right side there is another eagle's head and a banner that says "BROWNING CLASSIC" or "BROWN-ING GOLD CLASSIC."

On the Gold Classic the portrait of John Browning, the eagle's head on both sides, and the banner lettering is inlaid in contrasting gold. Both models have 18 karat gold triggers and they are all signed by the engraver.

The walnut grips are very highly finished, and the checkering is surrounded by hand carved beads. Also, the Gold Classic has fleur-de-lis patterns carved on the bottom of each grip.

They were all sent in walnut presentation cases that are velvet lined.

Both of these were in the catalogs until 1988. At this time, I do not know how many were eventually sold.

SILVER CHROME MODEL

This model was introduced in 1982 and discontinued in 1984, only to be reintroduced in 1992.

The early versions are 100% chrome plated except for the hammer, sights, and minor parts. All have adjustable sights and Pachmayr rubber grips; the other features of the blued model are the same.

In the 1992 version, all are chrome plated except the sights, safety, hammer, extractor, and some pins. All have adjustable sights, ambidextrous safety, and rubber grips. All else is the same as the other models.

MATTE BLUE MODEL

From 1985 to 1986 Browning imported their High Power with a matte blue finish. The main features were fixed sights, Pachmayr grips, and single action.

DOUBLE ACTION

This model was available from 1985 to 1987.

They all were made with a matte blued finish, Pachmayr hard rubber grips, fixed sights, and a two-hand trigger guard. All other features were exactly the same as the other models other than the total width which was 1 1/2".

AMBIDEXTROUS SAFETY MODELS

This was designed to accommodate the left handed shooter or, I suppose, a person who has an injured right hand and has to use the gun with his left. It was introduced in 1987 and discontinued as a separate model in 1991. After this, all High Powers were changed, so that this feature was now on all of them.

The main features were fixed sights only and Pachmayr rubber grips.

HI-PRACTICAL MODEL

The 9mm HP Practical.

As introduced in 1991 the main features of this model are a chromed frame, ring hammer, trigger, ambidextrous safety, and minor parts. The slide is blued, as are the sights. Only Pachmayr rubber grips are supplied with a rubber magazine guard. All other features are the same as on the standard model except that the front sight is adjustable.

MARK III MODEL

This variation was introduced in 1991 and has fixed sights with Pachmayr rubber grips and a thumb rest. All other features are the same as the standard model.

SILVER CHROME MODEL

In 1992 Browning introduced yet another variation called the Silver Chrome model. All parts are chrome plated except the adjustable sights, hammer, ambidextrous safety, extractor, pins, and minor parts. The Pachmayr rubber grips have a Browning deer head medallion on both sides. The rubber magazine guard is also used; all other features of this model are the same as the standard model.

COMPETITION MODEL AND OTHER RARITIES

Always wanting to inform readers about strange guns they might run across, I am including information about the High Power Competition which was imported by Aeromarine of Birmingham, Alabama.

It was designed specifically for the target shooter. Acceptable accuracy was accomplished by lengthening the barrel to 6".

Other features are a matte blue finish, a new barrel bushing, barrel weights, a new tangent style rear sight, a new sear and hammer design, and a new magazine safety. The triggers have also been reworked to about 4 lbs. The rear sight is adjustable for both windage and elevation, and the grips are the Pachmayr rubber wrap around. F.N. says that they have been getting about 1 1/2" groups with these guns.

One of the innovative features of this gun is a spring in the top of the slide that exerts constant pressure on the barrel. The spring pressure assures that the barrel will be in the same position relative to the slide. This helps in maintaining the same point of impact.

Total shipments to this country are less then 300.

INTERAMERICAN SACTO CA

There are several firms importing High Powers besides the Browning Arms Company. These companies work with the F.N. Security Division and only service military and police agencies. They are not importing any arms for sporting purposes.

One of these is marked on the slide:
**FABRIQUE NATIONALE
INTERAMERICAN SACTO CA**

The barrel is marked Caliber 7mm. 65.

It is parkerized and not blued.

SERIAL NUMBERS AND MODEL CODES

Serial numbers for post-war guns shipped to this country are mixed with guns intended for shipment to other parts of the world. Therefore, the serial numbers you see here are valid for guns with F.N. slide markings as well as for U.S. marked guns.

The latest serial number codes consist of model code, year code, and the serial number. The codes number 215 and 1304M stand for a standard military High Power, and code 245 stands for the Sport Model. This began in 1977. The letters "C" and "T" also stand for the model.

From 1954 through 1958 years of production are estimated. After 1958 better records are available. These serial number are shown here. From 1971 to 1976 each years serial numbers began with 0001.

1954	70000	72250	1969	69C——
1955	72251	75000	1970	T258001 T261000
1956	75001	77250	There were some brought
1957	77251	80000	into this country with "T"
1958	80001	85267	serial numbers as high as
1959	85268	89687	3 6 4 , 2 8 0
1960	89688	93027	1970	70C——
1961	93028	109145	1971	71C——
1962	109146	113548	1972	72C——
1963	113349	115822	1973	73C——
1964	115823	T136568	1974	74C——
1965	T136569	T146372	1975	75C——
1966	T146373	T173285	1976	76C
1967	T173286	T213999	Some had the new style
1968	T214000	T258000	number codes
1969	T258001	T261000	1977	77C——

Since 1979 F.N. has adopted a four digit model number on all High Powers designed for sporting purposes.

The first digit is for the sight:
1 Fixed
2 Tangent (no longer available)
3 Sport adjustable
4 Competition

The second digit is for the engraving:
0 none
1 Renaissance hand engraved
2 Louis XVI photo etched

The third digit is for the grips:
0 Checkered black plastic with lanyard ring cut
1 Checkered black plastic with no lanyard ring cut
2 Pearlite
3 Standard checkered walnut
4 Fine checkered walnut
5 Pachmayr rubber

The fourth digit is for the finish:
0 Gold
1 Phosphate
2 Old silver
3 Standard blue
4 Sandblast blue(Matte)
5 Matte chrome
6 Nickel
7 Bright chrome
8 Black anodized for alloy frames

For year codes after 1976, please refer to the General Information section in the front of this book.

THE BDA 380, 9MM, 38 SUPER, AND 45 CALIBER PISTOLS

The BDA 380 Nickel.

GENERAL INFORMATION

With the termination of the Nomad, Challenger and Medalist pistols in 1975 and the earlier cancellation of the 25 and 380 Autos, Browning was left with nothing but the old reliable High Power and the Challanger II. To get back into the lucrative handgun market, they made arrangements with SIG-Arms, Inc. of Germany to produce four different guns: the BDA 380, 9mm, 38 Super, and the 45 A.C.P. These were also imported by other companies in a slightly different configuration and known as the SIG-Arms Model P220.

Production on the 38 Super, 9mm, and 45 A.C.P. began in 1976, but shipments didn't start until 1977. The 380 production started in 1978. They were outstanding guns, for the 9mm was the official sidearm of the Swiss military where they are known as the M75.

As we all know, John M. Browning originated the principles by which almost all modern handguns operate. These were no different, for they operated on the short recoil principle which was a mainstay of his thinking and design almost 100 years ago.

As they perhaps were ahead of their time, acceptance by the public was not good and they were cancelled, the 9mm in 1978 and the 45 in 1980. The 380 is still being made as of 1992. Some people are now collecting them, for production was slim. Browning has confirmed a total of 2,740 for the 9mm, 852 for the 38 Super, and 9,597 for the 45 Auto. I do not know the production on the 380 at this time.

Frames were alloy, and the slide and all other parts besides the grips were steel. For the 45 A.C.P., the magazine capacity was 7 rounds, overall length 8 1/16'', barrel length 4 1/4'', height 5 1/2'', weight 29 oz., and the sight radius was 6 1/4''. All grips were black plastic. The only sights available were fixed with a white dot and square notch. Talk about rare — there were only two nickeled 45 Autos produced; all the rest were blued. There were none offered engraved nor were there any variations in finish. Of course all were double action, the most appealing thing about them.

On the left side of the slide markings are the words:
**BROWNING ARMS CO
MORGAN, UTAH & MONTREAL P.Q.**

On the right side of the slide you will find:
**FABRIQUE NATIONALE HERSTAL
MADE IN W. GERMANY**

The BDA 380 Automatic was made in Italy by Beretta. Its magazine capacity was 12, overall length 6 3/4'', barrel length 3 13/16'', height 4 3/4'', weight 23 oz., and sight radius 4 15/16''. All grips were walnut with a Browning metal medallion inlaid. The only sights available were fixed, and there were none offered other then the plain blued until 1982 when a nickel plated version became available.

On the left side of the slide markings are the words:
**BROWNING ARMS CO
MORGAN, UTAH & MONTREAL P.Q.**

On the right side of the slide you will find:
**FABRIQUE NATIONALE HERSTAL
PB(In a circle)MADE IN ITALY**

As advertised, they were extremely safe and quick to shoot. All had a safety block that was built into the slide and prevented forward movement of the firing pin until the trigger was pulled. This meant you could safely carry the weapon with a round in the chamber and on half cock. To fire you only had to point and pull the trigger. Also, to lower a cocked hammer, you only had to press the decocking lever and it was lowered to half cock.

SERIAL NUMBERS AND MODEL CODES

All serial numbers are of the new type adopted in 1976. Even though they were not cataloged until 1977, you will see some with 1976 serial number codes.

The numbers ran separately for each caliber. All numbers started with 1000 at the beginning of the year, so if you have a pistol that is numbered 375RT1000, 345RT1000 or 395RT1000, you have the first one ever made beside the four samples sent to Browning.

Refer to the year codes in the General Information section at the front of this book.

The model codes are 375 for the .38 Super, 345 for the 9MM and 395 for the .45ACP.

BDM DOUBLE AUTOMATIC

The BDM is Browning's latest innovation and an excellent handgun.

GENERAL INFORMATION

BDM stands for Browning Double Mode. This innovative 9mm handgun was introduced at the 1991 Shot Show as a completely new innovation. It is still being made in 1992 in Salt Lake City, Utah, at Arms Technology, which is the same company that has been making the Buckmark 22 pistol.

The design was by the Czechoslovakian designer, Peter Sadoma, who travelled all over the shooting matches and law enforcement meetings to get as much input about all the features shooters wanted in a new gun.

The U.S. Secret Service was to get the first production in 1991 and the public thereafter. Production was held up because of many design changes. By the time these changes were made and the bugs were worked out, the contract, as of May 1992, had expired. We will know more about this in the future. I have no doubt that many police departments will be interested in the gun, for it has so many features and is so advanced that it stands head and shoulders above all others. The only pistol that can come remotely close to it is the Walther P88, which costs three times as much.

The basic feature of the gun is its capability of changing from double action on every shot to double action on the first shot and single action thereafter. This is accomplished by turning a screw adjustment with the extended magazine lip. In the double action mode when you lower the hammer, you have the advantage of a shorter trigger pull to fire the gun; when you chamber a round and every round thereafter, the hammer is lowered to the decocked position. This will to give you a consistent double action mechanism that increases accuracy for double action shooters.

The basis of the operation of this gun is as follows: The mode selector has two positions: "P" for pistol and "R" for revolver. When in the pistol mode, the actuator lever serves as a hammer drop. It will pull the sear out of engagement with the hammer if you pull it down while the hammer is cocked. This precocked position will shorten the trigger pull by .15" with the same amount of weight. When in the revolver mode, the selector presses down on the mode actuator as the slide closes which in turn presses down the sear and at the same time blocks the hammer from falling all the way down. Each time the weapon is fired, the hammer is stopped by the hammer block and is in the precocked position.

The overall look of the gun says that it means business. With its matted surface, black rubber grips, contoured surface and rounded sights that won't catch on anything, two hand trigger guard and removable front sight, it is a genuine combat handgun.

Browning loaded down the BDM with many features. Some of these are an ambidextrous safety, 15 round magazine, all steel frame and slide, slim proportions, windage adjustable rear sight, recurved trigger guard, no magazine safety, reversible magazine release for left or right handed shooters, firing pin safety, takedown lever, and a hammer block

safety. The grips are wrap around black rubber with the Browning logo and 18 lines per inch molded checkering. As far as looks are concerned, there isn't a "bright spot" on the whole gun, for even the logo is left plainly molded and not highlighted with a gold insert like other Browning guns. The basic idea is a combat handgun that won't stand out and be noticed too easily by anyone.

The takedown lever is very handy, for you don't have to pull it all the way out of the gun to remove the slide for cleaning; you only have to rotate it down 90 degrees clockwise. This is a great feature for two reasons. First, you won't lose it if you don't remove it; and second, when reassmbling you don't have to search for one or more holes to align the pin up with before it will go in properly. This is one more convenience when considering the problems some shooters have with models such as the 1911.

When the pistol is loaded, the cartridge can be seen in the chamber just above the extractor. It is difficult to feel, but when loaded, the extractor protrudes slightly, and you can feel it to see if there is a round loaded.

The proportions are 4.73" barrel length, 7.85" long, 1.34" wide, and 5.45" high. Even with its staggered magazine, the width of the gun is .1" thinner then the Glock 17. Folks with an average size hand will appreciate this even though it doesn't sound like much. The thumb rests molded into the grips do not protrude any further then the safety, a feature that shows extra care in its design.

The markings are as follows:
On the left side of the slide are the words:

BROWNING ARMS COMPANY
MORGAN,UTAH & MONTREAL P.Q.

On the barrel over the chamber you will find:
9MM LUGER

On the right side of the slide ahead of the chamber is written:

BDM 9MM LUGER
MADE IN U.S.A.

The BDM shoots all factory loads and is an innovative handgun that should sell well. We will see.

For serial number information please refer to the General Information section in the front of this book.

Chapter Seventeen

Semi Automatic
22 Rimfire Pistols

Medalist
.22 Automatic Pistol
Long Rifle Caliber

Nomad
.22 Automatic Pistol
Long Rifle Caliber

Challenger
.22 Automatic Pistol
Long Rifle Caliber

BROWNING. AUTOMATIC PISTOLS

The Browning name and automatic pistols have been synonymous since 1899. A Browning was the first ever produced in America, and most American models since are Browning inventions though many have appeared under other names. An indication of their broad recognition and acceptance is the fact that arms authorities generally agree that more pistols of Browning design have been manufactured throughout the world than the totals of all other automatic makes combined.

Three new models in .22 Long Rifle caliber now join the Browning line. They are fully representative of other Browning pistols in quality and performance and embrace the same functional simplicity so essential to dependability and long life. Throughout rigorous testing over a two year period, more rounds have been fired through these new models than most owners would fire in a lifetime.

The NOMAD

This model was named NOMAD because it is an ideal pistol for the person who likes to roam the fields and hills for all-round shooting pleasure. Its strong but lightweight alloy frame makes it pleasant to carry, and also shooting contributes to its fast shooting characteristics. Fine materials and workmanship throughout afford it the durability an outdoorsman expects.

The Nomad has the balance and feel of a target model and is capable of exacting performance. It possesses a wide, crisp trigger and a comfortable, hand-filling, wrap-around grip of strong Novadur plastic.

An unusually unique feature of the rear sight greatly enhances accuracy. The sight is independently fixed and does not move rearward and forward with the operating slide. It is precision, screw adjustable for both horizontal and vertical correction. Both the front and rear sights are scientifically contoured to prevent light reflection.

Another distinctive feature is the facility to quickly interchange barrels. Fitting is not required and just one retainer screw need be loosened. Thus the handier 4½ inch barrel can be used for general plinking sport and, when maximum accuracy is desired, quickly replaced with a 6¾ inch barrel. A new patented V-way-wedge locking system prevents the slightest instability or loosening of the barrel so accuracy is never affected.

A positive safety is positioned where the thumb naturally rests as the pistol is gripped. The ten round magazine with follower button adds ease and speed to the loading procedure.

The CHALLENGER

The Challenger offers additional features to those described for the Nomad which permits even more flexibility toward satisfying the preferences of the enthusiastic pistol fancier.

It possesses a heavier all steel frame which provides extra steadiness for precision shooting. Its select walnut wrap-around grip, finely hand-checkered and finished, provides the feel of a target model and a beauty none but a custom artisan could duplicate. A convenient stop-open latch which operates manually as well as automatically, after the last shot has been fired, permits easier loading and cleaning and supports handling safety.

Each owner can easily regulate trigger pull to his preference by a screw adjustment on the rear face of the frame, thereby conveniently reducing the weight of pull for the more meticulous type of target shooting and then, in seconds, increasing to a safer degree for general shooting.

The Challenger, as the Nomad, is offered with either a 4½ inch or 6¾ inch barrel and will also accept the Medalist barrel for the most precise shooting. Interchanging barrels takes mere seconds; no special fitting is required.

The fine steel portions of the Challenger are exquisitely hand-polished and blued to justly complement its carefully machined and hand-fitted mechanism. The wide, grooved trigger is gold plated.

The Challenger and Medalist are also offered in striking gold inlaid models, discreetly adorned in keeping with the character of a .22 caliber. The modern, straight line style of engraving produces a startling beauty against the rich blue-black body of the pistol.

35

1. Stationary rear sight on all models enhances accuracy. Rear sight completely adjustable — vertical and horizontal.

2. Stop open latch on Challenger and Medalist models.

3. Convenient thumb safety on all models.

Barrels quickly interchangeable without fitting. Just one retainer screw need be loosened.

Micrometer rear sight.

Dry fire mechanism on Medalist is integral with safety latch.

Trigger pull can be set by screw adjustment on Challenger and Medalist.

Hand-filling wrap-around grip. Specially contoured with thumb rest on Medalist.

Pages 386 and 387 are from the 1964 catalog showing variations of the Nomad, Challenger, and Medalist .22 rimfire pistols.

NOMAD 22 PISTOL

Being introduced in 1962 to 1963, the Nomad was the first of the 22 pistols.

A photo of the 4½" Nomad from an early catalog.

GENERAL INFORMATION

This model was based on the Medalist, which was designed by Bruce W. Browning in the fall of 1961. F.N. used its basic design to produce this simplified version.

The early frames were made of aluminum but changed to steel about 1966 between serial numbers 60091P6 and 64538P6. The balance of the parts were all steel except the grips. I was not able to pin the receiver composition change any closer then this so if you have a Nomad between these serial numbers it would be appreciated by the author if you would direct any additional information about this to me, it will be included in any future publications of this book.

Triggers were all blued and shipped pre-adjusted from F.N. with a 3 1/2 pound pull.

Magazine capacity for all Nomads were 10 rounds plus one in the chamber. Originally, the Nomad was introduced to be used as an economical 22 caliber handgun for plinking and small game hunting. The magazine capacity was more then enough to satisfy the needs of all shooters.

Two barrel lengths were made, 4 1/2" and 6 3/4" and fully interchangeable without fitting. Overall length with the 4 1/2" barrel was 8 7/8" and with the 6 3/4" barrel 11 1/8". I have never seen any other made, but it is possible a special order was accepted; this would be rare. The figures show about 27,966 4 1/2" and 34,113 6 3/4" guns were made for a total of 62,079 Nomads. The information I have suggests that about 218,137 were made in all three of the 22 models for world wide sales; please note that this is not U.S. sales only.

On the very early, 1962, guns you will sometimes find a very narrow groove cut into the side of the barrel flats. These grooves were originally intended to be used with scope mounts that were, as far as I know, never produced. In addition, these rare barrels may have been originally intended for use on the Challenger.

1966 CATALOG DESCRIPTION

"The Nomad was so named because it is the ideal pistol for the person who likes to roam the fields and hills for all-around shooting pleasure. Its strong but lightweight alloy frame makes it pleasant to carry and contributes to its fast shooting characteristics. Fine materials throughout afford it the durability an outdoorsman expects.

The Nomad has good balance and feel and is capable of exacting performance. It possesses a wide, crisp trigger and a comfortable, hand-filling, wrap-around grip of strong Novadur plastic. Its precision rear sight is screw adjustable for both horizontal and vertical correction. Both front and rear sights are scientifically contoured to prevent light reflection.

As with the Challenger, barrels are quickly interchangeable. A positive safety is positioned where the thumb naturally rests as the pistol is gripped. The ten round magazine with follower button adds ease and speed to the loading procedure."

Above is the description given to the Nomad in 1966 by Browning.

From 1 to 22,000 the markings on the left side are:

**BROWNING ARMS COMPANY
ST LOUIS MO & MONTREAL P.Q.**

Sometimes you will find a line under the "T" in St. Louis and no ".".in Mo.

On the right side you will find:
**MADE IN BELGIUM
22 LONG RIFLE**

After 22,000 the markings change on the left as follows:

BROWNING ARMS COMPANY

On the right side:
**MADE IN BELGIUM
22 LONG RIFLE**

In 1970 at about serial number 37,000 the markings changed as follows:
On the left side you will find:
**BROWNING ARMS COMPANY
MORGAN, UTAH & MONTREAL P.Q.
MADE IN BELGIUM**

On the right side:
CALIBER .22 LONG RIFLE
PATENT NO 3,150,458

Sights varied from the "high post" front sight until late 1968, when a ramp with the blade attached came into use. Rear sights were fully adjustable for both windage and elevation.

When introduced in 1962 Browning called the standard grips for the Nomad checkered Novadur plastic, they were black throughout production with "BROWNING" on each side at the top. Do not accept any Nomad with other then these grips and don't be fooled by someone who tries to sell you a Nomad with checkered walnit grips and calls it a Challanger.

The standard shipping policy was to send all Nomads in a hinged red and black plastic box or vinyl pouch; the pouch was used most often. There are three different pouch variations, one for each barrel length.

SERIAL NUMBERS AND MODEL CODES

The serial numbers of all the 22 models ran together and commingled. I do not, therefore, believe we will ever find out exactly how many of each model were made; but, as noted above, we do know approximately how many were produced.

The serial numbers on the very first gun shipped into this country were stamped on the bottom of the barrel instead of on the frame. After about the first one thousand or so, the numbers will always be found on the front grip strap.

From 1962 - 1968 the serial numbers ran continuously, but from 1969 until the end of U.S. sales the serial numbers started with 0001 each year. Serial numbers from 1962 to 1975, the end of production, are as follows:

Nomad

1962 --P 2	1965 --P 5	1968 ---P8	1971 ---P71
1963 --P 3	1966 --P 6	1969 ---P69 or P9	1972 ---P72
1964 --P 4	1967 --P 7	1970 ---P70	1973 ---P73

The "P" in the serial number denotes the Nomad model. Some year codes may be reversed.

CHALLENGER 22 PISTOL

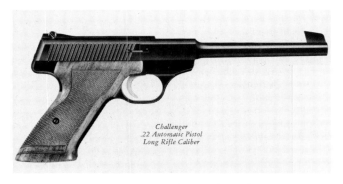

Another photo from an early catalog showing a 6¾"
Challenger.

GENERAL INFORMATION

As introduced in 1962 to 1963, the Challenger was based on the Medalist, which was designed by Bruce W. Browning in the fall of 1961. Some people will argue that this model was introduced in 1963, but according to Browning, it was 1962. You decide! Some of these were made as early as June, 1962, and will show their early production dates in the serial number. It was the second model 22 pistol that Browning brought into the U.S. This fine gun was discontinued in 1975 and replaced by the Challenger II.

The frame was the same as that used on the Nomad except that none had an aluminum receiver as far as I know.

The two barrel lengths made were 4 1/2" and 6 3/4". I have never seen any others, but it is possible a special order was accepted; this would be rare.

The information at hand suggests that about 218,137 were made in all three of the 22 models for world wide sales.

This breaks down as follows for all variations on the Challengers only:

4½"	21,070
6¾"	41,049
Gold 4½"	147
Gold 6¾"	146
Renaissance 4½"	121
Renaissance 6¾"	316

1966 CATALOG DESCRIPTION

"The Challenger offers many of the features described for the Medalist. It possesses an all steel frame for good steadiness in precision shooting and its select walnut wrap-around grip, finely hand-checkered, provides the feel and balance of a target model. A convenient stop-open latch which operates manually as well as automatically, after the last shot has been fired, permits easier loading and cleaning and supports handling safety.

The shooter can regulate trigger pull to his preference by a screw adjustment on the rear face of the frame, thereby conveniently reducing the weight of pull for target shooting, then, in seconds, increasing to a safer degree for general shooting.

The Challenger is offered with either 4½-inch or 6¾-inch barrels and will also accept the Medalist barrel. Barrels are interchangeable in mere seconds and no fitting is required. A patented V-way-wedge locking system prevents the slightest instability or loosening so accuracy is never affected. Its independently fixed rear sight does not move with the operating slide.

The steel portions of the Challenger are exquisitely hand-polished and blued to justly compliment its carefully machined and hand-fitted mechanism. The wide, grooved trigger is gold plated."

The Challenger description beginning on the previous page, and continued above, is also from the 1966 catalog.

On the very early 1962 guns, you will sometimes find a very narrow groove cut into the side of the barrel flats. These grooves were originally intended to be used with scope mounts that were, as far as I know, never produced. You will also find these on the Nomads, but they were originally intended for this model.

From 1 to 22,000 the marking on the left side are:
**BROWNING ARMS COMPANY
ST LOUIS Mo & MONTREAL P.Q.**

You will sometimes see a line under the "T" in St. Louis and no "." after Mo.

On the right side you will find:
**MADE IN BELGIUM
22 LONG RIFLE**

Sometime during the 1962 production the markings remained the same but the letters size is slightly smaller.

After about 22,000 the markings changed on the left as follows:
BROWNING ARMS COMPANY

On the right side:
**MADE IN BELGIUM
22 LONG RIFLE**

Rear sights were adjustable for windage and elevation and were positive. Front sights varied from the "high post" front sight until late 1968, when a ramp with the blade attached came into use.

The standard blue Challenger grips were walnut fully checkered 18 lines per inch and of a much fuller design then the Nomad. There were as many as four to five variations in the checkering designs with at least three different grip configurations. The early grips are the slimmest. Of course, the Gold Line and Renaissance grips are checkered as well as carved. From 1973 to 1975, there were some Challengers made in 1973 through 1975 with grips made of a brown mottled plastic material. These will also be found in at least two variations. It has been conveyed to me that the reason for this was that Browning was trying to hold down costs on this model. Some dealers complained at the time to

Browning and some of these grips were replaced free of charge with the more common wood grips. It would indeed be a nice variation to have one of these in any Challanger collection.

There were at least four different magazine variations, but they will all work in any given pistol. The magazine capacity was 10 in all models.

The overall length is 8 7/8" to 11 1/8" depending on the barrel length, the height is 4 7/8", and the weight empty is 26 oz.

The standard shipping policy was to send all Challengers in a hinged red and black plastic box or vinyl pouch; the pouch was used most often. There were five different pouch variations for each barrel length.

For all the 22 models, a total of about 218,137 were made for world wide sales, of which about 85,267 were Challengers.

GOLD LINE MODEL

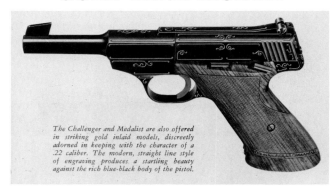

The Gold Line Challenger in the 1966 catalog.

The Gold Line Challengers were introduced in 1962, so it was the first of the high grade 22's made. They are the rarest of all, as only 147 were made in 4 1/2" and 146 in 6 3/4" and all were discontinued in 1974.

These are very difficult to find, for almost all are in collector's hands and are not put on the market very often. If you have a chance to purchase one at a decent price, do it.

All visible parts are richly blued and gold inlaid in the same manner as the Medalist. I know that this a very brief description, but how else can you describe it? The gold line is hand inlaid on both sides of the frame, down the barrel, and on the grip straps. In addition all of the triggers were gold plated.

The standard grips for the Gold Line were carved and checkered French walnut. The carving was a very nice fleur-de-lis pattern on the top 1/3, and the checkering on the bottom 2/3's was about 24 lines per inch. This was surrounded by carved beads and a high gloss finish. All were of outstanding quality.

RENAISSANCE

Introduced in 1970 and discontinued in 1975, all were chrome finished in a soft luster. The Renaissance models are very rare, for only 121 were made in the 4½" barrel length and 316 in the 6¾' length.

The engraving was fantastic to say the least. All parts were covered with at least 95% engraving. The standard Renaissance style is scroll and leaves in a very appealing style. Triggers, barrels beyond the flats, and sights were not engraved. All triggers were gold plated.

The standard grips for the Renaissance were carved and checkered French walnut. The carving was a very nice fleur-de-lis pattern on the top 1/3; the checkering on the bottom 2/3's was about 24 lines per inch. This was surrounded by carved beads and a high gloss finish, all of outstanding quality.

SERIAL NUMBERS AND MODEL CODES

The serial numbers of all three models of the 22's ran together and commingled. I do not, therefore, believe we will ever find out exactly how many of each model were made, but the figures above were taken from actual sales records and should be pretty close.

The Challengers had a "U" in their serial numbers for the model code. From 1962 - 1968, the serial numbers ran continuous from year to year. In 1969 to the end of U.S. sales, the serial numbers started with 0001 at the beginning of each year.

Serial numbers from 1962 - 1975, the end of production, are as follows:

Challenger

1962 —U 2	1967 —U 7	1972 —U72
1963 —U 3	1968 —U 8	1973 —U73
1964 —U 4	1969 —U69	1974 —U74
1965 —U 5	1970 —U70	1975 —U75
1966 —U 6	1971 —U71	some are reversed re: U47

CHALLENGER II AND III

The Micro Buck Mark Standard with 4 inch barrel.

CHALLENGER II
GENERAL INFORMATION

This model was introduced in 1976 after the termination of the original Challenger and was discontinued in 1982 after the introduction of the Challenger III. Like the original Challenger, this was also based on the Medalist action and frame as designed by Bruce W. Browning.

As far as I know, this was the first attempt by Browning to have a pistol produced in the U.S. Both the Challenger II and III were manufactured by Arms Technology based in Salt Lake City, Utah.

Browning advertised both a new wedge locking system which prevented the barrel from coming loose, they also had a recessed muzzle. All frames were steel and blued. There were no high grades produced, but all triggers were gold plated.

Grips were what Browning called "impregnated hardwood" with a metal Browning medallion inlaid on both sides; they were not checkered. Barrel length was

6¾", weight 38 oz., height 5¼", overall length 10⅞", and sight radius 9 ⅛"; the magazine capacity was 10 rounds of 22 Long Rifle only. Sights were fully adjustable for windage and elevation and were positive. They were mounted on a barrel rib, which was not attached to the slide. This makes for more consistent sight stability.

The markings on the left side of the barrel were:
BROWNING ARMS COMPANY
MORGAN, UTAH & MONTREAL P.Q. CANADA

On the right side were the words:
22 LONG RIFLE
CHALLENGER II
MADE IN U.S.A.

For year codes after 1972, please refer to General Information section in the front of this book.

CHALLENGER III

The Challenger III was introduced in 1982 and discontinued in 1990. It was touted as the target version of the Challenger II. The main features were an alloy frame made from 7075-T6 aircraft aluminum, which lightened the gun from 38 to 35 oz., improved sights, a bull flat sided barrel 5½" long, and adjustable trigger.

The markings on the left side of the barrel were:
BROWNING ARMS COMPANY
MORGAN,UTAH & MONTREAL P.Q. CANADA

On the right side you will find:
22 LONG RIFLE
CHALLENGER III
MADE IN U.S.A.

In 1983 a Sporter version was introduced, it is the same as above except the barrel is slimmer and 6¾" long.

The serial numbers appear on the front strap. They are all of the new type and can be found in the General Information section in the front of this book.

BROWNING® AUTOMATIC PISTOLS

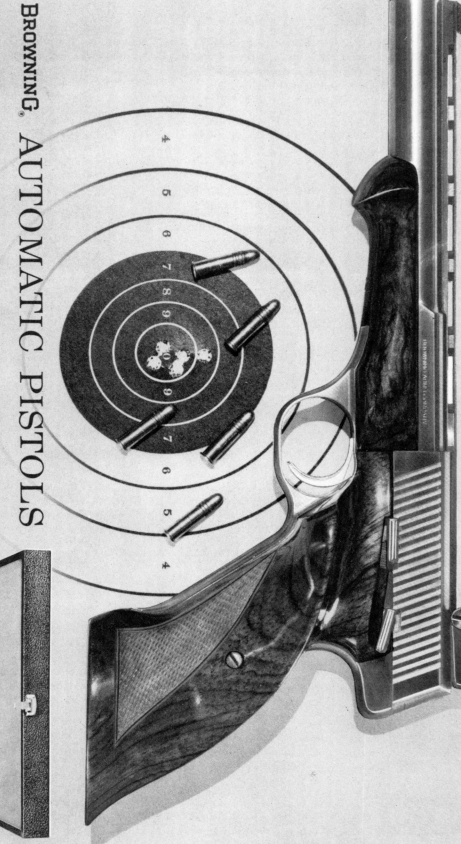

The Browning name and automatic pistols have been synonymous since 1899. A Browning was the first ever produced in America, and most American models since are Browning inventions though many have appeared under other names. An indication of their broad recognition and acceptance is the fact that more pistols of Browning design have been manufactured throughout the world than the totals of all other automatic makes combined.

Twelve different models are illustrated herein which range from the classic to richly hand-en-graved and gold inlaid designs. All, above any other consideration, are made for precision and dependability.

THE MEDALIST

The Medalist was designed for the serious competitor who demands faultless accuracy. Meticulous attention is accorded the fitting of every part to assure smooth, precision function.

Its fine walnut grip with thumb rest is scientifically contoured to permit the most sensitive control while firing. The medium heavy barrel with non-glare ventilated rib is proportioned for

(Continued from previous page.)

maximum steadiness and balance. A trim walnut forearm attaches to the barrel and is interchangeable with variable weights to permit further refinement in the amount of forward ballast.

Trigger pull is exceptionally clean and crisp and broadly and easily adjustable in weight of pull as well as backlash. The wide, gold plated finger piece is grooved and contoured for more precise, straight rearward pull. The recoil proof, micrometer rear sight is stationary, not moving rearward and forward with the operating slide and is click adjustable, both lateral and vertical. It remains in rigid alignment with a non-glare, removable front blade. Sight radius is a full 9½ inches.

An inimitable feature, especially appreciated by the target specialist, is a DRY-FIRE mechanism integral with the thumb safety. With the safety latch in its rearward position, it operates solely as a manual safety. In its forward position, however, the safety secures the hammer but allows a partial hammer fall with each pull of the trigger. A slight pressure on the safety latch, after each trigger realease, quickly recocks the hammer. Thus a shooter may dry fire with ease as long as desired. Trigger let-off is identical to actually firing; the firing pin remains inert; mechanical parts are unburdened by extensive practice; recocking is effortless and accomplished without disturbing aim. The pistol is on full safe throughout a practice session.

The Medalist possesses a stop-open latch which operates manually and also automatically after the chamber and magazine are clear. The special target grip is also available for left-handed shooters.

The Medalist is as much a masterpiece in fit and finish as it is in mechanical perfection. It is presented in a lifetime fitted case with lock and brass name plate and includes variable weights, disassembly tool and shell block.

The introduction for the Medalist, shown on the previous page and continued above, is from an early Browning catalog.

MEDALIST 22 PISTOL

GENERAL INFORMATION

The Medalist was designed by Bruce W. Browning in the fall of 1961 and introduced to this country in 1962. It was such a great design that Browning decided to introduce two other less expensive versions called the Nomad and the Challenger, which are covered under their own sections.

Only plain blued models were originally introduced; all were highly polished and blued. In July of 1962 the Gold Line entered the scene and in 1970 the Renaissance.

The only barrel length offered was 6 3/4''.

From 1 to 22,000 the marking on the left side are:
**BROWNING ARMS COMPANY
ST LOUIS Mo & MONTREAL P.Q.**

On the right side were the words:
**MADE IN BELGIUM
22 LONG RIFLE**

After 22,000 the markings changed on the left as follows:
**BROWNING ARMS COMPANY
MORGAN,UTAH & MONTREAL P.Q.**

The right side was now marked:
**22 L.R. BROWNING PATENTS
MADE IN BELGIUM**

There are two front and rear barrel sight variations. In the first four years, the front sight blade was shorter then those made after 1966. The rear sight adjustment screws were changed from the dished-out variation to straight sided in 1963.

The Medalist was a deluxe target pistol. The grips had a thumb rest and wrapped completely around the grip frame. The safety had a unique dry firing position that allowed you to fire the gun without harming neither the firing pin nor the chamber. This is an excellent feature; as an old competitor I can tell you the way to learn how to shoot a good score is to do plenty of dry firing.

There are two checkering pattern variations on the grips; the only difference is some have a little more checkering. I would think that this is due more to the whims of the worker than a manufacturing change. Of course, the Gold Line and Renaissance grips are checkered as well as carved. You could order this model either right or left handed; the left hand grips are a little rarer but not impossible to find.

The standard Medalists were finished in a highly polished dark blue, and all had gold plated triggers. There weren't any nickel or chrome plated guns produced unless a special order gun was made of which I have never seen or heard.

Medalists were shipped in a black leatherette case with key, cartridge block, barrel weights, and cartridge deflector pin. The only two variations are right or left hand and the hinges may or may not be brass.

I do not believe we will ever find out how many of each model were made, but the total was about

218,137 made for world sale. There was a total of about 25,552 Medalists manufactured as follows:

24,001 were in blue with 6 3/4'' barrels.
407 were blue with gold line inlays.
390 were chrome plated with Renaissance engraving.
60 were made for the Browning Collectors Association.
2 were Renaissance International models.
681 were Internationals with blue or dull parkerized finish and 5 7/8'' barrels

In addition, there were about eleven full coverage Renaissance guns made from 1962 to 1967. These are very rare, for the engraving goes all the way down the barrels.

INTERNATIONAL MEDALIST 1 & 2

The International Medalist I advertising started in 1970, though some were being made as early as 1969. Production ended in 1974 with about 681 made; they are still being produced for other countries. The second model, which is called the International Medalist 2, was made starting in 1975.

The original intention was to build a gun that would qualify under both N.R.A. and International Shooting Union regulations.

The medium heavy barrel has a non-glare ventilated rib. They were only made with barrels 5.9'' long, giving a sight radius of 8.6''. All the micrometer rear sights were adjustable for both windage and elevation and are positive.

Barrel markings on the left side are as follows:
**BROWNING ARMS COMPANY
MORGAN,UTAH & MONTREAL P.Q.**

On the right side were the words:
**22 LONG RIFLE
MADE IN BELGIUM**

The grips were made of walnut and have a thumb rest; they are not adjustable like the second model and are checkered 18 line per inch.

The grooved triggers were fully adjustable for weight of pull and backlash. As in the Medalist there is a dry fire mechanism as standard.

All were shipped in a leatherette pistol case lined in red velvet.

The second version of the International Medalist was only sold in this country in 1980. It is generally referred to by collectors as the International Medalist 2.

It has a heavy barrel that is bored and rifled to a high standard of excellence to assure accuracy and consistency. Under the barrel, a weight is fitted that can be slid forward or backward so that the shooter can alter the balance as he sees fit.

The most apparent difference with the first variation are the checkered walnut adjustable grips that have a palm rest you can move to make them as comfortable as possible.

The front sight is interchangeable with different types and sizes of blades, and the rear sight has positive click adjustments for both windage and elevation.

Triggers are gold plated and adjustable so that the shooter can adapt it to the type of shooting and his own preferences.

All were matte finished to cut down on the glare. These are strictly functional target pistols that were made for competitors. They are rare and very collectable, for only about 200 were shipped to this country. They are still being made for sales outside of the U.S.

All barrels were 5 15/16'' and marked with both F.N. and Browning Arms Company names as follows:
On the left side:
**BROWNING ARMS COMPANY
MORGAN,UTAH & MONTREAL P.Q.
MADE IN BELGIUM
BY FABRIQUE NATIONALE HERSTAL**

On the right side:
**22 LONG RIFLE
MADE IN BELGIUM**

The ones made in France were marked with a "P" in the serial number, markings on the barrel are as follows:
On one side:
**MADE IN FRANCE
BY FABRIQUE NATIONALE HERSTAL**

On the other side:
BROWNING ARMS COMPANY

On one side:
**22 LONG RIFLE
MADE IN BELGIUM**

It was delivered in a deluxe zippered case.

GOLD LINE

The Gold Line Medalist was introduced along with the Challenger in 1962, so they were also the first of the high grade 22's to be introduced. They are the rarest of all for only 407 were made; all were discontinued in 1974.

There are two types of Gold Lines models made. One was the earlier type like those shown in the catalogs in the 1960's, and the other is like those made for Jay's Guns in Florida at a later date.

All visible parts are richly blued and gold inlaid in the same manner as the Challenger. The gold line work is hand inlaid on both sides of the frame, on the rear sight, down the barrel flats, on the rear of the frame, and on the grip straps. All line work consists of straight lines which are finished off with little swirls or angles up or down. In addition all triggers were gold plated.

The grips for the Gold Line were carved and checkered French walnut finished in a high gloss. The checkering was 24 lines per inch and covered almost the entire surface. The carving consisted of beads carved along the bottom of the grip. All workmanship was outstanding.

These are very difficult to find for almost all are in collector's hands and are not put on the market very often. If you have a chance to purchase one at a decent price, do it.

A Renaissance Medalist with 100% coverage.

RENAISSANCE

The Renaissance model was introduced in 1970. It is truly a beautiful 22 auto and probably the nicest engraved 22 ever built by anyone. Prior to the official introduction of this model, Browning brought in less the 10 of these that were more elaborately engraved then the later guns and finished in a "bright" coin nickel. The engraving went all the way down the barrels. The later guns had a satin chrome finish that was not as bright.

All had 6 3/4" barrels that were marked as follows:
On the left side:
BROWNING ARMS COMPANY
MORGAN,UTAH & MONTREAL P.Q.

On the right side:
22 LONG RIFLE
MADE IN BELGIUM

In 1986, Browning had made 60 full coverage Renaissance Medalists for the B.C.A.. These had serial numbers 655PT0001 through 655PT0060 and the markings were as follows:

On the left side of the barrel:
BROWNING ARMS COMPANY
CALIBER .22 LONG RIFLE

On the right side:
MADE IN BELGIUM
BY FABRIQUE NATIONALE HERSTAL

On the Medalists engraving was fantastic to say the least. All parts were covered with at least 95% engraving. The standard Renaissance style is scroll and leaves in a very appealing style. Triggers, barrels, and sights were not engraved; all triggers were gold plated.

The grips are French walnut with a high gloss finish checkered 24 lines per inch; the checkering is on panels on both side. All this checkering is surrounded by hand-carved beads. About 1/3 of the surface of the grips and forearm is carved in a fleur-de-lis pattern.

There were about 390 of the standard pattern and about 10 of the earlier guns; all were made between 1970 and 1975.

SERIAL NUMBERS AND MODEL CODES

The serial numbers of all three of the 22 models ran together and commingled. From 1962 - 1968, the serial numbers ran continuously from year to year. From 1969 until the end of U.S. sales, the serial numbers started with 0001 at the beginning of each year.

The Medalist had a "T" and the International Medalist II had an "I" in the serial number and later a model code of 665 to distinguish the model.

Serial numbers from 1962 - 1975, the end of production, are as follows:

	Medalist	International		Medalist	International
1962	-T 2		1970	-T70	—I70
1963	-T 3		1971	-T71	—I71
1964	-T 4		1972	-T72	—I72
1965	-T 5		1973	-T73	—I73
1966	-T 6		1974	-T74	—I74
1967	-T 7		1975	-T75	—I75
1968	-T 8		1986	655PT0001 to 0060	
1969	-T69	—I69			

For information about yearly codes after 1975 please refer to the General Information section in the front of this book.

BUCK MARK .22

GENERAL INFORMATION

The Buck Mark model was introduced in 1985 as an economy model Challenger III and is still being made as of 1992 in several variations.

This is the third variation by Browning of the original Challenger II, which was produced in the U.S. The Challenger II and III and the Buck Mark were all manufactured by Arms Technology based in Salt Lake City, Utah.

BUCK MARK STANDARD

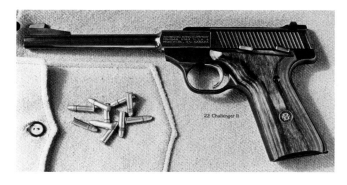

The Challenger II as shown in the 1981 catalog.

The Buck Mark features the same frame as the Challenger II including the wedge locking system which prevented the barrel from coming loose. All frames were steel and blued until 1991 when the BUCK MARK NICKEL was introduced with checkered rubber grips. There were no high grades produced, and all triggers were gold plated. The slides were machined differently than the Challenger III with a finger grip on the back which made opening much easier. Also, a new button magazine release was introduced, which, unlike the Challenger II and III's release on the bottom of the grip, was much handier.

Grips were black plastic with a metal Browning medallion inlaid on both sides; they were checkered.

The barrel length was 5 1/2" and it had a recessed muzzle; in 1992 a 4" barrel MICRO BUCK MARK was introduced. The weight was 32 oz., the height was 5 3/8", overall length was 9 1/2", sight radius was 8"m and the magazine capacity was 10 rounds of 22 Long Rifle only. Sights were fully adjustable for windage and elevation and were positive. They were mounted on a barrel rib which was not attached to the slide. This makes for more consistent sight stability.

The markings on the left side of the barrel were:
BROWNING ARMS COMPANY
MORGAN,UTAH & MONTREAL P.Q. CANADA

On the right side were the words:
22 LONG RIFLE
BUCK MARK
MADE IN U.S.A.

In 1987 three new variations were introduced: the Plus, the Varmint and the Silhouette.

BUCK MARK PLUS

The Buck Mark Plus has the same features as the Standard model except the grips are impregnated hardwood like the original Challenger II. In addition they have a "Buck Mark" medallion inlaid. The MICRO PLUS was introduced in 1992, which is the same gun except with a 4" barrel. Blueing is a high lustre on the barrel in contrast to the frame and slide which have a flat finish.

BUCK MARK SILHOUETTE

This is the same as the Standard variation except it has a 9 7/8" bull barrel which is 9/10" at the muzzle, the finish is a matte blue, overall length is 14", width 1 5/8", height 5 5/16", and weight is 53 oz. The sights are mounted on a grooved sighting plane screwed to the top of the barrel. The rear sight is a Millet Gold Cup™ 360 SIL and the front sight consists of interchangeable posts of various widths that are adjustable for height. Both the rear and front sight are hooded. One more feature is a forearm that mounts on the barrel. It is made of laminated wood as are the grips; in 1988 these were changed to walnut.

BUCK MARK VARMINT

This model also features a 9 7/8" bull barrel like the Silhouette. The finish is a matte blue, overall length is 14", width 1 5/8", height 5 5/16", and weight is 48 oz. The sighting plane is grooved all the way down so a scope can be moved front or back for various amounts of eye relief. The grips are the same as the Silhouette and a forearm is available as an option, both of which were also changed to walnut in 1988.

BUCK MARK TARGET 5.5

This variation has a 5 1/2" barrel made of the same stock as the Silhouette. It has hooded variable sights, walnut grips, and a matte finish. The overall length is 9 5/8", width 1 5/8", height 5 5/16", and weight is 35 1/2 oz. In 1992 the grips were changed to a fuller style with finger grooves on the front.

In 1991 the TARGET GOLD 5 1/2" was introduced; it has all the same features as the standard target gun. This is the same in all features except that the frame and top barrel plane are gold anodized.

BUCK MARK FIELD 5.5

This variation was introduced in 1991 and is the same as the Target 5.5 except the front and rear sights are of a lower contour.

BUCK MARK NICKEL

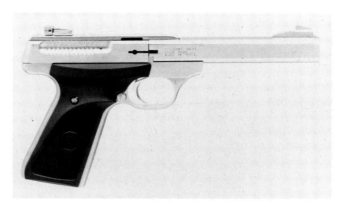

The Buck Mark Nickel.

This was introduced in 1991 with a 5 1/2" barrel and checkered rubber grips. In 1992 it was also offered with a 4" barrel and named the MICRO NICKEL. As first introduced, the entire gun was nickel plated except for the gold plated triggers. In 1992 the front sight and ramp and the rear sight and base was changed to a matte blue.

BUCK MARK UNLIMITED MATCH

As introduced in 1991 this is the same in every way as the Silhouette variation except it has a 14" barrel. The overall length is 18 1/8", width 1 5/8", height 5 15/16", and weight is 64 oz. It comes shipped in a Browning carrying case that is black with gold letters and a red stripe.

SERIAL NUMBERS

For yearly codes please refer to the General Information section in the front of this book.

Chapter Eighteen

Special Editions

1878 - 1978 CENTENNIAL COMMEMORATIVE SET

Produced to commemorate 100 years of Browning firearms, this set consisted of four guns and one set of knives.

(1) The first was a Superposed Continental Set with two sets of barrels, .30/06 24" long and 20 gauge 26 1/2", which was full and modified only. These had special presentation grade engravings with gold inlays. The engravings consisted of a bull elk head on one side and a bob white quail on the other. All this was shipped in a walnut presentatios case. Serial numbers were 1878C-001 through 1878C-500. The cost at retail was $6,500.00.

(2) The Jonathan Browning Mountain Rifle was shipped with a powder horn with matching serial numbers, which ran from 1878A-001 through 1878A-1000. The cost at retail was $650.00.

(3) The third was a B-92 rifle in 44 magnum caliber, which had a 20" round barrel, straight stock, saddle ring, iron sights, and crescent butt plate, serial numbers 1878B-001 through 1878B-6000. The cost at retail was $219.95.

(4) The fourth was a High Power 9MM chrome plated with walnut specially-checkered grips and fixed sights, which was shipped in a presentations case. The serial numbers ran from 1878D-001 through 1878D-3500 and the cost at retail was $495.00.

(5) A matched set of three knives included the Stalker II, the Canoe double blade, and the Stockman 3 blade all shipped in a walnut presentation case, serial numbers 001 through 2000. The cost at retail was $149.95.

All were engraved with the Centennial inscription.

For year codes refer to the General Information section in the front of the book.

BICENTENNIAL SETS

In 1976, F.N. produced 1,000 Bicentennial Sets to celebrate this country's Bi-Centennial.

These consisted of a B-78 with an octagon barrel in 45/70 that was specially engraved in Belgium, the stock was also checkered. The engraving was designed by Louis Vrancken.

The other half of the set was a fixed blade hunting knife made in Utah as described in the knife section and also engraved in Belgium on the pommel and handguard; the grip of the knife was also checkered in Belgium. The inscription on the blade was etched.

You will not find this set in any Browning catalog, since they were offered to gun shops through direct sales.

Both were cased in alder wood with a commemorative medallion. Serial numbers were from 1776-1 to 1776-1000. The retail price for these at the time was $1,500.00.

For year codes after 1976, refer the General Information section at the front of this book.

BROWNING COLLECTORS ASSOCIATION COMMEMORATIVE MODELS

The Browning Collectors Association has offered several unusual guns for distribution to members only. Listed below are the first seven guns and knives.

HIGH POWER

The High Power was first offered in 1979. It was limited to 100 pieces. Each piece was engraved and gold filled with the inscription "Browning Collectors

Association . . . First Edition. June 1980'' on the left side.

These were serial numbered B.C.A. 1-of-100 through 100-of-100.

They were sold with a walnut presentation case, the same used for the Browning 1878-1978 Centennial model; all were blued. The original price was $490.00.

STALKER II HUNTING KNIFE

In 1980 the commemorative piece offered was the Stalker II folding hunting knife, which was limited to 200 pieces.

On the left side of the blade was engraved "Browning Collectors Assn . . . Second Anniversary . . . June 1981.'' It was cased in a walnut presentation case.

All were serial numbered on the base of the heavily engraved bolster. The blade shape resembles the "Limited Edition Damascus'' model made in 1981. The scales are wood and the blades are stainless steel. The original price was $125.00 but was later discounted to $85.00.

B-92 RIFLE

In 1981 the B.C.A brought out the B-92 44 Magnum rifle.

On the left side of the receiver is engraved "Browning Collectors Ass'n . . . Third Anniversary . . . June 1982'' and some very light skimpy engraving.

On the right side is the inscription B C A NO. xxx. They were fully blued. I do not know how many were produced. The original price was $359.70. At an additional charge of $157.50, a red velvet-lined walnut presentation case was offered for this rifle. These cases are similar to the ones used for Presentation Superposed.

CHALLANGER II

In 1982 the Challanger II was utilized for the B.C.A. commemorative.

It has a 5 1/2'' barrel and adjustable sights. The right side of the barrel is machine engraved with the words, "Browning Collectors Ass'n . . . Fourth Anniversary . . . June 1983.'' They were fully blued. The original price was $305.00 and then lowered to $290.00; an optional walnut presentation case was available for $40.00. I do not know how many were produced.

AUTO-5

In 1983 the Fifth Anniversary Auto-5 was brought out.

These were all 3'' magnums with 30'' full choke vent rib barrels and round knob buttstocks. They are basically Belgium but not 100%, as some parts were made in Japan. On the left side is machine engraved and gold filled, "Browning Collectors Ass'n . . . Fifth Anniversary . . . June 1984.'' On the right side is B C A No. xxx. The balance of the receiver is engraved the same as all standard A-5's. Only 200 were made, so this is a rare A-5. The price was $595.00.

TROMBONE 22 RIFLE

In 1984 the B.C.A. offered 60 Model 1919 or Trombone .22 rifles to members as the sixth anniversary model for the Association. It is probably the nicest of all the B.C.A. guns.

This is truly a beautiful piece produced in the old Belgium tradition. The basis for this rifle is a gun produced for Mrs. John M. Browning in the 1920's. The original engraving pattern by Felix Funken was duplicated by Jose Baerten and is 100% coverage.

The engraving consists of elaborate scroll highlighted by animal figures. The stocks are of Group 4 or higher Claro Walnut, hand checkered, and finely finished. They were cased in an Italian luggage case. The serial numbers began with 1/60 and ended with 60/60 on the floor plate. The original issue price was $1325.00.

22 AUTO

In 1989 this little rifle was offered in 22 short only.

The left side of the receiver is engraved with a running fox surrounded by an engraved oval with some very light scroll engraving in a fleur-de-lis pattern. The corners of the receiver are also engraved in a similar manner.

On the right side is a sitting squirral eating within a wood scene; it is also encircled in an oval the same as the left side.

The top of the receiver is the same as the two sides except a rabbit is sitting within the oval. The entire receiver and trigger guard is finished greyed.

The wood is checkered and about group 2. These are known not to have the greatest wood and were a disapointment for the 155 members who purchased them.

The serial numbers ran 10BCA00001 to 10BCA00155, and the original price was around $900.00.

WYOMING GAME WARDEN SPECIAL EDITION

In early 1974, the Wyoming Game Warden's Association requested Browning to make up a set of items for them that consisted of a B-78 in 30/06 Springfield, a 20 or 12 gauge Citori Presentation grade, a 4018 folding knife, and a pair of Binoculars.

The total delivery consisted of eighty rifles, eighty shotguns consisting of seventy-eight 12 gauge 3'' magnums with 26'' mod/full barrels and two 20 gauges 3'' magnums with 26'' barrels choked Mod/Full, sixty-six sets of binoculars, and sixty-six knives.

The rifles and shotguns had on their left side a replica of their badges with their appropriate badge number from 1 through 80. Also on the left side was "WYOMING GAME WARDEN" engraved and gold filled. The knives and binoculars also had similar blades and inscriptions.

I don't know if you'll ever run across one of these, but at least you'll know what it is if you see one.

SOUTH DAKOTA CONSERVATION OFFICERS ASSOCIATION

In July 1976, Browning was commissioned to make 54 B-78 rifles in 22/250 with octagon barrels.

These had a gold filled inscription that said "South Dakota Game Conservation Officer" on one side and a badge with the numbers 1 to 54 on the other.

Two years later this group purchased thirty-four Citori shotguns, twenty-five 12 gauge and nine 20 gauge that were similarly inscribed.

THE AMERICAN HISTORICAL FOUNDATION

In 1992, The American Historical Foundation in Richmond Virginia issued a series of three shotguns. They consisted of 50 B25's, 100 B125's, and 200 Citori's. These were high grade guns, completely hand engraved as described.

The B25 and B125 engraving covered about 40% of the action and trigger guard with medium scroll. There were also 24 caret gold inlaid panels on the each side; the one on the left had King Elder ducks walking, one with head down and one with head up. On the right side were the same species in flight, both panels bordered with gold. On the bottom of the receiver is engraved what appears to be the head of a Labrador retriever, also bordered by the same scroll. Also appearing on the bottom are the words "FEDERAL DUCK STAMP." The trigger guard is scroll engraved and gold inlaid "1 of 50," "2 of 50," etc. In addition, the serial number under the top lever and the safety designation letters are gold inlaid. All these were engraved in Belgium.

The stocks are about group 5, round knob, standard forearm with a high gloss finish, and checkered 20 lines per inch. Stock options are the same as other B25's and include English style straight grip buttstock and a schnabel forearm.

The standard specifications were either 12 or 20 gauge with fixed full and modified chokes, but others were available.

The Citori version was engraved in the U.S. a little bit differently. The Elder ducks were enclosed in a scroll engraved oval on each side, but the ducks themselves were the same pattern. The balance of the engraving was the same but the only gold inlays were the serial numbers and the safety letters.

Hold on to your wallet, for the prices in 1992 were $4,995.00 for the Citori, $9,995.00 for the B125, and $14,500.00 for the B25.

In 1992, the Society advertised, without details, that future editions of these guns would be announced and that anyone purchasing one of these the first year would have the option to purchase others with the same serial numbers.

BROWNING ®

SALES OFFICE,
St. Louis 3, Mo.

BROWNING ARMS COMPANY

Dear Sir:

Thank you sincerely for your request for information on Browning guns.

It is a pleasure to send you our new descriptive brochure, together with a current price list.

We hope you will find this brochure informative and interesting enough that you will visit an Authorized Browning Dealer in your locality and actually examine the design, features and workmanship of our products.

If you do, we believe you will be impressed with their exceptional quality. They are made to serve you effectively with lasting performance and dependability. In terms of these things, we seriously doubt that there are many items of any type that cost so little.

Sales of Browning products are made only through our Authorized Browning Dealers. They will be happy to help you in your selection.

If we can be of further service, we shall be delighted to hear from you.

Yours very truly,

BROWNING ARMS COMPANY

The letter above and the four page price list that follows will give you an idea of the way Browning offered many options. Please pay attention on the last page to the "Engraving And Name Plates."

September 1, 1962

NEW
BROWNING®
PRODUCTS

RIFLESCOPES AND MOUNTS

2¾ X Cross Hair or Post and Cross Hair.......	$ 51.50
Range Finder......................	62.00
4 X Cross Hair or Post and Cross Hair.........	61.50
Range Finder......................	72.00
6 X Cross Hair or Post and Cross Hair.........	79.50
Range Finder......................	90.00
3 X — 9 X Variable Cross Hair...............	103.50
Dot Reticle—Optional at Extra Charge........	10.00
One-piece Base.....................	7.50
Split Rings (Pair)..................	14.00

BUCK SPECIAL
AUTOMATIC-5 SLUG SHOOTING SHOTGUN

Buck Special Complete With Accessories*

Standard 12 and 16 Gauge..............	$150.00
Lightweight 12, 16 and 20 Gauge.......	162.50
3″ Magnum 12 Gauge.................	162.50

Buck Special Without Accessories

Standard 12 and 16 Gauge.............	144.00
Lightweight 12, 16 and 20 Gauge.......	156.50
3″ Magnum 12 Gauge.................	156.50

Buck Special Deer Barrel Only

Standard 12 and 16 Gauge.............	53.50
Lightweight 12, 16 and 20 Gauge.......	59.50
3″ Magnum 12 Gauge.................	59.50

*Accessories consist of carrying sling, detachable swivels
and swivel attachments.*

ULTRA-FINE GUN OIL

Spout Can — 4 oz...................	$ .60
Aerosol Spray Can — 6 oz..............	1.00

PRINTED IN U.S.A.   9-62-30M

In 1962, Browning introduced several new additions. This is an enclosure with the catalog.

BROWNING®
PRICE LIST

Including the <u>new</u>
.22 Automatic Pistols

Prices effective
JUNE 1, 1962

World Famous BROWNING® Shotguns, Rifles, Pistols

For further information
see your
Browning Dealer

BROWNING ARMS COMPANY • 1706 Washington Ave. • ST. LOUIS 3, MO.

BROWNING®

AUTOMATIC-5 SHOTGUNS

HUNTING MODELS
Standard 12 and 16 Gauge
Plain Barrel $134.50
Ventilated Rib. 154.50

Light 12, Sweet 16 and Light 20 Ga.
Plain Matted Barrel. $147.00
Ventilated Rib 167.00

3″ Magnum 12 Gauge
Plain Barrel $147.00
Ventilated Rib. 167.00

SKEET MODELS
Light 12 and Light 20 Ga.
Plain Matted Barrel $147.00
Ventilated Rib. 167.00

TRAP MODELS
Standard 12 and Light 12 Ga.
Standard 12—Ventilated Rib. $154.50
Light 12—Ventilated Rib. 167.00

Right or Left Hand Safety Optional at No Extra Cost.

DOUBLE AUTOMATIC SHOTGUNS

HUNTING MODELS
Twelvette 12 Gauge
Plain Matted Barrel. $149.00
Ventilated Rib 169.00

Twentyweight 12 Gauge
Plain Matted Barrel. $155.50
Ventilated Rib 175.50

SKEET MODELS
Twelvette and Twentyweight 12 Ga.
Twelvette—Plain Matted Barrel. $149.00
Twelvette—Ventilated Rib. 169.00
Twentyweight—Plain Matted Barrel 155.50
Twentyweight—Ventilated Rib. 175.50

TRAP MODEL
Twelvette 12 Gauge
Ventilated Rib. $169.00

F. N. BROWNING
Semi-Automatic Rifles
Standard Model—Cal. .308W. $180.00
Lightweight Model—Cal. .308W 185.00

HIGH-POWER RIFLES
FAMOUS MAUSER BOLT ACTION
Safari Grade
.243 W, .264 WM, .270 W, 30-06, 308 W. . $175.00
.300 H&H, .338 WM, .375 H&H, .458 WM 180.00

Medallion Grade
All Calibers $295.00

Olympian Grade
All Calibers 495.00
Other standard calibers available by special order.

AUTOMATIC .22 RIFLES
Grade I   Long Rifle . . . . $ 69.50
Grade I   Short 69.50
Grade I   Gallery Model-Short. 72.50
Grade II   Long Rifle. 105.00
Grade III   Long Rifle. 170.00
Right or Left Hand Safety Optional at No Extra Cost.

AUTOMATIC PISTOLS
New .22 Caliber Long Rifle
Nomad Model. . . . . $ 49.95
Challenger Model. 64.95
Medalist Model. 112.95

.25 Caliber
Standard Model. 30.95
Lightweight Model. 42.50
Renaissance Model 75.00

.380 Caliber
Standard Model. 44.50
Renaissance Model 115.00

9mm Caliber
Standard Model. 74.50
Renaissance Model 200.00

Cased Set of 3 (.25, .380, 9mm)
Standard Models 149.95
Renaissance Models. 390.00

LIFETIME LUGGAGE GUN CASES
For Browning Shotguns (except next item) $35.00
For Superposed Shotguns with two extra
   sets of barrels. 50.00①
For Browning .22 Automatic Rifles. 20.00
For Browning High-Power Rifles. 45.00

① Add $20.00 if at least one set of barrels is 32″.

For maximum protection and safety, store and carry your new Browning gun in a well-made, specially fitted, luggage-type, Browning gun case. Models available for every Browning Shotgun and Rifle.

SUPERPOSED SHOTGUNS
All Models With Ventilated Rib
HUNTING MODELS
12 and 20 Gauge

	Weight	
Grade I	Standard	$ 315.00
Grade I	Lightning	335.00
Pigeon Grade	Lightning	475.00
Pointer Grade	Lightning	585.00
Diana Grade	Lightning	700.00
Midas Grade	Lightning	1,025.00*

3″ Magnum 12 Gauge

	Weight	
Grade I	Magnum	$ 320.00
Pigeon Grade	Magnum	475.00
Pointer Grade	Magnum	585.00
Diana Grade	Magnum	700.00
Midas Grade	Magnum	1,025.00*

28 and .410 Gauge

	Weight	
Grade I	Standard	$ 375.00
Pigeon Grade	Standard	500.00
Pointer Grade	Standard	610.00
Diana Grade	Standard	725.00
Midas Grade	Standard	1,050.00*

28 and .410 Gauge Barrels come in one weight only.

TRAP MODELS
12 Gauge

	Lightning	BROADway
Grade I	$ 335.00	$ 365.00
Pigeon Grade	475.00	500.00
Pointer Grade	585.00	615.00
Diana Grade	700.00	725.00
Midas Grade	1,025.00*	1,050.00*

SKEET MODELS
12 and 20 Gauge

	Weight	
Grade I	Standard	$ 315.00
Grade I	Lightning	335.00
Pigeon Grade	Lightning	475.00
Pointer Grade	Lightning	585.00
Diana Grade	Lightning	700.00
Midas Grade	Lightning	1,025.00*

28 and .410 Gauge

	Weight	
Grade I	Standard	$ 375.00
Pigeon Grade	Standard	500.00
Pointer Grade	Standard	610.00
Diana Grade	Standard	725.00
Midas Grade	Standard	1,050.00*

SUPERPOSED SHOTGUNS WITH EXTRA SETS OF BARRELS
All Models With Ventilated Rib

Any combinations of barrel weights and models can be provided. All prices include fitted luggage case. The 28 and .410 Gauge come in one weight only.

12 or 20 Gauge with one set of extra barrels of the same Gauge.①

Grade I	$ 530.00
Pigeon Grade	670.00
Pointer Grade	790.00
Diana Grade	905.00
Midas Grade	1,330.00*

12 Gauge with one set of extra barrels in 20 Gauge.①

Grade I	$ 565.00
Pigeon Grade	705.00
Pointer Grade	825.00
Diana Grade	940.00
Midas Grade	1,365.00*

12 or 20 Gauge with two sets of extra barrels of the same Gauge.①

Grade I	$ 705.00
Pigeon Grade	845.00
Pointer Grade	975.00
Diana Grade	1,090.00
Midas Grade	1,615.00*

20 Gauge with one set of extra barrels, either 28 or .410 Gauge.

Grade I	$ 585.00
Pigeon Grade	715.00
Pointer Grade	835.00
Diana Grade	950.00
Midas Grade	1,375.00*

20 Gauge with two sets of extra barrels, one 28 Gauge, one .410 Gauge.

Grade I	$ 815.00
Pigeon Grade	935.00
Pointer Grade	1,065.00
Diana Grade	1,180.00
Midas Grade	1,705.00*

28 Gauge with one set of extra barrels in .410 Gauge.

Grade I	$ 625.00
Pigeon Grade	740.00
Pointer Grade	860.00
Diana Grade	975.00
Midas Grade	1,400.00*

① For each set of BROADway Trap 32 inch barrels add $30.00 to prices listed above. Add $40.00 for each set of shorter length 12 gauge barrels with BROADway Rib.

* All prices shown for Midas Grade includes Retail Federal Excise Tax.

EXTRA BARRELS

An extra barrel for your Automatic gives you the equivalent of two guns in one.

Automatic-5 Standard 12 and 16 Gauge

Plain Barrel	$ 44.00
Hollow Matted Rib	54.00
Ventilated Rib	64.00

Automatic-5, Light 12, Sweet 16, Light 20 and 12 Ga. 3″ Magnum

Plain Matted Barrel	$ 50.00
Hollow Matted Rib†	60.00
Ventilated Rib	70.00

†Not available in 20 Ga. or 12 Ga. 3″ Magnum

Double Automatic Twelvette 12 Gauge

Plain Barrel	$ 45.00
Ventilated Rib	65.00

Double Automatic Twentyweight 12 Gauge

Plain Matted Barrel	$ 50.00
Ventilated Rib	70.00

EXTRA SET OF SUPERPOSED BARRELS STANDARD OR LIGHTNING WEIGHT FOR GUNS NOW IN USE

For a 12 or 20 Gauge set of extra barrels of the same gauge as the gun:

Grade I	$220.00
Pigeon	235.00
Pointer	250.00
Diana	265.00
Midas	370.00

For a 32″ BROADway rib set of extra barrels add $30.00 to prices listed above. For a shorter barrel length set of 12 ga. BROADway barrels add $40.00.

For a 20 Gauge set of extra barrels fitted to a 12 Gauge gun:

Grade I	$255.00
Pigeon	270.00
Pointer	285.00
Diana	300.00
Midas	405.00

For either 28 or .410 Gauge Barrels fitted to a 20 Gauge Gun add $55.00 to prices listed above.

TIME NECESSARY: 6 months from receipt of customer's gun. Pack carefully before shipping. Please state clearly all specifications desired.

CHOKING DEVICES

Cutts Compensator with spreader and full choke tubes	$ 24.50
Extra pattern control tubes, each	3.25
DeLuxe Polychoke, ventilated	24.75

SHORTENING STOCK—RECOIL PADS IVORY SIGHTS

Shortening stock, up to 1 inch:

On new Automatic Shotguns	$ 9.00
On new Superposed Shotguns	11.00

DeLuxe type recoil pad and fitting:

On new Automatic Shotguns	9.00
On new Superposed Shotguns	11.00
On new High-Power Rifles	9.00
Fit front ivory sight	2.25
Fit center ivory sight	2.25

ENGRAVING AND NAME PLATES

To fit in stock, between grip and toe, a one-inch 10 kt. gold oval name plate with three-letter monogram initial on any Browning shotgun or rifle $35.00

If one-inch nickel silver oval preferred .. 30.00

To engrave name in block or script or to engrave a three-letter monogram initial on the receiver of an Automatic shotgun or Grade I .22 rifle:

Three-letter Monogram	7.00
Name per letter (Minimum charge $5.00)	1.00

Style A..*MONOGRAM* Initials..
(P. R. Baker)

Style B..*MONOGRAM* Initials..
(J. R. Adams)

Style C..*Name*..
(Block letters ¼″ high)   **HENRY CHALMERS**

Style D..*Name*..
(Script letters ¼″ high)   *Helen D. Caston.*

The engraving on the receivers and trigger guards of the Superposed shotgun and Grade II and III .22 rifles covers all surfaces, prohibiting initial or name engraving unless provision is made at time of production. A special factory order is required. Name identification on a High-Power rifle is also limited to a name plate unless ordered specially from the factory. Please note—Olympian models are already provided with a gold medallion fitted in the grip cap.

Special factory order for engraving on trigger guards or receivers:

Style A or B—Three-letter monogram engraved	$ 7.00
Style A or B—Three-letter monogram gold inlaid	23.00
Style C or D—Name, cost per letter, engraved	1.00
Style C or D—Name, cost per letter, gold inlaid	2.00
Personalized signature, cost per letter, engraved	1.25
Personalized signature, cost per letter, gold inlaid	2.25

PRINTED IN U.S.A. 9-60 30M

Index

Illustrations and Tables
(By Chapter)

Subject
(People, Companies, and Miscellaneous)

Rifles — Shotguns — Handguns
(By Manufacturer)

ILLUSTRATIONS AND TABLES

PEOPLE, COMPANIES, AND MISCELLANEOUS

RIFLES — SHOTGUNS — HANDGUNS

RIFLE MODELS
FABRIQUE NATIONALE MANUFACTURED RIFLES

SPECIAL EDITIONS